FRANCE

B. Kaufmann/MICHELIN

Editorial Director   Cynthia Clayton Ochterbeck

THE GREEN GUIDE FRANCE

Editor   Gwen Cannon
Contributing Writer   Andrew Sanger
Production Coordinator   Natasha G. George
Cartography   Alain Baldet, Michèle Cana, Peter Wrenn
Photo Editor   Lydia Strong
Proofreader   Jonathan P. Gilbert
Layout & Design   Nicole D. Jordan and John Higginbottom
Cover Design   Laurent Muller and Frank Ladd

Contact Us: The Green Guide
                            Michelin Maps and Guides
                            One Parkway South
                            Greenville, SC 29615
                            USA
                            www.michelintravel.com
                            michelin.guides@us.michelin.com

                            Michelin Maps and Guides
                            Hannay House
                            39 Clarendon Road
                            Watford, Herts WD17 1JA
                            UK
                            ☎ (01923) 205 240
                            www.ViaMichelin.com
                            travelpubsales@uk.michelin.com

Special Sales: For information regarding bulk sales,
                            customized editions and premium sales,
                            please contact our Customer Service
                            Departments:
                            USA   1-800-432-6277
                            UK   (01923) 205 240
                            Canada 1-800-361-8236

Note to the Reader

One Team …
A Commitment to Quality

There's just one reason our team is dedicated to producing quality travel publications—you, our reader.

Throughout our guides we offer **practical information**, **touring tips** and **suggestions** for finding the best places for a break.

Michelin driving tours help you hit the highlights and quickly absorb the best of the region. Our descriptive **walking tours** make you your own guide, armed with directions, maps and expert information.

We scout out the attractions, classify them with **star ratings**, and describe in detail what you will find when you visit them.

Michelin maps featured throughout the guide offer vibrant, detailed and easy-to-follow outlines of everything from close-up museum plans to international maps.

Places to stay and eat are always a big part of travel, so we research **hotels and restaurants** that we think convey the essence of the destination and arrange them by geographic area and price. We walk you through the best shopping districts and point you towards the host of entertainment and recreation possibilities available.

We **test**, **retest**, **check and recheck** to make sure that our guidebooks are truly just that: a personalized guide to help you make the most of your visit. And if you still want a speaking guide, we list local tour guides who will lead you on all the boat, bus, guided, historical, culinary, and other tours you shouldn't miss.

In short, we remove the guesswork involved with travel. After all, we want you to enjoy exploring with Michelin as much as we do.

The Michelin Green Guide Teamm

PLANNING YOUR TRIP

INTRODUCTION TO FRANCE

SYMBOLS

🛈	**Tourist Information**
🕒	**Hours of Operation**
🕙	**Periods of Closure**
✍	**A Bit of Advice**
✎	**Details to Consider**
💳	**Entry Fees**
Kids	**Especially for Children**
🥾	**Tours**
♿	**Wheelchair Accessible**

DISCOVERING FRANCE

CONTENTS

HOW TO USE THIS GUIDE

Orientation

To help you grasp the "lay of the land" quickly and easily, so you'll feel confident and comfortable finding your way around the country, we offer the following tools in this guide:

- Detailed table of contents for an overview of what you'll find in the guide, and how the guide is organized.
- Map of Principal Sights at the front of the guide, with the Principal Sights highlighted for easy reference.
- Detailed maps for major cities and villages, including driving tour maps and larger-scale maps for walking tours.
- Floor plans of the major cathedrals, châteaux and museums.
- Principal Sights organized alphabetically for quick reference.

Practicalities

At the front of the guide, you'll see a section called "Planning Your Trip" that contains information about planning your trip, the best time to go, different ways of getting to the region and getting around, and basic facts and tips for making the most of your visit. You'll find driving and themed tours, and suggestions for outdoor fun. There's also a calendar of popular annual events. Information on shopping, sightseeing, kids' activities and sports and recreational opportunities is included as well.

WHERE TO STAY

We've made a selection of hotels and arranged them within the cities by price category to fit all budgets (*see the Legend on the cover flap for an explanation of the price categories*). For the most part, we've selected accommodations based on their unique regional quality, their French character, as it were. So, unless the individual hotel embodies local ambience, it's rare that we include chain properties, which typically have their own imprint. If you want a more comprehensive selection of accommodations, see the red-cover **Michelin Guide France**.

WHERE TO EAT

We thought you'd like to know the popular eating spots in the country. So we selected restaurants that capture the French experience—those that have a unique regional flavor and local atmosphere. We're not rating the quality of the food per se. As we did with the hotels, we selected restaurants for many towns and villages, categorized by price to appeal to all wallets (*see the Legend on the cover flap for an explanation of the price categories*). If you want a more comprehensive selection of dining recommendations, see the red-cover **Michelin Guide France**.

Attractions

Principal Sights are arranged alphabetically. Within each Principal Sight, attractions for each town, village, or geographical area are divided into local Sights or Walking Tours, nearby Excursions to sights outside the town, or detailed Driving Tours—suggested itineraries for seeing several attractions around a major town. Contact information, admission charges and hours of operation are given for the majority of attractions. Unless otherwise noted, admission prices shown are for a single adult only. Discounts for children, seniors, students, teachers, etc. may be available; be sure to ask. If no admission charge is shown, entrance to the attraction is free.
If you're pressed for time, we recommend you visit the three- and two-star sights first: the stars are your guide.

STAR RATINGS

Michelin has used stars as a rating tool for more than 100 years:

★★★	Highly recommended
★★	Recommended
★	Interesting

SYMBOLS IN THE TEXT

Besides the stars, other symbols in the text indicate sights that are closed to the public ⊶; on-site eating facilities ✕; also see ⓔ; breakfast included in the nightly rate ☕; on-site parking P; spa facilities Spa; camping facilities △; swimming pool ≋; beaches ⛱; and expect long lines/queues ‖‖‖.
See the box appearing on the Contents page and the Legend on the cover flap for other symbols used in the text.
See the Maps explanation below for symbols appearing on the maps.
Throughout the guide you will find peach-coloured text boxes or sidebars containing anecdotal or background information. Green-coloured boxes contain information to help you save time or money.

Maps

All maps in this guide are oriented north, unless otherwise indicated by a directional arrow. The term "Local Map" refers to a map within the chapter or Tourism Region. See the map Legend at the back of the guide for an explanation of other map symbols. A complete list of the maps found in the guide appears at the back of this book.

Addresses, phone numbers, opening hours and prices published in this guide are accurate at press time. We welcome corrections and suggestions that may assist us in preparing the next edition. Please send your comments to:

Michelin Maps and Guides
Hannay House
39 Clarendon Road
Watford, Herts WD17 1JA
UK
travelpubsales@uk.michelin.com
www.michelin.co.uk

Michelin Maps and Guides
Editorial Department
P.O. Box 19001
Greenville, SC 29602-9001
USA
michelin.guides@us.michelin.com
www.michelintravel.com

Principal sights

TOULOUSE ★★★ Highly recommended

Autun ★★ Recommended

Giverny ★ Interesting

Montélimar Other sights
described in this guide

Seaside resorts ≙, spas ✦ and winter resorts ❄ are classified
according to the quality and range of facilities offered.

Shown on this map are the towns and sights in the Discovering France section of the guide, with the
additional sights attached to them, as well as principal resorts.

A number of other places, monuments, historical events and natural sites appear in this guide
and may be found in the index.

0   100 km

Guernsey

Jersey

Perros-Guirec ≙≙

Île de Batz

Roscoff

Tréguier

CÔTE D'ÉMERAUDE

CAP FRÉHEL

DINARD ≙≙≙

D 788   D 786   D 767

N 12

Île d'Ouessant

Île de Molène

BREST   St.Thégonnec

ST-MALO

Guimiliau

Dinan

POINTE DE PENHIR

D 867   N 165

N 164

D 700   N 164

Douarnenez

Île de Sein   D 765

Locronan

POINTE DU RAZ

D 768

Quimper

Bénodet

Josselin

N 24

Concarneau

Îles de Glénau

N 165

Vannes

Île de Groix

Carnac

Golfe du
Morbihan

≙ Quiberon

Locmariaquer

Guérande   D 774

BELLE-ÎLE

Presqu'île
de Guérande

ST-
NAZAIRE

≙≙≙ LA BAULE

Île de Noirmoutier

A T L A N T I Q U E

Île d'Yeu

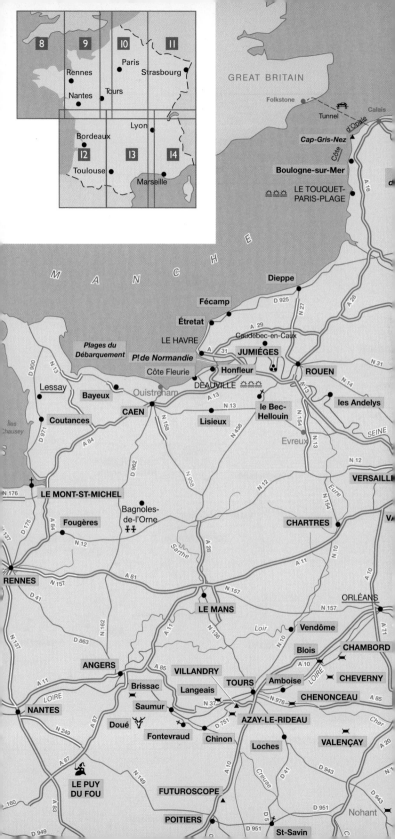

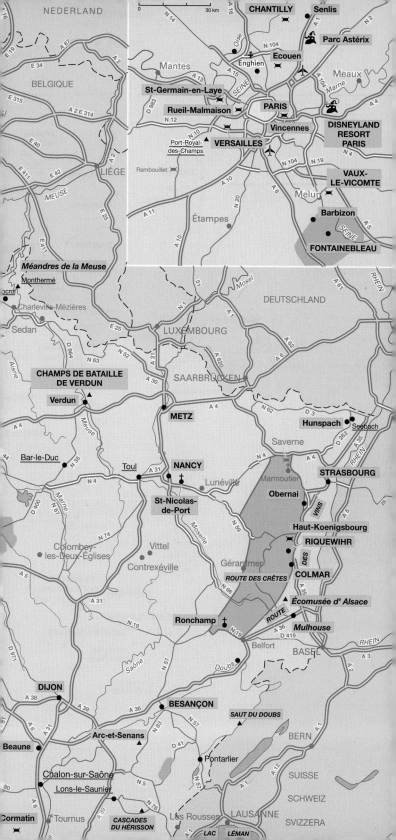

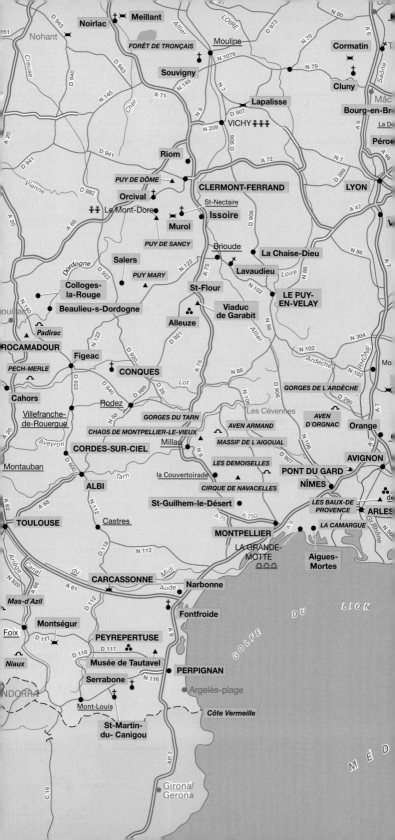

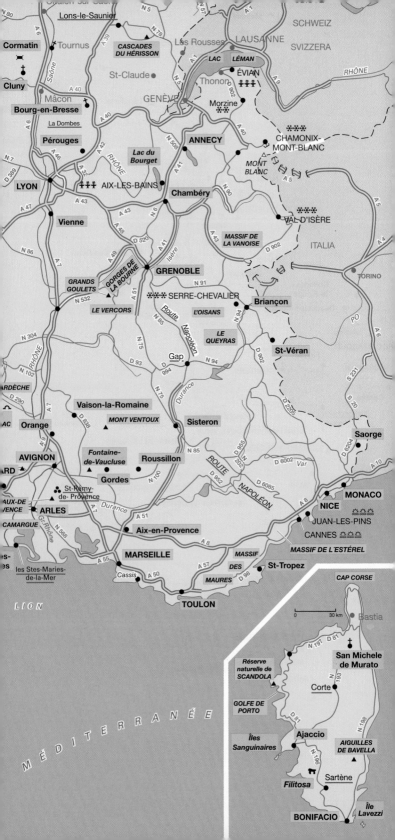

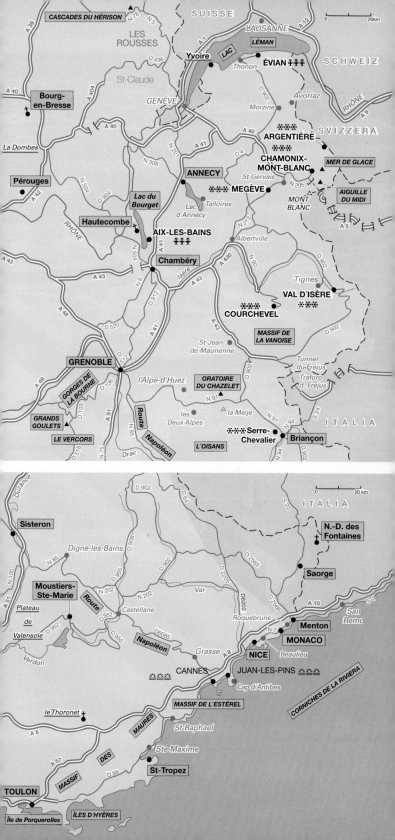

The gardens at Château de Villandry
Studio 3bis/MICHELIN

WHEN AND WHERE TO GO

When to Go

SEASONS

To give the visitor a general idea of the weather in France, below is a temperature chart that covers the entire country.

Depending on the purpose of your visit, **spring**, **summer** and **autumn** are generally the best seasons to visit France, each with its own appeal, and there is a region for every season. For **winter** sports, the season runs from December to April. For relaxing out of doors, high summer can be beautiful – and is called La Belle Saison – but resorts and sightseeing areas are much more crowded. it would be wise to travel if possible in May, June or September when French children are at school. Many visitors may prefer the more moderate warmth of these early and late summer months to the higher temperatures of July and August, especially in the southern half of the country.

CLIMATE

For an overview of the weather in a specific region of the country, see the **Michelin Green Guide** series, which covers 24 regions of France (13 of the guides are in English), such as Normandy, Brittany, the French Riviera, Provence, etc.

In general the French climate is a moderate one; extremes of either heat or cold are rare for the most part, so that outdoor activity of some kind is almost always possible. Inland the winters are chilly and darkness comes early, especially in the northern

Temperature chart throughout France												
	Jan	Feb	Mar	Apr	May	Jun	Jul	Aug	Sep	Oct	Nov	Dec
	9	10	15	17	20	23	25	25	23	18	12	8
Bordeaux	1	2	4	9	12	13	13	13	12	8	4	2
	8	9	11	13	15	18	19	20	18	15	11	9
Brest	4	3	4	7	8	11	12	13	11	8	6	4
	7	8	13	16	19	23	25	25	22	16	11	7
Clermont	-1	-1	2	5	7	11	13	12	10	6	3	0
	5	8	13	16	20	23	26	26	23	16	10	6
Grenoble	-3	-2	2	5	8	12	14	13	11	6	3	-1
	5	6	10	13	17	20	22	22	19	14	9	6
Lille	0	0	2	4	7	10	12	12	10	7	3	1
	12	13	14	17	20	23	26	26	24	20	16	13
Nice	4	4	5	9	12	16	18	16	12	8	5	
	7	7	12	15	19	22	24	24	21	15	10	6
Paris	1	1	3	6	9	12	14	14	11	8	4	2
	12	13	16	18	21	25	28	28	25	20	15	12
Perpig-nan	3	4	7	9	12	16	19	18	16	12	8	5
	3	5	11	15	19	23	24	25	20	14	8	4
Stras-bourg	-2	-1	1	4	6	11	13	13	10	5	2	-1
Maximum temperatures in red; minimum temperatures in black.												

latitudes. As spring turns to summer, the days become long and warm and by June the sun lingers well into the evening. Spring and autumn provide opportunities to explore the outdoors and enjoy the lovely countryside and coastal areas of France. In winter, snowfall throughout much of the interior of the country, as well as in the mountainous regions near Italy, permits a wide array of winter sports, including downhill skiing and snowboarding at many world-famous Alpine resorts. However, gray skies in this period are not unusual for much of the rest of the country, especially in Paris.

WEATHER FORECAST

National forecast: ☎32 50. Information about the weather is also available online at www.meteofrance. com.

WHAT TO PACK

Year-round, it is advisable to have a raincoat or hooded coat, and umbrella. Warmer wear, including a hat, neck scarf and gloves, is necessary in early spring, late autumn and winter. In summer it can be cool in the evening in some parts of the country, so taking some warmer clothing is recommended. Comfortable footwear is essential for sightseeing.

KNOW BEFORE YOU GO

Useful Websites

www.ambafrance-us.org, www.ambafrance-uk.org

The French Embassy has a website in the US and UK providing basic information (geography, demographics, history), a news digest and business-related information. It offers special pages for children, pages devoted to culture, language study and travel, and links to other selected French sites (regions, cities, ministries).

www.franceguide.com

The French Government Tourist Office/ Maison de la France site is packed with practical information, advice and tips for those travelling to France, including choosing package tours and even buying a property.

www.FranceKeys.com

This site has plenty of practical information for visiting France. It covers all the regions, with links to tourist offices and related sites. Very useful for planning all the details of your tour in France!

www.franceway.com

This is an online magazine that focuses on culture and heritage. For each region, there are also suggestions for activities and practical information on where to stay and how to get there.

www.ViaMichelin.com

This site has maps, tourist information, travel features, suggestions on hotels and restaurants, and a route planner for numerous locations in Europe. In addition, you can look up weather forecasts, traffic reports and service station location, particularly useful if you will be driving in France.

www.holidayfrance.org.uk/

The website of the Association of British Tour Operators to France features a holiday-finder, with a big selection of inclusive package deals.

Tourist Offices

For information, brochures, maps and assistance in planning a trip to France, travellers should contact the official tourist office in their own country:

AUSTRALIA-NEW ZEALAND

Level 13, 25 Bligh Street, 2000 NSW, Sydney, Australia
☏ 61 (0)2 9231 5244
Fax: 61 (0)2 9221 8682
Email: info.au@franceguide.com

CANADA

1800 Avenue McGill College, Suite 1010, Montreal, Quebec H3A 3J6
☏ (514) 288-2026
Fax: (514) 845-4868
Email: canada@franceguide.com

REPUBLIC OF IRELAND

No office
☏ (1) 560 235 235
Email: info.ie@franceguide.com

UNITED KINGDOM

178 Piccadilly, London W1V 0AL.
☏ 09068 244 123 (60p/min)
Fax (0171) 493 6594
Email: info.uk@franceguide.com

UNITED STATES

Three offices are available, but the quickest way to have a response to any question or request is by phone or email.

New York
444 Madison Av., New York 10022 NY
Los Angeles
9454 Wilshire Bld – Suite 715, Beverly Hills 90212 CA
Chicago
205 N.Michigan Ave, Suite 3770, Chicago 60601, IL
☏ (general inquiry line, use for all offices) 514 288 1904
Email: (all inquiries, use for all offices) info.us@franceguide.com

NATIONAL TOURIST OFFICES

France has a national network of regional and local tourist offices able to provide information useful in planning your trip and answering your questions.

Fédération nationale des comités régionaux de tourisme
17 av.de l'Opéra, 75001 Paris. ☏01 47 03 03 10. Email: contact@fncrt.com
www.fncrt.com

Fédération nationale des comités départementaux de tourisme
74-76 rue de Bercy, 75012 Paris.
☏(01) 44 11 10 20.
www.fncdt.net

Fédération nationale des offices de tourisme et syndicats d'initiative
11 rue du Faubourg Poissonniere, 75009 Paris. ☏(01) 44 11 10 30.
www.tourisme.fr

REGIONAL TOURIST OFFICES

Alsace Lorraine Champagne

Alsace
20a r. Berthe-Molly, BP 247, 68005 Colmar Cedex, ☏03 89 24 73 50.
www.tourisme-alsace.com

Lorraine
Abbaye des Prémontrés, BP 97, 54700 Pont-à-Mousson, ☏03 83 80 01 80.
www.tourisme-lorraine.fr

Champagne-Ardenne
15 av. Mar.-Leclerc, BP 319, 51013 Châlons-en-Champagne Cedex,
☏03 26 21 85 80.
www.tourisme-champagne-ardenne.com

Atlantic Coast

Aquitaine
Cité Mondiale, 23 parvis des Chartrons, 33074 Bordeaux, ☏05 56 01 70 00.
www.tourisme-aquitaine.info/

Poitou-Charentes
60 r. Jean-Jaurès, 86002 Poitiers,
☏05 49 50 10 50.
www.poitou-charentes-vacances.com

Auvergne – Rhone Valley

Auvergne
Parc Technologique Clermont-Ferrand
La Pardieu, 7 allée Pierre de Fermat,
63178 Aubière, ☏0810 827 828 .
www.maisondelauvergne.com

Rhône-Alpes
104 rte de Paris, 69260 Charbonnières-
les-Bains, ☏04 72 59 21 59.
www.rhonealpes-tourisme.com

Brittany

Bretagne
1 r. Raoul-Ponchon, 35069 Rennes
Cedex, ☏02 99 28 44 30.
Info ☏02 99 36 15 15.
www.touismebretagne.com

Burgundy Jura

Bourgogne
5, Avenue Garibaldi, 21006 Dijon
Cedex, ☏03 80 28 02 80.
www.bourgogne-tourisme.com

Franche-Comté
La City, 4 r. Gabriel-Plançon, 25044
Besançon Cedex, ☏03 81 25 08 08.
www.franche-comte.org

Chateaux of the Loire

Centre-Val de Loire
37 av. de Paris, 45000 Orléans,
☏02 38 79 95 00.
www.visaloire.com

Pays de la Loire
2 r. de la Loire, BP 20411, 44204 Nantes
Cedex 2, ☏02 40 48 24 20.
www..enpaysdelaloire.com

Corsica

Corse
ATC, 17 bd Roi-Jérôme, BP 19, 20181
Ajaccio, ☏04 95 51 00 00.
www.visit-corsica.com

Dordogne Berry Limousin

Limousin
30, cours Gay-Lussac , 87003 Limoges,
☏05 55 11 05 90.
www.tourismelimousin.com

French Alps

Rhone-Alpes
104, route de Paris, 69260 Charbonniè-
res- les-Bains, ☏04 72 59 21 59.
www.rhonealpes-tourisme.com

Provence-Alpes
10, place de la Joliette,
13567 Marseille, ☏04 91 56 47 00.
www.crt-paca.fr

French Riviera

Riviera-Côte d'Azur
400, Promenade des Anglais,
06203 Nice, ☏04 93 37 78 78.
www.guideriviera.com

Languedoc Roussillon Tarn Gorges

Languedoc-Roussillon
L'Acropole, 954 ave. Jean Mermoz,
CS79507, 34960 Montpellier Cedex 2,
☏04 67 200 220.
www.sunfrance.com

Midi-Pyrénées
54 bd de l'Embouchure, BP 2166,
31022 Toulouse Cedex 2,
☏05 61 13 55 55.
www.tourisme.midi-pyrenees.com

Normandy

Normandie
Le Doyenné, 14 r. Charles-Corbeau,
27000 Évreux, ☏02 32 33 79 00.
www.normandy-tourism.org

Northern France and the Paris Region

Île-de-France
11, rue du Faubourg Poissonnière
75009 Paris, ☏01 73 00 77 00.
www.pidf.com/

Nord-Pas-de-Calais
6 pl. Mendès-France, 59028 Lille
Cedex, ☎03 20 14 57 57.
www. crt-nordpasdecalais.fr

Paris
There are eight city tourist offices
in Paris, including:
127 av. des Champs-Élysées, 75008
Paris, ☎0892 683 000 (0.34 €/min).
www.parisinfo.com/

Picardie
3 r. Vincent-Auriol, 80011 Amiens
Cedex 1, ☎03 22 22 33 63
www.cr-picardie.fr/

Provence

Provence-Alpes-Côte d'Azur
Les Docks, Atrium 10.5, 10 pl. de la
Joliette, BP 46214, 13567 Marseille
Cedex 02, ☎04 91 56 47 00.
www.crt-paca.fr

International Visitors

EMBASSIES AND CONSULATES

Australia: Embassy, 4 rue Jean-Rey,
75015 Paris, ☎01 40 59 33 00,
Fax 01 40 59 33 10
www.france.embassy.gov.au

Canada: Embassy, 35 avenue Montaigne, 75008 Paris, ☎01 44 43 29 00,
Fax 01 44 43 29 99
www.international.gc.ca/canada-
europa/france/

Ireland: Embassy, 12 avenue Foch,
75116 Paris, ☎01 44 17 67 00,
Fax 01 44 17 67 50
www.embassyofirelandparis.com/

New Zealand: Embassy, 7 ter rue
Léonard-de-Vinci, 75016 Paris,
☎01 45 01 43 43, Fax: 01 45 01 43 44
www.nzembassy.com

UK: Embassy, 35 rue du Faubourg
St-Honoré, 75008 Paris,
☎01 44 51 31 00, Fax: 01 44 51 41 27
www.amb-grandebretagne.fr

Consulate, 16 r. d'Anjou, 75008 Paris,
☎01 44 51 31 00.

There are UK consular representatives
in Amiens, Bordeaux, Boulogne, Calais,
Cherbourg, Clermont-Ferrand, Dun-
kerque Le Havre, Lille, Lorient, Lyon,
Marseille, Montpellier, Nantes, Nice,
St Malo, Saumur, Toulouse and Tours.

USA: Embassy, 2 ave. Gabriel, 75008
Paris, ☎01 43 12 22 22,
Fax 01 42 66 97 83
http://france.usembassy.gov/

Consulates:
2 r. St-Florentin, 75001 Paris
(tel, fax and web as above).
15 ave. d'Alsace, 67082 Strasbourg,
☎03 88 35 31 04, Fax: 03 88 24 06 95.
Pl. Varian Fry, 13086 Marseille,
☎04 91 54 92 00, Fax: 04 91 55 56 95.
7 ave. Gustave V, 06000 Nice,
☎04 93 88 89 55 , Fax: 04 93 87 07 38.

There are American Presence Posts
in Bordeaux, Lille, Lyon, Rennes and
Toulouse.

ENTRY REQUIREMENTS

Passport – EU citizens entering
France from a Schengen Agreement
EU country do not need any documents. Those coming from all other
countries (including the UK) must be
in possession of a valid national passport or recognised identity document.
In case of loss or theft, report to the
embassy or consulate and the local
police.

Visa – Not required by EU, US,
Canadian, Australia and New Zealand
citizens for a stay in France of less than
90 days. Citizens of other countries
should check with a French consulate
or travel agent. US citizens are advised
to consult travel.state.gov for entry
requirements, security and other
information including contact numbers of US embassies and consulates.
In an emergency call the **Overseas
Citizens Services** ☎1-888-407-4747
(or 202-501-4444 from overseas).

CUSTOMS REGULATIONS

In the UK, **HM Revenue and Customs** (www.hmrc.gov.uk) publishes *A Guide for Travellers* on customs regulations and duty-free allowances. The **US Customs Service**, PO Box 7407, Washington, DC 20044, ☎202-927-5580, offers a free publication *Know Before You Go*. There are no customs formalities when bringing caravans, pleasure-boats and outboard motors into France for a stay of less than six months, but a boat's registration certificate should be kept on board.

HEALTH

It is advisable to take out comprehensive travel insurance cover, as tourists receiving medical treatment in French hospitals or clinics have to pay for it themselves. **Nationals of non-EU countries** should check with their insurance companies about policy limitations. Remember to keep all receipts.

British and Irish citizens, if they are not already in possession of an EHIC (European Health Insurance Card), should apply for one before travelling to France or any other EU country. The card entitles UK residents to be substantially reimbursed after paying for any medical treatment. The card can be applied for at UK post offices, by phoning 0845 606 2030, or at www. ehic.org.uk. Details of the health care available in France and how to claim the reimbursement are published in the leaflet *Health Advice for Travellers* available from post offices.

Accessibility

The sights described in this guide most easily accessible to people of reduced mobility are indicated in the Admission times and charges by the symbol ♿.

On French TGV and Corail trains there are wheelchair spaces in 1st class carriages available to holders of 2nd-class tickets. On Eurostar and Thalys special rates are available for accompanying adults. All airports are equipped to receive physically disabled passengers. Disabled drivers may use the EU blue card for free parking. Information about accessibility is available from French disability organizations such as **Comité National Français de Liaison pour la Réadaptation des Handicapés**, 236 bis rue de Tolbiac, 75013 Paris, ☎05 53 80 66 66.

There is information for slow walkers, mature travellers and others with special needs at www.access-able.com. The guide **Michelin Camping France** indicates camp sites with facilities suitable for the physically handicapped.

GETTING THERE

By Plane

Numerous airlines, from national carriers to budget operators, fly into **Paris** several times each day. The principal airports are Roissy-Charles de Gaulle, north of the city, and the smaller Orly, south of the city. Both airports have excellent transport links into the city. Many airlines, especially on shorter-haul journeys, also operate services to **Nice**, **Lyon** and **Marseille**, as well as other provincial cities, including **Bordeaux, Mulhouse, Nantes, Toulouse, Montpellier, Perpignan** and **Nimes.**

Most North American airlines fly to Paris only, but France's regional airports are well connected to both the Parisian airports and to each other. Many have several flights a day to Paris.

Many visitors from other European countries arrive on inclusive package-tour flights with a rail or coach link-up, as well as Fly-Drive schemes. Information, brochures and timetables are available from airlines, tour operators and travel agents.

Crossing the Channel

Drivers travelling from the British Isles to France have a wide choice of **cross-Channel services**. For bookings and information, visit the operators' websites, contact them on the UK numbers given below, or ask any travel agent.

Brittany Ferries
From Cork (Ireland), Plymouth, Poole and Portsmouth to Roscoff, Cherbourg, St Malo and Caen. ☎0870 9076 103. www.brittany-ferries.com

Eurotunnel
The fastest way across the English Channel – and you don't see the water. Drive straight onto a rail shuttle that travels through the Channel Tunnel between the M20 near Folkestone (junction 11A) and the A16 near Calais (junction 42). ☎08705 35 35 35 www.eurotunnel.com

Irish Ferries
Between Rosslare (Ireland) and Cherbourg or Roscoff. ☎0818 300 400. www.irishferries.com

Norfolk Line
Low cost Dover-Dunkerque car ferries. ☎0870 870 10 20. www.norfolkline-ferries.co.uk

P&O Ferries
Car ferries between Dover and Calais. ☎08705 980 333. www.poferries.com

SeaFrance
Car ferries between Dover and Calais. ☎0871 663 2546. www.seafrance.com

Speedferries
High-speed car ferries between Dover and Boulogne. ☎0870 220 0570 www.speedferries.com

To choose the most suitable route between one of the ports along the north coast of France and your destination, use the **Michelin France Tourist and Motoring Atlas**, **Michelin map 726** (which gives travel times and mileages) or **Michelin Local Maps** (with yellow covers).

By Coach/Bus

Eurolines, together with National Express, operate regular services between all parts of the UK and towns throughout France. The main UK terminus is Victoria Coach Station, in central London.
☎08705 808080 (in UK)
www.eurolines.com

By Car

France has an excellent network of major and minor roads covering long distances, including *autoroutes* – motorways or major highways, often with a toll to pay. Note that when entering the country at a land border, you may already be driving on an *autoroute*. After a short free section, a toll may be payable.

By Train

High-speed **Eurostar** trains run many times daily from London (St Pancras International) to **Paris** (Gare du Nord) via the Channel Tunnel. Some stop at Ebbsfleet (Kent), **Frethun** (near Calais) and **Lille**. The journey from London to Paris takes an average 2hrs22min.

Fast onward rail services connect with Eurostar at Lille, or can be reached in Paris by transferring to other stations. Eurostar also operates summer-only services from London to **Disneyland Paris** and to **Avignon**, in Provence. In winter, Eurostar **ski trains** run from London direct to the French Alps. Eurostar can book onward rail services, hotels and car hire if required.

Railways within France are run by state-owned **SNCF**, who offer a range of rail passes for seniors, families, young people, and friends travelling together, as well as InterRail passes for Europe-wide travel. SNCF's subsidiary outside France is **Rail Europe**.

For bookings and information contact

Eurostar
☎08705 186 186 (or +44 1233 617 575 from outside the UK).
www.eurostar.com.

Rail Europe
In the UK
Rail Europe Travel Centre,
178 Piccadilly, London W1V 0BA
☎08708 371 371.
www.raileurope.co.uk
In the US
Rail Europe Inc.
☎1-800-438-7245
or 1-800-4-EURAIL.
www.raileurope.com

SNCF – Information and bookings in English by phone and on the internet. Or buy rail tickets at any SNCF train station in France.
☎08 36 35 35 39 (in France)
www.sncf.com.

GETTING AROUND

By Train

Rail travel is a pleasure in France, where trains are comfortable, punctual and inexpensive. A comprehensive rail network, provided by the state's rail operator SNCF, covers almost the entire country.

Their sleek, fast TGV trains operate between main towns, with door-to-door journey times that easily rival air travel, especially Paris-Lyon (2 hours) and Paris-Marseille (3 hours). TGVs must always be booked in advance, and all seats are reserved. However, it is often possible to reserve a TGV seat up to just a few minutes before the train departs.

Apart from TGVs, the main city-to-city lines are also served by other comfortable modern trains which do not require advance booking. Away from these major lines, SNCF operates a reliable stopping service within each region, including a variety of smaller trains that reach into rural areas, sometimes supplemented by SNCFs bus services.

Before booking rail tickets, be sure to enquire at the station whether you are entitled to obtain one of the many rail discount passes. For example, groups of friends travelling together, or families with a young child, may be eligible.

When first starting any journey by train, remember that rail tickets must be validated (*composter*) by using the orange automatic date-stamping machines at the platform entrance (failure to do so may result in a fine).

By Car

Driving in France should present no difficulty. For British drivers unaccustomed to driving on the right, some care may be needed at first, but the rules of the road are otherwise similar to those in other Western countries. Road signs generally use easy-to-understand international visual symbols instead of words.

DOCUMENTS

When driving a motor vehicle in France, nationals of EU countries must be in possession of their own valid **national driving licence**. Nationals of non-EU countries should obtain an **international driving permit** (or IDP). In the US, the State Department

Fuel

In France the main types of petrol (US: gasoline) are:

sans plomb 95 – unleaded 95 octane

sans plomb 98 – unleaded 98 octane

diesel/gazole – diesel

Petrol is more expensive in France than in the USA or UK. However, diesel is less expensive. The French Tourist Office issues a map showing the location of cheaper petrol stations within a mile or so of motorway exits, usually in a hypermarket complex.

has authorised the American Automobile Association and the National Auto Club to provide the international permit. To apply for an international driving permit, you must at least 18 years old, and you will need to present two passport-size photographs and your valid U.S. license. The international driving permit costs under $20.00. The international permit does not replace your own driving licence but is simply an approved translation and should be used in conjuction with your licence – both should be carried. All drivers must also have with them the vehicle's registration papers and a current insurance certificate. The originals of all documents are required. Copies are not acceptable.

😊 Speed Limits 😊

Although liable to modification these are as follows:
– toll motorways *(péage)* 130kph/80mph (110kph/68mph when raining);
– dual carriage roads and motorways without tolls 110kph/68mph (100kph/62mph when raining);
– other roads 90kph/56mph (80kph/50mph when raining) and in towns 50kph/31mph;
– outside lane on motorways during daylight, on level ground and with good visibility – minimum speed limit of 80kph/50mph.

ENFORCEMENT

Police have wide powers to check documents at any time and to impose heavy on-the-spot fines for almost all driving offences. In the case of more serious offences, especially if alcohol is involved, they may at their own discretion confiscate the vehicle. If paying an on-the-spot fine, you should be given a copy of the officer's report form, a receipt for any money paid, and information on how to proceed if you wish to plead not guilty.

In addition to carrying the correct documentation, the driver of a vehicle registered outside France is expected to display a nationality plate of approved size close to the registration plate on the back of the vehicle, unless this already forms part of the registration plate.

INSURANCE

Insurance cover is compulsory and although an International Motor Insurance Certificate (known in the UK as a green card) is no longer a legal requirement in France for vehicles registered in the UK, it is still the most effective proof of insurance cover and is internationally recognised by the police and other authorities. If you have comprehensive insurance, you may want to check that your insurance cover is unaffected by driving abroad. Some insurers wish to be informed if you intend to take your vehicle abroad. Most British insurance policies give only the minimum third-party cover required while in France – but this amounts to less than it would in the UK. Therefore check with your insurance company before leaving to ensure you are fully covered in the event of an accident.

Ensure you have adequate breakdown cover before arriving in France. UK motoring organisations, for example the **AA** and the **RAC,** offer their own accident insurance and breakdown service programmes, either on all-year basis or for temporary periods, for both members and non-members. These offer an emergency phone number in the UK, and a reliable standard of service and workmanship provided locally but approved by the organisation.

Members of the **American Automobile Association** should obtain the free brochure *Offices To Serve You Abroad*. The affiliated organisation for France is the **Automobile Club National**, 5 rue Auber, 75009 Paris, ☎ (01) 44 51 53 99.

HIGHWAY CODE

The full text of the French Highway Code can be found online at www. legifrance.gouv.fr/.

Age limits
The minimum age to drive a car in France is 18 years old.

Priorité à Droite
On all two-way roads, traffic drives on the right. The rule of *priorité à droite* also means that priority must be given – in other words, you must give way – to **all vehicles coming from the right, even from minor roads (but not private property), unless signs indicate otherwise.** The principal sign indicating that you have priority over all other roads, even those on the right, is a yellow diamond. In practice, the yellow diamond normally gives priority to traffic on all main roads outside built-up areas. Traffic within a roundabout (traffic circle) has priority over vehicles entering the roundabout, unless signs indicate otherwise.

Traffic signals
Vehicles must always stop when the lights turn red at road junctions. They may filter to the right **only where indicated by a flashing amber arrow**.

Seat belts
It is compulsory for the front-seat and back-seat passengers to wear **seat belts** where they are fitted. Children under the age of 10 should not travel in the front of the car.

Lights
Full or dipped headlights must be switched on in rain, poor visibility and at night; use sidelights only when the vehicle is stationary. Headlight beams should be adjusted for driving on the right. It is illegal to drive with faulty lights in France, so it is advisable to take a spare set of bulbs with you.

Breakdown
In the case of a **breakdown**, a red warning triangle or hazard warning lights are obligatory.

Alcohol
The regulations on **drinking and driving** are strictly enforced. The maximum permissible blood alcohol content is currently 0.50g/litre.

PARKING REGULATIONS

In most town centres parking is either prohibited or metered; tickets should be obtained from the ticket machines (*horodateurs* – small change necessary) and displayed inside the windscreen on the driver's side; failure to display may result in a heavy fine (and, in extreme cases, removal of the offending vehicle!). A common arrangement is that parking is permitted on one side of the street only. In most large towns there are "blue" parking zones (**zone bleue**), marked by a blue line on the pavement, blue lines around parking spaces, or a blue signpost with a P and a small square underneath. In this particular case motorists should display a "parking disc" which can be adjusted to display their time of arrival and which allows a stay of up to 1hr 30min (2hr 30min over lunchtime) free. These discs are on sale in supermarkets, petrol stations or local kiosks (ask for a *disque de stationnement*).

ROUTE PLANNING

The road network is excellent and includes many motorways. The roads are very busy during the holiday period (particularly weekends in July and August), and to avoid traffic congestion it is advisable to follow the recommended secondary routes (signposted as *itinéraires bis*). The motorway network includes rest areas *(aires)* every 10-15km/5-10m and service areas, with fuel, restaurant and shopping, about every 40km/25m. For 24-hour motorway information dial 01 47 05 90 01. For general information on traffic and *itinéraires bis*, contact Bison Fute, ☎0826 022 022. www.bison-fute.equipement.gouv.fr

TOLLS

In France, most motorway sections are subject to a toll *(péage)*. Tolls can be paid in cash or with a credit card (Visa, Mastercard).

CAR RENTAL

There are car hire desks at airports, railway stations and in all large towns throughout France. The cars usually have manual transmission. Those wishing to rent a car with automatic transmission must book it in advance.

The minimum age for car rental is generally 20 years, and there may be a premium payable for drivers under 25. It is relatively expensive to rent a car in France; Americans in particular will notice the difference and should consider booking a car from home before leaving, or taking advantage of Fly-Drive schemes. Those who rent a car before leaving home should make sure that they inform the car rental company that they intend to take the car to France, so that their rental contract includes insurance while abroad.

Reservation Numbers in France:

Avis: ☎08 20 05 05 05.
www.avis.com

Europcar: ☎08 25 35 83 58
www.europcar.com

Budget: ☎08 25 00 35 64
www.budget.com

Hertz: ☎01 41 91 95 25
www.hertz.com

WHERE TO STAY AND EAT

Hotel and restaurant listings fall within the *Discovering France* section of the guide; they can be found in green boxes titled **Address Books**. To enhance your stay, hotel selections have been chosen for their location, comfort, value for the money, and in many cases, their charm. Prices indicate the cost of a standard room for two people in peak season. French cuisine is as varied as it is delicious. We have highlighted an array of eating places primarily for their atmosphere, location and regional delicacies. Prices indicate the average cost of a starter, main dish and dessert for one person. The Legend on the cover flap explains the symbols and abbreviations used in the Address Books.

Where to Stay

FINDING A HOTEL

The **Address Books** *(see opposite)* in this guide describe a number of lodgings arranged by price category. They appear in many of the cities and towns described in the guide. For an even greater selection, use the **Michelin Guide France**, with its famously reliable star-rating system and hundreds of establishments throughout France. The **Michelin Charming Places to Stay** guide contains a selection of 1 000 hotels and guest houses at reasonable prices. Be sure to book ahead to ensure that you get the accommodation you want, not only in the tourist season but year round, as many towns fill up during trade fairs, arts festivals etc. Some places require an advance deposit or a reconfirmation. Reconfirming is especially important if you plan to arrive after 6pm.

For further assistance, **Loisirs Accueil** is a booking service that has offices in some French départements. Contact: *280 blvd St-Germain – 75007 Paris ☎01 44 11 10 44 – www.resinfrance.com or www.loisirsaccueilfrance.com.*

The handbook of a respected federation of good-value, family-run hotels (most with restaurants), **Logis et Auberges de France**, is available from the French Tourist Office, as are lists of other kinds of accommodation such as hotel-châteaux, bed-and-breakfasts etc. Another resource, which publishes a catalog for each French *département*, for vacation villas, apartments or chalets is the **Fédération nationale Clévacances France** *(54 bd de l'Embouchure – BP 52166 – 31022 Toulouse Cedex – ☎05 61 13 55 66 – www.clevacances.com).*

Relais et Châteaux provides information on booking in luxury hotels with character: 15 rue Galvani, 75017 Paris, ☎01 45 72 90 00.

ECONOMY CHAIN HOTELS

If you need a place to stop en route, these lodgings can be useful, as they are inexpensive (around 35-45€ for a double room) and generally located near the main road. While a simple breakfast is available, there may not be a restaurant; rooms are small and functional, with a television and bathroom. All can be booked online.

For reservations:
– Akena ☎01 69 84 85 17.
www.hotels-akena.com
– Mister Bed ☎01 46 14 38 00.
www.misterbed.fr/
– Villages Hôtel ☎03 80 60 92 70.
www.villages-hotel.com

The hotels listed below are slightly more expensive (from 45€), and offer a few more amenities and services.

For reservations:
– Campanile, Climat de France, Kyriad ☎01 64 62 46 46.
www.campanile.com
– Etap ☎0892 688 900.
www.etaphotel.com
– Ibis ☎0825 012 011.
www.ibishotel.com.

RENTING A COTTAGE, BED AND BREAKFAST

The **Maison des Gîtes de France** is an information service on self-catering accommodation in France. Gîtes usually take the form of a cottage or apartment decorated in the local style where visitors can make themselves at home, or bed and breakfast accommodation (chambres d'hôtes) which consists of a room and breakfast at a reasonable price. Contact the Gîtes de France office in Paris: 59 rue St-Lazare, 75439 Paris Cedex 09, ☎ 01 49 70 75 75, or online at www.gites-de-france. fr, which has a good English version. From the site, you can choose and book a gîte, or order catalogues for different regions illustrated with photographs of the properties, as well as specialised catalogues (bed and breakfasts, farm stays etc).

Regional sites also have information about cottages in their area, for example www.loire-valley-holidays. com, on which you can view and book cottages in the Loire Valley chateaux country and contact the local tourist offices which may have lists of more properties and local bed and breakfast establishments.

HOSTELS, CAMPING

The international youth hostels movement, International Youth Hostel Federation or Hostelling International, has dozens of hostels in France. There is an online booking service on www. iyhf.org or www.hihostels.com, which you may use to reserve rooms as far as six months in advance. To stay in hostels, you may need a membership card. To obtain an IYHF or HI card (there is no age requirement) contact the IYHF or HI in your own country for information and membership applications (in the UK ☎ 01707 324170. In the US, there are many HI centres; check the website to find your nearest). There are two main youth hostel associations (auberges de jeunesse) in France, the **Ligue Française pour les Auberges de la Jeunesse** (67 rue Vergniaud, 75013 Paris, ☎01 44 16 78 78; www.auberges-de-jeunesse.com) and the **Fédération Unie des Auberges de Jeunesse** (4 boulevard Jules-Ferry, 75011 Paris, ☎01 43 57 02 60, Fax 01 43 57 53 90).

There are thousands of officially graded **campsites** with varying standards of facilities throughout the country. The **Michelin Camping France** guide lists a selection of camp sites. It is wise to reserve in advance.

Where to Eat

FINDING A RESTAURANT

Turn to the green-coloured Address Books within the *Discovering France* section for descriptions and prices of selected places to eat in the different locations covered in this guide. The Legend on the cover flap explains the symbols and abbreviations used in these Address. Books. Use the red **Michelin Guide France**, with its respected star-rating system and hundreds of establishments all over France, for an even greater choice. If you would like to experience a meal in a highly rated restaurant from the Michelin Guide, be sure to book ahead. Restaurants usually serve lunch between noon and 2pm and dinner between 7.30 and 10pm. It is not always easy to find something to eat at other times, except for a simple baguette sandwich in a café, or an ordinary hot dish in a brasserie. In French restaurants and cafés, the service charge and all taxes are included in the price, so tipping is not necessary. However, it is usual to leave any small change from the bill on the table when leaving.

For a glossary of gastronomic terms and for information on local specialities, ♿ see the section titled Food and Drink in the Introduction.

WHAT TO SEE AND DO

France offers a wide selection of leisure activities, from spa treatments and wine tours to a variety of outdoor sports and cruises. Below are suggestions of ways to enhance your visit.

Leisure Activities

Information and brochures for all sporting, special interest and outdoor facilities may be obtained from the French Government Tourist Office or from the local tourist information centres shown within the *Discovering France* section of this guide.

WINE TOURS

In most wine-making regions, wine tours taking in the main vineyards and wineries, or *caves*, are signposted. There are also many local guided tours in wine regions. For information apply to the local Tourist Information Centre. Buying your own wine directly from the grower can be an adventurous and satisfying holiday occupation. Signs announce farm-gate sales (*vins-vente directe*) or wine tasting and sales (*dégustation vente*).

CRAFTS

Many arts-and-crafts studios (weaving, wrought iron, cooking, painting, pottery) on the coast and inland give

River Cruise

S. Sauvignier/MICHELIN

vacation courses in summer. Apply to the Tourist Information Centre.

CYCLING HOLIDAYS

Many UK tour operators organise cycle touring holidays in France, for example Susi Madron's Cycling for Softies (www.cycling-for-softies.co.uk/) and Headwater (www.headwater.com). In France, the cyclists' touring association, Fédération Française de Cyclotourisme, organises cycle tours, provides itineraries detailing distances, difficulty of the routes, and sights to visit. 12 rue Louis Bertrand 94207 Ivry-sur-Seine Cedex, ☎01 56 20 88 88. www.ffct.org

Lists of local cycle hire shops are available from the Tourist Information Centres. The main railway stations also hire out cycles which can be returned at a different station.

HIKING

Short-, medium- and long-distance footpaths network the whole country. For the nationwide system of long-distance paths, Topo-Guides are published by the Fédération Française de la Randonnée Pédestre – Comité National des Sentiers de Grande Randonnée. These give detailed maps of the paths and offer valuable information to the hiker, and are on

sale at the Information Centre: 64, rue du Dessous des Berges, 75013 Paris, www.ffrandonnee.fr.

FISHING

Current brochures: folding map *Fishing in France* (*Pêche en France*) published and distributed by the Conseil Supérieur de la Pêche, 134 avenue de Malakoff, 75016 Paris, ☎01 45 02 20 20; also available from the departmental fishing organisations.

For information about regulations contact the Tourist Information Centres or the offices of the Water and Forest Authority (Eaux et Forêts).

RIVER AND CANAL CRUISING

The extensive network of navigable waterways in France can be explored at leisure (maximum speed 6km/h). Many tour operators offer touring vacations with motor cruisers. Information on boat hire companies is available from the Féderation des Industries Nautiques, ☎33 01 44 37 04 00. www.france-nautic.com.

Charges usually include boat hire, insurance, technical assistance. Some charter companies offer bicycles which enable visitors to go shopping and for rides or excursions along the towpath or to neighbouring villages. Visitors usually operate the locks on small canals by themselves; otherwise, it is customary to give a hand to the lock-keeper.

Two publishers produce collections of guides to cruising on French canals. Both series include numerous maps and useful information and are provided with English translations. The publishers are: Grafocarte, 125 rue J.-J. Rousseau, 92130 Issy-les-Moulineaux, ☎01 41 09 19 00;

Guides Vagnon, Les Éditions du Plaisancier, 100 avenue du Général-Leclerc, 69641 Caluire Cedex, ☎04 78 23 31 14.

SAILING

Many resorts have sailing clubs offering courses. In season it is possible to hire boats with or without crew; apply to the Fédération Française de Voile: 17 rue Henri Bocquillon, 75015 Paris, ☎01 40 60 37 00. www.ffvoile.net.

CANOEING

Apply to Fédération Française de Canoe-Kayak, 87 quai de la Marne, 94340 Joinville-le-Pont, ☎01 45 11 08 50. www.ffck.org. A guide is published annually indicating schools and places where canoeing may be practised.

MOTOR BOATING AND WATER-SKIING

Enquire at local Tourist Information Centres or at resorts waterfronts. Anyone who intends to drive a powered boat (6hp – 50hp) within five nautical miles of a French harbour must qualify for a sea certificate (*carte mer*). Beyond the five nautical mile limit an additional sea permit (*permis mer*) is required. Yachts and boats with engines of less than 6hp are exempt.

WIND SURFING

The sport, which is subject to certain regulations, is permitted on lakes, seafronts and in sports and leisure centres. Apply to sailing clubs. Boards may be hired on all major beaches.

SCUBA-DIVING

Apply to the Fédération Française d'Études et de Sports Sous-Marins, 24 quai de Rive Neuve, 13007 Marseille, ☎04 91 33 99 31. www.ffessm. fr. The federation publishes *Subaqua*, a bimestrial journal on diving in France.

RIDING AND PONY TREKKING

Apply to the Comité Nationale du Tourisme Équestre, 9 Boulevard MacDonald, 75019 Paris, ☎01 53 26 15 50, ww.ffe.com, which publishes an annual handbook covering the whole of France.

GOLF

For location, addresses and telephone numbers of golf courses in France, consult the map *Golfs, les Parcours français,* published by Edition Plein Sud based on **Michelin maps.** You can also contact the Fédération Française de Golf, 68, rue Anatole France, 92 300 Levallois-Perret, ☎01 41 49 77 00, www.ffgolf.org.

SKIING

The French Alps is one of the world's major ski and winter sports areas. There is also good skiing in the French Pyrenees. For all enquiries contact the Club Alpin Français, a national federation of 174 local moutain sports associations, based at 24 avenue de Laumière, 75019 Paris, ☎01 53 72 87 00, www.ffcam.fr.

CLIMBING

Excursions with qualified instructors are organised by sections of the Club Alpin Français (see Skiing above for address for information on regional sections) or by local guides. For information apply to the Tourist Information Centres or to the Fédération Française de la Montagne et de l'Escalade, 8 quai de la Marne, 75019 Paris, ☎01 40 18 75 50, www.ffme.fr.

SPELEOLOGY

Apply to the Speleology sections of the Club Alpin Français (see under Skiing and Mountaineering).

GLIDING

Apply to the Fédération Française de Vol à voile, 29 rue de Sèvres, 75006 Paris, ☎01 45 44 04 78, www.ffvv.org/

SPA AND WELL-BEING

Spas have long been part of French life. They are gradually become less medical, more pampering. Numerous coastal and mountain resorts offer treatments.

Activities for Children

In this guide, sights of particular interest to children are indicated with a KIDS symbol (Kids). Some attractions may offer discount fees for children.

Main Tourist Resorts

Most of the resort areas listed below have a wide range of accommodation and leisure facilities and are therefore characterised only in terms of their setting or other special features.

★★**Aix-en-Provence** – 🕭 *See Index* – Spa – Casino – 18C spa complex built next to site of Roman baths.

★★**Aix-les-Bains** – Spa – Palais de Savoie Casino and Nouveau Casino – prestigious "Season" – Parks – Lakeside esplanade★ – Dr Faure Museum★.

★★**Ajaccio** – 🕭 *See Index* – Sandy beach – Casino – Place Maréchal-Foch – other beaches around Ajaccio Bay.

★**L'Alpe-d'Huez** – Mountain resort (1 860-3 350m/6 100-10 990ft) with winter sports– Lac Blanc

Summit★★★ (*by cableway and cable-car*): view of Écrins Massif and Mont Blanc – Lake Besson★ (6.5km – 4mi).

★**Amélie-les-Bains** – Spa – Casino – Restored Roman baths – Montdony Gorges.

★★★**Annecy** – 🕭 *See Index* – Swimming in lake – Lakeside★★★ – Riverside walk.

★★**Arcachon** – 🕭 *See Index* – Sandy beach – Casino – Seafront with views over Arcachon Bay.

Argelès-Gazost – Spa – Panorama of the Pyrenees.

Argelès-Plage – Casino – Sandy beach at northern end of Côte Vermeille★★.

★★**Avoriaz** – Mountain resort (winter sports).

★**Ax-les-Thermes** – Spa – Mountain resort with winter sports (1 400-2 400m/4 590-7 870ft) – Ladres Valley – Bonascre Plateau★ (View★★ of Ariège heights and Andorra mountains).

★★**Bagnères-de-Bigorre** – Spa – Casino – Salut spa complex and park★.

★★**Bagnoles-de-l'Orne** – Spa – Casino – Lake★ – Park★ – Roc-au-Chien Walk★ (in Tessé-la-Madeleine).

★**Bandol** – Sandy beach – Casino – Jean-Moulin avenue★.

Barèges – Spa – Mountain resort with winter sports (1 250-2 350m/4 100-7 710ft) – Lienz Plateau – Font d'Ayré funicular.

★★★**La Baule** – 🕭 *See Index* – Sandy beach – Thalassotherapy centre – Casino – Seafront★★ – Dryades Park★ – La-Baule-les-Pins★★.

★★**Beaulieu-sur-Mer** – Sandy beach – Casino – Villa Kerylosa (setting★) – Fourmis Bay★.

★★**Belle-Ile** – 👜 *See Index* – Thalassotherapy centre.

★**Bénodet** – Sandy beach – Casino – Pyramide lighthouse (panorama★ over Cornouaille coast and Glénan islands).

★★★**Biarritz** – 👜 *See Index* – Sandy beach with rocks – Thalassotherapy centre – Casino – La Perspective viewpoint★★ – St-Martin Point (view★) – Vierge Rock★ – Museum of the Sea★.

Le Boulou – Spa – Casino – Setting at foot of Albères Mountains.

★★**La Bourboule** – Spa – Fenestre Park★ – Charlannes Plateau.

★★**Cabourg** – Sandy beach – Casino – Marcel-Proust Promenade.

Canet-Plage – Sandy beach – Casino – Active sports centre.

★★★**Cannes** – 👜 *See Index* – Sandy beach – Fleurs Casino, Palm Beach Casino, Casino Municipal) – Boulevard de la Croisette★★ – La Croisette Point★ – Super-Cannes Observatory (panorama★★★) – La Castre Museum★.

★★**Cap-d'Antibes** – Sandy beach with rocks – Round tour★★ – La Garoupe Plateau (panorama★★) – Thuret Gardens★.

★**Capvern-les-Bains** – Spa – View of Pyrenees.

Carnac – Thalassotherapy centre.

★**Cauterets** – Spa – Mountain resort with winter sports (930-2 340m/3 050-7 680ft) – Casino Esplanade – Espagne Bridge★★ – Lutour Valley★ and Falls★★; Jeret Valley★★.

★★★**Chamonix** – 👜 *See Index* – Mountain resort with winter sports (1 035-3 842m/3 400-12 604ft) – Setting at foot of Aiguille du Midi with view of Mont-Blanc.

★★**Châtelguyon** – Spa – Casino – Prades Valley★ – Enval Gorge★.

Chaudes-Aigues – Spa – Source of the River Par – Neighbourhood saints in niches.

★**Combloux** – Mountain resort with winter sports (1 000-1 853m/3 280-6 080ft) – View★ of Mont-Blanc.

★**Contrexéville** – Spa – Casino – La Folie Lake.

★★**Courchevel** – Mountain resort with winter sports (1 300-2 700m/4 260-8 860ft) – Panorama★ – La Saulire *(cableway and cable-car)*: panorama★★.

★**Dax** – Spa – Casino – Warm springs – *9km – 6mi northeast:* Buglose (birthplace of St Vincent de Paul).

★★★**Deauville** – 👜 *See Index* – Sandy beach – Summer and Winter Casinos – Boardwalk★ (Promenade des Planches).

★**Les Deux-Alpes** – Twin mountain resorts (L'Alpe-du-Mont-de-Lans and L'Alpe-de-Venosc) with winter sports (1 650-3 560m/5 410-11 680ft) – From L'Alpe-de-Venosc: La Croix viewpoint★ and Cimes viewpoint★ *(by cableway)*.

★★**Dieppe** – 👜 *See Index* – Pebble beach – Casino – Boulevard de la Mer (view★) – Boulevard du Maréchal-Foch.

★★★**Dinard** – 👜 *See Index* – Sandy beach with rocks – Thalassotherapy centre – Casino – Moulinet Point (view★★) – Grande Plage beach★ – Clair de Lune Promenade★.

★**Divonne** – Spa – Casino – Park.

★Douarnenez – Thalassotherapy centre.

★**Enghien** – Spa – Casino – Lake★.

★★★**Évian** – Spa – Casino – English Garden.

★★**Font-Romeu** – Mountain resort with winter sports (1 850-2 204m/6 070-7 230ft) – Casino – Hermitage★ (Camaril★★) – Calvary (panorama★★ over the Cerdagne).

★★**Gérardmer** – Spa – Mountain/ forest setting – Winter sports (870-1 130m/2 850-3 710ft) – Lake★.

★★★**La Grande-Motte** – Sandy beach – Casino – Modern resort architecture.

★**Hossegor** – Sandy beach – Casino – Lakeside Promenade★.

★★**Juan-les-Pins** – Sandy beach – Casino: Eden Beach – Fine coastal setting.

★★**Luchon** – Spa – Mountain setting with winter sports at Super-Bagnères (1 420-2 260m/4 660-7 420ft) – d'Étigny avenues.

★★★**Megève** – Alpine setting with winter sports (1 067-2 350/3 510-7 710ft) – Casino – Mont d'Arbois (by cable-car): panorama★★★ over Aravis mountains and Mont-Blanc.

★★**Menton** – ♿ See Index – Pebble beach – Casino du Soleil – Promenade du Soleil★★ – Carnolès Palace Museum★.

★★**Les Menuires** – Mountain resort with winter sports (1 067-2 350m/3 500-7 710ft) – Mont de la Chambre★★

★★**Le Mont-Dore** – Spa – Mountain resort with winter sports (1 350-1 850m/4 430-6 070ft) – Casino

– Promenade des Artistes★
– Salon du Capucin (funicular).

★★★**Monte-Carlo** – ♿ See Index – Sandy beach with rocks – Grand Casino, Casino du Sporting Club, Casino Loews – Museum of Dolls and Automata★.

★★**Morzine** – Mountain setting with winter sports (1 000-2 460m/3 280-8 070ft) – Meeting point of six valleys – Le Pléney (cable-car): panorama.

★★★**Nice** – ♿ See Index – Pebble beach – Casino-club.

★**Perros-Guirec** – Sandy beach – Thalassotherapy centre – Casino – Le Château Point (view★) – Viewing table (view★) – Douaniers Path★★.

★**Plombières** – Spa – Casino – Park designed by Haussmann.

★**Pornichet** – Sandy beach – Casino – Boulevard des Océanides.

★**Propriano** – Sandy beach – Valinco Bay★.

Quiberon – Sandy beach with rocks – Thalassotherapy centre – Casino – Côte Sauvage★★.

★★★**La Rochelle** – ♿ See Index – Sandy beach – Casino.

★**Roscoff** – ♿ See Index – Thalassotherapy centre – Sandy beaches with some pebbles – Aquarium★ – Notre-Dame-de-Kroaz-Betz Church★ (Belfry★, alabaster statues★).

★★**Royan** – Sandy beach – Casino (at Pontaillac) – Seafront★ – Notre-Dame Church★.

★★**Royat** – Spa – Casino – Set among foothills of Monts Dômes – Spa Park and Bargoin Park

★★**Les Sables-d'Olonne** – Sandy beach – Casino de la Plage

– Casino des Sports – Remblai promenade★ – Fishermen's quarter.

★★**St-Cast-le-Guildo** – Sandy beach – St-Cast Point (view★★) – La Garde Point (view★★).

★★**St-Gervais** – Spa – Mountain resort with winter sports (850-2 350m/2 790-7 710ft) – Bettex scenic route★★★ – Eagle's Nest and Bionassay glacier★★ (Mont-Blanc mountain railway).

★★**St-Jean-de-Luz** – *See Index* – Sandy beach – Casino.

★★★**St-Malo** – *See Index* – Sandy beach – Thalassotherapy centre – Casino.

★★**St-Nectaire** – *See Index* – Spa.

★**St-Raphaël** – Sandy beach – Casino – Sheltered setting at foot of Esterel Massif – Seafront.

St-Trojan – Sandy beach – Pinetum.

★★**St-Tropez** – *See Index* – Sandy beach – Harboura and quaysides – L'Annonciade Museum★★ – View★ from harbour wall – View★ from citadel.

★**Ste-Maxime** – Sandy beach – Casino – Panorama★ from semaphore.

★**Serre-Chevalier** – Winter sports.

★**Super-Lioran** – Mountain resort with winter sports (1 160-1 830m/3 810-6 000ft) – Plomb du Cantal★ *(cable-car)*: panorama★★.

★★**Talloires** – Bathing in the lake – Lakeside setting★★★ (Petit Lac d'Annecy).

★★**Thonon** – Spa.

★★★**Le Touquet-Paris-Plage** – *See Index* – Sandy beach – La Forêt and Quatre Saisons Casinos – Seafront promenade – Woodland – Lighthouse (view★★).

★★**Trégastel** – Sandy beach – Rocky coastline of the Breton Corniche★ – White Shore (La Grève blanche) footpath★.

★★**Trouville** – Sandy beach – Casino – Corniche road★ – Boardwalk (Promenade des Planches).

★★**Le Val-André** – Sandy beach – Casino – Pléneuf Pointa (View★★) – Promenade de la Guette★.

★★★**Val-d'Isère** – Mountain resort with winter sports (1 850-3 450m/6 070-11 320ft) – Rocher de Bellevarde *(cable-car)*: panorama★★★ – Tête du Solaise *(cable-car)*: panorama★★.

★★**Val-Thorens** – Mountain resort with winter sports (1 067-3 200m/7 546-10 499ft) – Cime de Carona★ (by cable-car).

★★★**Vichy** – *See Index* – Spa – Élysée Palace Casino, Grand Casino – Sources Park★ – Allier Park★.

★**Villard-de-Lans** – Mountain resort with winter sports (1 050-2 170m/3 450-7 120ft) – Vercors Regional Park setting – Bourne Gorge★★★.

★★★**Vittel** – Spa – Casino – Landscape park★.

The Islands of France

See also **Michelin Green Guides** to: *Normandy, Brittany, French Atlantic Coast, Provence, French Riviera, and Corse (in French)*.
France has an extensive coastline (2 700km - 1 678mi) along which are dotted idyllic islands, some as small as a field and others very large – Corsica is three times the size of a small country such as the Grand Duchy of Luxembourg. The islands are perfect destinations for a change of scenery and pace; their isolation as well as an air of mystery and charm add to the fascination of a way of life shaped by the sea.

The list below includes the principal islands ranging from north to south and west to east.

ÎLES DU PONANT

(English Channel-Atlantic Ocean)

Îles Chausey★: *65ha - 0.25sq mi* at high tide attached to **Granville**.

Île de Bréhat★: *318ha - 1.2sq mi; 10min* crossing from **Arcouest** near **Paimpol**.

Île de Batz: *357ha - 1.4sq mi; 15min* crossing from **Roscoff.**

Île d'Ouessant★★: the westernmost island off the Atlantic coast. *1 558ha - 6sq mi, highest point 60m - 197ft; 2hr 30min* crossing from **Brest** or *1hr 30min* from **Conquet**.

Île de Molène: *100ha - 0.38sq mi; 30min* crossing from **Pointe St-Matthieu.**

Île de Sein: *50ha - 0.19sq mi, highest point 6m - 20ft; 1hr* crossing from **Audierne.**

Îles de Glénan: a group of 10 islets, mostly uninhabited, attached to **Fouesnant**.

Île de Groix★: *1 770ha - 7sq mi, highest point 49m - 160ft; 45min* crossing from **Lorient.**

Îles du Golfe de Morbihan★★: Among the string of islets in the bay, the most noteworthy are **Île-aux-Moines**★, *310ha - 1.2sq mi*, and **Île d'Arz**, *324ha - 1.25sq mi.*

Belle-Île-en-Mer★★: *8 400ha - 48sq mi; 1hr* crossing from **Quiberon.**

Île d'Houat: *288ha - 1sq mi; 1hr* crossing from **Quiberon**.

Île d'Hoedic: *209ha - 0.8sq mi; 1hr 30min* crossing from **Quiberon** via **Houat.**

Île d'Yeu★★: *2 300ha - 9sq mi;* this island is the farthest from the mainland; *1hr 15min* crossing from **Fromentine.**

Île d'Aix★: *129ha - 0.5sq mi; 20min* crossing from **Fouras**.

Île de Noirmoutier, Île de Ré★ and **Île d'Oléron**★: These are linked to the mainland by a road bridge.

ÎLES DU LEVANT

(Mediterranean Sea)

Archipel du Frioul: Île de Pomègues and **Île Ratonneau** linked by Frioul harbour, **Îlot d'If**★★: *1hr 30min* excursion from **Marseille**.

Îles des Calanques: Maire, Jarre, Calseraigne, Riou are great spots for underwater fishing.

Île de Bendor★: *7min* from **Bandol**.

Îles d'Hyères★★★: **Porquerolles**★★★, *1 254ha - 5sq mi, 20min crossing from Giens; Port-Cros*★★, *640ha - 2.5sq mi, 45min* crossing from **Port-de-Miramar**; **Île du Levant**, *996ha - 3.8sq mi, 35min* crossing from **Le Lavandou.**

Îles de Lérins★★: **St-Honorat**★★, *60ha - 0.2sq mi;* **Ste-Marguerite**★★, *210ha - 0.8sq mi, 30min* crossing from **Cannes** or **Juan-les-Pins.**

Îles Sanguinaires★★: *60min* crossing from **Ajaccio.**

Îles Lavezzia: *30min* crossing from **Bonifacio.**

Calendar of Events

This list includes a selection of festivals and events likely to be of interest to the visitor, further details of which can be obtained from the telephone numbers shown after the name of the town.

RELIGIOUS AND CIVIC FESTIVALS

FEBRUARY

Nice ☎04 93 87 16 28, Carnival

Chalon-sur-Saône ☎03 85 48 39 79, Carnival, Winter Fur and Pelt Fair

Menton ☎04 92 10 76 76, Lemon Festival

Le Touquet ☎02 21 99 05 43, Motorbike Race along the beach

MAUNDY THURSDAY

Le Puy-en-Velay ☎04 71 09 38 41, White Penitents Procession

Saugues ☎04 71 77 84 46, White Penitents Procession (at nightfall)

GOOD FRIDAY

Arles-sur-Tech ☎04 68 39 11 99, Black Penitents Procession

Burzet ☎04 75 94 41 03, The Passion re-enacted

Collioure ☎04 68 82 15 47, Penitents Procession

Perpignan ☎04 68 66 30 30, Black Penitents Procession

Roquebrune-Cap-Martin ☎04 93 35 62 87, Procession of the Entombment of Christ

Sartène ☎04 95 77 05 11, U Catenacciu Procession

EASTER SUNDAY

St-Benoît-sur-Loire ☎02 38 35 72 43, Easter Service

EASTER MONDAY

Cassel ☎03 28 42 40 13, Carnival of the Giants Reuze-Papa and Reuze-Maman

APRIL

Chartres ☎02 37 21 54 03, Students' Pilgrimage

Gérardmer ☎03 29 63 00 80, Flower Festival

EARLY MAY

Orléans ☎02 38 79 23 86, Joan of Arc Festival

MID-MAY

St-Tropez ☎04 94 97 45 21, Procession in honour of St-Tropez (Bravade)

Tréguier ☎02 96 92 30 19, Pardon of St-Ives

Mont-St-Michel ☎02 33 60 14 30, Feast of St Michael in Spring

LATE MAY

Rouen ☎02 35 74 41 77, Joan of Arc Festival

Pomarez ☎05 58 89 33 32

Les Stes-Maries-de-la-Mer ☎04 90 47 82 55, Gypsy Pilgrimage

WHITSUN (PENTECOTE)

Honfleur ☎02 31 89 23 30, Seamen's Festival

EARLY JUNE

La Rochelle ☎05 46 44 62 44, International Regatta

Utah Beach-Omaha Beach ☎02 33
41 31 18, Commemoration of the
D-Day Landings (American sector)

Gold-Juno-Sword ☎02 31 86 53 30,
Commemoration of the D-Day
Landings (Anglo-Canadian sector).
*The two events are combined every
five years.*

MID-JUNE

Chambord ☎02 47 55 09 16,
Game Fair

Le Mans ☎03 43 40 24 24,
24-hour car race

EARLY JULY

Douai ☎03 27 88 26 76, Carnival of
the Giant Gayant and his family

MID-JULY

Carcassonne ☎04 68 25 07 04,
Illumination of the City

LATE JULY

Ste-Anne-d'Auray ☎02 97 57 68 80,
Great Pardon of Ste-Anne

EARLY AUGUST

Bayonne ☎05 59 59 31 31,
Corrida and Street Festival

Colmar ☎03 89 20 25 50,
Alsatian Wine Festival

MID-AUGUST

Béziers ☎04 67 36 73 73, Feria

Carcassonne ☎04 68 25 07 04,
Medieval Festival

Chamonix ☎04 50 53 00 88,
Mountain Guides Festival

Pomarez ☎05 58 89 33 32,
Running of the Cows

St-Palais ☎05 59 65 95 77,
Basque Festival

LATE AUGUST

Boulogne-sur-Mer ☎03 21 31 68 38,
Pilgrimage to Notre-Dame-de-
Boulogne

Concarneau ☎02 98 97 01 44,
Festival of the Blue Nets

Monteux ☎04 90 66 33 96,
Fireworks Festival

EARLY SEPTEMBER

Dinan ☎02 96 39 22 43, Ramparts
Festival (every two years)

Lille ☎03 20 30 81 00,
Grand jumble sale

Le Mas Soubeyran ☎04 66 85 02 72,
National Protestant Assembly

LATE SEPTEMBER

Mont-St-Michel ☎02 33 60 14 30,
Feast of the Archangel St Michael

MID-NOVEMBER

Beaune ☎03 80 22 24 51, Auction
sale of the wines of the Hospices
de Beaune

EARLY DECEMBER

Marseille ☎04 91 54 91 11,
Santons Fair

Mont-Ste-Odile ☎03 88 95 80 53,
Pilgrimage (the most important
in Alsace)

Strasbourg ☎03 88 52 28 28,
Christmas Market

DECEMBER 25

Les-Baux-de-Provence ☎04 90 97
34 39, Shepherds' Midnight Mass
Son et Lumière in the Loire Valley

Amboise ☎02 47 57 14 47,
"At The Court of King François"

Azay-le-Rideau ☎02 47 45 42 04,
"The Imaginary World of the
Château d'Azay-le-Rideau"

Blois ☎02 54 78 72 76,
"The Story of Blois"

Chenonceau ☎02 47 23 90 07,
"The Ladies of Chenonceau"

Cheverny ☎02 54 42 69 03,
"The River Loire down the ages"

Loches ☎02 47 59 07 98,
"The Strange Story of Bélisane"

Le Lude ☎02 43 94 60 09,
"Spectacular Historical Events"

Valençay ☎02 54 00 04 42,
"Esclarmonde"

CULTURAL FESTIVALS

Some of the more important annual
festivals around the country. Book
accommodation well in advance at
festival times, even out of season:

AIX-EN-PROVENCE

☎ 04 42 17 34 00, **July,** International
music Festival

ALBI

☎ 05 63 54 22 30, **June,** Theatre;
July, Music

ARLES

☎ 04 90 96 76 06, **2nd week July,**
International Photo Festival

AVIGNON

☎ 04 90 82 67 08, **2nd fortnight
July,** Dramatic art

BELFORT

☎ 03 84 54 24 24, **late November,**
Cinema

BELLAC

☎ 05 55 68 10 44, **late June/early
July,** Drama, music

BESANÇON

☎ 03 81 80 73 26, **September,** Classical music-Young
Conductors Competition

BÉZIERS

☎ 04 67 36 73 73, **1st fortnight
in July,** Classical music

BOURGES

☎ 02 48 70 61 11, **late April/early
May,** Music Festival

CANNES

☎ 04 42 66 92 20, **May,**
International Film Festival

CARCASSONNE

☎ 04 68 25 33 13, **July,**
Theatre, music and dance

CARPENTRAS

☎ 04 90 63 46 35, **2nd fortnight
in July,** Music and dance

LA CHAISE-DIEU

☎ 04 71 00 01 16, **late August/early
September,** Religious music

CHARTRES

☎ 02 37 21 54 03, **July and August,**
Religious music

CHAUMONT-SUR-LOIRE

☎ 02 54 20 99 22, **all summer,**
International Garden Festival

DEAUVILLE

1st fortnight in September,
American film Festival

DIVONNE

☏ 04 50 40 34 16, **2nd fortnight in June,** Chamber music

ENTRECASTEAUX

☏ 04 94 04 42 86, **2nd fortnight in August,** Chamber music

ÉVIAN

☏ 04 50 75 04 26, **mid-May,** Music

GANNAT

☏ 04 70 90 12 67, **2nd fortnight in July,** International folk music

JUAN-LES-PINS

☏ 04 93 33 95 64, **2nd fortnight in July,** World Jazz Festival

LANNION

☏ 02 96 37 07 35, **mid-July/late August,** Organ and choral music

LILLE

☏ 03 20 52 74 23, **October-November,** Music, dance and theatre

LORIENT

☏ 02 97 21 24 29, **early August,** Celtic festival

LYON

☏ 04 72 40 26 26, **2nd fortnight in September,** even years: dance; odd years: music and modern art

MONTAUBAN

☏ 05 63 63 60 60, **early August,** Choreography

MONTESQUIEU-VOLVESTRE

☏ 05 61 90 19 55, **mid August,** British Film Festival

NANTES

☏ 02 40 47 04 51, **early July,** Folkways

ORANGE

☏ 04 90 34 24 24, **2nd fortnight in July,** Music and opera

PAU

☏ 05 59 27 85 80, **mid-June/mid-July,** Theatre, music and dance

PRADES

☏ 04 68 96 33 07, **late July/mid-August,** Chamber music (Festival Pablo Casals)

LE PUY-EN-VELAY

☏ 04 71 09 38 41, **mid-September,** Renaissance Festival

QUIMPER

☏ 02 98 55 53 53, **4th Sunday in July,** Cornouaille Festival

RENNES

☏ 02 99 30 38 01, **early July,** Theatre, music, dance and poetry

ST-CÉRÉ

☏ 05 65 38 29 08, **mid-July/late August,** Music

ST-DONAT-SUR-L'HERBASSE

☏ 04 75 45 10 29, **late July/early August,** Bach Festival

ST-GUILHEM-LE-DÉSERT

☏ 04 67 63 14 99, **July/August,** Baroque Music

ST-MALO

☏ 02 99 40 42 50, **late October,** Comics Festival

ST-RÉMY-DE-PROVENCE

☏ 04 90 92 16 31, **mid-July/mid-September,** Organ music

SALON-DE-PROVENCE

☏ 04 90 42 12 12, **July,** Jazz/Rock

SARLAT

☏ 05 53 31 10 83, **late July/early August,** Theatre

SCEAUX

☏ 01 46 60 07 79, **mid-July/late September,** Classical music

TOULOUSE

☏ 05 61 11 02 22, **late June/late August,** Classical, Jazz and Folk Music

VAISON-LA-ROMAINE

☏ 04 90 36 12 92, **July and August,** Theatre and dance-Folklore

VANNES

☏ 02 97 47 24 34, **15 August,** Arvor Festival (folk music)

VERSAILLES

☏ 01 39 50 36 22, **May to October every Sunday,** Fountain display with music

☏ 01 39 50 36 22, **2 weekends July 2,** weekends, Illuminations of the Neptune Basin, fireworks display and fountain display with music

Shopping

OPENING HOURS

Ordinary shop hours in towns and villages are typically Tue-Sat 0900-1200 or 1230, 1500-1900. Note that they are closed on both Sunday and Monday. The lunch break is often longer in the South. Food shops may open earlier in the morning, but later in the afternoon, and some, especially bakeries, pastry shops (*pâtisseries*) and grocery stores, open on Sun am. In resorts shops may keep longer hours and stay open all day, seven days a week. Department stores are open Monday to Saturday, Mon-Sat 0900-18.30 (often with one or more later evenings per week). Hypermarkets are usually open until Mon-Sat 0900-2200.

WHAT YOU CAN TAKE HOME

There are no limits on the value of goods EU residents may take home from France, provided everything is for personal use. However, in the UK, HM Revenue and Customs attempt to limit the amount of alcohol and tobacco considered reasonable for personal use. These are: 3200 cigarettes, 200 cigars, 110 litres of beer, 90 litres of wine, 10 litres of spirits and 20 litres of fortified wine. More information at http://www.hmrc.gov.uk.
Anyone entering the USA cannot bring food and plant products. Americans are allowed to take home, tax-free, up to US$800 worth of goods, Canadians up to CND$750, Australians up to AUS$900 and New Zealanders up to NZ$700.

MARKETS

When travelling around France make sure you have a look around the different local markets – an important domestic institution – or the various agricultural fairs which are held regularly throughout the year.

VALUE-ADDED TAX

In France a sales tax (*TVA* or VAT) is added to all purchases. For non-EU residents (if aged over 15 years, and spending less than 6 months in France), this tax can be refunded as long as you have bought more than €175 worth of goods at the same time and in the same shop, and have completed the appropriate *Bordereau* form at the shop. The amount permitted may vary from time to time, so it is advisable to check first with the VAT-refund counter (*service de détaxe*). Present the *Bordereau* forms to Customs officials on leaving France for processing. Customs Information Centre: ☏ 08 25 30 82 63 or www.douane.gouv.fr.

Books

Some titles mentioned below may be out of print, but should be easily obtained through public libraries or online booksellers.

Politics and History

France in the New Century: Portrait of a Changing Society by John Ardagh *(Penguin 2001)*
> An acclaimed overview of the political landscape, by one of the most respected commentators on French life.

The French by T Zeldin *(Collins Harvill 1997)*
> A perceptive and entertaining look at the character of this enigmatic nation.

Searching for the New France by J Hollifield and G Ross *(Routledge 1998)*
> Why France is so anxious about its identity, its role and its future.

Betrayal: France, the Arabs and the Jews by David Pryce-Jones *(Encounter Books 2006)*
> How France's relations with the Arab world have led it into trouble.

Horrible Histories: France by Terry Deary (Author), Martin Brown (Illustrator) *(Scholastic Hippo 2002)*
> A comical cartoon summary of French history.

Culture

The Lost World of the Impressionists by A Bellony-Rewald *(Bulfinch Press 1988)*
> Beautiful art collection evocatively recapturing the past.

French Architecture by P Lavedan *(Penguin 1977)*
> The leading work on the development of the French style.

Touring

Exploring Rural France by Andrew Sanger *(A&C Black 1994)*
> Itineraries for off-the-beaten-track tourists.

The Wines and Winelands of France – Geological Journeys by L Pomerol *(Seven Hills Books 1989)*
> What lies behind the extraordinary diversity of the French wine list.

Green Guide to the Wine Regions of France by Michelin *(2007)*
> All you need to explore, visit, and taste your way around the country.

1000 Charming Hotels and Guesthouses by Michelin *(2005)*
> An appealing selection of places to stay.

Films

La Route Napoléon *(1953)*.
> Villagers in the Provence backcountry play along when a hotel claims the Emperor stopped there.

La Grande Illusion *(1937)*
> Prisoners of war strike up an unlikely friendship as they try to escape over the mountains.

Les Vacances de Monsieur Hulot, *Monsieur Hulot's Holidays (1951)*.
> Tati's gentle and comic view of the conventions of a respectable seaside resort in Brittany.

Au Revoir les Enfants (1988)
True story of a Catholic school which hides a Jewish boy from the Nazis. The name means "Goodbye children."

La Règle du Jeu (1939)
Renoir's classic on bourgeois France, set in a French château.

Les Misérables (1998)
Based on Victor Hugo's novel about a convict's struggle to redeem himself.

Germinal (1993)
The miners in a 19th-century northern town go on strike.

To Catch a Thief (1956); **Pierrot le Fou** (1965); **And God Created Woman** (1956)
Three great classic films set on the Riviera.

French Kiss (1995)
Comic romance as a Canadian out to save her marriage plans and a petty crook who is using her travel to Cannes together.

Les Parapluies de Cherbourg (1963)
Director J. Demy's remarkable love triangle set in this French port, in which every word is sung!

La Haine (1995)
Violence and racism as three youths – one black, one a Jew, one an Arab – get involved in riots in the Paris suburbs.

Le Fabuleux destin d'Amélie Poulain (2001)
Touching and lighthearted adventures of the naive Amélie as she looks for love in Paris.

Jean de Florette and **Manon des Sources** (1986)
Two peasants in rural Provence outwit the new owner of the neighbouring property. In the second movie, his death is poignantly avenged by his daughter Manon.

Le Retour de Martin Guerre (1982)
No one is sure of his identity when long-lost Martin returns to the village – not even his 'wife'.

Les Petites Vacances (2007)
Grandmother kidnaps the children and takes them on a crazy 'holiday' in the Alps.

USEFUL WORDS AND PHRASES

SIGHTS

abbaye	abbey
beffroi	belfry
chapelle	chapel
château	castle
cimetière	cemetery
cloître	cloisters
cour	courtyard
couvent	convent
écluse	lock (canal)
église	church
fontaine	fountain
halle	covered market
jardin	garden
mairie	town hall
maison	house
marché	market
monastère	monastery
moulin	windmill
musée	museum
parc	park
place	square
pont	bridge
port	port/harbour
porte	gateway
quai	quay
remparts	ramparts
rue	street
statue	statue
tour	tower

NATURAL SITES

abîme	chasm
aven	swallow-hole
barrage	dam
belvédère	viewpoint
cascade	waterfall
col	pass
corniche	ledge
côte	coast, hillside
forêt	forest
grotte	cave
lac	lake
plage	beach
rivière	river
ruisseau	stream
signal	beacon
source	spring
vallée	valley

ON THE ROAD

car park	parking
driving licence	permis de conduire
east	Est
garage (for repairs)	garage
left	gauche
motorway/highway	autoroute
north	Nord
parking meter	horodateur
petrol/gas	essence
petrol/gas station	station essence
right	droite
south	Sud
toll	péage
traffic lights	feu tricolore
tyre	pneu
west	Ouest
wheel clamp	sabot
zebra crossing	passage clouté

TIME

today	aujourd'hui
tomorrow	demain
yesterday	hier
winter	hiver
spring	printemps
summer	été
autumn/fall	automne
week	semaine
Monday	lundi
Tuesday	mardi
Wednesday	mercredi
Thursday	jeudi
Friday	vendredi
Saturday	samedi
Sunday	dimanche

NUMBERS

0	zéro
1	un
2	deux
3	trois
4	quatre
5	cinq
6	six
7	sept
8	huit
9	neuf
10	dix
11	onze
12	douze
13	treize
14	quatorze
15	quinze
16	seize
17	dix-sept
18	dix-huit
19	dix-neuf
20	vingt
30	trente
40	quarante
50	cinquante
60	soixante
70	soixante-dix
80	quatre-vingt
90	quatre-vingt-dix
100	cent
1000	mille

SHOPPING

bank	banque
baker's	boulangerie
big	grand
butcher's	boucherie
chemist's	pharmacie
closed	fermé
cough mixture	sirop pour la toux
cough sweets	cachets pour la gorge
entrance	entrée
exit	sortie
fishmonger's	poissonnerie
grocer's	épicerie
newsagent, bookshop	librairie
open	ouvert
post office	poste
push	pousser

pull	tirer
shop	magasin
small	petit
stamps	timbres

FOOD AND DRINK

beef	bœuf
beer	bière
butter	beurre
bread	pain
breakfast	petit-déjeuner
cheese	fromage
dessert	dessert
dinner	dîner
fish	poisson
fork	fourchette
fruit	fruits
glass	verre
chicken	poulet
ice cream	glace
ice cubes	glaçons
ham	jambon
knife	couteau
lamb	agneau
lunch	déjeuner
lettuce salad	salade
meat	viande
mineral water	eau minérale
mixed salad	salade composée
orange juice	jus d'orange
plate	assiette
pork	porc
restaurant	restaurant
red wine	vin rouge
salt	sel
spoon	cuillère
sugar	sucre
vegetables	légumes
water	de l'eau
white wine	vin blanc
yoghurt	yaourt

TRAVEL

airport	aéroport
credit card	carte de crédit
customs	douane
passport	passeport
platform	voie
railway station	gare
shuttle	navette
suitcase	valise
train ticket	billet de train
plane ticket	billet d'avion
wallet	portefeuille

CLOTHING

coat	manteau
jumper	pull
raincoat	imperméable
shirt	chemise
shoes	chaussures
socks	chaussettes
stockings	bas
suit	costume
tights	collants
trousers	pantalon

COMMON WORDS

goodbye	au revoir
hello/good morning	bonjour
how	comment
excuse me	excusez-moi
thank you	merci
yes/no	oui/non
I am sorry	pardon
why	pourquoi
when	quand
please	s'il vous plaît

USEFUL PHRASE

Do you speak English?.. Parlez-vous anglais?

I don't understand.. Je ne comprends pas

Talk slowly.. Parlez lentement

Where's...?.. Où est...?

When does the ... leave?.. A quelle heure part...?

When does the ... arrive?.. A quelle heure arrive...?

When does the museum open?.. A quelle heure ouvre le musée?

When is the show?..A quelle heure est la représentation?

When is breakfast served?.. A quelle heure sert-on le petit-déjeuner?

What does it cost? .. Combien cela coûte?

Where can I buy a newspaper in English? .. Où puis-je acheter un journal en anglais?

Where is the nearest petrol/gas station? .. Où se trouve la station essence la plus proche?

Where can I change traveller's cheques?.. Où puis-je échanger des **traveller's cheques?**

Where are the toilets?..Où sont les toilettes?
Do you accept credit cards?..Acceptez-vous vos les cartes de crédit?

♿*See Food and Drink in the Introduction.*

BASIC INFORMATION

Business Hours

Offices and other businesses are open Mon-Fri 0900-1200, 1400-1800. Many also open Saturday mornings. Town and village shops are generally closed Monday. There are many local variations. Midday breaks may be much longer in the South. However, in cities, tourist centres or resorts, businesses may keep longer hours or stay open all day, seven days a week, especially if they primarily serve the tourist.

Electricity

The electric current is 220 volts. Circular two-pin plugs are the rule. Adapters should be bought before you leave home; they are on sale in most airports.

Emergencies

♿*See Telephones in this section for a list of emergency numbers.* First aid, medical advice and chemists' night-service rotas are available from chemists/drugstores (*pharmacie* identified by a green cross sign).
All prescription drugs taken into France should be clearly labelled; it is recommended to carry a copy of prescriptions.
American Express offers its cardholders a service, "Global Assist", for any medical, legal or personal emergency: ☎01 47 16 25 29.

Post/Mail

Look for the bright yellow *La Poste* signs. Main post offices open Monday to Friday from 8am to 7pm, Saturday from 8am to noon. Smaller branch post offices generally close at lunchtime between noon and 2pm and finish for the day at 4pm. There are often automatic tellers (*guichets automatiques)* inside which allow you to weigh packages and buy postage and avoid a line. You may also find that you can use a Minitel, change money, make copies, send faxes and make phone calls in a post office. To mail a letter from the street look for the bright yellow post boxes. Stamps are also sold in newsagents and cafés that sell cigarettes (*tabac*). Stamp collectors should ask for *timbres de collection* in any post office (there is often a *philatélie* counter). France uses a five-digit postal code that precedes the name of the city or town on the last line of the address. The first two digits indicate the *département* and the last three digits identify the *commune* or local neighborhood. www.laposte.fr.

Airmail Postage Rates to:

UK: letter (20g) 0.50€;

North America: letter (20g) or postcard 0.90€;

Australia and New Zealand: letter (20g) or postcard 0.90€.

Money

CURRENCY

There are no restrictions on the amount of currency visitors can take into France. Visitors wishing to export currency in foreign banknotes in excess of the given allocation from France should complete a currency declaration form on arrival.

Coins and notes – The unit of currency in France is the **euro** (€). One euro is divided into 100 cents or *centimes d'euro*. Old franc notes can still be exchanged by the Banque de France until early 2012.

BANKS AND CURRENCY EXCHANGE

Banks are generally open from 9am to 4.30pm (smaller branches may close for lunch) and are closed on Monday or Saturday (except if market day). Some branches are open for limited transactions on Saturday. Banks close early on the day before a bank holiday. A passport or other ID may be necessary when cashing cheques (travellers' or ordinary) in banks. Commission charges vary and hotels usually charge considerably more than banks for cashing cheques, especially for non-residents.

By far the most convenient way of obtaining French currency is the **24-hr cash dispenser** or ATM (*distributeur automatique de billets* in French), found outside many banks and post offices and easily recognisable by the CB (Carte Bleue) logo. Most accept international credit cards (don't forget your PIN) and almost all also give instructions in English. Note that American Express cards can be used only in dispensers operated by the Crédit Lyonnais bank or by American Express. Foreign currency can also be exchanged in major banks, post offices, hotels or private exchange offices found in main cities and near popular tourist attractions.

CREDIT CARDS

American Express, Visa, Mastercard/Eurocard and Diners Club are widely accepted in shops, hotels, restaurants and petrol stations (however, pay-at-the-pump automatic gas stations normally only accept cards issued by French banks – foreign cards cannot be used.

If your card is lost or stolen call the appropriate 24-hour hotlines:

American Express
☏ (01) 47 77 72 00
Visa ☏ (08) 36 69 08 80
Mastercard/Eurocard
☏ (01) 45 67 84 84
Diners Club ☏ (01) 49 06 17 50

You should also report any loss or theft to the local police who will issue you with a certificate (useful proof to show the credit card company).

Telephones

The telephone system in France is still operated largely by the former state monopoly France Télécom. They offer an English-language enquiries service on 0800 364 775 (within France) or 00 33 1 55 78 60 56 (from outside France). The French **ringing tone** is a series of long tones; the engaged (busy) tone is a series of short beeps.

To use a **public phone** you need to buy a prepaid phone card (*télécartes*). Some telephone booths accept credit cards (Visa, Mastercard/Eurocard). *Télécartes* (50 or 120 units) can be bought in post offices, cafés that sell cigarettes *(tabac)* and newsagents, and can be used to make calls in France and abroad. Calls can be received at phone boxes where the blue bell sign is shown.

MOBILE/CELL PHONES

While in France, all visitors from other European countries should be able to use their cell phone just as normal. Visitors from some other countries notably the US, need to ensure before departure that their phone and service contract are compatible with the European system (GSM).

All the charges are given in the 'welcome' message you will receive on using your phone for the first time in France. The three main mobile phone operators in France are SFR, Orange and Bouygues.

If you do not have your cell phone with you, or you discovered it would not be compatible with the European system, depending on the length of your visit and on how often you plan on using the phone, it may be wise to consider buying or renting one with a coverage plan that fits your needs. There are a variety of options you can choose from making it less expensive than you might imagine.

Orange www.orange.com
Bouygues www.bouyguestelecom.fr
SFR www.sfr.com

NATIONAL CALLS

French telephone numbers have 10 digits. Numbers begin with 01 in Paris and the Paris region; 02 in northwest France; 03 in northeast France; 04 in southeast France and Corsica; 05 in southwest France. However, all 10 numbers must be dialled even with the local region. .

INTERNATIONAL CALLS

To call France from abroad, dial the country code 33, omit the initial zero of the French number, and dial the remaining 9-digit number. When calling abroad from France dial 00, followed by the country code (see below), followed by the local area code (usually without any initial zero), and the number of your correspondent.

International dialling codes:
Australia: 61
Eire: 353
United Kingdom: 44
Canada: 1
New Zealand: 64
United States: 1

Emergency Numbers
Police: 17
Fire (Pompiers): 18
Ambulance (SAMU): 15

International information, UK ☏00 33 12 44

International information, USA/Canada ☏00 33 12 11

International operator ☏00 33 12 + country code

Local directory assistance ☏12

To use the personal calling card of a telephone company, follow the instructions on the card, dialling the access code for the country you are in, eg: :
AT&T ☏0 800 99-0011
BT ☏0 800 99-0244
MCI/Verizon ☏0 800 99-0019
Sprint ☏0 800 99-0087
Canada Direct ☏0 800 99-0016

Cheap rates with 50% extra time are available from private telephones to the UK on weekdays between 9.30pm and 8am, from 2pm on Saturdays and all day on Sundays and holidays. Cheap rates to the USA and Canada are from 2am to noon all week, and to Australia between 9.30pm and 8am Monday to Saturday and all day Sunday.

Toll-free numbers in France (also known as Numero Verte) begin with 0800.

For more information about using the phone in France, see www.francetelecom.fr/en

Smoking Regulations

In February 2007, France banned smoking in public places such as offices, universities and railway stations. The law will become effective for restaurants, cafés, bars, nightclubs and casinos in January 2008.

Time

France is in the Central European time zone. During the winter months, from 0200 on the last Sunday in October to 0200 on the last Sunday in March, France is one hour ahead of GMT. From 0200 on the last Sunday in March to 0200 on the last Sunday in October, it adopts daylight saving time and is two hours ahead of GMT.

Because the UK changes its clocks to British Summer Time (i.e. daylight saving time) at the same times and on the same dates, France always remains one hour ahead of the UK.

When it is **noon in France,** it is:

- 11am in London
- 7pm in Perth
- 11am in Dublin
- 9pm in Sydney
- 6am in New York
- 11pm in Aucklan
- 3am in Los Angeles

In France "am" and "pm" are not used but the 24-hour clock is widely applied.

Tipping

Under French law, any service charge (as well as any taxes) is automatically included in the prices displayed for meals and accommodation. Any additional tipping in restaurants and hotels is therefore unnecessary and is entirely at the discretion of the visitor. However, in bars and cafes it is not unusual to leave any small change that remains after paying the bill, but this generally should not be more than 5%. Taxi drivers do not have to be tipped, but again is usual to give a small amount, not more than 10%. Attendants at public toilets should be given a few cents. Hairdressers are usually tipped 10-15%. Tour guides and tour drivers should be tipped according to the amount of service given: from 2 to 5 euros would not be unusual.

Public Holidays

There are 11 public holidays in France. In addition, there are other religious and national festivals days, and a number of local saints' days, etc. On all these days, museums and other monuments may be closed or may vary their hours of admission:

1 January	New Year's Day (Jour de l'An)
Mar-Apr	Easter Sunday and Monday (Pâques)
1 May	May Day
8 May	V E Day
Ascension Day	(Ascension)
Whit Sunday and Monday (Pentecôte)	
14 July	Jour National – France's National Day (or Bastille Day)
15 August	Assumption (Assomption)
1 November	All Saints' Day(Toussaint)
11 November	Armistice
25 December	Christmas Day (Noël)

School Holidays

French schools close for vacations five times a year. In these periods, all tourist sites and attractions, hotels, restaurants, and roads are busier than usual. These school holidays are one week at the end of October, two weeks at Christmas, two weeks in February, two weeks in spring, and the whole of July and August.

CONVERSION TABLES

Weights and Measures

1 kilogram (kg) 6.35 kilograms 0.45 kilograms	2.2 pounds (lb) 14 pounds 16 ounces (oz)	2.2 pounds 1 stone (st) 16 ounces	*To convert kilograms to pounds, multiply by 2.2*
1 metric ton (tn)	1.1 tons	1.1 tons	
1 litre (l) 3.79 litres 4.55 litres	2.11 pints (pt) 1 gallon (gal) 1.20 gallon	1.76 pints 0.83 gallon 1 gallon	*To convert litres to gallons, multiply by 0.26 (US) or 0.22 (UK)*
1 hectare (ha) 1 sq. kilometre (km²)	2.47 acres 0.38 sq. miles (sq.mi.)	2.47 acres 0.38 sq. miles	*To convert hectares to acres, multiply by 2.4*
1 centimetre (cm) 1 metre (m)	0.39 inches (in) 3.28 feet (ft) or 39.37 inches or 1.09 yards (yd)	0.39 inches	*To convert metres to feet, multiply by 3.28; for kilometres to miles, multiply by 0.6*
1 kilometre (km)	0.62 miles (mi)	0.62 miles	

Clothing

Women			
	35	4	2½
	36	5	3½
	37	6	4½
Shoes	38	7	5½
	39	8	6½
	40	9	7½
	41	10	8½
	36	6	8
	38	8	10
Dresses & suits	40	10	12
	42	12	14
	44	14	16
	46	16	18
	36	06	30
	38	08	32
Blouses & sweaters	40	10	34
	42	12	36
	44	14	38
	46	16	40

Men			
	40	7½	7
	41	8½	8
	42	9½	9
Shoes	43	10½	10
	44	11½	11
	45	12½	12
	46	13½	13
	46	36	36
	48	38	38
Suits	50	40	40
	52	42	42
	54	44	44
	56	46	48
	37	14½	14½
	38	15	15
Shirts	39	15½	15½
	40	15¾	15¾
	41	16	16
	42	16½	16½

Sizes often vary depending on the designer. These equivalents are given for guidance only.

Speed

KPH	10	30	50	70	80	90	100	110	120	130
MPH	6	19	31	43	50	56	62	68	75	81

Temperature

Celsius (°C)	0°	5°	10°	15°	20°	25°	30°	40°	60°	80°	100°
Fahrenheit (°F)	32°	41°	50°	59°	68°	77°	86°	104°	140°	176°	212°

To convert Celsius into Fahrenheit, multiply °C by 9, divide by 5, and add 32.
To convert Fahrenheit into Celsius, subtract 32 from °F, multiply by 5, and divide by 9.
NB: Conversion factors on this page are approximate.

East end of the old abbey in Issoire
S.Sauvignier/MICHELIN

NATURE

Topography

France has a fortunate location in the European continent – not detached from it like the British Isles, nor projecting away like Iberia or Greece, nor set deep in its interior like the countries of Central Europe, yet in touch with the resources and the life of the whole of Western Europe and the seas around it, Atlantic, Channel, Mediterranean and North Sea. These seas together with the other natural frontiers, the Alps and Pyrenees and the River Rhine, define the compact shape of the French "hexagon". Within this unified and robust framework there flourishes a geographical identity which is unmistakably French yet of an unrivalled local richness and variety. Less a paradox than a wonderful synthesis, this coexistence of unity and diversity is the work of both Nature and Man.

"La France est diversité"
(France is diversity)
Fernand Braudel

GEOLOGICAL HISTORY

It has been said that the whole of Earth's history – the building of the planet – can be traced within the confines of France. The country's complex geological history starts in the Primary Era (600 million years ago), when the Hercynian folding was responsible for the raising up of the great mountain ranges which were the ancestors of today's Massif Central, Armorican Peninsula, Vosges and Ardennes.

In Secondary Era times (beginning 200 million years ago), the Paris region, Aquitaine, the Rhône and Loire valleys and the southern part of the Massif Central all lay under the sea which gradually filled them with sedimentary deposits.

New mountain ranges reared up in the Tertiary Era (beginning 60 million years ago): the Alps, Pyrenees, the Jura and Corsica. The shock-waves of this violent mountain-building were felt far afield, particularly in the Massif Central where great volcanoes erupted.

The Quaternary age (2 million years ago) saw an alternation of warm and cold periods; glaciers advanced and retreated and rivers swelled and shrank, sculpting much of the land surface into its present forms.

CLIMATE AND RELIEF

In climatic terms too, France gathers into herself each of the contrasting patterns of the continent as a whole; Atlantic, Continental and Mediterranean influences are all present (in northern and western France, central and eastern parts of the country, and the south), contributing decisively to the formation of soils and their mantle of vegetation as well as to the processes which have shaped the geological foundation into the patterns of today's relief.

The north of the country is largely composed of great sedimentary basins, scarp *(côtes)* and vale country, drained by slow-flowing rivers like the Seine and the Loire. At the extremities of these lowlands are rugged areas formed of Primary rocks, the much-eroded granites of Brittany and the gneisses and schists of the Ardennes, and the higher massifs of the Vosges and the centre. Beyond lie the fertile plains of Aquitaine and Languedoc while the corridor carved by the Rhône and Saône links the north and south of the country. Finally come the "young" mountains of the Jura, Alps and Pyrenees; their high peaks and ranges, while forming fine natural frontiers, are by no means impermeable to political, commercial and cultural currents.

Regions of France

Few parts of the country are unfavourable to human settlement; France is still a largely rural country, with a relatively even spread of population. Great cities and conurbations exist, but beyond them spreads a spacious countryside, uncrowded but rarely deserted, created over the centuries by the efforts of its inhabitants, whose collective understanding of the places where they live is expressed in every detail of the local landscape. The layout of fields, the pattern of crops and woodlands, the grouping of the population in hamlets, villages and towns, the materials and styles of building, all combine to proclaim the individuality of the innumerable localities or *pays* which themselves contribute to the identity of the larger regions listed below and which form the subject of the 24 Michelin regional guides.

PARIS

The presence of a number of islands in the Seine made a convenient crossing point here for the prehistoric North-South trade route. Under the Gauls, urban development was confined to the Île de la Cité, though Roman Lutetia spread southwards over today's Latin Quarter. It was the Capetian kings who made Paris their capital, thereby giving it the dominant role in the country's political and cultural life which it has exercised ever since.

Until modern times, Paris tended to be tightly circumscribed by successive rings of fortifications (the wall of Philippe Auguste in the 13C, the wall of Charles V in the 14C, and the wall of the Farmers-General in the late 18C), giving the city a much more densely built-up character than, say, London. Within these boundaries, a succession of bold building and planning projects, spread over the centuries, has helped give the city its distinct identity.

Renaissance urbanism was responsible for the layout of the Marais district, centred on the Place des Vosges, where the French town mansion, the *hôtel*, took on its definitive form, while the Baroque sense of drama and movement in the townscape is seen in the grand perspectives opened up on the Invalides, Champ-de-Mars and above all the Champs-Élysées.

Neo-Classical monumentality was favoured by Napoleon I in his attempt to make Paris a fittingly Imperial capital, but the greatest planned transformation of all was undertaken in the 19C by Napoleon III and his Prefect, Baron Haussmann, who drove great axial boulevards through the dense web of ancient streets and laid out splendid green spaces like the Bois de Boulogne and the Parc Monceau. In the late 19C and early 20C it was the new institution of the international exhibition which gave the *"Ville Lumière"* some of its most characteristic monuments, the Eiffel Tower, the Grand Palais and Petit Palais, and the Palais de Chaillot.

Under the influence of Le Corbusier and many others, the aesthetics of Parisian architecture have been radically revamped since 1945: UNESCO (1957), the Palais de la Défense (CNIT, 1958), the Maison de la Radio et de la Télévision

Louvre exterior seen through the Pyramid, Paris

Allison M. Simpson/MICHELIN

(1963), the Montparnasse Tower (1973), the Palais des Congrès (1974). This trend was to be confirmed in subsequent years with the building in central Paris of several major landmarks, designed by prominent contemporary architects: the Palais Omnisports de Paris-Bercy (1984), the City of Science and Industry and the Géode Cinema at La Villette (1986), the Opera-Bastille (1989), La Grande Arche at La Défense (1989), the Louvre Pyramid (1989), the Ministry of Finance building at Bercy (1990), the Richelieu Wing (1994), an important stage of the "Grand Louvre" project (1981-98), the City of Music at La Villette (1995), the Bibliothèque de France (1997) and lately the Musée du Quai Branly (2006).

ILE-DE-FRANCE

This historic region, the kernel from which the French state has grown, is called Île-de-France (literally: Island of France) because of its location marked by the rivers Seine, Aisne, Oise and Marne. Where its limestone plateaux have been cut into by the rivers, lush valleys have been formed, contrasting with the vast arable tracts of the Beauce, Vexin and Brie. A girdle of greenery surrounds the capital; there are great forests like those of Fontainebleau, Halatte, Chantilly, Ermenonville and Rambouillet, into which merge the landscapes of leisure and pleasure with which the mighty surrounded their châteaux, the parks and gardens of Versailles, Chantilly, Vaux-le-Vicomte and others. The region's privileged position has left it an exceptional legacy of fine building, ranging from innumerable parish churches to the great monuments of the Gothic dawn, such as St-Denis, and Chartres.

From Corot's time, the landscapes of the Île-de-France have moved artists to render their subtleties in paint, the Seine valley above all becoming the great axis of Impressionist activity.

The capital has long burst its bounds to invigorate its region with urban activity of all kinds; its established towns have expanded rapidly to accommodate new populations, aided by new foundations, planned towns like St-Quentin-en-Yvelines, Marne-la-Vallée and Cergy-Ponto-

ise. One indication of the importance of the region in the country's economic life; covering only 2% of the area of France, it now employs 22% of the economically active population.

THE LOIRE VALLEY

This "garden of France" with its abundant horticultural crops, its flowers and its vineyards, has also been called "a home spun cloak with golden fringes", are ference to the contrast between the fertile valleys of the Loire and its tributaries and the low, somewhat bleak plateaux that separate them.

Rising far to the southeast in the Massif Central, France's longest (some 1 000km – 620 miles) river was once a busy waterway, connected as early as 1642 to the Seine basin by the Briare Canal. Many of the towns along its banks bear traces of this former activity, from Gien, rebuilt after its bombing in the Second World War, to Orléans, once the Loire's foremost port, Blois, Tours, Langeais, Saumur... But, as on the Rhône, navigation was never easy, and once the railways came, the Loire was left to its caprices. Below Gien, the valley opens out and the river describes a great bend partly enclosing the immense heathy tract of the Sologne, rich in game. But it is from Orléans onward that the Loire exercised, and continues to exercise, its greatest attraction; its gentle landscapes and soft light encouraged the kings, courtiers and magnates to build the Renaissance châteaux for which the region is famous, Blois, Chambord, Azay and others, their elegance and architectural exuberance contrasting with the sterner fortresses of an earlier age like the great castle at Angers. Other building has a distinctive character too, often with white walls of tufa and roofs of slate, while there are trogloditic dwellings, notably around Amboise and Tours.

BRITTANY

Populated by Celtic settlers who arrived here from Cornwall in the 5C, Brittany retains many affinities with the other Celtic lands fringing the Atlantic. Its identity, quite distinct from that of the rest of France, is expressed in language (Breton, akin to Welsh) and traditions as well as in its landscape.

The province turns its face towards the sea. Its extraordinarily indented coastline, 1 200km – 750 miles long, was given its name **Armor** ("country near the sea") by the Gauls. Its cliffs, reefs, rocky headlands and offshore islands are battered by Atlantic breakers, while its narrow drowned valleys *(abers)* and sandy bays are washed by tides of exceptional range (up to 15m – 49ft).

Much of France's fishing fleet operates from Brittany and there are naval bases, shipyards and commercial harbours too. All around the coast are resorts, some smart (Dinard), some simple.

Inland is the **Argoat** ("country of the wood"), once thickly afforested, now a mixture of bocage countryside and wilder landscapes of heath and moor rising to wind-blown granite heights (like **Trévezel Rock** 384m – 1 229ft and **Ménez Hom** 330m – 1 083ft) commanding vast prospects. The Monts d'Arrée and Montagnes Noires mark the natural boundaries of the Lake Guerlédan region and the Châteaulin basin.

From the Loire estuary to the Aulne valley, the **Atlantic coast** with its picturesque harbours, resorts, villages and distinctive geographical features (Gulf of Morbihan, Guérande and Crozon Peninsulas) is backed by a varied landscape: the Lanvaux moorlands, the Grande Brière, the Guérande salt flats and the Nantes region. The **Channel coast** from Fougères and the Rennes basin to the large harbour at Brest and the Ile d'Ouessant is punctuated by historic towns (Guingamp, Morlaix, Tréguier), elegant resorts and dramatic corniches and headlands (Cap Fréhel, Pointe St-Mathieu).

The province's long and mysterious past makes itself felt in the abundance of prehistoric remains, menhirs, dolmens, and the great lines of megaliths around Carnac. Granite, outcropping nearly everywhere, distinguishes Breton building, whether in church or chapel, castle or château, harbour wall or humble house, and is used to great effect in the robust and expressive forms of churchyard calvaries.

NORMANDY

Taking its name from the Norsemen or Normans, this old dukedom extends from the western edge of the Paris Basin towards the Breton peninsula. To many it is reminiscent of southern England, not only in its shared heritage of glorious Norman architecture, but also in the lush, pastoral countryside of the *bocage,* with its small hedged fields, abundant trees and woodlands, apple orchards, sunken lanes and scattered hamlets.

Lower Normandy (Basse-Normandie), like Brittany, is built of old rocks, the sandstones, granites and schists of the Primary era. The Cotentin peninsula projects into the English Channel dividing the Bay of the Seine from the Gulf of St-Malo with its dramatic tides washing Mont St-Michel and the rocky Channel Islands (Anglo-Norman Islands in French). To the southeast lies the *bocage* – its hedgebanks offered excellent cover to the German defence in 1944.

On either side of the Seine Valley extends **Upper Normandy** (Haute-Normandie) centred on the historic city of Rouen. To the south is the Pays d'**Auge**, quintessential *bocage* country, famous for its ciders, cheeses and Calvados. To the north stretches the vast chalk plain of the Pays de **Caux**, good arable land, bordered by the Channel coast with its white cliffs and hanging valleys.

A diversity of resources has given rise to an exceptional variety in the materials and styles of building; Norman masons fashioned the fine Caen limestone into great ecclesiastical edifices on both sides of the Channel, while humbler structures were built from cob, chalk, pebbles in mortar, brick, timber, shingles and thatch.

Normandy's coast is the nearest to Paris, and while much has changed since Marcel Proust watched Albertine playing at diabolo, its cliffs and beaches continue to attract visitors and holiday-makers.

FLANDERS, ARTOIS, PICARDY

Before the rising sea cut its way through the Straits of Dover at the end of the last Ice Age, the chalklands of southern England and the North of France were one; even today the broad fields of the old provinces of **Artois** (capital Arras) and **Picardy** (capital Amiens) recall the English downland, while a gap of only some 30km – 19 miles separates Cap Gris-Nez from the South Foreland and Shakespeare Cliff.

In the claylands of the Pays de Bray, the Vimeux and the Bas Boulonnais is *bocage* countryside, but most of the North's landscapes are open, with few field boundaries to check the view. This high-yielding arable land is broken by a number of valleys like that of the Somme making its way slowly to the sea, its alluvial soils intensively exploited by market gardeners whose tiny plots of land are linked by narrow canals. Many of the towns are sited by these sluggish streams, like Amiens, its superb cathedral a reminder that the region, together with the Île-de-France, was the cradle of Gothic architecture. With few dramatic hills, man-made verticals take on more importance, not only cathedral spires and church towers, but also the bright white concrete watertowers, the volcanic cones of pit-heaps or lines of electricity pylons marching majestically to the horizon. Much of the North is built of brick, from singlestoreyed roadside cabin to tall town house, though grander buildings may merit stone.

In close succession along the coast are the ports of Boulogne, Calais and Dunkirk, making this one of France's most important outlets to the sea. As well as chalk and limestone cliffs, there are extensive areas of land reclaimed from the sea, impressive dune systems and fine sandy beaches overlooked by resorts like Le Touquet.

The edges of the chalk country are marked by other, very different landscapes. Northeast is French **Flanders**, consisting largely of polderlands having much in common, including language, with the adjoining Low Countries. Inland is France's "Black country", the *pays noir* of the great coalfield stretching from Béthune to Valenciennes and running into the vast conurbation of a million people formed by Lille-Tourcoing-Roubaix. Farther eastward, the green pastures of the more hilly Thierarche and Avenois country anticipate the landscapes of the nearby Ardennes. As the Île-de-France is approached, extended wooded tracts appear, like the forest of Compiègne, impressive relics of the Gaulish forest which once extended from the Paris basin to the eastern frontier.

The North is indeed a frontier land, open to the Northern European Plain, an invasion route for successive waves of would-be conquerors, its countryside today studded with the memorials to the victims of two world wars, its place-names redolent of bloody struggles, defeats and victories.

CHAMPAGNE, ARDENNES

The eastern rim of the Paris Basin is formed by an outward-facing series of limestone escarpments pierced by rivers flowing northwest such as the Marne, Aube and Seine. Alluvial deposits carried by the watercourses have created the soft contours of the landscape.

Around Reims, the steep, sometimes cliff-like slopes of the Côte de l'Île-de-France carry the vineyards which since the days of Dom Pérignon have produced the world's most prestigious sparkling wine. Beyond stretch the sweeping Champagne chalklands, once notorious for their meagre soils, but now, with the use of artificial fertilisers, one of France's most productive agricultural regions. To the east are the Champagne claylands, an area of mostly mixed farming and woodlands, where great artificial lakes, designed to regulate the flow of Seine and Marne, have become important recreational areas.

Farther eastward still is the Barrois plateau and the escarpment of the Côte des Bars, a favoured site for towns like Bar-le-Duc, Bar-sur-Aube and Bar-sur-Seine, while to the north, forming a buffer between Champagne and Lorraine, is the vast Argonne forest.

The upper valleys of both Marne and Seine lead to an extensive and well-wooded limestone upland, the Plateau de Langres, named after the old fortified town sited on one of its spurs.

The French **Ardennes** form a small part of an ancient massif stretching away into southeastern Belgium and merging with the uplands of the German Eifel. This is one of Europe's most extensive areas of forest, with fine stands of oak and beech as well as conifers, all sheltering abundant game. Sometimes described as "impenetrable", the Ardennes have rarely proved a reliable barrier to the passage of armies, least of all in the spring of 1940. Below Charleville-Mézières the meandering Meuse cuts into the plateau, accompanied by a string of industrial towns.

ALSACE, LORRAINE, VOSGES

Alsace forms France's window onto Central Europe. Its capital, Strasbourg, was a free city, part of the Holy Roman Empire, until the days of Louis XIV; together with the other towns and villages along this left bank of the Rhine it has a picturesqueness of decidedly Germanic character. The Rhine itself is both a frontier and, with the Alsace Canal, a great international waterway, flowing through the broad rift valley defined by the Black Forest to the east, the Vosges uplands to the west.

The towns avoid the river and its once-unpredictable moods; its course leads it through a mysterious and little-frequented landscape of reed swamps, stagnant backwaters and old cut-offs. On the infertile sands and gravels brought down from the Alps grow forests like that of Haguenau, almost 140km2 – 54sq miles, 2/3 of which consists of Scots pine and the rest of hornbeam, beech and oak. But most of the Alsace countryside wears a cheerful air, particularly when the orchards are in blossom or when the grape-harvest is being collected in the famous vineyards of the foothills, where each eminence seems crowned by some ruined stronghold.

Above these lower slopes rise the **Vosges** themselves, their rounded granite summits in the south (the Ballons) contrasting with the more rugged forms of the red sandstone outcropping in the north. The latter is both attractive and easily worked, furnishing building material for many a castle, church or cathedral. In the valleys of these uplands, whose breadth rather than height once hindered communication, are glacial lakes, while the slopes are clad with splendid forests giving way near the summits to rich pastures, the Hautes Chaumes. Laid out for strategic puposes in the First World War, the high-level Route des Crêtes now forms a fine north-south tourist route.

Lorraine owes its name to ancient Lotharingia, central of the three kingdoms into which Charlemagne's inheritance was divided. To the west, the landscape is one of alternating outcrops of limestone and clay, the former giving rise to the escarpments of the Côte de Moselle and Côte de Meuse overlooking these northward-flowing rivers. Eastward to the foot of the Vosges extends the Lorraine plateau, a mixed-farming area of monotonous appearance.

Burgundy landscape

The presence of coal, iron-ore and salt led to the development of heavy industry in adjoining Luxembourg and Saarland as well as in Lorraine (Longwy, Thionville) itself. Fortress towns stud this much-contested province: Bitche, Metz, Verdun.

THE JURA

These limestone uplands, part of them in Switzerland, run in a great arc for some 240km – 150 miles from Rhine to Rhône, corresponding roughly to the old province known as the Franche-Comté. The limestones from which they were formed were folded along a northeast-southwest axis into long parallel ridges and valleys by the pressure exerted on them in the Alpine-building period; the exceptionally massive development of the limestone beds (they reach a maximum thickness of some 1 300m – 4 300ft) has led to the term "Jurassic" passing into geological usage for rocks of this age and type (compare the oolitic limestone of the English Cotswolds). Many characteristic features of limestone country occur, like great natural amphitheatres or *cirques* (Cirque de Baume), gorges, caves and chasms, while the regular pattern of valleys and ridges stepping down westwards can be easily appreciated from a number of high viewpoints like the Grand Colombier (1,571m – 5,151ft).

Owing to the high rainfall, extensive forests of beech and oak, firs and spruce (covering 40% of the land surface), and vast upland pastures, this is a verdant landscape. Water is everywhere present, rising from springs and resurgences to feed rushing torrents, spill over spectacular falls (like the Cascades du Hérisson) and fill some 70 lakes. Winters are harsh here, sometimes burying the sturdily-built isolated farmhouses to the eaves of their spreading roofs, and encouraging the development of woodcarving skills during the long months of enforced indoor activity. Woodmanship and forestry have long been supplemented by upland farming (the Jura is famous for its Comté and other cheeses) and at times by other occupations of an industrial character, salt production at Salins and Lons-le-Saunier, clock- and watch-making at Besançon, and metal-working, now mostly gone.

The margins of the upland have their own interest; where the westernmost and lowest ridge drops to the Bresse plain is the *Bon Pays*, an attractively variegated countryside including many vineyards, while at the foot of the great cliff falling away from the highest, east-ernmost ridge towards Geneva and its lake is the Pays de Gex, very much part of the hinterland of the great Swiss city.

BURGUNDY

Burgundy's unity is based more on history than on geography. Fortunately located on the great trade route linking northern Europe to the Mediterranean, the territory was consolidated in the 15C by the diplomatic skills of its great Dukes; it consists of a number of *pays* of varying character, though its heart-land lies in the limestone plateaux stretching eastward from the Auxerre area to the country around the ducal capital, Dijon.

The old dukedom's heritage of Roman-esque architecture is outstanding, but the village scene is characteristic too, the colours of the countryside repeated in the warm red roofs and mellow limestone walls of the houses clustered around a modest church made of the same materials.

Towards the east, the elevated land terminates in escarpments dropping down to the wide valley of the Saône. Of these, La Côte is the most renowned, its slopes producing some of the world's finest wines, its centuries of prosperity made manifest in the large and comfortable houses of the wine-growers. To the south lies the Mâconnais where the steep faces of the escarpment are turned towards the interior. This is a region of vine-covered hillsides and pastureland.

Standing apart from the province, and long isolated from the wider world through poor communications, is the **Morvan**, a granite massif of poor soils cut by a network of rivers, lonely farmsteads and scattered hamlets and extensive forests, its highest point being Haut-Folin (901m – 2 956ft). The lower slopes have been turned into pastureland. The region's unspoilt natural landscapes are a great attraction.

To the west and north of the Morvan are other pays, the plateaux and hills of the Nivernais stretching away to the Loire, the moorlands and pastures of the Gâtinais and Puisaye, while to the south the lower reaches of the Saône are bordered by the broad Bresse plain, famous for its beef, pork and delicately-fleshed poultry.

BERRY, LIMOUSIN

Little touched by industrialisation or mass tourism, these two regions seem to represent the quintessence of rural France.

Berry centres on Bourges, which with its great cathedral was once the seat of the French court. The vast limestone plateau which forms the area's heartland was settled as long ago as Neolithic times and is now devoted to large-scale arable farming. In contrast are the intimate *bocage* landscapes of the valleys of the Boischaut, the vines and orchards of the Sancerrois and the Brenne marshlands, a nature reserve of the first importance with innumerable ponds and little sandstone knolls covered in pine and broom.

Limousin is the name of the old province around Limoges forming the northwestern extremity of the Massif Central. Much of it is a quiet countryside of hedgerows, ponds and shady meadows, drained by rivers flowing westwards towards Saintonge and the Dordogne. In contrast is the Montagne, its name derived more from the rigour of its climate than from altitude since nowhere does it rise above 1,000m – about 3,300ft; the Plateau des Mille-vaches is a sparsely populated upland, grazed by sheep and cattle, blasted by wind and rain and with a high snowfall. The province's urban pattern is one of old market towns with solid, granite-walled and slate-roofed houses.

POITOU, VENDÉE, CHARENTES

Between the estuaries of the Loire and the Gironde, France faces the breezes and breakers of the Atlantic with a generally flat but otherwise fascinatingly varied coastline. There are great marshy tracts like the Marais Breton and above all the Marais Poitevin, low cliffs, vast mud-flats shimmering at low tide and dune systems bordering splendid sandy beaches. Landscapes inland are equally varied. Like Brittany, the **Vendée** has a granite foundation; its *bocage* countryside is one of deep lanes and scattered farmsteads, while its heaths and moors rise to 295m – 968ft at Puy Crapaud.

Poitou and **Charentes** are linked by the green valley of the Charente. Low limestone plateaux form the characteristic scenery of the region; on the right bank of the river are the vineyards of Cognac, whose product is distilled into the famous spirit, while farther north, stretching across the Gate of Poitou, the watershed between Loire and Charente, are extensive tracts of open, almost treeless farmland. In places the limestone forms spurs, good defensive sites for towns like Angoulême.

To the south is the Gironde, the name given to the estuary of the Garonne; its fine beaches extend from Meschers to the Coubre headland.

Off this western coast are a number of islands, each with a distinct identity. **Noirmoutier** is connected to the mainland by a causeway covered at high tide. **Yeu**, farther south, has an altogether more Breton character, with a wild, rocky coastline. The holiday island of **Ré** with its salt marshes is now linked to the mainland by a new road bridge. **Aix**, fortified by Vauban, was where Napoleon spent his last days on French soil, while **Oléron**, France's largest island apart from Corsica, enjoys a remarkably mild climate.

DORDOGNE
PÉRIGORD, QUERCY

With its hills, its mature and varied agricultural landscapes, its deciduous woodlands and its mellow stone

Château de Belcastel and the river Dordogne

buildings, this is a welcoming region, not unlike parts of southern England, albeit with a more genial climate and a general atmosphere of good living. Perhaps it is this pleasing synthesis of the familiar and the mildly exotic, more than the traces of the area's long association with the English Crown, that has led to its popularity with visitors from beyond the Channel.

Limestone underlies most of the area, in **Périgord** forming extensive plateaux deeply dissected by the Dordogne and other rivers; along the banks grow southern crops like maize, tobacco and sunflowers, as well as grass and cereals and numerous walnut trees. The soil is also suitable for the cultivation of strawberries.

On the higher land there are woodlands of oak and chestnut, and in the Périgord Noir, evergreen oaks too. The region is famous for the truffles which grow at the foot of oak trees.

In **Quercy** the thick layers of Jurassic limestone form *causses,* lying at a height of about 300m – 1 000ft, with a sparse cover of juniper, scrubby oaks and carob trees. These sheep-grazed uplands are dissected by dry valleys and spectacular canyons and there are caves and chasms and underground watercourses.

The area has been settled since very early times. Evidence of its attractiveness to prehistoric people extends beyond tools and implements to wall paintings and engravings, low reliefs and decorated bone, ivory and stone. As well as stunning examples of medieval settlement seeming to have grown organically from its site (Rocamadour, St-Cirq-Lapopie), there are numerous reminders of the Anglo-French struggle, from the geometrically planned towns *(bastides)* laid out by both parties to help consolidate their hold on the territory (Monpazier), to rugged strongholds like Beynac and Bonaguil. The medieval and later importance of the towns is expressed in a fine tradition of building in limestone (Sarlat).

AUVERGNE

The Auvergne forms the core of the **Massif Central**. It is a volcanic landscape, unique in France – its forms range from the classic cones of the Monts Dômes to the rugged shapes of the much-eroded Monts Dore and the great Cantal volcano, and to the lava flows which seem to have only just cooled into immobility. In the Cézallier area, the streams of lava have piled up on one another to surround the flattened dome of the Signal du Luguet; at La Cheire d'Aydat, the molten torrent has taken on a crystalline pattern, while around St-Flour it has formed the great stretches of upland known locally as *planèzes.* Elsewhere, the lava has filled valley floors, protecting them from the erosion wearing away the hills around and giving rise to the phenomenon of relief inversion (Polignac, Carlat, Gergovie). At Bort-les-Orgues and Le Puy there are curious crystalline formations resembling organ-pipes.

The volcanic activity has created an array of lakes and other water-bodies; at Aydat and Guéry a lava flow has blocked a valley, trapping its waters, while the same effect has been produced at Chambon and Montcineyre by a volcano erupting in the valley itself. Elsewhere, as at Chauvet, the hollows produced by a series of volcanic exposions have filled with water. Lakes have also formed inside a crater (Bouchet, Servière) or within the steep walls of an explosion crater (Gour de Tazenat, Pavin).

This great variety of relief makes for fine upland walking country, while the towns and villages of sombre granite have their own allure, heightened by the presence of some of France's finest Romanesque churches. The Auvergne is a mainly agricultural region, the grazing grounds of the higher land complemented by the rich alluvial soils of the series of basins through which the Allier flows northward towards the **Bourbonnais** with its *bocage* countryside of rich pasturelands. Industry is present too, notably at Clermont-Ferrand (Michelin), the provincial capital overlooked from a height of 1 465m – 4 806ft by the old volcano of the Puy de Dôme.

The area is famous for its springs, the spas which have grown up around them (Vichy) and for the bottling and marketing of mineral water.

THE RHÔNE VALLEY

Together with its tributary, the Saône, which joins it at Lyon, this great river has long served as a communications corridor of the first importance, linking northwestern Europe to the Mediterranean. Though its valley seems to divide the ancient uplands to the west from the younger, folded rocks of the Alps to the east, its geological structure is of some complexity; at Vienne and St-Vallier the river carves its way through some of the outermost granitic bastions of the Massif Central, while at Valence it flows between one of the last terraces of the Dauphiné and the limestone ridge of Crussol backing onto the granite mass of the Vivarais.

The area around the great city of Lyon itself is marked by centuries of industrial activity. Downstream, the river's course takes it through a succession of narrow gorges and broad basins, where châteaux perched on spurs alternate with an attractive pattern of red-roofed villages set among vineyards (some of them first planted in pre-Roman times) and orchards, though industry is present too. The southern character of the landscape becomes ever more pronounced, olives and evergreen oaks appearing just below Montélimar.

Fed by Alpine thaws, the Rhône's currents could be dangerously swift, its level unpredictable, its bed mobile. Until the incorporation of the Dauphiné, Dromme and the Papal lands around Avignon into the French kingdom, it was a frontier too, a further obstacle to easy commerce. Towns tended to develop in pairs, one on the east "foreign" bank, one on the west "French" bank, like Vienne/Ste-Colombe, Valence/St-Péray, Avignon/Villeneuve-lès-Avignon... The very diverse character of the river's banks and the frequency with which it is joined by wide tributaries made it difficult to form a satisfactorily continuous towpath, and later to engineer railway lines. But the Rhône has been tamed; decades of construction (18 dams, 13 power stations and locks) now allow 2 000-tonne barges to reach Lyon. Nevertheless, the improved waterway carries only a fraction of the total traffic using its corridor; it is supplemented by the A6 motorway, two national highways, a main-line railway on each bank (one carrying TGV traffic), a gas pipeline, and an oil pipeline.

To the west of the river runs an escarpment marking the edge of the Massif Central. Close to the old industrial area centred on St-Étienne is Mont Pilat (1 432m – 4,698ft) offering a number of splendid viewpoints over the Rhône valley (Crêt de l'Oeillon). Southward lie the basalt plateaux of the Velay and the lava flows and limestone country of the Vivarais, cut by the spectacular Ardèche gorges.

PROVENCE AND THE RHÔNE DELTA

The Rhône flows into the sea in the centre of France's Mediterranean coastline, the Midi (South). Here, "the climate has imposed a unifying stamp reflected in both the landscape and the way of life" (J Sion) and Mediterranean influences are supreme, from the extensive remains of the six centuries of Roman occupation to the traditional triumvirate of wheat, vine and olive alternating with the remnants of the natural forest (evergreen oaks, pines) and the infertile but wonderfully aromatic *garrigues* (arid scrubland).

Among the fertile Provençal plains stand the *mas,* shallow-roofed pantiled farmsteads protected from the fierce sun by stone walls with few window openings. Crops and buildings are shielded from the violence of the master-wind from the north, the *mistral,* by serried ranks of cypresses. The plains are flanked by ranges of limestone hills running east-west, including the picturesque Alpilles, the rugged Luberon range and the Vaucluse plateau with its chasms, gorges and great resurgent spring at Fontaine-de-Vaucluse.

The Provençal landscape and the intensity of the light have played a key role in the evolution of modern painting; Mt Ste-Victoire never ceased to fascinate Paul Cézanne, while Arles and the countryside around was made to reflect the tormented spirit of Vincent van Gogh.

The 20 million cubic metres of sand, gravel and silt brought down annually by the Rhône has created the vast deltaic plain of the **Camargue**, a lonely place of salt marshes and lagoons, populated by herdsmen and wildfowl. Before it changed its course to join the Rhône, the Durance too flowed directly into the sea through the Lamanon Gap, depositing vast quantities of boulders and pebbles to form the Grande Crau, a stony wasteland scorched by summer sun and blasted by the *mistral* in winter and increasingly invaded by the industries spawned by Marseille, France's great Mediterranean port and second city.

TARN GORGES: CÉVENNES, LOWER LANGUEDOC

Along the southern edge of the Massif Central stretch the **Grands Causses**, vast limestone tablelands of striking severity. They are laced with corniche roads offering unforgettable views over the deep canyons and gorges hollowed out by the Tarn and its tributaries. Below the surface is a "speleologist's paradise" of caves and chasms, and the endlessly weird forms produced by dissolution and deposition. Where dolomite occurs, weathering has resulted in the fantastic pinnacles and castellations of the rocky chaos known as Montpellier-le-Vieux.

The *causses* are bounded by landscapes of surprising diversity. The lava flows of the Aubrac area have given rise to a countryside of immensely

Vineyard at the foot of the Dentelles de Montmirail

B.Kaufmann/MICHELIN

broad horizons, one of France's least-populated areas. The **Cévennes**, mostly designated a National Park, consist of lowering granite summits overlooking deep and narrow valleys separated by crests *(serres)*, a secret and long-impenetrable area that merges southward with the Mediterranean vegetation of the *garrigues*.

The central plain of **Lower Languedoc** (capital: Montpellier) with its vast and highly productive vineyards, is bordered by a chain of brackish lakes, separated from the sea by sandy bars. Old towns like Sète (created in the 17C by Louis XIV) are complemented by planned modern resorts such as La Grande Motte with its modern apartment buildings in ziggurat form.

Far to the southwest, the ancient rocks of the Montagne Noire form the last outpost of the Massif Central. Behind it stretches the varied countryside of the Segalas and the great granite block of the Sidobre.

THE PYRENEES

Dividing France from Spain, these mountains, the "most satisfactory of France's frontiers", run some 400km – 250 miles from Atlantic to Mediterranean.

In the west is the **Basque country**, topographically and linguistically distinct, though many of the valleys descending northwards at right angles to the main crestline form *pays* (**Béarn, Bigorre**) with their own character and traditions. Here is spectacular mountain scenery: jagged ridges, great natural amphitheatres streaked with waterfalls, high-altitude lakes and rushing torrents, all in contrast to the well-cultivated valley bottoms with their scattering of white houses.

The centre of the range is formed by the splendid Maladetta Massif rising high above the **Comminges** country and the most venerable of the Pyrenees' many spas, Luchon. Northwards, a vast fan-shaped area of ridges and valleys has been formed from glacial debris brought down from the mountains and by subsequent river action. Prolonged westwards by the valleys of the turbulent Adour and its tributaries,

this landscape gives way to varied cropland along the course of **Aquitaine's** principal river, the Garonne. Here, the kindly climate and rich alluvial soils have allowed each town to develop its own specialised product, like the plums of Agen, which, dried, become delicious prunes. The ancient English province of **Guyenne** grew up around the confluence of Garonne and Dordogne, an area devoted then as now to the production of the world's most coveted wines. Beyond the provincial capital of Bordeaux, the Garonne widens out into the broad estuary of the Gironde.

The Atlantic coast (Côte d'Argent) south of Grave Point at the mouth of the estuary runs in a straight line almost to the Spanish border, interrupted only by the great Bay of Arcachon. Behind the vast sandy beaches rise the highest sand dunes in Europe, while inland are the **Landes**, once an immense, ill-drained waste, now successfully planted with profitable pinewoods.

Among the former statelets of the Pyrenees like the Pays de Foix, Andorra alone preserves its independence. The watershed between Atlantic and Mediterranean is crossed by the Canal du Midi, built as early as 1680 to link sea to ocean. The former capital of Languedoc, Toulouse, is France's sixth largest city, an important industrial centre. All around and northward in the **Albigeois** too, lies rich farming country, the granary of Southern France.

At the Mediterranean extremity of the Pyrenees lies **Roussillon**, France's Catalan province, the often snow-covered peak of Canigou (2 784m – 9 134ft) a symbol to Catalans on both sides of the border. At a lower level lie the upland basins of the Cerdagne and the Capcir, then come the forests and pastures of the Vallespir (Tech valley), the rugged Aspres hills, and finally the plain of Roussillon itself, a great market-garden with its vines and abundant fruit and vegetable crops. The province is bounded to the south by the rocky Côte Vermeille, where the Albères mountains descend to the sea through the Banyuls vineyards and scattered cork oaks clinging to the steep slopes. Few contrasts could be greater than the one between this charmingly irregular coastline with its ancient port-resort of Collioure and the sweeping beaches to the north, backed by the planned modern tourist developments of Languedoc-Roussillon.

THE FRENCH ALPS

Stretching 370km – 230 miles from the Mediterranean to Lake Geneva, the French Alps display all the varieties of mountain scenery, from the sublimity of bare rock and eternal snow to the animation of densely-settled valleys. Nowhere more than among these incomparable mountains does human habitat show such close adaptation to natural conditions. Centuries of endurance and ingenuity have overcome formidable obstacles and brought all possible resources into play, not only settling valley floors, but pushing grazing and cultivation to its highest limits and developing widely-varied local traditions of living and building. Whether grouped sociably in village or hamlet or standing proudly in isolation, the traditional farmhouse combines under a single roof, with a minimum of openings, virtually all the functions of the farm (residence, barn, storage, drying). Building form, orientation and choice of materials (stone, slate, timber, shingles) all reflect the resources of the locality, reinforcing a sense of place which is already strong in these valley *pays*.

In modern times the Alps have become a vast playground, welcoming visitors at all seasons to sophisticated resort and remote cabin alike. The mountains have never discouraged communication, rather channelling it through valleys linked by pass routes where necessary. The grandiose works of the railway engineers have been followed by steady improvement of the road network, opening up to the touring motorist such spectacular itineraries as the Route des Grandes Alpes.

The northern boundary of the French Alps and part of the country's frontier with Switzerland is marked by the great sweep of **Lake Geneva**. To the south of the superb lake rise the Alps of Savoy, first the Chablais and Faucigny country, then the famous peaks and glaciers around the great white mountain, Mont-Blanc. Westward lie other graceful stretches of water, Lake Annecy, Le Bourget Lake, still in a mountain setting, but bordered by flower-bedecked resorts and villages and a countryside of human scale, patterned by woodlands, fruit and nut trees, crops and pasture, a landscape in cheerful contrast to the sometimes severe countenance of the higher land.

An important southwest-northeast communication route is formed by the Sub-Alpine Furrow, a broad and prosperous valley in which Grenoble, the metropolis of the Alps, sits at the confluence of Isère and Drac. The latter

Villefranche-sur-Mer

river and its tributaries rise among the crystalline rocks of the **Écrins** mountains, while the headwaters of the Isère flow through the **Vanoise** massif, with its deep valleys and vast pastures the site of France's first National Park.

The western rampart of the Alps is formed by a succession of massifs, **Bauges, Vercors**—the latter an extraordinary natural fortress of giddy limestone cliffs.

Beyond Briançon, hard up against the Italian border, the mountains are lit by the strong light of the Mediterranean. Here, among splendid forests of larch and high grazing grounds, settlement reaches its maximum altitude in Europe in villages like St-Véran (2 040m – 6 693ft); the houses exhibit extreme adaptation to rigours of site and climate.

Farther south still, the scene is often one of striking severity, bare rock rising from vegetation of increasingly Mediterranean character, the olive tree making its appearance in the middle reaches of the Durance, the main watercourse of the Southern Alps.

The stark summit of Mount Ventoux overlooks the Comtat plain, while eastwards lie the most desolate tracts of the whole Alpine region, the Pre-Alps and high plateaux of Provence; here torrential streams have scored deep gorges like that of the Grand Canyon of the Verdon.

In **Upper Provence** (Haute-Provence), and particularly in the Maritime Alps which form the backdrop to the French Riviera, the proximity of the Mediterranean world makes itself felt again in the numerous fortified hill-top villages, with their houses of stone, pantiled roofs and fountains splashing in shady squares.

The richness of the natural heritage of the French Alps is reflected in the number of National (Mercantour, Écrins as well as Vanoise) and Regional (Vercors, Queyras) Parks set up to protect these incomparable landscapes and enhance the visitors' experience of them.

THE FRENCH RIVIERA

The Riviera's brilliant light, abundant sunshine, exotic vegetation and drama-tic combination of sea and mountains have made it a fashionable place of pleasure since its "discovery" in the 19C; it is the archetypal holiday coast against which all others must be measured.

Between Nice and Menton, the Pre-Alps plunge almost sheer into the sea. The coast is densely built up, the resorts linked by triple corniche roads. Farther north are the Maritime Alps, dissected by the upper valleys of the Var, Tinée, Vésubie and Roya, and, on the Italian border, the great crystalline massif of the **Mercantour** (Cime du Gélas 3 143m – 10 312ft). To the west of Nice the coast flattens out, forming wide bays with fine beaches.

The bustle of the coast is in contrast to the quieter charm of the interior, with its valleys carpeted in olive groves, its spectacular gorges, and its many hill-villages built to protect the population from the perils which proximity to the coast might bring. The limestone plateaus of the Provence tableland are separated from the sea by two massifs, Esterel and Maures. The jagged rocks of brightly-coloured porphyry making up the **Esterel massif** are best appreciated from the coast road leading from St-Raphaël to Cannes. The Estérel has been largely denuded of its former forest, but to the west, the **Maures massif** retains much of its fine cover of pine, cork oak and chestnut. Its coastline has great promontories and narrow tongues of land extending into the sea, defining wide bays like that of the Gulf of St-Tropez. Offshore are the densely-vegetated Hyères Islands, detached from the mainland in geologically recent times.

The Toulon coast, with its outstanding roadstead, is characterised by vertical cliffs interrupted by a number of attractive beaches. To the north rise the rugged limestone heights of the Provençal Ranges; Mount Faron overlooks the great French naval port from an elevation of 584m – 1 916ft.

CORSICA

The mountainous "Island of Beauty", the name given to Corsica by the ancient Greeks, lies some 170km – just over 100 miles off the coast of mainland France. With its intense light, its superbly varied and dramatic coast and its wild and rugged interior, it is a place of utterly distinct natural identity, enhanced by the succession of peoples who have been attracted here to settle or to rule; these have included megalith builders and mysterious Torreans, Greeks and Romans, Pisans and Genoese, French and British, though the somewhat absurd interlude of the Anglo-Corsican Viceroyalty of 1794-96 seems to have left little trace.

The gulfs of Corsica's west coast are of extraordinary beauty, the jagged headlands and precipitous porphyry cliffs rising from the Golfe de Porto being especially memorable. The Cap Corse promontory prolongs the island's backbone of schistic rocks 40km – 25 miles northwards into the sea. The coastal plains of Bastia and Aléria to the east constitute the only substantial areas of flat land; their agricultural prosperity has revived in recent years, largely through the enterprise of resettled *pieds-noirs* from Algeria.

The interior is penetrated by a skeletal network of narrow and winding roads as well as by a remarkable one metre-gauge railway. Here are villages of tall granite houses overlooking deep gorges, as well as superb forests of oak, Corsican pine and sweet chestnut, *garrigue* and *maquis* vegetation. Above the tree line rise the high bare summits, all the more imposing because of their proximity to the sea. Much of inland Corsica is now protected as a Regional Nature Park, through which GR 20, one of Europe's finest long-distance footpaths, threads its way.

HISTORY

The great sweep of prehistory has left abundant traces in France, and it is to Frenchmen that much of our knowledge of prehistoric times is due. ♿ *See Les EYZIES-DE-TAYAC: Prehistory.*

Time Line

ANCIENT TIMES

BC 5000	Megalithic culture flourishes in Brittany (Carnac), then in Corsica, lasting for over 2 500 years.
8C	Celtic tribes from central Europe arrive in Gaul where they build the fortified settlements known as oppidums.
600	Greek traders found a number of cities, including Marseille, Glanum (♿ *see ST-RÉMY-DE-PROVENCE)* and Aléria in Corsica.
2C	Celtic culture, which had spread as far as Brittany, gives way to both Germanic and Roman influences. The port of Fréjus, on the Mediterranean coast, is founded in 154 by the Romans as a link on the sea-route to their possessions in Spain. By the year 122 they have established themselves at Aix, and four years later at Narbonne.
58-52	Julius Caesar's Gallic Wars. He defeats the Veneti in 56 BC (♿ *see VANVES),* then himself suffers defeat at the hands of Vercingetorix (♿ *see CLERMONT-FERRAND)* in 52 BC, though the latter's surrender comes only a few months later.
AD 1C	During the reign of Augustus Roman rule in Gaul is consolidated and expanded (♿ *see NÎMES).* Fréjus is converted into a naval base and fortified.
5C	The monasteries set up by St Martin at Ligugé and by St Honorat at Lérins reinforce Christian beliefs and mark the beginning of a wave of such foundations (by St Victor at Marseille, by St Loup at Troyes, by St Maxime at Riez).

THE MEROVINGIANS (418-751)

451	Merovius, king of the Salian Franks (from the Tournai area in present-day Belgium), defeats Attila the Hun (♿ *see CHÂLONS-EN-CHAMPAGNE).* It is to him that the dynasty owes its name.
476	Fall of the Roman Empire in the West; Gaul occupied by barbarian tribes.
496	Clovis, grandson of Merovius and King of the Franks, is baptised in Reims.
507	Defeat of the Visigoths under Alaric II at Vouillé (♿ *see POITIERS)* by Clovis.
6C	Accompanied by Christian missionaries, settlers from Britain arrive in the Breton peninsulas, displacing the original Celtic inhabitants. But they too are overcome, first by the Franks (in the 9C), then by the Angevins (11C).
732	The Arab armies invading France are defeated at Moussais-la-Bataille (♿ *see POITIERS)* by Charles Martel.

St-Martin cutting his cloak

E. Joly/Bibliothèque minicipale. Tours

THE CAROLINGIANS (751-986)

751	Pepin the Short has himself elected king by an assembly of magnates and bishops at Soissons, sending the powerless Childeric, last of the Merovingians, to a monastery.
800	Charlemagne is crowned Emperor of the West in Rome.
842	The Strasbourg Oaths.
843	By the Treaty of Verdun, the Carolingian Empire is divided between the sons of Louis I, Charles the Bald receiving the territories to the west, roughly corresponding to modern France.
850	Nominoé (*see VANNES*) wrests eastern Brittany and the Rais country south of the Loire from its Frankish rulers.
910	Foundation of the great abbey at Cluny.
911	By the Treaty of St-Clair-sur-Epte, Charles the Simple and the Viking chief Rollo create the Duchy of Normandy.

THE CAPETIANS (987-1789)

The Direct Capetians (987-1328)

987	A descendant of Robert the Strong, Hugh Capet, Duke of "France", ousts Charles of Lorraine and has himself elected. By having his son crowned during his own lifetime, he consolidated his family's rule, which nevertheless does not become truly hereditary until the accession of Philippe Auguste in 1180.
1066	**William Duke of Normandy** (*see BAYEUX and CAEN*) sets out for the English coast from Dives. His victory over Harold at the Battle of Hastings leads to his coronation as King of England, though technically speaking he is still a vassal of the French king.
1095	The First Crusade is preached at Clermont-Ferrand.

1137	Louis VII weds Eleanor of Aquitaine (*see BORDEAUX*); the annulment of their marriage 15 years later is a disaster for the dynasty. Foundation of the School of Medicine at Montpellier.
1204	Gaillard Castle falls to Philippe Auguste, who goes on to conquer Normandy, Maine, Touraine and Anjou.
1209	Start of the Albigensian Crusade.
1214	Victory at the Battle of Bouvines (*see LILLE*); for the first time, a genuinely French patriotism appears.
1244	Cathars burnt at the funeral pyre at Montségur.
1270	St Louis (Louis IX) dies aboard ship off Tunis on his way to the Eighth Crusade.

THE HOUSE OF VALOIS (1328-1589)

The Hundred Years War – 1337-1475

Extending over six reigns, the war was both a political and dynastic struggle between Plantagenets and Capetians over who should rule in France. Accompanied by plague (including the Black Death of 1348) and religious confusion, it was a time of tribulation for the people of France, harassed as they were by bands of outlaws as well as by the English soldiery.

In 1337, Philippe VI of Valois resisted the claims to his throne made by Edward III of England (the grandson on his mother's side of Philippe le Bel (the Fair). This marked the beginning of the war. Three years after the French defeat at Crécy, Philippe VI purchased the Dauphiné (up to then a territory of the Empire) from its ruler, Humbert II, thereby extending French rule far to the east of the Rhône.

In 1356 King John the Good was defeated by the Black Prince at the Battle of Poitiers (*see POITIERS*).

Under Charles V, Du Guesclin succeeded in restoring internal order. But at this point in their conflict, both adversaries were beset by problems of their own, caused in England by the minority of Richard II. In France, Charles VI too was under age, then affected by madness. The War between Armagnacs and Burgundians began and the Church was torn by the Great Schism (👉 see AVIGNON). Following the English victory at Agincourt (👉 see ST-OMER) and the assassination of John the Fearless of Burgundy at Montereau (👉 see DIJON), the Treaty of Troyes, promising the French crown to the English king, seemed to extinguish any hope of the future Charles VII succeeding.

In 1429, however, after having picked out the king from among the courtiers assembled at Chinon, Joan of Arc recaptured Orléans, thereby preventing Salisbury's army from crossing the Loire and meeting up with the English troops who had been stationed in central and southwestern France following the Treaty of Brétigny in 1360. On 17 July, Charles VII was crowned in Reims cathedral; in 1436 Paris was freed, followed by Normandy and Guyenne. In 1453, the French victory at Castillon-la-Bataille was the last important clash of arms in the war, which was formally brought to an end by the Treaty of Picquigny.

1515 Accession of François I; Battle of Marignano and the signing of peace in perpetuity with Switzerland.

1520 Meeting of François I and Henry VIII of England at the Field of the Cloth of Gold at Guînes.

1539 The Ordinance of **Villers-Cotterêts**, one of the bases of French law, is promulgated by François I. Among its 192 articles are ones decreeing the keeping of parish registers of births and deaths, as well as law reform outlawing the founding of guilds and instituting secret criminal investigation and the compulsory use of French instead of Latin in legal matters. By this time, provincialism was on the way out, supplanted by a truly national consciousness, the outcome of three

centuries of shared ordeals and triumphs.

1541 Calvin's "Institutes of the Christian Religion" is published. In it, this native Frenchman (born at Noyon) attempts to stem the fissiparous tendencies of the Reformation and to proclaim its universality. Style, structure and significance combine in this work to make it the first great classic of French literature.

1559 Treaty of Le Cateau-Cambrésis is signed.

1560 The Amboise Conspiracy, harbinger of the looming political and religious crisis.

The Wars of Religion – 1562-1598

This is the name given to the 36-year-long crisis marked by complex political as well as religious conflict. During the latter half of the 16C, the French monarchy was in poor shape to withstand the looming hegemony of Spain, with political life in chaos and debt reaching incredible dimensions. The firm stand taken on religion by Spain and Italy on the one hand and by the Protestant countries on the other was missing in the France of Catherine de' Medici's regency, where both parties jostled for favour and a policy of appeasement applied.

The nobility took advantage of the situation, seeking to bolster their power base in the provinces and, under cover of religion, to grasp the reins of government. The Catholic League was formed by the Guise and Montmorency families, supported by Spain and opposed by the Bourbon, Condé and Coligny factions, Huguenots all, with English backing.

Though historians distinguish eight wars separated by periods of peace or relative tranquillity, the troubles were continuous: in the country, endless assassinations, persecutions and general lawlessness; at court, intrigues, volte-faces and pursuit of particular interests. Actual warfare, threatened ever since the Amboise Conspiracy, began at Wassy in 1562, following a massacre of Protestants. The names of Dreux, Nîmes, Chartres, Longjumeau, Jarnac, Montcontour,

Richelieu during the siege of La Rochelle (H. Motte)

St-Lô, Valognes, Coutras, Arques, Ivry follow in bloody succession.

The Peace of St-Germain in 1570 demonstrated a general desire for reconciliation, but only two years later came the St Bartholomew's Day Massacre in which some 20 000 Huguenots died.

The States General were convened at Blois at the request of the supporters of the League who were opposed to the centralisation of power into royal hands. Fearful of the power enjoyed by Duke Henri of Guise, head of the Catholic League and the kingdom's best military commander, King Henri III had him assassinated in the château at Blois one cold morning in December 1588, only to be cut down himself by a fanatical monk the following year.

This left the succession open for the Huguenot Henry of Navarre, the future Henri IV. By formally adopting the Catholic faith in 1593 and by promulgating the Edict of Nantes in 1598, this able ruler succeeded in rallying all loyal Frenchmen to his standard, putting at least a temporary end to the long-drawn-out crisis.

THE BOURBONS (1589-1789)

Henri IV – 1589-1610

Though his political manœuvrings and his personal conduct did not endear him to everybody, Henri IV put France's affairs on a firm footing once more,

attaching the provinces of Bresse and Bugey to the kingdom and setting great architects like Du Cerceau and Métezeau to work on projects in Paris such as the Place des Vosges and the Louvre Gallery, and La Rochelle and Charleville in the provinces. Important economic reforms were undertaken, and the king's old Huguenot friend, Maximilien de Béthune, Duke of Sully, set the nation's finances in order, dug canals and laid out new roads and port facilities.

In 1600, the landowner Olivier de Serres published his great work on progressive farming technique "The Theatre of Agriculture and Field Husbandry", supporting Sully in his contention that "tilling and stock-keeping are the two breasts from which France feeds". The king's concern with his people's well-being found expression too in his famous statement "a chicken in the pot every Sunday".

1610	Louis XIII becomes King. The country's trade flourishes with the development of inland ports and there are fine planned expansions to a number of towns (Orléans, La Rochelle, Montargis, Langres). The reign is marked by an aristocratic rebellion, as well as by the pioneering work of St Vincent de Paul in social welfare (hospitals, Sisters of Mercy). In the field of ideas, Descartes publishes his "Discourse on Method" (1637), with its reasoning based on systematic questioning ("Cogito, ergo sum"), a starting point for the intellectual revolution which, among other achievements, led to the invention of analytical geometry.
1624	The King's First Minister, Richelieu (1585-1642), is successful in his attempts to reduce the power of a Protestantism over-inclined to seek foreign aid (La Rochelle) or to resist the unification of the kingdom (Montauban, Privas). A few exemplary executions

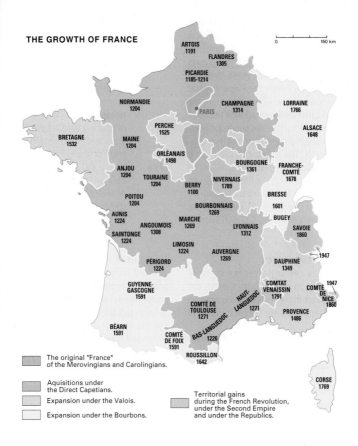

THE GROWTH OF FRANCE

0 — 150 km

ARTOIS
1191

FLANDRES
1305

PICARDIE
1185-1214

NORMANDIE
1204

CHAMPAGNE
1314

LORRAINE
1766

PARIS

PERCHE
1525

ALSACE
1648

BRETAGNE
1532

MAINE
1204

ORLÉANAIS
1498

BOURGOGNE
1361

FRANCHE-
COMTÉ
1678

ANJOU
1204

TOURAINE
1204

BERRY
1100

NIVERNAIS
1789

POITOU
1204

BRESSE
1601

AUNIS
1224

ANGOUMOIS
1308

MARCHE
1269

BOURBONNAIS
1269

LYONNAIS
1312

BUGEY

SAVOIE
1860

SAINTONGE
1224

LIMOSIN
1224

AUVERGNE
1269

1947

PÉRIGORD
1224

DAUPHINÉ
1349

GUYENNE-
GASCOGNE
1591

COMTAT
VENAISSIN
1791

HAUT-
LANGUEDOC

1947

COMTÉ
DE
NICE
1860

COMTÉ DE
TOULOUSE
1271

PROVENCE
1486

BÉARN
1591

COMTÉ
DE FOIX
1591

BAS-LANGUEDOC

1226

ROUSSILLON
1642

CORSE
1769

The original "France"
of the Merovingians and Carolingians.

Aquisitions under
the Direct Capetians.

Expansion under the Valois.

Expansion under the Bourbons.

Territorial gains
during the French Revolution,
under the Second Empire
and under the Republics.

serve to humble the nobility (Montmorency, Cinq-Mars), a process carried further by the demolition of castles. He strengthens France's role in Europe (Thirty Years War) and, in 1635, founds the Academy (Académie française).

Louis XIV – 1643-1715

The 72 years of the Sun King's reign marked both France and Europe with the force of his personality (🕯 *see PARIS and VERSAILLES*). At the time of his accession, the king was only five years old and Anne of Austria confirmed Mazarin in his role as first minister. Five days later, the French victory at Rocroi (1643) signalled the end of Spanish dominance of Europe's affairs. In 1648, the Peace of Westphalia ended the Thirty Years War, confirmed France's claim to Alsace

(apart from Strasbourg and Mulhouse) and established French as the language of diplomacy.

In 1657, while the king looked on, the two-month siege of Montmédy was brought to a triumphant conclusion by La Ferté and Vauban, thereby putting an end to Spanish rule in the Low Countries. In 1662, the king's first year of personal rule was crowned by the purchase of the port of Dunkirk, a result of the statesman Lionne's diplomacy; the place became a base for smugglers and for privateers like Jean Bart operating in the service of the king. Anglo-French rivalry for control of the seas (🕯 *see BELLE-ILE*) now became the main theme of international politics. In 1678, the Treaty of Nijmegen marked the end of the war with Holland, the giving-up of the Franche-Comté and of 12 strongholds in Flanders by Spain, and the reconquest of Alsace. This was a high point in Louis' reign and in French expansion, insured by Vauban's work in fortifying the country's new frontiers. The politics of religion were not always straightforward; for 20 years, the king was in conflict with the Pope in what was known as the Affair of the Régale; in 1685 came the Revocation of the Edict of Nantes with all its dire consequences, and in 1702, the suppression of the camisard revolt. The monarch's later years were clouded by the country's economic exhaustion, though the Battle of Denain in 1712 saved France from invasion by the Austro-Dutch armies and led to the end of the War of the Spanish Succession.

Oriental ventures

In 1664, a century after the voyages of Jean Ango and Jacques Cartier, the French East India Company was revived by Colbert, Louis XIV's great minister of finance.

Two years later he authorised it to set up bases both at **Port-Louis** (where the original East India Company had been) and on waste ground on the far side of the confluence of the Scorff and Blavet rivers. In 1671 the first great merchantman was fitted out for its journey to the East, and the new port was given the name of L'Orient in 1671 (**Lorient** in 1830). Anglo-French naval rivalry now began in earnest. Over a period of 47 years the Company put a total of 76 ships into use, which, in the course of their long and often dangerous voyages, would bring back cargoes of spices and porcelain (France alone importing over 12 million items of the latter). The initially fabulous profits eventually declined when the Company became a kind of state enterprise under the control of the bank run by the Scots financier Law. In the end, Lorient moved from a commercial role to a naval one.

1715   Louis XV succeeds to the crown at the age of five; the Duke of Orleans is Regent. The reign is marked by indecision, frivolity and corruption; many of France's colonies (Senegal, Québec, the Antilles, possessions in India) are lost. Inter-

nally, however, the country prospers, benefiting from a wise economic policy; the standard of living improves and a long period of stability favours agricultural development (introduction of the potato, artificial extension of grazing lands). Lorraine is absorbed into France in 1766, and Corsica in 1769.

1774   Louis XVI becomes King. Lafayette takes part in the American War of Independence, brought to an end by the Treaty of Versailles in 1783.

The spirit of scientific enquiry leads to rapid technological progress, the growth of industry (textiles, porcelain, steam power) and to endeavours such as Lalande's astronomical experiments and the Montgolfier brothers' balloon flights at Annonay in 1783.

THE FRENCH REVOLUTION (1789-1799)

1789   French Revolution begins in Paris.

The Revolution, opening up the continent of Europe to democracy, was the outcome of the long crisis affecting the Ancien Régime.

Hastened along by the teachings of the thinkers of the Enlightenment as much as by the inability of a still essentially feudal system to adapt itself to new social realities, the Revolution broke out following disastrous financial mismanagement and the emptying of the coffers of the state. The main events unfolded in Paris but their repercussions were felt in the provincial cities (Lyon, Nantes...) as well as in the countryside. The year 1789 heralded a number of major historical events for France. The Estates General were renamed the National Assembly, the Bastille was stormed, privileges were abolished (night of 4 July) and the Rights of Man were proclaimed. Two years later, in 1791, the king, fleeing with his family, was arrested in Varennes (22 June) and brought back to Paris, where he was suspended from office on 30 September. The following year the Convention (1792-95) was signed, while in Valmy (20 September) Kellermann and Dumouriez saved France from invasion by forcing the Prussians to retreat; on 22 September France is proclaimed a one and indivisible Republic. The major landmarks of 1793 were the execution of Louis XVI (21 January), the Vendée revolt, the crushing of the Lyon uprising and the siege of Toulon (July-December). In 1795 France adopted the metric system.

The Vendée

This is the name given to the Royalist-led but popular uprising in western France in 1793 in reaction to the excesses of the Convention. The bocage countryside of much of the area favoured the guerrilla warfare waged by the "Whites" (Catholic royalists) against "Blues" (Republicans), who brought in the Alsatian general Kléber. In the winter of 1794 thousands of Whites were executed at Nantes, Angers, Fontenay... while the countryside was ravaged by mobile columns of vengeful soldiery (known as the infernal columns of General Turreau). Still resistance continued, until finally put to an end by the more conciliatory policies of Hoche.

1799 Napoleon overthrows Revolutionary government, puts new constitution in place.

In 1799 Napoleon overthrew the **Directory** *(9 November)* and declared himself First Consul of the Republic. Finally, in 1801, the Code Napoléon was promulgated throughout the country

THE EMPIRE (1804-1815)

1804 On 2 December, Napoleon is crowned Emperor of the French in Notre-Dame by Pope Pius VII. The territorial acquisitions made in the course of the French Revolution now have to be defended against a whole series of coalitions formed by the country's numerous enemies.

La Marseillaise by Rude – Arc de Triomphe

A. Eïi/MICHELIN

1805 Napoleon gives up his plans for invasion of England, abandoning the great camp set up at Boulogne for that purpose. The Royal Navy's victory at Trafalgar gives Britain control of the seas, but France's armies win the Battles of Ulm and Austerlitz (Slavkov).

1806 Intended to bring about England's economic ruin, the Continental Blockade pushes France into further territorial acquisitions.

1808 Some of the best French forces bogged down in the Peninsular War.

1812 Napoleon invades Russia. The Retreat from Moscow.

1813 The Battle of Leipzig. The whole of Europe lines up against France. Not even Napoleon's military genius can prevent the fall of Paris and the Emperor's farewell at Fontainebleau (20 April 1814). Napoleon is exiled to the island of Elba.

THE RESTORATION (1815-1830)

1814 Louis XVIII returns from exile in England.

| 1815 | Battle of Waterloo. Napoleon is defeated. |

1815 proved a decisive year for France. Following the Hundred Days (20 March–22 June) - Napoleon's triumphalist journey back to Paris from his exile in Elba - his attempt to re-establish the Empire ended with the victory of the Allies (principally England and Prussia, under the leadership of England's Duke of Wellington) at Waterloo on 18 June. Louis XVIII was once more on the throne and France was now forced to withdraw into the frontiers of 1792. Talleyrand's efforts at the Congress of Vienna helped bring France back into the community of European nations. Marshal Ney was executed.

THE JULY MONARCHY (1830-1848)

| 1830 | Charles X's "Four Ordinances of St-Cloud" violate the Constitution and lead to the outbreak of revolution. There follow the "Three Glorious Days" (27, 28 and 29 July) and the flight of the Bourbons. Louis-Philippe becomes King. |
| 1837 | France's first passenger-carrying railway is opened between Paris and St-Germain-en-Laye. |

SECOND REPUBLIC AND SECOND EMPIRE (1848-1870)

1848	On 10 December, Louis Napoléon is elected President of the Republic by universal suffrage.
1851	On 2 December, Louis Napoléon dissolves the Legislative Assembly and declares himself President for a 10-year term.
1852	A plebiscite leads to the proclamation of the Second Empire (Napoleon III).
1855	The World Fair is held in Paris.
1860	Savoy and the county of Nice elect to become part of France.

| 1869 | Freedom of the Press is guaranteed. |
| 1870 | War declared on Prussia on 19 July. On 2 September, defeat at Sedan spells the end of the Second Empire. Two days later Paris rises and the Republic is proclaimed. But the way to the capital lies open, and soon Paris is under siege. |

THE REPUBLIC (1870-THE PRESENT DAY)

1870	Following the disaster at Sedan, the Third Republic is proclaimed on 4 September.
1871	The Paris Commune (21-28 May). By the Treaty of Frankfurt France gives up all of Alsace (with the exception of Belfort) and part of Lorraine.
1881	Jules Ferry secularises primary education, making it free and, later, compulsory.
1884	Trade unions gain formal recognition.
1885	Vaccination in the treatment of rabies (Pasteur). Inauguration of the Eiffel Tower (World Fair).
1894	The Dreyfus Affair divides the country. Forged evidence results in this Jewish General Staff captain being unfairly imprisoned for spying.
1897	Clément Ader's heavier-than-air machine takes to the air at Toulouse.
1904	Entente Cordiale.
1905	Separation of Church and State.
1914	Outbreak of the First World War. On 3 August the German armies attack through neutral Belgium but are thrown back in the Battle of the Marne. Four years of trench warfare follow, a bloody climax being reached in 1916-17 around the fortress city of Verdun, where the German offensive is held, at immense cost in lives on both sides.

In 1919 the signing of the Treaty of Versailles brings the First World War to an end.

1934 France is deeply divided; on 6 February, the National Assembly is attacked by right-wing demonstrators. Two years later, Léon Blum forms his Popular Front government.

1939 Outbreak of the Second World War.

1940 France invaded and concedes defeat.

In June 1940 France was overrun by the German army and Marshal Pétain's government requested an armistice. Much of the country was occupied (the north and the whole of the Atlantic seaboard), but the German puppet "French State" with its slogan of "Work, Family, Fatherland" is established at Vichy and collaborates closely with the Nazis. Almost all French Jews were rounded up by the French authorities and deported for extermination. France's honour was saved by General de Gaulle's Free French forces, active in many theatres of the war, and by the courage of the men and women of the Resistance.

1942 Whole country is occupied, and the French fleet scuttles itself at Toulon.

1944 In June the British and American Allies land in Normandy, and in the South of France in August. Paris is liberated.

1945 German surrender signed at Reims on 7 May 1945.

This major conflict (1939-1945), which inflamed all continents, is detailed in this guide under the places which it affected most in France.

1947 The Fourth Republic established. Its governments last an average of six months.

1954 Dien Bien Phu falls to the Vietminh. France abandons Indo-China and grants Morocco and Tunisia their independence (1956).

1958 The Algerian crisis leads to the downfall of the Fourth and the establishment of the Fifth Republic under De Gaulle. Civil war is narrowly averted. Nearly all its French population leaves Algeria, which becomes independent in 1962.

1958 The Fifth Republic established. The European Economic Community (EEC) comes into effect.

The new constitution inspired by General de Gaulle is voted by referendum.

1962 Referendum establishing that the future President of the Republic be elected by universal suffrage.

1967 Franco-British agreement to manufacture Airbus.

1968 The "events of May"; workers join students in mass protests, roughly put down by riot police. The Gaullists triumph in national elections, but it is a hollow victory and De Gaulle, defeated in the referendum of April 1969, retires to continue writing his memoirs.

1969 Georges Pompidou is elected President (16 June).

1974 Valéry Giscard d'Estaing is elected President (19 May).

Charles de Gaulle, 1967

© Hulton-Deutsch Collection/CORBIS

1981	François Mitterrand is elected President (10 May). Inauguration of the TGV line between Paris and Lyon (2h 40min); Paris-Marseille (1981); and Paris-Bordeaux (1990).
1994	Inauguration of the Channel Tunnel (6 May).
1995	Jacques Chirac is elected President (7 May).
1999	1 Jan, dubbed "€ Day," marks the beginning of circulation for Euro notes and coins
2002	French Franc withdrawn from circulation.
2003	11,000 die in heatwave.
2005	Proposed European Constitution rejected in referendum of French electorate (May). Ethnic minorities rioting in several cities (summer).
2007	Nicolas Sarkozy elected President of France (6 May).

CONTEMPORARY FRANCE

Although France is ranked among the industrialised nations and one of leading countries in the world in terms of international trade, it remains at the same time a nation with a strong **rural tradition.** Even if the number of people actually employed in farming is on the decline, the French continue to have close ties to the land. Many, wherever they live, maintain close contacts with their family's native region, either by acquiring a cottage in the country or by inheriting a family property.

For most French people, the qualities associated with this ancestral land are encapsulated in the traditional **village** – the village where one was born, where one has chosen to live or where one spends one's holidays. Leaving aside the differences attributed to climatic conditions and building materials, all villages feature common characteristics: the **main street** (Grand'rue) lined with small shops, the **marketplace,** where local cattle fairs used to be held, and of course, the **church**, whose chimes continue to herald the fortunes and misfortunes of the community. Although they see a surge of activity during municipal and trade fairs, French villages lead quiet, peaceful lives most of the year. Only the traditional **café** and the **boules playing ground** echo the conversations of the locals idly debating on the meaning of life.

This strong regionalism has led to frequent conflict with, and hostility to, the central government in Paris. To reseolve this long-standing problem, a series of decentralisation reforms was implemented in 1982, creating regional governments with considerable autonomy.

Regional capitals were established – in all cases a former historic seat of local power – to strike a balance between the capital and the countryside. Despite their long history and local tradition, these regional urban centres, well subsidised by Paris, tend to be resolutely turned towards the future and illustrate the thriving character of the French regions. In 2003, extensive further powers were devolved to the regions.

However, **Paris**, with her nine and a half million inhabitants, remains the administrative core of the country and a focal point for the whole nation. The seat of poliitical power, and an important centre for world trade , "the city of lights" is also an exceptional destination for visitors. In the country which attracts more tourists each year than any other, the capital is the main attraction, thanks to its wealth of architectural marvels, its extraordinary collection of world-class museums, and its high cultural standards.

This brief description would not be complete without mentioning the **French** themselves. Frequently misunderstood by foreign visitors, often condemned as brusque and unhelpful, they are nonetheless always ready to protect and safeguard their age-old traditions and support a cause in defence of the interests of France and the French way of life. To those who make the effort of going towards them, and who cherish that way of life as they do, the French will always extend a warm, genuine welcome.

ART AND CULTURE

ABC of Architecture

Art in France

Ecclesiastical architecture

CLERMONT FERRAND (Puy-de-Dôme) – Ground plan of Basilique Notre-Dame-du-Port (11C-12C)

Latin-cross plan, the transverse aisle forming the **transept**

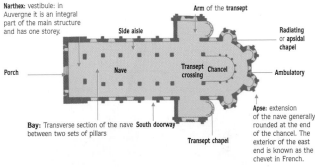

Narthex: vestibule: in Auvergne it is an integral part of the main structure and has one storey.

Arm of the **transept**

Side aisle

Radiating or **apsidal chapel**

Porch

Nave

Transept crossing Chancel

Ambulatory

Bay: Transverse section of the nave between two sets of pillars

South doorway

Apse: extension of the nave generally rounded at the end of the chancel. The exterior of the east end is known as the chevet in French.

Transept chapel

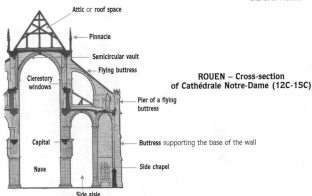

Attic or roof space

Pinnacle

Semicircular vault

Flying buttress

Clerestory windows

ROUEN – Cross-section of Cathédrale Notre-Dame (12C-15C)

Pier of a flying buttress

Capital

Buttress supporting the base of the wall

Nave

Side chapel

Side aisle

MOISSAC – South doorway of the 12C abbey church

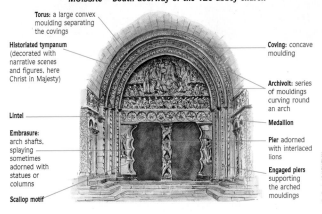

Torus: a large convex moulding separating the covings

Historiated tympanum (decorated with narrative scenes and figures, here Christ in Majesty)

Coving: concave moulding

Archivolt: series of mouldings curving round an arch

Lintel

Medallion

Embrasure: arch shafts, splaying sometimes adorned with statues or columns

Pier adorned with interlaced lions

Engaged piers supporting the arched mouldings

Scallop motif

R. Corbel/MICHELIN

79

ORCIVAL – Notre-Dame Basilica (12C)

Most of the Romanesque churches of the Auvergne belong to a school which developed in the 11C 12C and is considered one of the most unusual in the history of art in the western world

Relieving arch: releves the weight of the wall above an opening.

Twin windows

Transept

Gable-wall

Two storeyed **octagonal bell-tower:** its thrusts are but tressed by the chevet, nave and the arms of the transept.

Semicircular window

Window

Modillions: scroll shaped projecting mouldings supporting the cornice.

String-course with billet moulding: ornamental frieze consisting of bands of raised short cylindrical or square blocks placed at regular intervals.

Radiating or **apsidal** chapel

Buttress: external support for a wall, built against it.

Cornice adorned with chequered motif

Chevet: the east end is the most beautiful and most characteristic of the Auvergne churches owing to the original layout of the various levels.

R. Corbel/MICHELIN

CHARTRES – West front of Cathédrale Notre-Dame (12C-13C)

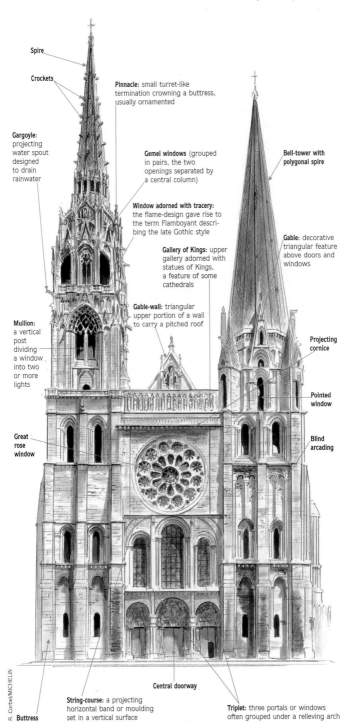

Spire

Crockets

Pinnacle: small turret-like termination crowning a buttress, usually ornamented

Gargoyle: projecting water spout designed to drain rainwater

Gemel windows (grouped in pairs, the two openings separated by a central column)

Bell-tower with polygonal spire

Window adorned with tracery: the flame-design gave rise to the term Flamboyant describing the late Gothic style

Gallery of Kings: upper gallery adorned with statues of Kings, a feature of some cathedrals

Gable: decorative triangular feature above doors and windows

Gable-wall: triangular upper portion of a wall to carry a pitched roof

Mullion: a vertical post dividing a window into two or more lights

Projecting cornice

Pointed window

Great rose window

Blind arcading

Central doorway

String-course: a projecting horizontal band or moulding set in a vertical surface

Triplet: three portals or windows often grouped under a relieving arch

Buttress

R. Corbel/MICHELIN

SENLIS – Cathédrale Notre-Dame (12C-13C)

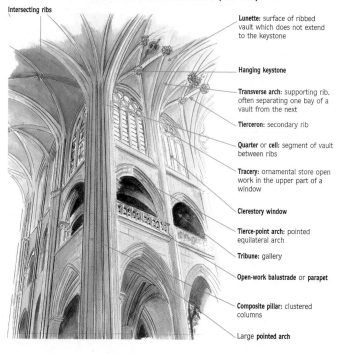

Intersecting ribs

Lunette: surface of ribbed vault which does not extend to the keystone

Hanging keystone

Transverse arch: supporting rib, often separating one bay of a vault from the next

Tierceron: secondary rib

Quarter or **cell:** segment of vault between ribs

Tracery: ornamental store open work in the upper part of a window

Clerestory window

Tierce-point arch: pointed equilateral arch

Tribune: gallery

Open-work balustrade or **parapet**

Composite pillar: clustered columns

Large **pointed arch**

JOUARRE – Crypte St-Paul (7C)

The crypts of Jouarre Abbey built in the Carollgian period are among the earliest examples of funerary religious architecture popular in the Middle Ages.

Groined vault

Ovolo moulding: egg and dart moulding

Abacus

Capitals generally with Classical orders: Corinthian style capitals enhanced by grooves, ovolo, beads

Recumbent figure

Cenotaph: funerary monument which does not contain remains

Fluting

Shell motif, symbol of immortality

Stone **sarcophagus**

Porphyry **shaft**

Torus: raised moulding

Base

R. Corbel/MICHELIN

THANN – Choir stalls in Collégiale St-Thiébaut (14C-early 16C)

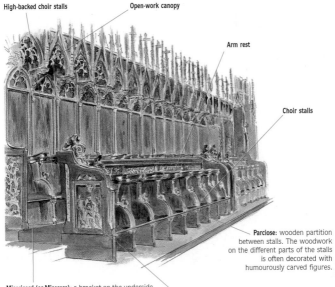

High-backed choir stalls

Open-work canopy

Arm rest

Choir stalls

Parclose: wooden partition between stalls. The woodwork on the different parts of the stalls is often decorated with humourously carved figures.

Misericord (or Miserere): a bracket on the underside of a hinged choir stall which can be turned up to give support to the occupant standing during long services (from the Latin "per misericordiam" in corn passion).

Cheek: a vertical panel at the end of a row of stalls

ALBI – Rood screen In Cathédrale Ste-Cécile (16C)

The **rood screen** was designed to separate the chancel (reserved for the clergy) from the nave (where the congregation gathered) and carry the Crucifix (rood). This example in Albi is typical of the Flamboyant Gothic style.

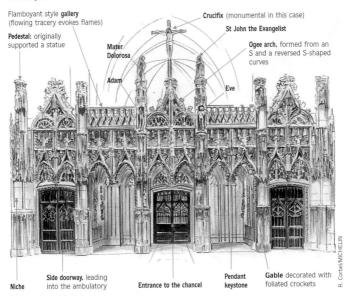

Flamboyant style **gallery** (flowing tracery evokes flames)

Pedestal: originally supported a statue

Mater Dolorosa

Adam

Crucifix (monumental in this case)

St John the Evangelist

Ogee arch, formed from an S and a reversed S-shaped curves

Eve

Niche

Side doorway, leading into the ambulatory

Entrance to the chancel

Pendant keystone

Gable decorated with foliated crockets

R. Corbel/MICHELIN

Military architecture

CARCASSONNE – East gateway of the Château Comtal (12C)

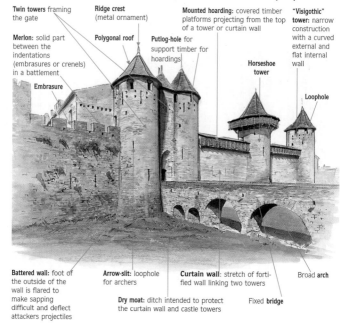

Twin towers framing the gate

Ridge crest (metal ornament)

Merlon: solid part between the indentations (embrasures or crenels) in a battlement

Polygonal roof

Embrasure

Mounted hoarding: covered timber platforms projecting from the top of a tower or curtain wall

Putlog-hole for support timber for hoardings

"Visigothic" tower: narrow construction with a curved external and flat internal wall

Horseshoe tower

Loophole

Battered wall: foot of the outside of the wall is flared to make sapping difficult and deflect attackers projectiles

Arrow-slit: loophole for archers

Dry moat: ditch intended to protect the curtain wall and castle towers

Curtain wall: stretch of fortified wall linking two towers

Fixed bridge

Broad **arch**

Château de BONAGUIL (13C – early 16C)

Bonaguil Castle, rebuilt from 1483 to 1510 by Béranger de Roquefeuil, is a good example of the Improvements made to a defensive stronghold to take account of the development of firearms.

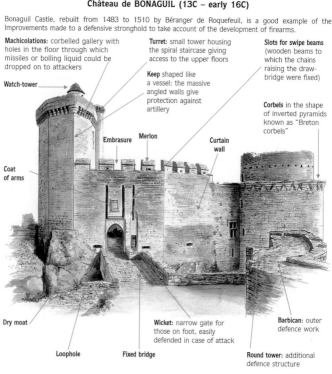

Machicolations: corbelled gallery with holes in the floor through which missiles or bolling liquid could be dropped on to attackers

Watch-tower

Turret: small tower housing the spiral staircase giving access to the upper floors

Keep shaped like a vessel: the massive angled walls give protection against artillery

Slots for swipe beams (wooden beams to which the chains raising the drawbridge were fixed)

Corbels in the shape of inverted pyramids known as "Breton corbels"

Coat of arms

Embrasure   **Merlon**

Curtain wall

Dry moat

Loophole

Fixed bridge

Wicket: narrow gate for those on foot, easily defended in case of attack

Barbican: outer defence work

Round tower: additional defence structure

R. Corbel/MICHELIN

NEUF-BRISACH (1698-1703)

The polygonal stronghold was developed in the early 16C as firearms became more common in warfare: the cannon mounted on one structure covered the "blind spot" of the neighbouring position. This stronghold was built by Vauban, opposite the formidable Breisach, handed back to the Hapsburgs under the Treaty of Ryswick (1697).

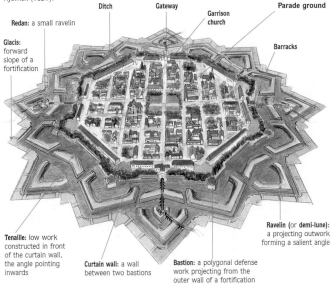

Redan: a small ravelin

Ditch

Gateway

Garrison church

Parade ground

Glacis: forward slope of a fortification

Barracks

Tenaille: low work constructed in front of the curtain wall, the angle pointing inwards

Curtain wall: a wall between two bastions

Bastion: a polygonal defense work projecting from the outer wall of a fortification

Ravelin (or demi-lune): a projecting outwork forming a salient angle

Civil architecture

BLOIS – Château, François-1er staircase (16C)

The spiral stairway is built inside an octagonal staircase half set into the façade. It opens onto the main courtyard in a series of balconies which form loggias. The king and his court would view all sorts of entertainment from here: the arrival of dignitaries, jousting, hunting or military displays.

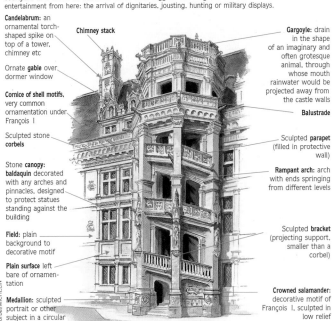

Candelabrum: an ornamental torch-shaped spike on top of a tower, chimney etc

Chimney stack

Gargoyle: drain in the shape of an imaginary and often grotesque animal, through whose mouth rainwater would be projected away from the castle walls

Ornate **gable** over dormer window

Cornice of shell motifs, very common ornamentation under François I

Balustrade

Sculpted stone **corbels**

Sculpted **parapet** (filled in protective wall)

Stone **canopy: baldaquin** decorated with any arches and pinnacles, designed to protect statues standing against the building

Rampant arch: arch with ends springing from different levels

Field: plain background to decorative motif

Sculpted **bracket** (projecting support, smaller than a corbel)

Plain surface left bare of ornamentation

Crowned salamander: decorative motif of François I, sculpted in low relief

Medallion: sculpted portrait or other subject in a circular frame

R. Corbel/MICHELIN

SERRANT – Château (16C-17C)

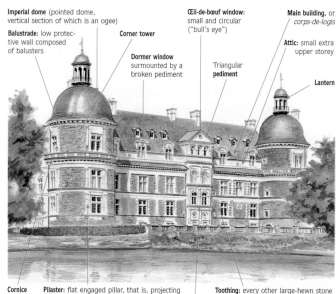

Imperial dome (pointed dome, vertical section of which is an ogee)

Balustrade: low protective wall composed of balusters

Corner tower

Dormer window surmounted by a broken pediment

Œil-de-bœuf window: small and circular ("bull's eye")

Triangular pediment

Main building, or *corps-de-logis*

Attic: small extra upper storey

Lantern

Cornice

Pilaster: flat engaged pillar, that is, projecting only slightly from the wall behind it

Avant-corps: part of a building projecting from the rest of the façade for the entire height of the building, roof included

Toothing: every other large-hewn stone is left projecting from the stone-work framing the windows for a more solid and more decorative bond with the adjoining schist walls

BORDEAUX – Palais de la Bourse (18C)

Flaming urn: a characteristic feature in Classical architecture

Triangular pediment with allegorical carving

Œil-de-bœuf: a small, circular window ("bull's-eye")

Trophy: decorative carving of arms grouped around a breast plate or helmet

Dentils: a frieze of small, rectangular blocks

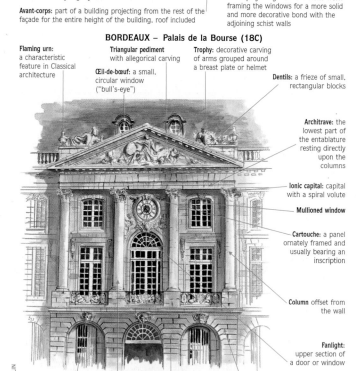

Architrave: the lowest part of the entablature resting directly upon the columns

Ionic capital: capital with a spiral volute

Mullioned window

Cartouche: a panel ornately framed and usually bearing an inscription

Column offset from the wall

Fanlight: upper section of a door or window

Mascaron: ornamental sculpture on keystone or voussoir

Colossal order spanning several storeys

Rusticated stonework: the massive blocks are dressed to a flat surface with chamfered edges

Groove marking the join between dressed stone blocks

R. Corbel/MICHELIN

A Survey of French Art

FROM PREHISTORY TO THE GALLO-ROMAN ERA

Prehistory

While stone and bone tools appeared in the Lower Paleolithic period, prehistoric art did not make its entrance until the Upper Paleolithic (350 to 100 centuries BC), and reached its peak in the Magdalenian Period (*see Les EYZIES-DE-TAYAC for the chronology of prehistoric eras*). The art of engraved wood and ivory objects together with votive statuettes developed alongside the art of wall decoration, as is well illustrated in France by caves in the Dordogne, the Pyrenees, the Ardèche and the Gard. Early artists used pigments with a mineral base for their cave paintings and sometimes took advantage of the natural shape of the rock itself to execute their work in low relief.

The Neolithic revolution (6500 BC), during which populations began to settle, brought with it the advent of pottery as well as a different use of land and a change in burial practices – some megaliths (dolmens and covered passageways) are ancient burial chambers. Menhirs, a type of megalith found in great numbers in Brittany (Carnac and Locmariaquer), are as yet of unknown origin.

The discovery of metal brought prehistoric civilisation into the Bronze Age (2300-1800 BC) and then into the Iron Age (750-450 BC). Celtic art showed perfect mastery of metalwork as in the tombs of Gorge-Meillet, Mailly-le-Camp, Bibracte and Vix in which the treasures consist of gold torques (necklaces) and other items of jewellery, various coins and bronzeware.

The Gallo-Roman Era and the Early Middle Ages

When the Romans conquered Gaul (2C-1C BC), they introduced the technique of building with stone. In cities, the Empire's administrative centres, the centralised power of Rome favoured a style of architecture that reflected its strength and prestige and imposed its culture. Theatres (Orange and Vienne), temples (the Square House or Maison Carrée in Nîmes), baths, basilicas and triumphal arches were constructed, while the local aristocracy took to building Roman villas with frescoes and mosaics (Vaison-la-Romaine and Grand). The presence of the Romans has had a lasting effect on the shape of France in terms of town-planning, roads, bridges and aqueducts (Pont du Gard). Towards the end of the late Empire, official recognition of the Christian church in the year 380 prompted the first examples of Christian architecture, among them the baptisteries of Fréjus, Riez, and Poitiers.

During the great barbarian invasions of the 5C, figurative art, unknown to Germanic peoples, gave place to abstract

Lagatjar Alignements at Camaret-sur-Mer, Brittany

B. Kaufmann/MICHELIN

(intertwining, circular shapes) and animal motifs. The technique of *cloisonné* gold and silverware (Childeric's treasure) became widespread.

Merovingian art (6C-8C), a synthesis of styles, included elements of antique, barbarian and Christian art (the Dunes hypogeum near Poitiers and the crypt in Jouarre) out of which evolved medieval art.

The **Carolingian Renaissance** (9C) was marked by a great flowering of illuminated manuscripts and ivory-carving (the Dagulf psalter in the Louvre) and by a deliberate return to imperial, antique art forms (Aix-la-Chapelle and the oratory of Germigny-des-Prés).

The altar in churches of the period is sometimes raised above a vaulted area of the chancel known as the crypt which was originally on the same level as the nave (St-Germain of Auxerre and St-Philibert-de-Grand-Lieu).

ROMANESQUE PERIOD (11C-12C)

In the early 11C, after the disturbances of the year 1000 (decadence of the Carolingian dynasty and struggles between feudal barons), the spiritual influence and power of the Church gave rise to the birth of Romanesque architecture.

Romanesque Architecture

Early Romanesque edifices were characterised by the widespread use of stone vaulting which replaced timber roofs, the use of buttresses and a return to architectural decoration (as in the churches of St-Martin-du-Canigou, and St-Bénigne in Dijon). The darkness of the nave was explained by the fact that for structural reasons wide openings could not be cut into the walls supporting the vaulting.

The basilica plan with nave and side aisles, sometimes preceded by a porch, predominated in France although some churches were built to a central plan (the church of Neuvy-St-Sépulcre). Depending on the church, the east end might have been flat or have had apsidal chapels; it was often semicircular with axial chapels (as in the church of Anzy-le-Duc) or may have featured radiating chapels.

More complex designs combined an ambulatory with radiating chapels (the churches of Conques and Cluny).

The first attempts at embellishment led to a revival of sculptural decoration of which the lintel of St-Genis-les-Fontaines Church is one of the earliest examples. Tympana, archivolts, arch shafts and piers were covered with carvings of a religious or profane nature (as in the illustration of the *Romance of Renart* in the church of St-Ursin in Bourges). Interior decoration consisted mainly of frescoes (the churches of St-Savin-sur-Gartempe and Berzé-la-Ville) and carved capitals with the occasional complex theme (as in the chancel capitals in Cluny).

The Romanesque decorative style drew largely upon three main models, the Oriental (griffins and imaginary animals) which was spread by the Crusades, the Byzantine (illustrations of Christ in Majesty and a particular style for folds) and the Islamic (stylised foliage and pseudo-Kufic script).

Regional Characteristics

The Romanesque style spread throughout France affecting some areas earlier than others and developing special stylistic features according to the region. It first appeared in the south and in Burgundy, reaching the east of France at a much later date.

Romanesque architecture in the **Languedoc** owes much to Toulouse's St-Sernin Basilica, whose tall lantern tower pierced by ornamental arcading served as a model for many local bell-towers. The sculptures on the Miége-ville doorway, completed in 1118, have a distinctive style, with highly expressive folds and a lengthening of the figures which is repeated in Moissac and, to a lesser extent, in St-Gilles-du-Gard.

In **Saintonge-Poitou**, the originality of the edifices derives from the great height of the aisles which serve to reinforce the walls of the nave and thus lend balance to the barrel vaulting. The gabled façades, flanked by lantern towers, are covered in ornamental arcading with statue niches and low relief (as in the church of Notre-Dame-la-Grande in Poitiers).

Detail on the tympanum of the Ste-Foy church doorway in Conques

S. Sauvignier/MICHELIN

In **Auvergne**, the transept crossing is often covered by a dome, buttressed by high, quadripartite vaulting and supported on diaphragm arches. This constitutes an oblong mass which juts out above the roof beneath the bell-tower. The use of lava, a particularly difficult stone to carve, explains the limited sculptural decoration (as in the churches of St-Nectaire, Notre-Dame-du-Port in Clermont-Ferrand and that of Orcival). The tympana lintels are gable-shaped. The development of the Romanesque in **Burgundy** was strongly influenced by the Abbey of Cluny (now destroyed) with its great chancel with radiating chapels, a double transept and the hint of direct lighting in the nave through slender openings at the base of the barrel vaulting. The churches of Paray-le-Monial and Notre-Dame in La Charité-sur-Loire were built on the Cluniac model.

The basilica of Sainte-Madeleine in Vézelay in the north of the Morvan, with its harmonious, simplified church body and its covering of groined vaults, was also to influence churches in the region.

In the **Rhine** and **Meuse** regions, architectural characteristics from the Carolingian era, with an Ottonian influence, tend to prevail. This is borne out by double chancels and transepts (as in Verdun) and a central plan and interior elevation like that of the Palatine Chapel in Aachen (as in Ottmarsheim).

Lastly, until a relatively late date the churches in **Normandy** faithfully retained the custom of a timber roof (as in Jumièges and Bayeux). As stone vaulting was introduced decorative ribs gradually came into use (as in St-Étienne in Caen). The monumental size of the edifices and their harmoniously proportioned façades with two towers, are also typical of the Anglo-Norman Romanesque style.

Apart from these regional features some buildings owe their individuality to their function. The **pilgrimage churches**, for instance, had an ambulatory around the chancel, transept aisles and two aisles on either side of the nave to give pilgrims easy access to the relics they wished to venerate. The main churches of this kind on the way to Santiago de Compostela were St Faith in Conques, St-Sernin in Toulouse, St-Martial in Limoges and St-Martin in Tours (the two latter have since been destroyed).

Romanesque Religious Art

Liturgical items at the time consisted of church plate, manuscripts, precious fabrics and reliquaries. Church treasure would often include a Virgin in Majesty made of polychrome wood or embossed metal decorated with precious stones. The blossoming of **Limousin enamelware** marked a great milestone in the history of the decorative arts during the Romanesque period when it was exported throughout Europe. The *cham-*

plevé method consisted of pouring the enamel into a grooved metal surface of gilded copper. Enamel was used in a number of ways to decorate items ranging from small objects such as crosses, ciboria and reliquaries to monumental works like altars (high altar of **Grandmont** abbey church and items in the Cluny Museum, Paris).

GOTHIC PERIOD (12C–15C)

Architecture

Transitional Gothic

In about 1140, important architectural innovations in St-Denis Cathedral, such as intersecting ribbed vaulting and pointed arches in the narthex and chancel, heralded the dawn of the Gothic style. In the late 12C, there were further innovations common to a group of buildings in Ile-de-France and in the north of France. They included ogives and mouldings which extended down from the vaulting into bundles of engaged slender columns around the pillars of great arches. Capitals were simplified, became smaller with time and gradually diminished in importance. New concepts of sculptural decorating, including the appearance of statue-columns, affected building façades. In

Flamboyant Gothic doorway, Avioth basilica

R.Mattès/MICHELIN

Sens Cathedral, the rectangular layout of the bays called for sexpartite vaulting with alternating major and minor pillars to support large arches. The major pillars supported three ribs while the minor ones supported a single intermediary rib. Apart from sexpartite vaulting with alternating supports, this early Gothic architecture typical of Sens, Noyon and Laon was also characterised by a four-storeyed elevation, great arches, tribunes, a triforium and tall bays.

In the years 1180-1200, in Notre-Dame Cathedral in Paris, raised vaults were reinforced by the addition of flying buttresses on the outside of the edifice while inside, alternating supports disappeared. These new measures gave rise to the emergence of a transitional style which led to Lanceolate Gothic.

Lanceolate Gothic

The Gothic style was at its peak during the reigns of Philippe Auguste (1180-1223) and St Louis (1226-70). The rebuilding of Chartres Cathedral (1210-30) gave rise to a model for what is known as the Chartres family of cathedrals (Reims, Amiens and Beauvais) which included oblong plan vaulting, a three-storeyed elevation (without tribunes) and flying buttresses. The chancel with its double ambulatory and the transept arms with side aisles made for a grandiose interior. The upper windows in the nave were divided into two lancets surmounted by a round opening.

The façades were subdivided into three horizontal registers, as in the cathedrals of Laon and Amiens. The doorways were set in deep porches with gables while above them was an openwork rose window with stained glass. A gallery of arches ran beneath the bell-towers.

There are a number of variations of Lanceolate Gothic in France. An example is Notre-Dame Church in Dijon where the ancient section of the sexpartite vaulting has been preserved.

Development of the Gothic Style to the 15C

The improvement in vaulting from a technical point of view, in particular the use of relieving arches, meant that the supporting function of walls was reduced and more space could be given over to windows and stone tracery as in St-Urbain's Basilica in Troyes and the Sainte-Chapelle in Paris (1248). This gave rise to the **High Gothic** style in the north of France from the end of the 13C to the late 14C. (Examples include the chancel in Beauvais Cathedral, Évreux Cathedral and the north transept of Rouen Cathedral.)

Gothic architecture in the centre and southwest of France developed along unusual lines in the late 13C. Jean Deschamps, master mason of Narbonne Cathedral, designed a massively proportioned building in which the vertical upsweep of the lines was interrupted by wide galleries above the aisles. St Cecilia's Cathedral in Albi diverged completely from Gothic models in the north of France through the use of brick and a buttress system inherited from the Romanesque period. Throughout the 14C, church interiors were filled with sculptural decoration in the form of rood screens, choir screens, monumental altarpieces and devotional statues.

From the late 14C, development of the main principles of Gothic architecture came to a halt but decorative devices grew apace giving rise to the elaborate **Flamboyant Gothic** style with its gables, lancet arches, pinnacles and exuberant foliage. This ornamentation, occasionally referred to as Baroque Gothic, also played a part in civil architecture. An example is the Great Hall in the Law Courts at Poitiers, carved by Guy de Dammartin in the last 10 years of the 14C. Riom's Sainte-Chapelle, built for the Duke Jean de Berry, is another early example. Flamboyant Gothic in France left its mark on a good number of public and religious edifices (Palais Jacques Cœur in Bourges and the façade of St-Maclou Church in Rouen) as well as on liturgical furnishings (the choir screen and rood screen in Ste-Cécile's Cathedral in Albi).

Throughout the Gothic period castle architecture remained faithful to feudal models (Angers Castle, the walled city of Cordes and the mountain fortress of Merle Towers) and did not develop further until the beginning of the Renaissance.

Sculpture, Decorative Arts and Painting

Gothic Sculpture

Progress towards naturalism and realism, the humanism of the Gothic style, can be seen in the statuary and sculptural decoration of the time. Statue-columns of doorways in the 12C tended still to be rigidly hieratic but in the 13C took on greater freedom of expression as may be seen in Amiens and Reims (the Smiling Angel). New themes emerged including the Coronation of the Virgin which first appeared in Senlis in 1191 and thereafter became a popular subject.

Stained Glass

The four main areas producing stained glass in France in the 12C were St-Denis, Champagne, the west (Le Mans, Vendôme and Poitiers) and a group of workshops in the Rhine area in eastern France. Master glassworkers developed an intense blue-coloured glass known as Chartres blue which was to become famous. The invention of silver yellow in 1300-10 led to a more translucent enamelled glass with a subtler range of colour.

The combination of stained glass and Gothic architecture gave rise to larger bays – formerly opaque wall space could be opened up and filled with glass, thanks to new support systems. The fragility of stained glass explains

Stained-Glass Window, Reims Cathedral

the fact that there are very few original medieval windows intact today; many have been replaced by copies or later works. The windows of Chartres, Évreux and the Sainte-Chapelle are precious testimonies to the art.

Illumination and Painting
The art of illumination reached its peak in the 14C when artists freed from University supervision produced sumptuous manuscripts, including Books of Hours, for private use. Among them were Jean Pucelle (Les Heures de Jeanne d'Évreux) and the Limbourg brothers (Les Très Riches Heures du Duc de Berry, dating from the early 15C).

Easel painting first made its appearance n 1350 (the portrait of John the Good, now in the Louvre, is an example). Italian and more particularly Flemish influences, evident as much in depiction of landscape as in attention to detail, may be seen in works by great 15C artists like **Jean Fouquet, Enguerrand Quarton** and the **Master of Moulins**.

THE RENAISSANCE

Gothic art persisted in many parts of France until the middle of the 16C. In the Loire region, however, there were signs of a break with medieval traditions as early as the beginning of the century.

Italian Style and Early Renaissance
Renaissance aesthetics in Lombardy, familiar in France since the military campaigns of Charles VIII and Louis XII at the end of the 15C, at first affected only architectural decoration, through the introduction of motifs from Antiquity such as pilasters, foliage and scallops (as in the tomb of Solesmes, Château de Gaillon). Little by little, however, feudal, military and defensive architecture gave way to a more comfortable style of seigniorial residence. The Château de Chenonceau (begun before 1515) and that of Azay-le-Rideau (1518-27) are examples of this development, particularly in their regular layout, the symmetry of the façades and the beginnings of a new type of architectural decoration. However, it was the great royal undertakings of the time that brought about the blossoming of the Renaissance style.

Architecture Under François I (1515-1547)
The Façade des Loges (1520-24) in the Château de Blois (begun in 1515) is a free replica of the Vatican loggia in Rome. While the castle's irregular fenestration recalls the old medieval style, its great novelty is the preoccupation with Italianate ornamentation. During the reign of François I, the Château de Chambord (1519-47) which combines French architectural traditions (corner towers, irregular roofs and dormer windows) with innovative elements (symmetrical façades, refined decoration and a monumental internal staircase) served as a model for a good many of the Loire castles including Chaumont, Le Lude and Ussé.

After his defeat at the Battle of Pavia in 1525, François I left his residences in the Loire valley to turn his attention to those in Ile-de-France. In 1527 building began on the Château de Fontainebleau under the supervision of Gilles Le Breton. The interior decoration by artists from the **First School of Fontainebleau** was to have a profound influence on the development of French art.

The Italian artist **Rosso** (1494-1540) introduced a new system of decoration to France that combined stuccowork, wood panelling and allegorical frescoes which drew upon humanistic, philosophical and literary references and were painted in acid colours. The Mannerist style, characterised by the influence of antique statuary, a lengthening of lines and overabundant ornamentation, became more pronounced after **Primaticcio** (1504-70) arrived at the court in 1532.

The influence of this art could be felt until the end of the century in works by sculptors such as **Pierre Bontemps, Jean Goujon** (reliefs on the Fountain of the Innocents in Paris) and **Germain Pilon** (monument for the heart of Henri II in the Louvre) and painters like Jean Cousin the Elder. Court portraitists, on the other hand (**Jean** and **François**

Clouet and **Corneille de Lyon**), were more influenced by Flemish traditions.

Henri IV and Pre-Classicism

After the Wars of Religion (1560-98) new artistic trends revived the arts and heralded the dawn of Classicism. Royal interest in town-planning gave rise to the regular, symmetrical layout of squares (Place des Vosges and Place Dauphine in Paris) and to the harmonisation of the buildings that surrounded them (ground-level arcades and brick and stone façades). These were copied in the provinces (Charleville and Montauban) foreshadowing the royal squares of the 17C, France's *Grand Siècle*.

The Fontainebleau style of adornment continued to develop under the auspices of the **Second School of Fontainebleau**. This was made up of all the court painters working during the reign of Henri IV and the regency of Marie de' Medici. The style was further shaped by decoration in other royal palaces including the Tuileries, the Louvre and Château-Neuf in St-Germain-en-Laye. **Toussaint Dubreuil** (1561-1602), **Ambroise Dubois** (1542-1614) and **Martin Fréminet** (1567-1619) continued the Mannerism of Fontainebleau (light effects, half-length figures and a lengthening of perspectives) in their works and at the same time sought greater classicism as well as a revival of themes from contemporary literature (*La Franciade* by Ronsard).

In the late 16C, castle architecture took on a new form with a single main building centred on a projecting section flanked by corner pavilions (Rosny-sur-Seine, and the Château de Gros-Bois). Right-angled wings were done away with and façades were given a brick facing with stone courses.

During the regency period, the architect Salomon de Brosse (Palais de Justice in Rennes, Palais du Luxembourg in Paris) designed sober, impressive monuments with a clarity of form which contained some of the characteristics of Classical architecture.

16C Decorative Arts

The 16C was a productive period for jewellery-making, in particular for small brooches fastened in the hair or hat and pendants which were used as articles of dress or simply as collectors' items. **Étienne Delaune** (1518-83) was one of the great goldsmiths of the time.

There was rich regional variety in ceramics. Beauvaisis produced famous blue-tinged stoneware. Following the example of Italy, Lyon and Nevers manufactured majolica (glazed and historiated earthenware). The decorative arts in Saintonge were dominated by **Bernard Palissy** (c 1510-c 1590) who, apart from making a great many plates covered in reptiles, fish and seaweed, all modelled from nature, also decorated the grotto at the Château d'Écouen and that of the Tuileries. Some of his ceramics (nymphs in a country setting) were influenced by engravings from the Fontainebleau School.

The technique for painted enamel on copper with permanent colours was developed in Limoges in the 15C during the reign of Louis XI. J C Pénicaud and especially **Léonard Limosin** (1501-75) excelled in the technique, which was favoured in portrait painting by the French court.

FRENCH CLASSICISM IN THE EARLY 17TH CENTURY

Architecture

Three famous architects, **Jacques Lemercier** (c 1585-1654), **François Mansart** (1598-1666) and **Louis le Vau** (1612-70), played an essential part in drawing up the standards for the French Classical architectural style.

J Lemercier, who built the Château de Rueil, the town of Richelieu and the Église de la Sorbonne in Paris, supported the Italian style which was particularly evident in religious architecture: two-storeyed façades and projecting central sections with columns and triangular pediments. F Mansart was even more inventive (**Château de Balleroy**, **Château de Maisons-Laffitte** and the Gaston of Orléans Wing in the Château de Blois). From his time on, castle plans with a central pavilion and projecting section, architectural decoration that accentuated horizontal and vertical lines, and the use of orders (Doric, Ionic and Corinthian), remained constant features of Classical architecture. Le Vau, who began his career before the reign of Louis XIV by designing town houses (Hôtel Lambert in Paris) for the nobility and the upper middle classes, favoured a grandiose style of architecture characteristic of Louis XIV Classicism (Château de Vaux-le-Vicomte).

Painting

The French school of painting blossomed as a result of Simon Vouet's (1590-1649) return to France in 1627 after a long stay in Rome and the foundation of the Royal Academy of Painting and Sculpture in 1648. References to Italian painting, in particular Venetian (richness of colour) and Roman (dynamism of composition), albeit tempered by a concern for order and clarity, are evident in the work of Vouet and that of his pupil **Eustache le Sueur** (1616-55). Painters such as **Poussin** (1595-1665) and **Philippe de Champaigne** (1602-74) produced highly intellectual works that drew upon philosophical, historical and theological themes – all emblematic of French Classicism.

Other trends in French painting flourished in the first half of the century. The realism of the Italian painter Caravaggio influenced the Toulouse school of which the major artist was **Nicolas Tournier** (1590-post 1660). In Lorraine, **Georges de la Tour** (1593-1652) was deeply affected by Caravaggio's style, notably in the use of light and shade and the portrayal of people from humble blackgrounds. The **Le Nain** brothers, Antoine (c 1588-1648), Louis (c 1593-1648) and Mathieu (c 1607-77), who painted first in Laon and then in Paris, belonged to a trend known as "painters of reality" that favoured genre scenes, drawing more upon the world of the landed upper-middle classes than that of peasant farmers. Their work bore the stamp of Flemish craftsmanship.

Sculpture

Sculpture in the early 17C was influenced by contemporary Italian models. **Jacques Sarrazin** (1588-1660), who studied in Rome, worked in a moderate, Classic mode that derived from Anti-

quity and also drew upon paintings by Poussin (decoration in the Château de Maisons-Laffitte and the tomb of Henri of Bourbon in the Château de Chantilly). François Anguier (Montmorency Mausoleum in the Lycée chapel in Moulins) and his brother Michel (sculptural decoration on the St-Denis gateway in Paris) showed a more Baroque tendency in their treatment of dynamism and the dramatic stances of their sculptures.

VERSAILLES CLASSICISM

During the reign of Louis XIV (1643-1715) the centralisation of authority and the all-powerful Royal Academy gave rise to an official art that reflected the taste and wishes of the sovereign. The Louis XIV style evolved in Versailles and spread throughout France where it was imitated to a lesser degree by the aristocracy in the late 17C.

The style was characterised by references to Antiquity and a concern for order and grandeur, whether in architecture, painting or sculpture. French resistance to Baroque, which had but a superficial effect on French architecture, was symbolised by the rejection of Bernini's projects for the Louvre. One of the rare examples of the style is Le Vau's College of Four Nations (today's Institute of France) which consists of a former chapel with a cupola and semicircular flanking buildings.

In Versailles **Louis le Vau** and later **Jules Hardouin-Mansart** (1646-1708) favoured a majestic type of architecture: rectangular buildings set off by projecting central sections with twin pillars, flat roofs and sculptural decoration inspired by Antiquity.

Charles le Brun (1619-90), the leading King's Painter, supervised all the interior decoration (paintings, tapestries, furniture and *objets d'art*), giving the palace remarkable homogeneity. There were dark fabrics and panelling, gilded stuccowork, painted coffered ceilings, and copies of Greco-Roman statues. The decoration became less abundant towards the end of the century.

In 1662, the founding of the **Gobelins**, the "Royal Manufactory for Crown Furniture", stimulated the decorative arts. A

Anne Marie de Mailly-Nesle, Duchess of Châteauroux, by J. -M. Nattier (1740)

team of painters, sculptors, goldsmiths, warp-weavers, marble-cutters, and cabinet-makers worked under Charles le Brun, achieving a high degree of technical perfection. Carpets were made at the Savonnerie factory in Chaillot. The massive furniture of the period was often carved and sometimes gilded. Boulle marquetry, a combination of brass, tortoiseshell and gilded bronze, was one of the most sumptuous of the decorative arts produced at the time.

Versailles park, laid out by **Le Nôtre** (1613-1700), fulfilled all the requirements of French landscape gardening with its emphasis on rigour and clarity. Its geometrically tailored greenery, long axial perspectives, fountains, carefully designed spinneys and allegorical sculptures reflect the ideal of perfect order and control over nature.

Sculptures were placed throughout the gardens. Many of the works were by the two major sculptors of the time, **François Girardon** (1628-1715) and **Antoine Coysevox** (1640-1720) who drew upon mythology from Antiquity. The work of **Pierre Puget** (1620-94), another important sculptor, was far more tortured and Baroque – an unusual style for the late 17C.

FRENCH ROCAILLE (1715-1750)

The 18C style in France grew from a reaction against the austerity and grandeur of the Louis XIV style, which was considered ill-adapted to the luxurious life and pleasures of the aristocracy and the upper-middle classes during the regency of Philippe of Orléans (1715-23) and the reign of Louis XV (1723-74). Rocaille was an 18C Rococo style or ornamentation based on rock and shell motifs.

Architecture

Rocaille architecture, at least on the outside, remained faithful to some of the principles of Classical composition – plain buildings with symmetrical façades and projecting central sections crowned by a triangular pediment – but the use of Classical orders became less rigid and systematic. The most representative examples of this new type of architecture were town houses such as the Hôtel de Soubise by **Delamair** and Hôtel Matignon by **Courtonne**, both in Paris.

The majestic formal apartments of the previous century gave way to smaller, more intimate rooms such as boudoirs and studies.

Inside, woodwork, often white and gold, covered the walls from top to bottom (Hôtel de Lassay in Paris and the Clock Room or Cabinet de la Pendule in Versailles). The repertoire of ornamentation included intertwining plant motifs, curved lines, shells and other natural objects. Paintings of landscapes and country scenes were inserted in the woodwork above doors or in the corners of ceilings. **Verberckt**, who worked in Versailles for Louis XV, was an exceptionally skilled interior decorator.

Painting

The generation of painters working at the turn of the century was influenced by Flemish art. Artists such as **Desportes** (1661-1743), **Largillière** (1656-1746) and **Rigaud** (1659-1743) painted sumptuously decorative still-lifes and formal portraits. Secular themes including scenes of gallantry *(fêtes galantes)*, and fashionable society life became popular. **Watteau** (1684-1721), **Boucher** (1703-70), **Natoire** (1700-77) and **Fragonard** (1732-1806) reflected the taste of the day in their elegant genre scenes, some with mythological overtones, of pastoral life and the game of love.

Religious painting was not neglected in spite of these trends. Charles de la Fosse (1636-1716), one of Le Brun's pupils, Antoine Coypel (1661-1722) and especially **Restout** (1692-1768) adapted it to the less stoical ideals of the 18C by stripping it of too strong a dogmatism. There was a revival in portraiture during the 18C. **Nattier** (1685-1766), official painter of Louis XV's daughters, produced likenesses in mythological guise or half-length portraits which were far less pompous than the usual court picture. The pastellist **Quentin de la Tour** (1704-88) excelled in portraying his subjects' individual temperament and psychology rather than their social rank by concentrating more on faces than dress and accessories.

The lesser genres (still-lifes and landscapes), scorned by the Academy but favoured by the middle classes for the decoration of their homes, blossomed considerably at the time. **Chardin** (1699-1779) painted simple still-lifes in muted tones and Flemish-inspired scenes of everyday life, giving them a realistic, picturesque quality.

Sculpture

Baroque influence swept through sculpture in the first half of the century. The **Adam** brothers (Neptune Basin at Versailles), **Coustou** (1677-1746) (Horses of Marly), and **Slodtz** (1705-64) introduced the style's expressiveness into their work to lend movement and feeling. The main characteristics of Baroque art were flowing garments, attention to detail and figures shown in action.

In contrast, the contemporary work of **Bouchardon** (1698-1762) who trained in Rome and was therefore influenced by Antique sculpture, tended to be more Classical (Fountain in the Rue de Grenelle in Paris).

Decorative Arts

The rise of fashionable society brought with it a great need for luxury furniture that matched the style of woodwork inside elegant homes. New types of furniture were created: after commodes (chests of drawers) came writing-desks – upright or inclined, escritoires, chiffoniers and countless small tables. For the comforts of conversation there were wing-chairs and deep easy chairs. There were also *voyeuses* or conversation chairs (special seats in gaming houses placed behind players to allow spectators to watch) and all manner of sofas and seats on which to recline (couches, lounging-chairs, divans and settees). Curved lines were favoured, as were rare and precious materials like exotic woods and lacquered panelling often set off by floral marquetry and finely chased gilded bronze. Among the great rocaille cabinet-makers were Cressent, Joubert and Migeon, while the principal

"Bachelier" vase, 19C, Sèvres

Ph. Gajic/MICHELIN

Le Panthéon

seat carpenters of the time were Foliot, Sené and Cresson.

The **Vincennes Porcelain Factory** moved to **Sèvres** in 1756 and produced luxury items of which some were decorated in deep blue known as Sèvres blue. Gilt ornamentation was theoretically used only for royal services. Rocaille gold and silver plate was adorned with reed motifs, crested waves, scroll-work and shells often arranged in asymmetrical patterns. **Thomas Germain** (1673-1748), one of the most prestigious names in the trade, supplied the princely tables of the time.

NEO-CLASSICAL REACTION

The middle of the century brought a reaction against rocaille on moral and aesthetic grounds. The style was considered to be too florid and frivolous, the result of decadence in both morals and the arts. Classical models from Antiquity and the 17C were then deemed the only recourse to revive proper artistic creation.

Architecture

The new style of architecture that emerged was more austere and tended towards the monumental. Sculptural decoration on façades grew more restrained and the Doric order became widespread (Église St-Philippe-du-Roule by J F Chardin in Paris). Some buildings, like the Église Ste-Geneviève (the present-day Panthéon) in Paris by **G Soufflot** (1713-80), were direct copies of Antique models. Louis XVI commissioned men like **Victor Louis** (1731-1802) who designed the Bordeaux theatre, **A T Brongniart** (1739-1813) and **J F Bélanger** (1744-1818) for most of the great architectural undertakings of the time. The philosophical influence of the Enlightenment led to a keen interest in the architecture of functional, public buildings such as the Royal Salt-works in Arc-et-Senans by **Claude-Nicolas Ledoux** (1736-1806).

Sculpture

Sculptors distanced themselves from rocaille extravagance by striving towards a natural portrayal of anatomy. E M Falconet (1716-91), P Julien (1731-1804) and G C Allegrain (1710-95) drew upon Greco-Roman models for their greatly admired sculptures of female bathers. **J A Houdon** (1741-1828), one of the greatest sculptors of the late 18C, made busts of his French and foreign contemporaries (Voltaire, Buffon and Madame Adélaïde for the first, and Benjamin Franklin and George Washington for the second) which constituted a veritable portrait gallery. The busts, executed in an extremely realistic manner, many without wigs or articles of dress to detract from the faces, were the culmination of modelled portraiture in France. Houdon also sculpted tombs and mythological statues. **J B Pigalle** (1714-85) maintained the style of sculpture predominant at the beginning of the century that the neo-Classical reaction had not managed to stifle entirely (mausoleum of the Marshal de Saxe in the Église St-Thomas in Strasbourg).

Painting

In the 1760s, attempts by the Royal Academy to restore a style of painting known as the grand manner encouraged the emergence of new themes such as antique history, civic heroism and 17C tragedies. These were adopted by painters like **J L David** (1748-1825), **J B M Pierre** (1714-89) and **J F P Peyron** (1744-1814). The style drew upon low-reliefs and statuary from Antiquity and followed the principles of composition used by painters like Poussin and other 17C masters.

Works by **J M Vien** (1716-1809) and **J B Greuze** (1725-1805) showed a less austere approach to painting, with more room for sensibility and emotion, that heralded the romanticism that was to blossom after the Revolution.

Decorative Arts

Louis XVI furniture kept some of the characteristics inherited from the beginning of the century such as the use of precious materials and chased gilt bronze ornamentation, but curves and sinuous shapes gave way to straight lines. As far as decoration was concerned, while the floral motifs and ribbons of the past were maintained, ovoli friezes, Greek fretwork and fasces were willingly introduced. **René Dubois** (1738-99) and **Louis Delanois** (1731-92) initiated the Greek style derived from Antique furniture seen in friezes at Herculaneum and Pompeii. Prestigious artists of the genre included Oeben and Riesener while Carlin followed by Beneman and Levasseur specialised in furniture adorned with plaques of painted porcelain.

At the end of the century new decorative motifs including lyres, ears of corn, wickerwork baskets and hot-air balloons were imported from England.

The technique of hard-paste porcelain that was introduced into France at the beginning of the 1770s took the lead over soft-paste porcelain in the factory at Sèvres. Figurines of **biscuit** porcelain (white, fired, unglazed pottery) shaped on models by Fragonard, Boucher and other artists, became very popular.

The iconoclasm that prevailed during the **Revolution** marked a break in the history of French art. The Louvre opened in 1793 paving the way for many more museums in France.

19TH CENTURY

Art During the First Empire

After his investiture in 1804, Napoleon favoured the emergence of an official style of art by commissioning palace decoration (Tuileries, destroyed in 1870, and Fontainebleau) and paintings that related the great events of the Empire. The artists to benefit from the Emperor's patronage were men like J L David and his pupils **A J Gros** (1771-1835) and **A L Girodet-Trioson** (1767-1824).

Paintings of the time took on new themes derived from the romanticism in contemporary literature, orientalism and an interest in the medieval. National historic anecdotes were painted by artists who, like the troubadours, praised heroic deeds and fine sentiment.

Artistic development in the realm of architecture was less innovative. Napoleon commissioned large edifices commemorating the glory of the *Grande Armée* including the Carrousel Arch, the column in Place Vendôme and the Temple de la Madeleine (now a church). The official architects **Percier** (1764-1838) and **Fontaine** (1762-1853) were responsible for the overall supervision of the undertakings, setting models not only for buildings but also for decoration at official ceremonies and guidelines for the decorative arts.

Ambitious town-planning projects like the reconstruction of Lyon were also completed under the Empire.

Former royal palaces were refurnished. The style of First Empire furniture derived from the neo-Classical with massive, quadrangular, commodes and jewel-cases made of mahogany with gilt bronze plating and Antique decorative motifs. **Desmalter** (1770-1841) was the main cabinet-maker of the imperial court. The sculptors **Chaudet** (1763-1810) and **Cartellier** (1757-1831) supplied models for furniture ornamentation in the neo-Classical style which also inspired their statues.

After the Egyptian Campaign motifs like sphinxes and lotuses began to appear in the decorative arts.

Restoration and the July Monarchy

Two major trends affected French art between 1815 and 1848. The first was the gradual disappearance of the neo-Classical style which, however, still influenced church building (Notre-Dame-de-Lorette and St-Vincent-de-Paul in Paris); and the second was the birth of historicism, a style that fostered regard for the architecture of the past, particularly of the medieval period (Église Notre-Dame in Boulogne-sur-Mer and Marseille Cathedral by Léon Vaudoyer). The trend was furthered by the founding of the *Monuments Historiques* (a body set up for the classification and preservation of the national heritage) in 1830 and the enthusiasm of **Viollet-le-Duc (1814-79)**.

The Second Empire

On the accession of Napoleon III the arts in general were affected by a spirit of **eclecticism**. The Louvre, completed by Percier's disciple Visconti (1791-1853) and **H Lefuel** (1810-80), and the Paris Opera by **Garnier** (1825-98) were among the greatest undertakings of the century. References to architectural styles of the past (16C, 17C and 18C) were present everywhere. Nevertheless, the introduction of new materials like glass and cast iron (the Gare du Nord by Hittorff and the Église St-Augustin by V Baltard) showed the influence of technological progress and a new rational approach to building.

Baron Haussmann (1809-91), Prefect of the *département* of the Seine, laid down the principles for a public works programme that was to modernise the capital. Prefect C M Vaïsse carried out a similar plan in Lyon.

Academicism reigned over the **painting** of the time. **Cabanel** (1823-83), **Bouguereau** (1825-1905) and the portraitist **Winterhalter** (1805-73) drew their inspiration just as easily from Antique statuary as from works by 16C Venetian masters or Rococo ornamentation. However, **Courbet** (1819-77), **Daumier** (1808-79) and **Millet** (1814-75) formed an avant-garde group that fostered realism in painting with subjects from town and country life.

Ingres (1780-1867) who represented the Classical trend, and **Delacroix** (1798-1863), the great romantic painter of the century, were both at the height of their powers.

Great architectural projects stimulated the production of **sculpture. Carpeaux** (1827-75), responsible for the high-relief of Dance on the façade of the Paris Opera, transcended the eclecticism of his time by developing a very personal style that was reminiscent of, and not simply a copy of, Flemish, Renaissance and 18C art. Dubois (1829-1905), Frémiet (1824-1910) and Guillaume (1822-1905) were more academic in their approach.

A taste for pastiche prevailed in the decorative arts. The shapes and ornamental motifs of the Renaissance, the 16C and 18C were reproduced on furniture and *objets d'art*. The advent of **industrialisation** affected certain fields. The goldsmith Christofle (1805-63) and the bronze-founder Barbedienne (1810-92) made luxury items for the imperial court as well as mass-produced articles for new clients among the rich upper-middle classes.

Late 19C Artistic trends

Architecture during the Third Republic was mainly marked by edifices built for

Argenteuil, by Claude Monet

Universal Exhibitions held in Paris (the former Palais du Trocadéro, the Eiffel Tower, the Grand-Palais and the Pont Alexandre-III). The pompous style of the buildings with their exotic ornamentation derived from the trend for eclecticism.

In the 1890s **Art Nouveau** architects, influenced by trends in England and Belgium, distanced themselves from the official style of the day. They harmonised decoration on façades with that inside their buildings and designed their creations as a whole – stained glass, tiles, furniture and wall-paper. Decoration included plant motifs, stylised flowers, Japanese influences and asymmetrical patterns. **Guimard** (1867-1942) was the main proponent of the style in France (Castel Béranger in Paris and entrances to the capital's metro stations).

The decorative arts followed the Art Nouveau movement with works by the cabinet-maker **Majorelle** (1859-1929) and the glass and ceramics artist **Gallé** (1846-1904) in Nancy.

In the field of painting, the **Impressionists** began exhibiting their work outside official salons in 1874. **Monet** (1840-1926), **Renoir** (1841-1919) and **Pissarro** (1830-1903) breathed new life into the technique and themes of landscape painting by working out of doors, studying the play of light in nature and introducing new subjects drawn from contemporary life. **Manet** (1832-83) and **Degas** (1834-1917) joined the group temporarily.

Between 1885 and 1890, Neo-Impressionists like **G Seurat** (1859-91) and **Signac** (1863-1935) brought the Pointillist (painting with small dots) technique known as divisionism to a climax. The Dutch painter **Van Gogh** (1853-90) settled in France in 1886. His technique of using pure and expressionist colours with broad swirling brushstrokes coupled with his belief that expression of emotional experience should override impressions of the external world were to have a great influence on early-20C painters. **Cézanne** (1839-1906) and **Gauguin** (1848-1903), who were influenced by primitive and Japanese art, partly dispensed with Impressionism to give more importance to volume. In

1886, seeking new inspiration, Gauguin moved to Pont-Aven, a small town east of Concarneau in Brittany that had often been visited by the painter Corot in the 1860s. Fellow artists **Émile Bernard** and **Paul Sérusier** formed the Pont-Aven School that favoured synthesist theories and symbolic subjects which paved the way for the **Nabis**.

Among the Nabis were artists like **Denis** (1870-1943), **Bonnard** (1867-1947) and **Vuillard** (1868-1940) who advocated the importance of colour over shape and meaning.

Sculpture at the end of the century was dominated by the genius of **Rodin** (1840-1917). His expressionistic, tormented, symbolic work stood free from formal academic conventions and was not always understood in his time.

20TH CENTURY

Avant-Garde Movements

At the beginning of the 20C, proponents of the avant-garde reacted against the many trends of the 19C including the restrictions laid down by official art, academicism in painting and Art Nouveau in architecture.

The **Stijl** movement was characterised in architecture by simple, geometric buildings adorned with sober low-reliefs. One of its most magnificent examples was the Théâtre des Champs-Élysées by the Perret brothers with sculptural decoration by **Bourdelle** (1861-1929). In the field of sculpture, the artists **Maillol** (1861-1944), **Bartholomé** (1848-1928) and **J Bernard** (1866-1931) opposed Rodin's aesthetic concepts and produced a very different type of art by simplifying their figures, in some cases to the point of schematic representation.

Fauvism was the great novelty at the Autumn Salon of painting in 1905. A Derain (1880-1964), **A Marquet** (1875-1947) and **M de Vlaminck** (1876-1958) broke up their subject-matter through the vivid and arbitrary use of colour, a technique which was to pave the way for non-figurative painting. After an early period with the fauvist movement, **Matisse** (1869-1904) went his own way developing a personal style based on the exploration of colour.

A further major avant-garde movement in painting followed on from **Cézanne's** (1839-1906) structural analysis in which he broke up his subject matter into specific shapes. The trend was taken up by artists like **Braque** (1882-1963) and **Picasso** (1881-1973) whose exploration led to **Cubism**, a new perception of reality based not on what the eye saw but on an analytical approach to objects, depicting them as a series of planes, usually in a restricted colour range. The style dominated their work from 1907 to 1914.

Members of the *Section d'Or* (golden section) Cubist group like **A Gleizes, J Metzinger** and **F Léger** (his early works) were less revolutionary and more figurative. The main contribution to French cubism in the field of sculpture came from **Henri Laurens** who was influenced by Braque.

Surrealism breathed new life into the art world in the 1920s and 1930s. It was a subversive art form that created an irrational, dreamlike, fantasy universe. For the first time chance and promptings from the subconscious were integrated into the creative process. **Duchamp** (1887-1968), **Masson** (b 1896), **Picabia** (1879-1953) and **Magritte** (1898-1967) all formed part of the movement.

Artistic Creation Since 1945

Abstract art began to affect the field of painting after the Second World War. **Herbin** defined it as the triumph of mind over matter. In 1949 he published *Non-figurative, Non-objective Art (L'Art non figuratif non objectif)* and greatly influenced young artists of the **geometric abstract** art movement. All his works from the 1950s onwards have been one-dimensional patterns of letters and simple geometric shapes painted in pure colours.

The **lyrical abstract** artists focused on the study of colour and texture. **Riopelle** applied his paint with a knife while **Mathieu** applied it directly from the tube. **Soulages**, who was influenced by art from the Far East, produced meditative, expressive work in shades of black. **Nicolas de Stael's** art constituted a link between abstract and figurative in that his abstract composi-

tions were the result of observations of real objects which could sometimes be distinguished in the final work.

There was an important revival in architecture with **Le Corbusier** (1897-1965) whose buildings fulfilled functional requirements with great clarity of form (Cité Radieuse in Marseille and Ronchamp Chapel).

In the 1960s, **New Realism** (*Nouveau Réalisme*), a form of pop art, with **Pierre Restany** as its leading theoretician, attempted to express the reality of daily life. Industrial items, the symbols of modern society, were broken up (by the artist **Arman**) and assembled (by **César**) or trapped in glass.

Yves Klein (1928-62) took his adherence to New Realism a step further in his *Monochromes* by trying to capture the universal essence of objects. He worked in pure colours and created I B K, or International Klein Blue. He rejected formal and traditional values as did **Dubuffet** (1901-85) who, in 1968, wrote a pamphlet entitled *Asphyxiating Culture (Asphyxiante culture)* which made a stand for permanent revolution. Dubuffet's later art consisted of puzzles of coloured or black and white units.

Since the 1960s, the problems posed by town-planning have led to a re-evaluation of the relationship between architecture and sculpture and an attempt to reconcile the two arts. Architects and sculptors often work together as in the case of the project by Ricardo Bofill and D Karavan in Cergy-Pontoise northwest of Paris. Artists are increasingly being asked to modify townscapes.

The **Support-Surface** movement (**Claude Viallet, Pagès** and **Daniel Dezeuze**) of the 1970s reduced painting to its pure material state by focusing on the way the paint was applied. Paintings were removed from their stretchers and cut up, suspended and folded.

The 1980s saw the return of **Figuration** in manifold ways. References to tradition are evident in the work of artists like **Gérard Garouste** and **Jean-Charles Blais**.

The great vitality of contemporary art can be seen in the extremely wide variety of styles and trends favoured by artists today.

FURNITURE FROM BASSE-NORMANDIE

Longcase clock (St Lô – 19C)

Box bed (Pays d'Auge – 18C)

Marriage wardrobe (Bayeux – 18C)

Dairy cupboard (Avranchin – 18C)

Sideboard (Vire – 19C)

Kitchen dresser (Cotentin – 19C)

Collection Musée du Meuble Normand, Villedieu-les-Poêles

THE COUNTRY TODAY

Economy and Government

France has both an entrenched bureaucracy and a vibrant democracy, with a parliament of 577 *députés* elected every 5 years and a president also elected every 5 years. The president has extensive personal powers. At the same time, France is divided into 22 regions with a high degree of autonomy, and within each region is a multitude of communes where there is a good deal of local self-determination under powerful mayors. Within the nation is a profound division between a disciplinarian right wing tendency and an equally authoritarian Socialist tradition. This authoritarianism goes hand in hand with an unruly streak that brings frequent strikes, demonstrations and even riots. In deference to the danger of unrest, the government frequently backs down in the face of popular protest, giving in to demands. Economically, France has followed its own path, favouring extensive employee rights, state monopolies, state intervention, heavy subsidies and protectionism. To date, despite fears of future problems, this path has not prevented France from becoming a prosperous modern nation. It is the world's 6th largest economy.

Food and Drink

France is the land of good food and good living and it has a host of regional specialities. In addition to the **Michelin Guide France**, which describes hundreds of hotels and restaurants throughout the country, here are examples of traditional fare.

FRENCH CUISINE

Soups and Consommés

The best-known are cream of asparagus *(velouté d'asperges)*, leek and potato *(soupe de poireaux-pommes de terre)*, onion *(soupe à l'oignon or gratinée)*, lobster *(bisque de homard)*, garbure (a thick soup with cabbage popular in southwestern France), and *cotriade* (Breton fish soup), all of which are served at the start of a meal.

Hors d'œuvres

There are countless ways to begin a meal and French chefs have boundless imagination in this respect. The following, though, deserve a special mention: *salade niçoise* (tomatoes, anchovies, onions, olives), *salade lyonnaise* (using various meats with seasoning and a dressing of oil, vinegar and shallots), and *salade cauchoise* (celery, potatoes and ham). Another good start to a meal is a *flamiche* (a leek quiche that is a speciality of Picardy), or a *ficelle* (a ham pancake with a mushroom sauce). *Tapenade* is one of the traditional dishes of Provence (black olive purée into which are blended capers, anchovies and tuna fish). Or you may prefer *quiche lorraine* (made with ham or bacon and cream) or *pissaladière* (provençal quiche with onions, tomatoes and anchovies). No mention of starters would be complete without seafood and shellfish, such as oysters from Belon, Cancale or Marennes, shrimps, prawns and clams.

Main Courses

There are two main "families" of main course – fish or meat accompanied by all sorts of vegetables depending on the season, or served with a *gratin dauphinois* (potatoes, eggs and milk), not to be confused with *gratin savoyard* (potatoes, eggs and stock). *Bouillabaisse* is the famous stew from Marseille made with three types of fish (scorpion fish, red gurnard and conger eel), seasoned with saffron, thyme, garlic, bay, sage and fennel. *Brandade* is a creamy blend of mashed cod with olive oil, milk and a few cloves of garlic; it is a speciality of Nîmes. In Brittany, what better than lobster *à l'armoricaine*, mussels in cream *(moules à la crème)*, shad or pike with Nantes-style "white butter sauce" *(brochet au beurre blanc)*, worthy rivals of Dieppe-style sole *(sole dieppoise)* or the shrimps *(crevettes)* and cockles (*coques*) of Honfleur in Normandy, and of the bass grilled with fennel (*loup grillé au fenouil*) or baked over a fire of vine shoots (*au sarment de vigne*), a dish that is popular in Provence and on the Riviera.

There are so many regional dishes that only a glimpse can be provided of the delights in store.

The best-known local meat dishes include Strasbourg sauerkraut (*choucroute* - cabbage, potatoes, pork, sausages and ham), Toulouse or Castelnaudary *cassoulet* (bean stew with pieces of goose or duck and pork-meat products), Caen-style tripe (*tripes à la mode de Caen*), Rouen pressed duck (*canard au sang*), Burgundy *meurette* (wine sauce) that is as good an accompaniment for poached eggs as for brains or beef – cooked Burgundy-style, of course! Also well worth a mention are Auvergne *potée* (cabbage, piece of pork, bacon and turnips) or its cousin from Franche-Comté (cabbage, Morteau or Montbéliard sausage), *aligot* (a creamy blend of fresh tomme cheese and mashed potato seasoned with garlic) from Chaudes-Aigues, *tripoux* from Aurillac, Basque-style chicken (*poulet basquaise* with tomatoes and pimentoes), rabbit (*lapin*) *chasseur* and rabbit *forestier* (with mushrooms and diced bacon).

Cheese

There is such a wide range of cheeses that it is difficult to know them all, so it is worth defining the main "families":

I – Soft cheeses

a) Cheese with surface mould (Brie de Meaux, Camembert, Chaource, etc)

b) Cheese with washed rind (Livarot, Reblochon, Munster, Vacherin, etc)

c) Cheese with natural rind (Tomme de Romans, Cendres de Bourgogne, Brie de Melun, etc)

II – Hard pressed non-boiled cheeses

(Cantal, Fourme de Laguiole, Gapron d'Auvergne, etc)

III – Hard pressed boiled cheeses

(Emmental de Savoie, Comté de Franche-Comté, Beaufort de Savoie, and Beaufort de Dauphiné, etc)

IV – Blue cheeses

a) Blue cheeses with natural crust (Bleu de Bresse, Bleu de Corse, Fourme de Montbrison, etc)

b) Scraped blue cheeses (Roquefort, Bleu d'Auvergne, Bleu des Causses, etc).

Bouillabaisse

S. Sauvignier/MICHELIN

V – Processed Cheeses

Such as Crème de Gruyère, spreads with grapes or walnuts, and a whole range of cheese spreads.

Fruit and Desserts

There are innumerable **desserts** to round off a meal. Apart from the baskets of fruit, strawberries and cream or strawberries in red wine, fruit salads and macedoines using all the orchard fruits, there are apple, pear, and peach compotes, and all sorts of cakes, such as *tarte Tatin* (a caramelised tart cooked with the filling underneath), Grenoble walnut cake (*gâteau aux noix*), Breton *far* (a baked custard dessert), gingerbread (*pain d'épices*) in the Gâtinais region, *clafoutis* (a blend of milk and eggs mixed with fruit and baked in the oven), and *kougelhopf* from Alsace baked in the form of a ring and served as a dessert or as an afternoon snack. Not to mention all the crème caramels, baked cream desserts, and soft meringues with custard sauce (*île flottante*) that are found in nearly every region of France.

THE WINES OF FRANCE

The wines of France encompass every variety of taste from the sweetest whites to the driest, from rich, full-bodied reds to light easy-drinking roses, from unpretentious, drinkable tables wines to the greatest names in the world, including

Galette de sarrasin with ham and egg

of course, the very symbol of celebration and delight, champagne.

For wine lovers, the **Michelin Guide The Wine Regions of France** offers a comprehensive introduction to French wine-making and features driving itineraries for the 14 main wine regions of the country: Alsace, Beaujolais, Le Bordelais (Bordeaux wines), Burgundy, Champagne, Cognac, Corse (Corsican wines), Jura, Languedoc-Roussillon, Loire Valley, Provence, Rhone Valley, Savoie-Bugey and the Southwest. Descriptions of over 500 restaurants, hotels and guest houses are included in this guide to enhance your journey through these regions.

See also the **Michelin Green Guide** for the specific region in which you are

A selection of French cheeses

interested, for example the *Green Guide Provence* describes Provençal wines. The official French wine website, www.wines-france.com, features information about grapes, wine labels, France's wine regions and more.

FOOD GLOSSARY

Aïoli............................Garlic mayonnaise
Andouille ... Large chitterling sausage
Andouillettes ..... Chitterling sausages
Anis..................... Aniseed confectionery
Asperges .... Asparagus
Bergamotes .... Orange-flavoured sweets
Berlingots................................Humbugs
Bêtises....................................Hard mints
Beurre blanc .... White butter sauce
Bouillabaisse...................Seafood stew
Bourride ....Fish soup
Brandade ....Creamed salt-cod
Cagouilles................................Snails
Calissons .... Almond and crystallised fruit sweetmeats
Canard au sang...............Pressed duck
Cassoulet ....Stew with haricot beans and pork rinds
Cedrats confits.................... Crystallised citrus fruit
Cèpes ....Cèpe mushrooms
Charcuterie ....Smoked, cured or dried meats
Chipirones................... Small cuttlefish, often stuffed
Choucroute ....Sauerkraut
Confiseries .... Confectionery
Confits...............Goose preserved in fat
Crêpes dentelles.......... Thin pancakes
Dragées .... Sugared almonds
Escargots ....Snails
Esturgeons ....Sturgeon
Far ....Flan with prunes
Ficelles picardes ....Ham pancakes with mushroom sauce
Foie gras...................... Goose liver
Fouace............................Dough cakes
Fraises .... Strawberries
Fruits confits.............. Crystallised fruit
Galettes ....Thick pancakes or waffles
Gâteau d'amandes.........Almond cake
Garbure ...... Meat and vegetable stew
Gratins .... Dishes with a crusty topping
Jambon...Ham

Jambon cru des Ardennes ....Ardennes cured ham
Kouign-Amam .... Cake
Kougelhopf..................Plain yeast cake
Lamproies ....Lampreys
Macarons ....Macaroons
Madeleines .... Small sponge cakes
Magrets ....Breast of duck
Marrons glacés .... Crystallised chestnuts
Massepains .... Marzipan cakes
Matelote................................Eel stew
Meurette ....Wine sauce
Mouclade .... Mussel stew
Moutarde....................................Mustard
Mouton de pré-salé......... Salt-pasture lamb
Noix ....Nuts
Nougat ....Sugar, honey and nut sweetmeat
Nougatine ....Caramel syrup and almond sweetmeat
Ortolans ....Buntings
Oursins.............................Sea urchins
Pain d'épice .... Spiced honey cake
Pâté d'alouette...............Lark paté
Pâté de merle ....Blackbird paté
Pauchouse............ Fish stew with wine
Pieds de cochon .... Pigs' trotters
Piperade...................Sweet pepper and tomato omelette
Poulardes....................................Chickens
Pralines.................Caramelised almond confectionery
Pruneaux .... Prunes
Quenelles................... Poached meat or fish dumplings
Quenelles de brochet............Poached Pike dumplings
Quiche (Lorraine) ....Egg, cream andbacon flan
Rillettes ....Potted pork
Rillons ....Potted chopped pork
Saupiquet...............Spiced wine sauce
Saucisse de Morteau............. Morteau sausage
Saucisson........................Dried sausage
Soupe au pistou ....Vegetable soup with basil
Touron...... Soft almond confectionery
Tourteau fromager ....Goats' cheese gateau
Tripes...Tripe
Tripoux..............................Stuffed tripe
Truffes..Truffles
Volailles.......................................Poultry

UNESCO World Heritage List

In 1972, the United Nations Educational, Scientific and Cultural Organization (UNESCO) adopted a Convention for the preservation of cultural and natural sites. To date, more than 150 States Parties have signed this international agreement, which has listed over 500 sites "of outstanding universal value" on the World Heritage List. Each year, a committee of representatives from 21 countries, assisted by technical organisations (ICOMOS – International Council on Monuments and Sites; IUCN – International Union for Conservation of Nature and Natural Resources; ICCROM – International Centre for the Study of the Preservation and Restoration of Cultural Property, the Rome Centre), evaluates the proposals for new sites to be included on the list, which grows longer as new nominations are accepted and more countries sign the Convention. To be considered, a site must be nominated by the country in which it is located.

The protected cultural heritage may be monuments (buildings, sculptures, archaeological structures etc) with unique historical, artistic or scientific features; groups of buildings (such as religious communities, ancient cities); or sites (human settlements, examples of exceptional landscapes, cultural landscapes) which are the combined works of man and nature of exceptional beauty. Natural sites may be a testimony to the stages of the earth's geological history or to the development of human cultures and creative genius or represent significant ongoing ecological processes, contain superlative natural phenomena or provide a habitat for threatened species.

Signatories of the Convention pledge to co-operate to preserve and protect these sites around the world as a common heritage to be shared by all humanity.

Some of the most well-known places which the World Heritage Committee has inscribed include: Australia's Great Barrier Reef (1981), the Canadian Rocky Mountain Parks (1984), The Great Wall of China (1987), the Statue of Liberty (1984), the Kremlin (1990), Mont-Saint-Michel and its Bay (France, 1979), Durham Castle and Cathedral (1986).

UNESCO World Heritage Sites iin France

1 – Mont-St-Michel and its bay. Green Guide Normandy.
2 – Chartres Cathedral. Green Guide Northern France.
3 – Versailles: Château and Gardens. Green Guide Northern France.
4 – Vézelay: Basilica and Hill. Green Guide Burgundy-Jura.
5 – Caves with prehistoric art in the Vallée de la Vézère. Green Guide Dordogne-Berry-Limousin.
6 – Fontainebleau: Palace and Gardens. Green Guide Northern France.
7 – Amiens Cathedral. Green Guide Northern France.
8 – Orange: Roman theatre and surrounding area, Triumphal Arch. Green Guide Provence.
9 – Arles: Roman and Romanesque monuments. Green Guide Provence.
10 – Fontenay Abbey. Green Guide Burgundy-Jura.
11 – Arc-et-Senans: Saline royale. Green Guide Burgundy-Jura.
12 – Nancy: Place Stanislas, Place de la Carrière, Place d'Alliance. Green Guide Alsace-Lorraine-Champagne.
13 – Saint-Savin-sur-Gartempe: Abbey church. Green Guide Atlantic Coast.
14 – Gulfs of Girolata and Porto, Scandola Nature Reserve, bays (calanches) in Piana, Corsica. Green Guide Corse (in French).
15 – Pont du Gard. Green Guide Provence.
16 – Strasbourg: Cathedral, Grande Île. Green Guide Alsace-Lorraine-Champagne.
17 – Reims: Cathedral, Palais du Tau, Basilique St-Rémi.Green Guide Alsace-Lorraine-Champagne.
18 – Paris: banks of the Seine from L'Arsenal to Pont d'Iéna (Île de la Cité, Île St-Louis), vistas and monuments (Place de la Concorde, Église de la Madeleine, Chambre des Députés, Pont Alexandre-III, Grand Palais, Petit Palais, Les Invalides, École Militaire, Champ-de-Mars, Palais de Chaillot). Green Guide Paris.
19 – Chambord: Château and Park. Green Guide Châteaux of the Loire.
20 – Bourges: Cathédrale St-Étienne. Green Guide Dordogne-Berry-Limousin.
21 – Avignon: Centre historique. Green Guide Provence.
22 – Canal du Midi. Green Guide Pyrénées-Languedoc-Roussillon.

Chateau de Chaumont
B. Kaufmann/MICHELIN

MASSIF DE L'AIGOUAL ★★★

MICHELIN MAP 339 G 4
GREEN GUIDE LANGUEDOC ROUSSILLON TARN GORGES

The immense forces involved in the formation of the Alps in the Tertiary era acted on the ancient granitic foundation of this landscape, uplifting it to form a massif which reaches its highest point at **Mont Aigoual**★★★ (1 567m – 5 141ft). Subsequent erosion, all the more vigorous because of high precipitation and the low elevation of the surrounding country, has created a landscape of long straight ridges cut by deep ravines. These well-watered highlands make a striking contrast to the arid landscapes of the neighbouring *causses* where any rainfall is immediately absorbed by the porous limestone.

- **Information:** Le Pont en Bois 30750 Camprieu, ☎04 67 82 64 67. www.causses-aigoual-cevennes.org
- ▶ **Orient Yourself:** Rising high at the heart of the Cévennes National Park, the Aigoual summit, 37km S of Florac, is reached on steep D118.
- ◔ **Organizing Your Time:** Choose a fine day for your visit – otherwise mist may reduce the view.

A Bit of History

From 1875 onwards a massive programme of reafforestation was undertaken by the state; the forest today covers some 14 000ha – 50 square miles. Tree growth is particularly vigorous on the more exposed western slopes. In the last 20 years conifers have been added to the beeches planted in the 19C, and there are sweet chestnuts too, the traditional tree of the Cévennes, growing at altitudes of 600-900m (2 000-3 000ft).

Visit

Panorama★★★

From the viewing table at the top of the meteorological station the view extends over the Causses and the Cévennes. The clearest days are in winter, when it is sometimes possible to see both Mont-Blanc and the Maladeta Massif in the Pyrenees.

AIGUES-MORTES ★★

MICHELIN MAP 339 K 7–POPULATION 6,012
GREEN GUIDE PROVENCE

Few places evoke the spirit of the Middle Ages as vividly as Aigues-Mortes sheltering behind its ramparts in a landscape of marshland, lakes and salt-pans.

- **Information:** Pl. St-Louis, b04 66 53 73 00. www.ot-aiguesmortes.fr.
- ▶ **Orient Yourself:** Take the tourist train around Aigues-Mortes for an overview of what there is to see and do. Shops, restaurants and hotels lie within the city walls. A traditional market can be found on Ave. Frederic-Mistral.
- **Don't Miss:** Climb to the top of the Tour de Constance (53 steps) for an impressive panorama over the town and surrounding flatlands.
- ◔ **Organizing Your Time:** See the fortifications first, allowing at least an hour.
- P **Parking:** Parking is available around the exterior of the ramparts.

D. Pazery/MICHELIN

Aigues-Mortes Ramparts

A Bit of History

In 1240, Louis IX (St Louis), then 26 years old, was troubled by the lack of French involvement in the kind of commerce undertaken by the merchant fleets of Pisa and Genoa. He was also taken by the idea of a Crusade, but lacked a Mediterranean port. A French king could not countenance sailing from a foreign harbour (at this time Provence was part of the Holy Roman Empire, Sète did not exist, and Narbonne was silting up). Louis' solution was to buy a site from a priory and grant a charter to the township which began to develop on what up to then had been virtually an island. The new settlement was laid out on the geometrical lines of a bastide and linked to the sea by an artificial channel.

On 28 August 1248, Louis IX set sail from here on the 7th Crusade, which was a failure. On 1 July 1270 he left from here again, on the 8th Crusade, which only reached Tunis, where Louis died.

By the 14C Aigues-Mortes' population totalled 15 000, but its waterways had begun to silt up; the Tour de Constance lost its military significance and instead became a prison. For more than a century after the revocation of the Edict of Nantes in 1665, Protestant rebels were held here, from 1715 to 1768 the Tour de Constance being reserved for women prisoners.

The silting up of the port and the incorporation of Marseilles into the French kingdom in 1481 pushed Aigues-Mortes into decline and the coup-de-grâce was the founding (17C) and subsequent development of Sète.

Visit

Tour de Constance★★

Access by place Anatole-France. ♿ ◷*May-Aug: daily 10am-7pm; Sep-Apr: daily 10am-5.30pm. Last admission 1hr before closing.* ◷ *Closed 1 Jan, 1 May, 1 and 11 Nov, and 25 Dec.* ⌦ *6.10€ (under 18 years: no charge).* ☎*04 66 53 61 55. www.monum.fr.*

The tower (1241-49) rests on wooden piles and was intended to be a symbol of royal power as much as a purely military installation. The layout of its elaborate internal defences (staircases, winding passageways, portcullises) is typical of the Capetian dynasty, and its fine walls of Beaucaire limestone stand out boldly against the surrounding sandy landscape. Its turret originally served as a lighthouse, the sea being only 3km – 2 miles away at the time.

Ramparts★★

◷ *Same hours as Tour de Constance.*

The ramparts were never seen by St Louis. They were begun in 1272 on the orders of Philippe le Hardi (the Bold) and their completion led to Aigues-Mortes becoming the Capetian kingdom's principal Mediterranean harbour.

At the end of the 13C Philippe le Bel (the Fair) improved the port and completed the defences, adding 20 massive towers to protect the gateways and provide enfilading fire along the walls themselves.

AIX-EN-PROVENCE★★

POPULATION 123 842
MICHELIN MAP 340 H-I 4
GREEN GUIDE PROVENCE

The old capital of Provence has kept much of its 17C and 18C character: the elegance of its mansions, the charm of its squares, the majesty of its avenues and the loveliness of its fountains. It is also a lively city whose large student population is much in evidence on the busy café terraces. The new part of town is rapidly expanding and attracting more and more residents; it has established itself as a city of the arts, a thermal spa and an important centre for industry and the tourist trade.

- **Information:** 2 pl. du Gén.-de-Gaulle, ☎04 42 16 11 61. www.aixenprovencetourism.com.
- **Orient Yourself:** For an overview of the city, join the 2hr guided tour (the tourist office has details).
- **Don't Miss**: Vieil Aix, the charming medieval heart of the city.
- **Organizing Your Time:** Even if you take the guided tour, the first thing to do in Aix is walk along the majestic Cours Mirabeau under its handsome plane trees, pause for a drink at one of the many cafés, then stroll through Vieil Aix. Allow at least four hours.
- **Also See: Thermes Sextius**, Aix's thermal spa (day tickets available, 55 Cours Sextius ☎0 800 639 699, toll-free within France; www.thermes-sextius.com; Mon-Fri 8.30am-7.30pm, Sat 8.30am-1.30pm and 2.30-6.30pm).

A Bit of History

The Aix of today is the legacy of Good King René (1409-80). The Roman city Aquae Sextiae had long before destroyed by the Lombards (AD 574) and by Saracens; its deserted buildings served as a quarry for building materials for a good six centuries. Then in the 12C its fortunes were restored by the Counts of Provence who made it their place of residence. The last and most illustrious of the line was René, Duke of Anjou, Lorraine and Bar, King of Naples, and the ally of Charles VII of France against the English and Burgundians. This enlightened monarch supported literature and the arts and completed Aix cathedral. Though a benevolent ruler, he was also a strict administrator. Towards the end of his life he made Charles of Maine his heir; Charles however was to die childless, enabling Louis XI to incorporate Provence into France (1486).

Harsh times intervened; invasion by Imperial troops, feuding, and religious conflict. While the Aix Parliament was putting up a strong resistance to Richelieu's centralising policies, an administrative class grew and prospered. The peaceful period ushered in by Cardinal Mazarin saw the extension and rebuilding of the city on Classical lines; judges, lawyers and other notables built sober but distinguished residences that contribute so much to the charm of the Old Town (Vieil Aix) today (rusticated doorways, mask and scroll decoration, stucco-work, ornate staircases).

The intellectual life fostered by King René continued to flourish and the roll-call of great men who were born or who lived in Aix is a long one. It includes the 17C astronomer Fabri de Peiresc who in 1636 drew the first map of the moon. In the 18C there was the elegant portrait-painter Jean-Baptiste van Loo; the essayist Vauvenargues; and the orator **Count Mirabeau**. The latter, meeting only contempt and rejection from his peers, gained election to the Estates-General in 1789 as a representative, not of the nobility, but of the Third Estate. Finally there is Paul Cézanne (1839-1906), one of the founders of modern painting; his many studies of Mount Ste-Victoire are

Address Book

Cézanne Tour – Mid-Mar to mid-Oct, Thur, 10am (details from the tourist office). Visit all the site associated with the artist.

For coin ranges, see the Legend on the cover flap.

WHERE TO EAT

Chez Charlotte – *32 r. des Bernardines* ☎04 42 26 77 56 – Open for *lunch and dinner.* Closed Aug, Sun, *and Mon.* Upon entering you are greeted with a nostalgic atmosphere. The main eating area's decor is dedicated to the cinema. Offering traditional and seasonal cuisine, the owner gives special attention to every dish.

Chez Féraud – *8 r. du Puits-Juif* - ☎ 04 42 63 07 27 – Aug, Sun and Mon. Tucked away in an Old Quarter lane , an appealing place with typical local cuisine (pistou, daube) and grills.

Chez Antoine "Côté Cour " – *19 cours Mirabeau* – ☎04 42 93 12 51 – Closed Mon lunch and Sun. This is a retreat with a luminous, verdant patio-veranda. All the flavours of Provence and Italy are at your fingertips. Try *aux aubergines à la parmesane* and *aux calamars farcis.* This is a place to be sure to visit.

WHERE TO STAY

The tourist office has its own accommodation desk, which finds vacancies and makes bookings free of charge.

Hôtel Cardinal – *24 r. Cardinale* -☎04 42 38 32 30 – 29 rooms. – 8€ In an 18C mansion in the calm of the Mazarin quarter, tasteful, marrying old-fashioned style with modern comfort. Well-placed for exploring the town centre on foot.

La Manoir – *8 rue d'Entrecasteaux* – ☎04 42 26 27 20 – www.hotelmanoir. com – Closed 7-30 Jan – 40 *rooms* – 11€. A lovely old building, formerly a hat factory. Part of an adjoining 14C cloister has been converted into a summer terrace, creating a unique atmosphere.

Hôtel St-Christophe – *2 avenue Victor-Hugo* – ☎04 42 26 01 24 – www.hotel-saintchristophe.com – – 47 rooms – 9€. This hotel is right in the centre of the city, near cours Mirabeau, and rooms are decorated in either a 1930s or Provençal style. Pavement terrace in fine weather.

Hôtel des Augustins – *3 rue Masse* – ☎04 42 27 28 59 – hotel-augustins.com –29 rooms – 10€. Stone vaulting and stained glass are reminders of the origins of this hotel, a stone's throw from cours Mirabeau, which was originally a 15C convent. The rooms, of which two have terraces with rooftop views, are decorated in a modern style.

ON THE TOWN

Café des Deux Garçons – *53 cours Mirabeau* – ☎04 42 26 00 51 – www. les2garcons.com – daily 7am-1am. Bordered by plane trees, cours Mirabeau throngs with locals and visitors come to relax at the outdoor tables of one of its many cafés. The Deux Garçons café, more familiarly known as "le 2 G", is the oldest and most famous of these cafés, dating from 1792. Cézanne and Zola were both regulars.

Château de la Pioline – *260 r. Guillaume-du-Vair, Les Milles* – ☎04 42 52 27 27 – www.chateaudelapioline.fr – daily 24hr. The bar of this hotel-restaurant (which dates from the 16C) is adorned with highly prestigious furnishings, such as those from the Medici hall (to commemorate the illustrious Catherine de' Medici) and the Louis XVI hall. Don't miss the large terrace overlooking the 4ha/10 acre French garden.

SHOPPING

Markets – Traditional market every morning in place Richelme and every Tuesday, Thursday, and Saturday in place des Prêcheurs and place de la Madeleine. Flower market every Tuesday, Thursday and Saturday in place de l'Hôtel de Ville, and in place des Prêcheurs on other days.

Antiques – Antique market every Tuesday, Thursday and Saturday in place Verdun. Antiques fairs take place in the centre of town throughout the year.

Crafts – Makers of vases, ceramics, fabrics, baskets and jewellery display their wares on cours Mirabeau at the end of

Mar, in mid-May, mid-Jun, mid-October, and mid-Nov.

Calissons du Roy René – *10 r. Clemenceau -* ☎ *04 42 26 67 86 – www. calisson.com –* ○ *Mon-Fri 8am-noon, 12.30pm-7pm, Sat 10am-noon, 2pm-7pm.* ○ *closed Sun, public holidays.* Buy your traditional local treats like calissons (almonds, sugar, candied melon) and nougat (white, dark or fruit) at this respected long-established shop.

Aperitifs – The definitive shop for Provençal liquors and aperitifs is **Liquoristerie de Provence**, *36 av. de la Grand-Bégude, 13770 Venelles –* ☎*04 42 54 94 65 – www.versinthe.net.* Free tour and tasting. ○ *closed Sun.*

Santons Fouque – *65 cours Gambetta,* ☎ *04 42 26 33 38 – www.santonsfouque. fr.* Visit the atelier where these figurines have been made by the same family for generations.

Books – Cité du Livre, *8-10 rue des Allumettes* bookstore is a haven for book lovers – ☎*04 42 91 98 88. www. citedulivre-aix.com*

EVENTS

International Opera and Music Festival Founded in 1948 by Gabriel Dussurget, this prestigious festival takes place every summer in the courtyard of the archiepiscopal palace which is converted into a theatre for the event. Concerts and recitals are held in the cathedral, the cloisters of St-Saveur and the Hôtel Maynier d'Oppède. The festival focuses on important operas (in particular those by Mozart) as well as Baroque opera and contemporary music. Among the many illustrious artists who have contributed to the high standards of the festival are conductors Hans Rosbaud and Carlo Maria Giulini and the acclaimed singer Teresa Berganza. Working alongside the musicians, world-famous directors (Jorge Lavelli, Pier Luigi Pozzi) and set designers (Balthus, Derain, Masson) have also contributed to the creation of some unforgettable performances.

Santon Fair – These figurines can be purchased from the end of November until the end of December along cours Mirabeau.

Wine Festival – Festivals des vins et Coteaux d'Aix – *cour Mirabeau – last Sunday in July.*

---

justly renowned. The room devoted to him in Aix's museum, the Musée Granet, houses among other paintings his *Still Life with Sugar-bowl, Nude at the Mirror* and the monumental *Bathers*. For a better understanding of the artist and his work, ask the tourist office for their leaflet on *les Sites Cézanniens.*

Sights

Vieux Aix★★

Elegant 17C-19C mansions with corner statues, pleasant squares and charming fountains combine to give the old town its distinctive character.

Cours Mirabeau★★

Fountains splash under the canopy of fine plane trees shading this most pleasant of Provençal boulevards. It was laid out on the line of the 15C ramparts by Mazarin's brother (also responsible for buidling the district immediately to the south). Planned deliberately to give the mansions a formal façade to the north and a sunny garden to the south, the grand residences line the south side of the Cours, distinguished by sculptured doorways and balconies of wrought iron held up by caryatids and atlantes.

Musee Granet ★

○ *Wed-Mon 10am-noon, 2-6pm. Closed Tue and public holidays. No charge.* ☎*04 42 52 87 80.*

In a 17th century mansion, the town's principal art museum displays collections left by F-M Granet (1775-1849), and rooms devoted to remnants of Roman Aix. On view, French art from the 16th to the 20th centuries, Italian and Flemish schools, and works by Cézanne.

Cathédrale St-Sauveur

G. Magnin/MICHELIN

Place d'Albertas★

A fine mansion of 1724 and fountain of 1745 are complemented by other 18C buildings with soaring first-floor pilasters and graceful balconies contrasting with the more robust appearance of the ground floor which has semicircular arches and rusticated stonework.

Cathédrale St-Sauveur★

The **baptistery**★ dates to the Merovingian period (4C). Eight ancient columns, probably from a Roman basilica nearby, hold up the 18C octagonal cupola crowning the Gallo-Roman structure. In the nave is the **Triptych of the Burning Bush**★★, painted around 1475 by Nicolas Froment, a masterpieces of the Second School of Avignon, integrating a religious subject, landscape and Flemish decorative elements. The **doorway panels**★ of 1500-08 *(masked by false doors)* represent Prophets and Sibyls. The roof of the Romanesque **cloisters**★ (🕑 *Guided tours* 🐾 *Apr-Nov: daily except during services 9am-noon and 2pm-6pm; Dec-Mar: daily except during services 10am-noon and 2.30pm-5.30pm;* ☎*04 42 23 98 90)* rests on delicate columns. In the time of the Emperor Augustus this was the site of the Forum of Aquae Sextiae.

▶ Hôtel de Ville – elegant facade and ironwork balcony, 17th-century Classical courtyard; Musée des Tapisseries – 17C-18C tapestries 🕑 *Wed-Mon 10am-5pm.* 🕑 *Closed Tue, 1 Jan, 1 May and 25 Dec.* ☞ *2€.* ☎*04 42 21 05 78.* **Église St-Jean-de-Malte – Nave**★. 🕑 daily, 10am-noon, 3pm-7pm. ☎04 42 38 25 70; **Église Ste-Marie-Madeleine – statue of Our Lady**★**, triptych**★ 🕑 *Weekdays 9am-noon, 3-6pm.* 🕑 *Closed Jul and Aug.* **Fondation Vasarely**★ 🕑 *Mon-Fri 10am-1pm, 2-6pm, Sat-Sun 10am-7pm (Nov-Mar: 6pm). Last admission 1hr before closing.* 🕑 *Closed 1 Jan, 1 May, 25 Dec.* ☞ *7€.* ☎*04 42 20 01 09. www.fondationvasarely.com.* **Fontaine des Quatre Dauphins**★. Hôtel Boyer d'Eguilles – houses Muséum d'histoire naturelle 🕑 *Open daily 10 am-noon, 1-5pm;* 🕑 *closed 1 Jan, 1 May, 25 Dec.* ☞ *2.50€.* ☎*04 42 27 91 27).* Atelier Paul Cézanne – the artist's studio just north of the city. 🕑 *10am-noon, 2.30pm-6pm (Oct-May closes 5pm);* 🕑 *Closed Tue.* ☎*04 42 21 06 53. www.atelier-cezanne.com.*

AJACCIO★★

POPULATION 60 000
MICHELIN MAP 345 A-B 7-8
GREEN GUIDE CORSE (IN FRENCH)

Ajaccio occupies a natural amphitheatre looking out over its splendid bay. The town was founded in 1492 by the Office of St George which governed Corsica on behalf of the Republic of Genoa. Native Corsicans were forbidden residence there until 1553, when, in the course of the first French intervention in the island, it was taken by the legendary military adventurer Sampierro Corso (1498-1567), born in the village of Bastelica 25km – 15 miles to the northeast.

- **Information:** 3 bd du Roi-Jérôme, 20181 Ajaccio (Aiacciu), ☎04 95 51 53 03. www.tourisme.fr/ajaccio.
- **Orient Yourself:** Place Foch is the heart of town, and most places of interest are nearby. In the square, the tourist office has information on guided tours.

A Bit of History

It was here, at 1am on 13 September 1943, that the first Free French forces to land on the territory of France disembarked from the submarine *Casabianca*, under Commander L'Herminier.

Ajaccio's historic importance is due above all to its being the birthplace of **Napoleon Bonaparte.** The town continues to revere the memory of its "glorious child prodigy". Born on 15 August 1769, the son of Charles-Marie Bonaparte and Letizia Romolino, he entered the military school at Brienne (*Aube*) at the age of 10. At 27 he married Josephine Tascher de la Pagerie, widow of General Beauharnais, before directing the Italian campaign (Battle of Arcole) and, two years later,

the expedition to Egypt. In 1804, taking the title of Napoleon I, he crowned himself Emperor of the French. On 26 August the following year he launched the Grand Army (*Grande Armée*) against Austria from the encampment at Boulogne whence he had threatened England with invasion. By 1807, at the age of 38, he dominated Europe.

It was then, however, that coalitions originally formed to resist the French Revolution were turned against the Empire. England was deeply involved in them all, in the colonies and on the high seas as well as in Europe. Though bloated and prematurely aged, Napoleon rose to the challenge, never more formidable than from 1809 on, the years of struggle against the Fifth and Sixth Coalitions. But France and her Emperor were out of touch with a changed Europe. There was now a strong desire for national independence among the peoples of Europe. The Napoleonic Age was brought to a close on 18 June 1815 by the Battle of Waterloo. On 15 July Bonaparte sailed to exile on St Helena, where he died on 5 May 1821.

Sights

Musée Fesch★★

🕐 *Jul-Aug: Mon 2-6pm, Tue-Thu 10am-6pm, Fri 2-9.30pm, Sat 10.30am-6pm. Apr-Sep (except Jul-Aug): Mon 1pm-5.15pm; rest of week 9.15am-12.15pm, 2.15-5.15pm.*

Napoleon statue on de Gaulle Square, Ajaccio

© Fotosearch Stock Photography

Oct-Mar: Tue-Sat 9.15am-12.15pm, 2.15-5.15pm. 🆓 *5.35€.* ♿ ☎*04 95 21 48 17 .* www.musee-fesch.com.

One of the leading art museums in France, the Fesche houses the greatest collections of **Italian paintings**★★ outside the Louvre, including 15C paintings by Jacopo Sellajo, Lorenzo di Credi, **Bellini** *(Mary with the Infant Jesus)* and **Botticelli** *(Virgin with Garland)*. There are two outstanding works from the 16C: Veronese's **Leda** and the second **Man with Glove** by Titian. There are also a number of French and Spanish works and temporary exhibits.

Maison Bonaparte

🕐 *Apr-Sep: Tue-Sun 9am-noon, 2-6pm; Oct-Mar: Tue-Sun 10am-noon, 2-5pm, .* 🆓 *4€* ☎*04 95 21 43 89.*

A typical house of the Genoese quarter, the Bonaparte family moved here from Italy in 1743. Napoleon is supposed to have been born on a couch in the antechamber on the first floor. The family enjoyed a reasonable standard of living. In May 1793, the Bonapartes, loyal to Republican ideas, were forced by the followers of Pascal Paoli to abandon the house, which was sacked and the adjoining family properties laid waste. On her return to Ajaccio in 1798, Napoleon's mother put the house back in order with the help of her half-brother, Abbot Fesch (a future cardinal). The work was financed in part by a grant from the Directory, in part by sums sent to his brother Joseph by Napoleon (now in Egypt), enabling him to acquire the upper storeys and the adjoining house. On his return from Egypt on 29 September 1799, Bonaparte stopped off at Ajaccio to see the family home. He is supposed to have slept in the alcove on the second floor. After six days he slipped away via a trap-door, never to see his birthplace again. A diverse collection of memorabilia is displayed.

Place Maréchal-Foch

This fine square, the focus of Ajaccio's outdoor social life, is shaded by palm trees; its upper part is dominated by a marble statue by Laboureur of Napoleon as First Consul.

ALBI★★★

MICHELIN MAP 338 D 6, E 7–POPULATION 47 800
GREEN GUIDE LANGUEDOC ROUSSILLON TARN GORGES

From the bridges spanning the Tarn to the extraordinary cathedral, Albi "the red" is made of brick which owes its rosy hue to the clays dug from the river's bed.

🛈 **Information:** Palais de la Berbie, pl. Ste-Cécile, 81000 Albi ☎05 63 49 48 80 www.albi-tourisme.fr

▶ **Orient Yourself:** To get a better idea of the massive proportions of the cathedral, take a look at it from a distance, preferably the bridge across the Tarn (the Pont du 22-Août), or from one of the streets of Old Albi, which opens onto the cathedral square.

🅐 **Don't Miss:** A boat trip on the Tarn (**Berges du Tarn** – *see Address Book*).

🕐 **Organizing Your Time:** Start the day at "la Berbie" on Place Ste-Cécile, opposite the cathedral. Drop in to sample some local specialities at "Pâtisserie Galy". Enjoy a boat trip on the river to appreciate the beauty of the city at its best. At the end of the day, this student town offers plenty of pleasant pubs to spend the evening, such as the "Connemara", "Estabar" or "Shamrock".

A Bit of History

At the beginning of the 13C the city was one of the centres of the dualist Cathar doctrine, dubbed the "Albigensian heresy" by a fearful Church. The subsequent "Albigensian Crusade" was directed on the spiritual side by St Dominic; on the

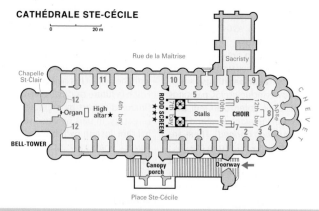

CATHÉDRALE STE-CÉCILE

1	Judith	5	Esther	9	Chapelle Sainte-Croix
2	Prophet Zephaniah	6	Charlemagne	10	Painting of the Holy Family
3	Prophet Isaiah	7	Constantine	11	Chapelle du Rosaire
4	Prophet Jeremiah	8	Statue of Virgin and child	12	Last Judgement

ground, armies moved in from north and east to commit the terrible atrocities of Béziers, Carcassonne, Minerve and Lavaur. The Capetian kings took advantage of the troubles, which lasted from 1208 to 1229, to gain a foothold in Languedoc, but Catharism itself was finally stamped out only by the Inquisition and the ghastly funeral pyre at Montségur (see Château de MONTSÉGUR).

Sights

Cathédrale Ste-Cécile★★★

Construction of the cathedral, extending over two centuries, began in 1282 at a time when work on the neighbouring Berbie Palace, the bishops' residence,

and on that of the Dominicans at Toulouse, was already well advanced. For the bishops, the status of the church was inextricably linked to its temporal power and they therefore gave their cathedral the appearance of a fortress. In the 19C the formidable edifice acquired the three upper storeys of its keep-like bell-tower, its machicolations and its inspection gallery.

Inside, the perfect simplicity of the single broad nave with its Southern French Gothic side chapels passes almost unnoticed, such is the exuberance of the Flamboyant decorative scheme. The rood screen (**jubé**★★★), one of the few to have survived, is also one of the most sumptuous. In the 15C and 16C all the greater churches possessed such a screen; it separated the clergy, in the

Albi "La Rouge"

©Alain Rezazadeh/SXC

Address Book

VISIT

Guided Tour of the Old Town *(45 min)* *organised by the Tourist Office, Jul-Aug: Mon-Sat except public holidays at 12 or 12.15pm. Book at the Tourist Office.* 4€ *(under 14s: no charge).*

Walks – Six walks allow the visitor to discover Albi : the circuit Pourpre (purple) goes through the heart of old Albi and takes in the main historic sites, characters and monuments; the circuit Or (gold) focuses on the growth of Albi over two thousand years; the circuit Azur (azure) leads along the banks of the Tarn, taking in the Pont Vieux and the Pont Neuf, and provides some fine views of the town (these routes marked by explanatory signposts in three languages); circuit of religious heritage; circuit of skilled craftsmen; and circuit of hidden gardens. Depart from the Tourist Office.

Albi Pass – This visitors' card gives numerous discounts at sites and monuments, shops and attractions. 5,50 € from the tourist office.

For coin ranges, see the Legend on the cover flap.

WHERE TO EAT

Le Poisson d'Avril – *17 r. d'Engueysse* – ☎*05 63 38 30 13* – *closed Mon midday and Sun Oct-Apr.* This restaurant in a typical old Albi house 200m/220yd from the cathedral has an unusual interior decor designed like the inside of a barrel, with wooden beams. Prices are moderate and food is not heavy.

Le Table du Sommelier – *20 r. Porta* – ☎*05 63 46 20 10* – *www.latabledusommelier.com/* – *closed Sun and Mon.* The proprietor sets the scene here perfectly, with cases of wine piled high in the entrance and rustic dining room with mezzanine floor. This wine-focused bistro serves refined cuisine using the freshest ingredients.

Le Robinson – *142 r. Édouard-Branly* – ☎*05 63 46 15 69* – *closed Nov-Feb, Tue noon and Mon.* This isle of green on the banks of the Tarn is acceible from the pont Neuf. Dating from the 1920's, the old-fashioned dance hall has an exuberant charm. The food is simple and the welcome warm. Dream away the evening!

Jardin des Quatre Saisons – *19 bd de Strasbourg* – ☎*05 63 60 77 76. www.lejardindes4saisons.fr.st* – *closed Sun evening and Mon.* A friendly welcome from the owners awaits, along with a good selection of wines and traditional cuisine. A little away from the centre, this remains a reliable favourite.

WHERE TO STAY

George V – *29 av. du Mar.-Joffre* – ☎*05 63 54 24 16* – *9 rms.* It is worth searching out this cosy establishment with its typical local style in the station district. Rooms are a generous size and some have a fireplace. At the first sign of fine weather, make the best of the pleasant shade of the little courtyard.

Chambre d'hôte à la Ferme "Naussens" – *81150 Castanet* – ☎*05 63 55 22 56.* *Dec-Mar.* 3 rooms. A warm and convivial welcome awaits at this farm in the midst of vines. Simple, traditional, family-style cooking using farm produce and washed down with their own wine.

Cantepau – *9 r. Cantepau* – ☎*05 63 60 75 80* – *closed 25 Dec-11 Jan* – *P* – *33 rms.* Wicker furniture, subdued hues and fans give this hotel a colonial feel following its recent revamp. Friendly welcome.

Hôtel Mercure – *41 bis r. Porta* – ☎*05 63 47 66 66* *P* – *56 rms.* This modern hotel has an original setting, in an old 18C red-brick mill on the banks of the Tarn. The functional rooms offer a view of the river and cathedral. Guests can enjoy the same view from the dining room.

SIT BACK AND RELAX

La Berbie – *17 pl. Ste-Cécile* – ☎*05 63 54 13 86* – *Jul-Aug: daily 9.30am-11pm; Sep-Jun: Wed-Mon 9.30am-8pm.* This attractive tea room on Place Ste-Cécile, opposite the cathedral, serves a wide range of tea, coffee, home-baked pastries, ice-cream sundaes and pancakes. Luncheon menu.

SHOPPING

In the streets of the Old Town (especially *rues Mariès, Ste-Cécile et Verdrusse*) are a variety of antique shops and boutiques. Also, visitors cannot miss the many shops selling local food and drink specialities, including foie gras, confits, anis biscuits and other pâtisserie.

L'Artisan Pastellier – 5 r. Puech-Bérenguier – ☎05 63 38 59 18 – artisan.pastellier@wanadoo.fr – ⏰Tue-Sat 10am-noon, 2-7pm, Mon mid-Jun to mid-Sep and Sun in Aug 3-6.30pm – ⏰closed 20 Jan-10 Feb, 14 Jul, 15 Aug, Sun and Mon out of season. Pastels were for centuries an important industry in Albi and its region. Near the Maison du vieil Alby, this shop is a poem in blue. Made from pastel leaves, this irresistable colour is used to shade local crafts and fabrics. Calligraphers and artists will also be in their element here among inks, paints and pastels of natural pigments.

Marché biologique (Organic market) – Pl. F.-Pelloutier – ⏰Tue 5-7pm. A big range of local organic produce.

Markets– Pl. Ste-Cécile. A big market is held on Saturday on place Ste-Cécile: fruit, vegetables, foie gras (in season), mushrooms, garlic from Lautrec, charcuterie from Lacaune et Gaillac wines.

Patisserie J.P. Galy – 7 r. Saunal – ☎05 63 54 13 37 – Tues -Sat 9.45am-7pm – ⏰closed 1 week in Feb and 4 weeks Sep-early Oct and holidays. One of the popular pastrycooks of the old quarter, with many local specialities (try out *navettes, gimblettes, croquants aux amandes, jeannots à l'anis, croissants aux pignons*).

RECREATION

Boat Trip on the Tarn (Berges du Tarn) ☎05 63 43 59 63 – www.albi-tourisme.fr ⏰ daily Jun-Sep. About 8 departures from 11.25am to 6pm – 🚌 5€ for 30min (children under 12 years: 3€); 15€ for 2hr, (children under 12 years: 10€); ⏰ closed Oct-Jun. 🚭. The boat is a flat-bottomed barge, a gabarre, used for transporting goods until the 19C and now used for pleasure trips. Leaving the old harbour at the foot of the ramparts of the Palais de la Berbie, the barge travels along the Tarn past the old Albi mills, and the locks at the Moulin de Gardès and Moulin de la Mothe.

CALENDAR OF EVENTS

Free Organ Concerts in the Cathedral -Wed and Sun afternoons in Jul and Aug.
Carnaval – Feb.
Le Grand Prix automobile d'Albi – Sep.

choir, from the lay worshippers in the nave; during services readings would be given from its gallery. This example dates from 1485, as does the screen closing off the choir (**chœur**)(⏰ daily Jun-Sep 9am-6.30pm, rest of year 9am-noon, 2-6.30pm; 🚌 1€; ♿ ☎05 63 43 23 43); its arches and gables, columns and arcading all show the extraordinary skill and attention to detail of the craftsmen who worked the white limestone. The naturalistic poses and facial expressions typical of Gothic art are here brought to a fine pitch. Old Testament figures are on the outside, those from the New Testament on the side of the choir, where there are two rows of 66 stalls. The vaults were painted from 1509 to 1512 by Bolognese artists; they repay study with binoculars.

The hallucinatory **Last Judgement** is a masterpiece of late-15C mural painting; it was unfortunately disfigured by the installation in the 17C of the great organ. But it is nevertheless possible to admire the upper part depicting the Heavenly Kingdom: on the left the Apostles, haloed in gold, and the saints as well as the elect bearing the book of their life held open; on the right the damned, punished by their sin itself.

Palais de la Berbie★

Restructuring scheduled to continue until 2009 may cause some changes to the displays. ⏰ Daily (except Oct-Mar). Jun-Sep: 9am-noon, 2-6pm, (Jul and Aug: no midday closing). Apr and May: 10am-noon, 2-6pm. Oct-Mar: Wed-Mon 10am-noon, 2-5pm (Mar and Oct: 5.30pm). ⏰ Closed 1 Jan, 1 May, 1 Nov, 25 Dec. 🚌 5€. 🐭 9 € ☎05 63 49 48 70. www.musee-toulouse-lautrec.com.

The former Bishops' Palace houses the **Musée Toulouse-Lautrec**★★devoted to the life and art of Henri de Toulouse-Lautrec (1864-1901). Born in Albi at the Hôtel du Bosc, Toulouse-Lautrec was crippled in early life by two accidents. He is revealed here as one of the great painters of everyday life; his vision of the depravity and decadence of late-19C Paris is communicated with restraint and compassion (*Jane Avril, Mademoiselle Lucie Bellanger, Au bal de l'Élysée-Montmartre*).

▶ **Vieil Albi**★★ (Old Town).

ECOMUSÉE D'**ALSACE**★★

MICHELIN MAP 315 H 9–ALSACE ECOMUSEUM

GREEN GUIDE ALSACE LORRAINE CHAMPAGNE

An open-air museum founded in 1984 to preserve local heritage comprises some 60 old buildings dotted over an area of 15 hectares – 37 acres. The old buildings dating from the 15C to 19C, which were saved from demolition and carefully dismantled and re-erected to create a village setting, are fine examples of rural habitat from the various regions of Alsace. The museum, which is constantly evolving, also includes industrial structures; next door to the museum are the restored buildings of a potassium mine which was worked from 1911 to 1930.

Information: 9 ave. Foch, pl. de la Réunion, 68100 Mulhouse, ☎03 89 35 48 48. www.tourisme-mulhouse.com

▶ **Orient Yourself:** The Ecomusée is in the countryside about 13km NW of the city of Mulhouse. Ten of the buildings are rented as holiday accommodation, and there is also a restaurant on the site.

Visit

🕐 *Mar-Sep: daily 10am-6pm; Jul and Aug: daily 9.30am-7pm; Jan-Feb and Oct to mid Nov: daily 10am-5pm; mid-Nov to mid-Dec: Sundays only.* 🚸 *12€.* ☎*03 89 74 44 74. www.ecomusee-alsace.com.*
Walk around the half-timbered buildings grouped by region (Sundgau, Reid, Kochersberg, Bas-Rhin) and complete with courtyards and gardens, to appreciate the development of building techniques and the varied architecture of farm buildings according to the regions and periods.

Specific buildings such as a fortified structure, a chapel, a school and a wash-house evoke community life in a traditional Alsatian village. Old plant varieties are grown in a typical field which also serves for farming demonstrations.
An area devoted to fun-fairs includes a rare merry-go-round (1909). Visitors will also discover the age-old crafts of carpenters and masons, as well as the evolution of living conditions, from the reconstructed interiors complete with kitchens, alcoves and "stube", the living area with its terracotta stove.

Alsatian dwellings

Potter's house in Outre-Forêt

Fisherman's house in the Reid

R. Corbel/MICHELIN – Source: Ecomusée d'Alsace

Farmstead in Kochersberg

House in the vineyards of Alsace

Farmhouse in the Sundgau

AMBOISE★★

MICHELIN MAP 317-O 4–POPULATION 11 460
GREEN GUIDE CHÂTEAUX OF THE LOIRE

Amboise is a bridge-town, built at the foot of an escarpment already fortified in Gallo-Roman times, on which stand the proud remains of its great château.

- **Information:** Quai du Gén.-de-Gaulle, 37400 Amboise, ☎02 47 57 09 28. www.amboise-valdeloire.com.
- ▶ **Orient Yourself:** The busy town centre rises from the south bank of the Loire.
- **Parking:** There is metered parking on Quai du Gén.-de-Gaulle, the main road beside the river.
- **Especially for Kids:** On the edge of town there are sights kids will love, including the Parc des Mini-Châteaux and the Chanteloup Pagoda.

Sights

Château★★

🕐 *Jul and Aug: daily 9am-7pm; Apr-Jun: daily 9am-6.30pm; Mid to end Mar, Sep and Oct: daily 9am-6pm; early to mid-Nov: daily 9am-5.30pm; mid-Nov to end Jan: daily 9am-noon, 2-4.45pm; early Feb to mid-Mar: daily 9am-noon, 1.30-5.30pm.*
🕐 *Closed 1 Jan, 25 Dec.* ◈ *8€.* ☎*08 20 20 50 50 – www.chateau-amboise.com.*

The 15C saw the Golden Age of Amboise. Charles VIII was born here in 1470; from his 22nd year onwards he carried on the work begun by his father, Louis XI. By the time he left on his Italian campaign, work was well in hand on a number of projects: the round towers, the great Gothic roof of the wing overlooking the Loire, and the Flamboyant St-Hubert Chapel, which served as an oratory for Anne of Brittany and has particularly fine Flemish door panels. In 1496 Charles returned from Italy, bringing with him not only works of art but a whole retinue of artists, architects, sculptors, cabinet-makers and gardeners.

With these Italians came a taste for Antiquity and a decorative sense unknown at the time in France (doorways resembling triumphal arches, inlaid ceilings, superimposed arches, etc). Charles' liking for luxury enhanced the prestige of the monarchy; his promotion of the artistic ideas of the Renaissance was continued by Louis XII and even more by François I, under whom château life became a whirl of princely gaiety with festivals, entertainments, hunting parties. However, this first French château of the Renaissance was destined to disappear; partly demolished by the troops of Louis XIII, it was further dismantled on the orders of Napoleon's Senate. Now it is known only from an engraving by Du Cerceau.

Tour – From the **terrace**, there is a fine view of the Loire. Inside, the **Royal Apartments** are the only part of the château that escaped demolition between 1806 and 1810. The tour of the interior takes in the **Salle des Gardes nobles**, or guard room; the **Salle des Tambourineurs**, which features interesting furniture and a 16C Brussels tapestry, **Homage to Alexander the Great**; the **Salle du Conseil**, also known as the Hall of State, where the king presided over the State Council (which decided policies of the realm); and **Henry II's bedchamber**, adorned with trompe-l'oeil decoration. Visit the two towers, **Tour des Minimes** and **Tour Herutault**, the latter of which leads directly to the town of Amboise.

Laid out in informal English style, the pleasant **gardens** are worth seeing.

Clos-Lucé★

500m from the Chateau. 🕐 *Jul and Aug: daily 9am-8pm; Apr-Jun and Sep-Oct: daily 10am-7pm; Feb-Mar and Nov-Dec: daily 10am-6pm; Jan: daily 10am-5pm.*
🕐 *Closed 1 Jan, 25 Dec.* ◈ *12€ (winter: 9€)* ☎*02 47 57 00 73. www.vinci-closluce. com.*

To this manor house of red brick with stone dressings François I invited **Leonardo da Vinci** in 1516. The great Florentine was then age 64. At Amboise he neither painted nor taught, devoting himself instead to organising royal festivities, designing a château at Romorantin, planning the drainage of the Sologne and amusing himself designing mechanical inventions, but some of which now have been constructed in a display of "fabuleuses machines".

The Château's Salle du Conseil

B.Kaufmann/MICHELIN

AMIENS★★

MICHELIN MAP 301 G 8–POPULATION 136 000
GREEN GUIDE NORTHERN FRANCE AND THE PARIS REGION

The largest Gothic cathedral in France, one of the finest in the world, is the majestic centrepiece of the historic capital of Picardy.

- **Information:** 6 bis r. Dusevel, 80000 Amiens, ☎03 22 71 60 50. www.amiens.com/tourisme.
- **Orient Yourself:** After visiting the cathedral (hire an audioguide for a guided tour in English), stroll the shopping streets, especially rue du Hocquet and place du Don. Walk across the River Somme to explore the narrow streets of Quartier St-Leu, which contain craft and antique shops, cafés and restaurants.
- **Parking:** Leave the car in place St. Michel, next to the cathedral, or in Saint-Leu underground car park.
- **Especially for Kids:** Within the Hortillonnages, the Île aux Fagots has an aquarium and insectarium that invites children to discover more about ecology. Amiens is famous for its tradition of puppets: enjoy a show at the **Chés Cabotans** puppet theatre."

A Bit of History

Amiens' great legend is that of the Roman soldier who, passing near Amiens, sliced his cloak in two and gave half to a wretched beggar. Later becoming Bishop of Tours, the former soldier was eventually canonised as St Martin, patron saint of France. In 1477, on the death of Charles le Téméraire (the Bold) this ancient capital of Picardy became subject to the French Crown. In the 17C its textile industry prospered (Amiens velvet). The city suffered in both World Wars, in 1918 during the Ludendorff Offensive, in 1940 during the Battle of France. Later attractively restored and becoming a university town, it is again a major centre for the arts and the economy.

Sights

Cathédrale Notre-Dame★★★
🕐 Apr- Sep: daily 8.30am-6.30pm; Oct-Mar: daily 8.30am-5.30pm. 🕐 Closed public holidays. ☎ 03 22 71 60 50.
The harmonious building was begun in 1220 and completed just 68 years later,. The architect, Robert de Luzarches, had all the stonework cut to its finished dimensions before it left the quarry, then simply assembled it on site.

Puppets

Amiens' puppet shows date back to about 1785. Known in Picardy dialect as **cabotans**, the puppets are carved out of wood and about 50cm – 19in tall. The main character **Lafleur** is The King of St-Leu (the medieval quarter) and undoubtedly embodies all the spirit and character of the Picardy people.

Since at least the 19C, this truculent, irreverent, bold character with his fiery temper has expressed plain common sense and acclaimed the proud nobility of the province in the language of his ancestors. Even from a distance, he is recognisable by his impressive stature, characteristic gait, and 18C valet's livery of fine red Amiens velvet. He is often accompanied by his wife Sandrine and his best friend Tchot Blaise. His motto is "Drink, walk and do nothing".

In the 19C each of the 20 quarters in the city had its own puppet theatre. With the arrival of the cinema and sporting events at the turn of the century, however, the theatres gradually closed down.

The cathedral is in Gothic Lanceo-late style, with three-storey elevations including a blind triforium in nave and transept. The wonderfully elegant nave is the highest in France (42.5m – 140ft).

At an early date problems arose through water from the Somme penetrating the foundations; movement occurred along the length of the building, evidence of which can be seen in cracks in the nave near the transept. The weight of the vaults aggravated the effect; to remedy it, in the 16C a brace of Toledo steel was inserted into the triforium, heated red-hot, and allowed to cool. For four centuries it has served its purpose admirably. The building was further strengthened by increasing the number of buttresses at the east end and by adding side chapels in the form of double aisles to the nave in order to spread the downward forces as widely as possible.

The famous slender steeple rising above the crossing was built by the master carpenter Cardon in two years (1528-29).

Much of the cathedral's decoration is of very high quality indeed: the sculpture of the west front (including the noble figure of Christ known as the "Beau Dieu"), and the rose windows of the main façade, including the 16C Sea Window (rose de la Mer), of the north transept; the 14C Window of the Winds (rose des Vents); and of the south transept, the 15C Window of Heaven (rose du Ciel). Inside, the wrought-iron choir screen dates from the 18C and the oak choir stalls from the beginning of the 16C. The third chapel of the north aisle houses a remarkable Romanesque Crucifixion probably influenced by oriental art. Christ's feet are nailed to the Cross separately; clad in a long robe, He wears His royal crown in glory. The figure was carved before the arrival in Paris of the relics of the Passion (including the Crown of Thorns) purchased by St Louis.

Hortillonnages★

Maison des hortillonnages, 54, bd Beau-villé. ⌂ 5.30€ (children 2.60€). ⌂ (50min) Apr to end Oct: by boat, 2pm onwards. ☎03 22 92 12 18.

The small allotments known as **aires** which stretch over an area of 300ha – 749 acres amid a network of canals or **rieux** fed by the many arms of the Somme, have been worked since the Middle Ages by market gardeners or *hortillons*. At present, fruit trees and flowers are tending to replace vegetables and the gardeners' sheds are becoming weekend holiday homes.

▶ **Musée de Picardie**★★ – archeology, painting ⌂ ⌂ *Tue-Sun 10am-12.30pm, 2-6pm.* ⌂ *Closed Mon,1 Jan, 1 and 8 May, 14 Jul, 11 Nov, 25 Dec.* ⌂ *4.50€, no charge 1st Sunday in the month.* ☎03 22 97 14 00.

Central doorway, Cathedral Notre-Dame

Address Book

For coin ranges, see the Legend on the cover flap.

TOURS

📞 Contact the tourist office for guided tours of the town in French, several times daily.

City Pass – from the tourist office, for discounts on entry fees and tours.
Barge tours – explore the canals of St-Leu in traditional style. Depart from bd du Cange, ☎03 22 22 30 90.

WHERE TO EAT

🍽 **Le Bouchon** – *10, rue Alexandre Fatton* – ☎*03 22 92 14 32. www.lebouchon. fr* 🕐 *closed Sun evening Sep to Jun.* A Parisian-style bistro near the railway station specialising in typically Lyonnais dishes and traditional cuisine of the region; a relaxed, "no fuss" atmosphere.

🍽🍽 **Les Marissons** – *Pont de la Dodane* – ☎*03 22 92 96 66 – les-marissons@les-marissons.fr* – 🕐 *closed Sat lunch, Sun and Wed lunch.* The place to be in the Saint-Leu quarter is this old marine workshop transformed into a restaurant. The flowery mini-garden becomes a terrace in summer, while in winter diners sit under the sloping wooden frame in a pleasant decor of handsome beams and round tables.

🍽 **Le Petit Poucet** – *52 rue des Trois-Cailloux* – ☎*03 22 91 42 32.* 🕐 *daily except Mon, 8am – 7.30pm (Sun 7pm).* 🕐 *closed 9 Jul-9 Aug.* This attractive establishment is very popular with the people of Amiens who come for a slice of quiche, a ficelle picarde (baked crepes, stuffed and rolled), or a mixed salad for lunch, a delectable chocolate for tea, or a box of divine pastries to enjoy at home.

WHERE TO STAY

🛏 **Hôtel Alsace-Lorraine** – *18 rue de la Morlière* – ☎*03 22 91 35 71 – www. alsace-lorraine.fr.st* –*14 rms:* 🍽 *7€.* This comfortable, likeable little hotel hides behind an imposing carriage entrance a five-minute walk from the town centre and train station. Bedrooms, brightened with colourful fabrics, give onto the charming inner courtyard.

🛏🛏 **Hôtel Carlton** – *42 rue de Noyon* – ☎ *03 22 97 72 22 – www.lecarlton.fr* – *24 rms:* 🍽 *8.50€.* Behind the attractive 19C facade discover a modern, plush interior. Every room features waxed furniture and murals. Their simple restaurant, Le Bistrot, serves grilled meats.

🛏🛏 **Le Petit Chateau (Bed and Breakfast)** – *2 rue Grimaux, 80480 Dury – 6km/3.6mi S of Amiens via N 1 dir. Beauvais* – ☎*03 22 95 29 52 –* 🛏 *4 rms.* In countryside 10 minutes from central Amiens, a massive 19C residence whose comfortable guest rooms are housed in an outbuilding. The owner is happy to show his collection of old automobiles.

ON THE TOWN

After dark, the Quai Belu canalside area in the St Leu quarter is the place for pubs, discos and nightlife.

Texas Café – *13 rue des Francs-Mûriers, Quartier Saint-Leu* – ☎*03 22 72 19 79 –* 🕐 *Tue-Sat 10pm-5am;* 🕐 *closed Sun-Mon.* This enormous Confederate-themed 'saloon' of brick and wood is always crowded and popular. Before midnight, drink (beer and cocktails), dance and sing (karaoke). After midnight, it's a disco and dance venue.

SHOWTIME AND ART

"The cathedral in living colour" – The artist Skertzò uses lighting to highlight the colourful entrance on the cathedral's west side. The presentation is held from mid-June to September at dusk, and from mid-December to early January at 8pm. Commentary in French and then English.

Comédie de Picardie – *62 rue des Jacobins* – ☎*03 22 22 20 20 –www. comdepic.com –* 🕐 *Mon-Fri 1pm-7pm, Sat 1pm-6pm. Closed Aug, public holidays, Sun except performance days. 11 to 46€.* This venerable old manor, entirely restored, houses a very pretty 400-seat theatre. The region's creative and dramatic hub, it produces 15 different shows for a total of 250 performances per season.

Maison de la Culture d'Amiens – *Pl. Léon-Gontier* – ☎*03 22 97 79 77 – www. maisondelaculture-amiens.com.* 🕐 *Tue-Fri noon-7pm, Sat-Sun 2pm-7pm* – 🕐 *closed public holidays and Mon.* Two halls (1070 and 300 seats), a movie theatre devoted to art and experimental films and two exhibition rooms. This complex offers an unusually interesting and eclectic selection of events.

Kids **Théâtre de Marionnettes** – *Chés Cabotans d'Amiens* – *31 rue Édouard-David, quartier St-Leu* – ☎03 22 22 30 90. www.ches-cabotans-damiens.com. ⏱ *Exhibitions: Apr-Aug from Tue to Sun 10am-noon, 2pm-6pm except Sun morning; mid-Oct to Mar from Tue to Sun 2pm-6pm. Performances: mid-Jul-mid-Aug from Tue to Sun: 6pm; 15 Oct to end Mar: Sun (except public holidays and Christmas week) 3pm; additional shows on school holiday weekdays at 2.30pm* – ☜ *10 € (children: 5 €)*. This fascinating show for all takes place in a veritable miniature theatre with a beautifully designed set. The puppets all have their own history and language (French or Picard) plus remarkably expressive faces that can also be admired in the ground-floor exhibition. .

SHOPPING

Atelier de Jean-Pierre Facquier – *67 rue du Don* – ☎03 22 92 49 52 or 03 22 39 21 74 – ⏱ *Tue-Fri 2pm-6.30pm, Sat 10am-noon, 2pm-6pm* – ⏱ *closed 1 Jan, 25 Dec*. Transforming them into traditional and invented wooden figurines, Monsieur Facquier carves life into pieces of wood before your eyes. Madame Facquier sews their clothes using fabric chosen with care. Each unique character is a genuine work of art.

Jean Trogneux – ☎03 22 71 17 17. www.trogneux.fr – The city's speciality since the 16C, the Amiens macaroon, with its blend of almonds and honey, is ever popular. The Trogneux family, confectioners and chocolatiers for five generations, sell more than two million of them every year! The shop also carries a nice selection of local products.

Marché des hortillons – The local market gardeners, who grow their produce in canal-bordered wetlands (*hortillonnages*), come to market Saturday mornings, pl. Parmentier. Once a year, on 3rd Sunday in June, market is held as in years gone by. The gardeners, wearing traditional attire, come in flat-bottomed punts and unload their produce onto the docks.

CHÂTEAU D'**ANCY-LE-FRANC**★★

MICHELIN MAP 319

GREEN GUIDE BURGUNDY JURA

This dignified château marks the end of the early, Italian-influenced French Renaissance in all its brilliance.

- **Information:** 59 Grande rue, ☎03 86 75 03 15. www.cc-ancylefranc.net.
- ▶ **Orient Yourself:** The chateau stands in north Burgundy countryside, south-east of Tonnerre.

Visit

🎧 *Guided tours (50 min) Apr to mid-Nov: daily except Mon 10.30am, 11.30am, 2pm, 3pm, 4pm and (except Oct-Nov) 5pm.* ⏱ *Closed Nov to Easter.* ☜ *8€.* ☎03 86 75 14 63. www.chateau-ancy.com. Designed by Sebastian Serlio, Italian architect invited to France in 1541 by François I, the château was begun in 1546 and completed 50 years later. The exterior gives an impression of great order, combining symmetry with a masterly handling of spaces and surfaces according to the rules of the Golden Section. The courtyard is particularly subtle, with deeply-sunken twin pilasters topped by Corinthian capitals and separating scalloped niches.

The interior is equally fine. The Judith Room has a coffered ceiling painted by a pupil of Primaticcio, Cornelius van Haarlem. There are ancient bindings in the library, secret cabinets from Italy, dell'Abbate's *Battle of Pharsalus* and oval medallions by Primaticcio representing the Liberal Arts.

LES **ANDELYS**★★

MICHELIN MAP 304–POPULATION 9 047

GREEN GUIDE NORMANDY

The white castle rising beside Les Andelys commanded the Seine valley on the border of Normandy. Its strategic position was valued by Richard the Lionheart, Duke of Normandy as well as King of England. In 1196 he decided to break his agreement with the king of France, and construct a mighty fortress of his own. Within the year, so legend has it, the work was complete, and Richard was able to cry aloud "See my fine yearling!"

🖹 **Information:** R. Philippe-Auguste, Grand Andelys, ☎02 32 54 41 93. www.ville-andelys.fr

▶ **Orient Yourself:** The château rises beside picturesque waterside Petit Andelys. Grand Andelys extends away from the river.

Visit

Château Gaillard★★

Accessible by car from Grand Andelys or on foot (30 min climb) from Petit Andelys. 🕐 *Mid-Mar to mid-Nov: Wed-Mon 10am-1pm, 2-6pm. Last admission 1hr before closing.* 🕐 *Closed Tue, 1 May.* ☜ *3€.*

The clifftop stronghold must have been an impressive sight; with 17 towers, eight-foot-thick walls, and three rings of defences and moats. Yet King Philippe Auguste succeeded in taking it in 1274 after a siege of eight months. This victory enabled him to incorporate Normandy, Maine, Anjou and Touraine into the French kingdom. In 1419, four years after Agincourt, Henry V of England took it back. La Hire, companion to Joan of Arc, won it again for France 10 years later, only to lose it to Henry once more. It finally passed into French possession under Charles VII in 1449.

PRINCIPAT D'**ANDORRA**★★

PRINCIPALITY OF ANDORRA

MICHELIN MAP 343 G-H-I 9-10–POPULATION 78 550

GREEN GUIDE LANGUEDOC ROUSSILLON TARN GORGES

No mere tax-free shopping haven, this tiny Catalan-speaking nation in the high Pyrenees is also a wild, scenic land of lofty plateaus and precipitous valleys.

🖹 **Information:** 26 av. de l'Opéra 75001 Paris, ☎01 42 61 50 55. www.tourisme-andorre.net.

▶ **Orient Yourself:** There are few towns or roads. A single highway crosses the territory passing through the capital, Andorra La Vella.

A Bit of History

Andorra (with an area of just 464 sq. km / 179 sq. mi) was through the centuries a possession of Catalan counts and bishops, and from 1278 was shared between the Count of Foix and the Bishop of Urgell ('co-principality'). In 1993 it was given the freedom to abandon its former feudal status and become an independent state. Despite a remote location, It is prospering with hydro-electric power and all-year-round tourism.

Sights

Andorra la Vella

The capital of the Andorran valleys is a bustling commercial town. Away from the main road, however, the heart of Andorra la Vella preserves quiet old streets. To the east Andorra-la-Vella merges with the lively town of Escales.

Port d'Envalira★★

This pass, highest in the Pyrenees (2 407m – 7 823ft), marks the watershed between the Mediterranean and the Atlantic. There is a superb **panorama**.

ANGERS★★★

MICHELIN MAPS 317 E-F-G 4–POPULATION 226 843
GREEN GUIDE CHÂTEAUX OF THE LOIRE

This dynamic and cultured city on the river Maine was once the capital of a mighty Plantagenet kingdom encompassing all of England and half of France.

- 🅸 **Information:** 7 pl. du Président-Kennedy, ☎02 41 23 50 00. www.angers-tourisme.com.
- ▶ **Orient Yourself**: A fun way to discover the city is a tour on the Petit Train which drives around to all the main sights. There are also Taxi Tours, and guided Discovery Tours on foot. Ask at the tourist office for details.
- 🅿 **Parking**: Parking is available by the château on Esplanade du Port-Ligny.
- 👁 **Don't Miss**: The 14C Tenture de l'Apocalypse and other historic tapestries.
- 🕐 **Organizing Your Time:** After visiting the Château (2hr), allow at least half a day to walk through the steets of the Old Town.

A Bit of History

On 9 June 1129, Geoffrey Plantagenet married William the Conqueror's granddaughter Mathilda, whose inheritance of both Normandy and England made her the most desirable of brides. Twenty-

three years later another significant marriage took place, between Henry II, Geoffrey's son, and Eleanor of Aquitaine, the divorced wife of Louis VII. Two months later Henry became King of England, thereby extending the frontiers of the Angevin state to Scotland in the north

Château d'Angers

Address Book

For coin ranges, see the Legend on the cover flap.

WHERE TO EAT

⊜ **La Ferme** – *2 pl. Freppel* – ☎*02 41 87 09 90* – *www.la-ferme.fr* – ⏱*closed 20 Jul-12 Aug, Sun evening and Wed* – *reservations required.* A well-known restaurant near the cathedral, where you can enjoy traditional local cooking in a simple setting. The terrace is one of the nicest in town.

⊜⊜ **Provence Caffé** – *9 pl. du Ralliement* – ☎*02 41 87 44 15* – ⏱*closed 3 Jan, 1 Aug-24 Aug, 19 Dec, Sun and Mon* – *reservations required.* This popular restaurant next to the Hôtel St-Julien is often full both at lunchtime and in the evenings. The patron is from the south of France and the menu reflects this, with its Mediterranean flavours. The dining room has a Provençal atmosphere too. Carefully prepared cuisine at moderate prices.

⊜⊜ **Le Relais** – *9 r. de la Gare* – ☎*02 41 88 42 51* – ⏱*closed 22 Aug-13 Sep, 24 Dec-4 Jan, Sun and Mon.* The woodwork and the murals in this charming tavern recall the vineyard and the harvest. The traditional cooking is satisfying and simple, at affordable prices.

WHERE TO STAY

⊜⊜ **Hôtel Mail** – *8 r. des Ursules* – ☎*02 41 25 05 25* – *www.hotel-du-mail.com* – 🅿 *– 26 rooms* – ⊡ *10€.* The thick walls of this former Ursuline convent in a peaceful street prevent the noise from the nearby town centre from penetrating. The fairly spacious rooms have a personal touch and are under the sloping roof on the top floor.

⊜⊜ **Chambre d'hôte Grand Talon** – *3 rte des Chapelles – 49800 Andard – 11km/6.8mi E of Angers on N 147 (towards Saumur) then D 113* – ☎*02 41 80 42 85* – ⤧ *– 3 rooms.* This elegant 18C house just outside Angers, decked out with leafy vines of Virginia creeper, is a haven of peace. You can picnic in the park, or relax in the lovely square courtyard. The rooms are pretty and the owners extend a very warm welcome.

⊜⊜ **Le Progrès** – *26 r. Denis-Papin* – ☎ *02 41 88 10 14* – ⏱*closed 7-15 Aug, 24 Dec-1 Jan. 41 rooms* – ⊡ *7.50€.* Conveniently located near the train station, this is a friendly place with modern, well-lit and practical rooms. Before setting out to tour the château, enjoy your coffee in the breakfast room, with its decor inspired by the bright colours of Provence.

⊜⊜ **Hôtel Cavier** – *La Croix-Cadeau – 49240 Avrillé – 8km/5mi NW of Angers on N 162 –* b*02 41 42 30 45 – lecavier@ lacroixcadeau.fr –* 🅿 *– 43 rooms* – ⊡ *10€.* The sails of this 18C windmill still turn! Inside its old stone walls is the dining room, near the original machinery. Modern bedrooms in a recent wing. Terrace next to the outdoor pool.

SHOPPING

La Petite Marquise – *22 r. des Lices -* b*02 41 87 43 01.* Does *Quernons d'Ardoise* mean anything to you? If you don't know about this delicious local speciality of nougatine and chocolate made to look like roof slates, head to this little shop where they were born.

Maison du vin de l'Anjou – *5 bis pl. Kennedy* – ☎*02 41 88 81 13 – www. interloire.com* – ⏱*May-Sept: Tue-Sun 9am-1pm, 3-6.30pm; Oct-Apr Dec: Tue-Sat. 9am-1pm, 3-6.30pm -* ⏱*closed Jan-Feb and public holidays.* In the centre of town, near the château, this wine shop offers a good selection of Anjou and Saumur wines, which you can taste.

OUTDOOR LEISURE ACTIVITIES

Maison de l'Environnement – This nature information centre organises various activities including environment-awareness courses.

Public Gardens and Parks – They are usually open from 8am to 8pm in summer and from 8am to 5.30pm in winter: Jardin des Plantes, Jardin du Mail (bandstand), Jardin Médiéval (at the foot of the castle), French-style gardens in the moat and Parcs de l'étang St-Nicolas on the outskirts of town.

Boat Trips – Various possibilities including a combined tourist-train ride and mini boat trip on the River Maine and a dinner/cruise by candlelight. *Batellerie promenade l'Union, cale de la Savatte, 49100 Angers,* ☎*02 41 42 12 12.*

and the Basque country in the south. By contrast, the Capetian kingdom to the east cut a sorry figure, its capital, Paris, seeming little more than an overgrown village in comparison with Angers.

In 1203, with the 81-year-old Eleanor living in retirement at Fontevraud, King Philippe Auguste succeeded in incorporating Anjou into the French kingdom, together with Normandy, Maine, Touraine and Poitou, all territories of John Lackland. In 1471, King **René** let Anjou pass into the hands of Louis XI.

Sights

Château★★★

🕐 *daily; May to early Sep: 9.30am-6.30pm; early Sep to end Apr:10am-5.30pm. Last admission 45min before closing.* 🕐 *Closed 1 Jan, 1 May, 1 and 11 Nov, 25 Dec.* ⟿ *Guided tours available (2hr).* ⊜ *7.50€ (18-25 years: 4.80€), no charge 1st Sunday in the month from Oct to Mar.* ☏*02 41 87 43 47. www.monum.fr.*

Built by Louis IX from 1228 to 1238 on the surviving Roman foundations, this splendid fortress was intended to counter any threat from the nearby Dukes of Brittany. With 17 towers in alternating courses of dark schist and white freestone they must have constituted a formidable deterrent. The moats were dug in 1485 by Louis XI. During the Wars of Religion, the towers were reduced in height and terraces added to give the defenders a clear field of fire.

A purpose-built gallery at the heart of the château displays the **Tenture de l'Apocalypse★★★**, a tapestry, originally 168m – 550ft long and 5m – 16ft high, the oldest and most important to have been preserved. Jean Lurçat (1892-1966) who discovered it in 1938 and whose artistic career was inspired by it, called it "one of the greatest works of Western art". The 76 extant scenes are based on the Apocalypse of St John, and are impressive in their masterly scale, composition and design. Commissioned by the Duke of Anjou Louis I, this superb

tapestry was executed in 1375-1380 by master weaver **Nicolas Bataille**.

In the Governor's Lodging, a fine collection of Flemish tapestries includes the 16C *Lady at the Organ* and *Penthesilea* and the richly coloured late 15C three-part *Tenture de la Passion et Tapisseries mille-fleurs★★* with graceful angels carrying the instruments of the Passion.

Cathédrale St-Maurice★★

The cathedral stands in a charming district of old houses. The characteristically elegant Angevin vault is notable in the 12C vaulting of the nave, with its transverse arches with double roll mouldings by Normand le Doué. By the end of the century the vaulting has become lighter; the number of ribs increases, springing from slender columns, as in the choir and transepts. At the beginning of the 13C it reaches its peak of development: lateral support is dispensed with; the structure dissolves into a graceful web of liernes, as in the hospital ward of the former **hôpital St-Jean★** (St John's Hospital), resting on a small number of slim columns, as in the early-13C ceiling of the choir of the Église St-Serge .

Musée Jean-Lurçat et de la Tapisserie contemporaine★★

4 bd Arago 🕐 *Jun-Sep: daily 10am-7pm; Oct-Jun: daily except Mon 10am-noon, 2-6pm;* 🕐 *closed 1 Jan, 1 May, 14 Jul, 1 and 11 Nov, 25 Dec;* ♿ ⊜ *4€;* ☏*02 41 05 38 00 – www.angers.fr.*

The former St John's Hospital, founded 1174 and in use for 680 years, now houses the **Musée Jean-Lurçat**. In the hospital ward with its Angevin vaulting is Lurçat's series of tapestries known as **Le Chant du Monde★★** (The Song of the World), 10 huge compositions symbolising the contradictions of the modern world. Lurçat's achievement marked the revival of the art of tapestry.

▸ **Romanesque arcade★★**
(in the Prefecture)

ANGOULÊME★★

MICHELIN MAP 324 K-L-M 5-6–POPULATION 43 170
GREEN GUIDE FRENCH ATLANTIC COAST

Narrow streets lace through the lofty Upper Town, lined with beautiful old buildings, and the ramparts give immense views. Angouleme is France's 'Cartoon Capital', and everywhere in town you'll see the influence of its celebrated Festival international de la bande dessinée, devoted to the art of the strip-cartoon.

- **Information:** 7 bis r. du Chat, ☎05 45 95 16 84. www.angouleme-tourisme.com
- ▶ **Orient Yourself:** Angoulême has a walled historic Upper Town, which rises high above a more industrial modern Lower Town. The tourist office has information on guided tours of the Upper Town.
- Kids In this cartoon-crazy city, there are brilliant graffiti and trompe l'oeil everywhere. The tourist office have a map of some of the best, or find their locations online at www.toutenbd.com/murs_peints/

A Bit of History

The town boasts **two Balzacs**. Guez de Balzac (1597-1654), one of the original members of the Académie Française and a champion of literary French, and Honoré Balzac (1799-1850), who added to the city's renown when he made Angoulême his home.

In 1806 a daring exploit was carried out on the city's northern ramparts: 77-year-old General Resnier launched himself into the void in a **flying-machine** of his own invention. The general suffered a broken leg, and a plan for the invasion of England by this method was shelved.

Bande Dessinée (strip cartoon, often known simply as BD) is an important entertainment for adults and kids alike in France. Angoulême's cartoon festival owes its origins to an exhibition in

1972, "Dix Millions d'images". In 1974, a regular Salon de la bande dessinée was started, that attracted many top cartoonists. In 1996, it became the popular international festival held in January each year.

Visit

Cathédrale St-Pierre★

Extensively destroyed by the Calvinists, the cathedral was restored in 1634 and again from 1866 onwards. The early-12C statuary of the west front **(façade★★)** is mostly intact; more elaborate than the other façades typical of the region around Angoulême, its themes include the Ascension (treated as at Cahors) and the Last Judgement.

Particularly noteworthy among the 70 statues and low-reliefs are the superb Christ in Majesty surrounded by the Evangelists, the medallions of saints and a battle scene inspired by the *Song of Roland* (lintel of the first doorway to the right).

▶ Kids **Centre National de la Bande Dessinée et de l'Image** – strip-cartoon centre ◷ *Jul-Aug: Mon-Fri 10am-7pm, Sat-Sun 2-7pm; rest of the year: daily except Mon 10am-6pm, Sat-Sun 2-6pm.* ◷ *Closed 1 Jan, 1 May, 25 Dec.* ❀ *5€ (children 7-18 years: 2.50€).* ☇ ☎*05 45 38 65 65. www.cnbdi.fr -*

The Cathedral façade

B. Kaufmann/MICHELIN

ANNECY★★★

MAP P 9 – MICHELIN MAP 328 J-K 5–POPULATION 50 350
GREEN GUIDE FRENCH ALPS

Lakeside Annecy enjoys an exquisitely beautiful setting of water and mountains, and has a picturesque old centre clustered around the river Thiou.

- **Information:** Centre Bonlieu, 1 r. J.-Jaurès, 74000 Annecy, ☎04 50 45 00 33. www.lac-annecy.com.
- **Orient Yourself:** The town is 61km / 38mi south of Geneva. The pedestrianised Old Annecy is the heart of the city. The tourist office has information on guided tours.
- **Don't miss:** A boat trip on the lake is a must.
- **Parking:** You won't need the car. Leave it at the central Bonlieu car park, or park at the train station.
- **Organising Your Time:** On market days, visit Old Annecy in the morning, when it is in full swing.

A Bit of History

Ancient lake settlement, then a hillside Gallo-Roman town, Annecy moved back downhill in the Middle Ages to its present site by the Thiou, whose rapid waters powered its many mills. In the 16C Annecy became the regional capital, displacing Geneva, and in the 17C was the home of the influential **St Francis of Sales**, bitter opponent of the Calvinism which had spread throughout the region.

Sights

Le Vieil Annecy (Old Annecy)★★

The picturesque old town, largely pedestrianised and renovated, lies on the banks of the Thiou as it flows from the lake. Its arcaded houses, Italianate wells and colourful markets (on Tue, Wed and Sun mornings) give immense charm. **Rue Ste-Claire**★ is especially attractive with arcades and gabled houses. The **Palais de l'Isle**★ rising from the midst of the river offers the most famous view of Old Annecy.

Overlooking the old town, the **château**★ (Jun-Sep: daily 10.30am-6pm; Oct-May:

Talloires

Fräsler/MICHELIN

daily except Tue 10am-noon, 2-5pm; last admission 45min before closing; ⏱ *closed main public hoidays;* ⊕ *4.70€;* ☎*04 50 33 87 30), former residence of the lords of Geneva, retains its defensive character. It houses a museum and an observatory.*

Le Lac (The Lake) ★★★

⏱ *Apr to end Oct: several types of boat trips with commentaries (1hr).* ⊕ *9.80€. May to mid-Sep: boats stopping at various places (2hr).* ⊕ *12.10€. Lunch trip and dinner-dance on board the MS Libellule. Times and reservations: Compagnie des*

Bateaux du lac d'Annecy, ☎*04 50 51 08 40. www.annecy-croisieres.com.*

A road runs around the edge of this lovely lake, giving wonderful views. Fine vista from the **Avenue d'Albigny**, in Annecy. There are several pleasant small resorts on the lakeside, notably **Talloires** ★★★, overlooking the narrows dividing the Grand Lac to the north from the Petit Lac to the south.

▸ **Jardins de l'Europe**★ – arboretum; **Musée de la Cloche**★ – 14C to 19C bells – at Sevrier *5km – 3mi south.*

ARCACHON★★

MICHELIN MAP 335 D 6-7–POPULATION 11 460
GREEN GUIDE FRENCH ATLANTIC COAST

A century and a half ago, the site of Arcachon was no more than a pinewood. Today, it is one of the most popular resorts on the French Atlantic.

🛈 **Information:** Esplanade G. Pompidou, ☎05 57 52 97 97. www.arcachon.com.
▸ **Orient Yourself**: The resort fronts onto the vast Bassin d'Arcachon inlet. The town centre is near the main beach on Blvd de la Plage and Av Gambetta.

A Bit of History

Arcachon was born when a couple of speculators, the Pereire brothers, laid a railway line to the coast in 1852. The resort quickly grew, and was popular for both winter and summer holidays. It is divided into 'seasons' – a winter resort (**ville d'hiver**★), with fine villas among

the pines; a summer resort (ville d'été), with the seafront and attractive **Boulevard de la Mer**★; and the fashionable autumn and spring districts (ville d'automne et ville de printemps) with opulent houses near Pereire park.

Sights

Bassin★ (Bay)

Bordered by the resorts of Arcachon, Andernos and the wooded dunes of the Cap Ferret peninsula, this vast airy bay, with Bird Island (Île aux Oiseaux) at its centre, extends over an area of 25 000ha – nearly 100sq miles, four-fifths of which is exposed at low tide. With its great stretches of oyster beds totalling 1 800ha – 4 500 acres in all, Arcachon is one of the main oyster-farming areas. Drive along the waterfront, or take a trip in a 'pinasse', one of the traditional boats used by the oyster farmers *(many excursions available from Thiers and Eyrac landing stages (Arcachon) and other land-*

Plage Pereire

J.Malburet/MICHELIN

ing stages around the Bassin. ☎*05 57 72 28 28. www.bateliers-arcachon.com).*

Dune du Pilat★★ *7.5km – 4.5mi south.* This huge hill of sand, the highest (114m – 374ft) and longest (2 800m – over 3 000yds) in Europe, drops on its landward side almost sheer to the pine woodland. Its summit offers a thrilling view along the long, straight sands of the 230km – 140 mile Silver Coast **(Côte d'Argent)** with its splendid Atlantic rollers. Every year the ocean deposits another 15 cubic metres of sand per metre of coastline, continually building up the dune which, in 1774, swallowed up the church at Soulac. The **panorama**★★ of ocean and forest is especially lovely at dusk.

ARC-ET-SENANS★★

MICHELIN MAP 321 E 4–POPULATION 1 277
GREEN GUIDE BURGUNDY JURA

Erected 1775-80, the Classical buildings of the former royal saltworks are an extraordinary essay in utopian town planning of the early Industrial Age. They are now on UNESCO's World Heritage List.

Information: Office of Tourism, Saline Royale, ☎03 81 57 43 21.

▶ **Orient Yourself:** The royal salt-works of Arc-et-Senans are located in Jura, not far from the River Loue. They are situated southwest of Besançon and north of Arbois.

A Bit of History

In 1773, the King's Counsel decreed the royal saltworks should be built at Arc-et-Senans, drawing on the salt waters of Salins. Only the cross-axis and half the first ring of buildings envisaged by the architect **Claude-Nicolas Ledoux** (1736-1806), inspector general of other saltworks, were actually completed; what we see today is however enough to evoke the idea of an ideal 18C city. His plan was ambitious; a whole town laid out in concentric circles with the Director's Residence at the centre, flanked by storehouses (Bâtiments des sels), offices and workshops, and extending out to include a church, a market, public baths and recreational facilities. Ledoux's vision makes him one of the forerunners of modern architecture and urban design.

Visit

Saline Royale
(Royal Saltworks)★★

The complex today consists of the gatehouse, Director's Residence, courtyard, coopers' building and salt storehouses. The **gatehouse**, which features a peristyle of eight Doric columns, now houses the reception and a book shop. Badly damaged by fire in 1918 and a subsequent dynamite attack, the **Director's Residence** has been the object of much needed restoration; its rooms are now used for conferences. Its basement contains a display on the saltwork operations. The semicircular **courtyard** is today a lawn; firewood was once unloaded for storage here. In the **coopers' building** architectural models, photographs and prints depict Ledoux' ideas about an ideal society. On the first floor, there is a display of toll-houses. The old **salt storehouses** have been converted into venues for concerts and other events.

GORGES DE L'ARDÈCHE★★★

ARDÈCHE GORGES
MICHELIN MAP 331 I-J 7-8
GREEN GUIDE PROVENCE

Overlooked by a dramatically engineered little road, the gorge of the tempera-mental Ardeche river ranks among the most imposing natural sites in France.

- **Information:** 1 pl. de l'Ancienne Gare, Vallon-Pont d'Arc, ☎04 75 88 04 01.
- ▶ **Orient Yourself:** The Ardèche gorge runs most of the way from Vallon Pont d'Arc to St Martin-d'Ardèche .
- **Warning:** To protect the gorge area – no fires, no litter, and no camping are allowed except at official sites.
- **Don't Miss:** The Haute Corniche scenic route links many of the best viewpoints.

Geography

The Ardèche rises at 1 467m – 4 813ft in hills to the north of the Col de la Chavade and flows 119km – 67 miles before join-ing the Rhône. It is notorious for spring floods and sudden spates which can increase its flow by as much as 3 000 per cent (the spate of 22 September 1890 brought down 28 bridges).

Vertical cliffs, dramatic meanders and rapids, alternating with calm stretches, are a lesson in the geography of river formation.

Prehistoric people settled here very early, and may have been the inventors of the bow, together with the domes-tication of the dog, and the making of pottery. Dolmens and cave-dwellings in the area date from the Bronze Age.

Visit

Aven d'Orgnac★★★
South bank. ⓒ *See Aven d'ORGNAC.*

Pont d'Arc

J.Damase/MICHELIN

Aven de Marzal★

North bank. At the bottom of this deep swallowhole, 130m – 426ft from the surface, the Gallery of Diamonds glitters with calcite crystals. A museum presents a display of equipment used by the great explorers of these caverns. Nearby, the popular **Prehistoric Zoo** features reproductions of prehistoric animals.

Gorges: From Vallon-Pont-d'Arc to Pont-St-Esprit

47km – 29mi. The meanders of the river mark the course it originally followed on the ancient surface of the plateau before cutting down through the rocks as they were uplifted during the Alpine-building Tertiary period. Great sweeps of vertical cliffs, dramatic meanders cut deep into the limestone, and rapids alternating with calm stretches of water combine to form a splendid object-lesson in the geography of river formation.

Pont-d'Arc★★

Spanning the full width of the river, the arch of this gigantic natural bridge is 34m – 112ft high and 59m – 194ft wide. In geological terms it is a recent phenomenon, caused by the action of the river, which, helped by the presence of fissures and cavities in the limestone, has succeeded in eroding away the base of a meander.

Haute Corniche (Scenic route)★★★

The road links a number of splendid viewpoints. From the Serre de Tourre can be seen the Pas du Mousse meander, where the river has still to cut through the wooded isthmus; the view from the Morsanne Needles (Aiguilles de Morsanne) gives a good idea of the structure of the plateau as it dips down to the south.

Limestone ridges can be viewed from Gournier, while the rock spires of the Cathedral Rock (Rocher de la Cathédrale) lend this natural monument the appearance of a ruined cathedral.

The Templars' Belvedere (Balcon des Templiers) commands a fine prospect of the Templars' Wall (Mur des Templiers), whose high cliffs (220m – 720ft) dominate the spectacular meander far below. On a rocky spur in the valley stand the ruins of a leper hospital built by the Templars.

ARLES★★★

MICHELIN MAP 340 C 3–POPULATION 50 510

GREEN GUIDE PROVENCE

Arles is one of the most important centres of Provençal culture, proud of its past and famed for an exceptional Roman and medieval heritage, yet vibrantly modern and forward looking. Van Gogh produced many of his greatest works here; what he loved was not the culture or history, but the brilliance of the light.

- **Information:** Esplanade Charles de Gaulle, blvd des Lices, ☎04 90 18 41 20. www.tourisme.ville-arles.fr
- ▶ **Orient Yourself:** Arles stands on the edge of the Camargue wetlands and the Rhone delta. As soon as you exit the highway into Arles (from any direction) you will find yourself on boulevard des Lices, the busy town center which skirts the edge of the historic district where most of the sights are located.
- **Don't Miss:** The most important sight is the Roman arena.
- **Organizing Your Time:** There are visitor passes available (13.50€) at the tourist office or any of the monuments and museums (except Museon Arlaten). This may be worth buying if you plan to visit the many artistic and historic sites. Expect to spend a couple of days if you want to see everything, but don't neglect the many enjoyable shops and cafés on the main boulevards.
- **Parking:** Park under the plane trees of boulevard Georges-Clemenceau. It is a mistake to venture into Old Arles' maze of alleyways by car!

A Bit of History

The ancient Celtic-Ligurian town was colonised by the Greeks of Marseille as early as the 6C BC and was already a thriving town when the Romans conquered the region. They built a canal linking it to the sea so that it could be supplied directly from Rome. Growing into a prosperous port town, and well placed on the major Roman highways, it became an administrative and political capital of Roman Gaul, with many magnificent buildings.

Sights

Théâtre antique★★

🕐 *May-Sep: 9am-6pm; Mar-Apr, and Oct: 9-11.30am, 2-5.30pm; Nov-Feb: 10-11.30am, 2-4.30pm.* 🕐 *Closed 1 jan, 1 May, 1 Nov and 25 Dec.* ⌦ *3€.* ☎*04 90 49 36 74.*

This is among the most important surviving Roman theatres, and dates from the end of the 1C BC. All that remains of its stage wall are two elegant columns in African breccia and Italian marble. The theatre began to be quarried for its stone as early as the 5C, and subsequently disappeared completely under houses and gardens. It was excavated in the 19C.

Arènes★★

🕐 *May-Sep: 9am-6pm (Wed to 1pm Jun-Aug); Mar,Apr,Oct: 9am-5.30pm; Nov-Feb: 10am-4.30pm.* 🕐 *Closed Easter (Thu-Mon), second weekend in Sep, 1 Jan, 1 May, 1 Nov, and 25 Dec.* ⌦ *5.50€.* ☎*08 91 70 03 70 (0.25 €/mn).*

Here as many as 20 000 spectators enjoyed a variety of games pitting men against wild animals, and gladiatorial combat. Dating from about AD 75, this amphitheatre (or arena) is even larger than the one in Nîmes. Its good state of preservation is due to being maintained as a fortress in the 5C and 6C when the Empire was crumbling under the barbarian assault. The sturdy structure was later filled in with as many as 200 houses and two chapels! The excavataion and restoration began in 1825.

Église St-Trophime★

🕐 *As for the Arènes.* 🕐 *Closed 1 Jan, 1 May, 1 Nov and 25 Dec.* ⌦ *3.50€*

Standing on even more ancient ruins, the church was rebuilt from 1080 onwards. Its porch (**portail★★**) is one of the masterpieces of late-12C Provençal Romanesque architecture. The arrangement of columns and design of the frieze hark back to Roman work like the municipal arch at Glanum (📖 *see ST-RÉMY-DE-PROVENCE*) and the 4C sarcophagi at nearby Alyscamps and Trinquetaille. The fact that the stone from which the church is

Roman Amphitheatre

Address Book

For coin ranges, see the Legend on the cover flap.

WHERE TO EAT

⊜⊜**Le Criquet** – *21 R. Porte-de-Laure – ☎ 04 90 96 80 51. Closed end of Dec to end of Feb and Wed.* Go for the charming dining room with its beams and exposed stonework rather than the terrace in this little restaurant near the amphitheatre. Once you're comfortably seated, savour local specialities like *bourride* (a kind of fish stew).

⊜⊜ **Jardin de Manon** – *14 avenue des Alyscamps, ☎04 90 93 38 68. Closed 4-24 Feb, 21 Oct-10 Nov.* This restaurant, situated just outside the city centre, is aptly named. Its interior courtyard terrace, full of trees and flowers, will appeal to lovers of alfresco dining. There are two dining rooms with wood panelling and the local cooking, which uses seasonal market produce, offers good value for money.

⊜⊜ **Lou Calèu** – *27 r. Porte-de-Laure, montée Vauban, ☎04 90 49 71 77. Closed 5 Jan- 15 Feb .* A real classic: fresh salads, *taureau* stew, lamb with rosemary. All Arle's delights are at your fingertips. An excellent wine list. The place for gourmets.

WHERE TO STAY

⊜ **Le Relais de Poste** – *2 r. Molière – ☎ 04 90 52 05 76. www.hotelrelaisde-poste.com. Closed Jan – 15 rooms – ⊑ 6€.* A couple steps from the boulevard des Lices and the espace Van-Gogh, this centrally-based hotel was once the 18C postal relay. The restaurant evokes its era, with beams and frescos. The rooms are simple and warmly decorated with Provençal textiles.

⊜⊜ **Hôtel du Musée** – *11 r. du Grand-Prieuré – ☎04 90 93 88 88 . www.hoteldumusee.com.fr. Closed Jan – 28 rooms – ⊑ 7€.* Facing the Musée Réattu, this is hotel was built in the 17C. It's a charming labyrinth of green pathways through intimate courtyards, with tranquil rooms.

⊜⊜ **Hôtel Muette** – *15 r. des Suisses, ☎04 90 96 15 39. www.hotel-muette. com. Closed Feb – 18 rooms – ⊑ 6€.* A beautiful building (originally 15C and 17C) in the heart of historic Arles.

Solid stone walls in authentic Provençal rooms guarantees they are soundproof.

⊜⊜⊜ **Hôtel Calendal** – *5 rue Porte-de-Laure – ☎04 90 96 11 89. www. lecalendal.com – 38 rooms – ⊑ 8€.* This hotel has all the stylishness of Provençal interiors with its colourful façade, pretty inner shaded garden and cosy sitting room. Blue and yellow make up the colour scheme of furniture, fabrics and ceramics. Small tearoom.

⊜⊜⊜ **Mireille** – *2 place St-Pierre, Trinquetaille – ☎04 90 93 70 74. Closed 4 Nov-14 Mar – 34 rooms – ⊑12€.* Dive into the swimming pool in total peace in this hotel situated outside the city centre. Good size rooms with vibrant colours and Provençal furniture. Airy dining room with red and yellow fabrics.

⊜⊜⊜⊜ **Hôtel d'Arlatan** – *26 rue Sauvage, ☎04 90 93 56 66. www.hotel-arlatan.fr – Closed 5 Jan to 8 Feb – 41 rooms ⊑ 12€.* Fall under the spell of this old mansion dating from the 15C, a stone's throw from place du Forum. Admire the underground Roman fragments through the glass floor of the bar and the drawing room. Rooms furnished with antiques and pretty fabrics. Small courtyard planted with trees where breakfast is served in the summer.

ON THE TOWN

Bar de l'Hôtel Nord Pinus – *place du Forum – ☎04 90 93 44 44 – www.nord-pinus.com –* An essential stop in Arles, the small bar of the Hotel Nord Pinus, dating from the 17C, has entertained artists, writers, film stars, and bullfighters, including Picasso, Jean Cocteau and Yves Montand. There's great charm in details such as its boat-shaped lamps, bullfighting bar, squat armchairs and a background of flamenco music.

Café Van Gogh – *11 pl. du Forum – ☎ 04 90 96 44 56 –* This bright, popular café with its large terrace was the subject of one of Vincent Van Gogh's most famous paintings.

L'Entrevue – *23 Quai Marx-Dormoy – ☎ 04 90 93 37 28 –* Arles is the birthplace of the flourishing Actes Sud publishing house, who also run this arty café-restaurant, a cultural hub of the town.

Le Méjan – *Pl. Nina-Berberova – ☎04 90 49 56 78.* Enjoy evening and afternoon musical performances, jazz concerts, lectures, conferences, and exhibitions in the chapel Saint-Martin-du-Méjan.

SHOPPING

Markets – Browse traditional markets every Wed in blvd Émile-Combes and every Sat in blvd des Lices and blvd Clemenceau. **Antique** market first Wed of the month in blvd des Lices.

Provençal Fabrics – Choose from wonderful colours at Les Étoffes de Romane, *10 boulevard des Lices, ☎04 90 93 53 70.*

Patisserie – Some of the best of local specialities, almond biscuits, breads, cakes and chocolates can be found at *De Moro, 24 rue du Prés.-Wilson, ☎04 90 93 14 43.*

Books and Music – A gold mine for music from the south is *La Boutique des Passionnés, 14 r. Réattu, ☎04 90 96 59 93. www.passion.toros.com.*

Olive Oil – Best quality Provençal olive oil, but also varieties from Spain, Greece and Italy, are found (together with other olive specialities) at *Fad'oli & Fad'ola, 46 r. des Arènes and pl. du Forum.*

EVENTS

Les Rencontres d'Arles – This international photography festival (*from July to mid-Sept*) is a feast of exhibitions, courses, talks, and activities in locations throughout the town centre, including the Roman Theatre. 🏛 *10 rond-point des Arènes, ☎04 90 96 76 06. www.rencontres-arles.com.*

Fête des Gardians – *1 May.* Mass is held in the Provençal dialect, with the blessing of horses, typical Camargue games, local folk music and dances, as well as beautiful girls competing for the title of "Queen" of Arles.

Festival Les Suds – *second half of July. www.suds-arles.com.* World music festival.

---

built was taken from the Roman Theatre further strengthens a sense of continuity with the Classical past.

The cloisters (**cloître★★**) were built after 1150 and are renowned for their sculpture. Particularly fine are the corner pillars of the north gallery and the capitals, foliated or decorated with Biblical scenes.

▸ **Musée d'Arles et de la Provence antique ★★** – the town's extensive collection of ancient art. 🕐 *Apr-*

Oct: 9am-7pm; Nov-Mar 10am-5pm. 🕐*Closed public holidays. ☎04 90 18 88 88.* – Museon Arlaten – Provençal culture and traditions 🕐 *Jun-Aug: Tue-Sun 9.30am-1pm and 2-6.30pm; Apr-May and Sep: Tue-Sun 9.30am-12.30pm and 2-6pm; Oct-Mar: Tue-Sun 9.30am-12.30pm and 2-5pm. Last admission 1hr before closing.* 🕐 *Closed Mon, Oct-Jun, 1 Jan, 1 May, 1 Nov, 25 Dec. ☎04 90 93 58 11.* **Musée Réattu★** – paintings, **Picasso Bequest★** 🕐 *May-Sep: daily 10am-12.30pm and 2-7pm; Mar-Apr and Oct: daily 10am-12.30pm and 2-5.30pm; Nov-Feb: daily 1-5.30pm. Last admission 30min before closing.* 🕐 *Closed 1 Jan, 1 May, 1 Nov, 25 Dec. ☎ 04 90 49 38 34.* **Palais Constantin★** – largest baths in Provence 🕐 *Same hours as for the Théâtre antique.* **Alyscamps★** – necropolis, *Allow half a day.* 🕐 *Same hours as the Théâtre antique. ☎ 04 90 49 35 67.*

Les Alyscamps – Allée des sarcophages

ARRAS★★

MICHELIN MAP 301 J 5-6–POPULATION 124 200

GREEN GUIDE NORTHERN FRANCE AND THE PARIS REGION

The Abbey of St-Vaast formed the nucleus around which the capital of Artois grew in the Middle Ages. Between the 12C and the 14C it gained privileges from the Counts of Artois encouraging an economy based on corn, banking and, especially, fabrics. The city prospered; poetic and literary societies thrived in which Arras' notables could enjoy hearing themselves lampooned by minstrels and entertainers. In the 15C, Artois passed into the hands of the Dukes of Burgundy, ensuring steady orders for its fine tapestries, which werenotable for dealing realistically with secular themes.

- **Information:** Hôtel de ville, pl. des Héros, 62000 Arras, ☎03 21 51 26 95. www.ot-arras.fr.
- **Orient Yourself:** Close to the English Channel, Arras is one of the main towns in northern France. Its centre is Place des Héros.
- **Don't Miss:** The 45-minute Historama film show at the town hall Belfry makes an interesting introduction to the town (☎*03 21 51 26 95*. ☜ *2.60€*).
- **Guided tours:** In summer the tourist office puts on walking tours of the town centre.

A Bit of History

The notorious Maximilian **Robespierre** was born in Arras in 1758 to a well-to-do legal family. He too was called to the Bar before becoming a Deputy in 1789, a Republican in 1792, and a prominent member of the feared Committee of Public Safety in 1793. Determined, indifferent to favours, "Robespierre the Incorruptible" embodied the spirit of the French Revolution. Backed by Saint-Just and Couthon, he harried plotters and crushed deviationists, going so far as to take part in the condemnation of his allies, the Girondins. Discredited in the end by the consequences of his extremist ideology, on 27 July 1794 he himself fell victim to the guillotine to which he had condemned so many others.

Sights

Les Places★★ (Main Squares)

Dating from the 11C, the **Grand'Place, Place des Héros** and the **Rue de la Taillerie** linking them celebrate the

Grand 'Place

B.Kaufmann/MICHELIN

city's status as an important regional market centre. Their present splendidly harmonious appearance is the fruit of the city fathers' purposeful civic design initiatives in the 17C and 18C. The existing Spanish Plateresque buildings of the 16C and 17C (Arras was effectively under Spanish rule from 1492 to 1640) were given Flemish Baroque façades from 1635 onward. The 155 brick and stone houses rest on 345 columns: their arcading sheltered traders and clients alike. With few projections, their regularly-proportioned façades give an impression of great unity, relieved by a rich variety of detail. This includes curvilinear gables, arcades with pilasters or corbelling, decorative tie-bars, and a number of sculpted merchants' signs (a whale, a harp and a bell, among others). To the north of the Grand'Place a brick building with a stone-built ground floor is topped by a stepped gable, the only one of its kind. Arras' civic pride was symbolised by the construction of its Town Hall, **Hôtel de Ville**★(🕐 *Jul and Aug: Wed and Sun 3pm;* 🐀 *2€*) in 1572; its bell-tower **(beffroi)** (🕐 *May-Sep: Tue- Sat 9am-6.30pm, Sun 10am-1pm, 2.30-6.30pm, Mon 9am-noon, 2-6pm; Oct-Apr: Tue-Sat 9am-noon, 2-6pm, Sun 10am-12.30pm, 2.30-6.30pm, Mon 10am-noon, 2-6pm;* 🐀 *2.30€.* 🕾*03 21 51 26 95*) blends Flemish Gothic with Henri II-style ornamentation. It was destroyed in the First World War but rebuilt using the original plans in 1919.

▸ **Ancienne abbaye St-Vaast**★★ *At its heart is the* **Musée des Beaux-Arts**★ 🕐 *Daily 9.30am-noon, 2-5.30pm, Thu 9.30am-5.30pm.* 🕐 *Closed Tue, 1 Jan, 1 and 8 May, 14 Jul, 1 and 11 Nov, 25 Dec.* 🐀 *4€, no charge 1st Wed and 1st Sun in the month.* 🕾*03 21 71 26 43.*

Excursions

Vimy Canadian Memorial★

10 km – 6mi north. A gripping sight that brings home some of the realities of the Great War. The summit of this chalky ridge was taken by the Canadian Expeditionary Force, part of the British Third Army, in April 1917. It is crowned by the Canadian Memorial. There are extensive views over a farmed landscape dotted with the conical tips of coal mines. To the west are the cemetery and basilica of Notre-Dame-de-Lorette, and nearby, entrenchments and pitted landforms left by trench warfare, which can be visited.

PARC ASTÉRIX★★
ASTERIX PARK
MICHELIN MAP 305 G 6
GREEN GUIDE NORTHERN FRANCE AND THE PARIS REGION

Asterix the Gaul, comical hero of the famous cartoon strip by Goscinny and Uderzo, is universally known and loved in France. He and his fellow characters provide the theme for this resort (50ha – 123 acres). It is a fantasy world for all ages which offers a madcap journey into the past: carefully reconstructed 'historical' sections, various attractions and shows, as well as audio-visual displays add to the fun.

▪ **Information:** 🛈*Paris.*
▸ **Orient Yourself:** The Parc is about 30 min from central Paris either on autoroute A1 or by RER train (line B, Roissy-Charles-de-Gaulle station).

Visit

Kids 🕐 *Opening times vary from year to year. Always check before making a booking to visit the park. Usual opening times are 10am-6pm or 9.30pm-7pm on popular dates.* 🕐 *Closed from approx. end Oct to end Mar.* 🐀 *33€ (children: 23€, children under 3 years: free).* 🕾*08 92 68 30 10. www.parcasterix.fr.*

To explore this enchanting world, start at the Via Antiqua lined with stalls symbolising Asterix's journeys across Europe. Six areas illustrate various themes: the **Village Astérix** is a veritable Gallic village with its huts; the **Menhir Express**★ is the highlight of a Stone Age village built on piles **(Domaine Lacustre)**; 10 centuries of history are illustrated in the **Rue de Paris**; a lake, **Grand Lac**, is a popular spot with thrilling attractions **(Goudurix★, Tonnerre de Zeus)**; Icarus's flight (Vol d'Icare) and performing dolphins in an auditorium, **Théâtre de Poséidon,** are the main interests of the section on Ancient Greece **(Grèce Antique)**; in the Roman city **(Cité Romaine)** contests between gladiators are held in the arena and there is an exciting descent into Hell **(Descente du Styx★).**

COL D'AUBISQUE★★
AUBISQUE PASS
MICHELIN MAP 342 J-K 5
GREEN GUIDE FRENCH ATLANTIC COAST

The main east-west axis of the Pyrenees is interrupted by a series of long narrow valleys running roughly north-south. Each of these valleys forms a distinct unit, with a characteristic landscape and way of life which often have more in common with the lowlands to the north or even with Spain than with the valleys on either side. A number of high passes permit east-west communication; the Tourmalet Pass at 2 114m – 6 936ft is the highest, but the Aubisque Pass (Col d'Aubisque – 1 709m – 5 608ft) separating the Béarn from the Bigorre country is the most spectacular.

▶ **Orient Yourself:** The Aubisque Pass lies in the Pyrenees region, southwest of Lourdes.

Visit

From the southern summit of the pass *(TV relay station – 30min return on foot)* the immense **panorama**★★★ extends over rocky slopes to the gentler, man-made landscape of the valleys far below, as well as taking in the magnificent rock formations of the Cirque de Gourette, marked from left to right by the Grand Gabizos, Pène Blanque and the Pic de Ger.

AUCH★
MICHELIN MAP 336 E 6-7, C-D-E-F 8–POPULATION 21 838
GREEN GUIDE LANGUEDOC ROUSSILLON TARN GORGES

Auch is an attractive, pleasantly busy local capital in the heart of Gascony.

▤ **Information:** 1 r. Dessoles, ☎05 62 05 22 89. www.mairie-auch.fr
▶ **Orient Yourself:** The main streets converge on central Place de la Liberation. The tourist office is on one corner of the square.
➥ **Guided tours:** In July and August, there's a guided tour of the town centre at 11am, Tue-Sat.
⊙ **Don't Miss:** The Escalier Monumental is a majestic flight of 232 steps linking the river to the town centre.

A Bit of History

Auch began in ancient times as a fortified Basque settlement beside the river Gers. For 2 000 years it served as a staging-post on the old Toulouse-Bordeaux highway; its position avoided the treacherously-shifting course of the River Garonne to the north. Its owes some fame to the story of *The Three Musketeers* – the real d'Artagnan, Charles de Batz, was from this district.

Sights

Cathédrale Ste-Marie★★

Closed at lunchtime (except mid-Jul to end Aug). Pre-recorded commentaries on the building available at the entrance. Audio tour of the gallery and windows available 2€, identity document retained as guarantee.

The cathedral's ambulatory contains a masterly series of Renaissance **stained-glass windows (vitraux)** ★★, completed in 1517, and remarkable for their sophisticated use of colour (subtle nuances and gradations and half-tones, all in strong contrast to the pure colours, rigidly separated, of the Gothic), and for the way in which the central figure of each window is surrounded by vignettes elucidating its symbolism and prefiguration (a characteristic humanist device of the time). Adam and Eve, Jonah, and the Nativity are exceptionally fine.

The **choir stalls (stalles)** ★★★(*Jul-Aug: 8.30am-6.30pm; Apr-Jul and Sep-Oct: 8.30-noon, 2-6pm; rest of year: 9.30-noon, 2-5pm. 2€*), are an inspired work completed in 1554, peopled by 1 500 different figures in an extraordinary wealth of detail. The backs are carved with representations of biblical and other personages; the faces crowding the dividers, elbow-rests, the panels and niches of the backs and the misericords provide an interest and stimulation which are inexhaustible. The opulence characteristic of the Flamboyant style survives in this work of the Renaissance.

AULNAY★★

MICHELIN MAP 322 G 3–POPULATION 1 462
GREEN GUIDE FRENCH ATLANTIC COAST

Originally in the province of Poitiers, Aulnay was apportioned to Saintonge by virtue of the division of France into *départements* by the Constituent Assembly on 22 December 1789. It is known for its magnificent 12C Romanesque church.

- **Information:** Office of Tourism, 290 av. de l'Église, ☎05 46 33 14 44.
- ▶ **Orient Yourself:** The village of Aulnay sits inland from Rochefort in the northern part of the Atlantic Coast region.

Sight

Église St-Pierre★★

This fine Romanesque church stands among the cypresses of its ancient burial ground with its Gothic Hosanna Cross. It was built between 1140 and 1170 at a time when Eleanor of Aquitaine ruled southwestern France as queen first to Louis VII, then to Henry II of England. Its structure, notably its tribune-less triple nave, is essentially in the Romanesque style typical of the Poitou area, while its sculpture is characteristic of Saintonge.

Although somewhat marred by massive 15C buttresses, the west front is remarkable for its sumptuously decorated arches and its large-scale figure sculptures. In the left portal is a poignant representation of St Peter hanging upside-down on his cross. Considering himself unworthy of the same treatment as his Master, he demanded this even crueller form of crucifixion for himself. This method of execution was not uncommon, even before the days of Nero; by lowering its centre of gravity, the cross could be made smaller, and thus less costly.

The doorway of the south transept has lofty corner columns and a great relieving arch; the second arch, supported by sitting atlantes and showing the Prophets and Apostles, is an achievement of the 13C Saintonge school of sculpture.

Within, the central window of the apse is famous for its unusually rich carving, characteristic of the level which decorative art had reached in the High Middle Ages. The capitals of the columns in the nave are also worthy of attention, as is the bell-tower with its 18C slate-clad spire; its lower levels are particularly attractive in spite of the insensitive addition of extra height in the 15C.

AUTUN★★

POPULATION 16 420
MICHELIN MAP 320 F 8
GREEN GUIDE BURGUNDY JURA

Flanked by wooded hills, this dignified country town in northern Burgundy has a cathedral, museums and Roman remains that bear witness to its past.

▸ **Information:** 2 av. Charles-de-Gaulle, 71400 Autun, ☎03 85 86 80 38. www.autun-tourisme.com/.

▸ **Orient Yourself:** The cathedral, ramparts and Roman remains are all within easy walking distance of the tourist office and central Place du Champs du Mars.

▸**Guided tours:** Ask the tourist office about guided tours of the town.

A Bit of History

Autun was founded by the Emperor Augustus, half a century after Caesar's conquest of Gaul. Rome itself was taken as the model for the new town; its walls (6km – 4mi in length) soon sheltered fine civic buildings (a theatre, an amphithea-

tre) and a thriving commercial life. From their stronghold at Bibracte on Mont Beuvray 29km – 18mi away to the west, the Gallic Aedui tribe watched the city's growth with fascination and ended up moving there themselves. In the Middle Ages the city consolidated itself on the upper part of its site.

Detail, Cathédrale St-Lazare

Visit

Cathédrale St-Lazare★★

The great sandstone edifice was built from 1120 to 1146 and named after the friend of Christ whom He raised from the dead and whose relics had supposedly been brought here from Marseille shortly before. Though its external appearance was altered by the addition of a tower and steeple in the 15C, it remains essentially a building of the Burgundian Romanesque style; its barrel-vaulted nave having slightly pointed arches (an early example) and a blind triforium designed to enliven an otherwise bare wall. With a gallery identical to that of the city's Roman Arroux Gate (Porte d'Arroux), this triforium is evidence of the continuing Roman influence well into the 12C.

The glory of the cathedral is its 12C Burgundian sculpture, most of it the achievement of Master Gislebertus, who came from Vézelay in 1125 and worked here for 20 years. The **tympanum (tympan)**★★★ over the central doorway dates from about 1135 and has the Last Judgement as its subject. It exhibits supreme mastery of technique and the boldness of its design outshines all other contemporary work. Look carefully for example at the joy of the saved, the agony of the damned and the use of scale in the treatment of the figure of Christ, the Apostles and other figures. The same mastery is evident in the **capitals (chapiteaux)**★★ in the nave and the chapter-house, where more capitals (originally in the choir) are displayed at eye-level.

▶ **Musée Rolin**★ – ⏱ *Apr-Sep: 9.30am-noon, 1.30-6pm; Oct-Mar: 10am-noon, 2-5pm.* ⏱ *Closed Tue, 1 Jan, 1 May, 14 Jul, 1 and 11 Nov, 25 Dec.* ⏺ *3.30€.* ☎*03 85 52 09 76–* Gallo-Roman collections, paintings, sculpture. **Porte St-André**★ – Gallo-Roman gate. **Roman Theatre** – vestiges of the largest theatre in Gaul.

AUXERRE★★

POPULATION 37 790
MICHELIN MAP 319 E-F-G 5
GREEN GUIDE BURGUNDY JURA

A port on the River Yonne, surrounded by rustic, wooded farm country and hillsides planted with vines and orchards, the city was once an important staging-post on the great Roman highway which led from Lyon to Boulogne via Autun and Lutetia (Paris).

🛈 **Information:** 1 quai de la République, 89000 Auxerre, ☎03 86 52 06 19. www.ot-auxerre.fr.

▶ **Orient Yourself:** Boulevard 11 Novembre encloses the central area where the sights are located.

🥾**Guided tours:** Painted marks on the ground lead the way on a self-guided tour.

🎯 **Don't Miss:** The 9C frescoes in St Germain abbey are among the oldest in France.

Visit

Abbaye St-Germain★

🥾*Self-guided tour of the museum, guided tour of the crypt (45min) Wed-Mon 10am-6.30pm (Oct-May: Wed-Mon 10am-noon, 2-6pm).* ⏱ *Closed Tue, 1 Jan, 1 and 8 May, 1 and 11 Nov, 25 Dec.* ⏺ *4.30€.* ☎*03 86 18 05 50.*

The city's famous Benedictine abbey is named after bishop St Germanus (378-448), born in Auxerre. A small basilica was probably erected over the saint's tomb in the 6C by Clothilde, the wife of King Clovis. It was extended in 841 to include an outer nave to the west and a crypt to the east; the relics were moved here on completion of the work 18 years later.

Auxerre on the bank of the River Yonne

The abbey crypt (**crypte** ★) houses a raised cavity which was hollowed out in the 9C to hide the tomb from raiding Norsemen. In addition there is a false tomb designed to lead them astray. In part of the crypt dating from Merovingian times (6C), there are two oak beams on Gallo-Roman columns and also a 5C monogram of Christ. From the Carolingian period (8C-10C) there is a **fresco** showing the bishops of Auxerre, floor-tiling, and most moving of all, a capital based crudely on the Ionian Order, proof of the aesthetic poverty of the time. The mid-12C bell-tower, a remarkable Romanesque structure, was isolated from the rest of the building by the destruction of several bays in the 19C. The eight sides of its squat spire have an almost imperceptible bulge.

▶ **Cathédrale St-Étienne★★** – ◷ *7.30am-6pm; Tour of the treasury and crypt from Easter to All Saint's Day (1 Nov) 9am-6pm, Fri 2-6pm; the rest of the year daily except Sun 10am-5pm.* ☎ *03 86 52 23 29* – crypt, **treasury**★, **stained glass**★.

AVEN ARMAND ★★★

MICHELIN MAP 338 M 5

GREEN GUIDE LANGUEDOC ROUSSILLON TARN GORGES

One of the wonders of underground world, this immense cavern is reached down a 200m tunnel in the bleak Causse Méjean.

🔢 **Information:** ♿Millau.
▶ **Orient Yourself:** 43km NE of Millau, Aven Armrand is in the plateau country S of the Gorge du Tarn.
😊 **Tip:** The temperature inside is 10C.

Visit

◷ *All visits are in guided groups only, Jul-Aug: 9.30am-6.15pm; Apr-Jun and Sep-Oct: 10am-5.45pm. Last entry 45 min before closing.* ◷ *closed: rest of year.* ⊙ *8€.* ☎ *04 66 45 61 31. www.aven-armand.com.*

Deep within the arid limestone of the Causse Méjean, subterranean waters have created a vast cavern, its floor littered with rock fallen from its roof. Four hundred stalagmites, the "Virgin Forest", make an extraordinary spectacle.

AVIGNON★★★

MICHELIN MAP 332 B-C 10–POPULATION 253 580

GREEN GUIDE PROVENCE

Protected by a ring of imposing ramparts, the historic core of Avignon is a lively centre of art and culture. For 68 years it was the residence first of seven French Popes, then of three others once Pope Gregory XI had returned to Rome in 1377; the Papal Legates remained until the city was united with France in 1791.

- ▣ **Information:** 41 cours Jean-Jaurès, b04 32 74 32 74. www.ot-avignon.fr.
- ▶ **Orient Yourself:** The major sights and city centre are inside the walled old city, where the main street is Rue de la République. This street runs straight to the main square, Place de l'Horloge and the adjacent Palais des Papes.
- ◉ **Guided tours:** The tourist office has details of numerous tour options. Marked itineraries also allow you to take a self-guided tour.
- 🄺 **Especially for kids:** There's a lovely old-fashioned carousel in Place de l'Horloge. And a fast, fun way to see the sights is via the 'Little Train' (45min), several times a day from Place du Palais (🕒 Nov-15 Mar. ☞ 7€, children 4€).
- ◉ **Don't Miss:** Get a great view of Avignon's skyline from across the Rhône, especially if you are approaching the city in the evening.
- 🕒 **Organizing Your Time:** With so much to do in Avignon, allow at least 3 hours to visit the Palais des Papes and Pont St-Bénézet before exploring the rest of the city. Many sights can be visited at a reduced rate by obtaining a "carte-pass" (available at any of the sights, or at the tourist office).
- 🅿 **Parking:** Parking is available in the Palais des Papes underground car park.

A Bit of History

At the beginning of the 14C the Popes felt the need to escape from the turbulent political life of Rome. Avignon formed part of the Papal territories, and occupied a central position in the Europe of the time. The case for moving there was put by Philippe le Bel (the Fair), possibly with a view to involving the Papacy in his own political manœuvrings. In 1309 Pope Clement V took the plunge, and Avignon became for most of a century the capital of Western Christendom.

When Pope Clement VI succeeded him in 1342, he greatly enlarged the papal palace, and brought to Avignon his love of the arts.

Avignon remains an influential cultural centre. It owes much to Jean Vilar, who in 1947 founded the prestigious annual event, **Festival d'Avignon**. This festival led to a blossoming of the arts: Avignon now hosts many different cultural events during the year.

Sights

Palais des Papes★★★

Place du Palais. 🕒 *During Festival (Jul): 9am-9pm; ; Aug-Sep: 9am-8pm; 15 Mar-Jun, and Oct: 9am-7pm; Nov-14 Mar: 9.30am-5.45pm. Last admission 1hr before closing.* ☞ *9.50€ (7.50€ early Nov to mid-Mar); 11.50€ combined ticket with pont St-Bénézet.* ☎*04 90 27 50 00. www.palais-des-papes.com.*

The huge feudal structure, fortress as well as palace, conveys an overwhelming impression of defensive strength with its high bare walls, its massive corbelled crenellations and stalwart buttresses. Inside, a maze of galleries, chambers, chapels and passages contains almost no furnishings. While the popes were in residence the palace was extremely luxuriously equipped.

Pont St-Bénézet★★

Accessed via ramparts. Rue Ferruce. 🕒 *Jul: daily 9am-9pm; Aug-Sep: daily 9am-8pm; mid-Mar-Jun and Oct: daily 9am-7pm; Nov to mid-Mar: daily 9.30am-5.45pm. Last admission 1hr before clos-*

Palais des Papes

ing. ⬥ 4€ *(low season: 3.50€); 11.50€ combined ticket with Palais des Papes.* ♿☎04 90 85 60 16.

Stepping out into the swirling Rhone, and coming to an abrupt end in midstream, this beautiful bridge was first built in 1177, according to legend, by a shepherd-boy called Bénézet. Until the Bridge Brotherhood (Frères Pontifes) built Pont-St-Esprit more than a century later this was the only stone bridge over the Rhône. It helped the economic development of Avignon long before becoming a useful link with Villeneuve when the Cardinals built their villas there. Eighteen of its arches were carried away by the floodwaters of the river in the 17C.

▸ **Petit Palais**★★ – ⏰ *Jun to end Sep: Wed-Mon 10am-1pm, 2-6pm. Oct to end May: Wed-Mon 9.30-1pm, 2-5.30pm.* ⏰ *Closed Tue, 1 Jan, 1 May, 14 Jul, 1 Nov, 25 Dec.* ⬥ 6€. ☎04 90 86 44 58. *Local and Italian paintings.* **Rocher des Doms**★★ – **views**★★. Cathédrale – **cupola**★. **Ramparts**★. **Musée Calvet**★ ⏰ *Wed-Mon 10am-1pm, 2-6pm.* ⏰ *Closed Tue, 1 Jan, 1 May, 25 Dec.* ⬥ 6€. ☎04 90 86 33 84 – *prehistory, metalwork, fine arts.* **Musée Louis-Vouland** ⏰ *May-Oct: Tue-Sat 10am-noon, 2-6pm, Sun and public holidays 2-6pm; Nov-Apr: Tue-Sun 2-6pm.* ⏰ *Closed Mon, 1 Jan, 1 May, 25 Dec.* ⬥ 4€. ☎04 90 86 03 79.– **faience**★. Hôtel des Monnaies

– **façade**★. **Musée lapidaire**★ ♿ ⏰ *Wed-Mon 10am-1pm, 2-6pm.* ⏰ *Closed Tue, 1 Jan, 1 May, 25 Dec.* ⬥ 2€ *(children under 12years: no charge).* ☎04 90 86 33 84 or 04 90 85 75 38. **Église St-Didier** – **frescoes**★.

Excursion

Villeneuve-lès-Avignon★
2km/1mi west, on the west bank of the river.

At the point where St Bénézet's bridge originally touched French territory Philippe le Bel built a small fort (only a tower remains). Half a century later, feeling hemmed in at Avignon, the Cardinals crossed the river and built themselves 15 fine houses (*livrées*) here.

At the same time, Jean le Bon (John the Good) erected the St-André fortress on the hill which was already crowned by an abbey. Protected by its walls and with a splendid twin-towered gatehouse, this vast building complex offers (from its Romanesque Chapel of Notre-Dame de Belvézet) one of the finest views over the Rhône valley. In the foreground is the gateway, Porte St-André, and beyond, on the far bank, the Palace of the Popes. In 1352 the General of the Carthusian Order had been elected Pope but humbly refused the throne. Pope Innocent VI, elected in his stead, founded a charterhouse, **Chartreuse du**

Address Book

For coin ranges, see the Legend on the cover flap.

WHERE TO EAT

⊖ **Le Mesclun – Le Petit Bistrot de Brunel** – *46 r. de la Balance – ☎04 90 86 14 60 -Closed evenings Sun, and Mon.* There's no better place for lunch, be it on the shaded terrace or inside. The daily dishes and menu mingle market freshness, Provence, and gastronomy with the zest of good cheer. The choice spot to take a pause between excursions.

⊖⊖ **Le Grand Café** – *cours Maria-Casares, La Manutention – ☎04 90 86 86 77 – Closed Jan, Sun and Mon except July-Aug – booking recommended.* Backing onto the buttresses of the Palais des Papes, these old barracks have become an essential part of local life. Locals and tourists all flock here to savour inventive cooking with Provençal accents. Pleasant décor that combines the styles of a Parisian bistro and a Viennese café. There is also an attractive terrace.

⊖⊖ **Au Coin des Halles** – *4 r. Grivolas – ☎04 90 82 93 49 – Closed Sun and public holidays.* Enjoy this central spot among the Avignonnais, with its reading space and two little dining areas, all infused with jazzy music. And check out the menu: simple dishes, like a delicious *reblochon* cheese tart, a *salade landaise*, a winter squash soup.

⊖⊖ **Entrée des Artistes** – *1 place des Carmes – ☎04 90 82 46 90 – Closed 23 Dec-3 Jan, 17 Aug-8 Sept, Sat and Sun.* The dining room of this restaurant is decorated in the style of a Parisian bistro, with its old posters and movie memorabilia. Tables are placed close together and the cooking is traditional. Service is friendly and there is a real scent of the Mediterranean in the air.

⊖⊖ **Le Moutardier** – *15 place du Palais-des-Papes – ☎04 90 85 34 76 – moutardier@wanadoo.fr – Closed 6-25 Jan, 24 Nov-19 Dec, and Wed from Oct-Mar.* This 18C building, listed in France's National Heritage, makes an exceptional setting for a simple, fresh meal. There is a pleasant atmosphere, both in the bistro room, where frescoes depict the story of "The Pope's mustard maker," and on the terrace facing the Palais des Papes.

⊖⊖⊖⊖ **Compagnie des Comptoirs** – *83 r. Joseph-Vernet, Le Cloître des Arts – ☎04 90 85 99 04 – jc.toussaint@lacompagniedescomptoirs.com – Closed Sun and Mon.* Inspired by the colonial trading posts of the French East Indies Company, this restaurant, situated in the 14C cloisters, is the "in" place to eat. The bar decor is glass and bamboo, there are colonial etchings in the dining rooms, and the terrace is decked out with a palm tree and straw huts. The menu combines the flavours of East Asia with those of southern France.

WHERE TO STAY

⊖ **Hôtel Le Provençal** – *13 r. Joseph-Vernet – ☎04 90 85 25 24 – hotel.leprovencal@wanadoo.fr – 11 rooms – ☕ 5€.* Le Provençal offers the advantage of being in the very heart of Avignon without being too pricey, a rare mix for this town. Moreover, the rooms are comfortable and decent.

⊖⊖ **Chambre d'hôte La Prévoté** – *354 chemin d'Exploitation – 84210 Althen-les-Paluds – 17km/10.5mi northeast of Avignon towards Carpentras – ☎04 90 62 17 06 – prevote@aol.com – Closed Nov-1 Mar – ⊠ – 5 rooms – ☕ 5€.* After a peaceful night spent in one of the spacious, colourful rooms of this *mas*, you will certainly enjoy breakfast, which is served in the shade of the vine arbour or under the chestnut tree. Let your gaze roam over the apple trees or have a dip in the swimming pool.

⊖⊖⊖ **Hôtel Garlande** – *20 rue Galante – ☎04 90 80 08 85 – hotel-de-garlande@wanadoo.fr –Closed Jan – 11 rooms – ☕ 7€.* Situated in two renovated old houses in a peaceful street, this small, family-run hotel is close to the church of St Didier. Colourful rooms with Provençal floral fabrics.

⊖⊖⊖⊖ **Hôtel Cloître St-Louis** – *20 rue Portail Boquier – ☎04 90 27 55 55 – hotel@cloitre-saint-louis.com – 77 rooms – ☕ 16€ – restaurant 38/55€.* Situated in 16C cloisters, part of this hotel was designed by the architect Jean Nouvel. The building uses a variety of materials including glass, steel, and stone. Rooms are stylishly minimalist. Pool and solarium on the roof. Sunday mass in the chapel at the heart of the hotel.

ON THE TOWN

Café In&Off – *place du Palais-des-Papes* – ☎04 90 85 48 95 – *www.cafeinoff.com* – *Open until 3am during the festival; rest of year: 7.30am-8pm – Closed from mid-Nov to the end of Feb.* Don't miss the only café that enjoys unbeatable views of the Palais des Papes. The interior is not lacking in appeal but the terrace is definitely the highpoint of this café.

SHOWTIME

Le Rouge Gorge – *10 bis rue Peyrolerie* – ☎04 90 14 02 54 – *www.le.rougegorge. fr – Open Tues-Sun 8.30pm-3am. Closed July-Aug.* The only cabaret in Avignon, the Rouge-Gorge, modestly sheltered by the Palais des Papes, unveils the sensual charms of its show every Friday and Saturday from 8.30pm, while two Sundays a month there is an operetta lunch. During the week the atmosphere remains lively with numerous themed evenings (Corsican, Latino, Oriental).

SHOPPING

Markets – **Les Halles Centrales,** *Place Pie, traditional covered market, Daily except Mon.* **Flower market** every Saturday in *place des Carmes.* **Fair** Sat and Sun, *rempart St-Michel.* **Flea market** every Sunday in *place des Carmes.*
Honey – **Miellerie des Butineuses**, *189 rue de la Source, 84450 St-Saturnin-lès-Avignon,* ☎04 90 22 47 52 – *www. miellerie.fr.* Honey, pollen, and royal jelly, as well as honey-based products.
Home decor – **Terre è Provence** – *26 r. de la République –* ☎04 90 85 56 45 – *terre-provence@waandoo.fr –* In the same family for several generations, this shop is dedicated to all that is Provence:

table settings, textiles with Provençal prints, pottery, and porcelain and many lovely ideas for your home.

EVENTS

The Avignon Festival – a huge programme of Mainstream and Fringe Events is put on in July each year. Theatre, dance, lectures, exhibitions, meetings, and concerts given in the main courtyard of the Palais des Papes, in the municipal theatre, in the many cloisters and churches of the town, as well as at Villeneuve-lès-Avignon and other outlying areas, such as the Boulbon quarry (Carrière de Boulbon), Montfavet or Châteaublanc. Fringe events are dotted around the town. **Booking** – Programmes and tickets are available at the Bureau du Festival d'Avignon, Cloître Saint-Louis – *20 r. du Portail-Boquier – 84000 Avignon,* ☎04 90 27 66 50 – *réservations* ☎04 90 14 14 14. From the first two weeks of June onwards it is also possible to make reservations by internet (*www.festival-avignon.com*), by minitel 3615 FNAC, at FNAC booking counters, and at the main office located at St-Louis d'Avignon (*20 rue Portail-Bocquier*). Festival programmes are available by mail: send a check for 5€ to: *Avignon Public Off, BP 5, 75521 Paris Cedex 11* (☎ *01 48 05 01 19, contact@ avignon-off.org, www.avignon-off.org*).
Hivernales d'Avignon – This modern choreography festival takes place in February but it never attains the atmosphere of the summer festival as the shows (luckily) take place indoors. ☎04 90 82 33 12. *www.hivernales-avi-gnon.com.*
Horse Festival – In January this event includes dressage, show jumping, competitions, and shows at the sports stadium. ☎04 90 84 02 04. *www.cheval-passion.com.*

Val de Bénédiction★ to commemorate the gesture. It soon became the greatest charterhouse in France. It has a monumental 17C gateway, small cloisters and graveyard cloisters, the latter fringed by the cells of the Fathers. The church contains the founder's tomb.

CHÂTEAU **D'AZAY-LE-RIDEAU**★★★

MICHELIN MAP 31 L 5
GREEN GUIDE CHÂTEAUX OF THE LOIRE

Sitting in a verdant setting where the waters of the Indre act as reflecting pools, this castle was built for financier Gilles Berthelot from 1518 to 1529.

- 🅸 **Information:** 4 rue du Château, ☎02 47 45 44 40. www.ot-paysazaylerideau.fr.
- ▶ **Orient Yourself:** Azay lies about 25km from Tours in the direction of Chinon.
- 🕓 **Organizing Your Time:** Allow 45min for the castle and 1hr for the park.

Visit

🕓 Apr-Sep: daily 9.30am-6pm (Jul and Aug: 7pm); Oct-Mar: daily 10am-12.30pm, 2-5.30pm. Last admission 45min before closing. 🕓 Closed 1 Jan, 1 May, 25 Dec. ⊗ 7.50€ (under 18 years: no charge). ☎02 47 45 42 04. www.monum.fr.

The château d'Azay-le-Rideau was built from 1518 to 1529 in French Gothic style. Its defences (machicolated cornice, pepperpot towers and turrets) are purely decorative. By contrast, the interior shows Italianate influences. The decoration includes Florentine shells in the gable of the great dormer window, pilasters, moulded entablatures and above all the grand staircase with straight flights and rectangular landings. The interior is also notable for the French-style ceiling in the dining room and the chimney piece in the François I Room.

B. Kaufmann/MICHELIN

Château d'Azay-le-Rideau

BAR-LE-DUC★

MICHELIN MAP 307 B6, E 5–POPULATION 16 950
GREEN GUIDE ALSACE LORRAINE CHAMPAGNE

This old capital of the Duchy of Bar is divided into two sections. The historic Ville Haut rests on a plateau, while the industrial Ville Basse is laid out along the River Ornain and the Rhine-Marne canal.

- 🅸 **Information:** 7 rue Jeanne-d'Arc,☎03 29 79 11 13. www.barleduc.fr
- ▶ **Orient Yourself:** The town sits half-way between Strasbourg and Paris

Sight

Ville haute★ (Upper Town)

Wonderfully aristocratic and grand, this Renaissance quarter is a beautiful ensemble of 16C-18C houses, especially notable in the triangular Place St-Pierre. Église St-Étienne has a curious late-18C belfry-porch in the medieval style; within are two works by the 16C master Ligier Richier, including the famous **Transi**★★ which owes much to advances in dissection technique and is far removed from the serene recumbent figures of the Middle Ages.

LA BAULE ★★★

MICHELIN MAP 316 B4–POPULATION 15 830
GREEN GUIDE BRITTANY

Perhaps the ultimate in modern seafront development on the French Atlantic, the resort of La Baule is today one of Europe's major resorts and considered to have one of its most beautiful beaches. It was only in 1879 that construction of the town began, after 400ha – 1000 acres of maritime pines had been planted to halt the steady encroachment of sand dunes. The older houses retain much of their original charm and stand mostly hidden behind the more recent constructions along the shaded and well laid-out avenues.

- **Information:** 8 pl. de la Victoire, ☎02 40 24 34 44. www.labaule.fr.
- ▶ **Orient Yourself:** The resort stands on the north bank of the wide Loire estuary. It is reached on autoroute A11 and then by expressway from Nantes.

Visit

Miles of beautiful and well-frequented sandy beaches are protected by the headlands, Pointes de **Penchâteau** and **Chémoulin** to the northwest and southeast respectively. Numerous hotels and apartment complexes, some comfortable, others luxurious in the proximity of delightful resorts such as **Le Croisica, Le Pouliguen**★ and **Pornichet**★, with their pleasure-boat harbours, make La Baule, together with its neighbour **La Baule-les-Pins**★★, the ideal spot for discovering the splendour of the **"Côte d'Amour"** and the **Guérande Peninsula.**

LES **BAUX-DE-PROVENCE** ★★★

MICHELIN MAP 340 D 3–POPULATION 437
GREEN GUIDE PROVENCE

With its ruined castle and deserted houses capping an arid rocky spur plunging abruptly to steep ravines on either side, the old village of Baux has the most spectacular of **sites**. Baux has also given its name to bauxite, a mineral first discovered here in 1822 that led to the development of aluminium.

- **Information:** Maison du Roy, rue Porte-Mage, ☎04 90 54 34 39. www.lesbauxdeprovence.com.
- ▶ **Orient Yourself:** Les Baux is south of St-Rémy-de-Provence, in the midst of the beautiful rocky hills of the Chaîne des Alpilles. The D78 approaches from Fontvielle and the first few houses of the old village clinging to the hillsides come into view suddenly in a bend.
- ◐ **Organizing Your Time:** A walk through the streets of Les Baux is a magical experience, as long as they are not too crowded or full of souvenir sellers (unavoidable in the summer months). Give yourself an hour to take in the village and at least 45 minutes for the château.
- **Parking:** Park the car in one of the car parks *(fee: 4€)* at the foot of the escarpment, before the road up to the village (where cars are not usually allowed). However in high season the car parks can be full, so it will probably be necessary to park by the side of the road some way down from the village and climb the rest of the hill on foot.

Sights

Town

The original entrance into the town is guarded by a gate (Porte Eyguières). Go through the fortified gateway into the town, and simply wander in the old streets. The **Place St-Vincent**★, pleasantly shaded by elms and lotus-trees, has a terrace giving views of the small Fontaine Valley and Val d'Enfer. The 17C former Town Hall (Hôtel de ville) has rooms with ribbed vaulting. The church (Église St-Vincent) dates from the 12C; dressed in their long capes, the shepherds from the Alpilles hills come here for their **Christmas festival**★★, celebrated at Midnight Mass. The **Rue du Trencat**★ was carved into the solid rock which has subsequently been pitted and eroded by wind and rain.

Château

🕐 Jun-Aug: daily 9am-7.30pm; Mar-May and Sep-Nov: daily 9am-6.30pm; Dec-Feb: daily 9am-5pm. ⊘ 7.50€. ☎04 90 54 55 56. www.chateau-baux-provence.com.
By the 11C the lords of Baux, "that race of eagles", were among the most powerful rulers in the south of France. Their turbulent ways, together with their support for the Reformation, were a great irritant

to Louis XIII who in 1632 ordered the castle and ramparts to be dismantled; this was the town's death-blow.

From the remains of the 13C keep a fine **panorama**★★ unfolds over the Alpilles with the windmills of Fontvieille to the west. One of them is Daudet's Mill (Moulin de Daudet). It was here that **Alphonse Daudet**, the Nîmes-born author very popular in France (and available in English translation), is supposed to have written his delightful *Letters from My Mill*, creating the characters of the Woman of Arles (*L'Arlésienne*), Monsieur Seguin's goat, the Pope's grumpy mule and Dom Balaguère the gourmand.

▶ **Cathédrale d'images**★ – 300m north of the village on D27. 🕐 Apr-Sep: daily 10am-7pm; Oct-Dec: daily 10am-6pm. 🕐 Closed 8 Jan to mid-Feb. ⊘ 7.50€ (children: 3.50€). ☎04 90 54 38 65. www.cathedrale-images. com – audio-visual show. **Musée Yves Brayer**★ 🕐 Apr-Sep: daily 10am-12.30pm, 2-6.30pm; Oct-Dec and mid-Feb to end Mar: daily except Tue. 10am-12.30pm, 2-5.30pm. ⊘ 4€. ☎04 90 54 36 99. www.yvesbrayer. com. – retrospective collection of the local artist.

Château and Chapelle Ste-Blaise

AIGUILLES DE **BAVELLA**★★★

MICHELIN MAP 345 E 9
GREEN GUIDE CORSE (IN FRENCH)

This is one of the most dramatic locations in Corsica. From the Bavella Pass, Col de Bavella, there is a awesome view of the jagged Bavella or Asinao Peaks in a spectacular, stark setting; the changing light plays on the sheer rock walls rising above the pine trees at the base.

- **Information:** There is no tourist office nearby, but the Mairie (town hall, ☎04 95 78 66 87) in Zonza can assist with information. For more on this region of Corsica, see www.alta-rocca.com/.
- ▶ **Orient Yourself:** The Aiguilles rise above the Col de Bavella, the mountain pass on D268, which runs from Satrene in south-west Corsica to Solenzara on the south-east coast. The nearest community is Zonza.
- **Walks:** The Bavella Pass is the starting point for many walks and trails for all levels of ability, and is on the long-distance path GR20, which traverses the island.

Visit

Forêt de Bavella★★

The dense forest growing at an altitude of 500m to 1 300m (1 640ft – 4 265ft) has been repeatedly damaged by fire and has been extensively replanted with maritime and laricio pines, cedars and fir trees. A hunting preserve shelters herds of wild sheep which can be glimpsed perched high up on the sheer rocks. Just before the pass are low buildings formerly used as sheep-pens, and an inn, **Auberge du Col**, which is the starting-point for hikes around the pass to the Trou de la Bombe and La Pianona.

Col de Bavella

The mountain ridge crowning the island is indented by the Bavella Pass (alt 1 218m – 3 996ft) marked by a cross and the statue of **Notre-Dame-des Neiges.** The setting and the panorama over the summits are spectacular. To the west the Bavella Peaks rise above the forest of twisted pine trees while to the east the rock wall of Calanca Murata and the jagged ridge of red rock of Punta Tafonata di Paliri stand out against the backdrop of the Tyrrhenian Sea.

BAYEUX★★

MICHELIN MAP 303 H 4–POPULATION 14 960
GREEN GUIDE NORMANDY

Charming with its half-timbered or stone houses, and known for its famous tapestry, Bayeux was also the first French town to be liberated at the end of WW2.

- **Information:** Pont St-Jean, ☎02 31 51 28 28. www.bayeux-tourism.com.
- ▶ **Orient Yourself:** 30km from Caen, the town is just inland from the Omaha and Arromanches Landing Beaches.
- **Especially for kids:** Special child-friendly audioguides are available to help youngsters enjoy the Bayeux Tapestry.

A Bit of History

A Roman town, an early episcopal city, a Viking city from 9C, Bayeux was the 'cradle of the Dukes of Normandy' and home of William, who invaded and conquered England. The invasion came the other way in 1944; Bayeux was liberated

The Norman Conquest

Edward the Confessor died without issue. His favourite, Harold, had sworn on sacred relics at Bayeux to honour the claim to the English throne of William the Bastard, Duke of Normandy (Edward's cousin). Whether through weakness or because of ambition, he reneged on his pledge. Secure in the support of the Pope and the neutrality of the King of France, encouraged by his barons and with the resources of the rich cities of Caen and Rouen at his disposal, William organised a punitive expedition in the space of seven months.

The main part of the Norman fleet was assembled at **Dives** (48km – 30mi east); its 3 000 ships carried 50 000 soldiers and cavalry who were landed on the coast of Sussex on 28 September 1066. Within a few days, battle had been joined just inland from Hastings and the Saxon army routed. Duke William had become the Conqueror.

Shortly after his great victory, at a coronation ceremony in Westminster Abbey on 25 December, he accepted the crown of England.

Though in accordance with feudal law, the situation was an ambiguous one: William was both King of England and Duke of Normandy; the latter title made him a vassal of the King of France. Difficulties soon arose, becoming even more serious in 1152 as a result of the divorce of Louis VII and Eleanor of Aquitaine, and were to be resolved only at the end of the Hundred Years War.

on 7 June. Here on D-Day + 7, General de Gaulle made his first speech on French soil.

Sights

The Bayeux Tapestry (Tapisserie de la Reine Mathilde)★★★

🕐 Mid-Mar to early Nov: daily 9am-6.30pm; May-Aug: daily 9am-7pm; early Nov to mid-Mar: daily 9.30am-12.30pm, 2-6pm. 🕐 Closed 1 Jan, 2 nd week in Jan, 25 Dec. ⌾ 7.50€ , children 3€ (ticket combined with the Baron-Gérard Museum and the Museum of Religious Art). ♿ ☎02 31 51 25 50.

Beautifully displayed in specially designed premises, this extraordinary masterpiece of embroidery was probably made in England soon after the

Conquest. Using a style similar to today's strip cartoon, its 58 captioned scenes recount the epic of the Norman invasion with striking truthfulness; in addition it is an irreplaceable source of information on the ships, weapons, clothes and way of life of the middle of the 11C.

Cathédrale Notre-Dame★★

Numerous changes contributed to this impressive edifice. The Romanesque vaulted crypt and lower nave date from the 11C. The 12C added intricate stonework including profusely decorated walls and cornerstonesand and rib-vaulting in the aisles. In the 13C, high point of Gothic, the superb chancel with radiating chapels and transepts with three-pointed arches and gallery with a fretwork design, were among many elegant additions. Later

Duke William knights Harold. They set out together for Bayeux
(detail of the Bayeux Tapestry)

Address Book

For coin ranges see the Legend on the cover flap.

WHERE TO EAT

⊝ **La Cassonade** – *35 r. du Bienvenu – ☎02 31 92 47 32 – Closed end of Dec.* Located in the heart of old Bayeux, this place is a must. Crepes and buckwheat *galettes*, salads and omelettes will satisfy the hungry and not-so hungry. Colourful dining room and reasonable prices.

⊝⊜ **Le Pommier** – *40 r. des Cuisiniers – ☎02 31 21 52 10 – Open Tue evening and Wed, except during July-Aug – Closed 7 – 28 Feb, 21 Nov – 2Dec.* No place could be more centrally located, near the Cathedral, its inviting apple-green façade announcing its rich Norman cuisine: smoked ham, *tripes à la mode de Caen*, cream sauces and of course apples. There are also vegetarian dishes. The vaulted dining-room with stone walls adds charming authenticity.

⊝⊜ **Hostellerie St-Martin** – *14480 Creully – ☎02 31 80 10 11 hostellerie. stmartin@ wanadoo.fr.* Today it's a restaurant, but in olden times the large vaulted rooms dating from the 16C housed the village market. Exposed stone, a fireplace, sculptures and a view of the wine cellar make up the curious decor. Classic cuisine. A few bedrooms.

⊝⊜ **Le Petit Bistrot** – *2 r. du Bienvenu – ☎02 31 51 85 40 – Closed Jan, Sun and Mon – reserv. advisable .* An inventive cuisine prepared by a keen chef is the main attraction of this small establishment facing the cathedral. Original dishes inspired by Mediterranean cuisine are served in a Provençal-style decor with an ochre colour scheme, water colours and drawings.

WHERE TO STAY

⊝ **La Ferme des Châtaigniers Bed and Breakfast** – *14400 Vienne-en-Bessin – 7.5km/4.6mi E of Bayeux via D 126 – ☎02 31 92 54 70 – ⤍ – 3 rooms.* Set apart from the farmhouse, this converted farm building contains simple yet pleasant, comfortable rooms. Guests have the use of a fitted kitchen. Peace and quiet is guaranteed in this house set in the fields.

⊝ **Le Grand Fumichon Bed and Breakfast** – *14400 Vaux-sur-Aure – 3km/1.9mi N of Bayeux via D 104 – ☎02 31 21 78 51 – duyckja@wanadoo.fr – ⤍ – 4 rooms.* Once part of Longues-sur-Mer Abbey, this fortified 17C farm, with its square courtyard and characteristic porch, is today a dairy and cider-making farm. The attic rooms are plain but pleasant.

⊝⊜ **Hôtel Reine Mathilde** – *23 r. Larcher – ☎02 31 92 08 13 hotel-reinemathilde@wanadoo.fr , www.hotel-reinemathilde.com – Closed 15 Nov to 15 Feb – 16 rooms: ⬚8 €.* If you wish to stay in the old town, this small family hotel is conveniently situated a stone's throw from the cathedral and the famous tapestry. Exposed beams and light-wood furniture. Plain rooms, some of them with sloping ceilings.

⊝⊜ **Le Manoir de Crépon Bed and Breakfast** – *14480 Crépon – ☎02 31 22 21 manoirdecrepon@wanadoo.fr – Closed 10 Jan to 10 Feb – 5 rooms.* This 17C and 18C house is typical of the area, with its oxblood-coloured roughcast. You will like the stone floors and fireplaces, the vast, tastefully furnished bedrooms and the authentic atmosphere of the former kitchen converted into a breakfast room.

SHOPPING

Naphtaline – *16 parvis de la Cathédrale – ☎02 31 21 50 03 – Open Apr-3 Oct: 10am-7pm; Nov: 2-6.60pm; Mar and Dec: 11am-12.30pm, 2-6.30pm. Closed Jan and Feb, Sundays and holidays off-season.* Two boutiques housed in a fine 18C building offer antique and modern lace, Bayeux porcelain and reproductions of traditional tapestries woven on Jaquard looms.

ON THE TOWN

Café Inn – *67 r. St-Martin – ☎02 31 21 11 37- Open daily 9am-7pm. Closed Sundays and holidays.* Coffee beans are roasted on the spot and 75 sorts of tea are served in a bustling ambiance. Light meals of salads, omelettes and quiches are offered as prelude to the delicious *Tarte Tatin*, an upside-down apple pie.

additions included side chapels (14C), frescoes, an octagonal storey over the crossing (15C).

▶ **Musée mémorial de la Bataille de Normandie**★ – ◐ *May to mid-Sep: daily 9.30am-6.30pm; mid-Sep to end Apr: daily 10am-12.30pm, 2-6pm. ◐ Closed mid to end Jan, 1 Jan, 25 Dec. ☞ 5.50 € ☍ ☎02 31*

51 46 90– Musée Baron Gérard (☍ temporarily in the Hôtel du Doyen) ◐ *Jul-Aug: daily 10am-12.30pm and 2-7pm; Sep-Jun: daily 10am-12.30pm and 2-6pm. ◐ Closed 1 Jan and 25 Dec. ☞ 2.60€ (ticket combined with the Bayeux Tapestry Museum and the Museum of Religious Art).* ☎02 31 92 14 21.

BEAULIEU-SUR-DORDOGNE★★

MICHELIN MAP 329 M-6–POPULATION 1 265
GREEN GUIDE DORDOGNE BERRY LIMOUSIN

Rising from the RIver Dordogne, picturesque Beaulieu has a fine church and former abbey.

🔲 **Information:** Place Marbot, ☎05 55 91 09 94. www.otbeaulieu19.fr .
▶ **Orient Yourself:** Beaulieu is in the Limousin region, some distance upriver from the popular Dordogne resorts.

Sight

Église St-Pierre★★

◐ *Daily 8am-7pm (summer: 7am-8pm).* ☎*05 55 91 18 78.* ☞ *Guided tours available Jul-Aug: 10am-noon, 2.30-6pm.* ☎*01 46 51 39 30. www.guidecasa.com.*
This is the beautiful church of a former Benedictine abbey. Its **doorway (portail)**★★, dating from 1125, has as its theme the opening stages of the Last

Judgement, with the dead being summoned from their graves. The ecstasy of the Apostles, the magnificence of the Cross and of the instruments of the Passion, the display of Christ's wounds and the subjugation of Evil represented by monsters, all proclaim the imminence of judgement. The Treaury in the north transept houses a remarkable 12C Romanesque **figure of the Virgin**★ in a 13C shrine.

BEAUNE★★

MICHELIN MAP 320 I-J 6-7–POPULATION 21 289
GREEN GUIDE BURGUNDY JURA

At the heart of one of the world's greatest wine regions, Beaune is also renowned for its artistic heritage. Fortified in 1368, it was the residence of the Dukes of Burgundy before they moved to Dijon.

🔲 **Information:** 1 r. de l'Hôtel-Dieu, ☎03 80 26 21 30. www.ot-beaune.fr.
▶ **Orient Yourself:** Central Beaune is enclosed by a fast-moving ring-road in anti-clockwise direction – so any turn on the left leads into the centre. Focal point is the Hôtel-Dieu and the main square in front of it, Place des Halles.
🅿 **Parking:** It's easier to park just outside the ramparts than try to find a space within the walled town.
☞**Walks and Tours:** The tourist office has information about many different tours and excursions in town and to the vineyards.

Address Book

For coin ranges, see the Legend on the cover flap.

EATING OUT

⊜⊜ **Le Bénaton** – *25 R. du Fg-Bretonnière* – ☎*03 80 22 00 26* – *lebenaton@club-internet.fr* – *Closed 30 Nov to 8 Dec, Wed and Thu except in high season.* Small restaurant far from the madding crowd with a pretty covered terrace for the summer days. Pleasant dining room with stone walls and bright decorative hues. Attractive quality/price ratio for light yet delicious meals made with fresh seasonal produce.

⊜⊜ **Le P'tit Paradis** – *25 R. Paradis* – ☎*03 80 24 91 00* – *Closed 8-16 Mar, 9-17 Aug, 21 Nov to-14 Dec, Mon and Tue.* The pretty dining room and terrace border a flowering garden. Contemporary cuisine incorporates regional flourishes, and wines are selected from boutique producers.

⊜⊜ **Ma cuisine** – *Passage Ste-Hélène* – ☎*03 80 22 30 22* – *cave-sainte-helene@wanadoo.fr* – *Closed August, Christmas holidays, Wed, Sat and Sun.* Located along a tiny street, this small dining room sports the colours of Provence. Regional wines on the wine list.

⊜⊜ **Le Caveau des Arches** – *10 Bd Perpreuil* – ☎*03 80 22 10 37* – *restaurant.caveau.des.arches@wanadoo.fr* – *Closed 24 Jul to 25 Aug, 23 Dec-17 Jan Sun and Mon.* In summer remember to bring a cardigan with you as the vaulted dining rooms of this restaurant set up on the ramparts can be somewhat chilly. Admire the ruins of an old bridge which once gave access to the city. Traditional Burgundy cooking.

WHERE TO STAY

⊜ **Chambre d'Hôte Le Meix des Hospices** – *R. Basse (near the church)* – *71150 Demigny* – *10km/6.2mi S of Beaune by D 18* – ☎*03 85 49 98 49* – ⌁ – *3 rooms.* This former hospice annexe consists of several outbuildings arranged around a square courtyard. The quiet, simple rooms, one of which is set up beneath the eaves, are sparsely appointed with modern furniture. The dining room features exposed beams, stone flooring and a fireplace.

⊜⊜ **Hôtel du Parc** – *21200 Levernois* – *5km/3.1mi SW of Beaune by rte de Verdun-sur-le-Doubs, D 970 then D 111L* – ☎*03 80 24 63 00* – *hotel.le.parc@wanadoo.fr* – *Closed 28 Nov-27 Jan* – *25 rooms* – ⌑ *7.50€.* Covered with Virginia creeper and bursting with flowers in summertime, this hotel is quite simply charming. The two buildings are separated by a small patio. Bright, sober accommodation. The park at the back looks out over peaceful meadows.

⊜⊜⊜ **Hôtel Le Cep** – *27 R. Maufoux* – ☎*03 80 22 35 48* – *resa@hotel-cep-beaune.com* – *61 rooms* – ⌑ *18€.* Ravishing 16C house in the old quarter. The bedrooms, decorated in old-fashioned style, carry the names of famous vintages from the Côte-d'Or. Breakfast is served in the vaulted cellar or, weather permitting, in the courtyard with its pretty Renaissance arcades and medallions.

⊜⊜⊜ **Hostellerie du Château de Bellecroix** – *Rte de Chalon* – *71150 Chagny* – *18km/11.2mi SW of Beaune by N 74 then N 6* – ☎*03 85 87 13 86* – *chateau.de.bellecroix@wanadoo.fr* – *Closed 19 Dec-13 Feb and Wed out of season* – *20 rooms* – ⌑ *17€.* The two towers of this 18C château stand amid wooded parkland. Nearby lie the turrets of a former 12C Knights Templar commandery belonging to the Order of Malta. The bedrooms are appointed with antique furniture. There are some fine replicas of medieval wainscoting in the dining hall.

SIT BACK AND RELAX

Bouché – *1 pl. Monge* – ☎*03 80 22 10 35* . *www.chocolatier-bouche.com. Closed Mon.* Step inside this pretty tearoom and you'll find lovely gift boxes ready to fill with tantalizing house specialties, among them chocolate "snails", candied chestnuts and candied fruits. At table, you'll have to chose between *tarte vigneronne, millefeuille,* or any of the 20 or so specially created sweets.

Palais des gourmets – *14 Pl. Carnot* – ☎*03 80 22 13 39* – *Closed. Tue Oct-Apr.* This delightful *patisserie*-tea room serves many a local delicacy, including *cassissines* (blackcurrant fruit jelly flavoured with blackcurrant liqueur), *roulés au cointreau* (pancakes with a Cointreau filling) and chocolate medallions depicting the Hôtel-Dieu.

ON THE TOWN

Le Bistrot Bourguignon – *8 R. Monge – ☎03 80 22 23 24 – le.bistrot.bourguignon@wanadoo.fr – Open Tue-Sat 11am-3pm, 6-11pm – Closed mid-Feb to mid-Mar.* Relax on the charming terrace or sink into one of the comfortable armchairs inside this old house, sipping a glass of excellent wine to the strains of a few popular songs.

Place Carnot – This large, recently restored square has many outdoor cafés where you can sit in the sun all day. The perfect place to have breakfast, lunch or dinner!

FOR WINELOVERS

L'Athenaeum de la Vigne et du Vin – *5 r. de l'Hôtel-Dieu – ☎03 80 25 08 30 – althenaeum@wanadoo.fr – Open daily 10am-7pm – Closed 25 Dec and 1 Jan.* This bookshop has earned quite a reputation as the ultimate authority on the art of oenology, Burgundy and fine gastronomy. It also presents a collection of miscellaneous items related to wine: corkscrews, glasses and cellarman's knives.

Cave Patriarche Père & Fils – *5-7 R. du Collège – ☎03 80 24 53 78 – www.patriarche.com – Open daily. Closed 25 Dec and 1 Jan.* Burgundy's largest cellars (15 000m2/18 000sq yd) are housed in a former convent dating from the 14C and 16C. Guided tours and tasting sessions of 13 different wines.

Cordeliers wine cellar

B.Kaufmann/MICHELIN

Caves de La Reine Pédauque – *Porte St-Nicolas – ☎03 80 22 23 11 – www.reine-pedauque.com – Open daily. Closed Christmas and Jan.* After exploring the 18C vaulted cellars, visitors may take part in a wine tasting session around an imposing round marble table! An opportunity not to be missed!

La Cave des Cordeliers – *6 R. de l'Hôtel-Dieu – ☎03 80 25 o8 85 – Open daily. Closed 25 Dec and 1Jan.* The Couvent des Cordeliers, built in 1242, provides a splendid backdrop to these wine cellars, which you can visit before tasting six fine Burgundy wines. In the courtyard, note the 1580 low relief depicting the Adoration of the Magi.

Le Comptoir Viticole – *1 R. Samuel-Legay – ☎03 80 22 15 73 – 222.comptoir-viticole.com – Open Mon 9am-noon, 2-7pm; Tue-Sat 8am-noon, 2-7pm.* Wine buffs and amateur vignerons will adore this shop, which sells all manner of devices related to winemaking: bottling machines, corkscrews, bottle racks, jeroboams, balthasars...

Marché aux Vins – *2 R. Nicolas-Rolin – ☎03 80 25 08 20 – www.marcheaux-vins.com – Open mid-Jun to late Aug: daily 9.30am-7pm; Sep to mid-Jun: 9.30am-noon, 2-6.30pm – Closed 25-26 Dec and 1-2 Jan.* Housed in Beaune's oldest church (13C and 14C) opposite the famous hospice, this wine market offers 18 wines of between 3 and 15 years of age, to be sipped and relished slowly. If requested, a cellar containing some extremely rare vintages, which have been maturing since 1911, can also be opened to visitors.

Vins de Bourgogne Denis-Perret – *40 R. Carnot – ☎03 80 22 35 47 – contact@denisperret.fr – Open May-Oct: Mon-Sat 9am-7pm, Sun 9am-noon; the rest of the year Mon-Sat 9am-noon, 2-7pm, Closed public holiday afternoons and Sun out of season.* Five wine-growers and a group of landowners have teamed up to offer you some of the most prestigious names from the Burgundy region—Romanée-Conti, Clos-Vougeot, Montrachet, Chambertin. Such a rich selection could easily leave you speechless but, not to worry, for several young oenologists are there to help you make your choice and to suggest the best dishes to go with each wine.

A Bit of History

The vine was first planted here in Gallo-Roman times; the area devoted to it increased in the Middle Ages thanks to the clearing of woodland by the monasteries. The reputation of Burgundy wines grew in the 15C along with the rise of its Ducal court.

Few careers have been as meteoric as that of **Nicolas Rolin** (1377-1461). Born into a bourgeois family, he became a successful lawyer, then counsellor to John the Fearless. In 1422 he was promoted to Chancellor by Duke Philip the Good. While expertly promoting the interests of his master, he also acquired fortune and power for himself to an unprecedented degree. It was he who detached Burgundy from its alliance with England, reconciling her with France by the Treaty of Arras. In 1443, Rolin and his wife founded the Hôtel-Dieu to be a free hospital and guaranteed it an income from 1 300ha – 3 200-acre of land between Aloxe-Corton and Meursault. Yet in 1457 Rolin fell from favour; he died at Autun four years later.

Sight

Hôtel-Dieu (Hospices de Beaune)★★★

🕐 End Mar to mid-Nov: daily 9am-6.30pm; mid-Nov to end Mar: daily 9-11.30am, 2-5.30pm. 🐌 5.40€. ♿ ☎03 80 24 45 00. www.hospices-de-beaune-tm.fr.

For 520 years, Rolin's foundation cared for the sick, from 1451 to 1971. It has come down to us intact. With its fine architecture, its elegant decoration (ironwork, gabled dormers, weathervanes), its multi-coloured glazed tiles and its old well, it seems more a palace than a place for the poor. Although the internal courtyard in Flemish-Burgundian style, the pharmacy, the nuns' quarters, the kitchens are fascinating, it is the Great Hall (Grand'Salle) which most completely evokes the spiritual dimension of the hospitals of yesteryear. It remained in service up to 1959.

One end of the Grand' Salle is arranged as a place of worship, so that the sick could attend services without leaving their beds. The **Polyptych of the Last Judgement**★★★ was displayed here. Rolin himself commissioned this work from Rogier van der Weyden to go over the altar of the Great Hall. The master, with the help of assistants, completed it between 1443 and 1451. In its expression of emotion at this crucial moment and in its perfection of detail (which can be inspected with the aid of a giant magnifying-glass), it is one of the greatest of Gothic paintings. At the time, its masterly evocation of the outcome to be expected from the living of a blameless life must have been reassuring too.

Ph. Gajic/MICHELIN

The Grand'Salle, Hôtel-Dieu

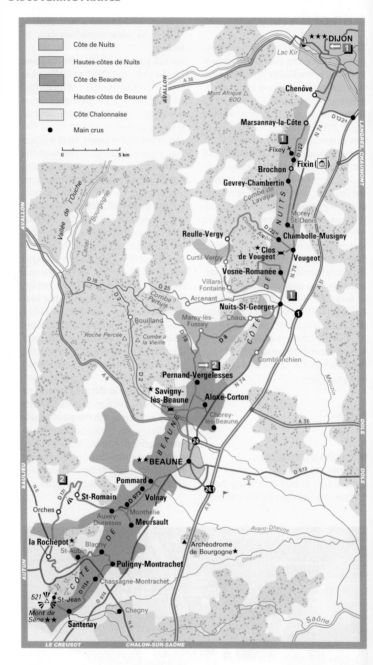

	Côte de Nuits
	Hautes-côtes de Nuits
	Côte de Beaune
	Hautes-côtes de Beaune
	Côte Chalonnaise
●	Main crus

0   5 km

On the third Sunday in November the auction takes place in Beaune of the wines of the Hospices.

▶ **Musée du vin de Bourgogne★** – 🕙 9.30am-6pm (Dec-Mar: 5pm).

Last admission 30min before closing. 🕙 *Closed Tue, 1 Jan and 25 Dec.* 📷 *5.40€.* ☎ *03 80 22 08 19–* relates the history of Burgundian vineyards. **Collégiale Notre-Dame★** – tapestries★★. **Hôtel de la Rochepot★**.

Excursion

Vineyard road★
Map opposite. The prestigious vine-yards of the Côte d'Or stretch mainly north and (much less) south from Beaune. Explore the famous names, and stop for tastings, on picturesque back roads, for example at Meursault, Vougeot and Gevrey-Chambertin.

BEAUVAIS★★

MICHELIN MAP 305 D 4–POPULATION 59 000
GREEN GUIDE NORTHERN FRANCE AND THE PARIS REGION

An extraordinary Gothic cathedral stands at the centre of this fortified city.

- **Information:** 1 r. Beauregard, 60000 Beauvais, ☎03 44 15 30 30. www.beauvaistourisme.fr
- **Orient Yourself:** Beauvais lies on the A16 in southern Picardy.
- **Guided tours:** The tourist office offers discovery tours (2hr) from Apr-Sep on Sun at 3pm. 4€.
- **Don't Miss:** The astronomical clock in the cathedral, which puts on a display at 40min past the hour several times daily. ☜ *4€ (children: 1€).*

Sights

Cathédrale St-Pierre★★★
🕐 *Daily. Jul-Aug 9am-6.15pm; May-Jun and Sep-Oct: 9am-12.15pm, 12-5.30pm; Nov-Apr: 9am-12h15pm, 2-6.15pm.* 🕐 *Closed 1 Jan.* ☎*03 44 48 11 60.*

The strange spireless building is the result of a long effort, technical and financial, which eventually ended in failure. In 1225 the Bishop of Beauvais decided to build the biggest and high-est cathedral of the age in honour of St Peter. Its vaults were to top 48 metres – 157ft. But in 1272, ten years after completion, the vault collapsed; it was rebuilt but fell again in 1284. Work had to start immediately on strengthening the walls, increasing the number of fly-ing buttresses at the east end and using tem like external struts at the very base of the roof, 40m – 131ft above ground, concealing the sheer daring of the origi-nal enterprise.

The interior was treated similarly. In the southern bays, additional pillars undepinned the structure above. The windows were given more lancets to subdivide and strengthen them, glazing was added to the elevation, lightening it considerably.

After the Hundred Years War, Martin Chambiges began the construction of the transepts and crossing. He designed the great gable and rose window of the south transept, then, instead of starting on the nave, he built the crossing tower. It was completed in 1539, a century later, but 11m – 36ft higher, than the tower of Strasbourg Cathedral. With no nave to buttress it, however, the great structure collapsed in 1573.

The dizzying height of the vaults is still most impressive and there is much decorative work to admire, from the Renaissance doors of the south por-tal, to the **stained-glass windows (vitraux)**★★ created by the Beauvais workshops founded by Ingrand Lep-rince. The south transept has beautiful hues of green in the triforium and a rose window by Nicolas Leprince. There's also a remarkable **astronomical clock (hor-loge astronomique)**★.

- **Église St-Étienne★ – Jesse Window (vitrail de l'Arbre de Jessé)**★★★, masterpiece of glass-work. **Musée Départemental de l'Oise★ –** 🕐 *Jul to Sep: Wed-Mon 10am-6pm; Sep to end Jun: Wed-Mon 10am-noon, 2-6pm.* 🕐 *Closed Tue, 1 Jan, Easter, Whitsun, 1 May, 1 Nov, 25 Dec.* ☜ *2€, no charge Wed.* ☎*03 44 11 43 83* – paintings, sculpture and tapestries.

ABBAYE DU **BEC-HELLOUIN**★★

MICHELIN MAP 304 E 6

GREEN GUIDE NORMANDY

This once-prestigious abbey produced two great archbishops of Canterbury.

- **Information:** 1 r. du Général de Gaulle, Brionne, ☎02 32 45 70 51. www.tourismecantondebrionne.com
- ▶ **Orient Yourself:** The abbey sits beside the Risle, south of the Seine, about 40km from Rouen.

A Bit of History

In 1042 **Lanfranc** (1005-89) appeared at the abbey. This great yet humble man had been a distinguished teacher. Three years later, he started teaching again, making Le Bec one of the intellectual centres of the West. After the Conquest, Lanfranc, who had become Duke William's Counsellor, was made Archbishop of Canterbury and Primate of all England.

His successor at Le Bec was **St Anselm** (1033-1109), philosopher and theologian. His *Proslogion*, written here in 1078, is considered a great source of Western thought. In 1093 he became Archbishop of Canterbury.

At the Revolution, the building was vandalised and the monks expelled. They returned in 1948.

Visit

🕐 *7am-9pm. ⊗5 €. 🗨 (45min) several times daily except Tue, eg. 10.30, 3 and 4pm, but possible additional times. ☎02 32 43 72 60.*

Since 1948, when Bec-Hellouin became a functioning abbey again, considerable reconstruction has taken place, particularly of the St-Nicolas Tower of 1467 and the Abbot's Lodging of 1735. But the great Abbey Church, whose 42m – 140ft choir was one of the wonders of the Christian world, has gone, though its spiritual power is undiminished.

BELLE-ÎLE★★★

MICHELIN MAP 308 L-M 10-11–POPULATION 4 489

GREEN GUIDE BRITTANY

The name alone is enticing, but the island's beauty surpasses expectations. Valleys cut deep into the high rocks, forming beaches and harbours. Farmland alternates with wild heath, and whitewashed houses stand in lush fields.

- **Information:** Quai Bonnelle, Le Palais. ☎02 97 31 81 93. www.belle-ile.com.
- ▶ **Orient Yourself:** Regular car ferries linking Quibéron (Brittany) and Le Palais in 45min are operated by SMN, ☎08 20 05 60 00. www.smn-navigation.fr. Passenger-only speedboats operate in summer between Le Palais and Lorient (Brittany) in 60min.

A Bit of History

Belle-Île's interest lies as much in its history as in its wonderful coastline. It is a story of constant attack and defence.

In the Middle Ages the island belonged to the Counts of Cornouaille and was often raided by pirates (French as well as Dutch and English) because of its wealth in grain.

Aiguilles de Port-Coton

From 16C the island was constantly in danger of an English attack, and the fortifications were substantially increased. The island's proximity to the mouth of the Loire and the Breton seaports gave it great strategic importance. In 1682, the military engineer Vauban modernised the citadel to deal with the latest war techniques. Yet in 1696, the English took the nearby islands of Houat and Hoëdic, at one point landed on Belle-Île itself. Over the next decades, the English fleet was a ceaseless threat, and eventually took Belle-Île's citadel in the Seven Years War. The island became a virtual English colony. By the 1763 Treaty of Paris, England gave back Belle-Île

Sights

Le Palais

This is the island's capital, known to locals simply as 'Palais'. Most of the island's amenities are to be found here. The natural harbour is dominated by the imposing citadel and fortifications, known as **Citadelle Vauban**★ (Apr-Oct: daily 9.30am-6pm; Jul and Aug: daily 9am-7pm; Nov-Mar: daily 9.30am-noon, 2-5pm. 6.10€ (children: 3.05€) no charge 3rd Sat-Sun in Sep ✆02 97 31 84 17). The proximity of Belle-Ile to the ports of the south coast of Brittany and the mouth of the Loire gave it great importance in the fight for the control of

the high seas conducted by England and France. In 1658, the island came into the hands of chancellor Fouquet. He consolidated the defences and installed 200 new batteries.

From 1682, the great military engineer Vauban was adapted the citadel to the needs arising from improvement in the technology of war, converting an old chapel (Henri II Tower) into a powder-magazine with a projecting roof to fend off broadsides, rebuilding the old arsenal as well as laying out an officers' walk (Promenade des Officiers) with a gallery giving fine seaviews.

Côte Sauvage★★★

The Côte Sauvage, literally "wild coast", runs from the Pointe des Poulains to the Pointe de Talud. Battered by the Atlantic waves, the schists of which the island's plateau is composed have been formed into spectacular coastal scenes.

Port-Donnant★★ has a splendid sandy beach between high cliffs but is known for its great rollers and perilous currents.

The **Aiguilles de Port-Coton**★★ are pyramids hollowed out into caverns and grottoes. The different colours of the rock have been exposed by the action of the sea.

▶ **Sauzon**★; **Pointe des Poulains**★★; **Port-Goulphar**★.

BESANÇON ★★

POPULATION 122 623

MICHELIN MAP 321 G 3

GREEN GUIDE BURGUNDY JURA

The capital of the Franche-Comté occupies a superb site★★★ on a meander of the River Doubs, overlooked by a rocky outcrop on which Vauban built a fortress.

- **Information:** 2 pl. de la 1re-Armée-Française, ☎03 81 80 92 00. www.besancon. tourisme.com.
- ▶ **Orient Yourself:** The historic centre of town lies within the circle (la boucle) of the Doubs river. Shops and restaurants can be found on Grande-Rue, near the bridges. The modern town is on lower ground across the river.
- ⏱ **Organizing Your Time:** There's a lot to see at the citadel, which could take several hours.

A Bit of History

A 2C triumphal arch called the Black Gate (Porte Noire) survives from a Gallo-Roman settlement (Vesontio): the modern Grande-Rue still follows the course of its main street in the heart of old Besançon. Later the town became an important archbishopric.

Through inheritance and marriages, in 15-16C the town – like the rest of Franche-Comté – became part of the Austro-Spanish empire. It marked a high point in the province's commercial life, illustrated by the rise of the Granvelle family. Although born into the humblest of peasant families, the son Perrenot was given an education, rose rapidly, becoming Chancellor to Charles V, and built himself the Palais Granvelle. In 1674 Louis XIV conquered the Franche-Comté, made Besançon its capital and had Vauban construct the citadel.

Sights

Palais Granvelle★

Grande-Rue. This fine example of civil architecture of the 16C has a three-storey façade, divided by five horizontal bands of decoration, and a high mansard roof with crowstep gables. Its proportions and decorative details are those of the Early Renaissance (basket-handle arches, mouldings) while other features are quite new (Tuscan columns,

and the superposition of Ionic and composite orders).

Citadel and Museums★★

99 r. des Fusillés-de-la-Résistance, ☎03 81 87 83 33. www.citadelle.com. ⏱*Jul-Aug: 9am-7pm. Apr-Jun, Sep-Oct: 9am-6pm. Rest of year: 10am-5pm.* ⏱*Closed Mar.* ⌨*7.80€ (low season 7.20€). Ticket valid for all the Citadel's museums.*

From 1675 to 1711 Vauban constructed this mighty fortress. Its great mass is best appreciated from the sentry-walk along the encircling ramparts. The building houses a zoo and several museums: Musée d'Histoire naturelle, Aquarium, Insectarium, Climatorium, Noctarium.

Musée des Beaux-Arts et d'Archéologie★★

1 pl. de la Révolution – ☎03 81 87 80 49 – www.besancon.fr ⏱*9.30am-noon, 2-6pm.* ⏱*Closed Mar., public holidays.* ⌨*5€ (free on Sun).*

The musuem houses a diverse collection of artistic, historical and archaeological displays. Most important is the priceless 14C-17C art collection of the Granvelle family. A room on the first floor provides plenty of evidence of the long tradition of clock-and-watch-making in the Franche-Comté. Most of the great clock-making firms are represented at Besançon. Many of the important advances in the art from 17C to the present have been made here or nearby.

Address Book

For coin ranges, see the Legend on the cover flap.

WHERE TO EAT

Au Petit Polonais – *81 R. Granges – ☎03 81 81 23 67 – jean-michel.vien-not@wanadoo.fr – Closed 14 Jul-15 Aug, Sat evenings and Sun.* In 1870 this restaurant was founded by a Pole, whose story is recounted on the menu. Simple, unpretentious setting. Traditional and regional cuisine. Warm, congenial atmosphere.

Le Cavalier Rouge – *3 R. Mégevand – ☎03 81 83 41 02 – fermé dim. et lun. soir.* A trendy urban atmosphere welcomes groups of regulars, who talk shop over specialties of the day. Quick service.

Le Chaland – *Prom. Micaud, near Pont Brégille – ☎03 81 80 61 61 – chaland@chaland.com – Closed Sat lunchtime.* Settle into the restaurant on this charming old barge moored along the Doubs, offering views of the old town and the Promenade Micaud. In fair weather, meals are served on the upper deck, from where you can see the cormorants circling above the water.

Barthod – *22 R. Bersot – ☎03 81 82 27 14 – Closed Sun and Mon.* Sit down on the charming terrace bursting with bushes and potted plants and admire the view of the nearby waterfall. The owner is a wine buff who proposes lovingly prepared menus (prices include wine) washed down by an interesting selection of vintages. Don't forget to drop by the shop on your way out.

WHERE TO STAY

Hôtel du Nord – *8 R. Moncey – ☎03 81 81 34 56 – ☐ 5.50€.* Situated in the historic quarter, this hotel is a perfect base for venturing out into the old town. The spacious, traditional rooms are equipped with all modern conveniences.

Relais des Vallières – *3 R. P.-Rubens – 4km/2.5mi from Besançon by Bd. de l'O – ☎03 81 52 02 02 – relaisvallieres@wanadoo.fr – 49 rooms – ☐ 7.50€.* Near the Micropolis expo park, this hotel offers clean, comfortable rooms (those at the rear are quieter); a few boast balconies. Buffet-style meals in the bistrot-style restaurant.

Hôtel Citotel Granville – *13 R. du Gén.-Lecourbe – ☎03 81 81 33 92 – 28 rooms – ☐7€.* This stone building boasts an ideal location just steps from the historic town centre. Comfortable rooms giving onto a paved interior courtyard. Buffet breakfast.

SIT BACK AND RELAX

Brasserie du Commerce – *31 R des Granges – ☎03 81 81 33 11 –* This brasserie founded back in 1873 has retained its original decor and has become something of an institution. Its old-fashioned atmosphere is indeed charming but its popularity is such that, on some evenings, it is almost impossible to find a table, or a seat!

SHOPPING

Le Vin et l'Assiette – *97 R. Battant – ☎03 81 81 48 18 – Closed 2 weeks in Aug, Sun and Mon.* This former wine-grower's cellar in the old quarter is housed in a 14C building which is an officially listed site. Wine buffs will be able to taste wine by the glass, accompanied by a plate of *rosette* (dry pork sausage) or Comté cheese.

Baud – *4 Grande-Rue – ☎03 81 81 20 12 –* This family business has literally become an institution in Besançon on account of the delicious food it provides: cakes and pastries, ice cream, take-away dishes. If the terrace is crowded, just grin and bear it: it's definitely worth the wait.

▶ **Cathédrale St-Jean** – ○*Daily except Tue 9am-6pm–* **Painting of the Virgin with Saints★**, **St-Jean Rose Window★** (Rose de St-Jean). **Astronomical Clock★** (Horloge astronomique) – 🔢 ○*Guided tours ⬤⬤ (30min) Apr-Sep: Wed-Mon* 9.50am, 10.50am, 11.50am, 2.50pm, 3.50pm, 4.50pm, and 5.50pm; Oct-Mar: Wed-Mon 9.50am, 10.50am, 11.50am, 2.50pm, 3.50pm, 4.50pm and 5.50pm. ○*Closed Tue, Jan, 1 May, 1 and 11 Nov, 25 Dec. ⬤ 2.50€ (under 18 years: no charge).* ☎03 81 81 12 76.

Folk Museum (Musée comtois) and Resistance and Deportation Museum, ⓞsame hours as Natural History Museum, except ⓞclosed Tue Nov-Mar. ⌦ 7€, ticket valid for all citadel museums (children: 4€).

☏03 81 87 83 33. www.citadelle.com. **Préfecture★**. **Bibliothèque municipale★** –Temporary exhibits. ☏03 81 83 26 63– manuscripts, incunabula, drawings, etc.

BEYNAC-ET-CAZENAC★★

MICHELIN MAP 329 H 6
GREEN GUIDE DORDOGNE BERRY LIMOUSIN

One of the great castles of Périgord, **Château de Beynac** is famous for its history, its architecture and for its panoramic setting on top of a rugged rock face.

- 🛈 **Information:** ℅See Sarlat-le-Caneda.
- ▶ **Orient Yourself:** The castle and village are on the north bank of the Dordogne, 12km south of Sarlat.
- ☺ **Don't Miss:** As well as the château, the beautiful Renaissance village at the foot of the cliff is also worth visiting.

Visit

ⓞJun-Sep: daily 10am-6.30pm; Oct-Feb: daily 10am to dusk, Dec-Feb: daily noon-dusk. Call for admission price information. ☏05 53 29 50 40.

Defended on the north side by double walls, the castle looms over the river from a precipitous height of 150m – 500ft. Crouching benath its cliff is a tiny village, once the home of poet Paul Eluard. A square keep existed here as early as 1115; it was strengthened at the time of the great rivalry between the Capetians and the Plantagenets. During the Hundred Years War, the Dordogne frequently marked the border between French and English territory; stirring times for Beynac, face to face with its rival Castelnaud on the cliffs opposite. The interior has much of interest, including the great Hall of State.

BIARRITZ★★★

MICHELIN MAP 324 C-D 2–POPULATION 30 055
GREEN GUIDE FRENCH ATLANTIC COAST

With its splendid beaches of fine sand and high-quality facilities, golf courses and luxury hotel, this Basque Coast resort enjoys an international reputation.

- 🛈 **Information:** 1 square d'Ixelles, ☏05 59 22 37 10. www.biarritz.fr
- ▶ **Orient Yourself:** Biarritz, Bayonne and Anglet form a single urban area, just north of the Spanish border.
- ☺ **Don't Miss:** The view of La Perspective, a promenade overlooking Plage des Basques, is one of the highlights of Biarritz.

A Bit of History

Over a century ago, Biarritz was a place of no particular distinction, its beaches attracting people from nearby Bay-onne. Fame came suddenly, with the visits of Empress Eugénie and Napoleon III, followed by many of the illustrious names of the period. Queen Victoria was here in 1889, and after 1906 Biarritz

Address Book

For coin ranges, see the Legend on the cover flap.

WHERE TO EAT

La Goélette – *4 r. du Port-Vieux – ☎05 59 24 84 65 – Closed 1 Dec-11 Jan.* Take a break from shopping and treat yourself to a meal in this pleasant restaurant surrounded by boutiques. The decor is inspired by the nearby sea – blue and white tones, fishing nets, and other nautical objects. Cuisine with an accent on fish and salads.

Tikia – *1 pl. Ste-Eugénie – ☎05 59 24 46 09. Tikia* means 'small' in Basque. It's true that there's not much space in this little restaurant, but its attractive ambience makes it a pleasant place to linger. The decor has a cabin-type feel, with varnished wood panelling on the walls, porthole-shaped mirrors and other marine knick-knacks. Giant kebabs on the menu.

La Pizzeria des Arceaux – *20-24 av. Édouard-VII – ☎05 59 24 11 47 – Closed 6-26 May, 14 Nov-6 Dec, Sun eve and Mon.* This lively pizzeria near the city hall is particularly popular with a young, trendy crowd. Attractive decor with tile frescos and mirrors and an excellent choice of desserts.

Le Clos Basque – *12 rue Louis-Barthou – ☎05 59 24 24 96 – Closed 16 Feb-5 Mar, 23 Jun-3 Jul, 19 Oct-6 Nov, Sun eve and Mon except in Jul-Aug.* Excellent local cuisine and a warm, friendly atmosphere mean that there's rarely a spare table in this popular restaurant. Exposed beams and *azulejos* tiles add an Iberian flavour to the decor.

Plaisir des Mets – *5 rue du Centre – ☎05 59 24 34 66 – Closed 15-30 Jun, 15-30 Nov, Mon noon and Tue noon in Jul and Aug, Tue eve and Wed from Sep-Jun.* This small restaurant is situated near the market hall, just a few hundred yards from the sea. The contemporary cuisine served here highlights seasonal, regional produce. Light, modern decor in restful shades of white and blue.

WHERE TO STAY

Hôtel Gardenia – *19 av. Carnot – ☎05 59 24 10 46 – www.hotel-garde-nia.com – Closed Dec-Feb. – 19 rooms.* This central hotel with a pink facade has all the charm of a private home. Its quiet, attractive rooms are regularly redecorated and its reception and salon have just been refurbished. Reasonable prices considering the location.

Hôtel Atalaye – *6 r. des Goëlands, Plateau de l'Atalaye – ☎05 59 24 06 76 – contact@hotelatalaye.com – Closed 14 Nov-15 Dec – 24 rooms.* This imposing turn-of-the-century villa owes its name to the superb Atalaye plateau overlooking the Atlantic ocean. The rooms here are gradually being refurbished – those with a sea view are the most attractive. Free parking nearby.

Chambre d'hôte Maison Berreterrenea – *Quartier Arrauntz – 64480 Ustaritz – 11km/6.6mi SE of Biarritz. Take the D 932, Arrauntz exit – ☎05 59 93 05 13 – 4 room.* Facing a cider apple orchard, this 17C Basque house dominates the Valley of the Nive. Now a bed and breakfast, the house has been sympathetically renovated in traditional style, with whitewashed stone walls. Simply furnished rooms adorned with beams and old doors.

Hôtel Maïtagaria – *34 av. Carnot – ☎05 59 24 26 65 – Closed 1-15 Dec – 17 rooms.* A warm, friendly reception in this little hotel near the garden, just 500m/550yd from the beach. The rooms, of varying sizes, are bright and functional and were recently renovated. Small flower-filled garden in the back.

Le Petit Hôtel – *11 r. Gardères – ☎05 59 24 87 00 – www.petithotel-biarritz.com – 12 rooms.* This appealing hotel is ideally located for exploring the town or spending time on the beach. Its soundproofed rooms have been renovated in tones of blue or yellow; all have Internet access. The hotel has a seminar room above its restaurant, just 100m/110yd from the hotel.

BARS AND CAFES

L'Impérial (Hôtel du Palais) – *1 av. de l'Impératrice – ☎05 59 41 64 00 – www.hotel-du-palais.com. Closed Feb.* "La Villa Eugénie", the scene of Napoleon III's love affair with the Empress Eugénie, me the majestic Hôtel du Palais in 3. Enjoy a glass of champagne and savour the atmosphere in the hotel's elegant bar, the Impérial, where a pianist makes the ambience complete from 8 to 11 every evening.

Le Caveau – *4 r. Gambetta* – ☎*05 59 24 16 17* – *Open nightly till 5am*. One of the trendiest disco bars in town, Le Caveau is popular with locals and visitors, as well as the inevitable stars on holiday. *The* place to be seen in Biarritz.

La Santa Maria – *Espl. du Port-Vieux* – ☎*05 59 24 92 25* – *Open 9am-3am*. The splendid view of the Rocher de la Vierge and the Port Vieux beach is one of the attractions of this little bar perched on a rock. A terrace, a few stools and a bar counter in a cave make this a pleasant, unpretentious spot where you can sample tapas while listening to the little orchestra.

ENTERTAINMENT

Gare du Midi – *21 bis av. du Mar.-Foch* – ☎*05 59 22 37 10* – *www.biarritz.tm.fr* – *tickets available from the tourist office:* The city's main theatre, with a seating capacity of 1 400, puts on a range of plays, music concerts and ballets. It is also the home of the Biarritz ballet company.

Casino de Biarritz – *1 av. Édouard-VII* – ☎*05 59 22 77 77* – *www.lucienbarriere. com* – *Open daily 10am-3am (4am at weekends)*. Located on Grande Plage, this enormous casino has a table games room (roulette, Black Jack) and 180 slot machines as well as Le Café de la Plage brasserie, Le Baccara restaurant, Le Flamingo discotheque, a show room (theatre, dance) and a ballroom.

SHOPPING

Cazaux et fils – *10 r. Broquedis* – ☎*05 59 22 36 03* – ⏰*Mon-Sat 10am-12.30pm and 3pm-7pm, public hols by appointment*. The Cazaux family has been involved in making ceramic pottery since the 18C. The boutique also offers personalised creations – every step can be undertaken according to the customer's wishes, from extracting the clay to hand-painting the finishing touches.

Fabrique de chistéras Gonzalez – *6 allée des Liserons* – *64600 Anglet* – ☎*05 59 03 85 04* – Founded in 1887, the Gonzalez company produces hand-made *cestas* (wicker scoops that prolong the protective *pelota* glove). In one hour, you'll learn everything there is to know about the history and manufacture of *pelotas* and *cestas*.

Chocolats Henriet – *Pl. Clemenceau* – ☎*05 59 24 24 15*. Established after WWII, Henriet is the local guiding light in chocolates and confectionery, featuring *calichous* (butter and cream caramels), and *rochers de Biarritz* (bitter chocolate, orange rinds, almonds). Propritor Serge Couzigou, maître chocolatier, also created the Musée du Chocolat (located 4 Ave. de la Marne).

Maison Arostéguy – *5 av. Victor-Hugo* – ☎*05 59 24 00 52* – *www.maison-arosteguy.com* – Founded in 1875, this famous Biarritz grocery store (formerly the 'Epicerie du Progrès') has kept its original walls, shelves and facade. The shop specialises in regional fare and also stocks many products difficult to find elsewhere: rare bottles of Bordeaux, prestigious Armagnacs, Basque products, flavoured teas and spices.

SPORT AND LEISURE

Euskal-Jaï Fernand Pujol – *R. Cino-del-duca* – ☎*05 59 23 91 09* – This pelota Basque school organizes competitions nearly every Wednesday and Saturday throughout summer.

Hippodrome des Fleurs – *Av. du Lac Marion* – ☎*05 59 43 91 56* – Horse races have been held here on July and August evenings for over fifty years. This trotters' hippodrome has an 800m cindered track with sharp bends.

Piscine municipale – *Bd du Gén.-de-Gaulle* – ☎*05 59 22 52 52*. Located on the shore, this municipal complex features heated seawater pools as well as a jacuzzi, a hammam and a sauna.

Thermes Marins – *80 r. de Madrid* – ☎*05 59 23 01 22* – *www.thermesmarins-biarritz.com* -This spa featuring a leisure pool and jacuzzi proposes various treatments, such as affusion or underwater showers, seaweed treatment booths, massages, sea-air bath booths.

Seafront

became one of the favourite resorts of Edward VII.

Now enhanced by modernisation, Biarritz continues to offer pleasures which never pall, its beaches, promenades and gardens to either side of the rocky promontory of the Plateau de l'Atalaye remaining as attractive as ever. The orientation of the beaches also produce Atlantic rollers that attract surfers.

Visit

Promenades

Pleasantly shaded and landscaped streets lead from the main beach (Grande Plage) to the Virgin's Rock (**Rocher de la Vierge**★). To the south is the viewpoint (Perspective de la Côte des Basques) offering an uninterrupted **view**★★ towards the mountain peaks of the Basque Country.

◗◗ **Musée Bonnat**★★ – ◔*Jul-Aug: daily 10am-6.30pm (Wed: 9.30pm); May-Jun and Sep-Oct: daily except Tue 10am-6.30pm; Nov-Apr: daily except Tue 10am-12.30, 2-6pm. ◔Closed public holidays (except Jul-Aug). ᓹ. ⊜5.50€, no charge 1st Sun in the month. ☎05 59 59 08 52.* **Musée Basque**★★ – ◔*Daily except Mon 10am-12.30pm, 2-6pm (May-*

Oct: daily 10am-6.30pm). ◔Closed public holidays. ⊜ 5.50€, no charge 1st Sun in the month. ☎05 59 46 61 90. www.musee-basque.com – one of the finest regional ethnographic museums in France. **Cathédrale Ste-Marie**★ (**Cloisters**★).

Excursions

Bayonne★★

Biarritz, Anglet and Bayonne merge with one another to form a single urban area of which Bayonne, with its busy quaysides and old streets, is the commercial centre. Its harbour on the estuary of te Adour handles maize, sulphur and chemical products.

The picturesque Rue du Pont-Neuf is flanked by arcades and tall houses. Among them are many excellent pastry-shops and confectioners emphasise the importance of the chocolate-making industry which began here in the 17C.

Route Impériale des cimes★

Bayonne to Hasparren 25km – 16mi. This section of Napoleon I's scenic highway was part of an overall project to link Bayonne with St-Jean-Pied-de-Port for strategic reasons. It follows a highly sinuous alignment and affords fine **views**★ of the Basque coast and countryside.

BLOIS★★

MICHELIN MAP 318 C-D-E-F 5-6-7–POPULATION 49 171
GREEN GUIDE CHÂTEAUX OF THE LOIRE

Blois looks northwards to the Beauce and south to the Sologne, and is situated at that point on the Loire at which the limestone landscapes around Orléans give way almost imperceptibly to the chalk country of Touraine downstream. Originally defended by a medieval castle, the town was transformed from 1503 onward when the kings moved there from Amboise, bringing in their train all the trades devoted to satisfying the royal taste for luxury.

- **Information:** 23 place du Château , ☎02 54 90 41 41. www.bloispaysdecham bord.com.
- ▶ **Orient Yourself:** The town climbs gently from the Loire, the château sitting at the very top.
- **Don't Miss:** Be sure to stroll in the old quarter, which rises behind the town centre.
- **Especially for Kids:** Across the square from the château, the Magic Museum will entertain young ones.

Sight

Château★★★

Apr-Sep: daily 9am-6pm; Sep-Mar: daily 9am-12.30pm, 2-5.30pm. Last admission 30min before closing. Closed 1 Jan and 25 Dec. 6.50€. ☎02 54 90 33 32. www.ville-blois.fr – for Illustration see Introduction: Art – Architecture.

The whole development of secular French architecture from feudalism to the Classicism of Louis XIII's reign can be traced at Blois.

The medieval remains include the round towers, spiral stairways and steep-pitched roofs of the Foix Tower and the Chamber of the States-General of 1205; with its panelled ceiling, this is where the States-General held its Assemblies in 1576 and 1588.

The transition from the Gothic to the Renaissance is evident in the Charles of Orléans Gallery and particularly in the Louis XII Wing of 1498-1501. Louis had been born at Blois in 1462 and, together with Anne of Brittany, carried out a number of improvements including the construction of a new wing. This was right up to date with its triumphal arch doorways, Italianate arabesque decoration applied to the three Gothic pillars on the courtyard side, and the use of galleries to link rooms rather than having them run directly into one another.

Built only 15 years later, possibly by Claude de France, the François I wing exemplifies the preoccupation with ornamentation that swept in with the first phase of the French Renaissance. The work remained incomplete but the new taste for sumptuous decoration is very apparent, not only in the Façade des Loges (built 7m – 23ft in front of the old rampart) with its still-irregular fenestration, but also in Pierre Trinquart's François I staircase; though somewhat over-restored in the view of some archeologists, this is a richly decorated masterpiece with openings between its buttresses forming a series of balconies. The much-modified interior includes, on the first floor, Catherine de Medici's study with its secret cupboards, and on the second floor, Henri III's apartments, scene of the murder of Henri de Guise. The style of Louis XIII appears in the Gaston of Orléans Wing (1632-37). The King's brother employed François Mansart, who, however, failed to deploy the full range of his talents, his work here being stiff rather than dignified. Building stopped when the birth of Louis XIV put paid to his uncle's hopes of succeeding to the throne.

Address Book

&For coin ranges, see the Legend on the cover flap.

WHERE TO EAT

🍴🍴 **Le Bistrot du Cuisinier** – 20 quai Villebois-Mareuil – ☎02 54 78 06 70 – bistrot.du.cuisinier@wanadoo.fr. Closed 24 Sep-4 Oct and 21 Dec-4 Jan. You'll find a real bistro atmosphere here, simple and relaxed, and from the front dining room there is a splendid view of Blois and the Loire.

🍴 **Au Bouchon Lyonnais** – 25 r. des Violettes – ☎02 54 74 12 87 – Closed Jan, Sun and Mon except public holidays – reservation recommended. Located just at the bottom of the hill crowned by the château, this restaurant is a favourite with residents of Blois, who enjoy the rustic decor with exposed beams and stone walls. The menu features regional fare.

🍴 **Au Rendez-vous des Pêcheurs** – 27 r. Foix – ☎02 54 74 67 48 – Closed 2-14 Jan, 29 Jul-20 Aug, Mon lunchtime and Sun – reservation recommended. A provincial-style bistro in the old part of Blois. Stained-glass windows filter the light in the quiet dining room. Fish features prominently among the fresh market produce on the menu.

WHERE TO STAY

🛏 **Hôtel Anne de Bretagne** – 31 av. J.-Laigret – ☎02 54 78 05 38 – Closed 9 Jan-6 Feb – 28 rooms – 🍽 6€. This small family hotel is near the castle and the terraced Jardin du Roi. The rooms are decorated in attractive colours and well soundproofed; those on the third floor are under the sloping roof.

🛏🛏 **Chambre d'hôte La Villa Médicis** – 1 r. St-Denis, Macé – 41000 St-Denis-sur-Loire – 4km/2.5mi NE of Blois on N 152 towards Orléans – ☎02 54 74 46 38 – reservation required in winter – 6 rooms. Marie de Medici came to take the waters at the springs in the park in which this 19C villa was built, as a hotel for spa patrons at the time.

SHOPPING

Rue du Commerce and the adjacent streets in the pleasant pedestrian-only town centre (rue du Rebrousse-Pénil, rue St-Martin) offer all kinds of shos.

SON ET LUMIÈRE

Shows are put on nightly at the château from Easter to the end of Sep, starting at 10pm (10.30pm in Jun-Jul). The Wed show is in English. 7 € (children 3 €). ☎02 54 90 33 32. www.ville-blois.fr -

Alain Decaux of the Académie Française wrote the texts that retrace the history of Blois – "a thousand years' history spanning 10 centuries of splendour" – and they are read by famous French actors including Michael Lonsdale, Fabrice Luchini, Robert Hossein, Pierre Arditi and Henri Virlojeux. Enormous projectors, combining photographs with special lighting effects, and the very latest in sound transmission systems make for a lively, entertaining and visually stimulating show, despite there being no live actors participating in the show.

CHÂTEAU DE **BONAGUIL**★★

MICHELIN MAP 336 I 2
GREEN GUIDE DORDOGNE BERRY LIMOUSIN

This majestic fortress on the border of Périgord Noir (Black Périgord, so-called because of its extensive woods) and Quercy, makes a stunning sight. It exemplifies the state of military architecture of the late 15C and of the 16C.

- **Information:** Place de la Truffière, Puy-l'Eveque. ☎05 65 21 37 63.
- **Orient Yourself:** The château is in the countryside, about a 70km drive west from Cahors.

Visit

🕐 *Open Jun-Aug: daily 10am-6pm; Apr-May: daily 10.30am-1pm, 2.30pm-5.30pm; Sep: daily 10.30am-1pm, 2.30pm-5pm; Feb-Mar: daily 11am-1pm, 2.30pm-5.30pm; Oct: daily 11am-1pm, 2.30-5pm; Nov: Sun, school and public holidays 11am-1pm, 2.30-5pm; Dec: school holidays 2.30-5pm.* 🕐 *Closed Jan, 25 Dec.* 🎫 *4.50€ (7-16 years: 3€).* ☎ *05 53 71 90 33.*

The castle *(illustration – 👁 see Introduction: Art – Architecture)* was enlarged in 1445 around the existing 13C keep, and further extended between 1482 and 1520. It is unusual in that underneath its old-fashioned appearance of a traditional stronghold it is actually remarkably well adapted to the new firearms then coming into use, and thus has loopholes for both cannon and muskets. Furthermore, it was conceived not as an offensive establishment to hold down territory or to threaten a rival, but as a place of refuge, able to withstand any attack, with its firearms used in a purely defensive role. In 1480-1520 this was something new, and anticipated the idea of the fort.

BONIFACIO★★★

MICHELIN MAP 345 D-E 11–POPULATION 2 683

GREEN GUIDE CORSE (IN FRENCH)

Projecting into the sea on Corsica's southern tip, the old town occupies the top of a high wedge of rock with exceptional views, while the harbour and new town at the foot of the cliff is the busy centre of commerce and actiivity.

🚹 **Information:** 2 rue Fred Scaramoni, ☎ 04 95 73 11 88. www.bonifacio.fr.

▶ **Orient Yourself:** From the harbour, steps lead up to Old Town.

A Bit of History

Greek and Roman remains have been found at Bonifacio and there is evidence that the site was occupied in prehistoric times, but the town's history really begins when Bonifacio, Marquis of Tuscany, gave it his name. The strategic position controlling of the Western Mediterranean was appreciated by the Genoese, who succeeded in taking it in 1187.

The town was besieged many times, most notably in 1420 by King Alfonso V of Aragon. Legend has it that his soldiers cut the famous stairway of 187 steps into the cliff-face in the course of a single night.

Visit

Site★★★

Bonifacio is magnificently sited on a long, narrow promontory protecting its "fjord" in the far south of Corsica and it is reached from the rest of the island across a vast, arid plain. The town is divided in two, the **"Marine"**★, the port quarter offering a safe anchorage for warships, fishing boats and pleasure craft, and the Upper Town **(Ville haute**★★**)** overlooking the sea from 60m – 200ft-high cliffs. Its old houses, many of them with four or five storeys, are joined together by what appear to be flying buttresses but are in fact rainwater channels feeding the town's cisterns.

The great loggia of the Church of Ste-Marie-Majeure is built over a cistern with a capacity of 650m3 – about 140 000 gallons; under Genoese rule this is where the affairs of the town were deliberated upon by four elders, who were elected for three months at a time. Twice a week the *podesta*, the mayor, who lived opposite, would mete out justice from here.

Upper town

Excursion

Grotte du Sdragonato★
45min by boat. The dragon's cave is dimly lit by a shaft in the shape of Corsica in reverse. 12km – 7 miles away across the sometimes choppy waters of the Bonifacio Straits (Bouches de Bonifacio) is Sardinia. The trip gives good views of the high limestone cliffs of the promontory and of the King of Aragon's steps.

BORDEAUX★★★

MICHELIN MAP 335 H 5–POPULATION 753 930
GREEN GUIDE FRENCH ATLANTIC COAST

"Take Versailles, add Antwerp, and you have Bordeaux" was Victor Hugo's description of the city, impressed as he was by its 18C grandeur and its splendid tidal river. Bordeaux had, however, played an important role in the affairs of France long before Versailles had been envisioned.

Information: 12 cours du 30-Juillet , ☎ 05 56 00 66 00. www.bordeaux-tourisme.com.

▶ **Orient Yourself:** Bordeaux is on the south bank of the wide River Gironde, about 48km/30mi from the Atlantic.

Guided walks: Jul-Aug, daily at 10am and 3pm; reso of the year, at 10am only. 6.70€. Enquire at the tourist office.

P **Parking:** There are car parks by the river, easily accessible from the ring road.

Don't Miss: The extensive collection of paintings in the Musée des Beaux-Arts.

Kids Especially For Kids: Croiseur Colbert– Take a tour of this anti-aircraft warship which was first launched in 1959 and has been berthed in Port de la Lune since 1993.

Also See: Of course, there are Bordeaux's world-famous wines. Take an excursion to the Bordeaux Vineyards, you won't regret it.

A Bit of History

A large settlement even before the Roman conquest, **Burdigala** (as it was called) was always an important trading port, but frequently attacked and seized by sea-going raiders. From 7C, Good King Dagobert took effective control of the town and its region, creating the Duchy of Aquitaine. In 1152, when **Eleanor of Aquitaine** married Henry Plantagenet, Duke of Normandy, Count of Anjou, ruler of Touraine and Maine, the bride's dowry consisted of practically the whole of southwestern France. Two months later her new husband inherited the English crown, becoming Henry II of England. Bordeaux thus became part of the English kingdom, and so remained for three centuries.

It was the English demand for wine that began the city's tradition of seafaring, and promoted the expansion of the Bordeaux **vineyards**. Even during the Hundred Years War claret continued to flow north to England,

In 1453, Bordeaux and Guyenne (Old English for Aquitaine) were won back for France in the final battle of the Hundred Years War.

The French crown appointed **Intendants** to rebuild and govern Bordeaux as a well-planned city to replace the tangle of medieval streets. In the course of the 18C they succeeded in transforming Bordeaux, giving it the Classical face it wears today, with grandiose set-pieces of urban design: the quaysides, the Place de la Bourse, the great avenues, the Town Hall (Hôtel de Ville), and the Grand Théâtre.

During the French Revolution the Bordeaux *députés* formed the group known as the **Girondins**. Accused of conspiring against the Revolution, twenty-two of them were tried in May 1793 and executed.

In the 18C, goods from the Caribbean added to the huge volume of trade, further stimulating the development of this great port lying 98km – 61 miles inland.

Sights

Vieux Bordeaux

The old town has been undergoing extensive restoration in an effort to return the ancient ochre stonework of its buildings to its original splendour. The 18C buildings scheduled for restoration include those along the **quayside** following the bend of the Garonne for over half a mile.

Grand Théâtre★★

1hr guided tours according to the rehearsal schedule, visitors must book. 5€. Tourist Office.

This theatre, one of the finest in France, has recently been restored. Its architect was Victor Louis (1731-1802), a proponent of the Louis XVI style; here he succeeded in creating a combined theatre and concert hall which recalls Antiquity not only in its sheer scale but also in its restrained use of decoration. A colonnade, one of his favourite devices, runs around the building; in front of the main façade, surmounted by 12 huge statues of muses and goddesses.

The interior too is a triumph, not only because of the great staircase, but also in the auditorium with its pillars, ramps and cantilevered boxes. The design of the balconies, including the type of wood chosen, was carried out with the acoustic quality of this magnificent space in mind.

A. Thuillier/MICHELIN

Fontaine des Girondins

Address Book

For coin ranges, see the Legend on the cover flap.

WHERE TO EAT

La Table du Pain – *6 pl. du Parlement* – ☎*05 56 81 01 00* – A wide selection of sandwiches, toasts and salads is offered at this restaurant with stone walls, old shelves and waxed pine furnishings.

Lou Magret – *62 r. St-Rémi* – ☎*05 56 44 77 94 – Closed 7-21 Jul, Sun and public holidays.* If overwhelmed by the choice of restaurants in this street, try this pleasant establishment whose speciality is canard de Chalosse, duck served grilled or with a delicious sauce. No-frills decor and outdoor terrace.

Bar Cave de la Monnaie – *34 r. Porte-la-Monnaie* – ☎*05 56 31 12 33 – www.latupinalatupina.com – Closed Sun.* This very young wine bar decorated with photos of old Bordeaux bistros has an original flair. Customers choose their dishes first (omelettes or salads), then they help themselves to a glass of Bordeaux from one of four taps in the wall. Affordable prices.

Chez Mémère – *11 r. de la Devise* – ☎*05 56 81 88 20.* Under the vaulted ceiling of this 16C workshop, discover the flavour and ambience of a fine meal chez mémère (at granny's): garbure landaise (soup), agneau de Pauillac, encornets frais aux piments d'Espelette... and, at the end of the week, la sanguette, a sort of black pudding made of poultry blood.

Le Bistro du Musée – *37 pl. Pey-Berland* – ☎*05 56 52 99 69 – Closed 2 weeks Christmas, 3 weeks in Aug and Sun.* This bistro with a pretty green wood entrance makes a promising impression from the start. Thoughtful decor with exposed stone walls, oak parquet, moleskin seats and wine paraphernalia. Southwest cuisine and a fine Bordeaux wine menu.

WHERE TO STAY

Hôtel Acanthe – *12 r. St-Rémi* – ☎*05 56 81 66 58 – www.acanthe-hotel-bordeaux.com -reserv. required – 20 rooms- ⊡ 5.50€.* A central location and very reasonable prices are strong points of this recently renovated hotel. The bright rooms are big enough and well sound-proofed, and the reception is agreeable.

Hôtel Opéra – *35 r. de l'Esprit-des-Lois* – ☎*05 56 81 41 27 – hotel.opera@wanadoo.fr – 27 rooms* – ⊡ 6€. Near the Grand Théâtre et the Allées de Tourny, here's a modest little family hotel. The reception is courteous and the rooms are functional. Those on the street are well sound-proofed. Good value for the euro.

Hôtel Notre-Dame – *36 r. Notre-Dame* – ☎*05 56 52 88 24 – hotelnotre-damefree.fr – 21 rooms* – ⊡ 6€. An unpretentious little family hotel in an 18C house just behind the Quai des Chatrons. Rooms small but well-kept; reasonable prices.

Hôtel Presse – *6 r. de la Porte-Dijeaux* – ☎*05 56 48 53 88 – infohotelde-lapresse.com – 27 rooms* - ⊡ 8€. In the pedestrian shopping quarter of the old city, this is a nice little hotel despite the rather difficult access by automobile. Superb stairway with crimson carpets. Modern, functional, yet cosy rooms.

Hôtel Continental – *10 r. Montesquieu* – ☎*05 56 52 66 00 – continentalhotel-le-ontinental.com – 50 rooms* - ⊡ 7€. In the old city, here's a venerable 18C mansion with a fine staircase in the hall. Breakfast room under a glass roof. Modern rooms with waxed wood furnishings.

SHOWTIME

L'Onyx – *11 r. Fernand-Philippart – Quartier St-Pierre* ☎*05 56 44 26 12 – www.theatreonyx.net – Closed Jul-Sep* – 12.5€. The city's oldest café-theatre, L'Onyx is an essential stop for local culture.

La Boîte à Jouer – *50 r. Lombard* – ☎*05 56 50 37 37 (reserv.) – Performances 8:30pm – Closed Jul-Sep.* This theatre has two small rooms (60 and 45 seats) where lesser regional, national or international troupes specialized in contemporary or musical theatre perform.

Opéra de Bordeaux-Grand théâtre – *Pl. de la Comédie,* ☎*05 56 00 85 95 – www.opera-bordeaux.com .* The Grand Théâtre de Bordeaux is one of the most handsome of France. Symphonies, operas and ballets are performed here under excellent acoustic conditions.

Théâtre Fémina – *20 r. de Grassi* – ☎*05 56 79 06 69*. With 1 100 seats, this handsome edifice sets the stage for plays, comedies, operettas, dance and concerts.

SHOPPING

Librairie Mollat – *15 r. Vital-Carles* – ☎*05 56 56 40 40 – www.mollat.com*. France's first independent bookstore is still a veritable regional institution.

Baillardran Canelés – *Galerie des Grands-Hommes* – ☎*05 56 79 05 89*. Located in the Grands-Hommes market, this boutique makes delicious *canelés*, the small brown Bordelais cakes, irresistibly delicate and caramelised, that take on the shape of the ribbed (canelé) cake tins they're baked in. Crisp outside, they're soft and spongy inside.

Confiserie Cadio-Badie – *26 allées de Tourny* – ☎*05 56 44 24 22 – www. cadiotbadie.com. Closed 2 weeks in Aug, Sun and, public holidays except Christmas and Easter*. You can't help but be charmed by the old-fashioned style of this appealing boutique founded in 1826. Their truffes and Armagnac-flavoured *bouchons bordelais* are worth a special trip.

Chocolaterie Saunion – *56 cours Georges-Clemenceau* – ☎*05 56 48 05 75 – Open Mon 2pm-7:15pm, Tue-Sat 9:30am-12:30pm, 1:30pm-7:15pm. Closed 15-22 Aug, Sun and Mon morning, public holidays except Christmas, New Year and Easter*. One of the most illustrious chocolate confectioners of Bordeaux – a must.

Conseil Interprofessionnel des Vins de Bordeaux – *1 cours du XXX Juillet* – ☎*05 56 00 22 66 – www.vins-bordeaux.fr – Closed weekends and public holidays*. This is where you'll find ample information about Bordeaux wines and vineyards – workshops, tastings. Several different wine cellars are to be found around this centre, including La Vinothèque Bordeaux (8 cours du XXX Juillet), L'Intendant (2 allées de Tourny) and Bordeaux Magnum (3 rue Gobineau).

Darricau – *7 pl. Gambetta* – ☎*05 56 44 21 49 – www.darricau.com – Closed 1 to 15 Aug and public holidays*. Since the turn of the century, this chocolatier pampers the city with the irresistible *pavé Gambetta* (praline with raisins soaked in wine), Bordeaux bottle-shaped chocolates (*confits de sauterne* or *de médoc*), la *cadichonne* (crunchy vanilla) and *niniches* (soft caramel with dark chocolate).

Place du Parlement★

A good example of the urban planning carried out in the reign of Louis XV, the square has a number of houses with groundfloor arcades, transom windows and decorative masks. The harmony and unity of the square is emphasised by the balcony running the whole length of the façades.

Quartier des Chartrons★

This old neighbourhood, behind the quayside devoted to the wine trade and ships' chandlers, became fashionable in the 18C when the city's great families built their town houses here. Some of the streets (Rue Notre-Dame, Cours de la Martinique, Cours Xavier Arnozan) have many fine dwellings with classical façades, attics, wrought-iron balconies (balconsa) and transom windows with entablatures.

Esplanade des Quinconces

The sheer size (about 126 000m2 – 150 700sq yds) of this esplanade is impressive. It was laid out on the site of the old Château de la Trompette during the Restoration (early 19C).

Monument aux Girondins

It consists of a column (50m – 164ft high) topped by Liberty casting off her chains and two bronze fountains (fontainesa) symbolising the Triumph of the Republic (facing the Grand Théâtre) and the Triumph of Concord.

▶▶ **Musée des Beaux-Arts**★★ – ♿
⊙ *Wed-Mon 11am-6pm.* ⊙ *Closed*

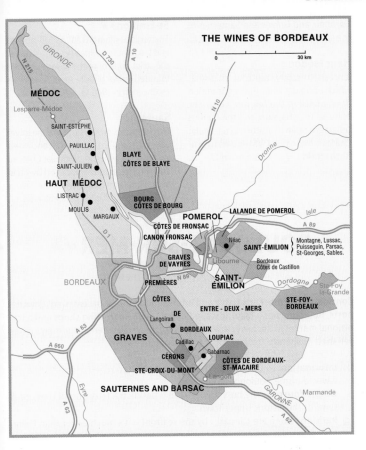

THE WINES OF BORDEAUX

0   30 km

MÉDOC

Lesparre-Médoc

SAINT-ESTÈPHE

PAUILLAC

SAINT-JULIEN

HAUT MÉDOC

LISTRAC

MOULIS

MARGAUX

BLAYE
CÔTES DE BLAYE

BOURG
CÔTES DE BOURG

POMEROL

CÔTES DE FRONSAC

CANON FRONSAC

LALANDE DE POMEROL

Néac

SAINT-ÉMILION   } Montagne, Lussac,
                  Puisseguin, Parsac,
                  St-Georges, Sables.

GRAVES
DE VAYRES

Libourne

Bordeaux
Côtes de Castillon

BORDEAUX

PREMIÈRES

CÔTES

DE

Langoiran

SAINT-
ÉMILION

ENTRE - DEUX - MERS

Ste-Foy
la-Grande

STE-FOY-
BORDEAUX

GRAVES

BORDEAUX

Cadillac

LOUPIAC

CÉRONS

Gabarnac

CÔTES DE BORDEAUX-
ST-MACAIRE

STE-CROIX-DU-MONT

Langon

SAUTERNES AND BARSAC

Marmande

Tue and public holidays. ⌾ 4€ (temporary exhibit: 5.50€), no charge 1st
Sunday in the month. ☎05 56 10 25
25. **Cathédrale St-André★**. **Basilique St-Michel★** ⌚ ⌯ Daily
guided tours 1st and 2nd Sun in the
month 3-5pm. ☎05 56 94 30 50. **Place
de la Bourse★★**. Église Ste-Croix –
façade★. **Musée d'Aquitaine★★** –
& ⌚ Tue-Sun 11am-6pm. ⌚ Closed
Mon and public holidays. ⌾ 6€, no
charge 1st Sunday in the month. ☎05
56 01 51 00. www.mairie-bordeaux.
fr. **Musée d'Art Contemporain★**
– & ⌚ Tue, Thu-Sun 11am-6pm, Wed
11am-8pm. ⌚ Closed Mon and public holidays. ⌾ 5.50 €, no charge 1st
Sunday in the month. ☎05 56 00 81
50 – **Entrepôt Lainé★★**. **Croiseur
Colbert★** – a post-WWII cruiser. 🄺🄸🄳🅂
⌚ Jul-Aug: daily 10am-8pm; Jun:
daily 10am-7pm; Apr-May and Sep:
Mon-Fri 10am-6pm, Sat-Sun, public

and school holidays 10am 7pm; Oct-
Mar and zone C school holidays: Wed,
Sat-Sun and school holidays: 10am-
6pm. Last admission 1hr before closing. ⌚Closed 1 Jan, 25 Dec. ⌾ 7.50€.
☎05 56 44 96 11.

Excursions

The Bordeaux Vineyards★

The Bordeaux wine region which
extends over approximately 135 000
hectares – 333 585 acres in the Gironde
département is the largest vineyard producing quality wines in the world.
The areas to the north produce red
wines: Médoc on the west bank of the
Gironde with Bourg on the east bank,
and St-Émilion and Pomerol north of
the Dordogne. The remaining area is
devoted to white wines: Entre-Deux-
Mers between the Dordogne and the

Garonne, and Graves and Sauternes to the south.

Haut Médoc

It boasts the most prestigious "châteaux" which uphold a wine-making tradition dating back to the reign of Louis XIV. Some of the châteaux and the famous cellars are open to visitors, in particular Château Margaux, **Château Mouton-Rothschild**★ and Château Lafite.

St-Émilion★★

The region is famous for its full-bodied and fragrant red wines produced under the strict control of the Jurade, a guild founded in the Middle Ages which was reconvened in 1948. *See ST-ÉMILION.*

Sauternes

The vineyards on the slopes of the lower valley of the Ciron produce renowned sweet white wines, in particular Château Yquem. The grapes are picked by hand at the "noble rot" stage when the flavour and richness is highly concentrated.

BOULOGNE-SUR-MER★★

MICHELIN MAP 301 C 3–POPULATION 135 120

GREEN GUIDE NORTHERN FRANCE AND THE PARIS REGION

Considered the most attractive and interesting of the 'short crossing' Channel ports, Boulogne has a historic walled upper town, interesting shops and a traditional market in the lower town and a busy quayside where fishermen's wives sell their husbands' fresh catch at traditional tiled stalls.

- ⓘ **Information:** 24 Quai Gambette, ☎03 21 10 88 10. www.tourisme-boulognesurmer.com.
- ▶ **Orient Yourself:** The busy town centre is beside the ferry port. It runs uphill towards the historic Upper Town.
- Ⓟ **Parking:** There are car parks by the seafront – it's much easier than trying to park in town.
- ☺ **Don't Miss:** The quiet streets of Ville Haute within its ring of sturdy ramparts.
- 🄺🄸🄳🅂 **Especially For Kids:** Nausicaa is certainly not only for kids – but they'll love it.

A Bit of History

Boulogne's location along the chalk cliffs facing the English coast made it a cross-Channel port at an early date. It was from here that Emperor Claudius set sail to conquer Britain; he even established regular boat services to Dover and built an enormous 12-storey landmark tower 200 Roman feet high which stood until the 16C.

Fishing has long been the town's principal activity, the ship-owners' guild being regulated as early as 1203. Today's fleet ties up alongside the Quai Gambetta, its catch of fresh fish the largest in continental Europe.

Sights

Nausicaa★★★

🄺🄸🄳🅂 *Blvd Ste-Beuve, beside the beach. Sep-Jun: daily 9.30am-6.30pm (Jul and Aug: 8pm). Last admission 1hr before closing. Closed first 3 weeks in Jan, 25 Dec (morning). 16.50€ (children: 10.80€). ☎03 21 30 99 99. www.nausicaa.fr*
Designated as the national sea life centre, Nausicaa is an extraordinary complex both educational and entertaining, with many serious elements, yet also with amusements such as highly trained sea lions. Also within the centre, a cinema, shops, restaurants and bar.

Ville haute★★

The upper town, Boulogne's historic district built on the site of the Roman fortress, is still surrounded by its 13C ramparts, which has a walkway on top with fine views.

▶ **Colonne de la Grande Armée**★★
3km/ 2mi north 🕐 *Summer: daily except Mon and Tue: 10am-12.30pm, 2.30-6.30pm; Winter: 10am-noon, 2-4pm. Closed the rest of the year.* – This monument commemorates the army assembled here by Napoleon in 1803 for the invasion of England.

Basilique Notre-Dame – **dome**★, **crypt**★ 🕐 *Tue-Sun 2-5pm* 🚫 *2€;* (☎ *03 21 99 75 98*) and **treasury**. **Château-Musée**★ 🕐 *Daily 10am-noon, 2-5pm (Sun and public holidays 5.30pm).* ☎*03 21 10 02 20.*

Excursion

Côte d'Opale★ – 🔓 *See CALAIS: Excursions.*

BOURG-EN-BRESSE★★

MICHELIN MAP 328 C-D-E 3-4–POPULATION 40 972

GREEN GUIDE BURGUNDY JURA

Bourg is the capital of the Bresse area, famous in France for its high-quality poultry, which bears its own label of authentification.

🛈 **Information:** Centre Albert Camus, 6 ave. Alsace Lorraine, ☎04 74 22 49 40. www.bourg-en-bresse.org.
▶ **Orient Yourself:** The main attraction is the church at Brou, about 2km/1mi SE of the town centre.

A Bit of History

"Fortune infortune fort une" – The sad motto of **Margaret of Austria** (1480-1530) can be translated (less poetically) as "Fate very hard on one woman." As a child of two, Margaret lost her mother, Mary of Burgundy. At three, she was chosen by Louis XI as the wife of the Dauphin Charles VIII because of her Burgundian inheritance; a form of wedding took place. Then, at the age of 11, she was repudiated by the Crown and the marriage annulled. At the age of 21 she married John of Castile who died after less than a year. At 24 she re-married, this time to Philibert le Beau. He too soon died. From then on Margaret's life was devoted to prayer and to quietly caring for the domains she had inherited. Her rule was marked by diplomacy, prudence and wisdom. As a result, in 1508 her father, the Emperor Maximilian, made her Regent of the Low Countries. Margaret, still only 26 years old, moved to Brussels, but also set about transforming the humble priory of Brou into a monastery, partly to fulfill a vow made 24 years earlier by her mother-in-law, Margaret of Bourbon, partly to symbolise her love for her husband.

Margaret of Austria, stained-glass window in Brou Church

Ph.Gajic/MICHELIN

Sight

Églis de Brou★★

🕐 Apr-Sep: daily 9am-12.30pm, 2-6pm; mid-Jun to mid-Sep: daily 9am-6pm; Oct-Mar: daily 9am-noon, 2-5pm. 🕐 Closed 1 Jan, 1 May, 1 and 11 Nov, 25 Dec. 🕾 6.10€ (combined ticket includes a visit to the museum and the cloister) ⚞ Guided tours available. ☎04 74 22 83 83.

The church – now deconsecrated – was built from 1513-32 in exuberant Flaboyant Gothic style. The work was undertaken by a Flemish master builder and a team of artists and craftsmen, mostly from Flanders, where Margeret was now living. The interior decoration was already much influenced by the Renaissance. In the elegant nave built of pale stone from the Jura, a finely sculptured balustrade was substituted for the more usual triforium. The stone rood screen (jubé★★) has three basket-handle arches and is profusely decorated with leaves, cable-moulding and scrolls.

The 74 choir stalls (stalles★★) were built by local carpenters. An array of statuettes represents Biblical figures. In the Margaret of Austria chapel (Oratoire★★★) an altarpiece is a masterwork of amazing craftsmanship. There are also superb stained-glass windows (vitraux★★). The three tombs (tombeaux★★★) give the church its truly regal character. On the right is that of Margaret of Bourbon, in a Gothic niche with Flamboyant decoration. Philibert the Fair's elaborate tomb is completely Renaissance in character. Margaret of Austria's tomb forms part of the parclose screen; she is first shown lying in state on a black marble slab, then, underneath, in her shroud. Its richly carved canopy incorporates her motto.

🕐🕐 **Musée★** (in the monastery) – 🕐 Apr-Sep: daily 9am-12.30pm, 2-6pm; Jun to mid-Sep: daily 9am-6pm; Oct-Mar: daily 9am-noon, 2-5pm. 🕐 Closed 1 Jan, 1 May, 1 and 11 Nov, 25 Dec. 🕾 6.10€. ☎04 74 22 83 83.– painting, sculpture, decorative arts.

BOURGES★★★

MICHELIN MAP 323 K 4-6–POPULATION 94 731
GREEN GUIDE DORDOGNE BERRY LIMOUSIN

The centre of Bourges is a majestic ensemble of dignified medieval buildings, dominated by the magnificent cathedral, a striking symbol of the town's rich past.

🛈 **Information:** 21 r. Victor Hugo, ☎02 48 23 02 60. www.bourges-tourisme.com.
▸ **Orient Yourself:** A 45min ride on the P'tit train touristique gives you a good look at the city's history and architecture. (🕐 Apr to mid-Nov: daily, train leaves every 15min in front of the Tourist Office). There are also 2hr guided tours offered by the tourist office, 5.50€.

A Bit of History

Bourges was already a place of some importance at the time of the conquest of Gaul; in 52 BC it was sacked by Julius Caesar, who is supposed to have massacred 40 000 of its inhabitants. In the 4C the city became the capital of the Roman province of Avaricum. Its significance increased over the years, but only at the end of the 14C did it take on a national role, under Jean de Berry. He made Bourges a centre of the arts to rival Dijon and Avignon, commissioning works like the Très Riches Heures, perhaps the most exquisite miniatures ever painted.

Address Book

For coin ranges, see the Legend on the cover flap.

WHERE TO EAT

🍽 **Le Bourbonnoux** – *44 r. Bourbonnoux* – ☎02 48 24 14 76 – *restaurant. bourbonnoux@wanadoo.fr – Closed 11-21 Feb, 16-26 Apr, 16 Aug-3 Sep, Sun eve Nov-Jun, Sat lunchtime and Fri.* The restaurant is in a street lined with craft shops, just a few steps away from St-Étienne Cathedral. The welcome is warm and the dining room is pleasantly decorated with bright colours and exposed beams. Popular with locals.

🍽 **Le Bistro Gourmand** – *5 pl. de la Barre* – ☎02 48 70 63 37 – *reservation recommended.* A delightful bistro specialising in regional and Lyonnais cuisine. The sober decor here is enhanced by gentle candlelight. The terrace looks onto the Église Notre-Dame.

🍽 **La Table Savoyarde** – *14 r. Florentin-Labbé* – ☎02 48 24 57 94 – *Closed first 3 weeks in Aug, Sun lunchtime and Mon.* As the name suggests, the focus here is on the cuisine of Savoy, with a menu that includes cheese fondues, *raclettes, tartiflettes* etc. Wooden skis, clogs, cow bells and other typically Savoyard objects adorn the cool stone vaults of this former coal cellar.

🍽 **La Courcillière** – *R. de Babylone* – ☎02 48 24 41 91 – *Closed Wed, Sun eve and Tue eve.* Located in the Les Marais district just a stone's throw from the city centre, this pleasant, rustic restaurant has a terrace by the water facing the gardens. Down-to-earth and reasonably priced cuisine.

🍽 **D'Antan Sancerrois** – *50 r. Bourbounnoux* – ☎02 48 65 96 26 – *Closed 1 Jan, 1-20 Aug, 25 Dec, Sun and Mon.* This pretty bistro used to be home to a 15C alderman who kept company with the Duchesse de Berry. The handsome rustic decor features an amusing collection of porcelain tureen lids. Traditional fare and good service.

WHERE TO STAY

🛏 **Chambre d'hôte Château de Bel Air** – *Lieu-dit le Grand-Chemin – 18340 Arcay – 16km/10mi S of Bourges on the D 73* – ☎02 48 25 36 72 – *6 rooms.* Surrounded by spacious grounds, this 19C château is both calm and comfortable. The vast entrance hall leads to the dining room with its massive fireplace. Large rooms on the upper floor. Mountain bikes available for rent.

🛏 **Hôtel Christina** – *5 r. Halle* – ☎02 48 70 56 50 – *info@le-christina.com – 71 rooms.* This hotel is the perfect base for discovering the city centre. Two categories of well-maintained bedrooms are available: cosy and chic, or smaller and functional.

🛏 **Hôtel Les Tilleuls** – *7 pl. Pyrotechnie* – ☎02 48 20 49 04 – *lestilleuls. bourges@wanadoo.fr – 39 rooms.* Situated in a quiet part of town, this hotel offers guests accommodation in the main building and an annex, where the rooms are less spacious, more basic, but with the benefit of air-conditioning. Children's play area in the garden. Solarium.

🛏 **Best Western Hôtel d'Angleterre** – *1 pl. des Quatre-Piliers* – ☎02 48 24 68 51. *30 rooms.* The city's former court of justice is located close to the Palais Jacques-Cœur. All necessary creature comforts in the bedrooms (most with air-conditioning), where the decor is sober yet modern. Buffet breakfast. Friendly staff.

BARS AND CAFÉS

Pub des Jacobins – *Enclos des Jacobins* – ☎02 48 24 61 78 – *Open Mon-Sat, 4pm-3am. Closed Sun.* This piano-bar is whole-heartedly devoted to jazz, as demonstrated by the photos of musicians covering the walls. Top-quality concerts are held here once a month. The pub specialises in cocktails.

Pub Jacques Cœur – *1 r. d'Auron* – ☎02 48 70 72 88 – This 16C half-timbered residence, now a pub, was built on the site where Jacques Cœur, a wealthy and influential 15C merchant and councillor to King Charles VII, was born. Sloping and lopsided, this antique building is the most photographed of Bourges. Concerts are frequently held here.

ENTERTAINMENT

Maison de la Culture de Bourges – *Pl. André-Malraux* – ☎02 48 67 74

70 – www.mcbourges.com – Closed 13 Jul-20 Aug and 1 May. Opened by André Malraux, then Minister of Culture, this was the first Maison de la Culture in France. This lively and popular venue hosts plays, dance performances and classical music and jazz concerts. Cinema and café.

Les Nuits Lumières de Bourges – ☎02 48 23 02 60 – ⏱ Every evening in Jul-Aug and during the Printemps de Bourges festival; May-Jun and Sep: Thu-Sat. No charge. A walk through the historic city centre at night to view illuminated buildings (2hr 30min). Blue lanterns mark the way.

LEISURE ACTIVITIES

Base de Voile du Val-d'Auron – 23 chemin Grand Mazières – ☎02 48 20 07 65. Open 9am-noon and 2-6pm. Closed Oct-Apr and Mon. This watersports centre at the Val d'Auron Lake covering 85 ha/210 acres offers a range of activities, including swimming, canoeing, fishing and rowing.

SHOPPING

The main shopping area is in the pedestrianised area that includes rue Coursarlor and rue Mirebeau (near the palais Jacques-Cœur), and rue Bourbonnoux and rue Moyenne (near the cathedral).

Markets – Every Saturday morning, the listed Halle au Blé comes to life with 200 stallholders selling all types of food. A permanent daily market is also held at the Halle St-Bonnet, selling fresh seasonal produce, local cheeses and other regional specialities. On Sunday mornings, stalls selling bric-a-brac, inexpensive clothes etc add to the charm of this popular market.

La Maison des Forestines – 3 pl. Cujas – ☎02 48 24 00 24 – mdforestines@ wanadoo.fr – This chocolate/confectionery business founded in 1825 occupies an attractive Haussmann-style building. The shop, with its coffered ceiling and superb Gien china, produces irresistible house specialities such as the Forestine, a chocolate praline with a satiny sugar coating created in 1879, the Amandine and Noisette (created in 1885) and the Richelieu, a nougatine filled with an almond and pistachio creme, created in 1890.

Domaine de Coquin – ☎02 48 64 84 51 – Open Mon-Fri, 8am-7pm, Sun and public hols, 9am-noon. Francis Audiot is a wine-producer whose family has been producing excellent white wines for the past 150 years.

Épicerie du Berry – 41 r. Moyenne (îlot Victor-Hugo) – ☎02 48 70 02 38. This small boutique at the foot of the cathedral only sells regional products such as sablés de Nançais (a type of shortcake biscuit), pasta from La Chapelle de St-Ursin, tortillons (goat's cheese pastries) and Monin syrups.

Visit

Cathédrale St-Étienne★★★

☜☜ 45min guided tours: Jul-Aug: 9.45am, 11am, 12.15pm, 2.15pm, 3.15pm, 3.45pm, 4.15pm, 5pm and 5.45pm; May-Jun: 10am, 11.15am, 2.30pm, 3.45pm, 5pm; Apr-Sep: 10.15, 11.15pm, 2.30pm, 3.45pm, 5pm; Oct-Mar: 10am, 11.15pm, 2.30pm, 3.30pm, 4.30pm. ⏱ Closed 1 Jan, 1 May, 1 and 11 Nov, 25 Dec. ☜ 6.10€ (under 18 years: no charge), crypt and North tower. 8.50€ combined ticket with Palais Jacques-Cœur. ☎02 48 65 49 44.

In the 12C, Bourges was the seat of an archbishopric linked by tradition to the royal territories to the north, whereas the regions to the southwest came under the sphere of influence of the Angevin kingdom. The great new cathedrals of the Ile-de-France were taking shape, and the Archbishop, Henri de Sully, Primate of Aquitaine, dreamed of a similar great edifice for his city.

In drawing up his plans, the anonymous architect exploited all the new techniques of the Gothic in order to control and direct the thrusts exerted by and on his great structure. Other innovations of his included leaving out the transepts, retaining six sexpartite bays and incorporating the Romanesque portals of the old cathedral into the north and south doorways of the new building.

By 1200 the crypt was completed, by 1215, the choir. In 1220 the great nave with its splendid row of two-tiered flying buttresses was ready. Over-enthusiastic restoration at the start of the 19C included the remodelling of the external gables and the unfortunate addition of round windows, balustrades and pinnacles.

The huge west front has five doorways, anticipating the nave and four aisles adorned with the radiating motifs of the High Gothic (mid 13C-14C) style; they were begun in 1230. Ten years later the two right-hand portals were in place. By 1250, the central portal (Last Judgement) had been finished. But 60 years later, subsidence made it necessary to prop up the South Tower by means of a massive pillar-buttress and to strengthen the west front. This was to no avail; on 31 December 1506, the north tower fell in ruins. Guillaume Pellevoysin, the new architect, worked for 30 years on its replacement and on the construction of the two left-hand portals; he included many architectural and decorative features of the Early Renaissance.

The east end (**chevet**) has the Gothic windows of the lower church inserted between the base of the chapels and the buttresses. Three-sided chapels radiate out from the outer ambulatory, while the inner ambulatory is spanned by the first tier of the double flying buttresses; the upper spans pierce the structure to hold the vault of the choir in place. The Lanceolate Gothic style here reaches a high point in its development.

Inside, the nave and four aisles (**nefs**), completed in 1270, make a striking impression by virtue of their great height and the light filtering through the stained glass. The outer aisles, lined by chapels, are already 9m – 30ft from floor to vault, the inner aisles, with a blind triforium, reach 21m – 70ft, while the nave rises to a full 37.15m – 122ft. With no gallery, and limited by the great size of its arches it is covered by a sexpartite vault; the alternating sequence of major and minor piers is cunningly disguised by the shafts wrapped around the columns. This rare arrangement was to be repeated soon afterwards in the choir at Le Mans. Beneath the choir a crypt (**crypte**★★) of the same layout takes up a 6m – 20ft change in level of the ground. A fine example of a 13C crypt, it has an outer ambulatory with trian-

East end of Bourges Cathedral

gular vaulting and arcades mounted on twisted diagonal arches to allow the keystones to be set properly.

The stained glass (**vitraux**★★★) – some of the finest in the whole of France – demonstrates the whole evolution of the art of glass-making between the 12C and 17C. The 13C windows in the choir recall the techniques of the master glass-makers of Chartres. The great nave is illuminated by light streaming in through all its windows, from the lowest (in the side chapels), from the double windows in the inner aisles, and from the highest, which reach almost to the vaults of the central nave itself.

Palais Jacques Cœur★★

1hr guided tours: Jul and Aug: 9.30am-7pm; May-Jun: 9.30am-12.15pm, 2-6.15pm; Sep-Apr: 10am -12.15pm, 2-5.15pm. ○ *Closed 1 Jan, 1 May, 1 and 11 Nov, 25 Dec.* ⊜ *6.10€ (under 17 years: no charge)* ☎*02 48 24 79 41.*

The son of a Bourges fur-trader, Jacques Cœur (1395-1456) started out as a goldsmith, first at the court of Jean de Berry, then with Charles VII. He soon became aware of the economic recovery just beginning and of the opportunities opening up in the Mediterranean. Before long he had many commercial interests and he supplied the royal court with luxury goods and became the king's Minister of Finance. At the peak of his career at the age of 50 he decided to build himself a worthy residence.

His palace, begun in 1445, was completed in the short space of 10 years. It shows how the will to build had revived after the stagnation due to war and also demonstrates the success of the Flamboyant Gothic style. It is a sumptuous building, incorporating certain pioneering comforts like a bath-house and an arcaded courtyard. Other innovations it contributed to the evolution of late-medieval domestic architecture included the provision of a large number of rooms with independent access, sculptures indicating the purpose of the rooms served by the various staircases, and, in the chapel, two oratories reserved for the proprietor and his wife.

▶ **Hôtel Cujas★** (Berry Provincial Museum) *Jan-Mar: Mon, Wed-Sat 10am-noon, 2-5pm, Sun. 2-5pm; Apr-Jun and Sep-Dec: Mon, Wed-Sat 10-noon, 2-6pm, Sun 2-6pm; Jul and Aug: Mon, Wed-Sat 10am-12.30pm, 1.30-6pm, Sun 1.30-6.30pm. Closed Tue, 1 Jan, 1 May, 1 and 11 Nov, 25 Dec. No charge.* ☎02 48 57 81 15. **Hôtel Lallemant★** *Jan-Mar: Tue-Sat 10am-noon, 2-5pm, Sun 2-5pm; Apr-Jun and Sep-Dec: Tue-Sat 10-noon, 2-6pm, Sun 2-6pm; Jul and Aug: Tue-Sat 10am-12.30pm, 1.30-6pm, Sun 1.30-6.30pm. Closed Mon, 1 Jan, 1 May, 1 and 11 Nov, 25 Dec. No charge.* ☎02 48 57 81 17 – decorative arts. Hotel des Échevins (Musée Maurice-Estève★). Jardin des Prés-Fichaux★.

LAC DU **BOURGET**★★

MICHELIN MAP 333 H-I 3-4
GREEN GUIDE FRENCH ALPS

Enclosed within an impressive mountain setting, this is France's largest (4 500ha – 11 000 acres), deepest (145m/476ft) and most celebrated lake, lying in a glaciated valley between the Jura and the Alps. On its shore is the elegant spa town, Aix-les-Bains.

▣ **Information:** Place Maurice Mollard, Aix-les-Bains, ☎04 79 88 68 00. www.aixlesbains.com

▶ **Orient Yourself:** The ideal base for a tour of the lake is Aix-les-Bains, a famous resort with lively streets, opulent hotels near the spa baths, and an attractive lake shore.

A Bit of History

The lake and its banks form a rich and unusual habitat for wildlife. In its waters live pollans, migratory members of the salmon family, together with crayfish, originally imported a century ago from New England. Its varied birdlife includes 300 cormorants which winter on the west bank at La grande Cale. The poet Lamartine (1790-1867) wrote movingly about the beauty of the lake, and of Mme Lulie Charles Julie whom he met here in October 1816. The popular spa Aix-les-Bains is one of the best-equipped resorts in the Alps, and has been known for its health-giving waters for over 2000 years. Queen Victoria visited three times.

Visit

Abbaye royale de Hautecombe★★

Jutting into the lake, the abbey houses the tombs of 42 princely members of the House of Savoy. The abbey's little harbour has an unusual 12C building (**grange batelière**) with covered moorings, allowing goods to be unloaded and stored under the same roof.

▶ **Tour du lac★★** (Lakeside road).

BRANTÔME★★

MICHELIN MAP 329 E 3–POPULATION 2 080
GREEN GUIDE DORDOGNE BERRY LIMOUSIN

Brantôme lies in the midst of lush, smiling countryside, in the charming Vallée de la Dronne, north of the town of Périgueux. Its old abbey and picturesque setting make it one of the most delightful little places in Périgord.

Information: Abbaye de Brantôme, ☎05 53 05 80 52. www.ville-brantome.fr.

▶ **Orient Yourself:** A boat trip on the river is the perfect way to appreciate the town and its setting.

Guided Tour: Enjoy a one-hour tour of the abbey and its bell-tower. Mid-Jun to mid-Sep, daily except Tue. ☞ 6€. ☎05 53 05 80 63.

A Bit of History

Pierre de Bourdeilles (1540-1614) was commendatory abbot here. In 1589 he retired to the abbey after a fall from a horse, having also fallen from favour at court as the Bourbons replaced the Valois. Under the nom-de-plume of Brantôme, this former courtier and soldier of fortune amused himself with his memoirs, published posthumously as the *Lives (les Vies) of Illustrious Ladies, Illustrious Men, Great Leaders, and of Gallant Ladies*. These lively tales of licentious exploits have many piquant portraits penned by a chronicler whose own days of merry-making were sadly over.

Visit

This riverside village has old dwellings with slate roofs built like manor houses, a crooked bridge seen across the tranquil surface of the water, and great trees growing on the lawns of its lovely gardens. The 18C abbey has a fine west front and a Romanesque **bell-tower★★**.

East bank of the River Dronne

J.P Clapham/MICHELIN

CHÂTEAU DE LA **BRÈDE**★

MICHELIN MAP 335 H 6
GREEN GUIDE FRENCH ATLANTIC COAST

In the peaceful countryside of the Graves area along the Garonne River, this **château**, protected by its moat, still keeps its aristocratic 15C appearance. It was the birthplace of **Charles Montesquieu** (1689-1755), Baron de la Brède, a magistrate of Bordeaux.

- **Information:** ☎05 56 20 20 49. www.chateaulabrede.com.
- ▶ **Orient Yourself:** The castle lies south of Bordeaux.

A Bit of History

Montesquieu, a country gentleman, wrote extensively (*Persian Letters* – 1724) and travelled widely, notably to England, where he spent two decisive years (1729-31), returning with that somewhat idealised notion of English constitutionalism prevalent among French political thinkers of the 18C. Twenty years of hard writing led to the publication in 1748 of his *L'Esprit des lois* (The Nature of Laws), in which he expanded the theory of the separation of legislative, executive and judicial powers, sole guarantee of the citizen's liberty. Its 31 volumes are hardly read today but with them, political writings entered the mainstream of French literary history.

Visit

🦽 🕐 *Guided tours* ••• *(30min) Jul-Sep: daily except Tue 2-6.30pm; Easter to end Jun: Sat-Sun and public holidays 2-6pm; Oct to mid-Nov: Sat-Sun and public holidays 2-5.30pm.* ☞ 7€.

In the château, the bedroom **(chambre)** with its original furnishings and library **(bibliothèque)** comprising some 7 000 volumes help to evoke the life and work of this sympathetic figure.

BREST★

MICHELIN MAP 308 A 4, E 4-5–POPULATION 149 630
GREEN GUIDE BRITTANY

A very ancient port built on a magificent natural roadstead that, being nowhere less than 10m/33ft deep, is almost an inland sea, Brest remains wedded to its maritime tradition.

- **Information:** Place de la Liberté, ☎02 98 44 24 96. www.brest-metropole-tourisme.fr
- ▶ **Orient Yourself:** The town is 71km/42mi north of Quimper.
- **Especially for Kids:** One of the town's principal attractions is the giant Oceanopolis centre.

A Bit of History

Although used as a port by Gauls and then Romans, the importance of Brest was firmly established from 13C onwards. A French garrison moved in and has been there ever since. At the beginning of the 17C, Richelieu's wish was to have French naval forces which could be permanently ready for action. He founded the naval dockyard and its first warship was launched in 1634. The Rue de Siam, running in a straight line between the arsenal and Place de la Liberté, formed the main axis of the ancient town and its fame was spread worldwide by the sailors who frequented it. The town had to be completely rebuilt after the Second World War in which it suffered four years of air attack and a 43-day siege.

Sights

Oceanopolis★★★
Kids ⏱ *Apr-Sep: daily 9am-6pm (7pm at peak times); Sep -Mar: Tue-Sat 10am-5pm, Sun, public holidays, and school holidays 10am-6pm.* ⏱ *Closed Mon except in school holidays.* 🎟 *15€ (children 4-17 years: 10.50€).* ♿ ☎ *02 98 34 40 40. www.oceanopolis.com.*
In this ultra-modern building, shaped like a giant crab, visitors discover the marine life of Brittany's coastal waters in the saltwater aquariums (downstairs), and the many sea birds of the coast in their nesting places on the cliff face (entrance level).

Cours Dajot★
This fine promenade was laid out in 1769 on the old ramparts. It gives splendid **views**★★ of the activity of the port and of the great roadstead of 150km² – 58sq mi.

Musée des Beaux Arts★
⏱ *Mon, Wed-Sat 10-noon, 2-6pm, Sun. 2-6pm.* ⏱ *Closed Tue and public holidays (except 14 Jul and 15 Aug.* 🎟 *4€.* ☎ *02 98 00 87 96.*
The collections illustrate the advances made by the painters of the Pont-Aven School, for example *Yellow Sea (Mer jaune)* by Lacombe, as well as a curious study of the town of Ys (⏱ *see QUIMPER*), Manet's *Parrots*, and *Bouquet of Roses* by Suzanne Valadon.

Excursions

Calvaire de Plougastel-Daoulas★★
11km – 7 mi east, south of the church. The calvary was built from 1602 to 1604 by the Priget brothers to mark an outbreak of plague four years earlier. Its 180 fig-

Christ washing the disciples' feet, the Calvary, Plougastel-Daoulas

MICHELIN

ures are sculpted in the round; a certain stiffness of posture is set off by the size of the heads and the vigorous expressions. The 28 scenes illustrate the life of Christ (the Nativity, the Washing of Feet) and above all the Passion (Arrest and Scourging) and the Resurrection.

The Abers★
The term *aber* is of Celtic origin and is found in Scottish and Welsh place names such as Aberdeen, Aberdour, Aberystwyth, Abersoch. In Brittany *abers* are picturesque, fairly shallow estuaries on the low, rocky northwest coast of Finistère. Harbours are suitable only for yachts and other sailing craft.
The entrance to the **aber Wrac'h** is guarded by the small seaside resort of the same name near which there are fine views of the lighthouse on Vierge Island, the tallest in France (82.5m – 270ft). A **scenic road**★ runs along the rugged coastline through a number of charming resorts.

BRIANÇON★★

MICHELIN MAP 334 H 3–POPULATION 10 740

GREEN GUIDE FRENCH ALPS

The highest town in Europe (1 321m – 4 334ft), Briançon is best viewed from the terraces of the fortress (**citadelle**) where stands the 9m – 30ft-high statue of **France**★ sculpted by **Antoine Bourdelle**.

- ▮ **Information:** 1 pl. du Temple, ☏04 92 21 08 50. www.briancon.com.
- ▶ **Orient Yourself:** After arriving at the town, follow signs to 'Briançon Vauban' to find the old town.

A Bit of History

Since ancient times, two great routes into Italy have met here, one coming from the Romanche valley via the Col de Lautaret, the other following the Durance up from Embrun. The strategic value of the site was appreciated by the Gauls. It seems likely that the survivors of the Germanic tribes routed by the Roman general Marius outside Aix-en-Provence found their way here, and Briançon may have provided a refuge too for some of the persecuted members of the Vaudois, a 15C sect. The town played an important commercial and military role, the latter enhanced by the presence of great rock bars lending themselves naturally to fortification. The forts (Dauphin, Sallettes, les Trois-Têtes, Anjou, Randouillet) built by Vauban in the 17C proved their effectiveness in the year of Waterloo, when General Eberlé's triumphant resistance here held off the invading Austro-Sardinians for three months.

Sight

Ville haute ★★(Upper Town)

In January 1692, the War of the League of Augsburg had been raging for six years; mercenaries in the pay of Vittorio-Amadeo II, Duke of Savoy, invaded the Dauphiné and put Briançon to the torch – only two houses out of 258 escaped the conflagration. Vauban was working in Burgundy, but was immediately dispatched by Louis XIV to Briançon (which he knew already) with a brief to rebuild the town and make it impregnable. A week sufficed for the great engineer to draw up his plans, but age and ill health made it impossible for him to supervise their execution, and he was to deplore a number of modifications and compromises made to his project.

With its gate (Porte Pignerol) and its fortified church, Briançon-Vauban, in contrast to the lower town Briançon-Ste-Catherine, still has the look of a frontier town of Louis XIV's reign, while its narrow, steeply-sloping streets, especially the **Grande Gargouille**★ (also known as the Grande Rue), express the drama of its precipitous site.

- ▶ **Pont d'Asfeld**★. **Fort des Salettes**★. **Prorel**★★ ⏱ Jul-Aug: (25min, continuous) 9.45am-5.30pm. ⌗ 9€ round trip (pedestrian). ☏04 92 25 55 00.

Briançon: The Porte d'Embrun

BRIARE

MICHELIN MAP 318 N 6–POPULATION 6 070
GREEN GUIDE BURGUNDY JURA

Briare is a busy town on the banks of the Loire, known for its ceramic floor mosaics and its stoneware.

- **Information:** Place de la Liberté, ☎02 98 44 24 96. www.brest-metropole-tourisme.fr
- ▶ **Orient Yourself:** The Briare canal lies SE of Orleans and north of Bourges.

Sight

Pont-Canal★

The Loire was used by river traffic from the 14C to the 19C, but the navigation companies found it difficult to cope with the river's irregular flow on the one hand, and shallowness on the other. To rectify this, and as part of his policy of economic unification, Henri IV began building the Briare Canal in 1604; completed in 1642, it linked the basins of the Loire and the Seine via its junction with the River Loing at Montargis. It was the first connecting canal in Europe.

The Loire Lateral Canal (1822-38) extends it south to Digoin. It crosses the Loire at Briare on an aqueduct built 1890-94 (58 years after those at Le Guétin and Digoin). The channel is the longest in the world (662.68m – 2 174ft 2in). It rests on 15 granite piers designed by G Eiffel; their loading is constant, irrespective of the presence of barges or the weight of their cargo, a nice illustration of Archimedes' principle.

BRIOUDE ★

MICHELIN MAP 331 C 2–POPULATION 6 820
GREEN GUIDE AUVERGNE RHÔNE VALLEY

Brioude is a bustling market town overlooking the lush plain of the River Allier.

- **Information:** Pl. Lafayette, ☎04 71 74 97 49. www.ot-brioude.fr .
- ▶ **Orient Yourself:** The town is mid-way along the road from Clermont-Ferrand to Le Puy en Velay.

Sight

Basilique St-Julien★★

This vast Romanesque church was built at the spot where, according to tradition, Julian, a centurion of a Roman legion based at Vienne, was martyred in 304. For many years it attracted throngs of pilgrims on the road which, beyond Le Puy, passed through Langogne and Villefort, at the time the only route between the Auvergne and Languedoc. Work on the present building began with the narthex in 1060, and was completed in 1180 with the construction of the choir and east end. The nave was raised in height and given a ribvault in 1259.

The east end (**chevet★★**) is one of the final examples of Romanesque architecture in the Auvergne. Its five slate-roofed radiating chapels have richly-decorated cornices and capitals, above which runs a band of mosaic masonry. The south porch (**porche★**) has kept its typical Auvergne five-sided lintel, its wrought-iron strap-hinges and two fine bronze knockers. The warm colouring of the interior is due to the combination of sandstones and basalts of red, pink and brown hue. The nave is paved with cobblestones laid in the 16C and only recently exposed again.

The presence locally of both sandstones and marble was a distinct advantage to the four, possibly even six, masons' workshops responsible for the decoration of the church during the 12C and 13C. The capitals (**chapiteaux**★★) are exceptional; note particularly (in the south aisle near the entrance) an armed knight, perhaps a participant involved in the First Crusade (which had been preached at Clermont-Ferrand), together with a usurer (the sculptor's social comment on this curse of the Middle Ages). Further up the south aisle are two 14C works, the Virgin Birth and Our Lord as a Leper. There are murals too, not, unfortunately, very well preserved, but covering an area of 140m – about 1 300sq ft. There are two outstanding subjects, the figure of St Michael in the first bay of the nave, and the composition in the gallery of the narthex (south room): Christ in Glory, the Chosen and the Damned, the Virtues and the Vices and 100 angels, and, on the timber wall, a stunning 13C Fall of Satan.

Excursion

Lavaudieu★

10km – 6mi southeast. The 11C Benedictine priory, attached to the great abbey at La Chaise-Dieu, has charming cloisters (**cloître**★) with timber-built galleries and 14C **frescoes**★ in the chapel and refectory.

CHÂTEAU DE **BRISSAC**★★

MICHELIN MAP 317 G 4
GREEN GUIDE CHÂTEAUX OF THE LOIRE

The château, set in a fine park shaded by magnificent **cedar trees**★, is unusual both for its height and for the juxtaposition of two buildings, one of which was intended to replace the other rather than stand next to it.

- **Information:** 8 pl. de la République, Brissac-Quincé, ☎02 41 91 21 50. www.otbrissac-loire-aubance.fr.
- **Orient Yourself:** Brissac lies 18km from Angers.
- **Don't Miss:** Be sure to see the tapestries inside the chateau.

Visit

Guided tours (45min) Apr-Jun and mid-Sep to end Oct: daily except Tue 10am-noon, 2.15-5.15pm; Jul to mid-Sep: daily 10am-5.45pm. 8€. ☎02 41 91 22 21. www.brissac.net.

As the original building had been damaged during the Wars of Religion, Duke Charles de Cossé commissioned a new residence designed by Jacques Corbineau, the architect responsible for the citadel at Port-Louis in Lorient. Work ceased on his death in 1621 and the château was left as we see it today. There is an unfinished main façade flanked by medieval towers. The central pavilion and the left wing are abundantly ornamented with rusticated pilasters and statues in niches. The right wing, which would have replaced the Gothic tower, was never built.

The 17C French painted **ceilings** are often embellished with sculptures; the walls are hung with superb **tapestries**. The Louis XIII staircase leads to the imposing guard room (Salle des Gardes), to the bedchamber where Louis XIII and his mother, Marie de' Medici, had a short-lived reconciliation after the Battle of Ponts-de Cé (1620), and to the Hunt Room (Chambre des Chasses) hung with magnificent 16C Flemish tapestries.

North of Brissac, on the road to Angers, stands a fine windmill with a chamber hollowed out at ground level.

CAEN

MICHELIN MAP 303 E-J 3-4–POPULATION 199 500
GREEN GUIDE NORMANDY

Tough and enduring, the city of Caen rebuilt itself after being almost destroyed by bombing during WW2. Today the city proudly preserves an impressive historical legacy, while being committed to peace and the future.

- **Information:** 12 pl. St-Pierre, ☎02 31 27 14 14. www.ville-caen.fr
- ▶ **Orient Yourself:** The pedestrian precinct, between place St-Pierre and place de la République and bounded by rue St-Pierre and boulevard du Maréchal-Leclerc, is lively both day and night. Near the château, in the Vaugueux district, several pubs and restaurants have opened in fine houses spared by the war.
- **Don't Miss:** The Mémorial de la Paix and the Abbaye-aux-Hommes.
- **Organizing Your Time:** Allow 2 hours for the château and the nearby museums, 2 hours for the abbeys, and 2 hours for the Peace Memorial.
- **Parks and Gardens:** Caen is a "green city" with hundreds of acres of parks and gardens, open daily. Tours are available.

A Bit of History

Caen Stone

The light limestone quarried locally was used not only here but in great buildings of the Normans in England (Canterbury Cathedral, the White Tower at the Tower of London and Westminster Abbey).

The City of the Normans

After the invasions of the Norsemen in the 9C and 10C, and the establishment of the duchy of Normandy, Benedictines built the first major religious buildings in Normandy. Caen's architectural heritage is reveals the affection felt for the city by William, Duke of Normandy, and his wife Mathilda, who chose this as their residence. They married in about 1050, against Papal opposition which arose because of they were cousins. This led to their excommunication until they made amends by William founding the Abbey for Men and Mathilda the Abbey for Women. When William left to conquer England, Mathilda became Regent and ruled the duchy herself.

"Caen the Crucible"

Chester Wilmot's pithy epithet evokes the sufferings undergone by the city in summer 1944. The first shells fell on Caen on D-Day itself; the city burned for 11 days. Liberated by the Canadians on 9 July, it was then continuously bombarded for another month by the Germans. The inhabitants huddled in the abbey (Abbaye aux Hommes), the hospital (Hospice du Bon Sauveur) and the quarries at Fleury; the final shell fell on 20 August.

Sights

Église St-Étienne★★

The church of the **Abbey for Men** was founded by the Conqueror; it was begun in 1066 and took 12 years to build. The west front with its soaring towers (the octagonal spires were added in the 13C) dates from this time. The nave is vast; it is a fine example of Romanesque construction with great square bays divided in two by minor piers and with high galleries over the aisles. The clerestory was altered in the 12C when the timber roof was replaced by sexpartite vaulting.

The great lantern-tower over the crossing is probably the work of Lanfranc and William themselves; in its simple perfection it is a masterpiece of Romanesque art. The choir which was extended and altered in the 13C is a very early example of Norman Gothic which set the standard for buildings all over the duchy.

Château★

This great fortress perched on a bluff overlooking the city was built by William in 1060, and subsequently strengthened and extended. From its ramparts there are

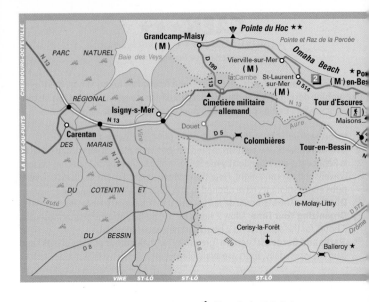

extensive views over Caen. The chateau houses Caen's **Musée des Beaux-Arts**★★ (🕐 Wed–Mon 9.30am–6pm. ♿ ⊗ 4€ (during exhibitions), call for prices during other periods. ☎02 31 30 47 70), displaying a good collection of paintings spanning 15C–20C.

Église de la Trinité★★

The Norman building with its nave of nine bays, round-headed arches, and blind arcades in the triforium was founded by Mathilda in 1062 as the church of the **Abbey for Women**. As

Address Book

For coin ranges, see the Legend on the cover flap.

and seafood dishes on the menu. Well-stocked cigar humidor.

WHERE TO EAT

🍽🍽 **P'tit B** – 15 r. Vaugueux – ☎02 31 93 50 76 -1eptitb@wanadoo.fr . Charming 17C house with a rustic interior artfully modernized, including a superb fireplace. Relaxed atmosphere, a view of the kitchen and seasonal dishes.

🍽🍽 **Le Bouchon du Vaugueux** – 12 r. Graindorge – ☎02 31 44 26 26 – Closed 3 weeks in Aug, Sun–Mon – reserv. required. This tavern (bouchon) is situated near the château and old Caen. Crowded tables add to the friendly ambience. Two fixed-price menus to be discovered on the slate menu du jour.

🍽🍽 **L'Insolite** – 16 r. du Vaugueux at the foot of the château – ☎02 31 43 83 87 – Closed Sun–Mon except Jul–Aug – reserv. advisable. Take the time to discover this half-timbered 16C house with its unusual decor combining rustic frescoes, mirrors and dried flowers. Fish

WHERE TO STAY

🛏 **Hôtel St-Étienne** – 2 r. de l'Académie – ☎02 31 86 35 82 – 11 rooms 🍽6€ . This house, going back to the 1789 Revolution, is located in a quiet district close to the Abbaye-aux-Hommes. Note the fine wooden staircase with its beautiful patined woodwork and the smart bedrooms, some of them with fireplaces. Breakfast served in the dining room.

🛏🛏 **Hôtel Bernières** – 50 r. de Bernières – ☎02 31 86 01 26 – hotelbernieres@wanadoo.fr – 17 rooms 🍽6€. Don't miss the discreet entrance of this hotel, with its convivial welcome, charming breakfast room and drawing room and delightful bedrooms. Dried-flower bouquets add a personal touch to the pleasant surroundings.

🛏🛏 **Le Bristol** – 31 r. du 11-Novembre – ☎ 02 31 84 59 76 – hotelbristol@wanadoo.fr – 24 rooms 🍽7€. Those who prefer to be at a distance from the

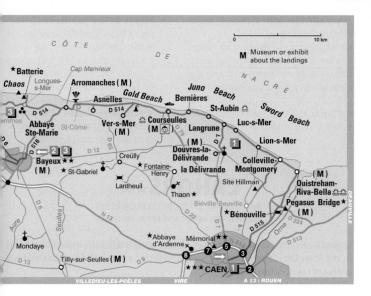

at St Stephen's, the upper storey was altered when the timber roof was replaced by sexpartite vaulting.

The choir with its spacious 11C groined vaults has Mathilda's tomb at its centre. The crypt is well preserved.

Le Mémorial★★★

Signposted from the city centre and the ring road. ⛱ – 🕐*Feb-Nov: 9am-7pm (last admission 1h15 before closing). Rest of year: daily exc Mon, 9.30am-6pm.* 🕐*Closed public holidays and 3 weeks in*

bustle of the centre will appreciate this hotel just a minute from the Orne and the racetrack. The bedrooms, recently updated, have yellow tones, modern furnishings, sound beds and efficient double-glazed windows.

A PLEASANT INTERLUDE

Stiffler – *72 r. St-Jean* – ☎*02 31 86 08 94-www.stifflertraiteur.com* – *Closed Mon.* This magnificent pastry shop offers such specialties as *charlotte aux fruits de saison, bavaroise au chocolat,* or *méringue aux amandes.* At the delicatessan counter, there are delicious prepared dishes and salads for a quick lunch as well.

SHOPPING

Librairie Guillaume – *98 r. St-Pierre* – ☎ *02 31 85 43 13* – *librairie.gen.calv.guillaume@wanadoo.fr* – The carved-wood façade of this splendid bookshop dates from 1902. There is a choice of books about the region and, on the upper floor, a first-rate selection of antique books. **Poupinet** – *8 r. St-Jean* – ☎*02 31 86 07 25-* *Closed July.* For authentic *tripes à la mode de Caen,* you must visit Poupinet,

where you can buy this specialty in jars. Other regional specialties include pâtés, terrines, black puddings, pork ears in jelly and more.

Markets – Marché St-Pierre (Sun), rue de Bayeux (Tue), boulevard Leroy (Wed & Sat), boulevard de la Guérinière (Thu), Marché St-Sauveur (Fri), Christmas Market (Dec).

LEISURE

Hippodrome de Caen – *La Prairie* – ☎*02 31 85 42 61* – *Closed Jul-Aug.* This racecourse, nearly 2km/1.2mi long, in located in the heart of Caen. On the second floor, the panoramic restaurant offers a lovely view of the city. Visits are organised on mornings when races are held (30 times a year).

Festyland – *Boulevard Péripherique 50 N, exit for Carpiquet, 14650 Carpiquet* – ☎*02 31 75 04 04* – *www.festyland.com* – *Closed Oct-Mar.* 10€ *(children under 12: 9€).* This family leisure park has some 30 attractions, including bumper boats, old bangers, babyland, old-style carrousel. Three daily shows (including a circus show) for young children. Food service available in the park.

Jan. – 17.50 €. 02 31 06 06 44. www. memorial-caen.fr
Le Mémorial is a "a museum for peace" housed in a former German command bunker. With numerous arresting displays about conflict and war past and present, with much material of the destruction of Caen during the Liberation, it is a place of contemplation.

▶ **Musée de Normandie**★★ ① *Wed-Mon 9.30am-6pm.* ① *Closed Tue and public holidays.* 02 31 30 47 60. *www.ville-caen.fr/mdn* – archeology and ethnography. **Église St-Pierre**★ ① *Daily 8.30am-noon, 2-6pm, Sun 12.30-6pm.* – **east end**★★. **Hotel d'Escoville**★. **Église St-Nicolas**★ (cemetery) ① *Mar-Oct: daily 8am-6pm; Nov-Feb: daily 8am-5pm.*

CAHORS

MICHELIN MAP 337 E 5–POPULATION 20 000
GREEN GUIDE DORDOGNE BERRY LIMOUSIN

Impressively sited on a promontory almost completely surrounded by a bend in the River Lot, Cahors enjoyed fame and fortune in the Middle Ages and is a pleasant country town today.

▪ **Information:** Pl. Mittérand, 05 65 53 20 65. www.quercy-tourisme.com/cahors.
▶ **Orient Yourself:** The ancient axis of Boulevard Gambetta is a lively central promenade. The old quarter lies on its east side. For a different perspective on the town, take a boat trip on the Lot.
🅿 **Parking:** There are several car parks around the town centre.
⊛ **Don't Miss:** Pont Valentré, the fortified bridge over the Lot.
① **Organizing Your Time:** Allow a full day to explore the town and the nearby villages and vistas of the Lot valley.

Pont Valentré

Address Book

For coin ranges, see the Legend on the cover flap.

WHERE TO EAT

Le Dousil – *124 r. Nationale – ☎05 65 53 19 67 – Closed 10 days in Feb, 10 days in Oct, Sun and Mon*. This wine bar near the town's covered market offers an extensive list of over 100 vintages. The decor includes a traditional zinc counter and stone walls. The menu includes a choice of sandwiches, *charcuterie* and daily specials.

Le Rendez-Vous – *49 r. Clément-Marot – ☎05 65 22 65 10 – Closed 29 Apr-14 May, 28 Oct-12 Nov, Sun and Mon – reserv. recommended*. Located close to the cathedral, Le Rendez-Vous has developed a reputation for modern cuisine. The mix of colourful contemporary decor and old stonework combine well in the dining room and mezzanine extension.

La Garenne – *In Saint-Henri, 7km/4.5mi N towards Brive – ☎05 65 35 40 67 – Closed Feb, 1-15 Mar, Mon eve and Tue eve (except Jul-Aug) and Wed*. This typically Quercy-style building once served as a stable. Cosy interior decor featuring exposed beams, stone walls, attractive, locally made furniture and typical country objects. The main attraction here is the delicious regional cuisine.

Auberge du Vieux Douelle – *46140 Douelle – 8km/5mi W of Cahors on the D 8 – ☎05 65 20 02 03 – auberged-edouelle@aol.com*. The dining room in the vaulted cellar of this popular inn, known locally as "Chez Malique", is decked out with bright red tablecloths. Meats are grilled over a wood fire; salads and a buffet are also available. Terrace and pool in the summer. A few rooms available.

WHERE TO STAY

Hôtel Les Chalets – *46090 Vers – 14km/8.7mi E of Cahors on the D 653 – ☎05 65 31 40 83 – les.chalets.vers@wanadoo.fr – Closed Jan Sun evenings and Mon Oct-Apr – 23 rooms*. This small modern hotel situated in an attractive leafy setting is particularly welcoming. The bedrooms, with balconies or small gardens, overlook the river. A quiet and peaceful retreat, with gentle background noise courtesy of a waterfall. Swimming pool in summer.

Chambre d'hôte Le Clos des Dryades – *46090 Vers – 19km/11.4mi NE of Cahors on the D 653, towards St-Cirq-Lapopie and the D 49 road to Cours – ☎05 65 31 44 50 – Closed 15 Nov-15 Feb – ⌂ – 5 rooms*. Nestled deep in the woods, this house with its tiled roof is the perfect place to get away from it all. The rooms are comfortable and the large swimming pool is a great place to cool off on a hot summer's day. Two self-catering cottages are also available.

Hôtel A l'Escargot – *5 bd Gambetta – ☎05 65 35 07 66 – Closed Feb school hols, Dec and Sun out of season – 9 rooms*. Near the Tour Jean-XXI, this hotel occupies the old palace built by the pontiff's family. Functional bedrooms with colourful furnishings, plus a renovated breakfast room.

SHOPPING

Market – *Pl. de la Halle*. A traditional market is held on Wednesday and Saturday mornings, with farmers' stalls selling a range of local produce.

Les Délices du Valentré – *21 bd Léon-Gambetta – ☎05 65 35 09 86*. Try the *Coque de Cahors*, a *brioche* with candied citron and flavoured with orange water, and *Cabecou*, a chocolate sweet.

LEISURE ACTIVITIES

L'Archipel – *Quai Ludo-Rollès. Water sports and leisure centre – ☎05 65 35 05 86 / 31 38 – Closed mid-Sep to mid-Jun*. This summer pool offers lots of fun activities, including slides, massage, bubble baths, fountains and games.

Alliance Nautique Cahors – *Port Bullier – ☎06 80 14 96 77 – Open Easter-15 Sep – 30min: 18€; 1hr: 28€*. Hire an easy-to-handle electric boat to explore the River Lot. No permit required.

EVENTS

Festival de Blues – *mid-Jul. ☎05 65 35 99 99*.

Festival du Quercy Blanc – *late-Jul to mid-Aug. ☎05 65 31 83 12*.

Sights

Pont Valentré★★

The city's merchants were responsible for building this superb six-arched stone bridge; its construction lasted from 1308 to 1378. Its fortifications are a reminder of the importance attached to the defence of Cahors by Philippe le Bel (the Fair), whose relationship with the city was based on an act of pariage (equality between a feudal lord and a town).

Cathédrale St-Étienne★

In these much-troubled lands it was wise to fortify a place of worship as was done here. The cathedral is one of the first of the domed churches of Aquitaine. The 13C north door (**portail nord**★★) shows the moment at which Christ is beginning to rise and the angels are stilling the fears of the disciples.

◖◗ **Barbacane et Tour St-Jean**★.

CALAIS

MICHELIN MAP 301 E 2–POPULATION 104 850

GREEN GUIDE NORTHERN FRANCE AND THE PARIS REGION

The proximity of the English coast a mere 38km – 24 miles away has always determined the destiny of Calais. The port handles more passengers than any other in France.

- **Information:** 12 bd Clemenceau, ☎03 21 96 62 40. www.ot-calais.fr.
- ▶ **Orient Yourself:** Calais is in two sections: the larger Calais-Sud is the modern commercial heart of town, while smaller Calais-Nord is the older maritime area close to the port and beach.
- **Parking:** There is plenty of metered street parking in Calais-Sud. Place d'Armes in Calais-Nord is a useful car parking area.
- **Don't Miss:** Rodin's remarkable *Burghers of Calais*, outside the town hall.
- **Organizing Your Time:** As well as the sights, allow plenty of time to browse Calais' excellent shops. For a more serious shopping spree, visit Cit Europe, a vast mall 3km south of town.

A Bit of History

In May 1347, eight months after his victory at Crécy over Philippe VI which marked the beginning of the Hundred Years War, Edward III succeeded in starving Calais into submission. The town was to remain English for more than two centuries until the Duke of Guise seized it in January 1558. The loss of England's last possession in France provoked Mary Tudor's sad comment "When I am dead and opened, you shall find 'Calais' lying in my heart."

Almost entirely destroyed in the WW2, Calais was rapidly rebuilt, and remained the principal entry point into France from Britain. The Channel Tunnel, passing beneath the sea from near Folkestone to Coquelles (3km south of Calais), was opened in 1994.

Sight

Monument des Bourgeois de Calais★★

In front of the Town Hall (Hôtel de ville). Rodin's group of bronze figures (1895) commemorates the self-sacrificing action of Eustache de Saint-Pierre and his five fellowcitizens; emaciated by the eight long months of siege, barefoot and clad in long robes, they came before Edward III offering themselves for execution provided the king spared their fellow-citizens. Edward accepted their plea and spared them too, doubtless with an eye to the governability of his new conquest. Rodin's huge talent comes over triumphantly in these vibrant figures, haughty in their humiliation.

Other examples of this sculpture may be seen in London (near the Houses of

Parliament), in Los Angeles (at the Norton Simon Inc. Museum of Art) and in Washington (at the Hirshhorn Museum and Sculpture Garden).

▶ **Views**★★ from the lighthouse (*Phare*). **Musée des Beaux Arts et de la Dentelle**★ ⚐ ⏰ *Mon, Wed-Fri 10am-noon, 2-5.30pm, Sat 10am-noon, 2-6.30pm, Sun 2-6.30pm.* ⏰ *Closed Tue and public holidays.* ⚐ *5€ during the summer exhibit, 3€ rest of the year, no charge Wed.* ☎*03 21 46 48 40.*– history and artistic development of the town.

Excursion

Côte d'Opale

The road linking Calais and Boulogne takes the visitor along the most spectacular part of this coastline with its high chalk cliffs, heathlands and vast sandy beaches backed by grassy dunes.

Blériot-Plage

The little resort has a fine beach stretching as far as Cap Blanc-Nez. On a cliff-top knoll is the obelisk commemorating the **Dover Patrol**, mounted continuously between 1914 and 1918 to protect the vital supply routes across the English Channel. At Les Baraques just to the west of the resort is a monument marking **Edouard Blériot's** flight across the Channel in 1909.

Cap Blanc-Nez★★

From the top of the white cliffs the **view**★ extends from Calais to Cap Gris-Nez and right across the Channel to the English coast.

Wissant

With its superb beach of fine hard sand, one of France's main centres for land yachting, Wissant enjoys its privileged position in the middle of the National Conservation Area which includes both Cap Gris-Nez and Cap Blanc-Nez.

Cap Gris-Nez★★

This lofty limestone headland makes a contrast with the chalk cliffs to the south. In fine weather, it gives a **view**★ of the white cliffs of the English coast.

Wimereux

This sizeable family resort is pleasantly situated between Cap d'Alprech to the south and the cliffs running up to Cap Gris-Nez in the north.

From the raised seafront promenade there are fine views over the Channel and along the coast from the monument **(Colonne de la Grande Armée)** to the port of Boulogne.

Boulogne-sur-Mer★ – ⚐ *See BOULOGNE-SUR-MER.*

LA **CAMARGUE**★★
MICHELIN MAP 340 A-E 4-5 AND 339 J-M 7-8
GREEN GUIDE PROVENCE

The Rhône delta forms an immense wetland plain of 95 000ha – 367sq miles. Product of the interaction of the Rhône, the Mediterranean and the winds, this remarkable area has a culture and history all its own, as well as distinctive flora and fauna. It is divided into three distinct regions: a cultivated region north of the delta, salt-marshes west of the Petit Rhône, and the watery nature reserve to the south.

▶ **Orient Yourself:** The main town in the Camargue is Les Saintes-Maries-de-la-Mer on the coast. The city of Arles lies on its northern edge.

⚐ **Don't Miss:** Try to catch sight of the three creatures that symbolise the Camargue – white horses, black bulls and pink flamingos.

⚐ **Caution:** Mosquitoes are a problem during the summer.

Boat in a roubine lined with reeds

Visit

Parc Naturel Régional de Camargue

🛈 *Parc Information Centre: Mas du Pont de Rousty, about 10 km from Arles and 30 km from Les Saintes-Maries-de-la-Mer on D570, b04 90 97 10 82. www.parc-camargue.fr.* 🕐 *Open daily (except Fri in winter).*

The nature park covers an area of 85 000ha – 328sq miles in the Rhône delta, including the communes of Arles and Stes-Maries-de-la-Mer. Together with the nature reserve, **Réserve Nationale de Camargue,** it aims to protect the fragile ecological system of the region with its exceptional variety of flora and fauna – there are some 400 bird species. The traditional image of the Camargue is associated with the herds **(manades)** and the horsemen **(gardians)**. Many horse owners hire out their mounts for organised rides among the animals.

The *manade* designates livestock and all that relates to the upkeep of the herd: herdsmen, pastureland, horses, etc. The *gardian*, an experienced rider, is the symbol of the *manade* with his large felt hat and long three-pronged stick; he watches over the herd, cares for the sick animals and selects the bulls for the bullfights.

Les-Stes-Maries-de-la-Mer

At the heart of the Camargue is situated Les-Stes-Maries-de-la-Mer , clustered around it fortified church. The town, which is now at some distance from the coastline of medieval times, is protected by dikes to counter the encroachment of the sea.

The church, and the name of the town, are deicated to a pious legend, according to which a boat carrying Mary, the mother of James, Mary Salome, the mother of James Major and John, Mary Magdalene, Martha and her brother Lazarus, came to rest on the shore where Les-Stes-Maries now stands. The two Marys and their black servant Sarah remained here; their burial place became a shrine, then a church. A large, colourful **Gypsy Pilgrimage**★★ in honour of Sarah, whom they consider as their patron, takes place 24-25 May, attracting thousands of gypsies.

◗◗ **Musée camarguais at Pont de Rousty** ♿ 🕐 *Jul and Aug: daily 10am-6pm; Apr-Jun and Sep: daily 9am-6pm; Oct-Mar: daily except Tue 10am-5pm. Last admission 1hr before closing.* 🕐 *Closed 1 Jan, 1 May, 25 Dec.* ⊛ *5€.* ☎*04 90 97 10 82. www.parc-camargue.fr.*

CANAL DU MIDI

MICHELIN MAP 343 H-I 4, J-K 5 AND 339 A-K 1-3, A-F 9

GREEN GUIDE LANGUEDOC ROUSSILLON TARN GORGES

It is hard to believe that this calm, beautiful, even elegant waterway, now so popular for leisurely boating holidays, was a daunting engineering achievement enabling the transport of industrial goods directly betweenthe Mediterranean and the Atlantic.

▶ **Orient Yourself:** The Canal runs from Sète on the Languedoc coast, to Bordeaux on the Atlantic.

A Bit of History

The Seuil de Naurouze pass (alt 194m – 636ft) forms the watershed between Atlantic and Mediterranean; the notion of a canal enabling shipping to avoid the long route via Gibraltar had preoccupied not only the Romans but also François I, Henri IV and Richelieu. The natural obstacles, however, seemed insurmountable.

Then in 1662, Pierre-Paul Riquet (1604-80) succeeded in interesting Colbert in overcoming them. The canal was to prove his ruin; all the work was carried out at his own expense and he died six months before the opening. The completed Canal du Midi is 240km – 149 miles long and has 103 locks; It proved a huge commercial success – too late for the great man.

Becoming obsolete in the late 19C, the canal provides a perfect illustration of pre-industrial techniques. It passed into state ownership in 1897 and today is used mainly by leisure craft. In 1996 it was named as a World Heritage site by UNESCO.

CANNES★★★

MICHELIN MAP 341 B-D 5 AND P-Q 5–POPULATION 67 304

GREEN GUIDE FRENCH RIVIERA

A charming old quarter, chic town centre and glamorous beachside promenade make Cannes one of the most enjoyable places on the Riviera. Spread out between the Suquet Heights and La Croisette Point on the shore of La Napoule Bay, Cannes also owes its popularity to an exceptionally beautiful **setting**.

🛈 **Information:** Palais des Festivals, 1 La Croisette, ☎04 93 39 24 53; and at the railway station (Gare SNCF), ☎04 93 99 19 77. www.cannes.fr.

▶ **Orient Yourself:** Cannes is surprisingly extensive. The heart of town, and most of the sights, are in a narrow strip close to the sea. The centre of the action is the Palais des Festivals.

🐾 **Don't Miss:** Make time to visit the superb covered market, near the Old Port, daily except Monday.

🕓 **Organizing Your Time:** Allow yourself at least 2hr to visit Le Suquet.

A Bit of History

In 1834, the former Lord Chancellor of Great Britain, Lord Brougham, was on his way to Italy when he was prevented from entering the County of Nice, then part of Italy, because of a cholera epidemic. Forced to wait, he made an overnight stop at a fishing village called Cannes. Enchanted by the place, he built a villa

Address Book

For coin ranges, see the Legend on the cover flap.

WHERE TO EAT

☞ **Côte d'Azur** – *3 Rue Jean-Daumos – ☎ 04 93 38 60 02 – Closed evenings and Sun.* Modest restaurant with a friendly ambience and cosy setting with period furnishings. The traditional cooking attracts a great many locals. Low prices guaranteed.

☞☞ **Aux Bons Enfants** – *80 Rue Meynadier – Closed Aug, 24 Dec-2 Jan, Sat evening Oct to Apr, and Sun – ⊟ – reservations highly recommended.* Simplicity, generosity and congeniality are the hallmarks of this informal establishment where there's no telephone and customers are required to pay in cash. A true locals' hangout since 1935, with tasty Mediterranean dishes.

☞☞ **Le Comptoir des Vins** – *13 Boulevard de la République – ☎04 93 68 13 26 – www.comptoirdesvins.com – Closed Feb, evenings Mon-Wed, Sun and public holidays.* This handsomely stocked wine boutique leads to a colorful dining area where light snacks can be served, washed down with a glass of wine.

☞☞ **Le Caveau 30** – *45 Rue F.-Faure – ☎ 04 93 39 06 33.* Large restaurant comprising two dining rooms done up in the style of a 1930 brasserie. The terrace overlooks a shaded square popular among boules players. Fish and seafood are the specialities of the house.

☞☞ **Au Poisson Grillé** – *8 Quai St-Pierre – Vieux Port – ☎04 93 39 44 68.* Appropriately located in the old port, this fish restaurant was opened back in 1949. It serves grilled fish alongside many other Mediterranean dishes, in a warm setting of varnished wood evoking the interior of a luxury cabin. Attentive service at affordable prices.

☞☞☞ **Fred L'Écailler** – *7 Place de l'Étang – ☎04 93 43 15 85 – http://fredlecailler.com.* A large neon sign marks the entrance to this rustic-style restaurant whose walls are draped with fishing nets. The tiny square affords a glimpse of village life with its bustling activity and daily games of pétanque. Fine selection of freshly caught fish and seafood.

WHERE TO STAY

☞ **Le Chanteclair** – *12 Rue Forville – ☎04 93 39 68 88 – Closed 15 Oct-3 Jan – ⊟ – 15 rooms – ⊡5.50€.* After walking through a building, you will discover this friendly hotel laid out on several floors, offering a selection of variously priced rooms depending on the level of comfort. Pleasant inner courtyard where breakfast is served in summer.

☞☞ **Hôtel Appia** – *6 Rue Marceau – ☎ 04 93 06 59 59 – www.appia-hotel.com – Closed 21 Nov-27 Dec – 31 rooms – ⊡6.50€.* Practicality takes precedence over comfort in this downtown hotel where the well-kept, smallish rooms are both air-conditioned and soundproofed. Pristine bathrooms.

☞☞☞ **Villa l'Églantier** – *14 Rue Campestra – ☎04 93 68 22 43 – ⊟ – 4 rooms.* Impressive white villa dating from 1920, surrounded by palm trees and other exotic species, dominating the city of Cannes. The large, peaceful rooms are all extended by a terrace or a balcony.

ON THE TOWN

The best way to get to know this glamorous city is to frequent its luxury hotel bars: order a cocktail on the terrace of the Carlton hotel, on the beach of the Majestic or in the piano-bar of the Martinez.

L'Amiral – *73 Boulevard de la Croisette – ☎ 04 92 98 73 00 – www.hotel.martinez.com – Daily 10am-2am.* Attached to the Martinez Hotel, this bar is by far the most popular meeting place along the coast. It owes its reputation to the head barman and to Jimmy, the American piano player. Live music every evening from 8pm.

SHOPPING

Market – Marché de Forville: *daily 7am-1pm except Mondays in low season;* fine stalls displaying fresh regional produce.
Allées de la Liberté – Flower market every morning. Popular flea market on Saturdays.
Shopping streets – Rue Meynadier: tempting window displays of food and craftwork in a lively pedestrian area. Rue d'Antibes: luxury clothes and luggage.

Cannolive – *16 Rue Vénizelos* – ☏*04 93 39 08 19* – *Closed Sun, Mon morning, and two weeks in Dec.* This shop boasts an incredible choice of Provençal products to take back home: household linen, *tapenades*, crockery, *santons*, soap, and even Lérina liqueur from the nearby islands for those who get seasick!

LEISURE ACTIVITIES

For sailing, deep-sea diving or water-ski-ing, contact the Tourism Office or visit www.france-nautisme.com.

Beaches – Not all the beaches on La Croisette charge a fee (details of prices are listed at the top of the steps), or belong to a hotel (located opposite). There are also three free beaches, one of which is located behind the Palais du Festival. The other public beaches lie west of the old port, on Boulevard Jean-Hibert and Boulevard du Midi, at Port Canto and on Boulevard Gazag-naire beyond La Pointe.

Ponton Majestic Ski Nautique – *Boulevard de la Croisette* – ☏*04 92 98 77 47/ 06 11 50 77 53* –*Open: Apr-Oct daily 8am until dusk.* If you want to get away from the bustling crowds, why not try your hand at water-skiing or parasailing?

TOURS AND TRANSPORTATION

TAM – *Gare routière, Place de l'Hôtel-de-Ville* – ☏*04 93 39 11 39* – *www.rca.tm.fr.* These buses operate between Cannes and Nice, including direct service to the airport.

Train Station – *SNCF Gare de Cannes* – ☏ *0 892 35 35 35* – *www.ter-sncf. com/paca.* This train station is served by local and national trains including TGV and regional TER trains (service between Mandelieu-La-Napoule and Vintimille).

Trans Côte d'Azur – *3 Quai des Îles* – ☏*04 92 98 71 30* – *Feb-Oct daily 8.30am-noon, 1.30-6pm (Jul-Aug 8am-7pm).* 🚢 *10€ (child 5€). www.trans-cote-azur.com.* Regular service to the Île Ste-Marguerite (15 minutes), plus seasonal tours to l'Île de Porquerolles, Monaco, Saint-Tropez, San Remo, la Corniche d'Or, etc.

CALENDAR OF EVENTS

International Film Festival – 10 days in May; free open-air cinema retro-spectives on the beach (official screen-ings open to accredited professionals only). *www.festival-cannes.org.*

Nuits Misicales du Suquet – End of July; classical concerts on the espla-nade in front of the Église du Suquet. ☏*04 92 99 33 83.*

here and returned to it every winter, establishing a trend among the English aristocracy and stimulating Cannes' first period of growth.

Sights

Boulevard de la Croisette ★★

Locals and visitors congregate along this wide, attractive seafront road, with delightful gardens along its centre. To one side extends the resort's splendid sandy beach and broad promenade, while the landward side of the boul-evard is lined with the dignified and impeccably maintained façades of four luxury 'palace' hotels and exclusive boutiques.

At the eastern end of La Croisette is a marina, busy with yachts and pleasure craft, and at its western end another,

overlooked by the Festival and Con-ference Centre (Palais des Festivals et des Congrès). It is here that the Cannes Film Festival is held every May, the town's most spectacular and prestig-ious event.

Le Suquet

Le Suquet, the old town of Cannes, climbs a steep hill beside the Old Port. The lower streets of this area are today the centre for nightlife and restaurants. From a terrace in front of the Tour du Mont Chevalier, there is a fine **view**★ over beach and bay, the Lérins Islands and the Esterel Heights .The 11C Cannes castle today houses the remarkable **Musée de la Castre** ★★, an eclectic 19C private collection of exceptional ethno-graphic artefacts taken from cultures around the world.

Excursion

Massif de L'Esterel★★★
40km – 24mi west by N98. The massif's jagged relief of volcanic rock (red porphyry) worn by erosion dips vertically into the deep blue sea between La Napoule and St-Raphael. The rugged coastline is fringed with rocks, islets and reefs. From **Mont Vinaigre**★★★, its highest peak (alt 618m – 2 027ft), a vast panorama unfolds over the surrounding area. The pine and cork-oak forests clothing the wild and lonely massif have been ravaged by fire in recent years.

CAP CORSE★★★
MICHELIN MAP 345 F 1-2
GREEN GUIDE CORSE (IN FRENCH)

Cap Corse is the finger of mountain range which prolongs the island's ridge of schistous rock 40km – 25 miles into the sea.

- ⓘ **Information:** Port de Plaisance, Macinaggio, ☎04 95 35 40 34. www.ot-rogliano-macinaggio.com.
- ▶ **Orient Yourself:** Cap Corse can be reached from either the east or the west coast. The city of Bastia stands at the base of the 'finger' on the east coast.
- ⊘ **Don't Miss:** Make time to visit the superb covered market, near the Old Port, daily except Monday.
- ⓧ **Organizing Your Time:** Take a picturesque corniche road to discover villages clinging to defensive sites, tiny sandy beaches, and marinas nestling in an inlet.

A Bit of History

A Seafaring People – In contrast to the rest of the Corsican population, local inhabitants responded to the call of the sea and took up trade and travel to distant lands. In the 19C they set up the first trading-posts in North Africa. A large number emigrated to South America; many became prosperous and built great houses in colonial or Renaissance style in their native village. These styles have influenced the architecture of the region.

CARCASSONNE★★★
MICHELIN MAP 344 E-F 3–POPULATION 43 470
GREEN GUIDE LANGUEDOC ROUSSILLON TARN GORGES

Like a picture in a story book, Carcassonne's walled **Cité seems to have been** preserved untouched since the end of the Middle Ages.

- ⓘ **Information:** 28 rue de Verdun, ☎04 68 10 24 30. www.carcassonne-tourisme.com .
- ▶ **Orient Yourself:** The walled medieval Cité stands on higher ground on the right bank of the River Aude. The Lower Town lies on lower ground on the left bank.
- ⊘ **Don't Miss:** The view of the Cité from a distance, especially from autoroute A61, is spectacular.
- ⓧ **Organizing Your Time:** Allow half a day to visit the fortified Cité.
- ⌁ **Walking tours:** There are several guided tour options in the Cité. Contact the tourist office for details. Château Comtal can only be visited as part of a guided tour.
- 🅿 **Parking:** When visiting the Cité, use the car parks outside the walls in front of the east gateway, Porte Narbonnaise.

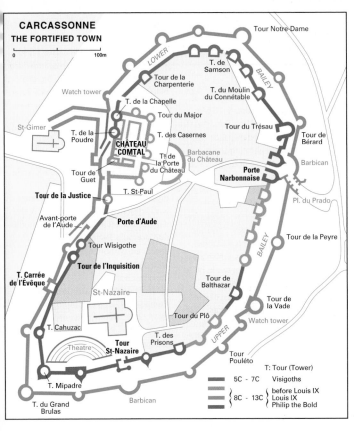

CARCASSONNE
THE FORTIFIED TOWN

0   100m

Tour Notre-Dame

LOWER

T. de Samson

Tour de la Charpenterie

T. du Moulin du Connétable

BAILEY

Watch tower

T. de la Chapelle

Tour du Major

Tour du Trésau

T. de la Poudre

T. des Casernes

St-Gimer

CHÂTEAU COMTAL

Tour de Bérard

Barbacane du Château

Tour de Guet

T. de la Porte du Château

Barbican

Porte Narbonnaise

Tour de la Justice

T. St-Paul

Pl. du Prado

Avant-porte de l'Aude

Porte d'Aude

Tour Wisigothe

Tour de la Peyre

Tour de l'Inquisition

BAILEY

T. Carrée de l'Évêque

St-Nazaire

Tour de Balthazar

Tour de la Vade

T. Cahuzac

Tour du Plô

Watch tower

Theatre

T. des Prisons

UPPER

Tour St-Nazaire

Tour Pouléto

T. Mipadre

Barbacan

T. du Grand Brulas

T: Tour (Tower)

5C - 7C	Visigoths
8C - 13C	before Louis IX / Louis IX / Philip the Bold

A Bit of History

The site of the Cité was first fortified by the Gauls; their entrenched camp served Roman, Visigoth and Frank in turn. In the 9C, Carcassonne became the capital of a county, then of a viscounty subject to the County of Toulouse. In common with the rest of the South of France it enjoyed a long period of prosperity which was brought to an end by the Crusade against the 'Albigensians' – Cathars.

On 1 August 1209 the army of crusaders under Simon de Montfort arrived at the walls of Carcassonne and besieged the city. Within a fortnight, the attackers had seized the Viscount, Raymond-Roger Trencavel, and the town capitulated. In 1240 his son tried to recapture his inheritance with the aid of the towns-people, but the attempt failed; Louis IX razed the fortifications and sentenced the inhabitants to seven years of exile for their treachery. After serving their term they were allowed to settle here again, but only on the far bank of the River Aude, which became today's Lower Town (Ville Basse). This was laid out in typical *bastide* fashion and the line of its ramparts is now marked by the ring of boulevards.

Visit

La Cité★★★

The Cité is the upper town within its impressive ramparts. Louis IX restored and reinforced the Cité both to hold down France's new territorial acquisitions and to defend the kingdom against Spain. His son Philippe le Hardi (the Bold) strengthened the defences still further, making Carcassonne "the Virgin of Languedoc," in other words, impregnable. During the Hundred Years War the Black Prince, unwilling to risk a frontal

Address Book

For coin ranges, see the Legend on the cover flap.

WHERE TO EAT

⊜ **Le Bar à Vins** – *6 r. du Plo* – ☎*04 68 47 38 38* – *mhrc@wanadoo.fr* – *Open daily 9am-2am. Closed Nov-Feb.* Situated at the heart of the medieval Cité, this wine bar enjoys a charming shady garden offering a view of the St-Nazaire basilica. Tapas and fast food.

⊜⊜ **La Tête de l'Art** – *37 bis r. Trivalle* – ☎ *04 68 47 36 36* – *tilcke@tele2.fr* – *Closed Sun in winter* – ✄ – *reservation recommended on weekends.* Food and art go hand in hand in this restaurant specializing in pork dishes, which are served in rooms displaying works of modern painting and sculpture, in between figurines of the mascot itself.

⊜⊜ **Auberge de Dame Carcas** – *3 pl. du Château* – ☎*04 68 71 23 23* – *Closed Jan, noon and Wed.* A friendly establishment in the medieval Cité. The good-natured atmosphere and generous menu no doubt contribute to its success – the dining rooms on four levels are regularly packed with people. Carvery on ground floor.

⊜⊜ **Chez Fred** – *31 bd O.-Sarraut* – ☎*04 68 72 02 23* – *contact@chez-fred. fr* – *Closed 9 Feb-2Mar, 20 Oct-3 Nov, Sat noon, Tue evening and Wed in winter.* This modern bistro not far from the station in the lower town is full of life. The cuisine vascillates between Andalusian dishes and daily menus. Food is served in a white-washed room or on the terrace in summer.

⊜⊜⊜ **L'Écurie** – *43 bd Barbès* – ☎*04 68 72 04 04* – *Closed Sun evening.* This restaurant serving fine fare is located in magnificent old stables, where the old horses' stalls now separate the guests. This original setting and the garden-court which is pleasant in summer are popular with local residents, who count it among their favourite places to go.

WHERE TO STAY

⊜⊜ **Chambre d'hôte La Maison sur la Colline** – *Lieu-dit Ste-Croix* – *1km/0.6mi S of la Cité on rte de Ste-*

Croix – ☎*04 68 47 57 94* – *Closed 1 Dec – 15 Feb* – ✄ – *reservation recommended in season* – *5 rms.* Perched on top of a hill, this restored old farm offers a spectacular view of the Cité from its garden. Rooms are spacious and furnished with old dyed objects, in a different colour for each room: blue, yellow, beige, white.Breakfast by the pool in summer.

⊜⊜ **Hôtel Espace Cité** – *132 r. Trivalle* – ☎*04 68 25 24 24* – *infos@hotel-espacecite.com* – *48 rms.* Modern hotel with attractive façade at the foot of the citadel. It offers a "budget accommodation" formula. Rooms are functional and clean, without grand luxury but with plenty of light. Warm welcome. Breakfast buffet.

⊜⊜⊜⊜ **Hôtel Le Donjon and les Remparts** – *2 r. du Comte-Roger* – ☎*04 68 11 23 00* – *info@bestwestern-donjon. com* – *62 rms.* Partly occupying a 15C orphanage at the heart of the Cité, this hotel combining old stonework and renovated decor offers three kinds of room to choose from: with white or rustic furniture in the main building, and modern style in the "Remparts" annex. Brasserie.

SHOPPING

Cabanel – *72 allée d'Iéna* – ☎*04 68 25 02 58* – *cabanel@wanadoo.fr* – ⊙ *Mon-Sat 8am-noon, 2-7pm.* This liqueur specialist has been here since 1868, selling a wide variety of unusual brews including Or-Kina (made from spices and plants), Micheline (its origins lost in medieval times), and Audoise (called the Cathars' liqueur). Selection of regional wines also available.

Marché aux fleurs. légumes and fruits – *Pl. Carnot* – ☎*04 68 10 24 30* – ⊙ *Tues, Thu and Sat 8am-12.30pm.* Flowers, fruit and vegetables.

CALENDAR OF EVENTS

Spectacles médiévaux "Carcassonne, terre d'histoire" – *Aug.* Medieval festival.

Tournois de chevalerie – *Aug.* Jousting tournament.

assault, contented himself with burning the Lower Town to the ground.

In 1659 Roussillon was incorporated into France, pushing the vulnerable frontier zone southward. This, together with the invention of modern artillery, meant that Carcassonne's strategic significance was now nil; abandonment and decay followed. Then, in the 19C, Romanticism brought the Middle Ages back into fashion; the writer **Prosper Mérimée**, with his taste for ruins, was made Government Inspector of Ancient Monuments; the architect **Viollet-le-Duc** surveyed the remains and in 1844 was put in charge of reconstructing the city. The restoration process lasted until 1910, but – although visually impressive – was much criticised as historically inaccurate. Recent alterations, especially to the towers, are intended to correct some of these mistakes.

Fortifications

See Introduction: Art – Architecture.
Carcassonne's remarkable defences enable us to imagine what medieval siege warfare was like; they are a veritable catalogue of the architectural ingenuity that went into resisting an attack. There are drawbridges and fixed bridges with portcullises, towers with projecting "beaks" or open on the inside, protected at the top by hoardings and at the base by flared footings, curtain walls with a sentry-walk behind the crenellations, watch-turrets, arrow-slits, machicolations... Even if the attackers succeeded in breaking in, they could be pinned down by covering fire.

Château Comtal

Guided tours only. (30min) Apr-Sep: daily 9.30am-6pm; Oct-Mar: daily 9.30am-5pm. Closed 1 Jan, 1 May, 1 and 11 Nov, 25 Dec. 6.50€. No charge 1st Sun in the month. 04 68 11 70 70. www.monum.fr.
Butting onto the Gallo-Roman ramparts, this was built in the 12C by the Viscounts, the Trencavels. A deep ditch and a barbican separate it from the interior.

Enceinte intérieure

The inner ramparts were first built in the 6C by the Visigoths, though altered and given extra height in the 13C. The original towers can be identified easily; they are slender, rounded on the outside and flat on the inside. The 13C additions include the remarkable "beaked" towers.

Enceinte extérieure

The outer ramparts were begun by Louis IX and completed by Philippe le Hardi (the Bold). Most of the towers are open on the inside; if taken by the attackers they would be difficult to defend against a counter-attack from within.

There are also completely enclosed towers acting as redoubts from which the defence could harass any attackers who had succeeded in gaining entry to the inner ward.

It is possible to date the fortifications by the way in which materials are used. The Gallo-Roman foundations are made up of large blocks fitted together without the use of mortar. The work of the Visigoths is characterised by the use of cube-shaped stones alternating with brick courses often laid in herring-bone fashion.

The Viscounts' buildings are constructed from yellowish sandstone laid rather crudely. The walls built by the kings of France are made up of rectangular stones laid in a regular fashion, smooth-faced under Louis IX, rusticated at the time of Philip the Bold in order to withstand impacts more easily. The curtain-walls and towers of the outer ramparts are unusual in that Roman or Visigothic work is visible at a higher level than the 13C walling. This is because additional work had to be carried out on the foundations when the ground level was lowered to form the outer ward.

▶ **Basilique St-Nazaire**★ – **stained glass**★★, **statues**★★.

CARNAC★

MICHELIN MAP 308 M 9–POPULATION 4 450
GREEN GUIDE BRITTANY

In the bleak Breton countryside just north of the little town of Carnac are some of the world's most remarkable megalithic remains.

🛈 **Information:** 74 ave. des Druides, ☎02 97 52 13 52. www.ot-carnac.fr .

▶ **Orient Yourself:** Although its fame is considerable, the site is surprisingly small. It is located at the base of the Quiberon Peninsula.

Visit

Megaliths★★

The area containing the megaliths is divided up by roads and a number of stones have been lost, but altogether it comprises 2 792 menhirs, arranged in 10 or 11 lines – *alignements* – including the **alignements du Ménec**★★ with 1 169 menhirs, the **alignements de Kermario**★ with 1 029 and the **alignements de Kerlescan**★ with 594. There are also dolmens (burial places), cromlechs (semicircles) and tumuli (mounds).

Megalithic culture flourished from about 4670 to 2000 BC. It was the creation of a settled population growing crops and with domestic animals (in contrast to the hunter-gatherers of Paleolithic times), who produced polished objects, pottery and basket-work and who traded in flints. The inhabitants of Carnac had commercial relations with people from Belgium and from Grand-Pressigny in the north of Poitou.

Markings on the megaliths resemble abstract art in contrast to the figurative cave-art of the Upper Paleolithic, and the orientation of the lines in a west-north-east direction adds to their enigmatic character. Various theories have been advanced about their likely religious or astronomical significance. The tumuli and dolmens which appeared 40 centuries before the birth of Christ are collective burial-places, and the mounds covering them, a thousand years older than the pyramids, may be "Mankind's most ancient built monuments."

Four thousand centuries previously, the Carnac area was inhabited by prehistoric people, and, during the Lower Paleolithic, by nomads, contemporaries of the nomads of Tautavel, Terra Amata and the Ardèche Valley. In 5C BC, the Celts moved here. In Gallo-Roman times there was the great villa of the Bosseno. Later, the area was repopulated by immigrants from Britain and by monks from Ireland.

◖◗ **Église St-Cornély**★ – fine 17C Renaissance church In the centre of the village with good 17-19C decoration. **Musée de Préhistoire J.-Miln-Z.-Le-Rouzic**★★ ♿ ◷ *Jun-Sep: daily 10am-12.30pm, 1.30-7pm; Oct-May: daily 10am-12.30pm, 1.30-6pm.* ◷ *Closed Wed morning, Jan, 1 May, 25 Dec.* ⊜ *5€ (children: 2.50€).* ☎*02 97 52 22 04. www.museedecarnac.com.* **Tumulus St-Michel**★ ◷ *Daily 9am-7pm. No charge.*

The Ménec Alignments

J. Malburet/MICHELIN

CASSIS

MICHELIN MAP 340 I 6–POPULATION 8 000
GREEN GUIDE PROVENCE

The little resort has a bustling harbour and an attractive **setting**. At the beginning of the 20C, artists like Derain, Vlaminck, Matisse and Dufy were attracted here by the quality of the light.

🛈 **Information:** Oustau Calendal, Quai des Moulins, ☎0892 259 892. www.ot-cassis.com.

▶ **Orient Yourself:** Cassis is the nearest beach resort to Marseille, 22km away.

Excursion

The coast
Choice of boat excursions – enquire at tourist office. West of Cassis the Puget Massif is incised by steep-sided inlets known as **Calanques**★★, which make pleasant bathing-places. East of Cassis lies **Cap Canaille**★★★, at 362m – 1 188ft the highest sea-cliff in France.

The Cosquer Cave

The submarine cave situated near the tip of the headland at Cap Morgiou was discovered in 1985 by Henri Cosquer, a local diver. The sensational news of its painted decoration and engravings dating from the Paleolithic Age broke on 3 September 1991 and it was acclaimed as one of the high spots for rock art. Carbon dating techniques date the **hand prints** to c 27 000 BC and the animal drawings to c 17 000 BC, making them 1 000 to 2 000 years earlier than those at Lascaux, which are similar in style and technique. The marine fauna (seals, penguins, fish) is a rare feature which adds to the interest of this decorated cave, the oldest of this type in the world.

The cave was submerged as the level of the sea rose and its treasures were preserved. It will not be open to view owing to its inaccessibility. However, an exhibition on the site is presented at La Joliette docks in Marseille.

The Port of Cassis

G.Magnin/MICHELIN

CASTRES★

MICHELIN MAP 338 E-F 9-10–POPULATION 43 5000
GREEN GUIDE LANGUEDOC ROUSSILLON TARN GORGES

This industrial town on the **Agout** river has fine 16-17C mansions and a famous Goya museum, and makes a good base for exploring the Lacaune and Montagne Noire hill country.

🛈 **Information:** 3 r. Milhau-Ducommun, ☎05 63 62 63 62. www.tourisme-castres.fr
▶ **Orient Yourself:** Castres is 70km east of Toulouse.

Sight

Musée Goya★

🕐 Jul and Aug: daily 10am-6pm; Apr-Jun, Sep: daily except Mon 9am-noon, 2-6pm, Sun and public holidays 10am-noon, 2-6pm; Oct-Mar: daily except Mon 9am-noon, 2-5pm, Sun 10-noon, 2-5pm. 🕐 Closed 1 Jan, 1 May, 1 Nov, 25 Dec. ⊜ 3€

summer, 2.30€ winter, no charge 1st Sun in the month (Oct-May). ☎05 63 71 59 30.
Set up on the second floor of the former episcopal palace (presently the Town Hall), this museum specialises in Spanish painting and possesses several outstanding works by Goya, namely *Self-Portrait, The Disasters of War, Francisco del Mazo* and *The Junta of the Philippines led by Ferdinand VII.*

LA **CHAISE-DIEU**★★

MICHELIN MAP 331 E 2–POPULATION 778
GREEN GUIDE AUVERGNE THE RHÔNE VALLEY

Set amid lush green countryside and rolling hills, the ornate abbey comes as a magnificent surprise.

🛈 **Information:** Place de la Mairie, ☎04 71 00 01 16.
▶ **Orient Yourself:** The village is 40km from Le Puy.

Eglise abbatiale de St-Robert

J.Damase/MICHELIN

Visit

Église abbatiale de St-Robert★★

Over 1 000m – 3 300ft up on the high granite plateau of Livradois, La Chaise-Dieu Abbey was already famous in the 11C. In the 12C its importance was second only to that of Cluny and by the 13C it had 300 dependent congregations. The abbey's decline set in after 1518, when abbots were henceforth appointed by the king, with fiscal, rather than religious, considerations taking first place.

The granite west front with its twin towers (the spires have disappeared) speaks strongly of the abbey's former grandeur and austerity. Within, the structure is of a noble simplicity, a single-storeyed elevation. The **Monks' chancel★★** was built from 1344 to 1352 by Pope Clement VI, a former monk here, who is also buried here. The 14 Flemish **tapestries★★★** (1500-18) of wool, linen and silk, came from Arras and Brussels. The tapestries are hung over the 15C richly carved **stalls★★**, 144 in number. In the **Dance macabre (Dance of Death)★** figures of the mighty, of great ladies, or of clergymen are shown next to their likeness in death.

A great organ was installed at the west end in 1683 and enlarged in 1726; the organ-case (**buffet★**) is elaborately sculpted and contrasts with the spirit prevailing in the architecture of the choir.

▶ **Cloisters** ★.

CHÂLONS-EN-CHAMPAGNE★★

MICHELIN MAP 306 I 9–POPULATION 47 340
GREEN GUIDE ALSACE LORRAINE CHAMPAGNE

Its centre traversed by the River Marne and two canals, Châlons is a dignified and attractive commercial town with some fine buildings.

🚩 **Information:** 3 quai des Arts, ☎03 26 65 17 89. www.chalons-tourisme.com

▶ **Orient Yourself:** The town is in eastern Champagne, close to both the A26 and A4 autoroutes.

😊 **Don't Miss:** The town has some good restaurants.

A Bit of History

The valley of the Aube to the south-west of the town was the setting in 451 for the series of battles known as the Catalaunian Fields (**Champs catalauniques**). Having given up his intention of sacking Paris, then known as Lutetia, because of the intervention of St Genevieve, Attila the Hun was engaged here by the Roman army under Aetius; after fierce fighting, he quit the battlefield and fled eastwards.

Châlons was the birthplace in 1749 of Nicolas Appert, a pioneer of the food industry and the inventor of a system of preserving food by sterilisation.

Sights

Cathédrale St-Étienne★★

The present building was begun around 1235 in the Lanceolate Gothic style invented 40 years previously at Chartres, though there is little evidence of stylistic development having taken place.

The cathedral is famous for its stained glass (**vitraux**), Renaissance as well as medieval. The 13C glass includes the tall windows in the choir, the north transept (with the wonderful hues of green characteristic of the region), and the first bay on the north side (the Tanners' window – note the hanging skins). The finest windows however are those of Renaissance date, in the side chapels of the south aisle, showing scenes from the Creation, the earthly Paradise, the

Passion, the Life of Christ and the Lives of the Saints.

Église Notre-Dame-en-Vaux★

🕒 *Jun to mid-Sep: daily 10-noon, 2-6pm, Sun 2.30-6pm; mid-Sep to Jun: daily except Sun 10am-noon, 2-6pm.* ☏ *03 26 65 63 17.* A typical early-Gothic church with a characteristic four-tier elevation. Particularly noteworthy is the ambulatory, inspired by the one at St-Rémi in Reims, together with the stained glass in the windows of the north aisle, again showing superb skill in the use of green. To the left of the church, the **Musée du Cloître de Notre-Dame-en-Vaux**★★ (🕒 *Apr-Sep: Wed-Mon 10am-noon, 2-6pm; Oct-Mar: Mon, Wed-Fri 10-noon, 2-5pm, Sat-Sun 10am-noon, 2-6pm;* 🕒 *closed Tue, 1 Jan, 1 May, 1 and 11 Nov, 25 Dec;* ✆ *4.60€, no charge 1st Sun in the month Oct-May, call to verify;* ☏ *03 26 64 03 87)* houses **sculptures**★★ from the old Romanesque cloisters.

CHALON-SUR-SAÔNE★

MICHELIN MAP 320 J 9–POPULATION 62 452
GREEN GUIDE BURGUNDY JURA

Chalon is the urban centre for the fertile lowlands bordering the Saône River as it makes its way between the Jura and the Massif Central.

▶ **Orient Yourself:** Chalon-sur-Saône, which is listed as a "Town of Art and History," offers discovery tours conducted by guide-lecturers approved by the Ministry of Culture and Communication. Information at the tourist office or on www.vpah.culture.fr.

A Bit of History

The river is fed by a number of canals; at Corre it is joined by the Eastern Canal (Canal de l'Est – completed 1882), at Pontailler by the canal from the Marne (1907), at St-Jean-de-Losne by both the Rhine-Rhône Canal (1833) and the Burgundy Canal (1832). But it is only at Chalon, where it is joined by the Central Canal (completed 1790), that it becomes one of Europe's great commercial waterways, flowing south to join the Rhône at Lyon. Long before the present age, however, the Saône had been an important commercial route; a large number of amphora bases were found at Chalon, proof that wine was imported here from Naples before the introduction of the vine to Burgundy by the Romans.

Since the 18C the banks of the river have been a favoured site for industry, which includes the heavy engineering firm Schneider du Creusot as well as electrical works and nuclear power plants.

The Origins of Photography – Joseph Nicéphore Niepce (1765-1833) was a native of Chalon. His restlessly inventive disposition had already led him to design an internal combustion engine in 1807. He lacked talent as a draughtsman, but was fascinated by lithography. At the age of 48 he set himself the task of recording images through the spontaneous action of light. He was already familiar with the optics of the camera obscura which had been studied by the Arab physicist El Hazen (11C), by Leonardo da Vinci and by various 18C men of science, among them Jacques Charles, the husband of Lamartine's Elvire.

After three years' work he succeeded in making and fixing a positive image, and on 28 May 1816 he sent his brother a print made at his home in St-Loup-de-Varennes (7km – 4mi south); this was the very first photograph. **Daguerre** popularised Niepce's discovery and others developed it (e.g. Fox Talbot and Bayard).

Progressive refinement and invention have led from Niepce's simple apparatus to photography as an art form, to the Hasselblad used in lunar exploration and to the snapshots in the family album.

Sight

Musée Nicéphore Niépce★★

Kids ○ Jul and Aug: daily 10-12.30pm,1.30-6pm; Sep-Jun: daily 9.30-11.45am, 2-5.45pm. ○ Closed public holidays. ⊗ 3.10€, no charge Wed and 1st Sun in the month. ☎ 03 85 48 41 98. ww.museeniepce.com.

The museum is housed in the 18C Hôtel des Messageries on the banks of the Saône. The rich collection comprises photographs and early photographic equipment, including the earliest cameras ever made which were used by Joseph Nicéphore Niepce, as well as his first heliographs. There are also works by well-known contemporaries of Niepce in the world of photography.

◗◗ **Musée Denon★** ○ Wed-Mon 9.30am-noon, 2-5.30pm. ○ Closed Tue, 1 Jan, Easter Mon, 1 and 8 May, Ascension Day, Pentecost Mon, 14 Jul, 15 Aug, 1 and 11 Nov, 25 Dec. ⊗ 3.10€, no charge Wed and 1st Sun in the month. ☎ 03 85 94 74 41.– paintings and archeological collections.

CHAMBÉRY★★

MICHELIN MAP 333 I 3-4–POPULATION 113 460
GREEN GUIDE FRENCH ALPS

The well-restored old centre recaptures something of Chambéry's past splendour as the capital of Savoy.

- **Information:** 24 blvd de la Colonne, ☎04 79 33 42 47. www.chambery-tourisme.com
- ▶ **Orient Yourself:** The town is in the Alps, 10km south of Lac du Bourget.
- **Don't Miss:** The many trompe-l'œil decorations around the town will fascinate kids and adults alike.
- **Also See:** Lac du Bourget.

◗◗ The **Fontaine des Éléphants** rue de Boigne; **Sainte-Chapelle★**, part of the **château★** (⚲ 1hr guided tours daily; ⊗ 4€ ☎04 79 70 15 94)- Flamboyant architecture, Renaissance stained glass and trompe-l'œil painted vaults; **Vieille ville★**. **Château★**. **Musée Savoisien★** (○ Wed-Mon 10am-noon, 2-6pm. ○ Closed Tue and public holidays. ⊗ 3.10€, no charge 1st Sun in the month. ☎04 79 33 44 48) – prehistory, religious art, regional ethnography.

CHÂTEAU DE CHAMBORD★★★

MICHELIN MAP 318 G 6
GREEN GUIDE CHÂTEAUX OF THE LOIRE

The first of France's great Classical palaces, Chambord stands in a vast park enclosed by a 32km – 20 mile wall. Beyond stretches the forest of Sologne, teeming with the game that the rulers of France have long loved to hunt.

- **Information:** pl. Saint Louis, Chambord, ☎02 54 33 39 16.
- ▶ **Orient Yourself:** The château is south of the Loire, between Beaugency and Blois, at the end of a long avenue through woodland.
- ○ **Organising Your Time:** Allow at least 2 hours for the château.
- **Don't Miss:** Two particularly outstanding features of this immense château are the double spiral staircase and the roof terrace.

A Bit of History

At the age of 21, François I had just returned in triumph from his victory over the Swiss at Marignano which had given him possession of the Duchy of Milan. Dissatisfied with the old royal residence at Blois in spite of the improvements he had made, he had a vision of a dream castle to be built four leagues away on the forest edge. Leonardo da Vinci may have helped with the plans for this fabulous edifice; its feudal keep and corner towers belied its purpose as a palace of pleasure and status symbol for a Renaissance prince. The château was begun in 1519; later Philibert Delorme, Jean Bullant and the great Mansart all worked on it.

Hardly had Chambord started to rise from its foundations when the king suffered defeat and captivity at Pavia in 1525. On his return to France he judged it more suitable for a monarch to live close to his capital, at either Fontainebleau or St-Germain-en-Laye.

Visit

🕐 Apr-Sep: 9am-6.15pm, except 14 Jul-20 Aug: 9am-7.30pm. Rest of year: 9am-5.15pm. Last entry 30min before closing. 🕐 Closed public holidays. ⟜ Guided visits available. ⟹ 9.50 P in Jul-Aug, rest of year 8.50 P. ☎02 54 50 40 00. www.chambord.org

The château's double staircase is justly famous for its interlocking spirals opening onto internal loggias and for its vaults adorned with salamanders, François' crest.

The extraordinary roof terrace was where the king and his entourage spent much of their time watching tournaments and festivals or the start and return of the hunt; its nooks and crannies lent themselves to the confidences, intrigues and assignations of courtly life, played out against this fantastic background of pepperpot turrets, chimney stacks, dormers peeping from the roofs, false windows embellished with shells, all decorated with inset slatework and dominated by the splendid lantern.

The state rooms contain rich furnishings: wood panelling, tapestries, furniture, portraits, hunting collections.

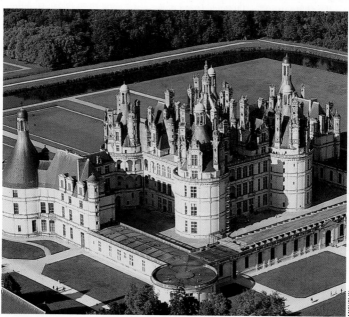

Château de Chambord

MICHELIN

CHAMONIX-MONT-BLANC★★★

MICHELIN MAP 328 M-O 5–POPULATION 9 830

GREEN GUIDE FRENCH ALPS

Chamonix is France's mountaineering capital. It lies at the foot of the famous 3 000m – 10 000ft Chamonix Needles (Aiguilles de Chamonix) at a point where the glacial valley of the Arve widens out. All around are the high mountains of the Mont Blanc Massif; this is the most renowned of the massifs of the French Alps, because of its dramatic relief, crystalline rocks and glacial morphology. The dome of the great White Mountain is visible from the town.

- **Information:** 85, Place du Triangle de l'Amitié , ☎04 50 53 00 24. www.chamonix.com.
- ▶ **Orient Yourself:** Chamonix is 101km/63mi east of Annecy.
- ◷ **Organising Your Time:** The resort is very crowded during school holidays, so try to come at some other time. Always reserve your rides up the Aiguille du Midi and Montenvers, and be sure to check the weather in advance.

Site

The tongue of the 7km – 4 mile-long Glacier des Bossons hangs 500m – 1 650ft above the valley on the approach to Chamonix.

The Geneva naturalist **Horace Benedict de Saussure** based himself here in the course of his scientific studies in Savoy. In 1760, he offered a reward for the first ascent of Mont-Blanc. On 8 August 1786 Dr Michel Paccard and Jacques Balmat reached the summit, thereby inaugurating the age of mountaineering, as well as the development of the town as an Alpine resort.

The Mer de Glace

J.-L. Gallo/MICHELIN

Excursions

🚠 *By cable-car or rack railway*

Aiguille du Midi ★★★

🕐 *Jul-Aug: daily 7.10am-5pm; May-Jun and Sep-Oct: daily 8.10am-4pm; Nov-Apr: daily 8.10am-3.30pm. Trip in two stages: Chamonix-Plan de l'Aiguille and Plan de l'Aiguille-Aiguille du Midi. (departures every 30min).* 🎫 *36€ round trip.* ☎04 50 53 22 75, reservation possible in summer, call ☎08 36 68 00 67. Allow at least 2hr round trip on the cable-car.*

The **panorama★★★**, especially from the central peak (3 842m – 12 605ft), is staggering, taking in Mont-Blanc, Mont-Maudit, the Grandes Jorasses, and the dome of the Goûter whose buttresses are buried in 30m – 100ft of ice.

The **Vallée Blanche**, also known as the Giant's Glacier (Glacier du Géant), can be reached by taking the cable-car (*teleferique*) to Pointe Helbronner. From here can be seen the glacial cirques with their flanks worn down by the incessant attacks of the ice.

Mer de Glace★★★

2hr30min by rack railway and teleferique.

The view from the upper station of the railway built in 1908 takes in the whole of this "sea of ice". The glacier is 14km – 9 miles long, in places 400m – 1 300ft thick, and moves 90m – 300ft a year. The rocky material it carries with it scores and scratches the mountain walls on either side as well as giving the glacier its characteristic rather grimy appearance (as the ice evaporates grit is left on the surface). At the foot of the glacier this material is deposited, forming a terminal moraine.

Beyond, the eye is led from one peak to another; this **panorama★★★** is one of the most beautiful in the region.

◐◑ Summit of the Brévent★★★

🕐 *Jun and Sep: daily 9am-4pm; Jul-Aug: daily 8am-5pm; Oct-May: daily 8.45am-5pm. Chamonix-Planpraz by rack railway (10min), Planpraz-Brévent by teleferique (10min).* 🕐 *Closed May and Oct to mid-Dec.* 🎫 *20€ round trip* ☎04 50 53 22 75. **La Flégère viewpoint★★** By teleferique* 🕐 *Jul and Aug: daily 7.40am-5.30pm; Jun and Sep: daily 8.40am-4.30pm; mid-Dec to mid-Apr: daily 8.45am-5pm.* 🕐 *Closed end Apr-May.* 🎫 *18€ round trip.* ☎04 50 53 22 75.

Summit of the **Aiguille des Grands-Montets★★★**; **Bellevue★★** (Les Houches) and the **Nid d'Aigle★★** (glacier de Bionnassay – leave from St-Gervais-les-Bains).

CHÂTEAU DE **CHANTILLY**★★★

MICHELIN MAP 305 F-G 6
GREEN GUIDE NORTHERN FRANCE AND THE PARIS REGION

A synonym for elegance, Chantilly evokes wonderful art collections, a great park and forest, and the cult of the horse as well as the château itself.

- 🅸 **Information:** 60 av. du Mar.-Joffre, Chantilly, ☎03 44 67 37 37. www.chantilly-tourisme.com.
- ▶ **Orient Yourself:** Chantilly is 50km north of Paris. When you arrive, the château is well signposted.
- 🕐 **Organising Your Time:** Allow at least 2 hours for the château.

Visit

Château

Anne de Montmorency, the great Constable of France who served six monarchs (from Louis XII to Charles IX), had a Renaissance castle built here in 1528. The foundations of an earlier building (1386) were re-used. In 1560 the architect Jean Bullant designed a charming little château (Petit Château) to the south of the main building.

The Great Condé and his descendants later made the state rooms of the Petit Château into their living quarters; today, there is much to delight the eye, including Rococo woodwork, manuscripts, silver caskets and icons. The greatest treasure is in the Library (Cabinet des Livres); this is the **Limbourg** brothers' sumptuously illuminated *Book of Hours for the Duke of Berry (Les Très Riches Heures du Duc de Berry)* of about 1415, completed 60 years later by Jean Colombe (on display in reproduction).

Under Louis II of Bourbon, known as the Great Condé, Le Nôtre laid out the park and gardens; François Mansart redesigned the principal façade and the layout of the rooms

At the French Revolution, the château was dismantled to first-floor level, the Petit Château was ruined and the park laid waste.

On the death of Louis-Joseph de Condé, the estate passed into the hands of the Duke of Aumale, who rebuilt the great edifice (1875-83) in a neo-Renaissance style.

The château houses a museum (**musée**★★) (🕒 *Mar-Oct: daily 10am-6pm; Nov-Feb: daily 10am-12.45pm, 2-5pm, Sat-Sun and public holidays 10.30am-5pm;* ✆ *7€, museum and park;* ☎ *03 44 62 62 62)* – manuscripts, furniture, paintings, sculpture – whose wealth would prove difficult to rival today.

Grandes Écuries★★

These stables were built in 1721 by Jean Aubert for Louis-Henri of Bourbon, the Great Condé's great-grandson. Much admired in its time, it is the finest example of 18C building at Chantilly to have come down to us. The stables house the **Musée vivant du Cheval et du Poney**★ (🕒 *Apr-Oct: daily 10.30am-6.30pm, Sat-Sun and public holidays 10.30am-7pm; Nov-Mar: daily except Tue 2-6pm, Sat-Sun and public holidays 10.30am-6.30pm; last admission 1hr before closing;* ✆ *8€, children 4-12 years: 5.50€;* ☎ *03 44 57 40 40, www. musee-vivant-du-cheval.fr)*, which has stalls from the time of the Duke of Aumale, historic harnessing, costumes, and all kinds of objects associated with equitation. Riding displays take place in the central rotunda.

More than 3 000 horses are stabled and trained in and around Chantilly; race-meetings and hunts both perpetuate the tradition begun on 15 May 1834 when France's first great official race-meeting was held, and maintain Chantilly's reputation as the country's thoroughbred capital.

▶▶ **Parc**★★ 🕒 *Mar-Oct: Wed-Mon 10am-6pm; Nov-Feb: Mon, Wed-Fri 10.30am-12.45pm, 2-5pm, Sat-Sun and public holidays 10.30am-5pm. 🕒 Closed Tue.* ♿ ✆ *3.50€.* ☎ *03 44 62 62 62. www.chateaudechantilly. com.* **Appartements des Princes**★. English gardens: 🕒 *Same hours as the park.*

CHARTRES★★★

MICHELIN MAP 311 E 5–POPULATION 40 361

GREEN GUIDE NORTHERN FRANCE AND THE PARIS REGION

Chartres' magnificent cathedral, the "Acropolis of France" (Rodin), still beckons to the pilgrim far off across the endless cornfields of the Beauce. The area was occupied by the Carnutes, and Druids once worshipped here; there is also evidence of the pagan cult of a holy spring, and possibly also of a mother-goddess, whom the first missionaries may have christianised as a forerunner of the Virgin Mary.

🛈 **Information:** Place de la Cathédrale, ☎02 37 18 26 26. www.chartres-tourisme.com

▶ **Orient Yourself:** The cathedral dominates the old quarter, known as Quartier St-André.

🕒 **Organising Your Time:** Allow at least 2 hours for the cathedral.

Address Book

For coin ranges, see the Legend on the cover flap.

WHERE TO EAT

Le Pichet – *19 r. du Cheval-Blanc.* ☎*02 37 21 08 35 – restaurant.pichet@ voila.fr. Closed Tue evening and Wed.* Just down the street from the cathedral, a very friendly little bistro that suits our tastes. Inside, there is a pleasant jumble of bric-a-brac: wooden chairs, a collection of coffeepots, pitchers, old street signs and other good stuff. The food is traditional French cuisine.

Le Café Serpente – *2 r. du Cloître Notre-Dame.* ☎*02 37 21 68 81.* A bicycle on the ceiling, posters on the walls and enamelled plaques in the stairwell comprise the decor of this thoroughly genial old café opposite the cathedral. On your plates: appetizing salads, brasserie fare and authentic cuisine at all hours.

Le Tripot – *11 pl. Jean-Moulin.* ☎ *02 37 36 60 11. Closed last 2 weeks of Aug, Sun-Mon.* This house built in 1553 used to accommodate a *jeu de paume* (real tennis court) called 'Le Tripot' whose Latin motto meaning 'Belligerents: stay away' may still be seen above the front door. A timeless ultimatum! Well-preserved rustic interior and contemporary cuisine.

WHERE TO STAY

La Ferme du Château (Bed and Breakfast) – *in Levesville, 28300 Bailleau-l'Évêque – 8km/5mi NW of Chartres via N 154 and D 134.* ☎*02 37 22 97 02. 3 rms.* This elegant Beauce farm offers pretty, comfortable rooms that have been decorated with a light hand. Neighbouring a small château, the farm is very quiet and its kind, hospitable owners are very discreet.

Le Grand Monarque – *22 pl. des Épars.* ☎*02 37 18 15 15, info@ bw-grand-monarque.com – 50 rms* – 🍽 *11€ – restaurant* 🍽🍽🍽🍽. A 16C coaching inn at the heart of the city. The comfortable rooms have a personal touch; some are embellished with cheerfully flowered patterns and canopies while others are more sober. Snug dining room with wood carvings and works of art.

SHOPPING

Marché aux légumes et volailles – *Pl. Billard.* Each Saturday morning, the covered Vegetable and Poultry Market displays colourful stands featuring authentic Beauce produce. This carrousel of sights, tastes and fragrances is one of the most popular markets in the area.

Atelier Loire – *16 r. d'Ouarville, 28300 Léves – Just north of Chartres on the way to Dreux, 2km/1.2mi from the cathedral* – ☎ *02 37 21 20 71 – www.galerie-du-vitrail.com –* 👓 *guided tours Fri pm. Closed Aug and public holidays.* A century-old, stately residence set amidst a park and adorned with stained-glass creations is the home of this atelier founded in 1946 by Gabriel Loire, and continued today by his grandchildren. The art and technique of making stained glass are carefully explained, beginning with artists' models (as designed by Adami, Miro or Fernand Léger, for example) and ending with the finished product created by master glass crafters. The visit, with its thousand hues and shades, is simply magical.

ON THE TOWN

Brûlerie les Rois Mages – *6 r. des Changes.* ☎*02 37 36 30 52 –* 🕐 *Tue-Sat 9:15am-12:15pm, 1:30-7:15pm.* Enter this "retro" coffee-roasting shop and choose among the wide variety of coffees roasted on site and the dozens of teas to enjoy in the brûlerie or take home.

La Chocolaterie – *14 pl. Marceau.* ☎*02 37 21 86 92 –* 🕐 *Tue-Sat, 8am-7:30pm; Sun-Mon 10am-7:30pm.* A highly useful address for stocking up on gourmet treats to take home as souvenirs, such as macaroons or Mentchikoffs, a local chocolate speciality. The very cosy tearoom offers sofas and a fireplace; there's a pleasant terrace in summer.

A Bit of History

The picturesque old town **(le Vieux Chartres ★)** lies at the point where the Eure cuts into the plain of the Beauce. Today, the old mill-races and laundry-houses have been restored, and a number of 17C houses have kept their embossed doorways topped by a bull's-eye. The most attractive townscape is to be found in the St-André quarter, by the riverbanks, and in Rue des Écuyers and Rue du Cygne. Loëns Granary (Grenier de Loëns) is a fine 12C building which once housed the tithes of grain and wine.

Chartres attracted pilgrims at an early date, first of all to Our Lady of the Underground Chapel (Notre-Dame-de-Sous-Terre), then to the cathedral which Bishop Fulbert built in the 11C but which was burnt down in 1194.

Sight

Cathédrale Notre-Dame★★★

👆 See *Introduction: Art – Architecture*. Reconstruction began immediately and was completed in the short space of 25 years. The north and south porches were added only 20 years later and the building consequently has a unity of style possessed by few other Gothic churches. Pilgrims have been coming here for eight centuries. .

The new cathedral raised the Transitional Gothic style to new levels. The bays of the nave, previously square in plan, are now oblong and have sexpartite vaults; the arches of arcades and windows are more pointed; a round opening is inserted in the space above the highest windows; the structural functions of galleries are taken over by flying buttresses, and a narrow triforium (still windowless) forms an inspection gallery.

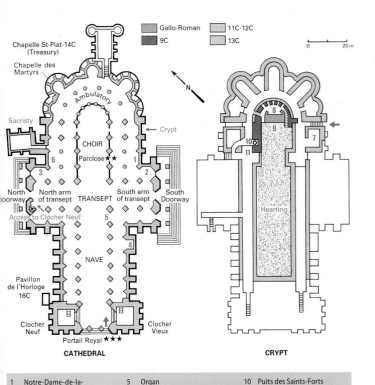

| | Gallo-Roman | | 11C-12C |
| | 9C | | 13C |

0   20 m

Chapelle St-Piat-14C
(Treasury)

Chapelle des
Martyrs

Ambulatory

Sacristy

← Crypt

CHOIR

Parclose ★★

6   1

3   2

North   North arm   South arm   South
Doorway   of transept   TRANSEPT   of transept   Doorway

Access to Clocher Neuf   5

NAVE

Pavillon
de l'Horloge
16C

Clocher   Clocher
Neuf   Vieux

Portail Royal ★★★

CATHEDRAL

8

9

10

11

7

Hearting

CRYPT

1	Notre-Dame-de-la-Belle-Verrière	5	Organ	10	Puits des Saints-Forts
2	St Fulbert's window	6	Vierge du Pilier	11	Chapelle Notre-Dame-de-Sous-Terre
3	Window of Peace	7	Chapelle St-Martin		
4	Chapelle Vendôme	8	Crypte St-Lubin		
		9	Gallo-Roman wall		

Gothic verticality reigns outside too, but the architect wisely kept two Romanesque masterworks, the Old Bell Tower (Clocher vieux) of 1145, a marvel of audacity and lightness, and the Royal Doorway, **Portail Royal**★★★, of the west front, with its long-bodied but intensely expressive sculpted figures. The cathedral's interior is subtly lit by its superb stained glass (**vitraux**★★★) which covers a total area of 2 700m2 – 25 000sq ft and depicts 5 000 figures. Most of the windows date from the 12C and 13C and are the greatest achievement of this art form. "Chartres blue" is famous for its clarity and depth; its full range can best be seen in the wonderful Notre-Dame-de-la-Belle-Verrière Window (*first window on the south side of the ambulatory*). In 1964, the American Society of Architects gave a window (in the south transept) and in 1971 the German Friends of the Cathedral did likewise (*north transept*).

◖◖ Musée des Beaux-Arts – **enamels**★ ◷ *May-Oct: Mon, Wed-Sat 10am-noon, 2-6pm, Sun 2-6pm; Nov-Apr: Mon, Wed-Sat 10am-noon, 2-5pm, Sun 2-5pm.* ◷ *Closed Tue, 1 Jan, 1 and 8 May, 1 and 11 Nov, 25 Dec.* ⊕ *2.60€.* ☎ *02 37 36 41 39.* **Église St-Pierre**★ – **stained glass**★.

CHÂTILLON-SUR-SEINE★

MICHELIN MAP 320 H 2–POPULATION 6 269
GREEN GUIDE BURGUNDY JURA

Châtillon occupied a strategic location on the ancient north-south trade route. It was here that the Seine ceased to be navigable; as a result, the place developed all the facilities that transhipment needed, and grew prosperous on the merchandise being exchanged between Cornwall and Etruria – amber, tin, coral, ceramics.

🛈 **Information:** Place Marmont, ☎03 80 91 13 19. www.pays-chatillonnais.fr
▶ **Orient Yourself:** The town is in a rural area 83km north of Dijon.

Sight

Trésor de Vix★★
Found in the tomb of a young Celtic queen, 1C grave goods (the treasure of Vix) can be seen in the town museum.

CHÂTEAU DE **CHENONCEAU**★★★

MICHELIN MAP 317 P 5
GREEN GUIDE CHÂTEAUX OF THE LOIRE

Chenonceau is a jewel of Renaissance architecture built 1513-21 on the site of a fortified mill on the River Cher by Thomas Bohier, François I's treasurer. It is a rectangular building with corner-towers; it stands on two piers of the former mill resting on the bed of the Cher. The library and the chapel are projecting structures to the left. Catherine de Medici's two-storeyed gallery is built on the bridge spanning the river.

🛈 **Information:** 1 r. Bretonneau, ☎02 47 23 94 45
▶ **Orient Yourself:** 14km south of Amboise, the château straddles the River Cher. The main entrance is on the north bank.
◷ **Organising Your Time:** Allow at least 2 hours for the château, the gardens and a riverbank stroll.

A Bit of History

Over the years the place has been in the charge of six women, of whom three marked it strongly with their personality.

Catherine Briçonnet was the wife of Thomas Bohier. In his absence she supervised much of the building work. It is to her that we owe the central hall giving onto all the other rooms; its axial vault, broken by keystones, is a masterpiece. Another innovation is the introduction into the Loire Valley of an Italian staircase, that is, one that substitutes ramps for Gothic spirals, and is consequently much better adapted for receptions. However, here the returns are still curved and provided with steps.

In 1556 **Diane de Poitiers** commissioned Philibert Delorme, who had previously worked for her at Anet, to design the flower garden (to the east) as well as the bridge across the Cher.

Three years later, on the death of Henri II, **Catherine de' Medici** humiliated the former favourite by forcing her to exchange Chenonceau for Chaumont.

Later, she added the two extra storeys to the bridge, laid out the gardens to the west and gave the windows their elaborate pediments.

Visit

Jul-Aug and public holidays: 9am-8pm. Otherwise, mid-Mar to mid-Sep: daily 9am-7pm; mid to end Sep: daily 9am-6.30pm; early to mid-Mar and early to mid-Oct: daily 9am-6pm; mid to end Oct and mid to end Feb: daily 9am-5.30pm; early to mid-Feb and early to mid-Nov: daily 9am-5pm; mid-Nov to end Jan: daily 9am-4.30pm. 9.50€ (children 7-18 years: 8€). 08 20 20 90 90. www.chenonceau.com.

There is much to see within the château; a fine fireplace by **Jean Goujon** (in the Salle Diane de Poitiers), the Library of 1521, the ceiling of the Green Cabinet (Cabinet Vert), the portrait of Diane by Primaticcio, the tapestries and mantelpiece of the Salon Louis XIV, a fine Renaissance creation with its wealth of scrolls, baskets of fruit, cornucopias and fantastic beasts.

CHÂTEAU DE **CHEVERNY**★★★

MICHELIN MAP 318 F 7

GREEN GUIDE CHÂTEAUX OF THE LOIRE

Cheverny was built between 1604 and 1634 with that simplicity and distinction characteristic of the Classical architecture of the reigns of Henri IV and Louis XIII.

▪ **Information:** 12 r. des Chenes des Dames, Cour-Cheverny, 02 54 79 95 63.

▸ **Orient Yourself:** 17km south of Blois, the château can be seen from afar.

◔ **Organising Your Time:** It'll take about 1 hour to visit the château, but if the weather is fine, allow some time to walk and relax in the beautiful gardens.

Kids Especially for Kids: There's a permanent exhibition on the cartoon character Tintin.

Visit

Allow 45min. Jul-Aug: daily 9.15am-6.45pm; Apr-Jun and Sep: daily 9.15am-6.15pm; Oct and Mar: daily 9.15am-5pm; Nov-Feb: daily 9.45am-5pm; "feeding the dogs" early Apr to mid-Sep: daily 5pm; mid-Sep to end Mar: daily except Tue, Sat-Sun and public holidays 3pm. 6.50€ (château and park). 02 54 79 96 29. www.chateau-cheverny.com.

The main façade is built in stone from **Bourré** (28km – 1mi southwest) which whitens and hardens with age. The elevation is strictly symmetrical, extending to either side of the well containing the staircase, and terminated by massive corner pavilions with square domes. The

Main façade, Chateau de Cheverny

prominent slate roofs are in Louis XIII style, pierced with mansards and bull's-eye windows. The first-floor windows are crowned with scrolls; between them are medallions of Roman emperors (Julius Caesar in the central pediment). The elegant doorway is adorned with two concentric collars. The state rooms, served by a majestic Louis XIII ramped staircase with massive balustrades and rich sculptural decoration, contain a fine collection of furniture from the 17C to the 19C.

CHINON★★

MICHELIN MAP 317 J 5–POPULATION 8 716
GREEN GUIDE CHÂTEAUX OF THE LOIRE

Chinon occupies a sunny site on the Vienne, surrounded by the fertile Veron countryside, and known for the mildness of its climate.

- **Information:** Place d'Hofheim, ☎02 47 93 17 85. www.chinon.com
- ▶ **Orient Yourself:** Chinon is 45km west of Tours.
- ◷ **Organising Your Time:** Allow at least 2 hours to explore the château and the town.

Sights

Le Vieux Chinon★★

The old town has kept its medieval and Renaissance appearance. The old gabled houses with corner turrets and the 16C and 17C mansions, most of them in white tufa, make up a most evocative townscape. Many fine old buildings stand in its main street Rue Voltaire, including the Gothic dwelling where Richard the Lionheart is supposed to have died in 1199. At the crossroads **(Grand Carroi★★)** the oldest houses of all press closely together. On her arrival from Vaucouleurs on Sunday 6 March 1429, **Joan of Arc** is thought to have used the coping of the well-head here to dismount from her horse. The following day she picked out the Dauphin hiding among his courtiers, and declared, "You are the heir of France and true son of the king, Lieutenant of the King of Heaven who is King of France".

Château★★

◷ Apr-Sep: daily 9am-7pm; Oct-Mar: daily 9.30am-5pm. ◷ Closed 1 Jan and 25 Dec. ☞ 6€ (12-18 years: 4.50€). ☎02 47 93 13 45.

The River Vienne at Chinon

The spur overlooking the town was the site of a Gallic oppidum, then of a fortress, long before Henry II of England (born at Le Mans in 1133) built the present castle to protect Anjou from Capetian designs. The castle was taken by Philippe Auguste in 1205 from John Lackland; it subsequently became a royal residence, was strengthened by Charles VII, but then abandoned by the court at the end of the 15C and gradually dismantled.

The remians of the castle include, to the east, St George's Fort (Fort St-Georges), watching over the most vulnerable approach, the Middle Castle (Château du Milieu) which has a 14C clock tower, the royal apartments and gardens, and finally the Coudray Fort (Fort de Coudray) at the far end of the spur.

CLERMONT-FERRAND★★

MICHELIN MAP 326 E-G 7-10–POPULATION 258 541

GREEN GUIDE AUVERGNE THE RHÔNE VALLEY

The site★★ of Clermont is unique; the old town, including the cathedral, is built on a volcano, whose black lava makes for an unusual townscape. To the north are the plateaux of Chanturgue and Les Côtes, once the site of a Gallic oppidum, and an example of the phenomenon known as relief inversion, which has protected them from erosion and left them standing out from the surrounding country. To the west are the summits of the Puys, the mountain range that gives Clermont its incomparable setting, perhaps best viewed from the Place de la Poterne with its pretty fountain (**Fontaine d'Amboise★**) of 1515.

- **Information:** Place de la Victoire, ☎04 73 62 71 00. www.clermont-fd.com.
- **Orient Yourself:** Place de Jaude is the focal point for everything that's happening in the city, and is a good place to start.
- **Organising Your Time:** Allow at least 2 hours for the cathedral.
- **Walking tours:** The tourist office organises 2hr discovery tours of Clermont from early Jul to mid-Sep on Mon, Wed, and Fri at 3pm, and on Tue and Thur at 8.30pm. Tours of Montferrand are on Tue, Thurs and Sat at 3pm. There are also theme tours, possibilities for a Sun visit to a museum or special temporary exhibits, and excursions. The cost is 5.70€.

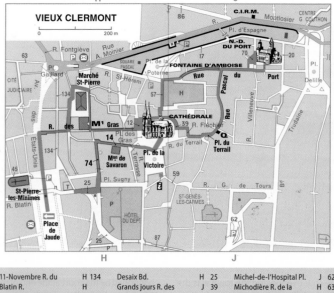

VIEUX CLERMONT

11-Novembre R. du	H	134	Desaix Bd.	H	25	Michel-de-l'Hospital Pl.	J	62
Blatin R.	H		Grands jours R. des	J	39	Michodière R. de la	H	63
Bourse Pl. de la	H	12	Gras R. des	H		Notre-Dame du Port Pl.	J	70
Chaussetiers R. des	H	14	Lamartine R.	H	45	Petit Gras R. des	H	74
Claussmann R.	J	17	Marcombes R. Ph.	H	57	Richepin R. Jean	J	86
Couronne R.	J	20	Massillon R.	J	59	St-Esprit R. R.	H	87

Hôtel M. de Chazerat	J	Q	Musée du Ranquet	H	M¹

A Bit of History

Clermont was the great oppidum of the Arverni (the Celts who gave their name to the Auvergne). Here in 52BC, Julius Caesar and his legions were roundly defeated by the forces of the Gallic chieftain **Vercingétorix**, whose spirited equestrian statue by Bartholdi stands at one end of Clermont's Place de Jaude . Caesar soon returned, this time winning a decisive battle, and captured Vercingétorix who was taken to Rome to be executed.

Notre-Dame Cathedral: Virgin and Child in the first south aisle

The Capital of the Motor Tyre

Two men, Aristide Barbier and Édouard Daubrée came together around 1830 to make agricultural machinery as well as gunshot, and rubber belts and tubes. In 1889, their factory was taken over by the brothers **André** and **Édouard Michelin**, the grandsons of Barbier. Building on their tradition of applying scientific method to the work of industry, the company has subsequently flourished through study of the client's real needs, scrupulous observation of reality and the consolidation of previous experience. This process has led via the detachable bicycle tyre of 1891, the car tyre of 1895, the low pressure "Confort" tyre of 1923, the "Metalic" of 1937 (its steel-reinforced casing helped heavy road transport come of age), the radial tyre of 1946 (given the designation "X" in 1949), to today's achievements, with the introduction in the early 1990's of the new Michelin Energy tyre. This new "green" tyre technology – based on reduced rolling resistance – will enable the driver to make considerable savings on fuel.

PARIS-BORDEAUX 1895 / 1ᵉˢ VOITURE sur PNEUS MICHELIN

It was at Clermont on 28 November 1095 Pope Urban II called for the reconquest of the Holy Land, and launched **The First Crusade**. Thousands of men set off from here, only to perish. Clermont was also the town of the remarkable writer, mathematician, thinker and inventor **Blaise Pascal** ("The heart has its reasons that reason knows not" – Blaise Pascal 1623-62). Among other things, at 19 he invented an adding machine (*on display in Musée du Ranquet*).

Sights

Basilique Notre-Dame du Port★★

  See Introduction: Art – Architecture. This is the finest of the larger Romanesque churches of the Lower Auvergne, unforgettable in its beautiful simplicity. It was built around 1150 over a crypt of the 11C.

Inside, the raised chancel (**chœur★★★**), admirably proportioned, is divided from the ambulatory by eight slender columns; their capitals (**chapiteaux★★**), together with those of the wall of the ambulatory, are among the finest in Auvergne because of their good state of preservation, their fascinating subjects, and their expressiveness.

In the crypt is an ancient, possibly Celto-Gallic well, together with a Black Virgin,

a copy of a Byzantine icon, which has been worshipped here since the 13C.

Rue Pascal

Lined with lava-built residences of somewhat severe aspect, this is one of the typical streets of the old town (**Vieux Clermont★★**).

Cathédrale Notre-Dame-de-l'Assomption★★

Compare this building with Notre-Dame-du-Port: a revolutionary change in architectural style had occurred in the 100 years which separates the two. This recalls the High Gothic of northern France. The west front, spires and first two bays of the nave are the work of **Viollet-le-Duc** in 1865. The stained-glass medallions (**vitraux★★**) of the 12C-15C are copies of those in the Sainte-Chapelle in Paris. The **Treasury★** (*early Jul to mid-Sep: Mon-Sat 2.30-5pm; min. 10 people required. ☎04 73 92 46 61*) displays 12C-19C collections of gold, silver and enamel ware.

▸ **Vieux Montferrand★★** (old town). **Musée d'Art Roger-Quilliot★★**(*Tue-Sun 10am-6pm. Closed Mon, 1 Jan, 1 May, 1 Nov, 25 Dec. 4.20€, no charge 1st Sun in the month. ☎04 73 16 11 30.*) **Église St-Léger★** (fortified church at Royat).

CLUNY★★

MICHELIN MAP 320 H 11–POPULATION 4 376

GREEN GUIDE BURGUNDY JURA

The conditions for the future renown and prosperity of the great **Abbaye de Cluny**★★ existed at the very moment of its foundation.

- 🛈 **Information:** 6 r. Merciere, ☎03 85 59 05 34. www.cluny-tourisme.com.
- ▶ **Orient Yourself:** A climb to the top of the Tour des Fromage gives the best view of the town and its historic structures.
- 🕓 **Organising Your Time:** Start with a guided tour of the abbey, then stroll in the town.
- 🚶**Walking Tours:** The tourist office has details of a choice of guided tours.
- 🅿 **Parking:** Plenty of parking available at pl. de l'Abbaye and pl. du Marche.

A Bit of History

The abbey, founded 910, deep in forest, far removed from the centres of power in either France or Germany, was subject to no authority other than that of the Pope himself. it answered – like its daughter houses and other dependencies – to no one but its elected abbot. It thus became a powerful instrument for the Papacy.

Cluny's development was rapid, its prestige immense, and its influence pre-eminent. In under a century, the abbey had amassed considerable power as well as much property and already had 1 184 daughter and dependent houses. One hundred and fifty years later their numbers had risen to 3 000, scattered all over Europe. For two and a half centuries this capital of monasticism found leaders of exceptional calibre, some of whom ruled for up to 60 years. The decline of the order began in the 13C, but its prosperity lasted until the 18C.

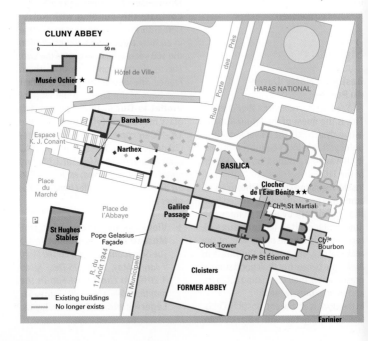

CLUNY ABBEY

Musée Ochier ★
Hôtel de Ville
HARAS NATIONAL
Rue Porte des Prés
Espace K. J. Conant
Barabans
Narthex
BASILICA
Place du Marché
Clocher de l'Eau Bénite ★★
Ch¹¹ᵉ St Martial
Place de l'Abbaye
Galilee Passage
St Hughes' Stables
Pope Gelasius Façade
Clock Tower
Ch¹¹ᵉ St Étienne
Ch¹¹ᵉ Bourbon
R. du 11 Août 1944
R. Municipale
Cloisters
FORMER ABBEY
Existing buildings
No longer exists
Farinier

Sight

Église Abbatiale

The abbey church, started 1088, was completed in 1130. It was destroyed during the Revolution. All that remains are the lower parts of two towers; the bell-tower known as "the Holy Water" (**Eau bénite★★**), a superb octagon, and another known as the Clock Tower (Tour de l'Horloge); of the great transept, the south arm with its two chapels and an octagonal vault (32m – 105ft high); of the minor transept, the chapel (Chapelle de Bourbon) with sculpted heads of the Prophets. Reduced in height, the flour store (Farinier) has a fine 13C timber roof, and eight capitals from the abbey. The abbey buildings were rebuilt in the 18C.

▶ **Musée Ochier★** – sculpture.

Excursion

Château de Cormatin★★

13km – 8mi north. Guided tours *(45min) early Apr to end May: 10am-noon, 2-5.30pm (Jun-Sep: 6.30pm), mid-Jul to mid-Aug: 10am-6.30pm). The park is open to the public even when the château is closed.* 6.50€. 03 85 50 16 55. The château (*4km – 2.5mi north of Taizé*), probably built by Jacques II Androuet du Cerceau, is a good example of the Henri IV style (late 16C-early 17C): the monumental gates framed by antique orders, the basement built of stone and the windows decorated with mouldings. The mannerist style which evolved in the literary salons under Louis XIII (1610-43) reached its peak with the gilding and the lapis-lazuli decoration of the St Cecilia Room (**Cabinet Ste-Cécile★★★**).

COGNAC★

MICHELIN MAP 324 I 5–POPULATION 19 534
GREEN GUIDE FRENCH ATLANTIC COAST

For many years Cognac was a river port on the calm waters of the Charente, exporting salt – the best in the world, so said the Scandinavians – and, from the 11C, wine. In 1570, it was one of the four strongholds conceded to the Protestants under the Treaty of St-Germain.

▣ **Information:** 16 r. du 14-juillet, ☎05 45 82 10 71. www.tourism-cognac.com.

▶ **Orient Yourself:** Place Francois I, a busy square with an ornamental fountain, links the old part of Cognac, on the slope above the River Charente, with the sprawling modern town.

☺ **Don't Miss:** Be sure to make time for a visit to one of the distilleries.

A Bit of History

Of all the different kinds of spirits, it is cognac which has acquired a universal reputation. Early in the 17C local vintners started to distil wines that travelled badly, in order to help turnover, reduce excise dues and facilitate storage. The taste for the product spread to Holland, Scandinavia and Britain, whose long association with brandy is reflected in some of the great names of Cognac, Hine, Martell, Hennessy.

A century later it was realised that ageing improved the quality of the spirit.

Cognac was divided into regions in 1887; today they comprise Grande Champagne, Petite Champagne, Borderies, Fins Bois, Bons Bois and Bois Ordinaires, reflecting, in that order, a decreasing proportion of chalk in the soil, an increasing earthiness of taste – *goût de terroir* – and ability to mature rapidly.

The production of cognac is the result of a two-stage distillation process, using the special still of the region. The 90 000ha – 220 000 acres of vineyards yield a white wine which is light, flowery and quite acid; it takes nine litres of it to make

Hennessy distillery

one of brandy. It is then kept in barrels made of porous oak from the Limoges district for at least two and a half years, during which time the brandy absorbs tannin and resins from the wood, and oxygen from the atmosphere, to which it loses 2 1/2% of its volume per annum – the "angels' portion", equivalent to 2 million bottles a year!

The making of cognac has given rise to a very distinct way of life. People here have a fine sense of irony and a love of independence which has expressed itself in revolts against salt-tax, in peasant rebellions at the time of Louis XIV and in the disturbances of the Wars of Religion; the chais where the cognac is stored, is the repository of the greater part of a family's savings.

Sights

Quartier Ancien

In the streets of the old part of the town on the west bank are a number of fascinating buildings. The Grande-Rue has a fine half-timbered example dating from the 15C, the Rue Saulnier a number of 16C houses with rusticated stonework and elaborate doorways and windows, while in the Rue de l'Îsle d'Or is the Hôtel de l'Échevinage (House of

the Magistrates), distinguished by its corner niches.

The château was rebuilt by John the Good in 1450; its riverside façade has an austere air, enlivened somewhat by the King's Balcony of 1515, a grand loggia resting on a bracket carved in the shape of a salamander, the emblem of François I who was born here in 1494.

Les chais

All tours are guided (45min–1hr30min).

The cellars and storerooms (chais) spread out along the riverside quays, near the port and in the suburbs, house the casks in which the slow alchemy between spirit and oak occurs, bestowing its distinctive subtlety to the brandy of Cognac.

Hennessy

Guided tours (1hr15min) Jun-Sep: daily 10am-6pm; Mar-May and Oct-Dec: daily 10am-5pm; Closed 1 May. 6€ (under 16 years: no charge). 05 45 35 72 68. www.hennessy.com.

The business was founded in 1765 by a captain of Irish origin serving in Louis XV's Irish Brigade. His descendants still head the company today. A Cooperage Museum (Musée de la Tonnellerie) is devoted to the manufacture of brandy casks by craftsmen.

Rémy Martin

🕐 🚂 *Guided tours by train (1hr30min) Jul-Aug: daily 10am-5.30pm; Apr-Jun and Sep-Oct: daily 10-11am, 1.30-4.30pm.* 🕐 *Closed 1 May. Reservations recommended.* ✍ *5€.* ☎*05 45 35 76 66. www.remy.com.*

The distillery, founded in 1724, creates its cognac exclusively from the prestigious Grande Champagne and Petite Champagne vintages. A little train takes visitors on a tour of the plant.

Martell

🕐 *Guided tours* 🚂 *(1hr) Apr-Oct: 9.30am-5pm, Sat-Sun and public holidays 11am-5pm.* ✍ *4€.* ☎*05 45 36 34 98. www.visitez-martell.com.*

Founded in 1715 it is the oldest of the famous cognac distilleries. Three rooms of the founder's residence have been restored and convey the working environment of an entrepreneur in the early 18C.

👆 Other cognac houses open their cellars to visitors: Camus, Otard, Prince Hubert de Polignac.

◗◗ **Musée du Cognac**. – 🕐 *Jun-Sep: daily except Tue 10am-noon, 2-6pm: Oct-May: daily except Tue 2-5.30pm.* 🕐 *Closed 1 Jan, 1 and 8 May, Ascension, 14 Jul,15 Aug, 1 and 11 Nov, 25 Dec. 4€.* ☎*05 45 32 07 25.*

COLLONGES-LA-ROUGE★★

MICHELIN MAP 329 K 5–POPULATION 379
GREEN GUIDE DORDOGNE BERRY LIMOUSIN

Collonges-la-Rouge boasts mansions, old houses and a Romanesque church built of red sandstone; rabbits thrive in the surrounding countryside dotted with nut orchards and vineyards. In the 13C the original simple village was granted franchises and other privileges by the county of Turenne. Later in the 16C it became a holiday centre favoured by the county dignitaries who built charming mansions and residences flanked by towers and turrets which give Collonges its special character.

🛈 **Information:** Place de l'Ancienne-Gare, ☎05 55 25 47 57.

▶ **Orient Yourself:** Collonges is a village 20km south-east of Brive, in the Limousin region.

🅿 **Parking:** Cars are not allowed in the village in summer. Use the car park by the old station.

Visit

The exclusive use of the traditional building stone and the balanced proportions of the various structures give a harmonious character to the town. Some are of special interest: the **Maison de la Sirène** (🕐 *Easter to All Saints: 10am-noon, 3-6pm;* ✍ *2€; contact Mme Foucher* ☎*05 55 84 08 03)* with an elegant carved porch; the imposing mansion **Hôtel des Ramades de Friac;** the **Château de Benge;** and the elegant **Castel de Vassinhac**★ bristling with massive towers and pepperpot turrets.

Église

The church dates back to the 11C and 12C; it was fortified in the 16C during the Wars of Religion. The tympanum **(tympan**★) carved from the local white limestone is an unusual feature of this structure built of red sandstone. The bell-tower **(clocher**★) is a fine example of the Limousin Romanesque style.

COLMAR★★★

MICHELIN MAP 315 I 8–POPULATION 65 136
GREEN GUIDE ALSACE LORRAINE CHAMPAGNE

The capital of Upper Alsace is situated at the point where the Munster valley widens out into the broad plain of the Rhine. Since the 13C the town has prospered on the proceeds of the wine trade and boasts fine monuments. More recently, industries have spread along the Logelbach Canal.

- **Information:** 4 r. des Hunterlinden, ☎03 89 20 68 92, www.ot-colmar.fr
- ▶ **Orient Yourself:** Locate the center of the Old Town at the Place de l'Ancienne Douane. The museum lies to your north, while south along the rue des Tanneurs you'll find picturesque flower-decked houses lining the canal of "Little Venice."
- **Guided Tours:** Tours of the old town are organised from Jul-Sep. €4. Enquire at the tourist office.
- **Don't Miss:** The **Retable d'Issenheim**, the 16C masterpiece of **Matthias Grünewald** on display at the Musée Unterlinden; **Colmar by Night** – The town's most beautiful buildings are lit up at night; a **Boat Trip** – *See Little Venice.*
- **Especially For Kids: Musée animé du Jouet et des Petits Trains** is housed in a former cinema, and its collections include numerous railway engines, trains, and dolls in many different materials (*Jul-Sep: daily 9am-6pm; Oct-Jun: daily except Tue 10am-noon, 2-6pm; last admission 30min before closing; closed 10 days in Jan, 1 Jan, 1 May, 1 Nov and 25 Dec; 4€; ☎03 89 41 93 10*).

A Bit of History

In 1834 **Frédéric Bartholdi** was born here, the patriotic sculptor responsible not only for many striking works, including New York's Statue of Liberty.
Between 1871-1918 Alsace and Lorraine were part of Germany. A particular irritant to authority was the Colmar writer and caricaturist Jean-Jacques Waltz (1872-1951), known as "Hansi", who was imprisoned at the outbreak of war in 1914, but escaped to enlist in the French army.
In early February 1945, the French army under General de Lattre de Tassigny launched an attack on Colmar to eliminate German resistance. On 1

A quiet canal in old Colmar

Address Book

For coin ranges, see the Legend on the cover flap.

WHERE TO EAT

Winstub La Krutenau – *1 r. de la Poissonnerie* – ☎ 03 89 41 18 80 – *Closed Christmas to end Jan, Sun and Mon out of season* . At this winstub beside the River Lauch you can go boating in Little Venice and eat a *flammekueche* on the flower-decked terrace beside the canal in summer. A fun way, with no obligations, to learn about this lovely part of Colmar – recommended.

Le Caveau St-Pierre – *24 r. de la Herse (Little Venice)* - ☎ 03 89 41 99 33 – *michel.francois@caveaustpierre.com* – *Closed in Jan – booking advisable.* A pretty wooden footbridge across the Lauch leads to this 17C house, which offers a little slice of paradise with its rustic, local-style decor and a terrace stretching out over the water. Local cuisine.

Schwendi Bier-U-Wistub – *23-25 Grand'Rue* - ☎ 03 89 23 66 26 – You will instantly warm to this charming winstub with its ideal location in the heart of old Colmar. The principally wooden decor and the cooking, which is good quality and served in generous portions, are a tribute to Alsace. Huge terrace to be enjoyed in summer.

La Maison Rouge – *9 rue des Écoles* - ☎ 03 89 23 53 22 – The somewhat ordinary façade hides a delightful rustic interior. Regional and home-made cooking take pride of place.

Chez Bacchus – *2 Grand'Rue – 68230 Katzenthal – 5km/3mi NW of Colmar, Kaysersberg direction, then D 10* – ☎ 03 89 27 32 25 – *Closed 7-31 Jan, 1 week in Jul and in Nov, open Thu-Sat evening from 1 Oct-14 Jul, Sun and 15 Jul-30 Sep every evening except Tue – booking advisable at weekends*. There's a lovely friendly atmosphere in this wine bar dating from 1789 in a winemaking village. Massive exposed beams and helpings of Alsatian cuisine to match – guaranteed to satisfy the healthiest of appetites. Automated puppets will entertain the children with a lively show.

Winstub Brenner – *1 r. de Turenne* – ☎ 03 89 41 42 33 – *Closed 17 Feb-3 Mar, 23 Jun-3 Jul, 17-26 No, 24 Dec-2 Jan, Tue and Wed*. The terrace by the Lauch in Little Venice is very popular on fine days. Not surprising, as the setting is ideal and the food, though simple, is served in generous portions. The whole of Colmar meets here with obvious enjoyment.

WHERE TO STAY

Colbert – *2 r. des Trois-Épis* - ☎ 03 89 41 31 05 - *50 rooms* - ⌑ €6. This functional hotel near the station provides a comfortable place to stay for those travelling by train. The rooms are well equipped with new bedding, effective soundproofing and air conditioning, and some have a balcony. Bar and disco for those in search of nightlife.

Chambre d'hôte Les Framboises – *128 r. des Trois-Épis – 68230 Katzenthal – 5km/3mi NW of Colmar, Kaysersberg direction from D 10* – ☎ 03 89 27 48 85 – *sarl.amrein@wanadoo.fr – 4 rooms*. Leave Colmar behind and head for the open countryside and this village among the vines. The proprietor distils his own *marc* (grape brandy) from Gewürztraminer and provides accommodation in wood-panelled attic rooms. Don't miss the puppet show in the mornings!

Hôtel Au Moulin – *Rte d'Herrlisheim – 68127 Ste-Croix-en-Plaine – 10km/6.2mi S of Colmar on A 35 and D 1* – ☎ 03 89 49 31 20 – *Closed 5 Nov-31 Mar – 17 rooms* - ⌑ €8. This old mill deep in the country is perfect for those seeking peace and quiet. Its spacious rooms are all the same but nicely arranged. A small museum of old local objects has been created in a neighbouring building.

Hôtel Turenne – *10 rte de Bâle* – ☎ 03 89 41 12 26 – *helmlinger@turenne.com – 82 rooms* - ⌑ €7.60. On the edge of the old town, this hotel occupies a large, pleasing building with a pink and yellow façade. Its rooms have been nicely renovated and are well soundproofed. A few small but neat and reasonably priced single rooms are available.

◎◎◎ **Hôtel Le Colombier** – *7 r. de Turenne* – ☎ *03 89 23 96 00* – *www.hotel-le-colombier.com* – *24 rooms* – ▭ *€10.* This lovely 15C house in old Colmar combines old stone and contemporary decor by retaining elements from its past, such as the superb Renaissance staircase. Contemporary furniture, modern paintings and carefully arranged rooms.

ON THE TOWN

La Manufacture – *6 rte d'Ingersheim* – ☎*03 89 24 31 78.* Programme of contemporary theatre, as well as music and dance.

Folk nights – *Pl. de l'Ancienne Douane* – *May-Sep: Tue at 8.30pm.*

Théâtre municipal – *Pl. du 18-Novembre* – ☎ *03 89 20 29 01. culture@ville-colmar. com.* Classic plays, comedy and opera.

SHOPPING

Domaine viticole de la Ville de Colmar – *2 r. Stauffen* – ☎*03 89 79 11 87* – *www.domaineviticolecolmar.com* – Founded in 1895, this estate grows seven *cépages* and boasts a host of *grands crus* in addition to sparkling wines.

Caveau Robert-Karcher – *11 r. de l'Ours* – ☎ *03 89 41 14 42* – *www.vins-karcher.com* – The vineyards of this family business are north-west of Colmar, but the cellar, dating from 1602, is in a pedestrian street in the town centre. You can taste the whole range of Alsace wines and be shown around the cellar.

Fortwenger – *32 r. des Marchands* – ☎*03 89 41 06 93* – *www.fortwenger. fr* – It was in Gertwiller in 1768 that Charles Fortwenger founded his gingerbread factory, but this Colmar shop sells a wide range of delicious products, made with chocolate, honey, icing sugar, aniseed and cinnamon.

Maison des Vins d'Alsace – *Civa – 12 av. de la Foire-aux-Vins – BP1217* – ☎*03 89 20 16 20* – *www.vinsalsace.com* – Five important local organisations concerned with Alsace wines are based in this centre. The visitor can study a map six metres (nearly 20 feet) long, showing all the winemaking villages and grands crus, as well as learn about the process of winemaking from hands-on models and a film.

February the German lines north of Colmar were overrun by American troops, who stood aside to let the French 5th armoured division of General Schlesser enter Colmar.

Sights

Musée Unterlinden★★★
🕐 *May-Oct: daily 9am-6pm; Nov-Apr: daily except Tue 9-noon, 2-5pm.* 🕐 *Closed 1 Jan, 1 May, 1 Nov, 25 Dec.* ◎ *7€ (ages 12-17: 5€).* ☎*03 89 20 15 50. www.musee-unterlinden.com*
It is housed in a former 13C monastery. The ground floor is devoted to religious art and presents rich collections of paintings and sculpture dating from the late Middle Ages and the Renaissance.

Retable d'Issenheim★★★
In the chapel. In 1512 **Matthias Grünewald** was called to Issenheim 22km – 14mi south of Colmar to paint the **Issenheim altarpiece** for the chapel of the Antonite convent. This extraordinary work should be seen, not as a collection of separate masterpieces, but as an integrated whole, conceived and executed as a programme whose logic, while still puzzling to the specialist of today, probably lies in the convent superior's particular vision of the meaning of suffering. Everything contributes to the overall effect, not only the choice of themes and their relationship to one another, but also the pose and expression of the figures, the symbolic meaning of the various themes, animals and monsters, and even the use of colour. Note for example the figure of Mary Magdalene at the foot of the cross; her pose conveys both the attraction exercised over her by the figure of Christ as well as the revulsion she feels in the face of His agony. Note too the way contrast is handled, with the generally gloomy tone of the paintings shot through with flashes of light.

Grünewald's stature as one of the truly great masters of Western religious painting is fully revealed in the central panel of the altarpiece, the harrowing Crucifixion.

Ville Ancienne★★

The heart of the old town comprises the Place de l'Ancienne Douane, Rue des Marchands and Rue Mercière (Haberdasher Street). There are many picturesque old houses, with corner turrets, oriel windows and half-timbering, and balconies gay with flowers. Particularly striking are the **Maison Pfister**★★, with

frescoes and medallions and a pyramidal roof, and the Old Customs House, **Ancienne Douane**★ of 1480 with a timber gallery and canted staircase tower.

▶▶ **Église des Dominicains** ◷ Apr-Dec: 10am-1pm, 3-6pm. ◉ 1.50€ (children 0.50€) – **stained glass**★ and **Virgin in the Rose Bower**★★. **Ancien Corps de Garde**★ (Old Guard House). **"Little Venice"**★. **Maison des Têtes**★. Église St-Matthieu Call in advance for guided tour. ☎03 89 41 44 96– **Crucifixion window**★.

COMPIÈGNE★★★

MICHELIN MAP 305 H 4–POPULATION 41 254

GREEN GUIDE NORTHERN FRANCE AND THE PARIS REGION

The site of Compiègne had been appreciated by the Merovingians, long before Charles the Bald built a château here in the 9C. A fortified town grew up around this nucleus. In 1429, Philippe le Bon (the Good), Duke of Burgundy, had designs on Picardy, which he hoped to incorporate into his realm by means of a joint operation with the English. The French line of defence along the Oise was reinforced on the orders of Joan of Arc; disgusted with the inertia prevailing at Sully-sur-Loire where the French Court had established itself, she had come to Compiègne on her own initiative. But on the evening of 23 May 1430, she was seized by the Burgundians. Wary of possible consequences, Philip the Good sold her on to the English; one year later she was burnt at the stake in Rouen.

🅸 **Information:** Pl. de l'Hôtel-de-Ville, 60200 Compiègne, ☎03 44 40 01 00. www.mairie.compiegne.fr.

▶ **Orient Yourself:** Hidden in the Forest of Compiegne, the town is 60km east of Beauvais, in southern Picardy.

👁 **Don't Miss:** The royal private apartments in the palace; the forest surrounding the town, one of the most beautiful of its type in France..

🌿**Walking Tours:** Compiègne offers themed discovery tours from mid-May to mid-Jul and mid-Aug to mid-Oct on Sat-Sun and public holidays. Enquire at the tourist office.

◷ **Organizing Your Time:** The Palace will take about 2hr to visit.

Sights

Le Palais★★★

◷ Guided tours 🌿 (1hr) Wed-Sun 10am-6pm. ◷ Closed Tue, 1 Jan, 1 May, 1 Nov, 25 Dec. Last admission 45 min before closing. ◉ 5€ (under 18 years: no charge), no charge 1st Sun in the month. ☎03 44 38 47 02. www.musee-chateau-compiegne.fr.

Compiègne had been a royal residence since the time of the later Capetians, but Louis XV was dissatisfied with the ill-assorted and crumbling buildings inherited from his great-grandfather, and in 1738 he gave orders for the château to be reconstructed. The architect was **Ange-Jacques Gabriel,** who succeeded in building one of the great monuments of the Louis XV style. Begun in 1751, the great edifice made use of the foundations of the previous structure, partly for reasons of economy, partly because the site was pitted with old quarries. Gabriel chose to emphasise the horizontality of his buildings, stretching them out and providing them with flattened roofs with balustrades, themes he took up again in the Place de la Concorde and École Militaire in Paris. The palace was 40 years a-building; after Gabriel's retirement the work was carried on by his draughtsman, and a general movement in the direction of greater simplicity is very evident, with features like entablatures, ornamental window-brackets and attic floors tending to disappear. This evolution can be traced in the left wing of the main courtyard (1755), the principal façade facing the park, which was designed in 1775 and completed 10 years later (Napoleon's staircase of 1801 spoils the effect wished for by Gabriel), and the peristyle of 1783.

While the place was still a building site, it formed the background to the first meeting (1770) between Louis XVI and Marie-Antoinette; then in 1810, it was where Napoleon met Marie-Louise, the latter's great-niece.

During the Second Empire, Napoleon III made Compiègne his favourite residence, where he took much pleasure in the house-parties to which like-minded celebrities would be invited, some 80 at a time.

Inside, the palace is decorated and furnished in 18C and Empire style (chests of drawers, applied ornament, wall-cupboards, tapestries).

Musée de la Voiture et du Tourisme★★

Within the Palace

In addition to 18C and 19C coaches, the vehicles exhibited include: the **Mancelle** of 1898, a steam mail-coach designed by Amédée Bollée; a No 2 **Panhard**; a Type **A Renault** of 1899 with direct drive; the **Jamais Contente** ("Never Satisfied") of 1899, an electric car with tyres by Michelin, the first to reach 100km/h-62.1mph; a Type C **Renault** of 1900, one of the first cars to have enclosed bodywork (by Labourdette); a **Citroën** half-track of 1924.

⊙⊙ **Hôtel de ville**★. **Musée de la Figurine historique**★ & ⊙ *Mar-Oct: Tue-Sat 9am-noon, 2-6pm, Sun and public holidays 2-6pm; Nov-Feb: Tue-Sat 9am-noon, 2-5pm, Sun and public holidays 2-5pm.* ⊙ *Closed Mon, 1 Jan, 1 May, 14 Jul, 1 Nov, 25 Dec.* ⊚ *2€ (under 18 years: no charge), no charge 1st Sun in the month.* ☎*03 44 40 72 55.* Musée Vivenel – **Greek vases**★★ *Mar-Oct:* ⊙ *Tue-Sat 9am-noon, 2-6pm, Sun 2-6pm; Nov-Feb: Tue-Sat 9am-noon, 2-5pm, Sun 2-5pm.* ⊙ *Closed Mon, 1 Jan, 1 May, 14 Jul, 1 Nov, 25 Dec.* ⊚ *2€ (under 18 years: no charge), no charge 1st Sun in the month.* ☎*03 44 20 26 04* – archeology, fine arts.

Le Palais

Address Book

For coin ranges, see the Legend on the cover flap.

WHERE TO EAT

🍽 **Le Bistrot des Arts** – *35 cours Guynemer.* ☎ *03 44 20 10 10. Closed Sat lunch and Sun.* Located on the ground floor of the Hôtel des Beaux-Arts, an appealing, authentic bistro decorated with various objects and etchings. In the kitchen, the chef concocts appetizing dishes using market-fresh produce.

🍽 **Auberge du Buissonnet** – *825 r. Vineux, 60750 Choisy-au-Bac – 5km/3mi NE of Compiègne via N 31 and D 66.* ☎ *03 44 40 17 41. Closed Sun evening, Tue evening and Mon.* Ask for a table near the bay windows of the dining room or on the terrace, weather permitting, and watch ducks and swans glide peacefully over the pond, then shake themselves off and waddle proudly toward the garden.

🍽 **Le Palais Gourmand** – *8 r. Dahomey –* ☎ *03 44 40 13 13. Closed 1 to 7 Mar, 2-23 Aug, 24-28 Dec, Sun evening and Mon.* This spruce timbered house (1890) has a string of rooms and an attractive verandah where heaters, Moorish pictures and mosaics create an agreeable atmosphere. Traditional cuisine.

🍽 **Le Nord** – *Pl de la Gare.* ☎ *03 44 83 22 30. Closed 25 Jul - 17 Aug, Sat lunch and Sun evening.* This has become quite an institution locally for its seafood dishes. The dining room is modern and bright.

WHERE TO STAY

🛏 **Auberge de la Vieille Ferme** – *60880 Meux.* ☎ *03 44 41 58 54 – auberge.vieille.ferme@wanadoo.fr. Closed 28 Jul to 19 Aug, 22 Dec to 7 Jan and Sun evening – 14 rms –* 🍴 *9.50€ – restaurant* 🍽. This old farmhouse built of Oise Valley brick offers rooms that are simple but well-kept and practical. The restaurant sports exposed beams, rustic furniture, a tile floor and gleaming copperware. The menu offers traditional and regional cuisine.

🛏 **Hôtel Les Beaux Arts** – *33 cours Guynemer.* ☎ *03 44 92 26 26 – hotel@bw-lesbeauxarts.com – 35 rms –* 🍴 *10€.* Located along the Oise waterfront, here's a contemporary hotel whose modern, well-soundproofed rooms have been furnished in teak or laminated wood. Some are larger and have a kitchenette.

Excursions

Clairière de l'Armistice★★

8km – 5mi east. This is the place where, at 5.15am on 11 November 1918, the armistice was signed which put an end to the First World War at 11am on the same day. At the time the site was sheltered by forest trees. A restaurant-car identical to the carriage **(wagon-bureau)** (🕐 *Apr to mid-Oct: Wed-Mon 9am-12.30pm, 2-6pm; mid-Oct to end Mar: Wed-Mon 10am-noon, 2-5pm;* ☏ *call in advance for guided tour;* 🕐 *closed Tue, 1 Jan, 25 Dec.* 🎫 *4€;* ☎ *03 44 85 14 18)* used by Marshal Foch displays the original objects handled by the delegates in 1918. **Ferdinand Foch** (1851-1929) is generally held to have been the architect of Allied victory in the Great War of 1914-18. He was born in Tarbes in the Pyrénées in an 18C middle-class home (now a museum). He taught strategy at the Military Academy (École de Guerre), then became its commandant. In 1914 he distinguished himself both in the Battle of the Frontiers in Lorraine and in the "Miracle of the Marne". After the German breakthrough in the Ludendorff offensive of early 1918, Foch was appointed supreme commander of the French and British armies. Promoted to marshal, it was he who launched the final Allied offensive on 8 August.

After the Battle of France in 1940, it was the turn of a French delegation to present itself here to the dignitaries of the Nazi regime in order to hear the victors' terms for an armistice. It was signed on the evening of 22 June. The clearing and its historic monuments were then ransacked by the occupation forces;

only the statue of Marshal Foch was spared.

Château de Pierrefonds★★

14km – 9mi southeast. The stronghold seems to embody everything that a medieval castle should be as it looms over the village crouching at its feet. For the most part, however, it is a creation of the 19C.

Pierrefonds was part of the Duchy of Valois, and its castle, whose origins go back as far as Carolingian times, was rebuilt in the middle of the Hundred Years War by Louis d'Orléans, the brother of Charles VI, as part of a chain of defences between the rivers Oise and Ourcq. It was dismantled during the reign of Louis XIII. The castle ruins were bought by Napoleon I. In 1857 Louis Napoleon inspired by romantic ideals commissioned **Viollet-le-Duc** (1814-79) to restore the keep; four years later he was entrusted with a complete rebuilding of the castle for use as an Imperial residence and a picturesque place for receptions given to entertain the Emperor's guests at Compiègne. From the ramparts the view extends over the Vallée de Pierrefonds.

Little of Louis d'Orléans' building is left save the base of the walls and the towers visible from the track leading to the castle. Viollet-le-Duc's contributions, in the neo-Gothic style, are not without merit, but are notable more for originality than for strict historical accuracy, in terms of both architecture and decoration (arcading and gallery of the main façade in the courtyard, tribune in the chapel, roof of the Salle des Preuses). Nevertheless, it gives an excellent idea of a castle's defensive system prior to the age of cannon (north rampart walk).

Château de Blérancourt

31km – 19mi northeast. In the First World War, the château was taken over by Ann Morgan, who set up a temporary hospital here. Blérancourt subsequently became the headquarters for the organisation of relief for the civilian population.

When the war was over, Miss Morgan's efforts were directed towards the establishment of a museum of Franco-American history. In 1929, she presented the place to the French state, whereupon its name was changed to the **Musée National de la Coopération Franco-Américaine**. About a dozen rooms in the left wing (at present closed for reconstruction) are devoted to the American War of Independence.

The exhibits on show in the right wing (Pavillon Florence Gould) illustrate aspects of the long and close relationship between the two countries; there are displays on the 1801 Treaty of Friendship, the Louisiana Purchase, emigration to the United States, the Gold Rush, etc. Other rooms evoke the two World Wars, notably by means of relics of the **La Fayette** Squadron and of the American Field Service.

CONCARNEAU★

MICHELIN MAP 308 H 7–POPULATION 19 453
GREEN GUIDE BRITTANY

The growth of Concarneau is based on its importance as a fishing port. Trawlers and cargo-boats moor in the inner harbour up the estuary of the Moros, while the outer harbour is lively with pleasure craft. There are many vegetable and fish canneries and plenty of bustle as the catch is sold in the early morning at the "criée" (fish auction market).

- ▪ **Information:** Quai d'Aiguillon, ☎02 98 97 0144. www.tourismeconcarneau.fr.
- ▸ **Orient Yourself:** The town is south of Quimper, in western Brittany.
- ⊛ **Don't Miss:** La Criée, the fish auction.

Sight

Ville close (Walled Town)★★

On its islet in the bay, this was one of the strongholds of the ancient county of Cornouaille; as at Dinan and Guérande, its walls proclaim the determination of the citizens to maintain their independence, particularly in times of trouble (as during the War of the Breton Succession in 1341).

The English nevertheless seized the place in 1342, and were thrown out only by Du Guesclin in 1373.

The granite ramparts **(remparts)** (🕐 *mid-Jun to mid-Sep: daily 10am-8pm; rest of year daily 10am-5pm;* 🚫 *access to the ramparts is prohibited if weather conditions are not favourable and during the Filets bleus festival;* 🎟 *0.80€ high season, no charge low season*) with their typically Breton corbelled machicolations, were started at the beginning of the 14C and completed at the end of the 15C. They were improved by Vauban at the end of the 17C at a time when England once more posed a threat to these coasts; he lowered the height of the towers and built gun emplacements into them.

The interior of the town gate is of the same period. It has impressive crenellations, regular stonework and gables. A Fishing Museum, **Musée de la Pêche**★ (♿ 🕐 *Jul-Aug: daily 9am-8pm; rest of the year: daily 10am-noon, 2-6pm;* 🕐 *closed last 3 weeks of Jan* 🎟 *6€, children 4€;* ☎ *02 98 97 10 20*), is nearby.

At the heart of the walled town, Rue Vauban and Rue St-Guénolé are a demonstration of how medieval marketplaces arose more or less spontaneously through a simple widening of the street.

CONQUES★★★

MICHELIN MAP 338 G 3–POPULATION 302
GREEN GUIDE LANGUEDOC ROUSSILLON TARN GORGES

This tiny medieval town has a splendid hillside site★★ best seen from the rock, Rocher du Bancarel (*3km – 2mi south*).

▪ **Information:** Rue Florent de Gonzague, ☎ 05 65 72 85 00.

▸ **Orient Yourself:** The village is just south of the River Lot, 43km east of Figeac.

Sights

Église St-Foy★★

Completely rebuilt between 1045 and 1060, this is one of the oldest Romanesque pilgrimage churches on the route to Santiago de Compostela. Its abbey had a chapel and hospice at Roncesvalles to serve the pilgrims as they made their way across the Pyrenees. Within, the spacious nave is flooded with light from the south tribune windows. The dimensions of the transept are exceptional and the ambulatory with its annular barrel vault is also remarkable.

The tympanum **(tympan**★★★**)** above the west door with its wealth of sculpture forms a striking contrast to the overall plainness of the west front. Traces of the original colouring can still be made out. It shows how sculpture had evolved away from the static solemnity characteristic of Burgundy and Languedoc, towards the greater freshness and spontaneity evident in the capitals of the churches of the Auvergne. It may be that the weighing of souls taking place below the figure of Christ is an expression of the idea – entirely new at the beginning of the 12C – of the personal nature of the Last Judgement.

It seems likely that the tympanum was moved forward by the length of a bay and integrated with the west front in the 15C in order to extend the nave; this move would have led to the displacement of the statues in the north transept.

Trésor★★★

🕐 *Apr-Sep: 9.30am-12.30pm, 2-6.30pm; rest of the year: 10-noon, 2-6pm.* 🕐 *Closed 1 Jan, 25 Dec.* ⊚ *5.50€.* ☎*08 20 82 08 03.*

The treasury is among the most important in Europe. Its most precious object is the reliquary statue of St Faith (Ste-Foy). The saint's relics had been brought to Conques at the end of the 9C, when they were venerated by prisoners and by the blind. The statue was put together and added to over a long period; some of its features probably go back as far as the last years of the Roman Empire and consist of reused elements of Roman date (face-mask, intaglio work in precious stones, jewels); the gold and engraved crystal are of the Merovingian and Carolingian periods (7C-9C). At the close of the 10C the revered statue was renovated here at Conques and adorned with enamels, cabochons and other precious stones.

Four more of the treasures are of exceptional significance: the initial "A" given to the abbey, it is said, by Charlemagne (a fragment of the Holy Cross decorated in the 11C with intaglio work and with chased and gilded silver); two portable altars, one, St Faith's, in alabaster and chased silver, the other, Abbot Begon's, from the beginning of the 12C, in porphyry and silver inlaid with niello; and the reliquary of Pope Pascal with filigree work and diadems, also from the early 12C.

CORDES-SUR-CIEL★★★
MICHELIN MAP 338 D 6–POPULATION 996
GREEN GUIDE LANGUEDOC ROUSSILLON TARN GORGES

Nestling at the top of the peak, Puech de Mordagne, Cordes occupies a most attractive site★★ overlooking the Cérou valley.

🄸 **Information:** Place Jeanne Ramel-Cals, ☎05 63 56 00 52.
   www.cordes-sur-ciel.org
▸ **Orient Yourself:** The village is 25km north-west of Albi.
🄿 **Parking:** Cars are not allowed in the Upper Town in summer. Park near the Porte de la Jane or the bottom of Grande Rue de l'Horloge.

Visit

The superb row of **Gothic houses (maisons gothiques★★)** dating from the 13C and 14C testify to the wealthy past of this quaint little town. Notice the **Maison du Grand Fauconnier★** and the **Maison du Grand Veneur★**. For more than 50 years, artists and craftsmen have contributed to preserving and restoring local tradition.

CORTE★
MICHELIN MAP 345 D 6–POPULATION 6 329
GREEN GUIDE CORSE (IN FRENCH)

Corte owes its fame to its site★ among gorges and ravines, as well as to two great men, Gaffori and Paoli, who were instrumental in making it one of the strongholds of Corsican patriotism.

🄸 **Information:** Citadelle de Corté, ☎04 95 46 26 70. ww.corte-tourisme.com
▸ **Orient Yourself:** Corte sits high in the rocky interior of the island.

A Bit of History

Jean-Pierre Gaffori (1704-53) was born here. He was a member of the Triumvirate elected as "Protectors of the Nation", who took up arms against Genoa. In 1746, supported by his indomitable wife Faustine, he succeeded in wresting the town from the Genoese. Four years later the latter returned, taking the citadel but failing to overcome the resolute defence of the old town; Gaffori's house still bears the marks made by the Genoese guns.

In June 1751, Gaffori was made "General of the Nation" and granted executive power. But two years later he was killed in an ambush, betrayed by his brother. After this assassination, an appeal was made for **Pascal Paoli** (1725-1807), then in exile in Italy, to return to his native land. He was proclaimed "General of the Nation" in his turn. By 1764, the island was united under his leadership, with only the Genoese coastal forts still able to hold out against him. For 14 years, watched closely by the European Powers, he made Corte his capital, drew up a constitution, founded a university, minted money, reformed the system of justice, encouraged industry and stimulated agricultural production.

Having failed to put down the Corsicans' long struggle for independence (1729-69) the Republic of Genoa requested the intervention of France. A mission of conciliation arrived, headed by the future French Governor, Marbeuf. Paoli, lacking somewhat in the skills of statesmanship, unwisely prevaricated, and was bypassed by events; on 15 May 1768, by the Treaty of Versailles, Genoa provisionally gave up its rights over the island to France. Paoli proclaimed a mass uprising, but was defeated at **Ponte Nuovo** on 8 May 1769.

Paoli went into exile, spent mostly in England, where he was lionised by the court of George III and was a friend of James Boswell. Amnestied at the outbreak of the French Revolution, he met with a triumphal reception in Paris before returning to Corsica. Later, after his denunciation as a counter-revolutionary, he sought aid from the English. Nelson's victories over the French at St-Florent, Bastia and Calvi did not however fulfil Paoli's hopes of independence under the English crown, but led to an Anglo-Corsican kingdom of limited duration (two years) and renewed exile in London for Paoli himself. He died there in 1807.

Sight

Ville haute★

Dominated by the citadel (**citadelle**★) perched high up on its rock, old Corte, with its cobbled and stepped streets and tall houses, still has the air of the island's capital it once was.

In the Place Paoli stands the statue of the great man, in bronze. Further up is the Place Gaffori, where, behind the monument to the General of the Nation, is his house, pitted with bullet holes from the siege of 1750. In the Rue de l'Ancien Collège is the old dwelling where Joseph Bonaparte was born. It was also the birthplace of Jean Thomas Arrighi de Casanova, one of the Empire's most brilliant generals.

A ramp opposite the National Palace (Palais National) leads to a viewpoint (**belvédère**★) on a peak standing out from the main promontory on which the citadel is built. It offers a fine view of the town in its setting bordered by the river valley, Gorges du Tavignano.

▶ **Chapelle Ste-Croix**★. **Musée de la Corse**★★. **Gorges de la Restonic**★★.

COUTANCES★★

MICHELIN MAP 303 D5–POPULATION 9 522
GREEN GUIDE NORMANDY

On its hilltop overlooking the woodlands and pastures (*bocage*) of the Cotentin peninsula, Coutances is dominated by its remarkable cathedral.

🛈 **Information:** Place Georges Leclerc, ☏02 33 19 08 10. www.ville-coutances.fr.

▸ **Orient Yourself:** The town is in Normandy's far west, 76km south of Cherbourg.

Sight

Cathédrale★★★

The present building (1220-75) made use of some of the remains of Geoffroy de Montbray's Norman cathedral, as well as drawing on the experience gained in the recently-completed abbey at Fécamp.

The west front is framed by two towers, whose soaring lines are emphasised by the tall, narrow corner turrets. The great octagonal lantern rises imposingly over the crossing; it too is flanked by turrets, and has strikingly delicate ribbing and slender openings. Within, the nave has clustered piers and highly moulded arches, a triforium with double openings and tall windows behind the typically Norman balustraded inspection gallery.

The transept is in a more advanced style. Built in 1274, it is a masterpiece of ingenious construction. The columns of a second gallery support the ribs of the vault, and light floods in through 16 windows.

The elevation of the choir and the inner ambulatory and the six coupled columns of the apse show the High Gothic style in all its perfection.

▸ **Jardin des Plantes★**

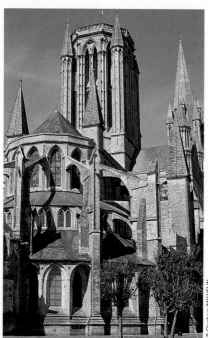

J.P. Clapham/MICHELIN

Lantern-tower of Coutances Cathedral

LA **COUVERTOIRADE**★
MICHELIN MAP 338 L 7–POPULATION 148
GREEN GUIDE LANGUEDOC ROUSSILLON TARN GORGES

High up on the lonely Larzac limestone plateau (*causse*), this old fortified settlement once belonged to the Knights Templar. It has many robustly-built houses, typical of the region, with cisterns, outside stairways leading to the main floor, and a vaulted sheep-pen at ground level. Most date from the 17C.

- **Information:** ☎05 65 58 55 59. www. lacouvertoirade.com
- ▶ **Orient Yourself:** The village stands to one side of the highway which crosses Larzac. Park outside the walls and walk through the main gateway. There may be a charge simply to enter the village on foot.

Visit

The towers and the sentry-walk of the **ramparts** are particularly interesting (🕐 *May-Aug: daily 10am-7pm; Mar-Jun and Sep-Nov: daily 10am-noon, 2-5pm.*

➾ *3€.* 👣 *5€.*). Also see the **fortified church** (🕐 *Jul-Aug: 10am-7pm; Apr-Jun: 10am-noon, 2-6pm; Mar and Sep to mid-Nov: 10am-noon, 2-5pm*), the old houses in Rue Droite, and the mansions, Hôtel de la Scipione and Hôtel de Grailhe.

DEAUVILLE★★★
MICHELIN MAP 303 M 3–POPULATION 4 261
GREEN GUIDE NORMANDY

Deauville owes its world-wide reputation as a luxury resort not only to its good facilities but also to the elegance of its social and sporting calendar.

- **Information:** Place de la Mairie, ☎02 31 14 40 00. www.deauville.org.
- ▶ **Orient Yourself:** Life in Deauville centres on Place de Morny, the yachting harbour and the seafront with its famous boardwalk and casino and Port Deauville.
- ⊛ **Don't Miss:** There are festive events all year long, especially in summer, with regattas, golf and tennis championships, galas, the American Film Festival, international yearling horse sales and horse racing culminating in the Deauville Grand Prix.

Excursions

Corniche Normande★★
From Deauville-Trouville to Honfleur via the D513 – *21km – 13mi*. This scenic route leads through typical Normandy countryside and affords fine views over the Seine Estuary.

Honfleur★★ – 🕐 *See HONFLEUR.*

Côte Fleurie★★
From Deauville-Trouville to Cabourg via the D513. – *19km – 12mi*. The road passes through a number of attractive small resorts with excellent recreational facilities, among them **Villers-sur-Mer**★★, **Houlgate**★★ and **Cabourg**★★.

LES PLAGES DU **DÉBARQUEMENT**★★
D-DAY LANDING BEACHES

MICHELIN MAP 303 F-K 3-4, LOCAL MAP PP194-195
GREEN GUIDE NORMANDY

A mighty Allied armada of over 4 000 specially made craft, together with hundreds of warships and naval escorts, sailed from the south coast of England on the night of 5 June 1944. The following morning they arrived: it was D-Day. The liberation of France, and of Europe, had begun.

- ⓘ **Information:** There are information offices at several of the towns along the coast, or ♿ *See Bayeux.*
- ▸ **Orient Yourself:** The Landing Beaches are the Normandy coast near Bayeux.

Visit

The Normandy invasion, and its significance in European and world history, is marked all along this coastline by cemeteries, monuments and museums

Omaha Beach
Here the US First Division made its first contact with French soil and here the bloodiest engagement of D-Day was fought. The film *The Longest Day* directed by D Zanuck gives a realistic account of these dramatic events.

Utah Beach
This beach northeast of Carentan entered history following the landing of American forces on 6 June 1944. Despite murderous fire from the Germans, the American 4th Division managed on 12 June to link up with the forces who had landed at Omaha Beach.

- ▸ **Pegasus Bridge** (near Caen) – where airborne landings took place; **Sword Beach** – where British and Free French troops landed, easternmost point of the invasion; **Pointe du Hoc**★★ – stormed by the Second Rangers Battalion early on D-Day; **Arromanches** – where the first Mulberry (artificial harbour) was in place by the end of D-Day; **St-Laurent military cemetery** – testimony to the thousands of young men who were cut down as they landed on the beaches.

GROTTE DES **DEMOISELLES**★★★

MICHELIN MAP 339 H 5
GREEN GUIDE LANGUEDOC ROUSSILLON TARN GORGES

The cave, discovered in 1770, contains an enthralling underground landscape.

- ⓘ **Information:** Plan de l'Ormeau, Ganges, ☎04 67 73 00 56.
- ▸ **Orient Yourself:** The caves are in the upper Hérault valley near the town of Ganges.
- ☺ The temperature in the caves is a constant 14 degrees centigrade.

Visit

🕐 *Guided tours* 🔊 *(1hr) Apr-Jun and Sep: daily 9.45am-noon, 1.30-5.30pm; Jul and Aug: daily 9.45am-7pm; Oct-Mar: daily 9.45am-noon, 1.30-5.30pm. Last departure 30min before closing time.* 🕐 *Closed 1 Jan and 25 Dec.* ⊛ *8€.* ☎04 67 73 70 02; www.demoiselles.com.

Deposition of calcium carbonate within the cave have produced extraordinary forms, from stalactites and stalagmites and translucent draperies, to the great columns and huge organ-case of this underground cathedral.

DIEPPE★★

MICHELIN MAP 304 G 2–POPULATION 34 653
GREEN GUIDE NORMANDY

Nearest seaside resort to Paris, Dieppe is also the most venerable. Its famous sea-front lawns were laid out in 1863 by Empress Eugénie and Napoleon III.

▪ **Information:** Pont Jehan Ango, Quai du Carenage, ☎02 32 14 40 60. www.dieppetourisme.com
▸ **Orient Yourself:** The town is on the Normandy coast close to the border with Picardy. The town centre is around the harbour.

A Bit of History

Dieppe's history as a major port goes back to the 11C, the English wool trade, and the import of spices from the Orient. Its mariners acquired a great reputation. As early as the 14C, Dieppe sailors were landing on the coast of the Gulf of Guinea and Jean Cousin was exploring the South Atlantic. In 1402 Jean de Bethencourt founded the first European colony on the Canary Islands. Jean Ango (1480-1541), whose privateers once captured a fleet of 300 Portuguese vessels, equipped many a voyage of discovery to remote shores. The Parmentier brothers reached Sumatra and drew up charts of the globe. In the 16C the great explorer **Samuel de Champlain**, a Dieppe ship-owner, sailed out from Honfleur to found the French colony of Quebec.

▸ **Cité de la Mer**★. **Museum**★ at the château, collections of meticulously-crafted masterpieces of ivory carving are displayed. **Église St Jacques**★. Notre-Dame de Bon Secours Chapel – **view**★.

Excursions

Côte d'Albâtre (Alabaster Coast)★

From Dieppe to Etretat (104km – 65mi)

Sheer white cliffs cut into by dry valleys (valleuses), descend sandy beaches. Little resorts – **Pourville-sur-Mer, Ste-Marguerite-sur-Mer** and **Veules-les-Roses** – are sited at the seaward end of a succession of lush valleys, their half-timbered houses hidden among the hedgerows.

In **Varangeville-sur-Mer**, the graveyard of the 11-15C church which overlooks the sea and shelters the tomb of the Cubist painter, **Georges Braque**, and the stained glass of Chapelle St-Dominique (on the outskirts) by the artist are of interest.

In a gap in the cliffs halfway between Dieppe and Fécamp, **St-Valéry-en-Caux** is a fishing port and popular resort.

DIJON★★★

MICHELIN MAP 320 K 5-6–POPULATION 236 953

GREEN GUIDE BURGUNDY JURA

Close to some of the world's finest vineyards, Dijon, former capital city of the Dukes of Burgundy, straddles important north-south and east-west communication routes and has a remarkable artistic heritage.

- **Information:** 34 r. des Forges, ☎08 92 70 05 58. www.dijon-tourism.com
- **Orient Yourself:** The core of the city is around Place de la Liberation. Make use of the free shuttle buses called Diviaciti which run in the city centre from 7am to 8pm Monday to Saturday.
- **Parking:** There are plenty of car parks around the perimeter of the city centre, and metered street parking within the city.
- **Guided Tours:** There is a choice of guided tours; ask at the tourist office.

A Bit of History

Dijon had been the capital of Burgundy ever since the rule of Robert the Pious at the beginning of the 11C. In 1361 Philippe de Rouvres died without an heir, leaving the duchy without a ruler. In 1363, the French King Jean II le Bon (the Good) handed the duchy to his son Philippe, the first of an illustrious line of Valois Dukes who made the Burgundian court at Dijon one of the most brilliant of Europe.

Philippe became Duke in 1364, at the same time as his brother Charles V le Sage (the Wise) was acceding to the throne of France. Thus from this time Burgundy and France were closely entwined. Philippe stood out as the most able of four royal brothers; cool, analytical on the one hand, well-named "le Hardi" (the Bold) on the other. His marriage in 1369 to Margaret of Flanders made him the most powerful prince of Christian Europe. Anxious to provide a worthy burial place for himself and his successors, he founded the Champmol Charterhouse in Dijon in 1383, and set out to attract to the city the best sculptors, painters, goldsmiths and illuminators from his possessions in Flanders.

Address Book

For coin ranges, see the Legend on the cover flap.

WHERE TO EAT

◎◎ **La Mère Folle** – *102 R. Berbisey - ☎ 03 80 50 19 76 - Closed Tue.* This small restaurant in the town centre offers regional specialties on its menu such as *escargots, œufs en meurette,* and *sandre au Chablis.* Convivial atmosphere, good service and 1930s-style décor.

◎◎ **Les Deux Fontaines** – *16 Pl. de la République - ☎ 03 80 60 86 45 - Closed 1 Jan, 10-25 August, 25 Dec, Sun and Mon.* Whitwashed walls, old banquettes, wood tables plastered with advertisements of yesteryear: it all makes for a nostalgic trip to bistrots past. Nostalgia reigns over the menu as well.

◎◎ **Le Bistrot des Halles** – *10 R. Bannelier - ☎ 03 80 49 94 15 - Closed Sun and Mon.* A typical bistrot a stone's throw from the covered market. Choose one of the dishes chalked up on a slate and enjoy the warm and friendly ambience.

◎◎◎ **La Dame d'Aquitaine** – *23 Pl. Bossuet - ☎ 03 80 30 45 65 - dame.aquitaine@wanadoo.fr - Closed 1-6 Jan, Mon lunchtime and Sun.* In the town centre, a porch, a paved courtyard and a long flight of steps will take you down to a superb vaulted dining hall dating back to the 13C. The decor is typically medieval, complete with tapestries, stained glass, sculpted columns and imposing chandeliers. Regional cuisine.

WHERE TO STAY

Jacquemart – *32 R. Verrerie -* ☎ *03 80 60 09 60 - www.hotel-lejacquemart. fr - 31 rooms -* ☐ *6.50€*. The people of Dijon do love their Jacquemarts at Notre Dame. Simple, family-style rooms in a 17C building.

Hôtel Victor Hugo – *23 R. des Fleurs -* ☎ *03 80 43 63 45 -23 rooms -* ☐ *5€*. You will appreciate the thoughtful service at this traditional hotel. The rooms with their white roughcast walls are simple and quiet, despite their location near the town centre.

Hôtel Wilson – *Pl. Wilson -* ☎ *03 80 66 82 50 - hotelwilson@wanadoo. fr - 27 rooms -* ☐ *11€*. This former post house has retained its traditional charm and charisma. The rooms are prettily decorated with light wood furniture. The exposed beams and luminosity make for a cosy atmosphere where one immediately feels at home.

ON THE TOWN

Theatres and Opera – Comedians and actors regularly ply the stages of the Théâtre du Sablier *(R. Berbisey)*, the Théâtre du Parvis-St-Jean *(Pl. Bossuet)*, the Bistrot de la Scène *(R. D'Auxonne)*. In May the city hosts the Rencontres Internationales du Théâtre. The Théâtre National Dijon-Bourgogne is directed by Robert Cantarella. Classical music, opera and dance productions are held at the Auditorium and at the Opéra de Dijon *(Pl. du Théâtre)*.

L'Agora Café – *10 Pl. de la Libération -* ☎ *03 80 30 99 42 - Tue-Sat 11:30am-2am*. A piano-bar located in a former 16C convent chapel. Wide selection of whiskies, beers and cocktails in a quiet, convivial atmosphere. Piano performances on Sat. evenings. Patio open in summer.

Le Caveau de la Porte Guillaume – *Pl. Darcy - downtown -* ☎ *03 80 50 80 50 - www.bourgogne.net/hnord - daily 7am-2am. Closed 20 Dec-5 Jan*. Bordering the Hotel du Nord, this wine bar is an ideal spot for discussing (and sampling) the delights of the region, by the glass or by the bottle.

SIT BACK AND RELAX

Comptoir des Colonies – *12 Pl. François-Rude -* ☎ *03 80 30 28 22* - Teas, coffees roasted in-house and hot chocolate await you in this colonial-style tea shop, which also has a leather and mahogany salon and a large sunny terrace.

La Causerie des Mondes – *16 R. Vauban -* ☎ *03 80 49 96 59 - la.causerie. des.mondes@wanadoo.fr - Open Tue-Sat 11am-7pm, Sundays Oct-Mar 3-7pm. - Closed Mon*. Jute-covered walls, and Asiatic-themed decor, with a backdrop of mood music makes for an exotic atmosphere in this pleasant tearoom. More than 70 imported teas, 20 house-roasted coffees, chocolates and cakes to tempt you.

SHOPPING

Marché des Halles – *Center of town - Tue, Thu and Fri mornings, and Sat.*

Mulot et Petitjean – *13 Pl. Bossuet -* ☎ *03 80 30 07 10 - mulot.petitjean@ wanadoo.fr* . This long-standing establishment, which originated in 1796, specialises in all forms of gingerbread: round biscuits filled with jam, crunchy *gimblettes* with almonds, and sweetmeats shaped as snails, fish, hens, eggs or clogs. The half-timbered house contains a sumptuous decor with marble and wood furniture dating from 1901.

Nicot Yves – *48 R. Jean-Jacques-Rousseau -* ☎ *03 80 73 29 88 - nicotvins@ infonie.fr* . The proprietor, M Nicot, nurtures a veritable passion for wines in this shop. He also runs a school offering courses in wine tasting and oenology. Good selection of Burgundies.

Boutique Amora-Maille – *32 R. de la Liberté -* ☎ *03 80 30 41 02* . Founded in 1777, this shop specialises in Maille mustards and vinegars of Dijon. Take a look at the sign over the entrance.

L'Escargotière de Marsannay-le-Bois – *Rte d'Épagny - 21380 Marsannay-le-Bois -* ☎ *03 80 35 76 15 - sylvain-mansuy@wanadoo.fr* . In addition to sampling and purchasing snails, scallops and other fine prepared dishes, you can learn about how culinary snails are raised, harvested and transformed for consumption.

His successor **Jean sans Peur** (John the Fearless) was assassinated in 1419. **Philippe le Bon** (the Good) inherited the title. From this time on, Burgundy saw its cultural importance waning in favour of the Netherlands and Flanders, where Renaissance ideas were blossoming. Nevertheless, artistic production continued throughout his 48-year reign. At the same time, Nicolas Rolin, the Duke's Chancellor, was establishing the Hôtel-Dieu at Beaune.

The boundaries of the Burgundian state had never been more extensive nor the life of its court more exuberant; on his wedding-day in 1429, Philip founded the Order of the Golden Fleece; never had the French king and his court, lurking in relative obscurity at Bourges, been more pitiful.

But Burgundy's alliance with England had become unpopular just as Joan of Arc was awakening national sentiment. Philip decided it was prudent to submit himself to the authority of the French king, marking the beginning of the end of the Hundred Years War.

Charles le Téméraire (the Bold) succeeded in 1467; he was the last and perhaps the most renowned of all the Valois Dukes of Burgundy. He squandered its resources in the search for glory. Charles' death in 1477 marked the end of the great days of the Burgundian dynasty, but in the same year Mary of Burgundy, Charles' daughter, married Maximilian,

Holy Roman Emperor. She was to be the mother of **Philippe le Beau** (the Fair), who in turn fathered the future Emperor Charles V. The recovery of Burgundy and the other lands making up her dowry cost France more than two and a half centuries of struggle.

Sights

La Ville Ducale (The Ducal City)

Palais des ducs et des États de Bourgogne★★

The ducal palace had been neglected since the death of Charles the Bold. In the 17C, it was restored and adapted and given a setting of dignified Classical buildings. At the time the city was concerned to emphasise its parliamentary role and needed a suitable building in which the States-General of Burgundy could meet in session. Plans were drawn up by Mansart. The exterior of the Great Hall of the States-General (Salle des États) recalls the Marble Court (Cour de Marbre) at Versailles. By contrast, the east wing with its peristyle anticipates the architectural style of the 18C.

Mansart was also responsible for the semicircular Place de la Libération (formerly Place Royale). With its arcades crowned by an elegant stone balustrade, it is designed to show off the main courtyard of the palace.

Dijon

B. Kaufmann/MICHELIN

Musée des Beaux-Arts★★

♿ 🕐 *May-Oct: Wed-Mon 9.30am-6pm; Nov-Apr: Wed-Mon 10am-5pm.* 🕐 *Closed Tue, 1 Jan, 1 May, 25 Dec.* ∞ *3.40€, no charge Sun.* ☎*03 80 74 52 09 .*

The Fine Arts Museum is housed in the former ducal palace and in the east wing of the palace of the States-General.

Salle des Gardes★★★

On the first floor, in the former Banqueting Hall. This is the ducal palace's most important interior. Its centrepiece is formed by two tombs which before the French Revolution were in the chapel of the Champmol Charterhouse. The tomb of Philip the Bold was designed by Jean de Marville; its decoration was in the hands of Claus Sluter followed by his nephew Claus de Werve who succeeded in softening somewhat the severity of Marville's conception. Flamboyant Gothic inventiveness and exuberance are expressed in the procession of hooded mourners making its way around the cloisters formed by the four sides of the monument. Nearby, the tomb (**tombeau**★★★) of John the Fearless and Margaret of Bavaria is similar in style.

There are also two altarpieces dazzling in the richness of their decoration: one, sculpted by Jacques de Baerze and painted and gilded by Broederlam, shows **Saints and Martyrs**★★★; the other, depicting the Crucifixion, has famous paintings by Broederlam on the reverse side of its panels. A portrait of Philip the Good by Rogier van der Weyden (born in Tournai, a pupil of Van Eyck and perhaps of Campin too, then teacher to Memling) is remarkable for its psychological insight. In an adjoining room is a fine Nativity of 1425 by the Master of Flémalle.

Ancienne Chartreuse de Champmol★

Enter at 1 Boulevard Chanoine-Kir. Follow the signs reading "Puits de Moïse." 🕐 *Daily 10am-6pm.* ☎*03 80 42 48 01.*

All that is left of the Charterhouse is Moses' Well (**Puits de Moise**★★) and the chapel doorway (**portail de la chapelle**★), both the work of Claus Sluter, the foremost among the sculptors of the Dijon School. Born in Holland, he learnt his skills in Brabant and worked in Dijon from 1385 to 1404.

Moses' Well was originally the pedestal of a Calvary. The head of the figure of Christ is now in the Archeological Museum. Six great statues of Moses and the Prophets face outwards from the hexagonal base; their treatment shows a striking realism and sense of movement, notably in the folds of the clothing. The statues of Philip the Bold and Margaret of Flanders in the chapel doorway are thought to be actual portraits.

▶ **Rue des Forges**★. **Église Notre-Dame**★. Cathédrale St-Bénigne – **crypte**★ 🕐 *9am-6pm. Call in advance for guided tour information.* ∞ *1€ offering.* ☎*03 80 30 14 90.* **Musée Archéologique**★ 🕐 *Wed-Mon 9am-6pm.* 🕐 *Closed Tue, 1 Jan, 1 and 8 May, 14 Jul, 1 and 11 Nov, 25 Dec.* ∞ *2.20€, no charge Sun.* ☎*03 80 30 88 54.* **Église St-Michel**★.

DINAN★★

MICHELIN MAP 309 J 4–POPULATION 10 907

GREEN GUIDE BRITTANY

Dinan is a gem of a town, surrounded by ramparts and guarded by a castle.

🅘 **Information:** 9 rue du Château, ☎02 96 87 69 76. www.dinan-tourisme.com.

▶ **Orient Yourself:** Dinan is at the top of the Rance estuary, about 30km/18mi south of St-Malo.

A Bit of History

The great hero of the town is **Bertrand du Guesclin** (c 1315-80), redoubtable warrior. Jean le Bon (John the Good) had been taken prisoner by the English at the Battle of Poitiers in 1356. During the four years of captivity he spent in England he became aware of the extent to which feudal rights imposed limitations on royal power, and conceived the idea of a body of knights attached to the monarch. In pursuit of this aim, he took Du Guesclin into his service shortly after his release and return to France. This middle-aged knight had until then experienced little but rebuffs and difficulties due to his modest ancestry, lack of means and exceptionally ugly appearance. John's successor, Charles V, kept him on, doubtless in view of his great popularity and reckless bravery and his implacable hatred of the English (which at one point in his youth had led him to support Charles of Blois). In 1366, after ridding France of the "Free Companies" (marauding bands of mercenaries), he was made High Constable of France. He freed Périgord from English rule in 1370 and Normandy in 1378. In 1379 he handed his sword to the king rather than use it against his rebellious Breton compatriots. In 1380 he died beneath the walls of Châteauneuf-de-Randon in the south.

Sights

La Vieille Ville

The houses of the old town cluster together behind the 2.5km – 1 1/2 mile long circuit of walls, built by the Dukes of Brittany in the 14C in order to protect the place's commercial activity and to defend their domain against the Normans, the English, and, after the accession of Louis XI, the French.

Château★

🕐 Jun-Sep daily 10am-6.30pm; Oct-May: daily 1.30-5.30pm. 🕐 Closed Jan. ⊜ 4€. ☎ 02 96 87 58 72.

Begun by Duke John IV about the middle of the 14C. Its 15C towers project outwards in order to facilitate enfilading fire. The exceptionally fine machicolations of Duchess Anne's Keep (Donjon de la Duchesse Anne) are of interest.

Basilique St-Sauveur

The west front is much influenced by the Poitiers version of the Romanesque. In the north aisle is the Evangelists' Window, a fine example of late-15C Breton glass, famous for its yellows. In the north transept is the cenotaph containing the heart of Du Guesclin.

Vieilles maisons

Duke John was happy to let Dinan run its own affairs, and the town's consequent prosperity is reflected in the rebuilding of many old timber houses in stone. A most picturesque townscape results from the many buildings with overhanging upper storeys, angle-posts, halftimbering on stone footings, arcades carried on timber beams, and granite side-walls.

The most interesting houses are on Rue de l'Apport (the 15C Mère Pourcel House), **Place des Merciers★** (triangular gables and porches), **Rue du Jerzual★** which links the main part of the town with the port (15C and 16C shops where craftsmen have worked for six centuries) and on Place Du Guesclin (17C and 18C town houses).

DINARD ★★★

MICHELIN MAP 309 J 3–POPULATION 9 918

GREEN GUIDE BRITTANY

On the magnificent estuary of the River Rance, Dinard is an elegant resort with sheltered sandy beaches and luxuriant Mediterranean vegetation flourishing in the mild climate.

- **Information:** 2 blvd Féart, ☎02 99 46 94 12. www.ot-dinard.com
- **Orient Yourself:** This smart resort is on the left bank of the Rance across from St Malo.

A Bit of History

The resort came into being when a wealthy American called Coppinger built himself a château here in 1850. He was followed two years later by a British family, who in turn attracted many of their fellow-countrymen. By the end of the 19C its reputation rivalled that of Brighton; sumptuous villas and luxurious hotels abounded, frequented by an international smart set. Nowadays many of Dinard's grand hotels are no more than a memory, but plenty of well-tended villas remain to tell of past glories.

Visit

Seashore

Promenades lead from **Plage de l'Écluse**★ (or **Grande Plage**) to the Plage du Prieuré, giving fine views over the coast and the Rance estuary. From the **Pointe du Moulinet**★★, the view extends as far as Cap Fréhel to the west and the ramparts of St-Malo to the east. In summer, the **Promenade du Clair de Lune**★ with its pretty parterres and Mediterranean plants forms an attractive setting for evening concerts.

DISNEYLAND PARIS ★★★

MICHELIN MAP 312 F 2

GREEN GUIDE NORTHERN FRANCE AND THE PARIS REGION

Europe's only Disney resort, this huge complex, divided into Walt Disney Studios Parc and Disneyland Parc, has six hotels, a wide range of family attractions themed as five separate 'lands', a 27-hole golf course, entertainment centre, restaurants, shops and a disco.

- **Information:** ☎01 60 30 60 30. www.disneylandparis.com.
- **Orient Yourself:** The resort is 20 miles east from Paris, with excellent transport links. On arrival, find the information desk in City Hall (Disneyland Park) where a program of the attractions is provided.
- **Organizing Your Time:** To avoid long lines, visit popular attractions during the parade, at the end of the day or with a **Fast Pass** issued by distributors outside the most attractions; this ticket bears a time slot of one hour during which time you may have access to the attraction within a few minutes.
- **Especially for Kids:** As you know, there is something here for children of all ages.
- **Parking:** There is parking available in the northeast portion of the park, but with both train and bus terminals, Disneyland Paris is easily accessible by public transport.

Visit

Parc Disneyland Paris★★★

Kids ◷ Jul-Aug: daily 9am-11pm (9pm for Walt Disney Studios); Sep to mid-Jan: Mon-Fri 10am-8pm, Sat-Sun and public holidays 9am-8pm; low season: Sun-Fri10am-8pm, Sat 9am-8pm. ☎01 60 30 60 30. For guided tours, contact the City Hall on Town Square in Main Street, USA: 7.62€ (children: 4.57€). P Parking: Cars 6.86€, motorcycles 3.81€. Big range of price options starting from 25€ (same price both adults and children) for immediate entry up to 3 day pass at 128€ (children: 105€). 3-day passports allows entrance to both theme parks and can be used non-consecutively. Passes valid for 3 years. Readmission: to leave the park temporarily, visitors must have their hand stamped; visitors must keep passports and parking tickets.

DOMME★★

MICHELIN MAP 329 I 7–POPULATION 987
GREEN GUIDE DORDOGNE BERRY LIMOUSIN

One of the many medieval fortified towns (bastides) founded in southwest France by both French and English, Domme was laid out by Philippe le Hardi (the Bold) in 1281. The normal rectangular plan of such settlements was here distorted in order to fit it to the rocky crag overlooking the Dordogne 145m – 475ft below.

- **Information:** Place de la Halle, ☎05 53 31 71 00. www.ot-domme.com
- ▶ **Orient Yourself:** The village is south of the River Dordogne, 12km from Sarlat.

Visit

Panorama★★★

There are splendid views over the alluvial valley of the Dordogne from the Barre belvedere or, better still, from the cliff-top walk (Promenade des Falaises – no parapet) just below the public gardens.

All around is an opulent landscape of castles perched on heights, well-wooded slopes dotted with stone-built villages, lush meadows, walnut trees, and corn.

American writer Henry Miller described the area as perhaps the nearest thing to Paradise on earth.

LE DORAT★★

MICHELIN MAP 325 D3–POPULATION 1 963
GREEN GUIDE DORDOGNE BERRY LIMOUSIN

Le Dorat lies in the gently rolling countryside of the old province of Marche, whose patchwork of pastureland feeds the yellowish-fawn Limousin cattle bought and sold in the great market at **St-Yrieix-la-Perche** 41km – 25 miles south of Limoges. The little town has a collegiate church of impressive size and harmonious proportions.

- **Information:** 17 Place de la Collégiale, ☎05 55 60 76 81.
- ▶ **Orient Yourself:** Le Dorat is in a rural location 58km north of Limoges.

Sight

Collégiale St-Pierre★★

◷ Daily year-round. Guided tours: daily except Sun and public holidays 10am-noon, 2.30-6pm. Call in advance. No charge.

The great edifice was rebuilt in Romanesque style over a period of 50 years beginning in 1112. It is firmly rooted in its region by virtue of its siting, the coarse granite from which it is built, and by a number of characteristic Limousin features. These include the massive square west tower flanked by bell-turrets, the portal with its scalloped archivolts, the openwork lantern (inspired by the one built 50 years earlier at St-Junien 45km – 28 miles south but vastly more original),

and the mouldings used in the arches and arcades throughout the building. The late-11C crypt **(crypte)** dedicated to St Anne has crudely hewn columns and simple capitals, only one of which is sculpted, openwork barrel vaulting in granite in the ambulatory and groined vaults in the chapels. Compared with the crypt in the church at Uzerche it shows the architectural progress achieved within a period of 50 years.

DOUAI★

MICHELIN MAP 302 G 5–POPULATION 51 727
GREEN GUIDE NORTHERN FRANCE AND THE PARIS REGION

The town preserves the 18C layout and grand buildings that gave it the aristocratic look that Balzac evoked.

- **Information:** 70 place d'Armes, ☎03 27 88 26 79. www.ville-douai.fr
- **Orient Yourself:** The town is in French Flanders, close to the Belgian border.

A Bit of History

In the 11C and 12C, Douai provided winter quarters for merchants and merchandise using the great trading routes of Northern Europe. The painter Jean Bellegambe (1470-1534) was born here. His Polyptych of the Trinity (polyptyque d'Anchina – in the former Anchin charterhouse) is justly famous. Around 1605, a number of Benedictine monks from England and Wales came to Douai and established the monastery of St Gregory the Great. It was here that the "Douai Bible", an English version of the Old Testament, was published in 1609. The monastery buildings were destroyed at the time of the French Revolution, and the community recrossed the Channel, eventually settling at Stratton-on-the-Fosse in Somerset, where they founded Downside Abbey.

Sights

Cortège des Gayants (Parade)
On the Sunday after 5 July, five giant figures of the Gayant family, dressed in medieval costume, are paraded though the town accompanied by folk groups: Gayant, the father (7.50m – 25ft tall, weighing 370kg – 816lbs), his wife Marie Cagenon (6.50m – 21ft tall) and their children Jacquot, Fillion and Binbin. The giants appear in town on the next two days. Gayant , the oldest giant in northern France (1530), is also the most popular. The inhabitants of Douai refer to themselves in jest as "Gayant's children".

Beffroi★
🕐 *Guided tours* 👣 *(1hr) Jul and Aug: Mon-Sat 10am, 11am, 2pm, 3pm, 4pm and 5pm; Sep-Jun: Mon-Sat 11am, 3pm, 4pm and 5pm.* 🕐 *Closed Sun, 1 Jan and 25 Dec.* ⊚ *3.50€.* ☎*03 27 88 26 79. www.ville-douai.fr.*
The is one of the best belfries of its kind in the North of France. Both Victor Hugo and Corot were much taken by the Gothic tower of 1390 with its elaborate crown. The Flemish Renaissance courtyard front was rebuilt in 1860.

SAUT DU **DOUBS**★★★

MICHELIN MAP 321 K 4

GREEN GUIDE BURGUNDY JURA

The gorges of the River Doubs downstream from Villers-le-Lac mark the frontier between France and Switzerland. The river has cut down deeply into the highly folded Jurassic limestone, but here its course has been blocked by eroded material to form Lake Chaillexon (Lac de Chaillexon). Its waters escape from the lake over the 28m – 92ft high Doubs Falls (Saut de Doubs).

- **Information:** Rue Berçot, Villers-le-Lac, ☎03 81 68 00 98. www.villiers-le-lac-info.org.
- ▶ **Orient Yourself:** The falls are in eastern Burgundy, close to the Swiss border.
- **Caution:** The falls are less interesting after a long period of dry weather.
- **Organizing Your Time:** Follow a footpath through the woods to reach the main viewpoint (*45min return*); beyond, a very steep path descends to the lake itself, from where there is another most impressive view of the falls crashing down into the narrow defile.

Saut du Doubs

DUNKERQUE
DUNKIRK

MICHELIN MAP 302 C 1–POPULATION 191 173
GREEN GUIDE NORTHERN FRANCE AND THE PARIS REGION

Almost entirely destroyed in WW2, the rebuilt town has an attractive centre with a pleasant atmosphere, appealing bars and good shops and museums.

- **Information:** Beffroi, r. de l'Amiral-Ronarc'h, ☎03 28 66 79 21. www.ot-dunkerque.fr.
- ▶ **Orient Yourself:** Dunkerque is an extensive urban area – the centre is close to the port, on its east side. Further east is the resort area of Malo-les-Bains.

A Bit of History

Dunkirk (Church of the Dunes in Flemish) was originally a fishing village, whose transformation into the principal port of Flanders began as early as the 14C. It was taken by Turenne after his victory in the Battle of the Dunes in 1658, and given to England in recognition of her help in the struggle against Spain. The town was repurchased by France in 1662. It was now that Dunkirk became the abode of smugglers and of pirates pressed into the service of the king. In the course of Louis XIV's reign, a total of 3 000 foreign ships were captured or destroyed and the trade of the Netherlands completely wrecked. The most intrepid of these privateers was **Jean Bart** (1651-1702). Despite his vocation, the town is proud of him: his statue of 1848 by David d'Angers stands in the square named after him.

Demolition of the fortifications in 1713 (one of the conditions of the Treaty of Utrecht) brought about a decline in Dunkirk's fortunes, notwithstanding improvements in the port facilities. The German breakthrough at Sedan in mid-May 1940 and subsequent dash to the coast near Abbeville had led to the Allied forces in the north being trapped with their backs to the sea.

Defeat and retreat was turned into the "Miracle of Dunkirk", the name given to the successful evacuation between 27 May and 2 June of more than 300,000 troops from the beaches of Dunkirk and its resorts of Malo, Zuydcoote and Bray-Dunes, an operation carried out in the face of intense bombardment on land and from the air.

Jean Bart, "the king's official privateer"

During the wars fought by Louis XIV, the privateers of Dunkirk destroyed and captured 3 000 ships, took 30 000 prisoners and wiped out Dutch trade. The most intrepid of all the privateers was Jean Bart (1651-1702).

He was as famous as the privateers from St-Malo, Duguay-Trouin and Surcouf, and was a past master at raiding on the North Sea trade routes. Unlike pirates, who were outlaws attacking any and every passing ship, privateers were granted "letters patent" by the sovereign entitling them to attack warships or merchant vessels. In 1694 Jean Bart saved the kingdom from famine by capturing 130 ships loaded with wheat. His success owed much to the existence of an ultra-modern arsenal and the constant presence of a royal fleet. He was a simple, plain-spoken man but his exploits were many and varied. As a result, he was raised to the nobility in 1694, then three years later given the rank of Commodore. The following year he avoided a combat with nine large ships while taking the Prince de Conti to Poland. Once the threat was past, the prince commented that had they been attacked they would have been captured. Jean Bart replied that there had been no such danger as his son was in the munitions hold and the latter had orders to set light to a powder keg as soon as he gave the command.

Sight

Le port★★

Dunkirk is the third largest port in France with a total of over 37 million tonnes of traffic in 1994. A vast industrial zone has emerged, based on shipbuilding, steelworks, refineries and petrochemicals.

▶ **Lieu d'Art Contemporain**★ – ⏰ *Daily except Tue 10am-12.15pm, 1.45-6pm.* ⏰ *Closed 1 Jan, carnival Sunday, 1 May, 1 Nov, 25 Dec.*

4€, no charge 1st Sunday in the month. ☎03 28 59 21 65. **Musée des Beaux-Arts**★ – ⏰ *Daily except Tue 10am-12.15pm, 1.45-6pm.* ⏰ *Closed 1 Jan, Sunday of the Dunkirk carnival, 1 May, 1 Nov, 25 Dec.* 4.50€; no charge 1st Sunday in the month. ☎03 28 59 21 65. **Musée Portuaire**★ – ⏰ *10am-12.45pm, 1.30-6pm (Jul and Aug: 10am-6pm).* ⏰ *Closed 1 Jan, eve of Shrove Tuesday, 1 May, 25 Dec.* 4€. ☎03 28 63 33 39.

ÉTRETAT★★

MICHELIN MAP 304 B3–POPULATION 1 615
GREEN GUIDE NORMANDY

Sited where a dry valley in the chalk country of the Caux region meets the sea, Étretat was a humble fishing village well into the 19C. It was then favoured by writers such as Maupassant and painters like Courbet and Eugène Isabey.

▯ **Information:** Place Maurice Guillard, ☎02 35 27 05 21. www.etretat.net
▶ **Orient Yourself:** The town is 30km up the Normandy coast from Le Havre.
◉ **Don't Miss:** The amazing cliff views.

Sights

Falaise d'Aval★★★

🚶 *1hr round trip on foot from the end of the promenade.*

▶ Take the steps and then the path to the clifftop known as Porte d'Aval.

There are fine views of the magnificent Manneport Arch, the solitary 70m – 200ft Needle (Aiguille), the long shingle beach and the Amont Cliff on the far side of the bay. The play of colours changes constantly with the time of day and conditions of sky and sea.

Cliffs at Étretat

Falaise d'Amont★★

1hr round trip on foot from the end of the promenade.

At the end of the promenade, the memorial was put up to mark the spot from which two aviators, Nungesser and Coli, were last glimpsed as they set out in their "White Bird" (*Oiseau Blanc*) on their attempt to make a non-stop westward crossing of the Atlantic (8 May 1927). It is not known whether these brave men perished under the ocean's waves or in the forests of New England.

ÉVREUX★★

MICHELIN MAP 304 G 7–POPULATION 51 198

GREEN GUIDE NORMANDY

The history of Évreux could read like a series of unmitigated disasters, from the burnings and sackings perpetrated by Vandals, Vikings and Plantagenets, to the more recent devastation wreaked from the air by Luftwaffe (in 1940) and Allied air forces (in 1944). But after each disaster, the townspeople have re-created prosperity from ruin. Evidence of this spirit can be seen in the promenade laid out on the old Roman rampart on the banks of the River Iton, and in the treatment of the Clock Tower (Tour de l'Horloge) which was built by Henry V in 1417, two years after his victory over the French at Agincourt.

- **Information:** 1 ter, Place de Gaulle, ☎02 32 24 04 43. www.ot-pays-evreux.fr .
- **Orient Yourself:** The town is 56km south of Rouen.

Sight

Cathédrale Notre-Dame★

The cathedral, begun in the 12C under Henry II of England and continued under the Norman and Plantagenet dynasties (the choir was completed in about 1260), is essentially a harmonious Gothic building of the 13C.

It did not escape the troubles which beset the town, much restoration having to take place for example after John the Good's siege in 1356 and during the reign of Louis XI (1461-83). In the 16C the aisles of the nave were rebuilt in Flamboyant style, and after the Second World War much of the upper part of the cathedral was replaced.

Its many beautiful 13-14C **stained-glass windows★** (*See illustration Introduction: Art – Architecture*) give an excellent insight into the evolution of this art form.

- Ancien évêché – **Musée★★** *Tue-Sun 10am-noon, 2-6pm. Closed Mon,1 Jan, 1 May, 1 and 11 Nov, 25 Dec. 4€, no charge first Sun in th month. ☎02 32 31 81 90 – archeology, medieval religious art. Église St Taurin –* **Châsse de St Taurin★★** *(reliquary).*

255

LES **EYZIES-DE-TAYAC**★★

MICHELIN MAP 329 H 6–POPULATION 909

GREEN GUIDE DORDOGNE BERRY LIMOUSIN

The village occupies a grandiose setting of steep cliffs crowned with evergreen oak and juniper, at the confluence of two rivers. In the base of the cliffs are caves that were prehistoric habitations, where the art and crafts of our distant ancestors can still be seen.

- 🗐 **Information:** Pl. de la Mairie, ☎05 53 06 97 05. www.leseyzies.com.
- ▶ **Orient Yourself:** The village is in the heart of the Dordogne region, 20km from Sarlat.
- 🖎 **Don't Miss:** The best of the many fascinating sites are Grotte de Font-de-Gaume, Grotte du Grand Roc, and the Musée National de la Préhistoire.
- 🕔 **Organizing Your Time:** The sites are not all in the village – they are mostly spread along the Vézère valley. It is rewarding to spend a full day in the area.
- **Kids Especially for Kids:** Prehistory is just fun and games at Prehisto-Parc near Les Eyzies.

Prehistory

The **Upper Paleolithic** is the period from 35 000 to 10 000 years BC. Skeletons dating from the early part of this period were found at Cro-Magnon in the Dordogne in 1868. Cro-Magnon people were tall, with nimble hands and clearly possessed of great inventiveness, the first examples of modern man, Homo sapiens. Another branch of the same species were the people known as the Chancelade race, remains of whom were discovered at Chancelade near Périgueux in 1888.

The Aurignacian and **Perigordian** cultures – the latter is marked by long migration periods – though contemporary, do not seem to have been in contact with each other and differ in a number of respects, although both are characterised by a continuous improvement in tool-making and the development of hunting techniques which allowed time to be set aside for the creation of works of art (line-drawings and paintings). Aurignacian industry (🕭 see **Aurignac**, *Green Guide Atlantic Coast*) brought forth very finely knapped flints, gravers and scrapers and perforated batons made from reindeer horn.

Outside the National Museum of Prehistory

The culture reached its peak about 25 000 years ago; its achievements can be seen in the in the cave at La Grèze and in the shelter **(Abri du Poisson)**, all of which mark the beginnings of human activity in the lower Vézère valley. Solutrean culture, named after the rock near Mâcon (Roche de **Solutré**★★, *& see Green Guide Burgundy Jura*), is well represented in the Dordogne. It is characterised by the manufacture of fine flint blades and weapons with serrated points and by the appearance of needles with eyes.

Capital of Prehistory

There are almost 200 prehistoric sites in the Dordogne, more than half of them in the vicinity of Les Eyzies. The area has easily-accessible natural **caves** and shelters as well as rock projections forming a natural habitat. Prehistoric people have left many traces of their activities. Two hundred centuries before civilisations arose along the Tigris and the Nile, the valley of the Vézère was inhabited by accomplished artists who carved in ivory and reindeer horn and painted on the walls of caves.

Visit

▶ **Grotte du Grand-Roc**★★ *Guided tours* (30min) Apr-Oct: daily 10am-6pm; Jul and Aug: daily 9.30am-7pm; Nov-Mar: daily 10am-5pm. *Closed Jan and 25 Dec.* 7€ (children: 3.50€). *05 53 06 92 70.* – Amazing rock formations.

Musée National de la Préhistoire★ *Jul and Aug: daily 9.30am-6.30pm; Jun and Sep: daily except Tue 9.30am-6pm; Oct-May: daily except Tue 9.30am-12.30pm, 2-5.30pm. Call in advance for guided tour. Closed 1 Jan and 25 Dec.* 4.50€ Mon-Sat, 3€ Sun (under 18 years: no charge), no charge 1st Sun in the month. *05 53 06 45 65.* – Comprehensive displays in an old 13C fortress with good views.

Grotte de Font-de-Gaume★ *(Just outside village on road to St-Cyprien; footpath to cave entrance)* *mid-May to mid-Sep: Sun-Fri 9.30am-5.30pm; mid-Sep to mid-May: Sun-Fri 9.30am-12.30pm, 2-5.30pm. Last departure 1hr30min before closing. guided tours, call in advance. Closed public holidays.* 6.10€. *05 53 06 86 00.* – Many multicoloured paintings.

Laugerie-Haute *(On D47 where it turns away from the Vézère)* *Open daily except Sat. Guided tours by appointment Closed public holidays.* 6.10€. *Information at the Grotte de Font-de-Gaume.* *05 53 06 86 00.)* – 7 000 years of civilisation.

FÉCAMP★★

MICHELIN MAP 304 C 3–POPULATION 21 027

GREEN GUIDE NORMANDY

Today the fishing industry dominates Fécamp, but as early as the 11C the town had seen considerable monastic activity. **Guy de Maupassant** (1850-93) used the town as the setting for many of his short stories.

🛈 **Information:** 13 rue Alexandre le Grand, 02 35 28 51 01.
▶ **Orient Yourself:** The town is on the north Normandy coast, 43km from Le Havre.
◉ **Don't Miss:** The abbey is the main attraction.

Sight

Abbatiale de la Trinité★★

As big as any cathedral, the ancient abbey church marks an important stage in the evolution of Gothic architecture in Normandy. Built for the most part between 1168 and 1219, it was much influenced by the developments taking place in the Île de France (use of tribunes

Dormition of the Virgin

as in the churches derived from St-Denis outside Paris, the combination of flying buttresses and triforium pioneered at Chartres, which made the tribunes redundant and which here is seen in the south wall of the chancel).

Norman regionalism reasserts itself however in a number of ways: in the slender lantern-tower high above the crossing, and in the inspection gallery at the base of the triforium windows.

In the south transept chapel is a beautiful **Dormition of the Virgin**★.

▶ **Palais Bénédictine**★★ ◷ *Mid-Jul to end Aug: 10am-7pm; end Mar to mid-Jul and Sep: 10am-1pm, 2-6.30pm; Feb-Mar and Oct-Dec: 10.30am-12.45pm, 2-6pm. Last admission 1hr before closing.* ◷ *Closed Jan and 25 Dec.* ⊕ *5.60€ (children under 12 years: no charge).* ☎ *02 35 10 26 10. www.benedictine.fr* – objets d'art, history and production of Benedictine. **Musée des Terres-Neuvas et de la Pêche**★ ♿ ◷ *Sep-Jun: daily except Tue 10am-noon, 2-5.30pm Jul-Aug: daily 10am-7pm.* ◷ *Closed 1 Jan, 1 May, 25 Dec.* ⊕ *3€ (under 18 years: no charge), ticket combined with the Musée des Arts et de l'Enfance.* ☎ *02 35 28 31 99.* **Musée Centre des Arts et de l'Enfance**★ ◷ *Sep-Jun: daily except Tue 10am-noon, 2-5.30pm; Jul-Aug: daily 10am-7pm.* ◷ *Closed 1 Jan, 1 May, 25 Dec.* ⊕ *3€ (under 18 years: no charge), ticket combined with the Musée des Terre-Neuvas et de la pêche.* ☎ *02 35 28 31 99* – ceramics, ivory, archeology, regional furniture.

FIGEAC★★

MICHELIN MAP 337 I 4–POPULATION 9 606
GREEN GUIDE DORDOGNE BERRY LIMOUSIN

A sprawling commercial town, Figeac had a prestigious past, shown in the architecture of its tall sandstone town houses.

🛈 **Information:** Hôtel de la Monnaie, place Vival, ☎ 05 65 34 06 25. www.tourisme-figeac.com

▶ **Orient Yourself:** The heart of town rises from the River Célé near Pont Gambetta.

Address Book

For coin ranges, see the Legend on the cover flap.

WHERE TO EAT

🍴 **À l'Escargot** – *2 bis av. Jean-Jaurès - ☎05 65 34 23 84 - Closed 21 Dec-10 Mar and Thu - reserv. recommended.* The regular clientele of this unassuming restaurant flock here for the simple, family-style fare and friendly ambience. Three generations of women have run the kitchen here.

🍴🍴🍴 **La Dînée du Viguier** – *R. Boutaric - ☎05 65 50 08 08 - Closed 23 Jan-15 Feb, 15-22 Nov, Sun eve out of season, Sat lunchtime and Mon.* The restaurant in the Château Viguier du Roy combines medieval decor (high ceilings, painted beams and stone fireplace) with contemporary cuisine.

🍴🍴🍴 **Ferme-Auberge Domaine des Villedieu** – *46100 Boussac - 8km/5mi SW of Figeac on the D 13 and then the D 41 - ☎05 65 40 06 63 - reserv. required.* An enchanting 18C farmhouse deep in the country. In keeping with their farming background, the owners serve their own produce in the wood-floored dining room and on the outdoor terrace. The restored farm buildings have been converted into a number of attractive guestrooms.

WHERE TO STAY

🛏 **Champollion** – *3 pl. Champollion - ☎05 65 34 04 37 - 10 rooms.* The memory of the famous Egyptologist is everywhere in the centre of town, including this hotel, the town's medieval meat market. Although on the small side, the bedrooms are modern and well-maintained.

🛏 **Le Pont d'Or** – *2, av Jean-Jaurès - ☎05 65 50 95 00 - www.hotelpontdor. com - 10 rooms.* A welcoming stone house on the banks of the Célé, with some rooms offering balconies overlooking the river. A yellow and orange colour scheme, contemporary furniture and immaculate bathrooms. Fitness room and rooftop swimming pool. In summer, breakfast is served on the riverside terrace.

LEISURE ACTIVITIES

Domaine de Loisirs du Surgié – *Chemin Moulin Surgie - ☎05 65 34 59 00 - www.domainedesurgie.com - Open May-Sep, 11am-8pm.* This large (14ha/34.5-acre) outdoor watersports and leisure area is on the banks of the River Célé to the northeast of Figeac.

SHOPPING

Market – The town's weekly market is held on Saturdays (the largest one is the last Saturday of the month). Evening markets are held on Thursdays in July and August.

A Bit of History

Jean-François Champollion – Champollion, the outstanding Orientalist, whose brilliance enabled Egyptology to make such great strides, was born at Figeac in December 1790. He set himself the task of deciphering a polished basalt tablet which had been discovered in 1799 by members of Napoleon's expedition to Egypt near Rosetta in the northwest Nile delta, from which it derives its name – the Rosetta Stone. In Figeac, at the **Place des Écritures**, a replica of the Rosetta Stone covers the square.

Sight

Le Vieux Figeac★

The old quarter, surrounded by boulevards which trace the line of the former moats, has kept its medieval town plan with its narrow and tortuous alleys.

The buildings, of elegant beige sandstone, exemplify the architecture of the 13C, 14C and 15C. Generally the ground floor was opened by large pointed arches and the first floor had a gallery of arcaded bays. Underneath the flat tiled roof was the soleilho, an open attic, which was used to dry laundry, store wood, grow plants, etc. Its

Place des Écritures

J.Damase/MICHELIN

even brick, which held up the roof. Other noticeable period architectural features to be discovered during your tour of the old quarter are: corbelled towers, doorways, spiral staircases and some of the top storeys, which are half-timbered and of brick.

▶ **Hôtel de la Monnaie**★ ⏰ *Jul-Aug. daily 10am-7.30pm; May-Jun and Sep. Mon-Sat 10am-noon, 2.30-6.30pm, Sun 10am-1pm; Oct-Apr: daily except Sun and public holidays 10am-noon, 2.30-6pm.* ⏺ *2€.* ☎*05 65 34 06 25.*
Musée Champollion★ ⏰ *Mar-Jun. daily except Mon (excluding public holidays) 10am-noon, 2.30-6.30pm; Jul and Aug: daily 10am-noon, 2.30-6.30pm; Nov-Feb: daily except Mon 2-6pm.* ⏰ *Closed 1 Jan, 1 May, 25 Dec.* ⏺ *3.09€ (children: 1.86€).* ☎*05 65 50 31 08.*

openings were separated by columns or pillars in wood or stone, sometimes

The Rosetta Stone

During the reigns of the first Ptolemaic kings (332-80 BC), Egyptian priests recorded the decrees issued at the end of their synods on basalt tablets which were then displayed in the main temples. The Rosetta Stone is one of these tablets, carved in 196 BC. By this time, the members of the clergy were the only people to be taught hieroglyphics, hence the need for a translation into three languages so that the decrees would be understood also by those people who used demotic script in Memphis and Greek in Alexandria. The content of the decrees was both political and economic, defining the respective powers of the clergy and the monarch, the extent of fiscal privileges and the nature of laws and taxes among other things. This is illustrated by the following extracts from the Rosetta Stone:

"whereas king PTOLEMY…, the son of King Ptolemy and Queen Arsinoe, the Gods Philopatores, has been a benefactor both to the temples and to those who dwell in them, … he has dedicated to the temples revenues in money and corn and has undertaken much outlay to bring Egypt into prosperity, and to establish the temples, and has been generous with all his own means; and of the revenues and taxes levied in Egypt some he has wholly remitted and others has lightened, in order that the people and the others might be in prosperity during his reign; …he has directed that the gods shall continue to enjoy the revenues of the temples and the yearly allowances given to them, both of corn and money, likewise also the revenues assigned to the gods from vine land and from gardens and other properties which belonged to the gods in his father's time."

Translation courtesy of the British Museum, London.

FILITOSA★★

MICHELIN MAP 345 C 9

GREEN GUIDE CORSE (IN FRENCH)

This fascinating site was discovered in 1946; the beginnings of Corsican history are all visible here, from the Neolithic (6000-2000 BC), to the Megalithic (3000-1000 BC) and the Torreen (1500-800 BC), and finally to the Roman.

Information: ☎04 95 74 01 11.

▶ **Orient Yourself:** The site, overlooking the Taravo valley, is located in the commune of Sollacaro, north of Propriano, in southern Corsica.

Visit

Station préhistorique★★

🕐 Apr to mid-Oct: 8am to dusk. Preferably in the middle of the day: good light to study the sculptures and engravings. Sound recordings in 4 languages. ✑ 5€. ☎04 95 74 00 91.

By the path leading to the prehistoric site stands the superb menhir known as Filitosa V bearing, in front, a long sword and an oblique dagger, and behind, anatomical or clothing details.

A stone wall built by the Megalithic people encloses the site. Within it, four striking groups of monuments testify to the domination exercised by the Torreens: the East Monument **(Monument Est)** which they filled in; the remains of huts **(cabanes)** which they re-used, the circular Central Monument **(Monument central)**, and the fragments of menhir-statues. The latter had been made by the Megalithic people; the Torreens cut them up and re-used them, face downwards, in the construction of the Central Monument, doubtless to signal their supremacy. Some of them, however, have been stood upright again, and Filitosa IX and XIII frame the way into the Central Monument. The West Monument **(Monument Ouest)** is Torreen, and is built on Megalithic foundations. The five menhir-statues near an age-old olive-tree on the far slope of the valley mark the end of the Megalithic period in this area.

FOIX★

MICHELIN MAP 343 H 7–POPULATION 9 109

GREEN GUIDE LANGUEDOC ROUSSILLON TARN GORGES

In the Middle Ages this hill town was important as the capital of the colourful Counts of Foix.

Information: 29, rue Delcassé, ☎05 61 65 12 12. www.ot-foix.fr.

▶ **Orient Yourself:** The town stands on the Ariège between the high hills of the Plantaurel and the Pyrenees proper.

A Bit of History

At the conclusion of the Albigensian Crusade, the Counts, who had favoured the heresy, were obliged to submit to the King of France. At the end of the 13C they inherited that other Pyrenean statelet, the Béarn, which still enjoyed its independence, and decided to reside there. Their fondness for Foix, their ancestral home, was undimmed, although they failed to maintain it properly, and in the end had to dismantle much of its massive fortifications. But the three great towers remained intact, symbols of their pride, property and power.

The greatest of the Counts was Gaston Febus (1331-91), a brilliant figure whose wide culture did not however stop him killing both his brother and his only son. Henri IV was a member of the family; his accession to the French throne in 1589 meant the formal union of the Pays de Foix with France.

Site

Panorama★

From the **Château** (🕐 Apr-Mai: 10.30am-noon, 2-5.30pm; Jun and Sep: 9.45am-noon, 2-6pm; Jul-Aug: 9.45am-6.30pm; Oct-Mar: daily except Mon and Tue, apart from school holidays, 10.30am-noon, 2-5.30pm; 🕐 closed Jan, 1st Mon in Sep, and 25 Dec; ⊛ 4€ , ages 6-18 2€; ☎ 05 34 09 83 83) rock high above the river there are extensive views over the surrounding region. To the southwest are the green Plantaurel hills, characterised by their remarkably regular relief. To the south are the Pyrenees themselves; among the many summits can be picked out the Trois Seigneurs (2 199m – 7 215ft) and St-Barthélemy (2 368m – 7 769ft). Eastward lies the high and windy Sault plateau from which rise a number of pointed peaks resembling the one on which the Cathar fortress of Montségur is built.

Excursions

Grotte de Niaux★★

Michelin map 343 H 8. Located in the Vicdessos valley, this cave is famed for its remarkably well-preserved prehistoric wall drawings, in particular those depicting animals in the "Black Hall" (Salon noir); the pure, sober lines and high craftsmanship mark the summit of Magdalenian art.

Parc pyrénéen de l'art préhistorique (Tarascon-sur-Ariège) ★★

At Lacombe, on the road to Banat. The park, devoted to cave paintings – there are some 12 decorated caves in the Ariège area – comprises a distinctive modern building housing a display area, the Grand Atelier, and an open space with exhibits featuring water and rock. An audio-tour of the Grand Atelier bringing into play the latest technological advances gives a comprehensive account of the discoveries of cave paintings.

FONTAINEBLEAU★★★

MICHELIN MAP 312 F 5–POPULATION 15 942

GREEN GUIDE NORTHERN FRANCE AND THE PARIS REGION

As early as the 12C, the Capetian kings had built a hunting lodge here, drawn by the abundant game which thrived in the vast forest. It was to become an extraordinarily majestic palace and park listed as a World Heritage site.

- 🛈 **Information:** 4 rue Royale, ☎ 01 60 74 99 99. www.fontainebleau-tourisme.com.
- ▶ **Orient Yourself:** Fontainebleau and its château are in the midst of a large forest, 64km south of Paris.
- 👁 **Don't Miss:** The Grand Apartments and famous horshoe staircase.
- 🕐 **Organizing Your Time:** The exterior of the Palace will take about an hour, the interior more than an hour.

A Bit of History

The woodland covers 25 000ha – 62 000 acres, much of it high forest of sessile oaks, Norway pines and beeches. It grows on the low east-west sandstone ridges, among the crags and boulders of stony wastelands, and in the sandy depressions between the ridges. The Forest is traversed by a network of well-signposted footpaths. Since the days of Colbert's Forestry Ordinance of 1669, "a masterpiece of forestry administration" (J L Reed), it has been carefully managed to ensure its long-term survival.

In spite of the forest's fame and popularity, it is the palace begun by François I which has made the reputation of Fontainebleau.

A taste for natural surroundings together with its role as a military base (notably for cavalry) led to the growth of the town of Fontainebleau in the 19C. Between 1947 and 1967 it was home to the headquarters of NATO.

Visit

Palais★★★

From the days of the Capetian kings to the time of Napoleon III, the Palace of Fontainebleau has been lived in, added to and altered by the sovereigns of France. Napoleon Bonaparte liked it; here, in contrast to Versailles, he was free of the overwhelming presence of Louis XIV, a formidable predecessor in the quest for glory. He called Fontainebleau "the house of Eternity", furnished it in Empire style and set about altering it for himself, for Josephine, and for Pope Pius VII.

In 1528, François I commissioned Gilles Le Breton to replace the existing medieval buildings with two structures linked by a gallery. Like his predecessor Charles VIII, while campaigning in Italy, François had acquired a taste for agreeable surroundings adorned with works of art. He brought in gifted and prolific artists who are known as the **First School of Fontainebleau**. They included Rosso (of Florence), Primaticcio (from Perugia), Niccolo dell'Abbate (from Parma), as well as architects, thinkers, cabinetmakers, goldsmiths, decorators... He also acquired works of art including Leonardo's Mona Lisa and paintings by Raphael. France was thus permeated by Renaissance taste, by Renaissance mathematics and by an appreciation of the rules of proportion derived from the architecture of Greece and Rome. The pleasures of life were savoured anew, and painters and sculptors abandoned religious subjects in favour of older divinities.

This era endowed the palace with many of its most splendid features: on the outside, the left wing and façade of the Court of the White Horse or Farewell Court (**Cour du Cheval-Blanc ou des Adieux★★**), the concave section of the Oval Court (**Cour Ovale★**), the Golden Gate (**Porte dorée★**) with its loggia painted by Primaticcio; and on the inside, the François I Gallery (**Galerie François I★★★**) by Rosso, the first important French interior to mix frescoes and stucco work, and the Ballroom (**Salle de bal★★★**) painted by Primaticcio and

Ballroom, Grands Appartements

Address Book

For coin ranges, see the Legend on the cover flap.

WHERE TO EAT

☕☕ **Croquembouche** – *43 r. de France –* ☎ *01 64 22 01 57. Closed Aug, Christmas school holidays, Sun evening, Thu lunch and Wed.* A plain and simple restaurant in centre city frequented by regular patrons who appreciate the warm reception, the inviting dining room decorated in soothing colours, and the traditional food prepared from fresh produce.

☕☕ **L'Île aux Truites** – *6 chemin de la Basse-Varenne, 77870 Vulaines-sur-Seine - 7km/4.2mi E of Fontainebleau dir. Samoreau.* ☎ *01 64 23 71 87. Closed 20 Dec to 25 Jan, Thu lunch and Wed – reserv. required.* A pretty thatched-roof country house well-situated on the banks of the Seine. Diners can savour trout and salmon culled from the restaurant's fish tank while enjoying an incomparable view of the river and forest. Summertime, meals are served outdoors.

WHERE TO STAY

☕ **Hôtel Victoria** – *112 r. de France.* ☎ *01 60 74 90 00 – resa@hotelvictoria.com – 20 rms: –* ☐ *7€.* This 19C building is a pleasant, relaxing place to stay. Most of the rooms on its three floors have been redone in shades of yellow and blue; five of them have a marble fireplace. Breakfast is served on the veranda or the terrace looking toward the garden.

☕ **Hôtel de la Chancellerie** – *1 r. de la Chancellerie.* ☎ *01 64 22 21 70 – hotel.chancellerie@gofornet.com – 25 rms – ☐ 5.50€.* This small hotel in the heart of the city is located in the former buildings of the chancellery. The small rooms are bright and practical and the reception is amiable. An appealing address for those on a budget.

ON THE TOWN

Le Franklin-Roosevelt – *20 r. Grande.* ☎ *01 64 22 28 73* – This wine bar aims to please. Note the inviting decor featuring mahogany furniture and red leatherette wall seats, the library dedicated to the period between 1890 and 1920, the intimate ambience with jazz in the background and some fine vintages on the wine menu. Heated terrace.

SHOPPING

La Ferme des Sablons – *19 r. des Sablons.* ☎ *01 64 22 67 25* – *Open Tue-Fri. Closed Aug.* A third of the 130 varieties of cheese sold by this cheese shop are matured on site, including the house speciality, le Fontainebleau, a soft white cheese with cream. There is also a selection of local products. A pleasant, pastoral setting.

SPORT

Jeu de Paume de Fontainebleau – *Château de Fontainebleau.* ☎ *01 64 22 47 67 – fontainebleau@wanadoo.fr – Open daily 11am-7pm.* The jeu de paume, a sport whose descendants include tennis and squash, has been played since 1601 in this indoor court of the Château de Fontainebleau. Visitors can watch a match or try a game themselves.

---

dell'Abbate and completed by Philibert Delorme in the reign of Henri II.

Henri II, Catherine de' Medici and Charles IX carried on the work initiated during this most creative and productive period.

Henri IV enlarged the palace further by building the real tennis court (Jeu de Paume), and the Diana Gallery (Galerie de Diane). He also completed the enclosure of the Oval Court. There was a change of style; the Second School of Fontainebleau looked to Flanders for its inspiration and found its artists in the Ile de France; oil was now the preferred medium for painting.

Louis XIII completed the Farewell Court. It was here, from the famous horse-shoe staircase built by Du Cerceau, that Napoleon bade his men farewell on 20 April 1814 following his abdication.

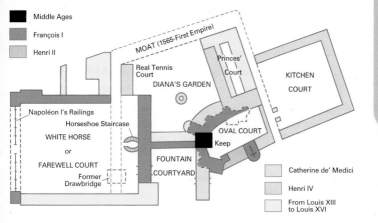

- Middle Ages
- François I
- Henri II

MOAT (1565-First Empire)

Real Tennis Court

DIANA'S GARDEN

Princes' Court

KITCHEN COURT

Napoléon I's Railings

Horseshoe Staircase

WHITE HORSE

or

FAREWELL COURT

Former Drawbridge

OVAL COURT

Keep

FOUNTAIN

COURTYARD

- Catherine de' Medici
- Henri IV
- From Louis XIII to Louis XVI

Ensemble des Grands Appartements★★★ *(First-floor State Rooms)* ♿ ① *Jun-Sep: Wed-Mon 9.30am-6pm; Oct-May: Wed-Mon 9.30am-5pm. Last admission 45min before closing.* ① *Closed Tue, 1 Jan, 1 May, 25 Dec.* ∞ *5.50€ (under 18 years: no charge), no charge 1st Sun in the month.* ☎ *01 60 71 50 60. www. musee-chateau-fontainebleau.fr.* **Petits Appartements**★ *(Ground-floor State Rooms)* 🚶 *Guided tours (1hr) daily. Call in advance the morn-*

ing of your visit. ① *Jun-Sep: Wed-Mon 9.30am-6pm. Oct-May: Wed-Mon 9.30am-5pm.* ① *Closed Tue, 1 Jan, 1 May, 25 Dec.* ∞ *3€. (under 18 years: no charge).* ☎ *01 60 71 50 60.* **Musée Napoléon**★ ♿ ① *Guided tours 🚶 (1hr) daily. Call in advance the morning of your visit. Jun-Sep: 9.30am-6pm; Oct-May: 9.30am-5pm.* ① *Closed 1 Jan, 1 May, 25 Dec.* ∞ *3€ (under 18 years: no charge).* ☎ *01 60 71 50 60.* **Gardens**★ *(Jardins).*

Châteaux in the Ile-de-France

Owing to its proximity to the seat of royal power and its immense prestige, the Ile-de-France was for many centuries a choice setting for architectural and artistic innovations. The quest for glory and love of art have inspired sovereigns and courtiers to build original and splendid mansions. Most of these are still extant and are a proud testimony to their past glory.

Highly recommended★★★

Palais de Versailles

Châteaux de Chantilly, Fontainebleau, Vaux-le-Vicomte

Recommended★★

Châteaux de Breteuil, Champs, Courances, Dampierre, Écouen, Malmaison, St-Germain-en-Laye, Sceaux, Thoiry

Interesting★

Châteaux de Ferrières, Fleury-en-Bière, Grosbois, Guermantes, Maintenon, Maisons-Laffitte, Marais, Rambouillet, La Roche-Guyon, Saussay

Also of Interest

Châteaux de Bourron, Blandy-les-Tours, Chevreuse, Courson, Malesherbes, St-Jean-de-Beauregard

LA **FONTAINE DE VAUCLUSE**

MICHELIN MAP 332 D 10
GREEN GUIDE PROVENCE

This impressive resurgent spring was famous enough to figure in Strabo's Geography 2000 years ago.

- 🛈 **Information:** Chemin de la Fontaine, ☎04 90 20 32 22.
- ▶ **Orient Yourself:** The village of Fontaine de Vaucluse (no "La") is at the end of a 7km country road from the town of L'Isle sur la Sorgue.
- 🕓 **Organising Your Time:** The fountain is much more impressive in spring than autumn.
- 🚶**Walk:** To reach the spring requires a walk on a paved path of about 1hr round trip from the village.

Visit

Gushing forth at the foot of a cliffs among treets, this is one of the most spectacular phenomena of its kind in the world. It is fed by rain falling high up on the Vaucluse hills. The water penetrates the limestone uplands with their 400-plus chasms (avens) and collects in a vast, still-unexplored cavern, from which it is forced out under pressure to the surface through a faultline.

In late winter, the flow can amount to 100 cubic meters– 3 631 cubic feet per second. At such times the waters foam and spray against the rocks, a magnificent natural spectacle.

ABBAYE DE FONTENAY★★★

MICHELIN MAP 320 G 4
GREEN GUIDE BURGUNDY-JURA

Tucked away in its lonely valley near the River Brenne, Fontenay is very evocative of the self-sufficient life of a Cistercian abbey of the 12C.

- 🛈 **Information:** Place Henri Vincenot, Montbard, ☎03 80 92 53 81. www.ot-Montbard.fr.
- ▶ **Orient Yourself:** The abbey is next to the small town of Montbard, in northern Burgundy.

A Bit of History

St Bernard (1091-1153), unhappy with the wealth and power of Cluny, found greater asceticism and spirituality at the abbey of **Cîteaux,** 23km – 14 miles south of Dijon. He was made responsible for establishing the abbey at **Clairvaux** on the River Aube; then, in 1118, at the age of 27, he founded **Fontenay,** his "second daughter." By the time of his death he had witnessed the founding of 167 Cistercian monasteries. At the end of the 13C their number had risen to 700.

Visit

Ancienne abbaye

&🕓 10am-noon, 2-5pm (Apr to mid-Nov 5.30pm). ◈ 8.50€. ☎03 80 92 15 00.

The abbey church (**église abbatiale)** was built between 1139 and 1147. It is the first example of the "monastic simplicity" characteristic of the architecture promoted by St Bernard, and is laid out in the most straightforward way, with a square chancel and chapels of square plan. The nave has a broken barrel vault, solidly supported by cross-vaulted aisles.

FONTEVRAUD L'ABBAYE★★

MICHELIN MAP 317 J 5

GREEN GUIDE CHÂTEAUX OF THE LOIRE

Fontevraud Abbey, close to the hearts of the Plantagenets, remains the largest group of monastic buildings in France.

- **Information:** Place Saint-Michel, ☎02 41 51 79 45.
  www.cote-saumuroise.com
- ▶ **Orient Yourself:** The abbey occupies the heart of the village, which is east of Saumur, close to the Loire and Vienne rivers.
- ◷ **Organising Your Time:** Allow 2 hours.

A Bit of History

The Order of Fontevraud was founded in 1099 as a result of the failure in France of Pope Gregory's reform which had been designed to enhance both the competence and the respectability of the clergy.

The Plantagenets chose the abbey as their last resting place. When Eleanor of Aquitaine died in 1204, her husband Henry II and her son Richard the Lionheart were already buried here.

The Order was aristocratic in nature and accommodated both sexes. It was presided over by an abbess (this at a time when the cult of the Virgin Mary was growing and influencing the status of womanhood).

Visit

Église abbatiale★★

In the transept crossing are a number of Plantagenet tombs (**gisants des Plantagenêts★**), good examples of Gothic funerary sculpture. The figures of Henry Plantagenet, of Richard the Lionheart and of Eleanor of Aquitaine are in painted tufa, while the figure of Isabel of Angoulême, John Lackland's wife, is of polychrome wood.

Cuisine (kitchen)★★

This highly individual structure, 27m – 89ft high, dates from around 1160 and was restored in 1902. It is a rare example of a Romanesque kitchen, with a tiled roof characteristic of the Poitiers area. Its fireplaces, arranged in pairs, could be lit according to the direction of the wind.

▶ **Église St-Michel★**

FOUGÈRES★★

MICHELIN MAP309 O4 –POPULATION 21 779

GREEN GUIDE BRITTANY

In the 19C Fougères was the most industrialised town in Brittany, having abandoned cloth-making in favour of shoe production. The area formed part of the frontier region taken from the Franks in AD 850 by Nominoé (◔ see VANNES).

- **Information:** 2 r. Nationale, ☎02 99 94 12 20.
- ▶ **Orient Yourself:** The town is on the eastern edge of Brittany.
- ◝ **Walking Tours:** Guided tours of the town: Information at the tourist office.
- ◷ **Organising Your Time:** Allow at least an hour to visit the castle, and another hour to enjoy the church and gardens.

Visit

Château de Fougères★★

🕐 *Apr-Sep: daily 9.30am-12.30pm, 2-6.30pm (mid-Jun to mid-Sep: 9am-7pm); Feb, Mar and Oct-Dec: 10am-12.30, 2-5pm.* 🕐 *Closed Jan and 25 Dec.* 💰 *4.10€.* ☎*02 99 99 79 59.* It is set on an easily defended rocky promontory protected by a meander. The first fortifications date from the 10C. Baron Raoul II began to rebuild in stone in 1173. In the 13C the castle's mighty towers served to protect Brittany from Capetian France. After its important role in the War of the Breton Succession (👐 *see JOSSELIN*) in the 14C, the castle was partly demolished by Richelieu in pursuit of his centralising policy designed to limit the power of the great feudal lords.

▶ **Église St-Sulpice**★; **Jardin public**★ (Gardens).

CAP **FRÉHEL**★★★

MICHELIN MAP 309 I 2
GREEN GUIDE BRITTANY

This is one of the grandest capes on the Breton coast, with red, black and grey cliffs rising sheer from reefs where the swell breaks heavily.

- 🛈 **Information:** 7 r. St-Gouéno, St-Brieuc, ☎08 25 00 22 22.
- ▶ **Orient Yourself:** It is between St-Brieuc and Dinard, on the Emerald Coast.
- 🚶 **Walk:** The cape is near the lighthouse – 30min there and back on foot.
- 🅿 **Parking:** There is vehicle access Jun-Sep, 8am-8pm (2€).

Visit

This cape is one of the most magnificent sights the Breton coast has to offer. The action of the waves has worn away the softer rocks around, and the great cliff of red sandstone rises 70m – 230ft above the reefs. Th**e panorama**★★★ from the clifftop is superb, taking in the Channel Islands and the Cotentin Peninsula.

FUTUROSCOPE★★

MICHELIN MAP 322 I 4
GREEN GUIDE FRENCH ATLANTIC COAST

This vast science-oriented leisure park offers a range of exciting shows, games and entertainments based on the theme of the screen image.

- 🛈 **Information:** ☎05 49 49 30 10. www.futuroscope.fr
- ▶ **Orient Yourself:** The Parc is on the northern outskirts of Poitiers.
- 🕐 **Organising Your Time:** Plenty to keep the family occupied for a couple of days.
- 👶 **Especially for Kids:** Much of the park is geared especially to youngsters.

Visit

🕐 *From 10am to 10pm or nightfall whichever is earlier.* 💰 *summer: 31€ (children: 23€); winter: 23€ (children: 17€).* Numerous attractions, both educational and purely entertaining, include **Lac enchanté** and its **Théâtre Alphanumérique** which present performances and productions incorporating the technology of the future. **Kinémax, Omnimax, Solido, Showscan** and **Imax 3D** show films using 3D films, hemispherical cinema, etc). **Images-Studio**★★★, a vast glass structure, shows what goes on behind the scenes.

CIRQUE DE **GAVARNIE**★★★

MICHELIN MAP 342 L-M 6

GREEN GUIDE LANGUEDOC ROUSSILLON TARN GORGES

Gavarnie's fame is due to its natural amphitheatre forming one of Europe's most magnificent mountain landscapes.

- **Information:** ☎05 62 92 49 10.
- ▶ **Orient Yourself:** Gavarnie is the upper end of a blind valley high in the Central Pyrenees.

Visit

2hr round trip on foot from the village; horses or donkeys can be hired.
The Cirque rises in a series of huge steps to a **crest** with a number of peaks over 3 000m – 10 000ft. Innumerable falls cascade down the rock walls, the greatest of them (the **Grande Cascade**) 422m – 1 385ft high. Downstream, the waters have carved a gorge; farther downstream the landscape has serenity and charm to it.

GORDES★

MICHELIN MAP 332 E 10–POPULATION 2 092

GREEN GUIDE PROVENCE

The **site**★ is spectacular, the charming village rising in tiers up rocky slopes.

- **Information:** Pl. du Château, ☎04 90 20 32 22. www.gordes-village.com.
- ▶ **Orient Yourself:** The village is in scenic back-country 40km east of Avignon.

Sight

Château

Daily 10am-noon, 2-6pm. Closed Jan 1 and 25 Dec. 4€. ☎04 90 72 02 75. www.gordes-village.com. The imposing Renaissance château stands dramatically on the village's highest point, facing Old Gordes. Today it houses the le Musée Pol Mara, displaying the work of this Flemish artist whoi lives in the village. There is a fine Renaissance **doorway** in the courtyard. In the great hall *(first floor)* is a splendid **chimneypiece** of 1541.

Excursions

Abbaye de Sénanque ★★

4km – 2.5mi north. Founded in 1148, this Cistercian abbey occupies a remote **site**★ conducive to contemplation. The abbey church is notable for its purity of line and lack of ornamentation.

Village des Bories★

3.5km – 2mi southwest. Curious drystone structures of this kind exist from Iceland to the Middle East. In Provence they were built in great numbers on the Vaucluse between the 14C and the 19C. The village consists of a number of dwellings as well as structures for threshing, baking, oil pressing, and housing animals.

GRAND COLOMBIER★★★

MICHELIN MAP 328 H 5

GREEN GUIDE BURGUNDY JURA

At 1 571m – 5 154ft the Grand Colombier forms the highest point in the Bugey area. The viewpoint at the summit is one of the finest in the whole of the Jura.

- **Information:** 6 r. de la Mairie, Culoz, ☎04 79 87 00 30.
- ▶ **Orient Yourself:** It's possible to drive almost to the top. Leave the car in the car park and continue to the summit on foot. It's a tough climb.
- ☻ **Don't Miss:** The road from Virieu-le-Petit to Culoz (29km – 18mi) road rises steeply (maximum gradient 19%) reaching a summit with the widest of panoramas, taking in the Jura, the Dombes plateau, the valley of the Rhône, the Massif Central and the Alps.

Visit

From Virieu-le-Petit to Culoz
29km - 18mi.

The road rises steeply (maximum gradient 19%), passing first through splendid fir-woods. At the summit, with its cross and triangulation-point, there is the widest of panoramas, taking in the Jura, the Dombes plateau, the valley of the Rhône, the Massif Central and the Alps. The features of the landscape read almost like a geological section, with the domes of anticlines and troughs of synclines clearly distinguishable.

In the distance the Grand Fenestrez, crowned by an observatory (**Observatoire**★★) rears up from the Culoz plain which can be reached by car via a boldly-designed hairpin road.

Diagram showing the typical structure of the folded Jura

The synclines form valleys (vals) running parallel to each other, separated by anticlinal ridges (monts).

Transversal valleys (cluses) cut across anticlines to link two main valleys.

A high-level depression (combe) occupies a hollowed-out ridge: it has steep inward-facing scarps (crêts).

GRENOBLE★★

MICHELIN MAP 336 H 6 -7–POPULATION 419 334
GREEN GUIDE FRENCH ALPS

Undisputed capital of the French Alps, Grenoble is a flourishing modern city of broad boulevards at the confluence of the Drac and Isère rivers.

- **Information:** 14 r. de la République, ☎04 76 42 41 41. www.grenoble-isere.info.
- ▶ **Orient Yourself:** Main routes into town follow the two rivers. The city centre is on the south bank of the Isère, about 2km/1mi east of the confluence.
- **Don't Miss:** A walk along the heights of the Bastille is a highlight of any trip.
- **Organizing Your Time:** The Notre-Dame district comes to life in the evening.

A Bit of History

The vast quantities of material brought down by the restless River Drac ("that most brutal, most violent of Alpine tributaries" R Blanchard) formed an alluvial fan on which by the late 3C a fortified Roman town was sited. Development of the town was held back by the precarious nature of its communication links; though Grenoble was well-sited on the roads leading from the Rhône valley to Turin and Cannes, frequent floods and challenging gradients made travelling an uncertain business.

In the reign of Henri IV the city was captured by Lesdiguières, commander of the armies of Piedmont and Savoy, who re-fortified it. Later fortifications, the Enceinte Haxo, doubled the area of the city to the south.

Sights

Fort de la Bastille

🚠 *Access by cable car. Allow 1 hr.* 🕐 *Jul-Aug: Tue-Sun 9.15am-12.15pm, Mon 11am-12.15pm; Jun and Sep: Tue-Sat 9.15am-11.45pm, Mon 11am-11.45pm, Sun 9.15am-7.25pm; Mar-May and Oct: Tue-Sat 9.30am-11.45pm, Mon 11am-7.25pm, Sun 9.15am-7.25pm. Nov-Feb: Tue-Sun 10.45am-6.30pm, Mon 11am-6.30pm.* 🕐 *Closed 2nd and 3rd week in Jan.* 🎫 *5.70€ round trip, 3.90€ single.* ☎04 76 44 33 65.

The fort was built in the 16C to protect the approaches to the city, and strengthened in the 19C. It has the best **view**★★★ over the town in its magnificent setting.

The Grenoble cable car: an unofficial emblem of the city

Fr. Isler/MICHELIN

Vieille ville (Old Town)★

The Roman town lay close to the present-day Place Granette (celebrated by Stendhal) and on either side of the Grande-Rue, itself a Roman road. By the 13C the town had spread northeastwards as far as the Isère, where today a number of courtyards and porches dating from the 16C can be found (no 8 Rue Brocherie, nos 8 and 10 Rue Chenoise).

Musée de Grenoble★★★

  Daily except Tue 10am-6.30pm. *Closed public holidays. 5€, no charge 1st Sun in the month.* ☎*04 76 63 44 44.* *www.museedegrenoble.fr.*

On the bank of the Isère in the heart of the old town, this Fine Arts museum has a remarkably plain and sober appearance. Huge windows look out on massive sculptures which enhance the parvis and the Parc Michallon, outside the north building.

This is one of France's most important provincial museums, with painting from 16C to 20C, including an exceptionally rich collection of modern art. The collections include fine modern works like Matisse's *Interior with Aubergines* and Picasso's *Woman Reading* as well as Old Masters like de Champaigne's *John the Baptist*, Rubens' *Pope Gregory surrounded by Saints* or de La Tour's *St Jerome*. Most art movements after 1945 are represented: Abstraction lyrique, New Realism, "Supports-surfaces", Pop Art and Minimalism.

▶ Église-musée St-Laurent (*on the outskirts*) – Merovingian **crypt**★;. Cathédrale – unusual 14C Flamboyant **ciborium**★ in polychrome stone; **Musée Dauphinois**★   *daily except Tue.* *Closed public holidays. No charge.* ☎*04 76 85 19 01.* *www.musee.dauphinois.fr*– popular art and traditions; **Musée de la Résistance et de la Déportation**★   *daily except Tue.* *Closed public holidays. No charge.* ☎*04 76 42 38 53;* **Palais de Justice (Law Courts)**★ – combining Renaissance and Flamboyant Gothic styles.

CHÂTEAU DE **GRIGNAN**★★

MICHELIN MAP 332 C 7
GREEN GUIDE PROVENCE

The old town of Grignan is dominated by its medieval château, which owes its fame to the delightful letters written in the 17C by Mme de **Sévigné** to her daughter Mme de Grignan.

▣ **Information:** Place Sévigné, Grignan, ☎04 75 46 56 75.
▶ **Orient Yourself:** Grignan is south-east of Montélimar, east of the Rhône.

Visit

 Guided tours *(1hr) daily 9.30-11.30am, 2-5.30pm (Jul-Aug: 6pm).* *Tue from Nov to Mar, and public holidays.. 5.50€.* ☎*04 75 91 83 55.*

The medieval castle was remodelled in the 16C. In 1669, the Count of Grignan married the daughter of Mme de Sévigné, who became a frequent visitor. The letters written by mother to daughter over a period of 27 years were to create a new literary genre; full of keen observation, wit and spontaneity.

The Renaissance south front of the château was restored early in the 20C following a fire. With its superimposed columns, moulded pilasters, mullioned windows and shell-decorated niches, it marks the arrival of Renaissance in Provence.

The original courtyard is flanked by a Gothic pavilion and opens out onto the terrace with a **view**★★ over the Tricastin area and Mont Ventoux. Inside are evocative furnishings (**mobilier**★) of many periods and Aubusson tapestries.

GUÉRANDE★

MICHELIN MAP 316 B4–POPULATION 13 603

GREEN GUIDE BRITTANY

Secure behind its circle of ramparts, Guérande has kept its appearance as a proud medieval town.

🛈 **Information:** 1 pl. du Marché au Bois, ☎02 40 24 96 71.

▶ **Orient Yourself:** The town lies behind beach resort La Baule.

🕐 **Organizing Your Time:** Explore this interesting district of salt-marshes, beaches and busy fishing ports.

Sights

Remparts★
Begun in 1343, the ramparts were completed in 1476 remain unbreached.

Collégiale St-Aubin★
Built between the 12C and the 16C, the church has a striking west front in granite. Embedded in a buttress on the right is an **outdoor pulpit**. Inside, the **capitals** are decorated with grotesque figures and foliage. The chancel is lit by a magnificent **stained-glass window**.

Presqu'île de Guérande★
In the Roman era, a great sea gulf stretched between the rocky island, Ile de Batz, and the Guérande ridge. Just a channel remains open opposite Le Croisic through which the sea flows at high tide.

ABBAYE D'HAMBYE★★

MICHELIN MAP 303 E 6

GREEN GUIDE NORMANDY

The 12C abbey of Hambye is charmingly sited in the green valley of the Sienne. Its ruins evoke the serenity of Benedictine life.

🛈 **Information:** Place des Costils, Villedieu-les-Poêles, ☎02 33 61 05 69. www.ot-villedieu.fr.

▶ **Orient Yourself:** The abbey is 12km/8mi north of the town of Villedieu, in western Normandy.

Visit

Église abbatiale★★
🕐 Apr-Oct: daily 10am-noon, 2-6pm. ⌦ 4€. ☎02 33 61 76 92.
The abbey buildings are dominated by the church, with slender columns and sharply pointed arches around the choir (1180-1200). The high bell-tower whose upper stage is pierced by round-headed arches was once crowned by a lantern. The monastic buildings frame former cloisters. The chapter-house is a masterpiece of Norman Gothic, divided into two by six central pillars, the final one gathers together the arches of the apse in a masterly way.

CHÂTEAU DE **HAUTEFORT**★★

MICHELIN MAP 329 H 4

GREEN GUIDE DORDOGNE BERRY LIMOUSIN

The elegant château rises up proudly on its hilltop site, overlooking its extensive and well-kept grounds.

- 🛈 **Information:** Pl. René-Lavaud, Hautefort, ☎05 53 50 40 27.
- ▶ **Orient Yourself:** The castle is 41km/25mi east of Périgueux.
- 👁 **Don't Miss:** Superb timberwork in the northwest tower.

Visit

🕐 Guided tours ☜ (1hr) Jun-Sep: daily 9.30am-7pm; Apr-May: daily 10am-12.30pm, 2pm-6.30pm; Feb-Mar and Oct-Nov: daily 2-6pm. Last admission 1hr before closing. 🖾 8€. Garden: self-guided visits. ♿☎ 05 53 50 51 23.

In the 16C, an ancient fortress was strengthened, and a century later, reconstructed in Renaissance and Classical style. It has been further restored since a fire in 1968. The interior has fine Flemish tapestries saved from the flames, a 17C Felletin landscape, good pieces of furniture and unusual paved floors. The tower has magnificent chestnut timberwork (**charpente**★★).

Château de Hautefort

CHÂTEAU DU
HAUT-KŒNIGSBOURG★★

MICHELIN MAP 315 I 7

GREEN GUIDE ALSACE LORRAINE CHAMPAGNE

This vast mock-medieval edifice in pink sandstone overlooks the Alsace plain from its lofty rock rising through the treetops of the Vosges forest.

- ▶ **Orient Yourself:** The castle is roughly 21km/13mi north of Colmar. It is reached on a steep winding access road in the hills between Sélestat and Ribeauvillé.
- 👁 **Don't Miss:** A superb **panorama**★★ from the tall bastion.

Visit

🕐 *Jun-Aug: 9.30am-6.30pm; Mar and Oct: 9.45am-5pm; Nov-Feb: 9.45am-noon, 1-5pm. Last admission 30min before closing.*
🕐 *Closed 1 Jan, 1 May, 25 Dec.* ♿ 🚹 *7.50€ (18-25 years: 4.80€), no charge 1st Sun in the month (Oct-Mar).* ☎*03 88 82 50 60.*

The present building is the outcome of an almost complete reconstruction in neo-feudal style carried out on the orders of Emperor William II between 1900 and 1908 during the period when Alsace and Lorraine had been reincorporated into Germany.

LE **HAVRE**★

MICHELIN MAP 304 A 5–POPULATION 250 000
GREEN GUIDE NORMANDY

Destroyed in WW2 and rebuilt in a very striking modern style, this city is one of Europe's most important ports.

- ℹ️ **Information:** 186 blvd Clemenceau, ☎02 32 74 04 04. www.lehavretourisme.com.
- ▶ **Orient Yourself:** The town consists of a large port and industrial area as well as the residential district of Ste-Adresse and the old port of Harfleur. The newer part of town centers around the Espace Niemeyer, which provides an ultra-modern architectural facelift to the urban landscape on place Gambetta.
- 👁 **Don't Miss:** Avenue Foch is a fine promenade bordered by lawns and shaded by trees which opens onto the seafront by the Porte Océane.
- 🕐 **Organizing Your Time:** Spend an hour walking around the modern town starting from the place du Général-de-Gaulle.
- 🅿 **Parking:** Between the Bassin du Commerce and the Espace Niemeyer (Place du Gén.-de-Gaulle).

A Bit of History

By 1517 the harbour at Harfleur had silted up. To remedy the situation, François I ordered the building of a new port which was to be called "Havre-de-Grâce" (Harbour of Grace). The marshy site selected by Admiral Bonnivet seemed unpromising, but his choice was a happy one since the tide remained at the flood two hours longer here than elsewhere. The port area has subsequently spread some 20km – 12 miles upstream with a parallel industrial development, mostly on the north bank,

Le Volcan by Oscar Niemeyer, Basin du Commerce

Pont de Normandie, from Le Havre

G. Targat/MICHELIN

of chemical, engineering and motor industries, shipyards and refineries.

The town and its region has an important **Impressionist** history and features in several Impressionist works, notably Claude Monet's Terrace at Ste-Adresse (in the Metropolitan Museum in New York), a key work. The old town and resort of **Ste-Adresse**★★ is still a pleasant place; from the clifftop at La Hève there are fine views out over the estuary and the English Channel.

Sights

Quartier moderne (Modern Town)★

During the bombing that preceded Le Havre's liberation on 13 September 1944, the old centre was obliterated and more than 4 000 people were killed; the besieged Germans completed the destruction by dynamiting the port.

The architect **Auguste Perret** (1874 1954), already famous for his innovating work with reinforced concrete, was given the task of rebuilding the devastated town from scratch. His initial concept involved a vast deck covering all the new city's services (energy, pipelines, gas, traffic). This bold scheme was rejection, so Perret laid out the town largely using the old street pattern, but in an uncompromisingly modern idiom which remains striking. Among the highlights of Perret's remarkable work are **Place de l'Hôtel de Ville**★, one of the largest squares in Europe; **Avenue Foch**★ with a vista down to the sea and **Église St-Joseph**★, whose interior walls are a lattice of stained glass.

▶ **Musée des Beaux-Arts André Malraux**★ (◔ *Daily except Tue 11am-6pm (Sat-Sun 7pm).* ◔ *Closed public holidays.* ⚅ ⬠ 5€) – built entirely of glass, houses work of **Eugène Boudin**★ (*Yellow Boats at Étretat, Breton Church Interior*) and Raoul Dufy (*Amphitrite, Sea Goddess*).

Excursion

To ⚘**Honfleur**★★ via the **Pont de Normandie**★★, soaring cable-stayed bridge crossing the Seine with a record breaking main span 856m (2 808ft) between 214m (705ft)-high towers.

CASCADE DU **HÉRISSON**★★★

MICHELIN MAP 321 F 7
GREEN GUIDE BURGUNDY JURA

High up at the foot of the cirque of Chaux-de-Dombief is little Lake Bonlieu drained by the River Hérisson (hedgehog). The river crosses the narrow Frasnois plateau, then, in the space of 3km – 2mi drops via a series of rapids and falls through its famous wooded gorge to the Champagnole plain 200m – 650ft below. The falls are dramatic after wet weather, much less so after a dry period.

🛈 **Information:** 36 Grande-Rue, Clairvaux-les-Lacs, ☎03 84 25 27 47.

▶ **Orient Yourself:** The falls are east of the town of Lons-le-Saunier. They are approached by road from the villages of Bonlieu, Doucier or Ilay, and then reached on foot.

🐾**Walking Tour:** The falls are reached by foot on the marked Sentier des Cascades footpath.

😊 **Don't Miss:** Most impressive of the falls is **Cascade du Grand Saut**★★.

- 🅿 **Parking:** From Doucier, parking is available at the Jacquard Mill (*fee*), from Ilay, you can leave the car near the Auberge du Hérisson.
- **Caution:** Wear a raincoat and take care not to slip on the wet ground.
- 🕐 **Organizing Your Time:** The hike takes a good three hours there and back.

Visit

▶ *Follow the footpath which starts 8km – 5mi east of Doucier as far as the Ilay crossroads – 3 hr there and back.*

The path climbs over a series of limestone outcrops rising above areas of alluvial deposits where lakes have formed and where a rich vegetation flourishes. The limestones were laid down over a period of 35 million years during Jurassic times; it is they that form the succession of splendid falls, the **Éventail**★★★ (Fan Falls), the **Grand Saut**★★ (Great Leap), Château Garnier, the **Saut de la Forge**★ and Saut Girard.

HONFLEUR★★

MICHELIN MAP 303 N 3–POPULATION 8 178
GREEN GUIDE NORMANDY

Honfleur lies at the foot of the **Côte de Grâce**★★ hill, overlooking the wide waters of the Seine estuary. With its characterful old houses and lanes, it is truly the most picturesque of ports.

- **Information:** Quai Lepaulmier, ☎02 31 89 23 30. www.ot-honfleur.fr
- ▶ **Orient Yourself:** The town is on the seafront at the mouth of the Seine. Its centre focuses on the old port.
- **Walking Tours:** The tourist office offers guided tours (5€) lasting 90 min.
- **Don't Miss:** The picturesque lanes of the old quarter.
- 🕐 **Organizing Your Time:** Make time in early morning or dusk to linger over the estuary views and the reflections of quayside houses in the harbour.

A Bit of History

Many maritime ventures began on the quayside at Honfleur. Paulmier de Gouneville sailed from here to Brazil in 1503, and in 1506 Jean Denis explored the mouth of the St Lawrence River. In 1608 Samuel de Champlain set out to found Quebec City and in 1681 La Salle started the voyage which was to make him the first European to descend the Mississippi all the way to the sea, thereby opening up those vast territories to which he gave the name Louisiana in honour of his king, Louis XIV.

Great artists have appreciated the soft light and breadth of sky over the Seine estuary as seen from Honfleur. The town appealed to English water-colourist Bonington, locally born Eugène Boudin and later to Claude Monet and the other Impressionists. Erik Satie composed some of his music in Honfleur, and several distinguished writers have lived and worked here.

Sight

Le vieux Honfleur
(Old Honfleur) ★★
The streets and quaysides of the ancient port are full of character. The old harbour (**Vieux bassin**★★) shelters a fishing fleet as well as yachts and pleasure-craft. A richly varied townscape is formed by the fine stone residences along the Quai St-Etienne, the narrow, slate-faced houses on the Quai Ste-Catherine, the church (Église St-Etienne), the Governor's House (Lieutenance), all seen against the foreground of masts and rigging.

Address Book

For coin ranges, see the Legend on the cover flap.

WHERE TO EAT

Le Bistrot des Artistes – *14 pl. Berthelot – ☎02 31 89 95 90 – Closed Jan and Mar, and Wed except July to Sept.* Antiques, paintings of the sea, photos of Honfleur and leatherette wall seats make up the decor of this restaurant with a Parisian bistro flair. Tables near the window have a lovely view of the Vieux Bassin. On the menu: salads and slices of bread with various toppings.

Au P'tit Mareyeur – *4 r. Haute – ☎ 02 31 98 84 23 – jule.rastacoop@freesbee.fr – Closed 5 Jan to 5 Feb, Mon and Tue.* This minuscule restaurant right near the harbour has a decided maritime slant, in the kitchen as well as the dining area. The bill of fare changes often, but between the fixed-price menu and the suggestions du jour, fish and seafood fans can look forward to a delightful meal.

Au Vieux Honfleur – *13 quai St-Étienne – ☎02 31 89 15 31.* This restaurant by the old harbour extends its terrace along the quay when the weather is fine. Al fresco or inside, nice and warm among bibelots, posters and paintings, you'll be able to savour Norman dishes and seafood while gazing upon the splendid basin.

WHERE TO STAY

Le Vieux Pressoir – *Hameau le Clos-Potier – 27210 Conteville – 13.5km/8.2mi from Honfleur via D 580, rte de Pont-Audemer then left on D 312 – ☎02 32 57 60 79 – 5 rooms.* Located in the heart of the countryside, this 18C wood-sided farm is meant for lovers of quietude and authenticity. Each room overflows with 19C and 20C furniture and objects discovered in second-hand shops. Children will be delighted with the duck pond.

Le Belvédère – *36 r. Émile-Renouf – ☎02 31 89 08 13 – Closed Jan – 9 rooms – 7€.* This venerable old house owes its name to the belvedere crowning the roof. The renovated bedrooms benefit from the ambient tranquillity. Mealtime, the glass-covered restaurant

and small terrace offer an unbeatable view of the Pont de Normandie.

Hôtel Otelinn – *62 cours A.-Manuel – ☎02 31 89 41 77 – 50 rooms - 7€.* At a distance from the city centre, this hotel has the considerable advantage of proposing rooms at reasonable prices. Small and functional, they make for an agreeable halt. A garden and a terrace give you the opportunity of basking in the gentle Norman sun.

Le Clos Deauville Saint-Gatien – *4 chemin des Brioleurs – 14130 St-Gatien-des-Bois – 9km/5.4mi S of Honfleur via D 579 – ☎02 31 65 16 08 -hotel@clos-st-gatien.fr – 60 rooms – 13€.* The charm of the Norman countryside a few short miles from the shore characterises this half-timbered house nestled in a verdant setting. Comfortable, cosy rooms. Three pools, one covered, a sauna and a fitness room: careful not to strain your muscles!

SPORT

Centre équestre du Ramier – *Chemin du Ramier – 14600 Équemauville – S of Honfleur, towards Équemauville, follow signs – ☎02 31 89 49 97 or 06 60 15 42 28 – Open Wed, Sat-Sun and public holidays 9am-5pm; other days by appointment.* Located in the heart of the (authentic!) Norman countryside, this lovely riding centre has 15 training horses available. Rides last for 1hr-1hr 30min.

TAKE A BREAK

Pom'cannelle – *60 quai Ste-Catherine – ☎ 02 31 89 55 25 –* These home-made ices are an absolute must. In addition to liquorice and apricot, you must try this blissfully anti-dietetic concoction: ice cream flavoured with "confiture de lait," a gooey milk caramel.

La Petite Chine – *14 r. du Dauphin – ☎02 31 89 36 52 – Closed Mon.* Decorated in blue and yellow, Monet's favourite colours, this pretty little pastry shop and tearoom looks out on the wharf. Try the regional specialities: gingerbread, *tarte paysanne* (farmers' pie) and apples in calvados. Music and a library are at the customers' disposal.

Nearby is the **Église Ste-Catherine**★ with its detached **bell-tower**★ (🕐 *mid-Mar to mid-Nov daily 10am-noon, 2-6pm;* 🕐 *closed Tue, 1 May, 14 Jul;* 🎫 *2.10€;* ☎ *02 31 89 54 00*). The church was rebuilt after the Hundred Years War by the shjips' carpenters. All around are houses built in like fashion, making up a fine group of timber buildings, unusual in Western Europe.

Rue Haute, a former pathway outside the fortifications, has kept many fine houses of brick, stone and timber once lived in by shipbuilders.

◖◖ Musée Eugène Boudin 🕐 *Mid-Mar to end Sep: Wed-Mon 10am-noon, 2-7pm: Oct to mid-Mar: Wed-Mon 11am-5pm.* 🕐 *Closed Tue, Jan to mid-Feb, 1 May, 14 Jul, 25 Dec.* 🎫 *5.20€.* ☎ *02 31 89 54 00* – paintings in the Honfleur tradition. **Pont de Normandie**★★ (🕐 *see LE HAVRE*).

HUNSPACH★★

MICHELIN MAP 315 L 3–POPULATION 615
GREEN GUIDE ALSACE LORRAINE CHAMPAGNE

Carefully preserved and free from incongruous modern additions, Hunspach is one of Alsace's most charming villages. Flowers fill the streets of timber-framed houses with their projecting roofs and bull's-eye windows (a Baroque feature). Many of the buildings are in fact old farmhouses, with yards opening off the street; orchards, vines and long-handled pumps complete the picturesque scene.

▸ **Orient Yourself:** Hunspach is in the extreme north-east of the country, close to the River Rhine and the border with Germany.

Excursion

Seebach★
5km – 3mi northeast by D 249. This is a wonderful example of the flower-decked Alsatian village with its half-timbered houses adorned with awnings and gardens.

ISSOIRE★★

MICHELIN MAP 326 G 9–POPULATION 13 559
GREEN GUIDE AUVERGNE THE RHÔNE VALLEY

This old Auvergne town is situated at the point where the Pavin valley meets the flatter fertile country of the southern Limagne. In 1540 the town became a notable centre of Protestantism. More recently it has acquired an industrial character, with important engineering works (heavy pressing machinery and aluminium alloys). But there is still an agreeable, provincial ambiance about the place that rewards even the shortest break.

🛈 **Information:** Place du Général de Gaulle, 63500 Issoire, ☎ 04 73 89 15 90, www. sejours-issoire.com

▸ **Orient Yourself:** Climb up the clocktower for a superb view of the town and surrounding countryside. Then start your tour of the town. Most shops, restaurants and bars cluster around the tower and along the Main street.

Visit

Ancienne abbatiale St-Austremoine★★

Built around 1135, this is the largest Romanesque church in the Auvergne. It was extensively restored in the 19C (west front, roof, bell-tower, many of the capitals, the polychrome interior decoration).

The east end (**chevet★★**) is a fine example of Auvergne Romanesque, generously and harmoniously proportioned and rich in detail (cornices, ornamental brackets, mosaic stonework and sculpture).

Inside, an impression of strength and solidity, characteristic of these Auvergne churches, is given by the four great arches at the crossing and by the ambulatory with its ribbed vault. The influence of the Mozac School of sculpture is clearly seen in the capitals (**chapiteaux★** – c 1140) carved from the local volcanic rock; particularly fine are those showing the Last Supper and Christ washing the feet of the disciples.

In the narthex is a 15C mural of the **Last Judgement★**, a favourite subject of the time, here treated with great verve and a degree of satire.

CHÂTEAU DE **JOSSELIN**★★

MICHELIN MAP 308 P 7
GREEN GUIDE BRITTANY

This stronghold has stood guard over the crossing of the Oust for 900 years, and seen many battles.

🛈 **Information:** Place de la Congregation, ☎02 97 22 36 43. www.pays-de-josselin-tourisme.com.

▶ **Orient Yourself:** The chateau is in the heart of the inland village of Josselin, west of Rennes.

A Bit of History

The **War of the Breton Succession**, which started in 1341, set rival heirs to the Duchy against each other, Jeanne de Penthièvre, granddaughter of Jean II of Brittany, and Jean de Montfort, Jean III's half-brother. The struggle, long and confused, overlapped with the early stages of the Hundred Years War. Jeanne was married to Charles de Blois and her claim, supported by the Valois rulers of France, was based on established Breton custom. The ousted De Montfort allied himself to the Plantagenets who had won the great naval battle of Sluys the previous year. He was able to persuade them to set a terrible example by laying waste the area around Tréguier; this action took place during the period which also saw the triumph of English arms at Crécy and Calais.

The garrison at Josselin faced the defenders of Ploërmel Castle, 12km – 8mi to the east; between them they ravaged the countryside without any decisive outcome. A solution to the impasse was sought by arranging a contest between 30 knights from each camp. The **Battle of the Thirty** took place in 1351, half-way between the two towns. Ploërmel's champions consisted of four Bretons, six Germans and 20 Englishmen. Josselin emerged victorious, but even this dramatic settling of accounts did not prove decisive.

The war was finally brought to an end in 1364 by the death of Charles de Blois at the Battle of Auray. In 1365 de Montfort was acknowledged as ruler of the Duchy, albeit subject to the Capetian kings of France.

Visit

🕒 *Guided tours* 👣 *(45min) mid-Jul to end Aug: daily 10am-6pm; Jun to mid-Jul and Sep: daily 2-6pm; Apr-May and Oct: Sat-Sun, public and school holidays 2-6pm.* 6.80€ *(children: 4.70€).* 02 97 22 36 45.

The medieval robustness of the massive walls overlooking the river contrasts with the refinement of the upper parts belonging to the reconstruction of the 15C-16C. The marriage of Anne of Brittany to Charles VIII of France in 1491 had led to a lessening of tension between the Duchy and the French kingdom, and John of Laval was able to rebuild the old castle in accordance with the new ideas of Renaissance architecture. What had been a fortress now became a palace. The transformation is particularly evident in the courtyard, where the **façade**★★ featuring an ornate roof **balustrade** has a splendid variety of motifs: pinnacles, tracery and mouldings. Inside there is an innovative staircase with straight ramps.

In the 17C the keep and five of the towers were demolished on the orders of Richelieu. A park was laid out in 1760, and in 1882 the castle was restored.

▶ **Basilique Notre-Dame-du-Roncier**★ – **Mausoleum**★ of Olivier de Clisson.

ABBAYE DE **JUMIÈGES**★★★

MICHELIN MAP 304 E 5
GREEN GUIDE NORMANDY

The great abbey in its splendid setting on the Lower Seine forms one of the most evocative groups of ruins in France.

- **Information:** Rue Guilllaume-le-Conquérant, Jumièges, 02 35 37 28 97. www.jumieges.fr.
- ▶ **Orient Yourself:** Jumièges is on a big loop of the River Seine just west of Rouen. The abbey is a ruin, in places open to the sky; consider this an outdoor venue and dress accordingly.
- **Don't Miss:** Enjoy the view from the terrace over the garden.
- **Organizing Your Time:** Allow at least an hour for the visit.

A Bit of History

It was founded in the 7C and within 50 years housed 700 monks and 1 500 lay-brothers. Its great wealth was based on the generosity of the Merovingian rulers and on tithes drawn from a vast area. Destroyed by the Vikings, the abbey was raised again in the early 11C, but suffered in the Wars of Religion. The monks were scattered at the outbreak of the French Revolution. In 1793 it was auctioned and a purchaser started dismantling it to re-use the stone, blowing up the chancel and lantern-tower in the process. In 1852 a new owner saved it from complete destruction but by then the great edifice was already a ruin.

Visit

Jul-Aug: daily 9.30am-6.30pm; mid-Apr to end Jun and early Sep to mid-Sep: Mon-Fri 9.30am-1pm, 2.30-6.30pm, Sat-Sun: 9.30am-6.30pm; mid-Sep to mid-Apr: daily 9.30am-1pm, 2.30-5.30pm. Closed public holidays. 5€, no charge 1st Sun in the month (Oct-Mar). 02 35 37 24 02. www.monum.fr.

The most striking feature of the abbey is the west front of the **Église Notre-Dame** with its two magnificent towers, 43m – 141ft high, the oldest and grandest of any Norman abbey.

The power of the building to move the beholder is enhanced by the absence of vaults which permits the eye to soar freely skywards; the ruins seem to express spiritual qualities.

KAYSERSBERG★★

MICHELIN MAP 315 H 8–POPULATION 2 755
GREEN GUIDE ALSACE LORRAINE CHAMPAGNE

A typically pretty Alsace village, its flower-bedecked streets have many old houses, several dating from the 16C, and behind the pretty little town rise the serried ranks of vines on the slopes of the Vosges hills.

- **Information:** 14 r. de la République, ☎04 76 42 41 41. www.grenoble-isere.info.
- **Orient Yourself:** Kaysersberg is 12 km north-west of Colmar.
- **Parking:** The village is completely pedestrianised, with car parks on its south, west and east approaches.
- **Don't Miss:** A few minutes inside the church.

A Bit of History

Kaysersberg was a Roman town, and in the Middle Ages it was one of the confederation of 10 free cities known as the Decapolis, set up to resist feudal demands on their burgeoning urban culture.

The great doctor, theologian and pioneer of Third World aid, Albert Schweitzer (1875-1965), was born, at no 12 Rue du Général de Gaulle (next to the Musée Albert-Schweitzer, open daily in summer, which contains memorabilia).

▶▶ **Église**★ (church) – **altarpiece**★★. **Hôtel de ville**★. **Vieilles maisons**★ (Old houses). **Pont fortifié**★ (bridge). **Maison Brief**★.

KERNASCLÉDEN★★

MICHELIN MAP 308 L 6–POPULATION 355
GREEN GUIDE BRITTANY

The small village has a beautiful church with remarkable 15C frescoes.

- **Orient Yourself:** The village is about 25km north of the coastal town of Lorient.

Sight

Church★★

Built in granite between 1430 and 1455, the church typifies the Breton version of Flamboyant Gothic. It has two **porches** on the south side (one of them with statues of the **Apostles**★). Inside there is a fine window at the east end. The **frescoes**★★ are striking: the choir vault depicts 24 scenes from the Life of the Virgin; in the north transept note particularly the folds of the clothes of the celestial choir; in the south transept is the Passion, and a Dance of Death.

CHÂTEAU DE **LANGEAIS**★★

MICHELIN MAP 317 L 5
GREEN GUIDE CHÂTEAUX OF THE LOIRE

The town's whitehouses nestle beneath the high walls of the château.

Information: Pl. du 14-juillet, Langeais, ☎02 47 96 58 22.

▶ **Orient Yourself:** The town and château are on the right bank of the Loire between Tours and Saumur, beautifully approached by taking the left bank road and crossing the river into the town.

A Bit of History

The great Angevin ruler Foulques Nerra built a sturdy keep to command the Loire Valley. Completed in 994, now in ruins in the park of the château, it is considered to be the oldest such building in the whole of France.

The château itself was built to protect France from Brittany. In 1491 the marriage of Charles Viii of France and Anne of Brittany ended the threat.

Visit

🕐 Apr to mid-Jul and Sep to mid-Oct: daily 9.30am-6.30pm; mid-Jul to end Aug: daily 9.30am-7pm; mid-Oct to end Mar: daily 10am-5.30pm. 🕐 Closed 25 Dec. ☜ 6.50€ (children: 4€). ☎02 47 96 72 60.

Seen from outside, the château still looks like a medieval fortress, with drawbridge, towers, battlemented sentry-walk and almost windowless walls. But the façade facing the courtyard has the features of a Renaissance country house, including pointed dormers, turrets, sculptures and mullioned windows. Inside, the apartments **(appartements**★★★**)** have kept their medieval layout, one room commanding the next through narrow doors and laid out along diagonal lines. The last owner, Jacques Siegfried (a mill- and ship-owner and banker from Le Havre), refurnished the interior very expertly, and Langeais gives a good impression of aristocratic life in the early Renaissance period. The rooms contain fine tapestries. In the Charles VIII Room is a 17C clock with a single hand.

LAON★★

MICHELIN MAP 306 D 5–POPULATION 26 265
GREEN GUIDE NORTHERN FRANCE AND THE PARIS REGION

This ancient town dominates the surrounding countryside from its magnificent hilltop site★★, a 100m – 330ft high limestone outlier rising abruptly from the plain. Its defensive potential was noted by the Carolingian kings who made it their capital for 150 years, from the reign of Charles le Chauve (the Bald) (840) to Louis V (987). It was only in the reign of Hugh Capet that the capital was moved to the Île-de-France.

Information: Place du Parvis Gautier de Mortagne, ☎03 23 20 28 62. www.tourisme-paysdelaon.com

▶ **Orient Yourself:** On arrival at Laon, head to the Upper Town, which is in two sections: la Cité, around the cathedral, et le Bourg.

Walking Tour: Guided tours on summer weekends. 5€. Information at the tourist office.

Ⓟ **Parking:** Driving and parking are difficult in the Upper Town.

🕐 **Organizing Your Time:** The quickest and most enjoyable way to reach the Upper Town is on the cable railway, called Poma (*Mon-Sat 8am-8pm, 1€*).

Sight

Cathédrale Notre-Dame★★

The present cathedral was begun in 1160 and completed towards 1230. It is in the early-Gothic style, still caught up in the Romanesque idiom (as in its Norman-style lantern-tower). The west front is a masterpiece, with its deep porches and stepped towers flanked by openwork turrets. The immensely long **nave**★★★ shows the persistence of Carolingian traditions, but "nowhere else did the development of 12C Gothic achieve such breadth and unity" (Henri Focillon). The elevation is four-storeyed, with great arches carried on circular columns, a gallery with bold double arches, a blind triforium and a clerestory. In the nave, transept and chancel the bays are marked – still in a less emphatic way than at either Sens (1140) or Senlis (1153) – by a pattern of major and minor clustered columns, the former with five, the latter with three engaged columns.

▶ **Quartier de la Cathédrale**★★ (cathedral area); **Rempart du Midi**★ (southern ramparts) – **views**★; **Musée**★ 🕐 *Jun-Sep: Tue-Sun 11am-6pm; Oct-May: Tue-Sun 2-6pm.* 🕐 *Closed Mon, 1 Jan, 1 May, 14 Jul, 25 Dec.* 🎟 *3.40€, no charge Sun (Oct-Mar).* ☎*03 23 20 19 87*– painting and archeology. **Chapelle des Templiers**★ 🕐 *Jun-Sep: Tue-Fri 9am-6pm, Sat-Sun and public holidays 11am-6pm; Oct-May: Tue-Fri 9am-6pm, Sat-Sun and public holidays 2-6pm.* 🕐 *Closed Mon, 1 Jan, 1 May, 14 Jul, 25 Dec.* ☎*03 23 20 19 87.* **Église St-Martin**★*Call tourist office or the church in advance for guided tour.* ☎*03 23 20 26 54.* **Porte de Soissons**★.

CHÂTEAU DE **LAPALISSE**★★

MICHELIN MAP 3 332
GREEN GUIDE AUVERGNE THE RHÔNE VALLEY

The little crossroads town has grown up at the foot of the château which has commanded the crossing of the Besbre since the 11C. Its most famous owner was Jacques II de Chabannes (1470-1525), a Marshal of France who distinguished himself in the conquest of Milan but who was killed by a blast from a harquebus received during the Battle of Pavia.

🛈 **Information:** 26 r. Winston Churchill, Lapalisse, ☎04 70 99 08 39.
▶ **Orient Yourself:** Town and château are 25km north-east of Vichy.

Visit

🕐 *Guided tours* 🔄 *(1hr) Apr-Oct: daily 9am-noon, 2pm-6pm. Last admission 1hr before closing.* 🎟 *5.50€* 🚻 ☎*04 70 99 37 58.*

Little remains of the medieval castle. The present building, started at the beginning of the 16C, is very much in the style of the early Renaissance, the work of Florentine craftsmen brought from Italy by Jacques. The courtyard façade is enlivened by heraldic motifs and polychrome brickwork, by sandstone courses on the towers and around the windows, by bracketed lintels and mullioned windows, by medallions in the portal of the central tower, by foliated scrolls, pilasters and Corinthian capitals. Inside, there is interesting Louis XIII furniture in the main reception room. The **Salon doré**★★ has a coffered ceiling and 15C Flemish tapestries. The chapel, built in granite, is in Flamboyant style, and there is a fine timber ceiling in the service range (**communs**).

GROTTE DE **LASCAUX**

MICHELIN MAP 329 I 5

GREEN GUIDE DORDOGNE BERRY LIMOUSIN

The world-famous cave paintings of Lascaux were discovered by accident on 12 September 1940 by a young man looking for his dog which had disappeared down a hole. Most of the paintings appear to date from the end of the Aurignacian period, others from the Magdalenian. They cover the walls and roofs of the cave with a bestiary of bulls, cows, horses, deer and bison, depicted with such skill as to justify Abbot Breuil's epithet "the Sistine Chapel of prehistoric times". Such damage was caused by visitors that the caves were closed to the public and a full-size replica was made nearby – Lascaux II.

- **Information:** Place Bertran-de-Born, Montignac, ☎05 53 51 82 60. www.bien-venue-montignac.com
- **Orient Yourself:** The cave is situated 2km/1.2mi south of the village of Montignac, and 26km/16mi north of Sarlat.
- **Caution:** In summer the ticket office is located at Montignac, next to the Tourist Office under the arcades.
- **Organizing Your Time:** Lascaux II is open for guided visits from about 9.30am to 6pm daily (*longer hours in Jul-Aug, shorter in winter*). The sale of tickets starts at 9am and closes when 2 000 tickets have been sold (which happens quite quickly). You will be allocated a visit time (☞ 8€, *children: 4.50€. ☎05 53 05 65 65.)*

LES ÎLES DE **LÉRINS**★★

MICHELIN MAP 341 D 6

GREEN GUIDE FRENCH RIVIERA

The peaceful **islands** (*boat service from Cannes*) are clad in a rich vegetation of pines, cypresses and eucalyptus and have a fascinating historic and archeological heritage. The fine view back to the coast of the mainland stretches from Cap Roux to Cap d'Antibes.

- **Information:** *See: Cannes.*
- **Orient Yourself:** The islands are just offshore from Cannes, with frequent boat departures (*no booking required*) from the Old Port.
- **Walking Tour:** Many wide paths criss-cross the larger island, Ste-Marguerite. Explore freely, or take a guided tour (*details from Office National des Forets*, ☎04 93 43 49 24).

Visit

Île Ste-Marguerite★★

Regular boat service from Cannes. ☞ 10€ (5-10 years: 5€). ☎04 93 39 11 82.
There are fine **forest walks** as well as through the botanical collection and along the avenue, Allée des Eucalyptus géants. Pines of many species soar above an undergrowth of arbutus, tree heathers, cistus, thyme and rosemary. **Fort Royal** was built for coastal defence by Richelieu. It served as a prison for Protestants, and also for the mysterious Man in the Iron Mask (1687-98). From the terrace there is an extensive **view**★ of the coast.

Île St-Honorat★★

Regular boat service from Cannes. 9€ *round trip (children: 5€).* 04 92 98 71 38.

St Honoratus founded one of the first monasteries of Roman Gaul here in the early years of the 5C. It became one of the most famous and powerful of the period, not least because Provence was not yet affected by the barbarian invasions. In 1073, the monks built a crenellated keep **(donjon★)** on a headland on the south side of the island. It was here that they took refuge from the raids of pirates from the Barbary Coast. It has two-storeyed cloisters, fine stonework and a remarkable **view★★** from its battlements. The monastery itself was rebuilt in the 19C in a Romanesque style.

LESSAY★

MICHELIN MAP 303 C 4–POPULATION 1 719
GREEN GUIDE NORMANDY

Lessay lies on the edge of moorland country whose harsh beauty was sung by Barbey d'Aurevilly (1808-89), who helped establish a distinct Norman literature. The town comes to life every September at the time of the Holy Cross Fair.

- **Information:** 11, place Saint-Cloud, 50430 Lessay, 02 33 45 14 34
- ▶ **Orient Yourself:** Lessay grew up round the Benedictine abbey.

Sight

Église abbatiale★★

Founded in 1056, this is not only one of the most perfect examples of Romanesque architecture in Normandy, but also a tribute to the extraordinary skill and devotion of the chief architect of the Historic Monuments Institute, Yves Froidevaux, who rebuilt the church after it had been blown up by the Wehrmacht in 1944.

From the east there is a fine view of the rounded apse backed by a flat gable and dominated by the massive tower.

Inside, there are the typically Norman features of great nave arches, triforium and inspection gallery running underneath the clerestory windows. But Lessay also marks the architectural transition from groined vaults (as used in the 11C aisles) to quadripartite vaults, used somewhat crudely in the choir (end of the 11C), then with greater confidence in the nave (beginning of the 12C). This revolutionary development led directly to the great achievements of Gothic architecture, with its high-flung vaults and walls of glass.

LILLE★★

MICHELIN MAP 302 G 4–POPULATION 1 000 900
GREEN GUIDE NORTHERN FRANCE AND THE PARIS REGION

Lively, convivial capital of French Flanders, the city successfully combines vibrant forward-looking appeal with its splendid Baroque heritage.

- **Information:** Palais Rihour, pl. Rihour, 08 91 562 004. www.lilletourism.com.
- ▶ **Orient Yourself:** Lille is a large city close to the Belgian border. It is easily reached by high-speed TGV and Eurostar trains which arrive in the centre, or by road on A1 from Paris and A25 from the English Channel. Place Géneral-de-Gaulle is the city centre. Lille is laid out on an axis stretching east to west, with the new town leading into the old town leading into the citadel.

- **Don't Miss:** The picturesque lanes and shops of the old quarter Le Vieux Lille; Centre Euralille, a huge indoor mall and more, with more than 130 shops, a hypermarket, private apartments, and a business school.
- **Walking Tours:** Tours of Old Lille are on Sat at 3pm and 5pm for 7€. Evening tours and beer tasting in Jul and Aug on two Wed per month at 8pm for 9€. Other theme tours are offered in the summer. Contact the tourist office.
- **Organizing Your Time:** Old Lille will take 2hr30min. The citadel, about 2hr. The tourist office publishes a weekly journal, *Sortir*, listing all of the city's current events, concerts and art exhibitions.

A Bit of History

A medieval trading city, Lille moved into manufacturing, wool and cloths predominating from the 14C. In the 15C Lille belonged to Burgundy, which held the whole of Flanders; in 1454 Duke Philippe le Bon (the Good) of Burgundy was responsible for the fine brick-built Palais Rihour. The marriage of Marie de Bourgogne to Charles V brought first Austrian, then Spanish rule. In 1667, after a nine-day siege, Lille fell to Louis XIV, subsequently becoming the capital of France's northern provinces. In October 1914 Lille, which was poorly defended, surrendered to the Germans. Some 900 buildings were destroyed. During the Second World War, the French troops capitulated on 1 June 1940.

From the 1960s to 1990s, a plan to restore the old district successfully preserved its artistic heritage, while modernisation has proceeded apace with new buildings.

Sights

La Citadelle★

The Citadel is a military base. Guided *tours only. Phone first for details.* ☎0891 562 004.

Within four months of Louis XIV's troops entering the town, Vauban began to reconstruct the citadel. The great complex is set in a marshy site of some 1 700ha – 4 200 acres which could be flooded when necessary. With its masterly handling of brick and sandstone, its

Vauban, a Military Genius

Sébastien Le Prestre (1633-1707) was born at St-Léger *(25km – 16mi southeast of Avallon in the Morvan)*. Better known as the Marquis de **Vauban**, he was one of the truly great figures of the age of Louis XIV, a soldier who personally conducted 53 sieges, an engineer who created the French army's corps of engineers and who studied the science of gunnery, and not least an architect and town planner who redesigned ports, dug canals, spanned the Eure at Maintenon with a fine aqueduct, and built from scratch 33 new fortresses as well as improving no fewer than 300 others (many have of course disappeared). Appointed Commissioner of Fortifications in 1678, he took his inspiration first of all from his predecessors, bringing their work to a new peak of perfection; in the case of Belfort he added a second external line of defences as well as strengthening the existing bastions by means of demilunes and a deep moat, while at Neuf-Brisach his innovations included supplementing the internal walls with bastions and placing demilunes in front of the redoubts. But above all he was able to assimilate new inventions and changes in tactics, and to adapt his designs to the particular characteristics of the site.

His main concern was to defend France's new, expanded frontiers. His work thus took him to Flanders, the Ardennes and Alsace, to the Franche-Comté, to the Pyrenees, the Alps and to many places along the country's coastline. Some of his fortresses proved their worth to the retreating French and British forces in 1940.

THE QUEEN OF CITADELS

—— : preserved or visible remains   ▨▨▨ : features no longer in existence

Place d'armes			
1 Arsenal	**a** Demi-lune redoubt	**e** Caponier
2 Governor's Residence	**b** Covered way	**f** Scarp
3 Chapel	**c** Curtain wall	**g** Counterscarp
	d Postern-gate	

economical design, its logical plan and its response to the geometry of artillery, it was the great engineer's masterpiece, the "queen of citadels".

Le Vieux Lille★★

Beautiful façades of 17C – 18C buildings line the bustling old streets where there are numerous good little shops and brasseries. The distinctive Lille stye combines brick and carved stonework.

Vieille Bourse

The Old Exchange built in 1650 is an example of the persistence of the Louis XIII style adapted to Flemish tastes (doors with broken pediments, caryatids supporting the entablatures, columns, pilasters and window-surrounds in sandstone, fruit and floral decoration and a little bell-tower). The whole building proclaims the importance of textile manufacturing in the life of the city as

Address Book

For coin ranges, see the Legend on the cover flap.

WHERE TO EAT

Domaine de Lintillac – *43 r. de Gand. ☎03 20 06 53 51. Closed 2 wks in Aug, Sun-Mon.* The red facade of the building will lead you directly to this rustic restaurant in old Lille. Wicker baskets hang from the beams and the walls are lined with pots of preserves from southwest France. The plentiful cuisine of the Périgord region is honoured here.

Le Passe-Porc – *155 r. de Solférino – ☎ 03 20 42 83 93. Closed 29 Jul to 19 Aug and Sun – reserv. required.* A bistro after our own hearts. The tiled floor, wall seats and enamelled plaques on the walls act as the backdrop for a remarkable collection of pigs. The hearty ambience and plentiful fare are in perfect harmony with the amusing surroundings.

Aux Moules – *34 r. de Béthune – ☎03 20 57 12 46.* A multitude of mussels (*moules*) and a few other Flemish specialities await customers in this 1930s style brasserie located in a lively pedestrian street. A must for bona fide shellfish fans and friends.

T Rijsel (Estaminet) – *25 r. de Gand, ☎ 03 20 15 01 59. Closed first 3 wks of Aug, Sun-Mon.* A sure bet, this *estaminet* is located in a street crowded with restaurants. The appealing Flemish décor features photos, posters and advertisements, while the appetizing regional menu is presented in the form of an old school notebook.

La Reine des Chants– *10 r. Faidherbe. ☎03 20 55 13 74.* This pretty yellow and blue restaurant in the town centre gives pride of place to the noble potato in its many guises. Whether your dish was originally concocted in Lille, Paris or rural France, your taste buds will surely be gratified.

La Tête de l'Art – *10 r. de l'Arc. ☎03 20 54 68 89. Closed first 3 wks of Aug, Sun and evenings except Fri-Sat – reserv. essential Sat-Sun.* A charming, lively restaurant is hidden behind the pink facade of this manor built in 1890. Follow the hallway to discover the inviting dining room where denizens of Lille gather for traditional meals. A good selection of wines at reasonable prices.

Restaurant La Cave aux Fioles –*39 r. de Gand. ☎03 20 55 18 43. Closed Sat lunch, Sun and public holidays – reserv. required evenings.* Don't be put off by the gloomy passageway that leads to this restaurant housed in two 17C and 18C residences – the interior is unexpectedly warm and pleasant: brick, wood, beams and paintings by area artists. Check out the collection of commodes upstairs. Convivial ambience; bistro cuisine.

WHERE TO STAY

b& b(Bed and Breakfast) – *78 r. Caumartin – ☎03 20 13 76 57. Closed 15 Jul-15 Aug – – 3 rms.* "B & B" as in Bed and Breakfast, as well as in Béatrice and Bernard, the current owners of this house built during the reign of Napoléon III. The comfortable rooms – non-smoking only – have been nicely refurbished; two of them have sloping ceilings. Cosy sitting room, breakfast room looking out onto the garden.

Hôtel Flandre Angleterre – *13 pl.de la Gare. ☎03 20 06 04 12, hotel-flandre-angleterre@wanadoo.fr – 44 rms – 7€.* Situated opposite the train station and near the pedestrian streets, this family-run hotel presents modern rooms that are comfortable and cosy. Recommended for its location and affordability.

Hôtel Brueghel – *5 parvisSt-Maurice ☎03 20 06 06 69, hotel.brueghel@wanadoo.fr – 60 rms – 8€.* This Flemish-style house is conveniently located in the pedestrian part of town quite near the train station. The rooms have old-fashioned charmand modern bathrooms. The lift, the woodwork and the knick-knacks givethe place a nostalgic appeal.

ON THE TOWN

L'Échiquier (Bar of the Alliance Hotel), *17 quai de Wault – ☎03 20 30 62 62. Mon-Sat 10am-1am, Sun and public holidays 10.30am-11pm. No musical events Jul-Aug.* This bar, installed in the majestic 17C setting of a former Minim convent, is attached to the Alliance

Hotel. A harpist performs Mon-Thu 7.30pm-9.30pm, followed by a pianist Mon-Thu 10pm-11.30pm, Fri and Sat 7.30pm-11.30pm, Sun 4pm-7pm. Rich selection of champagne and cocktails.

Les 3 Brasseurs – *22 pl. de la Gare (Opposite the Lille-Flandres train station),* ☎*03 20 06 46 29 – Closed Aug.* The pungent scent of hops greets visitors to this brasserie, a veritable Lille institution. Sample one or all of the four kinds on beer on draught drawn directly from the tuns behind the counter. Flammekueches, sauerkraut and regional fare are on hand for the pleasure of nibblers and the ravenous alike.

Pâtisserie Meert – *27 r. Esquermoise -* ☎*03 20 57 07 44 – www.meert.fr.* This pâtisserie-confiserie salon-de-thé founded in 1761 is a veritable Lille institution with mirrors, arabesques and gilt. The best of local specialities is offered, including its famed gaufre fourrée à la vanille de Madagascar, using the same recipe since 1849.

SHOWTIME

Useful tip: The Office de Tourisme publishes a weekly journal, *Sortir,* listing all of the city's current events, concerts and art exhibitions.

Théâtre Le Grand Bleu – *36 av. Max-Dormoy.* ☎*03 20 09 88 44, www.legrand-bleu.com – Ticket office 9am-noon, 2pm-6pm; performances 8pm, Wed and Sat 3pm, Sun 5pm. Closed Aug – adults: 10€ (children: 8.50€).* This performance hall caters to a young audience. Some of its events appeal to children as young as five years old, others are designed for teens. Dance, circus, theatre, storytelling, hip-hop and other nice surprises.

Orchestre National de Lille – *30 pl. Mendès-France, 59000 Armentières.* ☎*03 20 12 82 40, www.onlille.com – Closed Aug – tickets start at 10€.* Since 1976, The Orchestre National de Lille gives an average of 120 concerts per season. Performances are held in the Lille area, the Nord-Pas-de-Calais region and abroad (30 countries altogether). The varied repertoire, featuring performances for young audiences, original pieces, established musicians and fresh talent, exemplifies this orchestra's motto: 'taking music to all who would hear it.'

Théâtre de Marionnettes du Jardin Vauban – *R. Léon-Jouhaux, Chalet des Chèvres in the Jardin Vauban, 59000 Armentières.* ☎*03 20 42 09 95. Open Easter-Oct – tickets 4€.* An outdoors puppet show of the Guignol tradition starring characters of local repute, such as Jacques de Lille and Jean-Jean La Plume.

SHOPPING

Marché de Wazemmes – *59000 Armentières.* ☎*08 90 39 20 04.* Tues, Thur and especially Sun mornings, the Wazemmes market takes over the Placede la Nouvelle-Aventure and its great covered market built of red brick. Food stands alternate with second-hand bric-a-brac in a merry market for shoppers of all categories.

Rue de Gand – Paved, animated and highly colourful, La Rue de Gand is well worth a visit. Butcher shops, taverns, bars and especially restaurants serving various types of cuisine line the pavements.

VISIT IDEAS

Tourist packages – The Tourist Office offers themed packages (discovery, Christmas market, culture, Lille flea market, cabaret) that include oneor more nights in a hotel, a City Tour, museum admission or a show, etc.

Minibus Tour – A 1hr city tour in several languages – *May-Oct: schedule varies, but usually dep. hourly from 10am to 6pm. 9.50€.* Rendez-vous at Palais Rihour. Bus accessible to persons of reduced mobility. Schedule sometimes varies: enquire at the Office de Tourisme, ☎*03 20 21 94 21.*

Lille Métropole City Pass – This inclusive ticket gives you access to metropolitan Lille's public transportation network (Transpole) plus 25 interesting sites and tourist attractions in Lille, Roubaix, Tourcoing, Villeneuve-d'Ascq and Wattrelos. The passes are valid 1 day, 2 days or 3 days. Information and sales in the Offices de Tourisme of the cities cited, through the Comité Départemental du Tourisme du Nord, ☎*0820 42 40 40, www.transpole.f.r*

well as paying tribute to great men and their contributions to progress with the statues lining the arcades.

Musée des Beaux-Arts★★★

🕐 *daily except Mon am and Tue, 10am-6pm* 🕐 *Closed public holidays.* ♿ ⟨⟩ *5€, no charge 1st Sun in the month.* ☎*03 20 06 78 00.*

The imposing building (1885-92) has recently been renovated and extended. The collection includes many masterpieces of French painting, among them the *Mystical Fountain* by Jean Belle-

gambe (early 16C) with its symbolic treatment of renewal and redemption, a serenely Classical Nativity by Philippe de Champaigne (1674), a beautifully modelled portrait of Madame Pélerin by Quentin de la Tour, and another portrait, J Forest (1746), by Nicolas de Largillière.

▶ **Demeure de Gilles de la Boé**★. **Rue de la Monnaie**★, **Hospice Comtesse**★, **Église St-Maurice**★. **Porte de Paris**★.

LIMOGES★

MICHELIN MAP 325 E 5-6–POPULATION 173 299
GREEN GUIDE DORDOGNE BERRY LIMOUSIN

A dynamic regional capital with a long history, and a great tradition of high-quality enamel, ceramics and porcelain.

🅸 **Information:** 12 blvd de Fleurus, ☎05 55 34 46 87. www.tourismelimoges.com.
▶ **Orient Yourself:** The town is circled by an expressway. The town centre lies on the north bank of the River Vienne, and is divided into two districts, Ville and Cité. The centre of activity is Ville.
🢒**Walking Tours:** The tourist office has details of guided themed tours during school holidays.
⊙ **Don't Miss:** The picturesque Rue de la Boucherie area; the Adrien-Dubouchée porcelain museum.
🆔 **Especially for Kids:** The Aquarium de Limousin is not only for kids, but they'll love it (6.50€, children 4.50€; third child free).

A Bit of History

Limoges originated as a ford over the River Vienne at a meeting-point of Roman highways, but remained a small provincial centre, specialising in ceramics, until the early 19C, when the manufacture of porcelain moved here from St-Yrieix (40km – 25mi south) where there were kaolin deposits but no workforce. It became a prestigious industry, the town's name synonymous with the highest quality porcelain. Later, shoe-making also became established.

The town was the birthplace of Auguste Renoir (1841-1919), one of the initiators of Impressionism.

Jardins de l'Évêché

Address Book

For coin ranges, see the Legend on the cover flap.

WHERE TO EAT

⊜ **Chez Alphonse** – *5 pl. de la Motte – ☎ 05 55 34 34 14 – Closed Mon eve, Sun and public hols*. Tucked away behind the *halles*, this bistro is a popular local haunt. Tables decorated with chequered tablecloths and a menu which is written up on the blackboard.

⊜⊜ **Le Pont St-Étienne** – *8 pl. de Compostelle – ☎05 55 30 52 54 – reserv. required at weekends*. Attractive bay windows with views of the old stone bridge and the river. The à la carte menu features a number of imaginatively named dishes. Summer terrace.

⊜⊜ **Les Petits Ventres** – *20 r. de la Boucherie – ☎05 55 34 22 90 – Closed 8-15 Jan, 2-17 May, 5-22 Sep, Sun and Mon*. Classic French cuisine is to the fore in these two typical 15C houses, run by two young and enthusiastic owners. The cuisine is high on quality with traditional dishes based on liver, tongue, pig's trotters, tripe etc.

⊜⊜ **Le Bœuf à la Mode** – *60 r. François-Chenieux – ☎05 55 77 73 95 – Closed Aug, Sat lunchtime and Sun*. If you love eating meat, then this is definitely the place for you! Excellent cuisine served in a friendly and traditional ambience.

⊜⊜ **L'Escapade du Gourmet** – *5 r. des 71ème-Mobiles – ☎05 55 32 40 26 – Closed 10-26 August, Sat lunchtime, Sun eve and Mon*. A Belle-Époque decor of wood, frescoes, moulded ceilings and coloured glass is the backdrop to this popular traditional restaurant located between the château and the Cité Episcopale. Classical French cuisine. Good-value-for-money.

WHERE TO STAY

⊜ **Hôtel de la Paix** – *25 pl. Jourdan – ☎05 55 34 36 00 – 31 rooms*. This Napoléon III-style hotel in the heart of the city features an entertaining phonographic collection. Bright and airy bedrooms, some with wicker furnishings. Friendly atmosphere.

⊜⊜ **Hôtel Jeanne-d'Arc** – *17 av. du Gén.-de-Gaulle – ☎05 55 77 67 77 – hoteljeanned'arc.limoges@wanadoo. fr – Closed 20 Dec-7 Jan – 50 rooms*. This pleasant, well-located hotel is close to the city's famous train station. The well-mantained bedrooms and pleasant breakfast room have managed to retain their old French charm.

BARS AND CAFÉS

Brasserie Artisanale St Martial – *8 pl. Denis-Dussoubs – ☎05 55 79 37 98* – This brewery (in the true sense of the term), established over 10 years ago, perpetuates an old local tradition. Beer has been brewed in the region since the 18C; in the 19C there were no fewer than 50 brewers in the Limoges area.

Café des Anciennes Majorettes de la Baule – *27 r. Haute-Vienne – ☎05 55 34 34 16 – Closed Mon, and mid-Jul to mid-Aug*. This renowned local bar is the venue for regular concerts and plays.

L'Irlandais – *2 r. Haute-Cité – ☎05 55 32 46 47* – This lively Irish pub is run by a fisherman from Brittany who has travelled the world and has already established a bakery and a pub in Ireland, and a concert violinist who has played in royal circles. Over the past three years they've hosted jazz, Celtic music and other concerts here. Juggling shows on the terrace during the summer months.

SHOPPING

Most of the city's shops are located in the area around the castle. The main boutiques selling porcelain are along boulevard Louis-Blanc and along the streets heading west from the city centre.

Le Pavillon de la Porcelaine – *Av. du Prés.-John-Kennedy – ☎05 55 30 21 86 – pavillon-porcelaine@haviland-limoges. com*. This factory outlet of Haviland, makers of prestigious porcelain sets. A wide choice of tableware on sale.

Paul Buforn – *4 pl. de la Cité – ☎06 70 54 30 40*. Skilled enameller.

Buissières – *27, r. Jean-Jaurès – ☎05 55 34 10 44. At* this chic confectioner's, the Art-Deco decor is almost worth a visit on its own. Chocolates, pastries and desserts, including the house speciality black chocolate with cream.

Limoges Enamel

Enamel has been known since the days of Antiquity. In the 12C Limoges became an important centre of production, partly thanks to the variety of minerals to be found in the surrounding area; its exquisite wares were exported all over Europe. The technique consists of crushing leadglass, coloured with metal oxides, applying it to a metal surface, gold, silver or copper, then heating it to a temperature of up to 800 °C, resulting in a crystalline effect. In the 12C Limoges specialised in champlevé enamels, in which the enamel is poured into grooves let into a copper surface, then polished level with the metal. In the 14C painted enamels made their appearance.

In the reign of François I, Léonard Limosin was made Director of the Manufactory, which produced enamels of great brilliance and colour.

Sights

Musée de l'Évêché – Musée de l'Émail (Enamel Museum)★

🕐 Jul-Sep: daily 10am-noon, 2-6pm. Rest of year: closing at 5pm, and closed Tue. 🕐 Closed public holidays. ⊗ no charge. ☎05 55 45 98 10. The museum is housed in the former Bishops' Palace and features a stunning collection of some 300 champlevé or cloisonné enamels (ground floor) by Limoges masters. The palace gardens, **Jardins de l'Évêché★**, include a themed garden and a "wild" garden.

Musée Adrien-Dubouché★★

🕐 Daily except Tue 10am-12.25pm, 2-5.40pm (Jul and Aug: Open continuously). 🕐 Closed 1 Jan, 1 May, 25 Dec. ⊗ 4€, no charge 1st Sun in the month. ☎05 55 33 08 50. www.musee-adriendubouche.fr. This remarkable collection of international importance features items illustrating the evolution of pottery from ancient times to today, with many examples of the finest Limoges ware.

Ville and Cité

Early in its history, Limoges developed two rival centres, known as Cité and Ville (or Château). Overlooking the Vienne, **La Cité** is the historic core of Limoges. It spreads out around the **Cathédrale St-Étienne★** which has a fine portal **(portail St-Jean★)** and which has kept its **rood screen★** of 1533, now located at the west end of the nave. In the chancel are a number of **tombs★**.
The **Château** quarter, or Ville, serves as the modern centre of Limoges, with busy shopping streets. **St-Michel-des-Lions★** is an old hall-church that has retained its original rectangular plan.

LISIEUX★★

MICHELIN MAP 303 N 5–POPULATION 23 166
GREEN GUIDE NORMANDY

Lisieux is the market centre of the Auge region. With its closely-packed hedgerows, thatched cottages and old manors, this is a countryside of great charm.

▪ **Information:** 11 r. d'Alençon, ☎02 31 48 18 10
▸ **Orient Yourself:** The town is a short distance inland from Honfleur.

A Bit of History

The town is famous in France for **St Teresa of Lisieux** (1873-97), canonised in 1925. Devout pilgrims come to the town to see her house, or attend services at the vast basilica dedictaed to her, south-east of the town.

Excursions

Manor Houses of the Pays d'Auge

The farmhouses and manors of this tranquil landscape are set within an enclosure planted with apple trees and defined by a hedge. All the buildings are timber-framed, from the house itself, to the cider-press, apple-store, stables and dairy grouped around it. Among the finest are the moated site at **Coupesarte** *(16km – 10mi southwest)* and **Château Crèvecœur**★ *(18km – 11mi west)* with its museum devoted to the story of petroleum research (musée de la recherche pétrolière).

LOCHES★★

MICHELIN MAP 317 O 6–POPULATION 6 328
GREEN GUIDE CHÂTEAUX OF THE LOIRE

Modern Loches lies mostly on the left bank of the Indre, at the foot of the fortified bluff that dominates the valley and that set natural limits to the growth of the medieval town.

- **Information:** pl. de la Marne, ☎02 47 91 82 82.
- ▶ **Orient Yourself:** Loches is on the River Indre, south of Tours.
- **Don't Miss:** The public gardens by the Indre give a wonderful view of the fortress and château.

Sight

Cité médiévale★★

The medieval town is contained within a continuous wall some 1 000m – about 1 100 yd long in which there are only two gates.

To the south, the great square keep **(donjon★★)** (*Apr-Sep: daily 9am-7pm; Oct-Mar: daily 9.30am-5pm; closed 1 Jan and 25 Dec; ⊙ 7€. ☎02 47 59 07 86)* was built by the Counts of Anjou in the 11C on even earlier foundations. In the 13C, it was strengthened by wide ditches hewn into the solid rock, by buttress towers and the Martelet Tower with its impressive dungeons, then given additional accommodation including service buildings.

In the centre of the old town is a church, **Église St-Ours**★, with its Angevin porch built around a Romanesque portal, and pyramid vaults in its nave.

To the north is the **Château★★** (*Apr-Sep: daily 9am-7pm; Oct-Mar: daily 9.30am-5pm; closed 1 Jan, 25 Dec; ⊙ 7€. ☎02 47 59 01 32)*, begun at the end of the 14C as an extension of the 13C watchtower known as Agnes Sorèl's Tower **(Tour Agnès Sorel)**. Part of the royal apartments are medieval (Vieux logis), part Renaissance (Nouveau logis). It was in the great hall of the Vieux Logis on 3 and 5 June 1429 that Joan of Arc persuaded the Dauphin to undertake his coronation journey to Reims.

There is a tiny Flamboyant oratory dedicated to Anne of Brittany decorated with the ermine of Brittany and the girdle of St Francis and, in the Charles VIII Room, a recumbent figure **(gisant d'Agnès Sorel**★) of Charles VII's "Lady of Beauty".

▶ Porte Royale★ – Ramparts★ and walk round the outside of the ramparts.

LOCRONAN★★

MICHELIN MAP 308 F 6–POPULATION 799

GREEN GUIDE BRITTANY

The little town once flourished on the manufacture of sailcloth. Traces of its golden age are to be found in its fine main square.

- **Information:** Place de la Mairie, ☎02 98 91 70 14
- ▶ **Orient Yourself:** Locronan is sited at the foot of its granite hill at the meeting point of the roads from Quimper to Châteaulin and from Crozon to Douarnenez.
- **Don't Miss:** The beautiful main square is a must.
- **Parking:** Cars must be left outside the village.

Sights

Place de l'Église★★

This little square with its well is like many others in Brittany, having grown up over the centuries in a haphazard way without any overall plan, but with a unity due to the consistent use of granite. Because of the strength of the westerly winds, the walls on that side of the weavers' houses are windowless. In the 17C many of the houses were given an additional storey in stone. The lofts are lit by means of dormer windows let into the roof.

Église St-Ronan et Chapelle du Penity★★

This is a 15C pilgrimage church with stone vaults. Its architect endowed it with the plain east end current in Brittany at the time, thereby letting more light into what would otherwise be a somewhat dark interior. Behind the altar, the main window has fine 15C stained glass depicting scenes from the Passion. The pulpit (**chaire**★) of 1707 has panels illustrating the life of St Ronan.

The chapel (Chapelle du Penity) in the south aisle has a 16C altarpiece with a low relief (**bas-relief**★) of the Last Supper, a St Michael in armour (on the pillar) weighing souls, and an early-15C effigy of St Ronan, carved from the dark kersanton stone.

The buildings on the main square were once the homes of makers of sailcloth

LONS-LE-SAUNIER★

POPULATION 18 483

MICHELIN MAP 321 D 6

GREEN GUIDE BURGUNDY JURA

The capital of the Jura is a spa town with an interesting heritage, and makes a good base for excursions to the vineyards or the Jura plateau.

- **Information:** Pl. 11-novembre, ☎03 84 24 65 01. www.ville-lons-le-saunier.fr
- ▶ **Orient Yourself:** The town is in eastern France near the Swiss border. Its centre is Place de la Liberté.

Sight

Rue du Commerce★

The town was ravaged by fire between 25 June and 4 July 1636 when it was attacked by Condé on Richelieu's orders. Seven years later, the population was amnestied by Mazarin and allowed to return. The Rue du Commerce was rebuilt in accordance with a detailed plan in the second half of the 17C; it is elegantly laid out on a slight curve and is famous for its great variety of shops with their attractive displays.

What might have been a monotonous piece of planning reflects instead a local love of independence and appreciation of good design. Note particularly the high roofs with their mansards and tall chimneys, the 146 stone arcades (some of them of Romanesque date) of many different shapes and sizes, the trapdoors leading to the cellars, sculpted heads, and balconies and window decoration in wrought iron.

No 24 is the birthplace of Rouget de l'Isle, composer of the *Marseillaise*, the French national anthem. .

Excursion

Cirque de Baume★★★

19km – 12mi east. This is one of the most spectacular of the blind valleys characteristic of the western rim of the Jura. The action of water has been particularly significant here in undermining the upper beds of limestone, which have caved in, thus forming the impressive gorge we see today. The viewpoint at Roches de Baume *(near the D 471)* gives splendid prospects over this great natural amphitheatre with its 200m – 650ft walls marking the boundary between the high plateau of the western Jura and the Bresse plain.

LOURDES★★★

MICHELIN MAP 324 L 4–POPULATION 15 203

GREEN GUIDE LANGUEDOC ROUSSILLON TARN GORGES

This little market town, sited at the meeting point of mountain and plain, became a pilgrimage place of world renown in the 19C.

- **Information:** Place Peyramale, ☎05 62 42 77 40.
  www.lourdes-infotourismefrance.com.
- ▶ **Orient Yourself:** The town is in the central Pyrenees area, 20km south of the town of Tarbes.
- ☺ **Don't Miss:** The grotto where Beranadette Soubirous had her visions.

Geological Notes

The town's setting

The summit of the **Béout** mountain (*reached by cable car then 45min round trip on foot)* is littered with great erratic blocks that give some idea of the power of the Quaternary glaciers. The **view**★ is an object lesson in physical geography; it extends northwards from the exits of the Lavedan valleys over the morainic terraces through which the Pau torrent winds its sinuous course, to the glacial rock-bar on which the castle is sited, and finally to the great terminal moraine which forces the stream to make an abrupt turn to the west.

A Bit of History

On 11 February 1858, a poor, lonely and sickly **Bernadette Soubirous** (1844-79), while preparing for her First Communion, had the first of the 18 visions that led to Lourdes' becoming a world-famous centre of the cult of Mary, with the grotto and its surroundings attracting pilgrims from all five continents, with a special place reserved for the lame and the sick, who come in the hope of a miraculous cure.

In 1866, the building of the first sanctuary was begun, and in 1871 the upper basilica was constructed. The grandiose Basilica of the Rosary built in Romano-Byzantine style in 1889. Bernadette was canonised in 1933.

Visit

Grotto area

⊘ *Appropriate dress essential.*

In the summer months the great local, national and international pilgrimages are held here. The degree of spirituality is evident in the scale of the ceremonial and the devotion of the participants.

Esplanade

500m – 550 yards long, the site of daily processions.

Basilica of the Rosary

In neo-Byzantine style. The two curving approach ramps have fixed the image of the great building in the popular mind.

Crypt

A realm of devotion, contemplation and silence.

Upper Basilica

Dedicated to the Immaculate Conception and with a vast nave of five bays. St Pius X Underground Basilica: ellipse-shaped, one of the world's largest sanctuaries.

Grotto of the Miracles

The site of the visions, where the most moving manifestations of faith take place.

Fountains

Lourdes water collected by pilgrims.

Pools

Immersion of the sick.

A typical day during a pilgrimage

Until 5am the only access, Entrée des Lacets, is to the Way to the Cross (Chemin du Calvaire). At 9am pilgrims gather at Esplanade du Rosaire for a celebration of the Virgin in Majesty (Easter to 31 October). Then a ceremony for the sick is held in the grotto; a forest of candles twinkle along the alleyway and on the candelabrum in front of the grotto. Twenty outlets near the cave supply holy water to the faithful from the source which surged in front of Bernadette. The sick are immersed in marble pools. At 4.30pm a procession (Procession du Saint Sacrement) leaves from the grotto to the Esplanade du Rosaire, where the Blessing of the sick is celebrated. Finally at 8.45pm a candle-lit procession takes place from the grotto to the Esplanade and Parvis du Rosaire.

Address Book

For coin categories, see the Legend on the cover flap.

WHERE TO EAT

Pizza Da Marco – *R. de la Grotte – ☎05 62 94 03 59 – Closed Sun and Mon.* This is a pleasant place, decorated with photos and engravings. The pizzaïolo is set up in the front room, but it is nicer to sit in the other one. Crispy pizza and efficient service.

Brasserie de l'hôtel de la Grotte – *66 r. de la Grotte – ☎05 62 42 39 34 – booking@hoteldelagrotte.com – 1 Apr-31 Oct.* Agreeable contemporary surroundings comprising ochre coloured dining room, veranda and terrace, and a menu to suit all budgets. Extravagant diners can decamp to the more formal adjacent restaurant.

Le Magret – *10 r. 4 Frères-Soulas – ☎ 05 62 94 20 55 – pene.philippe@wanadoo.fr – Closed 5-26 Jan and Mon.* This little restaurant occupies a rustic style dining room with exposed beams and straw-bottomed chairs. Pilgrims and locals alike can enjoy traditional southwest cuisine without pretention.

WHERE TO STAY

Cazaux – *2 chemin Rochers – ☎05 62 94 22 65 – hotelcazaux@yahoo.fr – Closed end Oct-Easter – 20 rooms. ⊟5.50€.* This small hotel just outside the town centre offers scrupulously kept, fresh-looking rooms, a friendly welcome and reasonable prices among other things. It is near the market.

Chambre d'hôte M. and Mme Vives – *28 rte de Bartrès – 65100 Loubajac – 6km/4mi NW of Lourdes on D 940 towards Pau – ☎05 62 94 44 17 – nadine.vives@wanadoo.fr – Closed 11 Nov until Feb holidays – ⊟ – 6 rms.* If you like the countryside, peace and quiet and a farm atmosphere, then this is the place for you. Sheep, chickens and ducks are raised and consumed here against a stunning backdrop of the Pyrenees. Four rooms with beams and sloping ceilings, and two others with a terrace. Fine garden and children's play area.

Chambre d'hôte Le Grand Cèdre – *6 r. du Barry – 65270 St-Pé-de-Bigorre – ☎ 05 62 41 82 04 – chp@grandcedre.com – ⊟ – 4 rms.* This lovely 17C manor is sure to charm you. Each room is in a different style: Art déco, Louis XV, Henri II, Louis-Philippe. Dining room, music room and superb park with a glasshouese and a vegetable garden.

Chambre d'hôte Les Rocailles – *65100 Omex – 4.5km/3mi SW of Lourdes on D 13 then D 213 – ☎05 62 94 46 19 – muriellefanlou@aol.com – Closed 1 Nov-Easter – ⊟ – 3 rms.* We fell in love with this sweet little place! The owner used to be a costume designer at the Paris Opera and has decorated this small stone house with taste and refinement. Warm woods blend harmoniously with shimmering fabrics.

Hôtel Solitude – *3 passage St-Louis – ☎05 62 42 71 71 – contact@hotelsolitude.com – Closed 6 Nov-31 Mar – 281 rms. ⊟13€.* This large imposing modern hotel on the banks of the Pau, a Pyrenean stream, has a small rooftop swimming pool. The dining room is a rotunda and has a terrace overlooking the river. The rooms with their little red armchairs are comfortable. We recommend those on the side of the river.

Hôtel Impérial – *3 av. du Paradis – ☎05 62 94 06 30 – hotelimperial.lourdes.fr@gofornet.com – Closed 16 Dec-31 Jan – 93 rms. ⊟10€.* This 1935 hotel, which has been completely renovated in its original Art Deco style, is near the cave. The rooms are pleasant and furnished in soothing mahogany tones. Large classic style dining room and drawing room opening onto a small garden.

LEISURE ACTIVITIES

Lac de Lourdes – *Leave town W along D 940 and turn left onto the path leading to the edge of the lake via l'Embarcadère restaurant.* Lying at an altitude of 421m/1 381ft, the 11m/36ft-deep glacial lake offers water sports facilities (non-supervised bathing), fishing and golf (Lourdes 18-hole golf course to the south). From the shores of the lake there are fine views of the Pyrenean foothills. A footpath runs round the lake.

Stations of the Cross
Overlooking the basilicas and the Pau torrent.

▶ Château★ (Musée du Folklore Pyrénéen★). Musée Grévin de Lourdes (Wax museum).

Excursions

Grottes de Bétharram★★
14km – 9mi west. This is one of the most popular natural attractions in the Pyrenees area. The caves comprise five separate galleries, one above the other. The vast roofs of porous rock of the upper level, a striking column which is still growing and is a typical example of the evolution of stalagmites and stalactites, a collapsed pot-hole 80m – 262ft deep, a narrow fissure through which the river flows are fascinating examples of concretions and underground erosion.

Pic de Pibeste★★★
2hr20min climb from Ouzous on D 202. This peak – alt 1 349m – 4 426ft – provides one of the best viewpoints in the central Pyrénées.

▶ Parc des Bosquets★. Boiseries★ de l'Église St-Jacques (panelling).

LYON★★★

MICHELIN MAP 327 H-I 5–POPULATION 1 348 832
GREEN GUIDE AUVERGNE THE RHÔNE VALLEY

Two millennia of history, a site at the meeting point of the Rhône and Saône corridors and an exceptionally enterprising population have combined to make Lyon France's second city. Its past periods of greatness, in Roman and Renaissance times, are matched by its present industrial, commercial and cultural dynamism.

Information: Place Bellecour, ☎04 72 77 69 69. www.lyon-france.com.

▶ **Orient Yourself:** Truly the heart of the city, la Presqu'île offers great views of the quays of the Saône River and Vieux Lyon. Department stores, boutiques, movie theatres and bars line rue de la République, well-known for its 19C architecture. Stretching from north to south, rue du Président-Herriot and rue Paul-Chenavard are also good for shopping. Guided tours of Lyon are available from the tourist office.

🕐 **Organizing Your Time:** Check the tourist office for the **Lyon City Card,** which suggests possible itineraries for one, two and three day visits. A one day visit proposes spending the morning on foot in Vieux Lyon, then visiting the terrace on Fouvière and the Roman theatres by using the funicular railway (with the exception of the museums found there); in the afternoon, tour the musée des Beaux-Arts or take a walk in the Croix-Rousse neighborhood.

🅿 **Parking:** Lyon has many underground parking garages strategically placed throughout the city. Many have been designed by famous architects who truly made them into works of art worth visiting in their own right.

Don't Miss: Nip down a traboule, a special kind of short-cut in Lyon; the Renaissance old quarter, Vieux Lyon, on the right bank of the Saône.

Especially for Kids: A session with Guignol, the city's traditional Punch-and-Judy style puppet show is a sure success. But they are not only for kids – satirical Guignol shows for adults are also popular.

A Bit of History

A Celtic, then Gallic settlement, Lyon was chosen as a base camp by Julius Caesar for his conquest of Gaul. Under Augustus it became the capital of the Roman Empire's "Three Gauls" (Aquitaine, Belgium and the province around Lyon) complementing the older province centred on Narbonne. Agrippa was respon-

Basilique Notre-Dame, Colline de Fourviere

sible for choosing Lyon as the hub of the road system, constructed originally in pursuit of political ends. It was here that the great route coming north from Arles met the other highways from Saintes, Orléans and Rouen, from Geneva and Aosta, and from Chalon with its links to Amiens, Trier and Basle.

The manufacture of pottery became established here as early as the first century AD, only to move later to La Graufesenque on the Tarn (◉ *see MIL-LAU*). The Amphitheatre of the Three Gauls on the hill, Colline de la Croix-Rousse, was joined by the Temple of Rome and of Augustus and by the Federal Sanctuary where the noisy annual assembly of the 60 tribes of Gaul was held under Roman supervision.

Lampas Silk

Christianity reached Lyon via Vienne by the middle of the 2C, brought by soldiers, traders and Greek missionaries. In 177, there were riots on the occasion of the annual assembly, and Saints Pothinus and Blandina, along with 48 others, became the city's first Christian martyrs. Twenty years later, Saint Irenaeus, head of the Church in Lyon, was to meet the same fate. According to St Gregory of Tours, the Gospel was reintroduced to Lyon around 250 by Roman missionaries, and, under Constantine, Christianity is supposed to have flourished here as in the other cities of the Empire.

The era of invention – Lyon played a leading role in science and technology at this time. Among its eminent citizens should be noted the following:

Marie-Joseph Jaquard who built a power-loom in 1804; **André Ampère,** inventor of the galvanometer, electromagnetism, and electrodynamics; **Barthélemy Thimonnier**, who invented the sewing machine in 1829; **Jean-Baptiste Guimet**, who, in 1834, succeeded in making the dye ultramarine; the **Lumière brothers** (Auguste and Louis), the creators of cinematography; **Hector Guimard**, one of the founders of Art Nouveau in architecture, the designer of the entrances to the metro stations of Paris.

Basset, Cailliure/Courtesy Musée des Tissus, Lyon

Address Book

For coin categories, see the Legend on the cover flap.

WHERE TO EAT

⊜⊜ **La Brasserie Georges** – *30 cours de Verdun* - ☎ *04 72 56 54 54.* Open since 1836, this brasserie near the Perrache train station is still a favourite Lyon haunt. The enormous central room (listed as a historic property), with its red wall seats, Art Deco chandeliers and old frescoes, is worth a visit in itself. "Good beer, good food" is this eatery's motto.

⊜⊜ **Le St-Florent** – *106 cours Gambetta* - ☎ *04 78 72 32 68 - closed 3 wks in Aug, 1 wk at Christmas, Sat lunch, Mon lunch and Sun - reserv. recommended.* Pluck and cluck: the interior design of this restaurant – egg-yolk yellow, chair backs that look like feathers, etc – gives diners a good hint of what to expect from the menu, essentially devoted to the poultry of Bresse.

⊜⊜ **L'Est** – *14 pl. Jules-Ferry, Les Brotteaux station* - ☎ *04 37 24 25 26.* The last of Bocuse's bastions in Lyon: the Brotteaux train station. The decor is that of a big, old-fashioned brasserie where electric trains circumnavigate the dining room. As for the cuisine, the team serves dishes from the world over at very affordable prices – a highly successful concept.

⊜⊜ **Le Caro de Lyon** – *25 r. du Bât-d'Argent* - ☎ *04 78 39 58 58 - closed Sun.* This restaurant behind the Opera, designed to resemble a library, welcomes diners into an intimate atmosphere comprised of blond wood, Murano chandeliers, antique knick-knacks and coloured chairs. Savvy Lyonnais come here to enjoy a relaxed meal inspired by the spirits of the south and east.

WHERE TO STAY

⊜⊜ **Élysée Hôtel** – *92 r. du €rés.-Edouard-Herriot* - ☎ *04 78 42 03 15 - 29 rms* - ⊿ *8€.* A small family-run hotel where one can enjoy the vitality of the Presqu'île at affordable prices. The petite red and yellow rooms are modest but cheerful and well kept up; those facing onto the back are quieter.

⊜⊜ **Hôtel La Résidence** – *18 r. Victor-Hugo* - ☎ *04 78 42 63 28 - 67 rms* - ⊿ *6.50€.* This hotel borders on a pedestrian street quite near the Place Bellecour. Some rooms are more elegant than others; all are neat and clean.

⊜⊜ **Savoies** – *80 r. de la Charité* - ☎ *04 78 37 66 94 - hotel.des.savoies@wanadoo.fr - 46 rms: 63/67€* - ⊿ *5€.* Look for a façade decorated with the Savoie coat of arms in the Perrache train station quarter. The cleanliness of the standard, yet small rooms; the convenient garage; and reasonable prices make this a popular address with travellers.

Sights

La Colline de Fourvière (Fourvière Hill)

The name of the hill is derived from the old forum *(Forum vetus)* which was still here in the reign of King Louis I in the 9C. Its site is now occupied by the pilgrimage chapel (with its Black Virgin) next to the basilica of 1870. Roman Lyon had numerous public buildings, including the imperial palace (the Capitol) giving onto the forum, a theatre and an odeon (both rebuilt) on the slope of the hill, baths, a circus building and several temples, as well as the amphitheatre on the east bank of the river.

The terrace to the north of the basilica forms a splendid **viewpoint** overlooking the confluence of the Rhône and Saône and encompassing the hills and Dauphiné plain over which the great city has spread.

Musée de la Civilisation Gallo-Romaine★★

17 r. Cléberg. ⏲ *Mar-Oct: Tue-Sun 10am-6pm; Nov-Feb: Tue-Sun 10am-5pm.* *Guided tours Sun at 3pm.* ⏲ *Closed Mon, 1 Jan, 1 May, 1 Nov and 25 Dec. On other public holidays call in advance.* ♿ ⬡ *6€.* ☎ *04 72 38 49 30.*

The most striking exhibit is perhaps formed by the Claudian Tables **(Table Claudienne★★★)** of bronze, discovered in 1528. They record the speech made by Claudius in AD 48 which gave the citizens of Gaul the right to become senators. It is possible to compare this ponderous "official" version with the more witty and revealing transcription made by Tacitus.

Le Vieux Lyon (Old Lyon)★★★

The medieval and Renaissance quarter of Lyon, the precursor of today's city, extends along the west bank of the Saône at the foot of the Fourvière hill.

Of interest in the old town are the many passages or alleyways known as "traboules" – from the Latin trans ambulare meaning "walking through." The passageways run perpendicular to the streets and link the buildings by means of corridors with vaulted or coffered ceilings leading to inner courtyards.

Primatiale St-Jean★

Begun in 1192, today's church was preceded by a number of sanctuaries, including an early-Christian baptistery, remains of which are on the north side of the building. The cathedral was enlarged in the reigns of Philippe Auguste and St Louis, beginning with the Romanesque east end. The 280 medallions adorning the west front were begun in 1310; in their wealth of detail and great variety they are comparable with those of Rouen cathedral or the chapel of the Papal Palace at Avignon, though the juxtaposition of the sacred, profane and grotesque is sometimes disconcerting. Inside, the chancel **(chœur★★)**, together with the apse, is the oldest part of the church. The apse, with its fluted pilasters below a blind arcade and a frieze of palm-leaves, is typical of Romanesque architecture of the Rhône valley. It is lit by a 13C stained-glass axial window with a fine medallion depicting the Redemption. There is a 14C astronomical clock **(horloge astronomique★)** with original ironwork.

Quartier St-Jean★★

Lyon was incorporated into the French kingdom at the beginning of the 14C. In the Middle Ages it was a border town facing the Dauphiné, Savoy, and the Holy Roman Empire. Charles VII made it a trading centre of European importance when he founded the twice-yearly fair in 1419. Louis XI introduced the weaving of raw silk imported from the Levant and from Italy, but local opposition led the only silk-mill to transfer its operations to Tours. Forty-four years later, Louis doubled the number of fairs; long-distance trade was encouraged and patterns of commercial activity developed which were far in advance of the time; accommodation at inns and hostels was improved, and clearing houses were set up, forerunners of the great bank founded in the 16C.

Trade flourished, and with it came a period of great prosperity for the city, its merchants, bankers and high officials. Lyon seethed with activity and ideas; its streets were lined with elegant Flamboyant Gothic façades with

GALLO-ROMAIN LYON

0   600 m

Amphitheatre of the Three Gauls

CONDATE

Claudian Tables

ARAR

SAÔNE

Forum vetus Capitole

Pl. des Terreaux

Baths

Temple

St-Jean

Odeon

Theatre

RHODANUS

Pl. Bellecour

Circus

ISLAND OF THE CANABAE

LUGDUNUM

RHÔNE

SAÔNE

RHODANUS

symmetrical window patterns; behind them, down narrow alleys, lay courtyards like the ones at nos 11 and 58 in Rue St-Jean. More numerous are houses of Renaissance date, decorated with Italianate motifs (polygonal turrets, superimposed galleries, basket-handle arches and corner signs like the figure of the ox at the junction of Rue du Bœuf – Hôtel Paterin, 4 Rue de la Juiverie), sculpted in the 16C by John of Bologna.

The **Hôtel de Gadagne**★ houses the **Musée historique de Lyon**★ (www.museegadagne.com for latest information) and the **Musée international de la Marionnette**★ (as for the Musée historique de Lyon), the latter created by Laurent Mourget (1769-1844), whose **Guignol** is the very embodiment of the spirit of the Lyon populace.

With the development of the characteristic forms of the French Renaissance come superimposed orders, as in the Hôtel Bullioud (8 Rue de la Juiverie) with its gallery and corner pavilions by the local architect **Philibert Delorme**.

Printing had been invented in Korea in 1403, then again at Mainz in 1447. It made its first appearance on the banks of the Saône in 1485. The world of the transcriber or of the illuminator would never be the same again. The spread of books transformed Europe with its diffusion of learning, in literature, science and technology and accounts of voyages. The Reformation, born from widespread reading of the Bible, came about some 50 years after the invention of the printing press.

This was also the age of **Louise Labé**, known as la "Belle Cordière" (Ropemaker's wife), whose salon became a centre for literature and the arts; among those writing was the Lyon poet Maurice Scève.

By 1548 there were almost 400 printers working in the city, including Sébastien Gryphe, Guillaume Rouille and Étienne Dolet, the publisher of Marot and of Rabelais (◐ see CHINON); the latter served as a doctor at the Pont-du-Rhône hospital for three years, carrying on a correspondence with Erasmus and Du Bellay. It was Du Bellay who published **Rabelais**' Pantagruel in 1532 and Gargantua in 1534 to coincide with the Lyon fairs.

It was here that the Florentine Angelo Benedetto produced white porcelain. Other manufacturers were active too, including Julio Gambiu, who moved away to Nevers around 1565.

Musée de l'Imprimerie★★

13 r. de la Poulaillerie. ◐ *Wed-Sun 9.30am-noon, 2-6pm.* ◐ *Closed public holidays.* ♿ ☞ *4€.* ☎ *04 78 37 65 98.*
The museum traces the evolution of printing from its very beginnings in Lyon, from the first wood engravings to the discovery of typography and to photocomposition.

La Presqu'île (Lyon's Peninsula)

The modern centre of the city is sited on a long tongue of alluvial material brought down by the Rhône. The formation of the "Peninsula" has shifted the junction of the two rivers 4km – 2.5mi southwards since Roman times.

The area was first of all a military encampment, then its proximity to the two rivers made it a favourable place for trading and warehousing. Finally it became the very core of the city; its development along Classical lines begun under Henri IV and Louis XIII was continued in the 18C and 19C, until the urban area spread outwards to the modern suburbs and beyond. The great city's character comes across not only in the busy Rue de la République with its fine 19C façades and elegant shops, but also in the pleasantly shaded Place de la République (FT) with its trees and fountains.

Place Bellecour

Planned by Henri IV in 1609, the project could not be started until 50 years later, when the city had finally succeeded in purchasing the land.

The designer was Robert de Cotte, who arranged the avenues of trees on the south side of the square in such a way as to disguise its irregular shape. The buildings lining the square were razed during the Terror in retribution for the city's resistance to the Convention. "Lyon is no more," it was triumphantly proclaimed at the time, but the square was rebuilt in the 19C.

Hôtel-Dieu

The plans for this, one of the kingdom's most important buildings, were drawn up by Soufflot in 1740. It marks a significant stage in the evolution of French architecture with its long façade facing the Rhône, its projecting central section with Ionic columns and its dome rising from a square base and crowned with a square lantern. The way in which the transoms of the windows are decorated with linen motifs evokes its function as a hospital. A balustrade relieves the great length of the main façade and disguises the low roofs.

Place des Terreaux

This is sited where the Saône flowed into the Rhône in Roman times. The older inhabitants of the city are particularly fond of the square with its fountain (**fontaine**★) by Bartholdi, which has four eager horses representing rivers bounding oceanwards. The town hall dates from the reign of Louis XIII, although its façade was rebuilt by Robert de Cotte after a fire and is typically 18C, with a dome and a rounded tympanum supported by atlantes.

Musée des Beaux-Arts★★

20 pl. des Terreaux. ◷ *Daily except Tue 10am-6pm (Fri 10.30am-8pm).* ◷ *Closed public holidays.* ♿ . ☞ 6€. ☎04 72 10 17 40.

The museum presents a remarkable survey of art through the centuries throughout the world. Its collections are organised into five separate departments: painting, sculpture, art objects, antiquities and graphic art. The highlights of the selection of European painting include 35 **Impressionist** works, **The Ascension**★ by Perugino, an imposing *St Francis* by Zurbaràn, and *The Adoration of the Magi* by Rubens. Also illustrated is the evolution of French painting from the 17C (Philippe de Champaigne) to the 19C (*Femme au perroquet* by Delacroix) and 20C (*Corbeille de Fruit* by Chagall).

There is a very fine collection of ancien art: temple doors from Mehamoue (Egyptian section), a remarkable kore (statue of a young girl) from the Acropolis (Ancient Greece).

Musée des Tissus★★★

♿ ◷ *Tue-Sun 10am-5.30pm.* ◷ *Close public holidays, Easter and Pentecost.* ☞ 5€ (under 18 years: no charge). Ticket also valid for the musée des Arts décoratifs ☎04 78 38 42 00.

Apart from its exhibits devoted to very early examples of the weaver's art, the collection consists mostly of Lyon silk from the 17C onward, by masters such as Philippe de Lasalle. There are Louis XV lampas and embroidered satins, embroidery, and cut velvets of the Empire and Restoration periods. The museum also houses the **Centre International d'études des textiles anciens.**

On the slopes of the hill, Colline de la Croix-Rousse, is a network of covered passageways called *traboules*, once used to protect the precious sheets of silk from the weather. They proved their worth during the French Revolution too, and were much used by the Resistance in the Second World War.

▶ **Musée lyonnais des arts décoratifs**★★ (same ticket as the Musée des Tissus). **Museum d'Histoire Naturelle**★★ – Far Eastern and Egyptian art and remarkable specimens in the Paleontology section. **Centre d'Histoire de la Résistance et de la Déportation**★ – in the former HQ of the Gestapo, preserving the memory of the local Resistance and Jews. **Musée des Hospices civils – pharmacy**★. Basilique St-Martin d'Ainay – capitals★. **Église St-Nizier – Virgin with the Infant Jésus**★. **Église St-Paul – Lantern-tower**★. **Montée de Garillan**★ (hill). **Parc de la Tête d'Or**★. **Place Rouville – view**★.

LE MANS★★

MICHELIN MAP 310 K 6–POPULATION 189 107
GREEN GUIDE CHÂTEAUX OF THE LOIRE

Le Mans, a large modern provincial capital, hosts several fairs and events every year, most famously the 24-hour Grand Prix.

- **Information:** Hôtel des Ursulines, r. de l'Étoile, ☎02 43 28 17 22. www.ville-lemans.fr.
- **Orient Yourself:** The city centre is the old quarter on the left bank of the Sarthe.
- **Parking:** There is usually plenty of space in Place des Jacobins.

A Bit of History

An old town, enclosed by ramparts in the 4C, Le Mans was part of the Plantagenet estates. It has long been the site of trade fairs and festivals, which today include a Spring Fair (late March to early April), a great Four-Day Fair (mid-September), an Onion Fair (first Friday in September).

As a result, Le Mans has a long gastronomic tradition; local specialities include potted pork (rillettes), plump pullets (poulardes), capons (chapons) accompanied by sparkling cider, as well as the delicious reinette apple.

Sights

Vieux Mans★★

The historic centre of Le Mans stands on the site of a Celtic settlement, overlooking the lowlands on either side of the Sarthe. This part of the city is still enclosed within its 4C Gallo-Roman ramparts, some of the few extant in western France. See **Maison de la Reine Bérengère**★ (Queen Berengaria's House) and Red Pillar House – Maison du Pilier Rouge.

Cathédrale St-Julien★★

This magnificent building makes a fine spectacle from Place des Jacobins. Its Gothic **chevet**★★★, supported on intricate Y-shaped two-tier buttresses, is a

The River Sarthe at Le Mans

Studio 3bis/MICHELIN

spectacular demonstration of the boldness and ambition of its architect. The transition from nave to choir is one of the clearest demonstrations anywhere – even for the architecturally uninitiated – of the great technical and stylistic changes which took place over a period of some 160 years. The arches of the south porch are pleasingly decorated, and the doorway (**portail**★★) has splendid statue-columns. The Gothic choir was completed in 1254. The whole is lit on three levels by 13C stained-glass windows (**verrières**★★) ; in the chapels opening out onto the outer ambulatory, in the inner ambulatory and in the clerestory. Note how in the south transept (1385-92) the junction has been effected between the Gothic choir and the older, Romanesque transept.

Musée de l'Automobile de la Sarthe★★

5km – 3mi south, in the Le Mans circuit. Jun-Sep: daily 10am-7pm; Oct-May: daily 10am-6pm; Jan: Sat-Sun 10am-6pm. Last admission 1hr before closing. Closed 1 Jan, 25 Dec. ⚐ 6€. ☎02 43 72 72 24. www.sarthe.com/auto/museeint.htm.
The museum displays 115 vehicles in a modern and instructive setting. The section on racing cars, especially winners of the 24-hr Grand Prix race, presents a superb collection of outstanding cars.

▸ **Maison de la Reine Bérengère**★ – ethnographical collection. **Musée de Tessé**★ – paintings. **Église de la Couture**★. **Église Ste-Jeanne d'Arc**★. **Notre-Dame de L'Épau**★.

MARAIS POITEVIN★

MICHELIN MAP 316 H-L 8-9 AND 324 D-G 2
GREEN GUIDE ATLANTIC COAST

The vast Poitou marshlands occupy what was once a wide bay, the Golfe du Poitou. It is now a conservation area extending over three *départements.* **Under clear, luminous skies, its meadows are bordered by slender poplar and willow. The boats of the marshlanders glide on a network of waterways.**

▸ **Orient Yourself:** The region lies north and north-east of La Rochelle. It is divided into the Dry Marsh, where the Atlantic winds blow keenly, and the Wet Marsh, farther inland.
Especially for Kids: The aquarium at Coulon.
Don't Miss: Enjoy a boat trip on the waterchannels, or a walk in the Parc Ornithologique at Le Petit Buisson.

Geography

The marsh rests on a bed of hardened marine silts; it is drained by an extensive network of channels and protected from floods and high water by dikes and sluices. The bay is in the process of silting up and evolving into a marsh. The work of reclamation, involving the digging of drainage channels, the building of sluices and the parcelling out of the new-won lands, was begun by the monks from the abbeys as early as the 11C, and continued, once the Wars of Religion were over, by Henri IV.

Visit

The marsh is linked to the ocean by a bay (**anse d'Aiguillon**). It is protected from the waves by a headland (**Pointe d'Arçay**) and its sandbanks, and by the Aiguillon dike built by a team of Dutch engineers.
The bay makes a grand sight at high water, but only when the tide is out does the waterbody reveal its full interest.

MARSEILLE★★★

MICHELIN MAP 340 H 6–POPULATION 1 349 772
GREEN GUIDE PROVENCE

The 19C Romano-Byzantine Basilica of **Notre-Dame-de-la-Garde** stands in a commanding position overlooking this great Mediterranean seaport. The **view**★★★ from the church is immense, taking in the islands standing guard in the bay, the harbour, and the background of limestone hills as well as the sprawling city itself.

🛈 **Information:** 4 La Canabière, ☎04 91 13 89 00. www.marseille-tourisme.com.

▶ **Orient Yourself:** Marseille is centered on the magnificent **Vieux Port** (old port) with its lively quaysides and daily fish market on Quai des Belges. Main boulevard **Canebière** leads straight through the city centre to the old port. To gain an overview of the city, there are many guided tours – ask at the tourist office. A fun way to see the central district is on the **little tourist train** from quai du Port – choose the old town itinerary (the Panier and Vieille Charité quarters). **City Pass Marseille** (from the tourist office – 18 P/1 day, 25 P/2 days) is an all-included pass giving free access to the museums, public transport, a boat trip to the Château d'If, and even a ride on the little tourist train.

🅰 **Don't Miss:** The **Corniche Président -J.-F.-Kennedy** is a promenade that runs nearly 5km – 3mi. For a pleasant and timeless evening, choose an outdoor restaurant in the tiny fishing port called **Vallon des Auffes.** Marseille is famous for its *bouillabaisse* (full-flavoured seafood soup), the *aïoli* (garlic sauce) and *pieds-et-paquets* (stuffed tripe and sheep trotters).

🕐 **Organizing Your Time:** Starting from the Vieux Port, it takes about 2hr to walk along the Canebière. Afterwards, return along the Canebière, unless it is the season of the santon fair just before Christmas, to the shopping area which extends south of it. Also allow an hour for the lanes of the old Le Panier district, rising from the port. To get around more quickly, use the inexpensive bus network or two Metro lines (free network maps at ticket offices. ☎04 91 91 92 10).

🅿 **Parking:** Getting around by car is difficult, thanks to endless traffic jams and fellow motorists with short tempers (especially towards those who do not know their way around) and a fondness for sounding their horns. There are several underground car parks around town, most notably at place d'Estienne-d'Orves (reached via place aux Huiles, quai de Rive-Neuve or rue Breteuil). From here Old Marseille is easily accessed following quai de Rive-Neuve to quai des Belges.

View of port, Marseille

A Bit of History

Marseille began life as a trading post set up by Greeks from Asia Minor around 600 BC. Its inhabitants soon established other commercial bases both in the interior and on the coast, at Nice, Antibes, the Lérins Islands, Agde, Glanum (St-Rémy), and Arles. By the 3C-2C BC the city they called Massilia covered an area of some 50ha – 125 acres to the north of the Old Port, and the knolls rising above the busy streets were crowned with temples.

A cultural as well as a commercial centre, the city aroused the interest and envy of the Celto-Ligurians of Entremont, and in 123 BC Massilia found it prudent to conclude an alliance with Rome. The Senate took the opportunity to begin its programme of expansion into Provence and subsequently Gaul.

Seventy years later, when Caesar and Pompey were engaged in civil war, Marseille was obliged to take sides and had the ill fortune to choose the loser. The victorious Caesar besieged the city and sacked it in 49 BC. Narbonne, Arles and Fréjus grew prosperous on the spoils, and Marseille went into decline.

Even after its sack by Caesar, Marseille remained a free city. Its life as a port carried on, with many ups and downs, based on the "Horn" (corne), the original basin sited to the northeast of today's Old Port, which itself came more and more into use as an outer harbour. Nevertheless, the decline of the city as a whole made it difficult to maintain the installations and the original harbour gradually silted up, finally becoming completely blocked in the 11C.

The Crusades, together with the growth of the rivalry between Pisa and Genoa, led to a revival of the city's fortunes in the 12C. Further expansion followed, with the incorporation of Provence into the French kingdom in 1481 and even more with the construction of new quays under Louis XIII (a blow to its old rival Arles). In the 19C, the city's fortunes revived further with the expansion of French (and European) colonial activity in the Orient as well as in Africa.

Sights

Basilique St-Victor★

A Christian quarter grew up opposite the old Greco-Roman city. It was here that St Victor is supposed to have met a martyr's death at the very beginning of the 4C, and here too that a fortified abbey is said to have been built in his memory around AD 420.

La Marseillaise

On 20 April 1792, Revolutionary France declared war against Austria. In Strasbourg, General Kellerman asked Claude Joseph Rouget de l'Isle, a captain in the engineering corps and a composer-songwriter in his spare time, to write a "new piece of music to mark the departure of the volunteers"; the *Chant de guerre pour l'Armée du Rhin (War Song for the Rhine army)* was written during the night of 25 to 26 April. Soon adopted by a battalion from Rhône-et-Loire and carried south by commercial travellers, the Chant reached Montpellier on 17 June. On 20 June, a young patriot from Montpellier on assignment in Marseille, François Mineur, sang it at a banquet offered by the Marseille Jacobin club, located at rue Thubaneau. Enthusiasm was such that the words of the song were passed on to 500 national guards from Marseille, who had been called to arms for the defence of Paris. Renamed *Chant de guerre aux armées des Frontières (War song for the Border Armies)*, the anthem was sung at each of the 28 stages of the journey towards the capital, with growing success and virtuosity. On 30 July, the impassioned verses sung by the warm southern voices, ringing out across the St-Antoine district, was referred to by the electrified crowd as the Chant des Marseillais (Song of the people of Marseille). A few days later, on the storming of the Tuileries, the new anthem was given its definitive name. La Marseillaise became the national anthem on 26 Messidor an III (14 July 1795) of the Republican calendar, and again, after a long period of obscurity, on 14 July 1879.

Address Book

🍷 *For coin ranges, see the Legend on the cover flap.*

WHERE TO EAT

Specialities – As well as Marseilles' celebrated *bouillabaisse*, made with rockfish and found in most restaurants, and the famous *aioli* (garlic sauce), another speciality of Marseilles is a dish made with tripe called *pied-et-paquets*.

🍽 **Toinou** – *3 cours St-Louis* – *☎04 91 33 14 94. Closed Aug*. This is a real institution and inhabitants of Marseille aren't wrong about these things. They flock here to eat oysters and seafood. Platters are paraded on every floor of this contemporary style building with its wood and burnished metal decor. Reasonable prices a stone's throw from the Vieux Port.

🍽 **Couleur des Thés** – *24 rue Paradis* – *☎04 91 55 65 57 Closed 15 Aug-1Sept and Sun*. Located on the first floor of a building in the city centre, this tearoom has the intimacy of a plush apartment. On offer are a salad buffet, charcuterie, savoury tarts and homemade pastries. Fifty varieties of tea.

🍽🍽 **Les Arcenaulx** – *25 cours d'Estienne-d'Orves* – *☎04 91 59 80 30. Closed 11-19 Aug and Sun*. Dine surrounded by books which cover the walls of this restaurant which is combined with a bookshop and publishers, located in the orignal setting of the warehouses of the 17C Arsenal des Galères. Large terrace on cours d'Estienne-d'Orves.

🍽🍽 **Shabu Shabu** – *30 rue de la Paix-Marcel-Paul* – *☎04 91 54 15 00 . Closed 28 Jul-1Sept, Mon lunchtime and Sun – booking recommended at weekends*. Every kind of Mediterranean fish prepared as sushi right before your very eyes! The decor here is Japanese but the chef is French, and passionate about Japanese cooking.

🍽🍽 **Chez Fonfon** – *140 Vallon-des-Auffes* – *☎04 91 52 14 38 . Closed 2-24 Jan, Sun evening and Mon lunchtime*. The dining room of this renowned restaurant dominates the Vallon des Auffes harbour. Every morning fresh fish and seafood is brought in by "pointus", the local fishing boats.

🍽🍽 **L'Épuisette** – *156 Vallon-des-Auffes* – *☎04 91 52 17 82. Closed 7 Aug-7 Sept, Sun and Mon*. Get a front seat for stormy days! Located above the rocks and facing the Frioul islands, this restaurant almost feels like a ship advancing through the sea. Well-presented food with daily specials.

WHERE TO STAY

🏠 **Chambre d'hôte Villa Marie-Jeanne** – *4 rue Chicot* – *☎04 91 85 51 31 – 🏠 – 3 rooms*. A very special address in Marseille, this 19C building has been tastefully done up. Situated in a residential neighbourhood, it blends the traditional colours of Provence with antique furniture, wrought iron and contemporary paintings. Garden shaded by plane trees and a nettle tree.

🏠🏠 **New Hôtel Vieux Port** – *3 bis rue de la Reine-Élisabeth* – *☎04 91 90 51 42 – 42 rooms – 🍽 12€*. The building is an old one but has been internally renovated, and its setting, right beside the Vieux Port, is ideal. Some rooms have views of the harbour and the old city. Functional and well soundproofed.

🏠🏠🏠 **Tonic Hôtel** – *43 quai des Belges, ☎04 91 55 67 46. 🍽 13€*. In the centre of Marseille. The largest rooms overlook the Vieux Port. All have jacuzzi-style baths.

ENTERTAINMENT

Programmes are listed in local newspapers *(La Provence, La Marseillaise)*, in a free weekly paper, Taktik, distributed by the tourist office.

Classical music and dance – There's classical music and opera at the Opéra Municipal (2 rue Molière), dance at the Ballet National directed by Marie-Claude Pietragalla (20 bd de Gabès). A varied musical programme at the Cité de la Musique (4 rue Bernard-du-Bois) and at the Pharo auditorium.

Modern music – Rock concerts, jazz, reggae, etc. at the Espace Julien (39 cours Julien). Large concerts at the Marseille Dôme, with its huge cement arch: a vast room holding 8 000 where world-famous singers perform.

Art galleries – Art events take place in the old warehouses of the Friche de la Belle-de-Mai, rue Jobin. There are also several galleries in rue Sainte, rue Neuve-Ste-Catherine, in the Arcenaulx quarter and on cours Julien.

SHOPPING

Markets – Fish market: every morning on quai des Belges; food markets: every morning (except Sunday) in cours Pierre Puget, pl. Jean-Jaurès (la Plaine), pl. du Marché-des-Capucins and avenue du Prado. La Canebière has a flower market every Tuesday and Saturday morning; also on avenue Prado every Friday morning. Fleamarket: Sunday mornings in avenue du Cap- Pinède.

Le Cabanon des Accoules – 24 montée des Accoules – ☎04 91 90 49 66). Specialised in the manufacture of santons, in the picturesque Quartier du Panier.

Santons Marcel Carbonel – 47 rue Neuve-Ste-Catherine – ☎04 9154 26 58 – www.santonsmarcelcarbonel.com Visit the workshop where the famous santons are made, as well as the shop.

Herbalist – Au Père Blaize, 4-6 rue Méolan – ☎04 9154 04 01. This shop has remained unchanged since 1780 and sells a wide range of herbs: star anise,

thyme, marjoram, pesto, rosemary as well as medicinal plants.

La Compagnie de Provence – 1 r. Caisserie – ☎04 91 56 20 94. Marseille soap and natural products: bath products, body care, decorations for the home.

Four des Navettes – 136 rue Sainte – ☎04 91 33 32 12 . Impossible to celebrate Candlemas without "navette" which protect from sickness and catastrophe! In the oldest bakery of the city people buy these biscuits flavoured with orange blossom; their recipe has been jealousy guarded for two centuries. There is also lavender flavoured chocolate, replete with the scent of Provence.

Provençal fabrics – Souleïado, 101 rue Paradis and in the shops on rue Vacon.

EVENTS

In a very full annual calendar of events, highlights include:

Festival de Marseille – Theatre and dance around the city (June-July).

Fiesta des Suds – The big celebration of the city's melting-pot culture (October).

The basilica was rebuilt in 1040. Its crypt and nave altered in the early Gothic period. In the crypt (**crypte★★**) are a number of 4C sarcophagi, examples of the individualism which distinguishes Christian art from that of the Classical world. The sarcophagi showing the Council of the Apostles and the Companions of St Maurice are justly famous.

Vieux-Port (Old Port and surrounding area)★★

On the south side of the Old Port is the bust of Vincent Scotto (1876-1952), the composer of much-loved popular melodies, surveying what is almost always a highly animated scene. To the east is the **Canebière**, the city's busy main artery, whose fame has been spread around the world by the mariners of Marseille. For a glimpse into the long history of the port, visit **Musée des Docks romains★** (🕐 Jun-Sep: Tue-Sun 11am-6pm; Oct-May: Tue-Sun 10am-5pm; 🕐 closed Mon and

public holidays; 🎫 2€ ☎04 91 91 24 62), part of the **Musée d'Histoire de Marseille★**, known as the Garden of Ruins (Jardin des Vestiges – K). The "horn" formed by the first harbour is dramatically visible, and inside there is a 3C boat excavated from the mud.

Centre de la Vieille Charité★★

🕐 Jun-Sep: Tue-Sun 11am-6pm; Oct-May: Tue-Sun 10am-5pm. 🕐 Closed Mon and public holidays. 🎫 Musée d'Archéologie méditerranéenne: 2€; Musée des Arts Africains, Océaniens et Amérindiens: 2€; temporary exhibits: 3€; major event exhibits 5€. ☎04 91 14 58 80.

The old workhouse and hospice (1671 – 1749) has been carefully restored. The **chapel★** is a masterpiece by Pierre Puget, a Marseille man; it has a little ambulatory and recessed steps allowing the different categories of inmates to make their separate ways to the chapels and galleries, and a central, oval-shaped cupola resting on a drum and supported by Ionic columns and pilasters. The second-floor gallery affords unusual views of the oblong chapel dome.

The rich and varied collections of the **Musée d'Archéologie de Marseille,** comprising some 900 artefacts from the Near East, Greece, Etruria and Rome, make this one of the few provincial museums able to offer a comprehensive survey of ancient Mediterranean civilisations.

▶ **Musée du Vieux-Marseille**★ ◔ *Jun-Sep: Tue-Sun 11am-6pm; Oct-May: Tue-Sun 10am-5pm. ☞☜ Call in advance for a guided tour (1hr). ◔ Closed Mon and public holidays. ⊚ 3€. ☎04 91 55 28 68.*

Ancienne cathédrale de la Major★.

Musée Cantini★ ◔ *Jun-Sep: Tue-Sun 11am-6pm; Oct-May: Tue-Sun 10am-5pm. ◔ Closed Mon and public holidays. ⊚ 2€ (3€ during temporary exhibits). ☎04 91 54 77 75– Modern art. Corniche President J.-F.-Kennedy*★★.

Musée de la Faïence★ ◔ *Jun-Sep: daily except Mon 11am-6pm; Oct-May: daily 10am-5pm. ◔ Closed public holidays. ♿. ⊚ 2€. ☎04 91 72 43 47.*

Musée Grobet Labadié★★ ◔*Jun-Sep: Tue-Sun 11am-6pm; Oct-May: Tue-Sun 10am-5pm. ◔ Closed Mon and public holidays. ⊚ 2€. ☎04 91 62 21 82– decorative arts, painting.*

Palais Longchamp★ (Musée des Beaux Arts★) ☎04 91 14 58 80 ⊙━ *Closed for renovation until 2009.*

Château d'If★★ *About 1hr30min including boat trip and tour of the castle. ◔ Jun-Sep: 9.30-6.30; Oct-May: closes 5.30. ◔ Closed Mon from Sep to Mar, and public holidays. ⊚ 5€. Boat service every hour in the summer, every hour and a half in winter. 10€ for the île d'If, 15€ for both the îles du Frioul and the île d'If.*

GROTTE DU **MAS-D'AZIL**★★

MICHELIN MAP 343 G 6

GREEN GUIDE LANGUEDOC ROUSSILLON TARN GORGES

This cave is one of the outstanding natural phenomena of southwestern France as well as a prehistoric site of the first importance.

▶ **Orient Yourself:** The site lies in the Ariège hills north-west of Foix.

Visit

◔ *Guided visits only (45min) Jul-Aug: daily 10am-6pm; Jun and Sep: Tue-Sun 10am-noon, 2-6pm; Apr-May: Tue-Sat 2-6pm; Sun, public holidays and school holidays 10am-noon, 2-6pm; Mar and Oct-Nov: Sun and public holidays 2-6pm. ◔ Otherwise closed Mon. ⊚ 6.10€, includes museum visit. ☎05 61 69 97 71.*

The River Arize has hollowed out a 420m – 1 380ft tunnel through the Plantaurel heights which once barred its way; a meandering dry valley to the east testifies to its former course. The entrance to the tunnel is formed by a magnificent 65m – 213ft arch, the exit by a much lower opening made in a sheer rock rising to a height of 140m – 460ft. The site was first excavated by Edouard Piette (1827-1906), who in 1887, discovered a human habitat intermediate between the Magdalenian and the Neolithic, the Azilian. In this cave (grotte) that Azilian industry was studied. Practised between 11000 and 9500 BC, it is characterised by miniaturised tools, flat harpoons made from stags' antlers, and the making of flattened pebbles. The latter carry enigmatic markings done in a red paint made from calcinated ferric oxide; they have been interpreted to be lunar or menstrual calendars, or possibly the beginnings of abstract numbering.

The four floors of excavated galleries run for 2km – 1mi through limestone which is sufficiently homogeneous to prevent infiltration and propagation of moisture. Display cases contain artefacts from the Magdalenian (scrapers, chisels, needles, a moulding of a famous neighing horse) and Azilian periods (harpoons made from antlers – the reindeer had moved northwards as the climate became warmer – tips, coloured pebbles, miniature tools).

In the chamber, Salle Mandement, are the remains of animals (mammoths, bears) coated in rubble; these were probably reduced to a heap of bones by subterranean flooding.

CHÂTEAU DE **MEILLANT**★★

MICHELIN MAP 323 L 6
GREEN GUIDE DORDOGNE BERRY LIMOUSIN

This château is a fine example of how stylistic change was allied to the growing desire for domestic comfort towards the end of the 15C, to transform what had been a typical medieval castle into an agreeable country residence.

▶ **Orient Yourself:** The castle is located 39km/24mi south of Bourges.

Visit

🕐 *Guided tours* 🔊 *(45min) Jul-Aug: 9.30am-6pm; May-Jun and Sep: 9.30am-noon, 2-6pm; rest of the year: 9.30am-noon; 2-5.30pm.* 🎫 *7€.* ☎*02 48 63 32 05.* The medieval south front lapped by the waters of a moat is the only remnant of the old fortress built in the early 14C by Étienne de Sancerre; the towers retain their narrow loopholes although the wall-walk has been demolished. The ornate east façade, which is in a different style recalling that of the châteaux of the Loire, includes two projecting stair turrets in the late-Gothic style featuring a pierced balustrade at the base of the roof, dormer windows adorned with carvings, chimneys with elaborate Gothic balustrades, and in particular the splendidly decorated tower (Tour du Lion) by Giocondo, one of Michelangelo's assistants.

The interior, notably the formal dining room (Grande Salle à Manger) and the Bishop of Amboise's chamber (Chambre du Cardinal d'Amboise), is furnished with period pieces, fireplaces, tapestries and carpets.

MENTON★★

MICHELIN MAP 341 F 5–POPULATION 28 812
GREEN GUIDE FRENCH RIVIERA

Between mountain and Mediterranean, Menton stretches out agreeably on its sunny site★★ on the lower slopes of a picturesque natural amphitheatre of mountains. The town is known for its citrus groves, and its dazzling annual Lemon Festival (during Carnival).

🚹 **Information:** Avenue Boyer, ☎04 92 41 76 76. www.villedementon.com.
▶ **Orient Yourself:** Menton is the last town on the French Riviera before the Italian border. It is divided into a modern beach resort and, lying behind, an old town.
🌄 **Don't Miss:** The Tropical Garden (**jardin botanique exotique**★★) is outstanding. There are also many interesting Edwardian gardens in the **Garavan** district and nearby countryside.

A Bit of History

On the cliffs around are the remains of fortifications and human settlement going back to Neolithic times. The town was bought by the Grimaldi family of Monaco in the 14C, then incorporated into the French kingdom when the county of Nice was annexed.

Sights

Hôtel de ville

The town hall is a pretty building in Italianate style, with pilasters and Corinthian capitals and a cream-coloured cornice contrasting with the rosy rendering of the walls. The Registry Office **(Salle des mariages★)** was decorated by Cocteau in 1958 and can be visited duiring normal office hours (⊜ *1.50€*).

Vieille ville★★

Allow about 2hr.

The old town nestles underneath the hill just above Rue Longue and Rue St-Michel fragrant with orange trees, whose alignment marks the course of the Roman Via Giulia Augusta. **Parvis**

St-Michel★★ is a charming square in the Italian style, laid out on two levels by the Grimaldis, whose monogram can be seen in the pebble mosaic forming the paving. It is bordered by a number of houses in the local style, by a pink-walled chapel (Chapelle de la Conception), and by the **Église St-Michel★**, a fine Baroque building dating from the middle of the 17C, extensively restored after the earthquake of 1887.

▶ **Promenade du Soleil★★. Musée des Beaux Arts★** (Palais Carnolès) ◔ *Daily except Tue and public holidays. No charge.* ☎*04 93 35 49 71*– fine arts.

Excursion

Roquebrune-Cap Martin★★

2km – 1mi southwest. Roquebrune is a most picturesque hill-top village **(village perché★★)**, where the tourist can stroll through the small streets towards the keep **(donjon★)** From the top, wonderful **panorama★★** of the sea, Cap Martin, the Principality of Monaco and the Mont Agel.

View of Menton by night

METZ★★★

MICHELIN MAP 307 I 4–POPULATION 322 526
GREEN GUIDE ALSACE LORRAINE CHAMPAGNE

From the limestone escarpment of the Côtes de Moselle high above Metz, the Lorraine plateau can be seen stretching away eastwards towards the German frontier. The city itself lies at the meeting point of the Moselle with the Seille, a strategic site whose importance was appreciated by the Romans; it was here that their great highways leading from the Channel coast to the Rhine and from Trier to Italy were linked, their course marked today by Metz' busy shopping street, Rue Serpenoise.

- **Information:** Pl. d'Armes, ☎03 87 55 53 76. http://tourisme.mairie-metz.fr
- ▶ **Orient Yourself:** Metz is a major junction at the heart of Lorraine, with good rail, road and air links, only 50km/31mi from the German border. Much of the historic centre is traffic-free.
- **Parking:** Use one of the eight underground car parks, of which two are open 24 hours. .
- **Organizing Your Time:** Bus services (*from Pl. de la République,* ☎*03 87 76 31 11*) operates all over Metz and the vicinity. **Visi'Pass** is a one-day ticket (€3).
- **Guided Tours:** Daily except Sun and public holidays 3 and 4pm, P4 (1hr), P7 (2hr), enquire at the tourist office. The tourist office has designed a number of visits for disabled visitors so that they can discover the town, its monuments and museum. Wheelchairs loaned.
- **Especially for Kids:** The popular Walibi-Lorraine leisure park is just 15 minutes' drive from Metz.

A Bit of History

In the 4C, as a response to the threat posed by the Germanic tribes to the east, fortifications were built, together with a basilica which later became the church of a monastery, the original Church of St Peter of the Noviciates (St-Pierre-aux-Nonnains). In the early part of the Middle Ages, the city was the residence of the Merovingian rulers of Eastern Gaul (Austrasia); it then became

Metz Cathedral

Address Book

For coin ranges, see the Legend on the cover flap.

WHERE TO EAT

La Robe des Champs – *14 en Nouvelle rue* – ☎*03 87 36 32 19* . You can't miss the yellow façade and Provençal-style terrace of this pleasant bistro in a pedestrian town centre street. Potatoes, as the name infers ("In its jacket"), take pride of place in this friendly unpretentious establishment.

Restaurant du Pont-St-Marcel – *1 r. du Pont-St-Marcel* – ☎*03 87 30 12 29*. A 17C restaurant not far from St Étienne's cathedral, standing on piles beside a branch of the Moselle. Inside, an amusing contemporary fresco depicts a 17C fairground scene, complete with acrobats and theatre. The staff wear costumes to serve the local cuisine.

La Gargouille – *29 pl. de Chambre* – ☎*03 87 36 65 77. Closed Mon lunchtime, Tue evening and Wed*. Don't be fooled by the ordinary façade of this restaurant located down from the cathedral: behind it lies a sumptuous interior with velvet-covered seats, cosy little booths and 1900-style decor typical of the Nancy School, all making for a warm ambiance. The food is exceedingly refined: carpaccio de fois gras au sel de Guérande, or joue de bœuf sauce vigneronne. Highly professional service.

Restaurant du Fort – *Allée du Fort* – *57070 St-Julien-lès-Metz – 8km/5mi NE of Metz, Bouzonville direction on D 3, then a minor road* – ☎*03 87 75 71 16. Closed 1-10 Jan, 24 Jul-9 Aug, Sun evening and Wed – booking advisable at weekends*. At the end of a forest track you will be amazed to discover this 1870 fort, evidence of the Moselle's turbulent history. Part of it has been restored to create a restaurant offering Lorraine cuisine.

L'Écluse – *45 pl. de la Chambre* – ☎*03 87 75 42 38. Closed 1-15 Aug, Sat midday, and Sun and Mon eves*. Refined modern style, with art on display, and well-prepared contemporary dishes.

Maire – *1 r. du Pont-des-Morts* – ☎*03 87 32 43 12 – restaurant. maire@wanadoo.fr . Closed Wed lunchtimes and Tue*. There is a superb view of the Moselle from this town-centre restaurant. Enjoy the chef's carefully prepared dishes, whether in the salmon-pink dining room with its pale wood furniture or on the terrace.

WHERE TO STAY

Chambre d'hôte Bigare – *23 r. Principale – 57530 Ars-Laquenexy – 9km/5.6mi E of Metz, Château-Salins direction then D 999* – ☎*03 87 38 13 88* – ⊟ *– 2 rooms*. If the bustle of city life doesn't suit you, a short journey will bring you to this friendly local village house. Simple rooms and reasonable prices.

Hôtel de la Cathédrale – *25 pl. de la Chambre* – ☎*03 87 75 00 02*. €11. A charming hotel situated in a lovely 17C house, completely restored. The attractive rooms have cast iron or cane beds, old parquet flooring and furniture, some of which is oriental. Most rooms face the cathedral, just opposite.

---

the capital of the kingdom of Lotharingia (Lorraine), before being attached to the Holy Roman Empire. In the 12C Metz declared itself the capital of a republican city-state, with an elected High Magistrate as ruler. But in 1552, together with Verdun and Toul, it was annexed by a French kingdom seeking to push its frontier eastwards, and its role henceforth was that of a fortress-town standing guard over the border.

1871-1918-1944

On the 6 August 1870, the Prussian armies conquered the city, which became part of the newly-declared German Empire. The city lost a quarter of its population, people who chose to resettle in France; artists left and so did many businessmen, at the very moment when industry was expanding rapidly. Metz' loss was Nancy's gain.

The town began to take on a Germanic character. In 1898 the cathedral was given a neo-Gothic portal, complete with a statue of the Prophet Daniel looking uncommonly like Kaiser Wilhelm II (though his moustache was subsequently clipped). With its surrounding forts, Metz became the centre of the greatest fortified camp in the world. From 1902-08 the area around the station was rebuilt; the station itself was constructed in a style which mixed Rhenish neo-Romanesque and Second Reich symbolism (the Emperor himself designed the bell-tower); an imposing central post office rose nearby, together with hotels providing accomodation for the officers of the garrison and their guests. Metz was in fact the linchpin of the Schlieffen Plan, the strategy to be followed in the event of a future war with France; this plan envisaged the adoption of a defensive posture to the south of the city coupled with a vast turning movement to the northwest, which would sweep through Belgium and then descend on Paris. In 1914 this plan all but succeeded; the German armies marched steadily forward for six weeks, coming within 50km – 30mi of Paris, only to be thrown back by Marshal Joffre at the Miracle of the Marne.

In the inter-war period, the ring of forts around Metz was incorporated into the Maginot Line. Their defensive strength was such that the Allied armies took two and a half months to eject their German occupants in the autumn of 1944.

Sights

Cathédrale St-Étienne★★★

The cathedral grew out of the joining together around 1240 of two churches which up to then had been separated by an alley-way and had faced in different directions.

The 13C and 14C interior recalls the Gothic style of Champagne; its relative narrowness combines with the modest height of the aisles to exaggerate the loftiness of the nave, which does

in fact reach 41.77m – 137ft. The late Gothic chancel, crossing and transepts were completed at the beginning of the 16C.

The cathedral is known as "God's Lantern" (Lanterne du Bon Dieu) due to its stained-glass windows **(verrières★★★)**. They have a total area of 6 500m² – about 60 000sq ft. The rose window of the west front is 14C work, the lower part of the north transept window 15C, and the upper part of this window together with the glass of the south transept and the chancel, 16C. Contemporary glass can be seen beneath the towers (abstract designs by Bissière), and above all in the north ambulatory and on the southwest side of the north transept (the *Earthly Paradise* by Chagall).

Musées de la Cour d'Or★★

🕐 *Daily except Tue 9am-5pm, Sat-Sun 10am-5pm.* 🕐 *Closed certain public holidays.* 🎟 *4.60€ (under 18 years: no charge), no charge first Sun in the month.* ☎03 87 68 25 00.

The museums are housed in the buildings of a former Carmelite convent (17C), a 15C tithe barn (Grenier de Chèvrement), and several link rooms and extensions. In the basements are the remains of ancient baths.

The complex, which was extended in 1980, brings into play the latest display techniques to present a fascinating survey of times past.

Section archéologique★★★

On display in the archeological section are artefacts found in Metz and the surrounding area. The finds attest to the importance of the town, which was in turn Gaulish, a major crossroads in Gallo-Roman times, and a cultural centre under the Carolingian kings.

The **Grenier de Chèvrement**★ is a fine building (1457) used to store cereals given over as tithes.

▶ Porte des Allemands★. Place St-Louis★. Église St-Maximin★. Église St-Pierre-aux-Nonnains★

MASSIF DU **MÉZENC**★★★

MICHELIN MAP 331 H 4
GREEN GUIDE AUVERGNE THE RHÔNE VALLEY

These dramatic volcanic uplands in the southern part of the Velay region form the watershed between Atlantic and Mediterranean. They lie at the centre of a belt of igneous rocks cutting across the axis of the Cévennes.

▸ **Orient Yourself:** The Massif and the walks are featured under **LAC D'ISSARLÈS** in *Michelin Green Guide Auvergne Rhône Valley*. The area lies south-east of Le Puy-en-Velay.

Walking Tours

Mont Mézenc

🚶 *2hr round trip on foot from the Croix de Boutières pass.*

Two great lava flows extend downwards from the twin summits of the mountain, from which a vast **panorama**★★★ extends over the Velay. Quite close at hand can be seen the village of Les Estables.

Gerbier de Jonc★★

🚶 *1hr30min round trip on foot.*

Screes of bright phonolite clatter under the feet of the many who clamber to the summit of this lava pinnacle, from which there is a fine **view**★★.

Cascade du Ray-Pic★★

11km – 7mi south of the Gerbier de Jonc – 1hr 30min round trip on foot.

In a harsh setting formed by a succession of lava flows, the Bourges torrent drops in a series of falls. In the bed of the stream, dark basalt contrasts with lighter granite.

Lac d'Issarlès★

20km – 12mi east of the Gerbier de Jonc.

This pretty, rounded lake with its blue waters occupies the crater of an extinct volcano, 138m – 450ft deep.

Lac d'Issarlès

PIC DU **MIDI DE BIGORRE**★★★

MICHELIN MAP 342 M 5

GREEN GUIDE LANGUEDOC ROUSSILLON TARN GORGES

A vertiginous mountain road winds over the Tourmalet Pass (Col du Tourmalet). From the top (2 114m – 6 936ft) a toll road, one of the highest in Europe, leads to the place known as Les Laquets; from here a cable-car or a rough path *(2hr round trip)* gives access to the summit of the Pic du Midi de Bigorre, now reduced in level to the 2 865m – 9 400ft contour in order to accommodate the television transmitter.

- 🅸 **Information:** ☎05 62 56 71 14. www.picdumidi.com.
- ▶ **Orient Yourself:** The Pic is a landmark in the Gascon Pyrenees, rising south-east of Lourdes.
- 😊 **Don't Miss:** A glassed-in gallery and several terraces offer the most impressive **panorama**★★★ in the Pyrenees.

Visit

🕐 *High season: departures from La Mongie 9am-4.30pm, last descent from the summit at 7pm; low season: departures from La Mongie 10am-3.30pm, last descent from the summit at 5.30pm.* ⊜ *High season: 23€; low season: 20€ (under 18 years: 12€)* 🕐 *Closed end Apr to early May and early Nov to early Dec.*

Observatoire et Institut de physique du globe du Pic du Midi

The factors favouring the siting here of an observatory include the great height, the purity of the atmosphere and the all-round viewing possibilities. The observatory, founded by General Nansouty, was originally intended for botanical and meteorological studies, but the astronomical function was soon added. It was here in 1706 that the first observations were made of the solar corona during a total eclipse of the sun. At the beginning of the 20C, the great observatory dome and reflecting telescopes were added.

Today, it is used for lunar mapping and research into the solar corona, cosmic radiation and nocturnal luminescence.

MILLAU★

MICHELIN MAP 338 K 6–POPULATION 21 339

GREEN GUIDE LANGUEDOC ROUSSILLON TARN GORGES

Millau huddles between two high limestone plateaux, the Causse du Larzac and the Causse Noir, at the meeting-point of the Tarn and the Dourbie. The site of a ford in ancient times, it acquired a bridge in the Middle Ages and became a trading centre of some importance. Today it is a lively provincial town, with a southern air, close to a remarkable modern viaduct soaring over the Tarn valley.

- 🅸 **Information:** 1 pl du Beffroi, ☎05 65 60 02 42.
- ▶ **Orient Yourself:** Millau, beside the Tarn at the northern edge of the Larzac plateau, is on autoroute A75. All main roads lead directly into the busy centre of town.
- 😊 **Don't Miss:** Take a trip out of town to the Aire de Vision to see the beautiful 2.5km Millau Viaduct, part of the A75 autoroute.

A Bit of History

As early as the 2C AD, the milk of the Larzac ewes was made into a gourmet blue cheese in the nearby caves at Roquefort. Their wool and skins were also turned to advantage, including the manufacture of fine gloves at Millau. In a sheltered valley with a mild climate, Millau's streets are attractive with plane trees, fountains and a bustling air.

Excursions

Chaos de Montpellier-le-Vieux★★★
18km – 11mi northeast – 2hr round trip on foot.
This extraordinary 'ruined city' in fact made entirely of natural rocks extends over some 120ha – 300 acres and has a bewildering variety of rock formations (the Sphinx, the Elephant, the Gates of Mycaenae...). The contrasting properties of the different rocks are further expressed in the tremendous diversity of vegetation.

Caves de Roquefort★
25km – 15mi southwest
The name of the market town of Roquefort located between Millau and St-Affrique is synonymous with one of the most famous of French cheeses, the delicious blue-veined Roquefort. All production of the cheese takes place underground, in natural caves in which the temperature and humidity are constant. Roquefort is produced exclusively from full-fat, untreated ewes' milk. A minimum maturing period of three months is necessary for a good Roquefort.

MOISSAC★★

MICHELIN MAP 337 C 7–POPULATION 12 321
GREEN GUIDE LANGUEDOC ROUSSILLON TARN GORGES

Moissac is sited on a low rise overlooking the fertile flood plain near the meeting point of the Tarn with the Garonne. The place is famous for the white Chasselas dessert grape, which grows here in abundance.

- **Information:** 6 pl. Durand de Bredon, ☎05 63 04 01 85.
- ▶ **Orient Yourself:** Carefully follow the orange signs, which lead to the town's famous abbey.

Visit

Église St-Pierre★
⊙ *Illustration Art: Architecture.* The former Benedictine abbey church, founded in the 7C, was consecrated in 1063 and the **cloisters**★★ completed 35 years later. It subsequently served as a model for similar work all over Europe. The church's south doorway **(portail méridional**★★★**)** is one of the great triumphs of Romanesque sculpture.

PRINCIPAUTÉ DE MONACO★★★

MICHELIN MAP 341 F 5–POPULATION 31 800
GREEN GUIDE FRENCH RIVIERA

The Principality of Monaco, world-famous haunt of the super-rich, is a sovereign state covering an area of 192ha – less than a square mile. Inhabited since prehistoric times and later a Greek settlement (5C BC) and a Roman port (1C AD), its history really began when the Grimaldi family bought it from the Republic of Genoa in 1308. Prince Rainier III ruled the principality from 1949-2005 with the assistance of a National Council. His only son Prince Albert has taken power, but because he has no children, it seems certain that the line of succession will pass to the children of Rainier's daughter Caroline.

- **Information:** 2a, Boulevard des Moulins, ☎(from outside Monaco) 00 377 92 16 61 66; (from inside Monaco) 92 16 61 66. www.visitmonaco.com.
- **Orient Yourself:** The territory includes the Old Town or Monaco Ville on the Rock (Rocher de Monaco); the new town of Monte-Carlo; the port area at La Condamine linking the two; and the Fontvieille quarter. Either walk around or take the bus, as the whole Principality is so compact. Several big lifts connect the port areas and the loftier town streets.
- **Parking:** Park in the underground garage (parking des Pêcheurs creusé) of Le Rocher, and take the lift up to the Old Town on the Rock.
- **Guided tours:** Guided visits around Monaco and day-trips to the surrounding region can be booked at the tourist office. Also very enjoyable is the tour by 'Petit Train', starting from the Musée océanographique in Monaco Ville (*6€*).
- **Organizing Your Time:** With lots to do in the old town of Monaco, take about 3hr before visiting Monte-Carlo, where you can try your luck in the casino. Be aware that November is especially busy, especially around the 19th, Monaco's National Day.
- **Don't Miss:** Spot the differences – Monaco is not the same as France. For example, policemen have distinguishable uniforms, and letters mailed from the Principality must have Monégasque stamps.
- **Especially For Kids:** Check out the aquatic life inside the Musée Océanographique, vintage vehicles at the Collection des voitures anciennes, the displays of dolls from the 18C and automated figures from the 19C at the Musée des Poupées et Automates, or enjoy a boat trip on Aquavision.

Sea Dragon

Address Book

For coin ranges, see the Legend on the cover flap.

WHERE TO EAT

⊜⊜ **Polpetta** – *2 Rue Paradis* – *☎00 377 93 50 67 84. Closed 10-30 Jun, Sat for lunch and Tue*. A small Italian restaurant offering three different settings in which to enjoy a tasty tagliatelle alla carbonara or vitello al funghi: the verandah giving onto the street, the rustic-style dining hall or the cosy, intimate room at the back.

⊜⊜⊜ **La Maison du Caviar** – *1 Avenue St-Charles* – *☎00 377 93 30 80 06. Closed 20 Jul-20 Aug, Sat for lunch and Sun*. This prestigious house has been serving choice caviar to Monaco residents for the past 50 years. In an unusual setting made up of bottle racks and wooden panelling, you can also purchase salmon, foie gras or bœuf strogonoff. Definitely worth a visit.

⊜⊜⊜⊜ **Zebra Square** – *Grimaldi Forum, 10 Avenue Princesse Grace* – *☎00 377 99 99 25 50. Closed 6 Feb – 2 Mar*. This stylish restaurant has the same sleek decor as its Parisian namesake, featuring modern fusion cuisine and panoramic views over the sea from the terrace. At night the bar is packed with a young and trendy crowd.

⊜⊜⊜⊜ **Vistamar** – *Hôtel Hermitage, Place Beauarchais* – *☎00 377 92 16 40 00. Closed 24-26, 31 Dec, and lunch Jul-Aug*. An elegant restaurant specialising in fresh seafood, with one of the best panoramic views of the Principality from its top-floor terrace.

WHERE TO STAY

⊜⊜ **Hôtel de France** – *6 Rue de la Turbie – Near the train station* – *☎00 377 93 30 24 64 – www.monte-carlo. mc/france – 26 rooms – ⊡9€*. Charming, soundproofed rooms decorated in Provençal hues and a modern breakfast lounge enhanced with metal and wood furniture.

⊜⊜⊜⊜ **Columbus Hôtel** – *23 Avenue Papalins, ☎00 377 92 05 90 00. www.columbushotels.com – 153 rooms – ⊡*. Clean, contemporary lines and a soothing palette are combined with cozy fabrics and warm wood furnishings. A lounge bar and Italian-style

brasserie with terrace seating attract fashionable locals. Access to a private pool; the heliport is just a block away.

⊜⊜⊜⊜ **Metropôle** – *4 Avenue Madone – Above the Metropôle Shopping Centre, ☎00 377 93 15 15 15. www. metropole.com – 131 rooms – ⊡36€*. This 1886 hotel got a complete facelift by the hot Parisian designer Jacques Garcia, with luxurious fabrics and timeless style. The outdoor pool and solarium have views overlooking the rooftops of the Place du Casino. The restaurant is managed by leading French chef Joël Robuchon.

ON THE TOWN

Casino de Monte-Carlo – *Place du Casino* – *☎00 377 92 16 20 00 – www. casino-monte-carlo.com. Open daily from noon until the last client leaves*. This is Europe's leading casino, with over a million euros in profits, attributed to gambling and not to slot machines as is the case in other casinos. The gambling salons and lavish dining hall Le Train Bleu, decorated in the style of the Orient-Express, are truly impressive. The terrace overlooking the sea is a haven of tranquillity, whether or not you have broken the bank!

Bar du Vistamar – *Square Beaumarchais* – *☎00 377 92 16 40 00 – www. montecarloresort.com. Closed Jul-Aug at lunch*. This famous bar has been patronised by many celebrities over the years. Its superb terrace affords beautiful views of Monaco harbour. The specialities of the house are American cocktails, particularly with champagne!

Sass Café – *11 Avenue Princesse-Grace* – *☎ 00 377 93 25 52 00 – www.sasscafe. com. Open daily 8pm-2am (restaurant; until midnight in winter), 11pm to dawn (piano-bar)*. Exclusive bar-restaurant with a cosy atmosphere where members of the local jet set drop in for a fancy vodka or champagne cocktail before meeting up at Jimmy'z.

Le Jimmy'z – *Quai Princesse-Grace* – *☎00 377 92 16 22 77. Open daily 11pm to dawn. Reservations recommended*. Formal evening wear is expected in this legendary small but select club where the wealthy love to congregate, whether they come from banking, advertising, fashion, film or the entertainment world... A unique, magic experience.

Stars'N'Bars – *6 Quai Antoine-1 – ☎00 377 93 50 95 95 – www.starsnbars.com. Open daily 11am-midnight; 4am for the dance hall.* This is the great American bar of the moment, more relaxed than the Principality's other establishments, and catering to a younger clientele eager to drink beer, eat a hamburger or two, play billiards, surf on the Internet and dance away the night. The decoration features the paraphernalia of stars. Rock concerts are organised on a regular basis. Terrace with a view of Monaco harbour.

Le Cabaret – *Place du Casino – ☎00 377 92 16 36 36 – www.montecarloresort. com. Shows Wed-Sat from 10.30pm; bar/restaurant open from 8.30pm.* This cabaret run by the Monte-Carlo Casino presents three different shows, and international jazz and variety acts.

BOAT TRIPS

Aquavision – *Quai des Etats-Unis – ☎00 377 92 16 15 15 – www.aquavision-monaco.com. Departures several times daily throughout the season. ☞11€ (ages 3-18, 8€).* Views of the sea depths, and marine fauna and flora, with commentary in four languages.

SHOPPING

All the famous fashion brands have boutiques in Monte-Carlo. Find shops specialising in traditional goods in the narrow streets of the Rock *(Le Rocher)* opposite the palace. Boutique du Rocher in Avenue de la Madone is the official shop for local crafts.

CALENDAR OF EVENTS

Highlights of a packed calendar are

Monte-Carlo Rally – *held every year since 1911 (end of Jan).*

Feast of Ste-Dévote – *Monaco's Patron Saint feast (Jan 27).*

Sciaratù Carnival – *Monégasque festival (week of Mardi Gras).*

Spring Arts Festival – *Art, music, theatre and dance festival (Apr).*

Monaco Grand Prix – *3.145km/2mi race in the Principality's winding streets (May).*

National Day – *Picturesque procession and cultural displays (Nov 19).*

Sights

Le Rocher (The Rock)★★

This is the historic core of the principality, and its prestigious capital, the miniature city of Monaco. It is built on a rocky peninsula 60m – 200ft above the sea.

Musée Océanographique★★

Kids ⏰ *Jul-Aug: daily 9.30am-7.30pm; Apr-Jun and Sep: daily 9.30am-7pm; Oct-Mar: daily 10am-6pm. ☞ 11€ (6-18 years: 6€). ♿ ☎00 377 93 15 36 00. www. oceano.mc.*

The museum was founded by Prince Albert I who was a leading light in the early days of oceanography. The imposing rooms house the skeletons of large marine mammals (whale, sea-cow...) as well as stuffed specimens. A splendid **aquarium**★★ teems with rare tropical and Mediterranean species of marine life (sea dragon). A live coral reef from the Red Sea is a unique exhibit.

The museum is also a research centre, with exhibits of marine laboratories, the technology of underwater exploration and applied oceanography.

Cathédrale

The neo-Romanesque building contains a number of early paintings of the **Nice School**★★, including a St Nicholas altarpiece by Louis Bréa.

Palais Princier (Prince's Palace)★

⏰ *Audio guided tours (30min) Jun-Sep: daily 9.30am-6.30pm; Oct: daily 10am-5.30pm. ⏰ Closed Nov-May. ☞ 7€. ☎00 377 93 25 1831.*

The palace overlooks a square called the **Place du Palais**★, ornamented with cannon presented by Louis XIV. With its medieval battlements and walls strengthened by Vauban, the palace makes a most picturesque composition.

An imposing gateway leads into the Court of Honour with its arcades; inside the Palace is the Throne Room and state apartments decorated with fine furniture and hung with signed portraits by Old Masters.

Monte-Carlo★★★

Europe's gambling capital was launched by François Blanc, director of the casino in Bad Homburg in Germany. The place's success has led to building at a very high density indeed, but Monte-Carlo retains its attractiveness with its luxurious casino, its sumptuous villas, its de luxe shops and its pretty gardens.

From the fine terrace (**terrasse★★**) of the Casino, the view extends from Monaco to the Bordighera headland in Italy.

Jardin Exotique★★

🕐 *Mid-May to mid-Sep: daily 9am-7pm; mid-Sep to mid-May: 9am-6pm or until dusk, depending on the month.* 🕐 *Closed some public holidays.* ⊗ *6.90€ (ticket includes visits to the grotte de l'Observatoire and the musée d'Anthropologie préhistorique).* ☎ *00 377 93 15 29 80. www.monte-carlo.mc/jardinexotique.*

The gardens cascade down a steep rock-face which has its own microclimate supporting a luxuriant variety of vegetation; there are many semi-desert species together with plants from the southern hemisphere.

Collection des voitures anciennes★

Kids 🕐 *Daily 10am-6pm.* 🕐 *Closed 25 Dec.* ⊗ *6€ (children: 3€).* ♿ ☎ *00 377 92 05 28 56. www.palais.mc.*

Fine old carriages and vehicles from the royal collection are on display. There are also famous cars from the early 20C: Buick, Packard, etc...

▶▶ Grotte de l'Observatoire★ *As for visit to the Jardin exotique.*

Musée d'Anthropologie préhistorique★ *As for visit to the Jardin exotique.*

Musée Napoléonien★ 🕐 *Jun-Sep: daily 9.30am-6.30pm; Oct to mid-Nov: daily 10am-5.30pm; mid-Nov to end May: daily except Mon 10.30am-12.30pm, 2-5pm.* 🕐 *Closed 1 Jan, 25 Dec.* ⊗ *4€.* ☎ *00 377 93 25 18 31. www.palais.mc.*

Kids Musée des Poupées et Automates★ 🕐 *Easter to end Sep: 10am-6.30pm. Rest of year: 10am-12.15pm, 2.30-6.30pm.* 🕐 *Closed public holidays.* ⊗ *6€ (children 3.50€).* ☎ *00 377 93 30 91 26*

Musée des Timbres et des Monnaies. ♿ 🕐 *Jul-Sep: 10am-6pm; Oct-Jun: 10am-5pm.* ⊗ *3€.* ☎ *00 377 93 15 41 50.*

MONTAUBAN★

MICHELIN MAP 337 E 7–POPULATION 51 855
GREEN GUIDE LANGUEDOC ROUSSILLON TARN GORGES

On the boundary between the hillsides of Bas Quercy and the rich alluvial plains of the Garonne and the Tarn, the old bastide of Montauban, built with a geometric street layout, is an important crossroads and a good point of departure for excursions into the Aveyron gorges. It is an active market-town, selling fruit and vegetables from market gardens from all over the region. The almost exclusive use of pink brick lends the buildings here a distinctive character, which is also found in most of the towns and villages in Bas Quercy and the Toulouse area.

🛈 **Information:** 4 rue du Collège, ☎05 63 63 60 60. www.montauban-tourisme.com

▶ **Orient Yourself:** The town is on autoroute A20, north of Toulouse and east of Agen.

Sight

Place Nationale★

The square, formerly the Place Royale, dates from the foundation of the town in the 12C.

After fire destroyed the wooden roofs or *couverts* above the galleries in 1614 and again in 1649, the arcades were rebuilt in brick in the 17C. The square features a double set of arcades with pointed- or round-arched vaulting. The inner gallery was a covered passageway while the outer gallery was occupied by market stalls.

The ornate elements and warm tones of the brick soften the overall effect, which would otherwise be rather austere, without destroying the stylistic homogeneity.

Musée Ingres★

19 r. de l'Hôtel-de-Ville ◷ *Jul-Sep: daily 10am-6pm; Oct-Jun: daily except Mon 10am-noon, 2-6pm (mid-Oct to Palm Sunday: closed Sun morning).* ◷ *Closed public holidays.* ◌ *4€ (6€ during special exhibits).* ☎*05 63 22 12 91.*

Devoted to Jean-Auguste-Dominique Ingres' works, the museum is housed in a former bishop's palace. The first floor features some of the artist's best examples of his paintings: *Ruggiero freeing Angelica, Ossian's Dream, Jesus among the Doctors*, along with a selection of his 4 000 **drawings**, displayed in rotation.

▸ Vieille ville★ (old town).

MONTHERMÉ★

MICHELIN MAP 306 K 3–POPULATION 2 791
GREEN GUIDE ALSACE LORRAINE CHAMPAGNE

Monthermé has a spectacular site★ just downstream from the meeting-point of the Semoy with the Meuse, and makes a good starting point for walks or cycle rides into the Ardennes.

▪ **Information:** pl. J.-B. Clément, ☎03 24 54 46 73.
▸ **Orient Yourself:** The little town is close to Charleville-Mézières. The old and new parts of town are separated by the River Meuse.

Excursion

La Meuse Ardennaise★★ (The Meuse Gorge Through The Ardennes)

72km – 45mi. One of Europe's great rivers, 950km – 590 miles in length, the Meuse rises on the Langres uplands. It flows between the escarpment of the Côte des Bars and the dip-slope of the Côte de la Meuse, before penetrating the schists of the high plateau of the Ardennes in a deep gorge. Its meanders here mark the course it traced out in Tertiary times; since then the plateau has been uplifted, but the river has succeeded in entrenching itself in the schists, a process known as superimposition.

From Charleville-Mézières to Givet there is a succession of single meanders (Monthermé, Fumay, Chooz), double (Revin) and even triple ones (Charleville). The valley has long formed a corridor of human activity, with its water, rail and road communications, and with a skilled workforce producing engineering products and domestic appliances. At the beginning of the century, Monthermé was a centre of trade union activity, with considerable conflict between workers and employers.

Downstream from Monthermé the most interesting sites are: the **Roches de Laifour**★ and the **Dames de Meuse**★ opposite one another; Revin, where the old town and the industrial area each occupy their own peninsula; Fumay, with its old quarter, once famous for its quarries producing violet slate; Chooz, with its nuclear power stations; Givet, sited at the exit from a side valley originally fortified by Charles V and strengthened by Vauban. The composer Mehul (1763-1817) was born here, best known for his *Chant du Départ*, a patriotic song of the French Revolution.

MONT-LOUIS ★

MICHELIN MAP 344 D 7–POPULATION 270

GREEN GUIDE LANGUEDOC ROUSSILLON TARN GORGES

Mont-Louis occupies a strategic site at the meeting point of three valleys. To the north is the valley of the Aude; its broad upper course is known as the **Capcir**. To the southwest is the Sègre, a tributary of the Ebro, which here flows through the **Cerdagne**, an upland basin; its elevated position (1 200m – 4 000ft) diminishes the apparent height of the surrounding peaks, and its high sunshine level led to the construction here in 1949 of the first "solar oven" (**four solaire**) using parabolic mirrors. Finally, to the west, is the valley of the Têt, which flows out of the Lac des Bouillouses to form the **Conflent**, the major routeway linking the Cerdagne with Perpignan.

- **Information:** 3 rue Lieutenant Pruneta, ☎04 68 04 21 97.
- ▶ **Orient Yourself:** The town is high in the Pyrenees, east of Font-Romeu and Andorra. The tourist office organises guided tours daily in Jul-Aug.

A Bit of History

The site's importance was confirmed following the **Treaty of the Pyrenees** in 1659, which, by restoring Roussillon to the French crown, made the Pyrenees the legal as well as the natural boundary of France. Louis XIV set about giving his newly acquired lands some more solid protection than that afforded by a signature; the great Vauban carried out his survey of Roussillon and the Cerdagne in 1679 and, from 1681 onwards, directed the construction of Mont-Louis.

Thus came into being this austere little fortified town, completely contained by its massive ramparts (**remparts** ★) and protected by its citadel.

Sight

Four Solaire (Solar Furnace)

🕐 *Guided tours ➝ (40min) Jul-Aug: daily 10-11.30am, 2-5.30pm (last admission 6pm); Feb-Jun and Sep-Oct: daily 10-11am, 2-4pm (last admission 5pm); Nov-Jan: daily 10-11am, 2-3pm (last admission 4pm).* 🕐 *Closed 1 Jan, 25 Dec.* ⚆ *5.50€ (children: 4€). ☎04 68 04 14 89. www.four-solaire.fr.* Installed as long ago as 1953, the solar furnace uses the sun's reflected light to generate heat and power. Its 546 mirrors focus on one point, where the temperature can reach 3500ºC.

- ▶ Ramparts

MONTPELLIER ★★

MICHELIN MAP 339 I 7–POPULATION 207 936

GREEN GUIDE LANGUEDOC ROUSSILLON TARN GORGES

One of the most charming and agreeable of French provincial cities, lively, cultured Montpellier successfully combines beautiful historical districts, 17C mansions and modern architecture.

- **Information:** 30 allée De-Lattre-de-Tassigny (esplanade Comédie), ☎04 67 60 60 60. www.ot-montpellier.
- ▶ **Orient Yourself:** The heart of the town is the spacious traffic-free Place de la Comédie at its centre. Ask the tourist office about City Pass, giving free entry to many sites, discounts on leisure actiivities, and travel on local transport.
- Ⓟ **Parking:** The city centre is largely traffic free. Leave the car in one of the big underground car parks, such as Parkings Antigone or Esplanade.

Address Book

For coin categories, see the Legend on the cover flap.

WHERE TO EAT

Simple Simon – *1 r. des Trésoriers-de-France* – ☎04 67 66 03 43. *Closed Sun May-Oct and in the evening – reservation recommended*. Simply British, Simple Simon serves a medley of British pastries, an Indian or sweet and savoury dish for lunch, salads in summer and soup in winter. Perfectly cosy setting, with tablemats and a thick carpet. Languedoc wines by the glass, lest we forget our French!

Le Petit Jardin – *20 r. Jean-Jacques-Rousseau* – ☎04 67 60 78 78. *Closed Jan and Mon*. Located on a narrow street in the renovated Écusson quarter, this charming little house welcomes diners to its appealing terrace-garden whenever the weather obliges. Enjoy tasty regional fare as you admire the cathedral from your vantage point under the trees.

Les Bains de Montpellier – *6 r. Richelieu* – ☎04 67 60 70 87. *Closed in Feb, Toussaint and Christmas holidays, Mon lunchtime and Sun – reservation recommended*. Whether seated in the shade of the courtyard palm trees, beneath the large glass roof or in one of the little drawing rooms, there's an ambience to suit every guest in the wonderfully well-restored old 'Parisian baths'. Cuisine made from fresh market produce.

WHERE TO STAY

Hôtel de la Comédie – *1 bis r. Baudin* – ☎04 67 58 43 64 – *hotel-delacomedie@wanadoo.fr – 20 rms*. ☕6€Located just off of La Place de la Comédie, this hotel with a 19C facade offers pleasingly modern bedrooms. Located in a lively Montpellier neighbourhood, it is an excellent starting point for discovering the city. Relaxed ambience.

Hôtel du Palais – *3 r. du Palais* – ☎ 04 67 60 47 38 – *26 rms*. ☕12€. This family hotel near the Peyrou gardens and the Place de la Canourgue has small rooms that are stylish and well kept.

Sofitel Antigone – 11 r. Pertuisanes – ☎04 67 99 72 72 – *88 rms*. ☕22€ One of the best hotels in town is located in the Antigone quarter, modern rooms, good facilities, traditional regional dining.

SIT BACK AND RELAX

Dorian's Kawa – *12 r. Four-des-Flammes* – ☎04 67 66 18 71. A tearoom to make a note of – the coffee is excellent and the owner very friendly. The shop sells coffeepots, tea services and English china. Ideal for a break or a tête-à-tête.

Grand Café Riche – 8 pl. de la Comédie – ☎ 04 67 54 71 44. Oldest cafe in the city, and an institution in Montpellier. A wonderful place to linger and watch the passers-by.

L'Heure Bleue – *1 r. de la Carbonnerie* – ☎ 04 67 66 41 05 . This literary tearoom in an 18C mansion is also an art gallery and second-hand shop; as such its decor includes a lavish collection of sculptures and curios. Home-baked pastries and nearly 30 varieties of tea.

ON THE TOWN

In Montpellier, a student's city, many music bars stay close to new trends and it is quite common to discover a rap concert being performed round the corner from a bourgeois manor. The city's cultural landscape is very diverse, with its jazz enthusiasts, accordion fans and lovers of salsa or classical music.

Rockstore – *20 r. de Verdun* – ☎04 67 06 80 00 – www.rockstore.fr. Open: bars: Mon-Sat 6pm-4am; disco: 11pm-4am. This hotspot of Montpellier nightlife hosts numerous rock groups and organizes techno, rap and sound system evenings. With the huge red American car stuck above the entrance, the techno and rock bars and the disco, the decor mirrors the musical programming.

Centre dramatique national – *Domaine de Grammont, Avenue Albert-Einstein* – ☎ 04 67 99 25 25 : reserv. by phone: 04 67 60 05 45.

Opéra Comédie – *11 bd Victor-Hugo* – ☎ 04 67 60 19 99. Closed Aug. Traditional stage performances.

Zénith – *Av. Albert-Einstein* – ☎04 67 64 50 00 – www.zenith-montpellier.com – performance schedule variable – ⏱ closed Aug. Variety and rock shows.

🕐 **Organizing Your Time:** The main attraction is just strolling and relaxing – allow at least a couple of hours for the Old Town. Think about combining your stay in the city with a trip to the nearby Mediterranean resorts of La Grande Motte, Carnon and Palavas.

🔍 **Don't Miss:** The Jardin des Plantes (Botanic Gardens); a stroll in the **Antigone quarter**★; a ride on the modern trams; a drink at an outdoor table in Place de la Comédie.

A Bit of History

By the 11C, Montpellier was an inland port served by the Maguelone lagoon and the Camargue canal. At the time of the first Crusades, there was already considerable trade with the Levant and Near East. Directly and indirectly this led to the founding here in 1137 of Europe's first medical school. It became a university in 1289.

The town passed by marriage into the hands of the king of Aragon, but was bought back by Philippe VI de Valois in 1349. A centre of Protestantism, it was much damaged in the Religious Wars. Louis XIV made it the capital of Lower Languedoc, and encouraged reconstruction, opening a period of high architectural achievement. In recent years too it has been noted for striking architecture, especially in the neo-Classical Antigone district.

Sights

Promenade du Peyrou★★
This handsome central park constructed to conceal water works, first laid out in 1688, gives a fine view★ over the Garrigue and the Cévennes.

Le Vieux Montpellier★★
In the 17C and 18C the medieval town centre was embellished with numerous fine mansions (hôtels), each with its own character but all conforming to common rules of taste. Among the most impressive, **Hôtel des Trésoriers de la Bourse**★ has kept its fine staircase, and **Hôtel de Varennes**★ integrates Romanesque and Gothic elements.

▸ Montpellier has many interesting **museums**, including: Musée Fabre★★ – 17-20C fine arts, paintings; Musée Atger★ – fine art, 16-18C drawings; Musée Languedocien★ – regional art and architecture.
Planétarium Galilée (www.planetarium-galilee.com) – a good rainy day choice for kids.
Le jardin des Plantes de Montpellier – the oldest botanic gardens in France.

Façade of the Opera House, Montpellier

©iStockphotos.com/Diane White Rosier

LE **MONT-ST-MICHEL**★★★

MICHELIN MAP 303 C 8–POPULATION 46
GREEN GUIDE NORMANDY

Mont-St-Michel has been called "the Wonder of the Western World"; its extraordinary site, its rich and influential history and its glorious architecture combine to make it the most splendid of all the abbeys of France.

- **Information:** Corps de Garde des Bourgeois, ☎02 33 60 14 30.
  www.ot-montsaintmichel.com.
- ▶ **Orient Yourself:** Mont-St-Michel is a granite island about 900m – 984yd round and 80m – 262ft high. As the bay is already partially silted up, the mount is usually to be seen surrounded by huge sand banks which shift with the tides and often reshape the mouths of the neighbouring rivers. It is linked to the mainland by a causeway which was built in 1877.
- **Parking:** Parking is available outside the Tour du Roi near the Porte de l'Avancée.

A Bit of History

At the beginning of the 8C St Michael appeared to Aubert, the bishop of Avranches. Aubert founded an oratory on an island then known as Mont Tombe. This oratory was soon replaced by an abbey, which adopted the Benedictine Rule in the 10C, thereby assuring its importance. Two centuries later the Romanesque abbey reached its peak of development.

In the 13C, following a fire, a great rebuilding in Gothic style took place, known as *la Merveille* – the Marvel. Even though the English beseiged it during the Hundred Years War, the Mount did not fall into the invaders' hands.

Mont-St-Michel

Visit

L'Abbaye (Abbey)★★★

The architecture of the Abbey was determined by the constraints imposed by the rock on which it stands. Crowned as it is by the Abbey church and the buildings of the Merveille (c 1225), the result bears little resemblance to the conventionally-planned Benedictine monastery.

Église★★

There is a striking contrast between the stern character of the Romanesque nave and the well-lit Flamboyant choir. The axis of the sanctuary is aligned on the rising sun on 8 May, the spring Feast of St Michael under the Eastern calendar.

La Merveille★★★

This is the group of buildings on the north side of the mount. The Guests' Hall (**salle des Hôtes**★) is a masterpiece of High Gothic. Suspended between sea and sky, the cloisters (**cloître**★★★), with their slim columns in pink granite arranged in a quincunx pattern, make a magic garden conducive to serenity and inner joy. The Refectory (**Réfectoire**★) is filled with light from its recessed windows. It hangs 45m – 148ft high, a bold achievement on the part of its architect who was unable to use buttresses on the sheer rock-face. The vast Knights' Hall (**Salle des Chevaliers**★) is divided into

A. De Valroger/MICHELIN

Address Book

For coin ranges, see the Legend on the cover flap.

WHERE TO EAT

⊖⊜ **La Sirène** – ☎02 33 60 08 60 – *closed 10 Jan to 2 Feb, 15 Nov to 20 Dec and Fri*. Take the spiral staircase to enter the crêperie in this 14C house that was an inn for many years. The frosted-glass windows, their panes separated by metal mullions, confirm the genuine flavour of the place.

⊖⊜ **Pré Salé** – *Rest. belonging to the Hôtel Mercure – 2km/1.2mi S of Mont-St-Michel via D 976* – ☎02 33 60 14 18 – *contact@hotelmercure-montsaintmichel. com. Closed 12 Nov to 6 Feb*. Located along the River Couesnon at the start of the dike, the Hôtel Mercure welcomes you into its bright dining room, recently renovated with tables set comfortably apart from each other. Try the delicious salt-meadow (pré salé) meat from Mont-St-Michel Bay.

⊖⊜ **La Promenade** – *Pl. du Casino – 50610 Jullouville* – ☎02 33 90 80 20. *Closed Mon and Tue – reserv. advisable.* It would be difficult to find a better view of Mont-St-Michel Bay than that offered by this elegant restaurant-tea-room located on the ground floor of the former casino hotel (1881). Handsome antique furniture and tableware. Menu with an accent on seafood.

WHERE TO STAY

⊜ **Mme Gillet Hélène Bed and Breakfast** – *Le Val-St-Revert – 35610 Roz-sur-Couesnon – 15km/9.3mi SW of Mont-St-Michel via D 797, the coast road to St-Malo* – ☎02 99 80 27 85 – ⤳ – *3 rooms*. This family house overlooks the bay and offers a beautiful view of Mont-St-Michel and the surrounding countryside. Five rooms where an old world charm lingers on: three on the sea side and a more recent and brighter one with a terrace facing the garden.

⊜ **Amaryllis Bed and Breakfast** – *Le Bas-Pays – 50170 Beauvoir – 2.5km/1.5mi S of Mont-St-Michel dir. Pontorson* – ☎02 33 60 09 42 – ⤳ – *5 rooms* – ⊡4.70€. This recently built stone house was designed as a B&B. The impeccably clean rooms feature well-equipped bathrooms and a furnished terrace. An extra treat: you can visit the farm next door.

⊜ **La Tour Brette** – *8 r. Couesnon – 50170 Pontorson – 9km/5.4mi S of Mont-St-Michel* – ☎02 33 60 10 69. *Closed 14-22 Mar, 1-20 Dec and Wed except Jul-Aug – 10 rooms*- ⊡ *6.50€*. This small, centrally located hotel is named after the tower that used to protect Normandy from the Duchy of Brittany's assaults. The rooms are not very large but they've just been renovated. Restaurant in a simple setting with a long, traditional menu.

⊜ **La Bergerie Bed and Breakfast** – *La Poultière – 35610 Roz-sur-Couesnon – 16km/9.9mi SW of Mont-St-Michel via D 797, the coast road to St-Malo* – ☎02 99 80 29 68 – ⤳ – *5 rooms*. Located in the former sheepfold, these rooms are not particularly charming, but they are comfortable and benefit from the peaceful atmosphere of the small hamlet. The kitchen set aside for guests is very much appreciated as is the garden where sheep still graze. A self-catering cottage is also available.

⊖⊜ **Bretagne** – *R. Couesnon – 50170 Pontorson – 4km/2.4mi S of Mont-St-Michel via D 976* – ☎02 33 60 10 55. *Closed 20 Jan to 5 Feb – 16 rooms* – ⊡7€. Regional-style house. Admire the lovely 18C wood panels, the grey-marble fireplace and the plate-warming radiator (very unusual!) in the first room. Cosy, typically British bar and spacious, pleasantly furnished rooms.

⊖⊜ **Les Vieilles Digues** – *Rte du Mont-St-Michel – 50170 Beauvoir – 3km/1.8mi S of Mont-St-Michel dir. Pontorson* – ☎02 33 58 55 30. *Closed Jan – 7 rooms*. This pretty stone house boasts spacious rooms thoughtfully furnished with handsome pieces. The room with a view of Mont-St-Michel is, naturally, a favourite. Agreeable half-timbered breakfast room. Landscaped garden.

four parts. It may be so named after the chivalric Order established here.

Jardins de l'Abbaye★

From the gardens there is a view of the north face of the mount, the "most beautiful wall in all the world," according to Victor Hugo.

◖◗ La ville★★ (town) – Grande-Rue★, Remparts★★.

CHÂTEAU DE **MONTSÉGUR**★

MICHELIN MAP 343 POP 117
GREEN GUIDE LANGUEDOC ROUSSILLON TARN GORGES

It was on this fearsome peak that the last episode of the Albigensian Crusade took place, when its Cathar defenders were massacred and Languedoc eclipsed by the power of the French kingdom.

- **Information:** Syndicat d'Initiative, in the village, ☎05 61 03 03 03.
- **Orient Yourself:** The small village is north of Ax-les-Thermes, in the foothills of the eastern Pyrenees. It is dominated by the castle.

A Bit of History

Catharism – the name is derived from a Greek word meaning "pure" – was based on the principle of the total separation of Good and Evil, of the spiritual from the material. Its adherents comprised ordinary believers and the *"Perfecti,"* the latter living lives of exemplary purity in the light of God. Their austerity contrasted sharply with the venality and laxity of the Catholic clergy.

At the beginning of the 13C the local **Cathars** built a castle here to replace an old, since-demolished fortress. Forty years later, following the ravages of the Albigensian Crusade against the Cathars, the stronghold was occupied by some 400 adherents to the faith, from whose ranks was drawn the fierce band which marched on Avignonet *(70km – 44mi north)* to put to the sword the members of the Inquisition meeting there. This action sealed the fate of Montségur; in the absence of Louis IX who was dealing with disturbances in Saintonge, Blanche of Castille ordered the Crusaders to put the castle to siege. On 2 March 1244 the resistance of the defenders was overcome, but 200 of the faithful refused to retract their beliefs, even after being granted a fortnight in which to consider the matter. On 16 March, they were brought down from the mountain to be burnt on a huge pyre at a place known from then on as the "Field of the Burnt Ones" (Camp des Crémats).

Visit

Château

To reach the château requires a steep walk on a difficult path. ⏱ daily from about 9am or 10am to 4pm to 6pm depending on the season. ⏱ closed Jan. 4 €. ☎05 61 01 10 27. www.montsegur.fr – The climb, the view and the site all contribute to an evocative sense of the history which occured here. The rebuilding of the **château** was begun in the year following the siege, on the same **site**★★. It was the third stronghold to be built here, and its ruins crown the summit (pog) today. It later became part of the line of French defences facing the kingdom of Aragon. Its great keep and its fine staircase, concealed from the outside, bear witness to the skill of its builders.

- Musée archéologique, in the village.

MOULINS★

MICHELIN MAP 326 H 3–POPULATION 21 892

GREEN GUIDE AUVERGNE THE RHÔNE VALLEY

Moulins, on the River Allier, is the quiet, charming capital of the Bourbonnais region.

Information: 11 r. F. Péron, ☎04 70 44 14 14.

Orient Yourself: Moulins sits in the centre of the country, between Nevers and Vichy.

A Bit of History

The city was founded by the Bourbon lords at the end of the 11C. In time, the Bourbons rose to the rank of dukes. The 15C was the duchy's golden age, with many artists commissioned to work here. The independence of the Bourbonnais became an irritant to the king. François I took advantage of the supposed treason of Charles III, the Ninth Duke, to confiscate his estates. After a series of battles against the French forces, Charles was killed (1527) and the Bourbonnais attached to the French Crown.

Sight

Triptyque du Maître de Moulins★★★

🕐 *Guided tours* ☚ *(20min) mid-Mar to mid-Oct: daily 9.30am-noon, 2-6pm, Sun 2-6pm; mid-Oct to mid-Mar: daily except Tue 10-noon, 2-5.30pm, Sun 2-5.30pm. Last admission 30min before closing.* 🕐 *Closed 1 Jan, 1 May, 14 Jul, 25 Dec.* ☚ *2€ offering suggested.* ☎*04 70 20 89 65.*

The **Triptych by the Master of Moulins,** from about 1498, is a triumph of late-Gothic painting. The Master has never been conclusively identified. The poses of the figures depicted suggest the Flemish School, while their faces recall the work of Florentine masters. The figures of the donors are painted in a realistic manner, in contrast to the idealised treatment of the central panel. The painting appears to be rich in symbolism, the use of the numbers 7 and 12, in particular, representing the Gothic idea of perfection.

▶ Cathédrale★ – stained glass★★. Jaquemart★ (Belltower). Mausolée du Duc de Montmorency★

MULHOUSE★★

MICHELIN MAP 315 I 10–POPULATION 224 445

GREEN GUIDE ALSACE LORRAINE CHAMPAGNE

Mulhouse became a free Imperial city as early as the end of the 13C, and in the 16C formed part of the *Decapolis,* the league of 10 towns of Alsace.

Information: 9 avenue de Marechal Foch, ☎03 89 35 48 48.

Orient Yourself: This large city lies at the meeting point of France, Germany and Switzerland.

Especially for Kids: Those who love cars – old and new – will enjoy the Schlumpf motor museum.

Don't Miss: Find time for the fascinating textile museum, where beautiful fabrics with historic designs are on sale.

A Bit of History

A historic manufacturing and trading centre, the city's independent spirit led it into an association with the cantons of Switzerland. It joined France voluntarily in 1798. Mulhouse was already long established as a textile centre, when, in 1746, three of its citizens, J-J Schmaltzer, the painter J-H Dollfus and the merchant S Koechlin together founded the first mill producing calico cotton fabrics. Production advanced by leaps and bounds. In 1812 the Dollfus and Mieg mill was the first to install steam power.

Sights

Hôtel de Ville ★★

Since 1558, the City Hall has symbolised Mulhouse's civic and political liberties. It is a unique example in France of a building (1552) of the Rhineland Renaissance by a Basle architect; the exterior is decorated solely by artists from Konstanz. It was aptly described as a "splendid, golden palace" by the writer Montaigne. It was remodelled in 1698. It is this later decoration which has been restored to its former glory and can be admired today. The coats of arms of the Swiss cantons painted on the main façade on either side of the covered double flight of steps recall the historical link with Switzerland.

Musée de l'Automobile – Collection Schlumpf ★★★

Kids ♿ ⏰ *Apr-Oct: 10am-6pm; Feb-Mar and Nov-Dec: 10am-5pm; Jan: Mon-Fri 1-5pm, Sat-Sun 10am-5pm.* ⏰ *Closed 25 Dec.* ✆ *10€ (children 7-12 years: 5€).* ☎03 89 33 23 21. www.collection-schlumpf.com.

The splendid, definitive collection of 500 vehicles (including those in storage) was lovingly (and secretly) built up over the years by the mill-owning Schlumpf brothers – and led to their bankruptcy. The collection vividly evokes the history of the motor car over more than a century, from the steam-powered Jacquot (1878) to the latest and most exclusive models. Most are in working order; several had famous owners – Charlie Chaplin's Rolls-Royce Phantom III is here.

▶ **Musée français du Chemin de fer**★★★ – history of railways.
Musée de l'Impression sur Étoffes (Textile Museum) ★ – history of the printing of patterned cloths.
Musée Historique★★
Électropolis★ Kids – history of electric power.
Parc zoologique et botanique★★ – Zoological and Botanical Gardens.
Musée du Papier-peint★ (at Rixheim, 6km – 4mi east of Mulhouse) – all about wallpaper.

NANCY★★★

MICHELIN MAP 307 I 6–POPULATION 331 363
GREEN GUIDE ALSACE LORRAINE CHAMPAGNE

Capital of the industrial area of Lorraine, Nancy is sited on the low-lying land between the River Meurthe and the Moselle Heights (Côtes de Moselle).

▯ **Information:** 14 pl. Stanislas, ☎03 83 35 22 41. www.ot-nancy.com
▶ **Orient Yourself:** The city is reached on autoroutes A31 and A33 The Old Town is the historic heart of the city, centred on place St-Epvre. The handsome New Town is the area outside its original gates.
⏱ **Organizing Your Time:** Discover Nancy by taxi on one of five routes that features commentary recorded by the tourist office.
🔊 **Guided tour:** Audioguides with a recorded commentary are also available on the Art nouveau theme. *Enquire at tourist office.*
👁 **Don't Miss:** Place Stanislas.

A Bit of History

The city was founded in the 11C but its history really begins in the 15C, when the Dukes of Lorraine asserted their independence, added Renaissance ornament to their Flamboyant Gothic palace, and to the north of the Triumphal Arch – Arc de Triomphe – the district now known as Vieux Nancy began to take shape. In the 17C, the new town (ville neuve) was planned on a regular pattern by the artist Claude Gellée, known as **Claude Lorrain** (1600-82). Louis XIV 's architect Mansart designed the town hall **(Palais du Governement★)** in 1699.

Ever since the Treaty of Munster in 1648, the Duchy of Lorraine had been in a precarious situation; an independent enclave in French territory, it still formed part of the Holy Roman Empire. Though French in language and culture, its people were proud of their independence and much attached to their princes.

In 1738, following the War of the Polish Succession, Duke François I, son of Leopold and husband of Maria-Theresa of Austria, found himself having to cede Lorraine in exchange for Tuscany. In his place, Louis XV appointed, as ruler for life, his own father-in-law Stanislas Leszczynski, and by 1766 the Duchy had been painlessly incorporated into the French kingdom, a notable success for Cardinal Fleury's foreign policy. Stanislas was a man of peace, fond of his daughter the Queen of France, a lover of good living and of the opposite sex, and a passionate builder. He set out to join together the old quarter of Nancy with the "New Town" by means of a set-piece of civic design in honour of his son-in-law. The great project was completed in the short space of three years, between 1752 and 1755.

Detail, Place Stanislas

E. Baret/MICHELIN

Sight

Place Stanislas★★★

In charge of the work were the architect Emmanuel Héré (1705-63) and Jean **Lamour**, a metal-worker of genius. Héré designed the City Hall (Hôtel de ville) and the flanking buildings with their fine façades. To the north the square is defined by two further buildings, similar in general treatment, though with only one storey. The whole forms a space of exceptional elegance and clarity of structure, ornamented with urns and trophies and with balustrades to conceal the roofs. Further enclosure is achieved by Jean Lamour's brilliant ironwork. Perfectly integrated into the architectural concept, his **gilded railings** with their crests and floral decoration are of inimitable gracefulness.

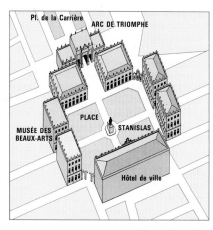

Address Book

For coin ranges, see the Legend on the cover flap.

WHERE TO EAT

Rue des Maréchaux, by place Stanislas, justly nicknamed "rue gourmande", has some 40 different restaurants to suit all tastes and budgets.

Les Pissenlits – *25 bis r. des Ponts – ☎03 83 37 43 97. Closed 1-16 Aug, Sun and Mon*. There's always a crowd in this bistro near the market. The atmosphere is relaxed, the cuisine innovative and diverse, and the decor pleasant with closely packed tables and blackboard.

Le Foy – *1 pl. Stanislas – ☎03 83 32 21 44. Closed 29 Jul-21 Aug, Sun evening, Tue evening and Wed*. Climb the lovely stone staircase to reach this first-floor restaurant above the café-brasserie of the same name in place Stanislas. The food is good and served in generous portions. Rustic decor with exposed beams.

Le V Four – *10 r. St-Michel – ☎03 83 32 49 48. Closed 1-7 Feb, 30 Aug-9 Sep, Sat lunchtime, Sun evening and Mon*. It may be small, but this restaurant in the heart of the old city is popular among the locals, who enjoy its simple modern decor and its trendy cuisine. Terrace.

Le Gastrolâtre – *1 pl. Vaudémont – ☎03 83 35 51 94. Closed 1-6 May, 15-30 Aug, Christmas holidays, Mon lunchtimes, Thu evenings and Sun*. This popular bistro just behind place Stanislas is run with a master's hand by a media boss. Its mouth-watering menu and characterful cuisine combine local flavours with those from the south of France.

Grenier à Sel – *28 r. Gustave-Simon – ☎03 83 32 31 98. Closed 23 Jul-15 Aug, Sun and Mon*. This restaurant is in a little-frequented street on the first floor of one of the oldest houses in town. In the large country-style dining room you can enjoy food with a modern flair.

WHERE TO STAY

Weekends in Nancy – Hotel stays of two nights and more are rewarded by a welcome gift and reductions on visits to the town. Ask at the tourist office for the list of hotels and reservation conditions.

Portes d'Or – *21 r. Stanislas – ☎03 83 35 42 34 – contact@hotel-lesportesdor.com – 20 rooms – ⚏ 9€*. The main advantage of this hotel is its proximity to the Place Stanislas. The pastel-coloured rooms are not very large, but have modern furniture and are reasonably well equipped.

Hôtel Crystal – *5 r. Chanzy – ☎03 83 17 54 00 – hotelcrystal.nancy@wanadoo.fr – 58 rooms – ⚏ 9€*. This entirely renovated hotel near the station is a good place to stay in Nancy. Its modern, spacious rooms have been nicely arranged and decorated and feel welcoming. Cosy bar-lounge.

ON THE TOWN

L'Arquebuse – *13 r. Héré – ☎03 83 32 11 99. Open Tue-Sun 6.30pm-4am, until 5am Fri and Sat*. This high-class bar with a refined decor has a good view of the place Stanislas. A wide choice of cocktails with atmospheric music and disco, attracting a mixed clientele of smart students and businessmen. The place to go after 2am.

L'Échanson – *9 r. de la Primatiale – ☎03 83 35 51 58. Open Tue-Sat noon-2.30pm, 5.30-9.30pm*. A pleasant little wine merchant that also serves as the local bistro. A dozen or so wines are available by the glass, which can be accompanied by a savoury snack.

SHOWTIME

Get hold of a programme! – The magazine *Spectacles à Nancy* will keep you informed. *Information from: www.spectacles-nancy.presse.fr*

Concerts and stage performances – The Opéra de Nancy et de Lorraine, Ballet de Nancy, Théâtre de la Manufacture, Centre dramatique national Nancy-Lorraine, Association de musique ancienne de Nancy, Ensemble Poirel, Orchestre symphonique et lyrique de Nancy, Association lorraine de musique de chambre, Gradus Ad Musicam, La Psalette de Lorraine all put on numerous concerts and shows throughout the year.

Gastronomie en musique – Ask the tourist office about these summer evening musical performances (*Thu, Fri and weekends in different areas of the city*).

Patrimoine en musique – Classical concerts in city-centre churches in the afternoons.

SHOPPING

Adam – *3 pl. St-Epvre* – ☎*03 83 32 04 69. Closed Mon.* This confectioner sells St-Epure, which is made of almond meringue, vanilla cream and crushed nougatine, together with a host of other sweet-tooth delights.

Confiserie Chocolaterie Alain Batt – *30 r. du Tapis-Vert* – ☎*03 83 35 70 00.* Before your very eyes, this confectioner will create macaroons and bergamotes de Nancy, plums in marzipan, Chardons de Lorraine, bergamot truffles and chocolates. Products to taste and buy.

Au Duché de Lorraine – *47 r. Henri-Poincaré* – ☎*03 83 30 13 83. Open daily.* Fans of the famous bergamotes de Nancy (hard sweets flavoured with citrus rind) and macarons des Dominicains will not be disappointed by this confectioner, established since 1840. Also on sale, delightful Lorraine gift boxes and baskets, all generously filled.

Maison des Sœurs Macarons – *21 r. Gambetta* – ☎*03 83 32 24 25* – *www.macaron-de-nancy.com.* The secret recipe for macaroons has been handed down within the family since the 18C. Other Lorraine specialities are available here: bergamots (a sweet made with essence of bergamot), Berg'amours (crystallized fruits), perles de Lorraine (crystallized fruits with plum liqueur centres), Florentines des sœurs, (fondant-encased praline chocolates) Babas du Roi, gingerbread, etc.

▶ Palais Ducal★★ and Musée Historique Lorrain★★★
Musée des Beaux-Arts★★
Arc de Triomphe★.
Place de la Carrière★.

Église★ and Couvent des Cordeliers Chapel★.
Porte de la Craffe★.
Musée de l'École de Nancy★★
Église de Notre-Dame-de-Bon-Secours★.

NANTES★★★

MICHELIN MAP 316 G 4–POPULATION 544 932
GREEN GUIDE BRITTANY

Nantes is Brittany's largest city, sited at the point at which the mighty Loire becomes tidal. The presence of islets (inhabited from the 17C on) in the river had long facilitated the building of bridges, making Nantes the focus of trade and movement between Lower Brittany and Poitou.

▸ **Information:** 3 cours Olivier de Clisson, ☎08 92 46 40 44. www.nantes-tourisme.com

▸ **Orient Yourself:** Three tramway lines and over 60 bus routes make for easy movement throughout the city.

◷ **Organizing Your Time:** You'll need at least 3hr to visit the château and the surrounding sights.

🅿 **Parking:** It is not easy to move around Nantes by car. Find parking in one of several lots surrounding the downtown area and move around the city by tramway, bus or foot.

☺ **Don't Miss:** Find a bar or restaurant in the Ste-Croix neighborhood for an authentic Nantes evening.

Kids **Especially for Kids:** The Safari Park at Port-St-Père.

Un bon vin blanc

This expression, well known for being part of a phonetics exercise for Anglo-Saxon learners of French – literally "a fine white wine" – adequately describes the local Muscadet, dry but not too sharp, perfect with seafood. The vineyards are located to the south and east of Nantes, alongside or near the Sèvre and towards Ancenis on the banks of the Loire.

A Bit of History

In the 9C, the city was disputed between Nominoé, the first Duke of Brittany, and the Franks to the east. In 939, it was chosen as his capital by King Alain Barbe-Torte (Crookbeard). By the 14C, Nantes had become a trading port, with a fleet of 1 300 ships, but it was only in the 15C, under Duke François II, that the city reached its full importance. It was in its cathedral, on 13 April 1598, that Henri IV signed the **Edict of Nantes**, establishing equality between Catholics and Protestants, and granting privileges to the latter regarding the right to maintain fortified strongholds. Louis XIV revoked the Edict in 1685, provoking the Huguenot exodus to England, Holland and Germany and depriving France of some of its most valuable craftsmen.

In the early 18C Nantes grew rich on the 'triangle' of trade importing sugar cane from the West Indies, exporting manufactured goods to Africa, and shipping of slaves from Africa to the West Indies. Nantes became France's premier port until the loss of French territories abroad and the abolition of slavery. The substitution of sugar-beet for cane sugar and the increasing size of ships further led to the old port's decline. However, in the 19C and 20C the construction of larger downstream harbour facilities has contributed towards Nantes' continuing prosperity.

Sights

Château des Ducs de Bretagne★★

4, place Marc Elder ⏰*Open daily. Castle courtyard and ramparts 9am-8pm; Museum 9.30am-7 pm (no admission after 6pm).* ⏰*Evening events: mid-May to mid-Sep, the courtyard, ramparts and moat gardens are open until 11 pm – a chance to enjoy the Castle's illuminations. From mid-Jul to mid-Aug, open air concerts on Tue at 8 pm.* ✆ *Entrance is free to the Castle courtyard, ramparts and moat gardens. Museum or temporary exhibition: €5 (free to under 18s).* ☎*0811 46 46 44 (when in France), 00 33 2 51 17 49 48 (from abroad).* www.chateau-nantes.fr

"God's teeth! No small beer, these dukes of Brittany!" exclaimed Henri IV on seeing this massive stronghold for the first time. The castle was much rebuilt and strengthened from 1466 on by Duke François II who saw in it the guarantee of his independence from Louis XI. His daughter Anne of Brittany continued the work.

The great edifice is defended by deep ditches of considerable width, which could be flooded when necessary, and by six stout towers with characteristically Breton pyramidal machicolations. The interior reflects the castle's role as a palace of government and residence, known for its high life of feasts and jousting.

Many of its features are of great interest, like the Golden Crown Tower (**Tour de la Couronne d'or★★**), the main building (Grand Logis) with its massive dormer windows, the Governor's Major Palace (Grand Gouvernement) rebuilt at the end of the 17C, and the well (**puits★★**) with its wrought-iron well-head incorporating ducal crown motifs.

There are two museums in the castle: the **Musée d'Art populaire★** featuring Breton coiffes, dress and furniture, the Musée des Salorges, a maritime museum *(reorganisation in progress)*. Temporary exhibitions of the latter's collections are held in the Horse-shoe Tower (Tour du Fer-à-Cheval).

Cathédrale St-Pierre et St-Paul

Although the building of the cathedral extended over a period of 450 years, it has a great unity of style. The use of a white calcareous tufa in the **interior**★★ enhances the impression of boldness and purity of line resulting from the mouldings of the pillars which soar without a break in their flight up into the keystones of the vaults.

In the south transept of the cathedral is the exceptionally fine tomb of François II (**tombeau de François II**★★ – 1502).

▶ Musée des Beaux-Arts★★
Muséum d'Histoire Naturelle★★
The 19C Town★ Palais Dobrée★

Musée Jules-Verne★
Musée archéologique★
Jardin des Plantes★.
Ancienne Île Feydeau.

Excursions

Safari africain de Port-St-Père★★

20km – 12mi southwest, on D 758. Kids
This safari park at the heart of the Pays de Retz has over 1 500 animals roaming free in its 140ha – 350-acre enclosure. The visit includes two circuits: one to be toured on foot, the other by car.

NARBONNE★★

MICHELIN MAP 344 I-J 3–POPULATION 46 510
GREEN GUIDE LANGUEDOC ROUSSILLON TARN GORGES

An agreeable provincial town near the Languedoc beaches, Narbonne retains vestiges of an exceptionally illustrious history.

🛈 **Information:** pl. Salengro, ☎04 68 65 15 60. www.mairie-narbonne.fr.

▶ **Orient Yourself:** The town is south-east of Béziers and east of Carcassonne.

🅿 **Parking:** The central area is a pedestrian zone. The two nearest car parks are on quai Victor-Hugo, and beneath cours Mirabeau.

🕐 **Organizing Your Time:** In summer, it's best to explore early in the morning before it's too hot for comfort, then spend the afternoon at indoor venues like the museums.

👁 **Don't Miss:** The Palais des Archevêques.

A Bit of History

The history of this ancient Mediterranean city is a long one, reaching back many centuries BC. After the defeat of Hannibal, the Roman Empire chose Narbonne to be the commercial centre of the Celtic province, with an artificial port created by diverting an arm of the river Aude. Finally it was made the capital of Gallia Narbonensis (today's Languedoc and Provence regions) and flourished right up to the end of the Empire and the arrival of the Visigoths, who made it the capital of their kingdom.

Trading activity continued (Muslim raiders found the city still worth looting in 793), and medieval shipping made use of the extensive shallow lagoons lining the coast behind the rampart of sand bars. However, in the 14C, the city's large and long-established Jewish community was expelled (as from the rest of France), the famous port silted up, and the town's prosperity came to an abrupt end. The construction of the Canal du Midi in the 17C, the coming of the railway in the 19C, and the development of tourism on the Languedoc coast in the 20C halted the process of decline.

Sights

Cathédrale St-Just★★

The present building was begun in 1272, but construction was halted 82 years later in order to preserve the ramparts which would otherwise have been breached to accommodate the nave. The choir remains, its vaulting reaching the dizzy height of 41m – 135ft. It is in the High Gothic style, with a fine triforium – its columns extend upwards into the lancets of the clerestory windows. The great arches of the apse are crowned with battlements and loopholes. The lofty cloisters (1349-1417) are built in crumbling limestone on the site of a Carolingian church. The cathedral **treasury** *(daily 2-6pm; Jul-Sep: 11am-6pm on Mon-Sat. ⊚ 2.20€)* has a wonderful late-15C **Flemish Tapestry**★★ in silk and gold thread, a 10C ivory missal plaque and a rare marriage casket in rock crystal with intaglio decoration.

Palais des Archevêques

Many building styles are represented here, from the 12C Old Palace (Palais Vieux), the 13C Madeleine Tower (donjon de la Madeleine) and Gilles Aycelin Tower **(donjon Gilles Aycelin★)** *(Jul-Sep: daily 10am-6pm; Oct-Jun: daily 9am-noon, 2-*6pm. ⊚ 2.20€)*, the 14C St Martial Tower (tour St-Martial) and New Palace (Palais Neuf), the 17C Archbishops' Residence (Résidence des archevêques) with its Louis XIII staircase to the City Hall (Hôtel de ville), with its 19C façade.

▶ Musée Archéologique★★
   Musée d'Art et d'Histoire★.
   Basilique St-Paul – chancel★
   Musée Lapidaire★

Excursion

Abbaye de Fontfroide★★

15 km – 9mi southwest. This former Cistercian abbey nestles in a quiet, restful corner of the countryside, planted with cypress trees. The fine flame-coloured shades of yellow ochre and pink in the Corbières sandstone used to build the abbey enhance the serenity of the sight, particularly at sunset. Most of the buildings date from the 12C and 13C.

CIRQUE DE NAVACELLES★★★

MICHELIN MAP 339 G 5

GREEN GUIDE LANGUEDOC ROUSSILLON TARN GORGES

This spectacular 300m – 1 000ft deep basin, separating the Causses – high plateaus – de Larzac and Blandas, marks the former course of the River Vis before it cut through the base of the meander.

▶ **Orient Yourself:** The site is reached by turning off the road between Lodève and Ganges, in the Hérault département.

Visit

On the outer sweep of the meander great screes have been formed; the upper parts of the cliffs are made up of exceptionally thick beds, thinning out at the lower levels where traces remain of old buildings and terraces on the marl and clay deposits. On the valley floor a pretty single-arched bridge leads to the village of Navacelles (which once had a priory). The little settlement clings to a rocky outcrop in order to conserve as much as possible of the belt of cultivable land in the former bed of the river.

In contrast to the harsh conditions prevailing on the arid, windswept causses, the valley floor has a mild microclimate which allows figs to be grown.

MASSIF DE NÉOUVIELLE★★★

MICHELIN MAP 342 M 5
GREEN GUIDE LANGUEDOC ROUSSILLON TARN GORGES

The Massif de Néouvielle, forming part of the high central spine of the Pyrenees, is a veritable museum of glacial topography, with virtually all the features characterising such landscapes, from high, ice-smoothed cliffs and cirques separated by narrow ridges, to hanging valleys, rock-steps and a multitude of lakes and erratic boulders.

- **Information:** 37 r. Vincent Mir, ☎05 62 39 50 81.
- **Orient Yourself:** This high mountain region is best approached from the town of Lanneman.

Driving Tour

The popular little mountain resort of St-Lary-Soulan★ is the starting-point for the spectacular scenic route *(46km – 29mi round trip)* rising up to 1 362m – 4 435ft and leading, via dark fir-woods and many hairpin bends, to a dam (Barrage de **Cap de Long**★), and lakes **(Lac d'Oredon**★ and **Lac d'Aumar**★).

NEVERS★

MICHELIN MAP 319 B10–POPULATION 100 556
GREEN GUIDE BURGUNDY JURA

From the red sandstone bridge spanning the Loire, there is a fine view of the old town of Nevers set in terraces on its limestone hill. Its tall town houses with their roofs of slate and tile are dominated by the high square tower of the great cathedral and the graceful silhouette of the ducal palace.

- **Information:** Palais Ducal, rue Sabatier, ☎03 86 68 46 00.
- **Orient Yourself:** Long established as a stopover on the upper Loire highway, the centre of town clusters on the east bank.

A Bit of History

Nevers was known for its pottery in the Middle Ages. Artistic pottery seems to have been brought here in the 1560s by Italian craftsmen. In the time of Louis XIII and Louis XIV the town was a centre of faience production, with 12 manufactories and producing some of the finest Blue Persian work ever made. There is a fine **collection**★ of Nevers pottery in the museum (**musée municipal**). Nevers flourished as a port until the 19C when the Loire ceased to be navigable. Following her visionary experiences at Lourdes, Bernadette Soubirous came to Nevers in 1866 to enter the convent of **St-Gildard**★ here.

Sights

Palais ducal★
The former residence of the Dukes of Nevers is a fine example of French Renaissance architecture.

Église St-Étienne★
This splendid Romanesque church has a magnificently tiered east end and a beautiful overall pattern of windows in the style of the great abbey church of Cluny. The height of the interior is particularly impressive for a building of its date (1063-97).

- Cathédrale St-Cyr-et-Ste-Julitte★★. Porte du Croux★.

NICE ★★★

MICHELIN MAP 341 E 5–POPULATION 888 784
GREEN GUIDE FRENCH RIVIERA

Enclosed by an amphitheatre of hills, extending around a beautiful blue bay, the capital of the Riviera has artistic treasures, countless attractions, distinctive cuisine, a wonderful climate and a magnificent setting that has long attracted visitors year round.

- **Information:** 5 Promenade des Anglais, and at main Train Station, ☎08 92 70 77 07. www.nicetourisme.com.
- **Orient Yourself:** Start with the Promenade des Anglais – most visitors arrive along this seafront highway. At its eastern end is the old town (Le Vieux Nice), the château hill and the old port. North of it spreads the modern town, reaching to the Cimiez, the ancient Roman settlement.
- **Guided Tours:** There's a choice of walking tours in the Old Town, and bus tours around the city. Ask for details at the tourist office. Ask too about Carte Passe-Musées, a 7-day museum pass (6€).
- **Don't Miss:** A stroll along the Promenade des Anglais; the panorama from the château hill.
- **Organizing Your Time:** At least a full day is necessary to discover Nice. Spend the morning on the oceanfront and in Vieux Nice; reserve the afternoon for Cimiez; and, if you have time, choose an art museum according to your taste – Matisse, Chagall, or the Musée des Beaux-Arts, the Musée d'Art moderne et d'Art Contemporain and the Musée des Arts Asiatiques.
- **Parking:** It is not difficult to drive in Nice (if you know the city), but parking is difficult. As soon as possible, park in one of the many large underground car parks.

A Bit of History

Some 400 000 years ago, bands of elephant hunters made their encampments on the fossil beach at Terra Amata, 26m – 85ft above the present level of the sea. In the 6C BC, Celto-Ligurians settled on the castle hill; a little later it was the turn of merchants and sailors from Marseille; they established themselves around the harbour, followed by the Romans, who favoured the Cimiez district. In 1388, aided and abetted by the **Grimaldi** family, Count Amadeus VII of Savoy incorporated Provence into his domain and made a triumphal entry into Nice.

As a result of the alliance of 1859 between France and Sardinia, Napoleon III undertook to help drive out the Austrians from Lombardy and the Veneto; in return, France was to receive from the House of Savoy the lands to the west of the Alps and around Nice which had once been hers. A plebiscite produced an overwhelming vote in favour of a return to France (25 743 for, 260 against) and the ceremony of annexation took place on 14 June 1860.

Sights

Le Vieux Nice★

The core of the city, huddling at the foot of the castle hill, has a lively, utterly Mediterranean character.

Château

The landscaped slopes of the castle hill with their umbrella pines shading pleasant walks reach a height of 92m – 300ft. The summit provided a place of refuge for the denizens of Cimiez at the time of the fall of the Roman Empire. In the 12C, the Counts of Provence built a castle here which was subsequently strengthened by the Angevin princes and the Dukes of Savoy but was demolished by Louis XIV in 1706. From the top there is a fine **view**★★ over the city, the Pre-Alps and the bay (Baie des Anges).

Place Garibaldi

The square is named after the great fighter for Italian unity who was born in Nice. The ochre walls and arcading of the buildings along its sides recall the urbane elegance characteristic of Piedmontese town planning in the 18C.

Cathédrale Ste-Reparate

This is a fine example of the Baroque style as it developed in Nice. The west front, a pleasant mixture of greens and yellows, is decorated with niches and medallions, topped by an imposing entablature and supported by buttress-pillars with composite capitals. The **interior**★ is enlivened by an elaborate cornice, and in the choir is a frieze outlined in white and gold and decorated with little figures of angels.

Église St-Jacques★

The west front recalls the Gesù church in Rome. Behind it lies a nave whose severity is relieved by an abundance of sculpture. The barrel vault opens into side chapels containing loggias where the local nobility once worshipped.

Place Masséna

The linear park laid out on what was once the bed of the river Paillon is interrupted by this square begun in 1815. Its buildings with their façades rendered in reddish ochre and their arcades recall the planned urban spaces of Turin.

Site archéologique gallo-romain★

Cimiez. 🕒 *Daily except Tue 10am-6pm. Last entry 30min before closing.* 🕒 *Closed 1 Jan, Easter, 1 May, 25 Dec.* 💶 *4€ (includes access to the museum), no charge 1st and 3rd Sun in the month.* ♿ ☎*04 93 81 59 57.*

The Cimiez district originated in the Roman settlement whose growth soon eclipsed that of the older town laid out around the harbour. The archeological site consists mostly of medium-size amphitheatres and the area around the baths.

Monastère★

Cimiez. The monastery church possesses a Pietà of 1475 *(to the right of the entrance)*; though an early work of Louis Bréa, and executed in Gothic style, it is one of his finest achievements, notably in its portrayal of the grieving Mary. To the left of the choir is a later work by the same artist, a Crucifixion (1512) which heralds the Renaissance.

Musée Matisse★★

Cimiez. 🕒 *Daily 10am-6pm.* 🕒 *Closed Tue, 1 Jan, Easter, 1 May, 25 Dec.* 💶 *4€, no charge 1st and 3rd Sun in the month.*

Hotel Negresco, Promenade des Anglais

Jonathan Ogilvie/SXC

Address Book

For coin ranges, see the Legend on the cover flap.

WHERE TO EAT

Salade niçoise, socca, pan-bagnat, poutine, tourte aux blettes, beignets de fleurs de courgettes are just some of the distinctive local specialities to look out for, especially in Le Vieux Nice, the main restaurant district .

La Table d'Alziari – *4 Rue François-Zannin* – ☎*04 93 80 34 03 – Closed 11-22 Jan, 9-20 Aug, 6-17 Dec, Sun and Mon.* Unpretentious family restaurant set up in a small alley of the old district. Typical dishes from Nice and the Provence area, chalked up on a slate, are served in a homey decor, together with wine recommended by the owner.

La Tapenade – *6 Rue Ste-Réparate* – ☎ *04 93 80 65 63* – . Curious decor re-creating a typical street from the south of France, with its shutters, terra-cotta flower pots and strings of garlic. Do not miss the surprising fresco painted on the ceiling. The warm, friendly owners will serve you a pizza, a tapenade or any other local speciality.

Le Pain Quotidien – *3 Rue St-François-de-Paul (Cours Saleya)* – ☎*04 93 62 94 32.* This country-style restaurant specializing in brunch has long wooden tables where guests sit side-by-side, an original formula conducive to a friendly, convivial atmosphere. In addition to the bread baskets and tatsy spreads of jam, honey and hazelnut, there is a wide selection of salads and open sandwiches.

Lou Balico – *22 Avenue St-Jean-Baptiste* – ☎*04 93 85 93 71 – Closed lunch in Jul-Aug.* Three generations of the same family have been serving classic Niçois dishes in this cosy dining room adorned with a piano and guest book with signatures from around the world.

Grand Café de Turin – *5 Place Garibaldi* – ☎*04 93 62 29 52.* This brasserie, which is over 200 years old, has become an institution in Nice. It serves seafood dishes à la carte at reasonable prices throughout the day. Pleasant, welcoming setting, although a bit noisy on the terrace.

L'Escalinada – *22 Rue Pairolière* – ☎*04 93 62 11 71.* – *Closed 15 Nov-15 Dec.* Nestling in the old quarter, this charming restaurant offers attractively presented regional cuisine in a spruce dining room with rustic overtones. Friendly service.

WHERE TO STAY

Star Hôtel – *14 Rue Biscarra* – ☎*04 93 85 19 03 – star-hotel@wanadoo. fr – Closed Nov – 24 rooms – ⌿6€.* Small hotel away from the bustling town center offering simple accommodations, some with a balcony. Close to the Etoile Shopping Center.

Clair Hotel – *23 Boulevard Carnot, Impasse Terra Amata* – ☎*04 93 89 69 89 – 10 rooms – ⌿7.50€.* This converted schoolhouse near the archeological museum has rooms all on one floor (in the old classrooms) and a Mediterranean garden terrace where breakfast is served in the summer. Quiet neighborhood, friendly, family-run atmosphere.

La Pérouse – *11 Quai Rauba-Capéu* – ☎*04 93 62 34 63 – 58 rooms – ⌿23€.* A prime seaside location overlooking the Baie des Anges from the foot of the Château hill, this cosy Provençal-style hotel features a heated swimming pool and grill restaurant set within a garden against the rocky hill. The top floor terrace has panoramic views over the sea, a hot tub and fitness room.

ON THE TOWN

Casino Ruhl – *1 Promenade des Anglais* – ☎*04 97 03 12 22 – Daily 10am to dawn.* The casino boasts 300 slot machines and has facilities for French and English roulette, blackjack, stud poker, etc. American bar. Dinner is coupled with live performances on Fridays. Themed evenings on Thursdays.

Le Mélisande – *Hôtel Palais Maeterlinck, 30 Boulevard Maurice-Maeterlinck, Cap de Nice* – ☎*04 92 00 72 00 – www. palais-maeterlinck.com – Daily 11am-midnight.* This bar attached to the luxury hotel whose terrace dominates the sea and offers splendid views of the Baie des Anges. Champagne cocktails, cigars. The Belgian writer Maurice

Maeterlinck, 1911 Nobel Prize for Literature, once lived on the premises.

Le Relais – *Hôtel Negresco, 37 Promenade des Anglais* – ☎04 93 16 64 00 – *Daily 11.30am-1am, until midnight in winter.* The sumptuous decoration of this bar belonging to the legendary Negresco Hotel has remained the same since 1913: Brussels tapestry (1683), 18C paintings, replicas of the wall lamps adorning the Ballroom in Fontainebleau Château and a rug similar to that chosen by Napoleon I for the King's Bedchamber in Rome. Piano bar every evening.

La Trappa – *Rue de la Préfecture and Rue Gilly* – ☎04 93 80 33 69 – *Daily 5pm-2am.* A lively tapas bar with deep, comfortable settees and red walls awaits you at La Trappa, open since 1886. Sip a Cuban cocktail while you listen to Latin American music (DJ weekends). Friendly atmosphere and local wine list.

SHOPPING

Shopping streets – The streets around Cathédrale Ste-Réparate have many shops selling typical Provençal fabrics *(Rue Paradis and Rue du Marché)*, arts and crafts *(Rue du Pont-Vieux and Rue de la Boucherie)*, olive oil and santons *(Rue St-François-de-Paul)*.

Markets – There are street markets all over town, including: **Fish market** – Pl. St-François *daily except Monday, 6am to 1pm;* **Flower market** – Cours Saleya *daily except Monday, 6am to 5.30pm;* **Marché aux Puces** (Flea market) – Pl. Robilante *daily except Monday 10am-6pm;* **Marché de la Brocante** (Antiques) – Cours Saleya *Mondays, 7.30am-6pm.*

Alziari – *14 Rue St-François-de-Paule* – ☎ 04 93 85 76 92 – www.alziari.com. fr. One of the best addresses in town for olive oil and regional specialities.

La Maison de l'Olive – *18 Rue Pairolière* – ☎04 93 80 01 61. Marseille soaps made from pure olive oil, lotions and scents for the body and home, and regional products such as dried tomatos, lemon jam, marinated capers and olives, and Provençal herbs and spices.

À l'Olivier – *7 Rue St-François-de-Paule* – ☎04 93 13 44 97 – www.olivier-on-line.com. Every brand of French olive oil with the AOC label is sold in this boutique, originally opened in 1822, in Nice since 2004. Also a fine selection of elegant glassware, dishes, tablecloths.

Confiserie Auer – *7 Rue St-François-de-Paule* – ☎04 93 85 77 98 – www.maison-auer.com. A gorgeous vintage boutique selling candied fruit and crystallised flowers from the Nice region, as well as chocolates, and calissons from Aix.

Confiserie Florian – *14 Quai Papacino, on the Port* – ☎04 93 55 43 50 – www.confiserieflorian.com. Guided tours of the factory 9am-noon, 2-6.30pm. Candied fruit, lemon, orange and grapefruit preserve, chocolates and sweets, crystallised petals and delicious jams made with rose, violet and jasmine blossom.

Maison Poilpot – Aux Parfums de Grasse – *10 Rue St-Gaétan* – ☎04 93 85 60 77. This traditional perfumery produces more than 80 different fragrances, including popular Mediterranean scents such as mimosa, rose, violet and lemon.

L'Art Gourmand – *21 Rue du Marché – Old Town* – ☎04 93 62 51 79 – www.nice-ville.com. This Old Nice boutique has nougats, calisson, candied fruit, cookies, pastries, ice cream and northern France specialities. There's a tea room decorated with murals.

CALENDAR OF EVENTS

There are many traditional festivals throughout the year. Ask at the Tourism Office for a complete schedule. Highlights include:

Nice Carnival – This colorful, 2-week extravaganza attracts huge crowds. Events, culminating at Mardi Gras (Shrove Tuesday), include fancy dress, processions, lavish floats, 'battles' where armfuls of flowers and confetti are thrown, and a firework display.

Cougourdons Festival – Cougourdons are dried, painted gourds. The city of Nice pays homage to these vegetables in early April.

Fête de la Mer et de la St-Pierre – Celebrating the sea and St-Peter on the port and Quai des Etats-Unis the last weekend in June.

Nice Jazz Festival – The Roman amphitheatre is the venue for the jazz festival in the last two weeks of July, attended by leading performers from all over the world. ☎0 892 707 407.

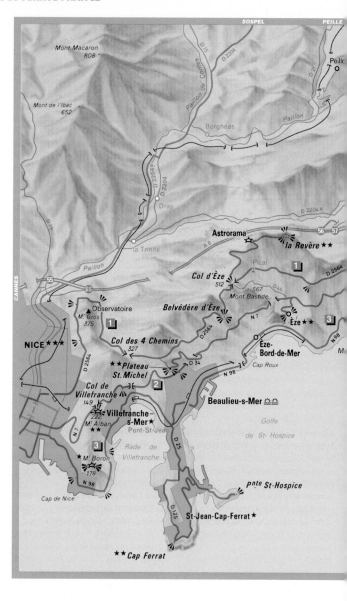

  ☏04 93 81 08 08. www.musee-mat-isse-nice.org.

The museum is housed in the Villa des Arènes; it traces the artist's evolution, from a still-life (*Nature morte aux livres, 1890*) to the *Rococo Armchair (Fauteuil de Rocaille, 1947*) and the *Blue Nude (Nu bleu, 1952)*.

Musée Marc-Chagall★★

At the bottom of Blvd de Cimiez. 🕐 *Jul-Sep: daily 10am-6pm; Oct-Jun: daily 10am-5pm. Last admission 30min before closing.* 🕐 *Closed Tue, 1 Jan, 1 May, 25 Dec.* ☜ *6.50€, no charge 1st Sun in the month.* ☏04 93 53 87 21. www.musee-chagall.fr.

The museum was designed to display the 17 great paintings making up

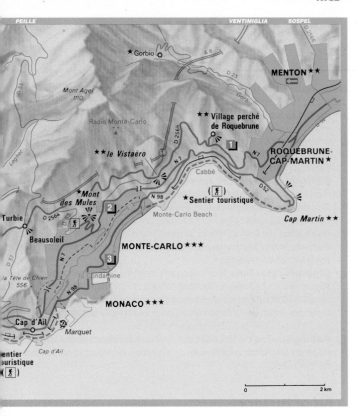

the artist's Biblical Message (painted between 1954 and 1967).

▶ Promenade des Anglais –
Front de mer★★ (seafront).
Musée des Beaux-Arts ★★.
Musée d'Art moderne et d'Art contemporain★★.
www.mamac-nice.org.
Musée Masséna★
Palais des Arts, du Tourisme et des Congrès★ (Acropolis).
Chapelle de la Miséricorde★.
Église St-Martin – St-Augustin – interior★.

Excursion

Corniches de la Riviera★★★
Circular tour of 41km – 26mi – allow 3 hours. The Lower Corniche road skirts the foot of Mont Boron, giving fine views over Villefranche-sur-Mer and its bay. The highly indented coastline is the result of the recent folding and subsequent drowning of the limestone Pre-Alps.

Both **Cap Ferrat**★★ and nearby headland, Pointe St-Hospice, offer splendid views of the Riviera with its corniche roads; the village of Èze-Bord-de-Mer, the fashionable resort of Beaulieu, Cap d'Ail can all be identified, and rising out of the sea in the distance is Cap Martin.

Clinging like an eagle's nest to its inaccessible rock spike, **Èze**★★ seems the very archetype of a hill village. It was inhabited by the Ligurians and by the Phoenicians, then fortified against raiders from the sea. In 1706 both the village and its castle were demolished on the orders of Louis XIV, but it was rebuilt after 1760.

NÎMES

MICHELIN MAP 339 L 5–POPULATION 148 889

GREEN GUIDE PROVENCE

Nîmes lies between the limestone hills of the Garrigue to the north and the alluvial plain of the Costière du Gard to the south. Its elegant and bustling boulevards are shaded by lotus-trees. The quality of its Roman remains is outstanding.

- **Information:** 6 r. Auguste, ☎04 66 58 38 00. www.ot-nimes.fr.
- ▶ **Orient Yourself:** Heading northwest along boulevard Victor-Hugo, the Maison Carrée appears in the centre of an elegant paved square separated from the Carré d'art by the boulevard itself. From here you can take the narrow rue de l'Horloge then turn right into place de l'Horloge and then left into rue de la Madeleine to find the main shopping street. Nîmes offers a range of guided tours – ask for details at the tourist office.
- **Don't Miss:** The Roman Arènes, Maison Carrée and Jardin de les Fontaines**.** *(A combined ticket ("Nîmes romaine") gives access to the Arènes, Maison Carrée and Tour Magne for just 9.50€).*
- **Organizing Your Time:** Those who can't stand the heat should avoid the city in August when it becomes an absolute furnace, even at night. Visitors who object to bull-fighting or crowds are advised not to come during the long weekend of Pentecost (Whitsun – 7th Sun after Easter) when entry just about anywhere is almost impossible, as is finding accomodation.
- **Parking:** Entering the city along the canal de la Fontaine and boulevard Victor-Hugo, go around the amphitheatre to get to the underground car park beneath the Esplanade.

A Bit of History

Emperor Augustus heaped privileges on Nîmes and allowed the building of fortifications. The town, situated on the Domitian Way, then proceeded to erect splendid buildings: the Maison Carrée along the south side of the forum, an amphitheatre able to hold 24 000 people, a circus, baths fed by an imposing aqueduct, the Pont du Gard. In the 2C the town won favour with Emperors Hadrian and Antoninus Pius (whose wife's family came from Nîmes); it continued to flourish and build and reached the peak of its glory.

Maison Carrée

Address Book

For coin ranges, see the Legend on the cover flap.

WHERE TO EAT

Bistrot des Arènes – *11 rue Bigot – ☎ 04 66 21 40 18. Closed Aug, Sat lunch and Sun.* Lyon specialities in a delightful setting crammed with objects including Lyonnais Guignol puppets.

Le Bistrot au Chapon Fin – *3 pl. du Château-Fadaise – ☎04 66 67 34 73. Closed Aug. Sat lunch and Sun.* Quirky bistro with feria and movie posters and daily dishes listed on a blackboard.

Le Bouchon et L'Assiette – *5 bis rue Sauve – ☎04 66 62 02 93. Closed 2-17 Jan, 29 Apr-2 May, 29 Jul-23 Aug, Tue lunch and Wed.* A carefully chosen decor, embellished with paintings and antiques, a warm welcome, and tasty seasonal cooking.

Aux Plaisirs des Halles – *4 rue Littré – ☎04 66 36 01 02 . Closed 12-20 Aug, Sun evenings and Mon except evenings in Jul-Aug.* Behind a discreet façade is an elegant room with armchairs draped in fabric, a pretty patio terrace, and good food and wine.

WHERE TO STAY

Hôtel Amphithéâtre – *4 rue des Arènes – ☎04 66 67 28 51. Closed 2-15 Jan – 16 rooms – ☐ 6.50€.* Near the amphitheatre in a pedestrian street, this small, family-run hotel with its slightly austere façade, is an excellent address for those travelling on a low budget. It offers quite spacious rooms decorated with rustic furniture.

New Hôtel la Baume – *21 rue Nationale – ☎04 66 76 28 42 – 34 rooms – ☐ 10€.* This 17C mansion successfully blends contemporary and antique styles. An interior stone staircase leads to the simple bedrooms, a few of which have pretty, French-style painted ceilings.

ON THE TOWN

The city is characterised by a huge number and variety of cafés including Café-concerts, bodegas, Irish pubs or the great fin-de-siècle cafés: each has its own following.

La Grand Bourse – *2 bd des Arènes – ☎ 04 66 67 21 91.* With its Napoleon III style coffered ceiling, a terrace facing the amphitheatre and deep comfortable rattan armchairs, this is the most prestigious café in Nîmes. Excellent, professional service attracts customers of all ages and backgrounds.

Bar Hemingway – *15 rue Gaston-Bois-sier – ☎02 66 21 90 30.* Opening onto a garden with redwood and cedar trees, a fountain and sculptures, the Hemingway bar of the Hotel Imperator Concorde is an oasis of calm and magic. Photographs evoke the presence in this bar of two lovers of tauromachy: Ava Gardner and Ernest Hemingway.

SHOPPING

Maison Villaret – *13 rue de la Madeleine – ☎04 66 67 41 79.* Crunchy almond biscuits known as *croquants*.

Wine – *La Vinothèque – 18 rue Jean-Rebou – ☎04 66 67 20 44.* Local wines.

Markets – Large market on Mon on bd Gambetta. Organic market Fri mornings on av Jean-Jaurès. Flea market Sun mornings in the Costières stadium car park. Evening market, Jul-Aug, Thur 6-10pm ('Les jeudis de Nîmes').

ENTERTAINMENT

Programmes – See the daily newspaper *Midi-Libre*, the weekly publication *La Semaine de Nîmes* or its rival the *Gazette de Nîmes,* or *Le César* (free from the tourist office).

Ferias and bullfighting – There are three major annual ferias: the "spring" feria which takes place in February, *novilladas* take place throughout the weekend; the Pentecost feria, the most well-known, across the Whitsun long weekend, includes a pégoulade along the boulevards, *abrivados, novilladas* and corridas throughout the day and evening as well as other entertainments all over the city; the harvest feria, the most traditional of all, takes place in mid-September.

Amphitheatre – As well as ferias, the amphitheatre also hosts rock and pop concerts, and all kinds of fairs, conventions and tournaments.

Le Printemps du jazz – (3rd week in March) Jazz concerts in a variety of venues around town.

Sights

Arènes★★★

🕐 Jun-Aug: 9am-7pm; Apr-May, Sep: 9am-6pm; Mar and Oct: 9am-5.30pm; Jan-Feb: 9.30am-4.30pm. 🕐Closed to visitors during bullfights and shows. Visit with audioguide ☜7.70€. ☎ 04 66 76 72 77.

This superb structure was built in the reign of Augustus, possibly some 80 years before the amphitheatre at Arles. The scale of the great structure is extraordinarily impressive, as is the achievement in cutting, transporting and placing stonework of such dimensions with such precision. The big, crowded bullfights still held here give a flavour of the original arena.

Maison Carrée★★★

🕐 Mid-Mar to mid-Oct: 9am-7pm; mid-Oct to mid-Mar: 10am-5pm. 🕐 Closed 1 Jan, 1 May, 25 Dec. No charge. ☎ 04 66 58 38 00.

This is the purest and best preserved of all Roman temples. It was built in the reign of Augustus (1C BC) – it is not known which cult was observed here. It was inspired by the Temple of Apollo in Rome.

Jardin de la Fontaine★★

In Roman times this site was occupied by a spring, a theatre, a temple and baths. Today's shady gardens exemplify the subtle use of water in the landscapes of Languedoc. They were laid out in the characteristic manner of the 18C, with pools leading into a canal, balustraded walks, and porticoes.

▶ Musée Archéologique★.
  Musée des Beaux-Arts★.
  Musée du Vieux-Nîmes★.
  Carré d'art★

ABBAYE DE **NOIRLAC**★★

MICHELIN MAP 323 K 6
GREEN GUIDE DORDOGNE BERRY LIMOUSIN

One of the best preserved medieval monasteries in France, Noirlac occupies an exceptional setting for the Gregorian chants, concerts and cultural events that take place here.

🛈 **Information:** pl. de la République, St Amand-Montrond,☎02 48 96 16 86.
▶ **Orient Yourself:** The abbey is just outside the town of St Amand-Montrond.

Visit

🕐 Jul and Aug: daily 9.45am-6.30pm; Apr-Jun and Sep: daily 9.45am-12.30pm, 2-6.30pm. Oct-Nov and Feb-Mar: daily 9.45am-12.30pm, 2-5pm. 🕐 Closed Dec-Jan (call for specific dates). Call for admission prices. ☎02 48 62 01 01.

The perfect simplicity of the abbey church (**église abbatiale**) dates from 1150-60. It follows the plan of the great abbey at Clairvaux. The modern glass is the work of Jean-Pierre Raynaud, aided by craftsmen from Chartres and Bourges. The Gothic cloisters were added in the 13C.

OBERNAI★★

MICHELIN MAP 315 I 6–POPULATION 9 610
GREEN GUIDE ALSACE LORRAINE CHAMPAGNE

Sited where the lower, vine-covered slopes of Mont Ste-Odile meet the plain, its ruined walls eloquent of its ancient independence and its narrow, winding streets lined with high-gabled houses, the little town of Obernai seems to represent the very essence of Alsace.

▸ **Information:** pl. du Beffroi, ☏03 88 95 64 13.
▸ **Orient Yourself:** Obernai is north of Colmar on the main highway to Strasbourg.

Sight

Place du Marché★★

With its cheerfully-coloured timber-framed buildings, the picturesque market-place is the centrepiece of Obernai, graced by a fountain of 1904 with a statue of St Odile. It has a Town Hall **(Hôtel de ville★)** of the 15C-16C with a fine oriel window and sculpted balcony, a 16C Corn Hall **(Ancienne halle aux blés★)** much restored but with a stork's nest above its doorway, and the Chapel Tower **(Tour de la Chapelle★)**, a 13C bell-tower topped by a spire 60m – nearly 200ft above the ground.

▸ Maisons anciennes★ (old houses).

L'OISANS★★★

MICHELIN MAP 333 J 7
GREEN GUIDE FRENCH ALPS

In this second highest massif in France after Mont Blanc, the population is grouped in villages sited on high terraces reached by spectacular narrow roads.

▸ **Orient Yourself:** The region is largely within the Parc National des Ecrins, between the rivers Romanche and Drac.

Excursions

Les Écrins

These bare mountains between the valleys of the Romanche, Drac and Durance look down on more than 100km2– some 40sq miles of glaciers. The Route des Grandes Alpes (👁 *see ROUTE DES GRANDES ALPES*) gives fine views of the north and east faces of the massif (from the Col du Galibier, the Oratoire du Chazelet, and from La Grave), cut by isolated valleys with their typical way of life and served by long cul-de-sac roads; the best-known is the valley of the Vénéon leading to La Bérarde.

Bassin du Bourg d'Oisans★

Until the 13C the fertile basin was a glacial lake, now filled in by material brought down by the Romanche and its tributary, the Vénéon. This is the economic centre of the region.

Vallée du Vénéon★★★

31km – 19mi from Bourg-d'Oisans to La Bérarde.

The road up to La Bérarde is a lesson in glacial geomorphology made more dramatic by the scale of the great U-shaped valley and the ruggedness of its high granite walls, moraines, waterfalls in hanging valleys, and compact little villages, before reaching La Bérarde, now a climbing centre.

ORADOUR-SUR-GLANE★★

MICHELIN MAP 325 D 5–POPULATION 2 025
GREEN GUIDE DORDOGNE BERRY LIMOUSIN

This small country town where the 642 inhabitants were massacred in a revenge attack by retreating Germans on 10 June 1944 is preserved unchanged as a fascinating and deeply moving memorial.

- **Information:** pl. du Champs-de-Foire, ☎05 55 03 13 73.
- **Orient Yourself:** The site is located 24km/15mi northwest of Limoges.
- **Don't Miss:** Take the time for a look around the Centre de la Mémoire, at the entrance to the ruined village.

Visit

Access to the ruins of the martyred village via the Centre de la Memoire. The centre offers a permanent exhibit dedicated to the rise of Nazism and the massacre of the villagers. ⊘ *Jul-Aug: 9am-7pm; Mar-Jun and Sep-Oct: 9am-6pm; Feb, Nov and early to mid-Dec: 9am-5pm. Last admission 1hr before closing.* ⊜ *6€.* ☎*05 55 43 04 30.*

The stark walls of the burnt-out village have been kept as an eloquent reminder. Harassed by the Resistance, the troops made a characteristically brutal example of this entirely innocent place, massacring its inhabitants (men, women and children), and laying waste the village itself. The victims are buried in the village cemetery; a memorial commemorates the terrible deed.

ORANGE★★

MICHELIN MAP 332 B9–POPULATION 27 989
GREEN GUIDE PROVENCE

Gateway to the Midi, Orange is famous for its remarkable Roman remains, including the triumphal arch and the Roman Theatre, as well as for its prestigious international music festival, Chorégies.

- **Information:** I5 cours Aristide Briand, ☎04 90 34 70 88. www.otorange.fr
- **Orient Yourself:** Orange, on the River Meyne, close to the Rhône, is at the meeting of autoroutes and other highways. The old city centre is on the left bank of the Meyne. By far the best approach is on the N7 (from Montélimar), which enters the town via its majestic triumphal arch.

A Bit of History

Orange flourished in the days of the Pax Romana as an important staging-post on the great highway between Arles and Lyon. In the 16C, it came into the possession of William the Silent, ruler of the German principality of Nassau, then Stadtholder of the United Provinces. He took the title of Prince of Orange and founded the Orange-Nassau line. Orange is still proud of its association with the royal house of the Netherlands, whose preferred title is Prince (or Princess) of Orange. In 1678 under the Treaty of Nijmegen, the town became French territory.

Sights

Théâtre antique★★★

⊘ *Jun, Jul, and Aug: 9am-7pm. Apr, May, Sep: 9am-6pm. Mar and Oct: 9am-5.30pm. Jan-Feb and Nov-Dec: 9.30am-4.30pm.* ⊜ *7.50€.* ☎*04 90 51 17 60. www.theatre-antique.com.*

Arc de Triomphe, Orange

B.Kaufmann/MICHELIN

Dating from the reign of Augustus, this theatre is the best-preserved structure of its type in the whole of the Roman world. The stage wall measures 103x36m – 340x120ft; Louis XIV called it "the finest wall in all the kingdom". Its outer face is of striking simplicity, interrupted only by the mounts for the poles supporting the awnings shading the audience from the sun.

On the auditorium side, the wall has lost its marble facing and mosaic decoration, its columns and its statues. The great statue of Augustus has been replaced in its central niche; together with some remaining hammer-finished granite blocks, it gives some idea of how the theatre must have appeared originally.

Arc de Triomphe★★

This was built between the years AD 21 and 26. On its north and east sides are reliefs depicting the exploits of the Second Legion in Gaul (weapons both of Gauls and of Amazons), the triumph of Rome (captured Gauls in chains) and Roman domination of the seas following the naval battle of Actium (anchors, oars, warships).

ORCIVAL★★

MICHELIN MAP 326 E 8–POPULATION 244

GREEN GUIDE AUVERGNE THE RHÔNE VALLEY

Many houses in this tiny Auvergne village, famed for its Romanesque basilica, still have their original roof coverings of tiles cut from the phonolitic lavas of the nearby Roche Tuilière, the core of an ancient volcano.

▯ **Information:** Le Bourg, ☎04 73 65 89 77. www.terresdomes-sancy.com

▶ **Orient Yourself:** The village is high in the Volcanoes Regional Park, south-west of Clermont-Ferrand.

Sights

Basilique Notre-Dame★★

Illustration ⚲ *see Introduction: Art – Architecture.* Completed around 1130, this basilica is a fine example of the Auvergne Romanesque, with a many-tiered apse, powerful buttresses and massive arches. Inside, the majestic crossing is lit by 14 windows, while both chancel and crypt, the latter with a spacious ambulatory, are masterpieces of their kind.

In the chancel is a **Virgin Enthroned**★ still with its original gilt ornamentation;

one side of the face (left) is that of an Auvergne peasant woman, the other (right) of a society lady.

AVEN D'**ORGNAC**★★★

MICHELIN MAP 331 I 8

GREEN GUIDE PROVENCE

This extraordinary chasm, Aven d'Orgnac, lies among the woods covering the Ardèche plateau. It was first explored by Robert de Joly (1887-1968) on 19 August 1935. Joly was an electrical engineer, fascinated by cars and planes but above all by speleology; it was due to his efforts that the mysteries of France's underground world were revealed, he himself being responsible for numerous "firsts".

▶ **Orient Yourself:** The site is in the Ardeche region, south of the river gorges.

Guided Tour: The cavern is visited in guided groups on a 1hr tour – simply arrive and wait until the next departure. Take a sweater, as the temperature inside the cavern is around 10.5°C. Also bear in mind that during the tour you will go up and down 788 steps.

Visit

🕐 Jul and Aug: daily 9.30am-6pm; Apr-Jun and Sep: daily 9.30am-5.30pm; Oct to mid-Nov: daily 9.30am-noon, 2-5.15pm; Feb-Mar and Christmas vacation: daily 10.30am-noon, 2-4.45pm. 🕐 Closed mid-Nov to end Jan. 🚌 9.40€ (children: 5.80€), ticket includes museum. ☎04 75 38 65 10.

Of the four caverns at Orgnac, only **Orgnac I** has so far been opened up to the public. The caverns owe their origin to an underground stream which linked up the Cèze and Ardèche rivers. Over the millennia the erosion and corrosion created extraordinary concretions. Smashed by gigantic earthquakes, the broken pieces formed the base for new stalagmites, which in the lower chamber developed a variety of forms: bayonet-like spikes, "stacks of plates" and "pinecones".

Orgnac III was inhabited 300 000 years ago; the museum **(musée)** has displays on the cultures which flourished in the region before the Bronze Age.

ORLÉANS★

MICHELIN MAP 318 I 4–POPULATION 263 292

GREEN GUIDE CHÂTEAUX OF THE LOIRE

Orléans grew up on the great bend in the Loire between the rich cornfields of the Beauce to the north and the heaths and forests of the Sologne to the south. For a time the city was the capital of France. Place du Martroi, with its statue of Joan of Arc, is the centre of the historic town.

▪ **Information:** 2 pl. de l'Etape, ☎02 38 24 05 05. www.tourisme-orleans.com.

▶ **Orient Yourself:** The city occupies a site at the Loire's closest point to Paris, and is easily reached by excellent road and rail links. The city centre is on the north bank.

A Bit of History

The **Siege of 1428-29** was one of the great episodes in the history of France, marking the country's rebirth after a period of despair. It began on 12 October 1428, as the Earl of Salisbury attempted to take the bridge over the Loire and thus link up with the other English forces in central and southern France. Lasting almost seven months, the siege was the scene of one of the first-ever (albeit inconclusive) artillery duels. On 29 April 1429, **Joan of Arc** arrived from Chinon (& see CHINON); she skirted Orléans to the south and entered the city by the Burgundy Gate (Porte de Bourgogne), several days in advance of the army advancing along the north bank of the river. By 7 May, victory seemed assured, and on the 8th the English capitulated. In Orléans, Joan enjoyed the hospitality of Jacques Boucher, whose fine half-timbered dwelling with its museum is now known as Joan of Arc House (**Maison de Jeanne d'Arc**★).

Statue of Joan of Arc

Sights

Musée des Beaux-Arts★★

Pl. Ste-Croix. ◑ *Daily except Mon 9.30am-12.15pm, 1.30-5.45pm, Sun and public holidays 1.30-6pm.* ◑ *Closed public holidays.* ◉ *3€ (under 16 years: no charge), no charge 1st Sun in the month.* ✆ 02 38 79 21 55. www.orleans.fr.
This museum houses some of the richest collections in France, especially of French painting from the 16C to the 20C, including Courbet, Boudin, Gauguin,

Soutine, and even Max Jacob (better known as a writer).

Cathédrale Ste-Croix★

Construction of the cathedral lasted from the 13C to the 16C. The nave was torn down by the Huguenots in 1568, but rebuilt in composite Gothic style by **Henri IV**, mindful of the city's loyalty to him.
The woodwork (**boiseries**★★) of the choir stalls (1706) includes splendidly carved medallions and panels adorning the high backs.
In the crypt (**crypte**) are traces of the three buildings which preceded the present cathedral.

◖◖ Musée historique★.
Musée des Sciences naturelles★
Parc Floral de la Source★★ (at Olivet).
www.parfloral-lasource.fr.

ÎLE D'OUESSANT★★

MICHELIN MAP 308 A 4–POPULATION 1 062

GREEN GUIDE BRITTANY

Most of the island's male residents are professional seamen, many in the Navy. The few fishermen trap lobsters. The population lives in scattered hamlets or in the little capital of Lampaul, with its tiny harbour and the mausoleum where the Proella crosses representing those lost at sea are assembled.

- **Information:** From the ferry operator or airline.
- ▶ **Orient Yourself:** The island is open to pedestrians and cyclists only, and reached from the coast of Brittany by a 15m flight from Brest or by ferry from Brest (2h15m), Le Conquet (30m-1h) or Camaret (1h15m).
- **Organizing Your Time:** Almost all ferry crossings are early in the morning.

Geography

The island is a fragment of the Léon plateau on the mainland, 25 km – 16mi away. Two outcrops of granite running northeast-southwest enclose a sunken area of mica-schist much eroded by the sea to form bays to the southwest (Baie de Lampaul) and to the northeast (Baie du Stiff).

Where there is shelter from the wind, camellias, aloes and agaves can grow, but the characteristic vegetation of the island is heather and dwarf gorse. The meagre grasses nourish a small flock of sheep. The cliffs of Ushant and its neighbouring islands house numbers of migrating and nesting birds.

Visit

For all ferry information, reservations, crossing times and prices, contact **Compagnie Maritime Penn Ar Bed** ☎02 98 80 80 80. www.pennarbed.com. *For flight information and bookings, contact* **Finistair**, ☎ 02 98 84 64 87. www.finistair.fr.

Côte Sauvage★★★

4hr round trip on foot starting at Lampaul. The headlands and inlets of Ushant's rocky northwestern coastline have a rugged and dramatic beauty. The most spectacular locations include Keller Island (Île de Keller), Penn-ar-Ru-Meur and the Cadoran islet (Îlot de Cadoran).

The 300 or so vessels which pass each day are guided by five great light-houses. The one at **Creac'h**, which houses the **Centre d'Interpretation des Phares et Balises** (open daily 10.30am-6.30pm (5pm in winter), ☎02 98 48 80 70), a historical museum on lighthouses and beacons, is the most powerful in the world; together wth its counterpart at Land's End in Cornwall it marks the western limit of the English Channel. The light at **Stiff** with its towers built by Vauban in 1695 gives a splendid **view**★★ over the roll-ing sea. The lighthouses play a vital role: over the last hundred years 54 wrecks have been recorded.

GOUFFRE DE PADIRAC★★

MICHELIN MAP 337 G 2
GREEN GUIDE DORDOGNE BERRY LIMOUSIN

Padirac Chasm (Gouffre de Padirac), hollowed out of the limestone mass of the Gramat plateau (Causse de Gramat), and reaching an underground river, is an astonishing natural phenomenon.

Information: All local tourist offices in the Dordogne and surrounding region have information about the Gouffre.

▶ **Orient Yourself:** The Gouffre lies about 2km/1mi from the village of Padirac, in the Lot département.

A Bit of History

The chasm served as a refuge for the people living on the causse during the Hundred Years War and the Wars of Religion, but it would appear that it was towards the end of the 19C, following a violent flooding of the river, that a practicable line of communication opened between the bottom of the well and the underground galleries.

The speleologist, **Edouard A Martel,** was the first to discover the passage, in 1892. He then undertook nine expeditions and finally reached the Hall of the Great Dome.

Padirac was opened to tourists for the first time, in 1898. Since then, numerous speleological expeditinos have uncovered 22km/13.5mi of underground galleries. The 1947 expedition proved by fluorescein colouring of the water that the Padirac river reappears above gound 11km/7mi away where the Lombard rises and at St George's spring in the Montvalent Amphitheatre near the Dordogne. During the expeditions of 1984 and 1985, a prehistoric site was discovered, with bones of mammoths, bison, bears and other animals, all of which were found to date from between 150 000 and 200 000 years ago. Among the bones were chipped flints dating from between 30 000 and 50 000 years ago.

Thanks to the efforts of **Guy de Lavaur** (1903-86), the total known length of the subterranean network at Padirac rose from 2km – 1.5mi to 15km – 9mi.

Visit

Exhibited in the entrance hall are copies of some of the bones found in the prehistoric site.

The chasm *(1hr 30min)* itself is like a gigantic well of striking width (99m – 325ft around its rim) and depth (75m – 246ft to the rubble cone formed by the collapse of the original roof). With its walls covered in vegetation and the overflow from stalagmites, it is one of the most atmospheric of France's underground domains.

The underground river flows 103m – 340ft beneath the surface of the plateau, to reappear on the surface near the natural amphitheatre at Montvalent 11km – 7mi away on the Dordogne. Some 5km – 3mi of its main channel and tributaries have been explored.

The Grand Pilier, Grande Pendeloque of the Lac de la Pluie and the **Salle du Grand Dôme** are among the most striking of all natural monuments of the underground world.

PARIS★★★

MICHELIN MAP 312 D 2–POPULATION 9 644 507
GREEN GUIDE NORTHERN FRANCE AND PARIS REGION

The brilliance and greatness of Paris—its evocative spirit, the imposing dignity of its avenues and squares, its vast cultural wealth and unique flair and style—are known the world over. The dominance of Paris in France's intellectual, artistic, scientific and political life can be traced back to the 12C when the Capetian kings made it their capital.

Information: There are several branches of the tourist office in the city. The main office is at 25, rue des Pyramides.

The other branches are Bureau d'accueil Gare de Lyon, Bureau d'accueil Gare du Nord, Bureau d'accueil Anvers, Bureau d'accueil Paris Expo / Porte de Versailles, Bureau d'accueil Clémenceau, Bureau d'accueil du Carrousel du Louvre (Ile-de-France) and the Syndicat d'Initiative de Montmartre.

☎0892 68 3000 (0.34 €/min). www.paris-touristoffice.com.

▶ **Orient Yourself:** The Seine River flows from east to west across the city. Places north of the river are on the *rive droite*, while those to the south are on the *rive gauche*. Paris is divided into 20 *arrondissements* (districts or neighbourhoods), each one with its own local government and characteristics. Each arrondissement is futher divided into a number of neighborhoods determined by history and the people who live there. The **metro** is the easiest and most economical way of moving around the city. Line 1, which crosses Paris from east to west, services many of the most famous attractions: the Louvre, the Champs-Élysées and the Arc de Triomphe. Line 4 is useful for travelling across the city from north to south. The metro also services the immediate suburbs of Paris, but for those a bit farther out, use the RER suburban trains.

Don't Miss: Many of the city's world-famous attractions are worth making an effort to see, among them the Arc de Triomphe, Place de la Concorde, Eiffel Tower, Notre-Dame Cathedral, the Champs-Élysées, the Latin Quarter, Montmartre, the Louvre and the Musée d'Orsay.

Especially For Kids: La Villette encompasses the child-friendly Cité des Sciences et l'Industrie, the spherical cinema La Géode and the Cité des Enfants, which has many interactive exhibits and presentations for youngsters.

✕ For comprehensive suggestions for Where to Stay and Where to Eat in Paris, consult the red-cover *Michelin Guide Paris* and the *Michelin Green Guide Paris*.

A Bit of History

Origins

At the time of the fall of the Roman Empire towards the end of the 5C, Paris was a modest township founded seven centuries previously by Gallic fishermen. Following its occupation by the **Romans**, the settlement had been extended south of the river to where the remains of the Cluny Baths and a 2C amphitheatre now stand (the "Latin Quarter"). In the 3C St Denis, Paris' first bishop, had met his martyrdom and the Barbarians had razed the place to the ground. This destruction, together with the threat posed by Attila's hordes (but supposedly averted by the intervention of St Genevieve), had caused the inhabitants to withdraw to the security of the Île de la Cité.

Clovis, King of **the Franks**, settled in Paris in 508. Two years later, he founded an abbey south of the Seine in honour of St Genevieve, just as 35 years previously a basilica had been erected over the tomb of St Denis. In 885, for the fifth time in 40 years, the Norsemen sailed up the river and attacked Paris; Eudes, son of Robert the Strong, bravely led the local resistance, and was elected king of "France" in 888; from then on, the town

Eiffel Tower

A. Eil/MICHELIN

became the royal seat, albeit with some interruptions.

The Capetian dynasty (987-1328)

In 1136, Abbot Suger rebuilt the abbey church of St-Denis in the revolutionary Gothic style, an example soon followed by Maurice de Sully at Notre-Dame. Between 1180 and 1210, **Philippe Auguste** surrounded the growing city with a continuous ring of fortifications anchored on the Louvre fortress. In 1215 France's first university was founded on the Ste-Geneviève hill.

The House of Valois (1328-1589)

On 22 February 1358, Étienne Marcel, the merchants' provost, succeeded in rousing the townsfolk to break into the Law Courts (Palais de Justice); entering the Dauphin's apartments, he slew two of the future Charles V's counsellors before his very eyes. On becoming king, **Charles V** quit this place of ill memory. In 1370, he built himself a stronghold in the eastern part of the city, the Bastille, which became the centrepiece of a new ring of fortifications.

Paris was taken by the English in 1418. **Joan of Arc** was wounded in front of Porte St-Honoré trying to retake the city in 1429. Paris was won back for France eight years later by Charles VII.

In 1492, the discovery of America marked the first beginnings of a new outlook and the modern age. The Neapolitan artists brought back by **Charles VIII** from his campaigns in Italy were introducing new trends in taste and thought; the influence of the Renaissance became apparent in many new buildings. In the 1560s, the brothers Androuet Du Cerceau drew up the plans for the Flore Pavilion abutting the Louvre to the west, then set about the construction of the Pont Neuf (New Bridge), which today is the city's oldest surviving bridge.

On 24 August 1572, the bells rang out from the tower of St-Germain-l'Auxerrois to signal the start of the St Bartholomew's Day Massacre (i.e. of Protestants). Henry of Navarre, the future Henri IV, just married to Marguerite of Valois, barely escaped with his life. In 1589 Henri III was assassinated at St-Cloud in 1589 by the monk Jacques Clément. This violent act marked the end of the Valois line.

The Bourbons (1589-1789)

In 1594 Paris opened its gates to **Henri IV**, the new king who had renounced his Protestant faith and succeeded in pacifying the country. But on 14 May 1610 in the Rue de la Ferronnerie, this monarch too fell victim to an assassin.

Under **Louis XIII** (1610-43), Métezeau designed an imposing Classical west front for St-Gervais Church, the first of its kind in Paris; Salomon de Brosse built the Luxembourg Palace for Marie de' Medici; Jean Androuet Du Cerceau laid out the courtyards and gardens of the Hôtel de Béthune-Sully; as well as erecting a church for the Sorbonne with Classical columns on its courtyard side, Lemercier built the Palais-Royal for Richelieu. On the king's death in 1643, Anne of Austria became Regent, acting in concert with Mazarin and continuing the policies of Richelieu. Paris fell prey to the series of disturbances caused by unrest among the nobility and known as the Fronde; the young king came to the conclusion that it might be advantageous to separate Court from city.

The 23-year-old **Louis XIV** began his long and highly personal reign in 1661. Even more than the splendour of court life, it was the extraordinary advancement of the arts and literature at this time that gave Paris and France such prestige in Europe. Under the protection of a king keen to encourage artistic endeavour and promote creative confidence, writers, painters, sculptors and

Seal of the Watermen's Guild (1210)

landscapers flourished as never before. In the space of 20 years, the great Le Nôtre redesigned the parterres of the Tuileries; Claude Perrault provided the Louvre with its fine colonnade and built the Observatory; Le Vau completed the greater part of both the Institut de France and the Louvre. France's "Century of Greatness" came to an end with Louis XIV's death in 1715.

The country now found itself, for the second time, under the rule of a five-year-old. The running of the country was therefore put into the hands of a regent, Philippe d'Orléans; the first action of the court was to pack its bags and quit the boredom of Versailles for the gaiety of the capital. A long period of peace accompanied the years of corruption; for 77 years France experienced no foreign incursions. Literary salons flourished, notably those of the Marquise de Lambert, Mme Du Deffand and Mme Geoffrin, all helping the spread of new ideas in what became known as the **Age of Enlightenment**. The Palais Bourbon (1722-28), which now houses the National Assembly, was erected at this time.

The personal rule exercised by **Louis XV** was discredited by his favourites, but Paris nevertheless witnessed a number of great personalities and important advances; such as Charles de la Condamine, a surveyor and naturalist responsible for the discovery of rubber (1751); Jussieu, incumbent of the Chair in Botany at the Botanical Gardens, responsible for a systematic classification of plants (1759) and for many advances in pharmacology; Diderot, author, together with d'Alambert, of the great *Encyclopaedia*, a splendid summary of the technology of the age; Chardin, who had lodgings in the Louvre, devoted himself to working in pastel; Robert Pothier, who wrote the *Treatise of Obligations*; Ange-Jacques Gabriel, the last and most famous of a line of architects linked to Mansart and Robert de Cotte, who between them gave France a hundred years of architectural unity; it was he who designed the magnificent façades fronting the Place de la Concorde, the west front of St-Roch Church and the École Militaire (Military Academy). Finally there was Soufflot, creator of the dome which crowns the Panthéon.

Distinguished furniture-makers were at work too: Lardin with his cabinets and commodes with rosewood inlay, and Boudin with his virtuoso marquetry and secret compartments; they anticipate the masters who were to emerge in the following reign.

Revolution and Empire (1789-1814)

In 1788, King **Louis XVI (1774-92)** decided to convene the States-General. The delegates assembled at Versailles on 5 May 1789. As a result, on 17 June, the States-General transformed itself into a **National Assembly** which styled itself the Constituent Assembly on 9 July; the monarchy would eventually become a constitutional one.

On **14 July 1789**, in the space of less than an hour, the people of Paris took over the Bastille in the hope of finding arms there; the outline of the demolished fortress can still be traced in the paving on the west side of the Place de la Bastille (14 July became a day of national celebration in 1879). On 17 July, in the City Hall (Hôtel de Ville), Louis XVI kissed the recently adopted tricolour cockade. The feudal system was abolished on 4 August, and the Declaration of the Rights of Man adopted on 26 August; on 5 October, the Assembly moved into the riding-school of the Tuileries, and the royal family was brought from Versailles and installed in the Tuileries Palace.

© The Gallery Collection/Corbis

Louis XVI by Antoine-Francois Callet (detail)

On 12 July 1790 the Church became subject to the Civil Constitution for the Clergy. Two days later, a great crowd gathered on the Champ-de-Mars to celebrate the anniversary of the fall of the Bastille; Talleyrand, Bishop of Autun as well as statesman and diplomat, celebrated mass on the altar of the nation and the king reaffirmed his oath of loyalty to the country.

After his attempt to join Bouillé's army at Metz had been foiled, Louis was brought back to Paris on 25 June 1791; on 30 September, he was forced to accept the constitution adopted by the Assembly which then dissolved itself.

The Legislative Assembly – The new deputies met the following day in the Tuileries Riding School. On 20 June 1792, encouraged by the moderate revolutionary faction known as the Girondins, rioters invaded the Tuileries and made Louis put on the red bonnet of liberty. On 11 July, the Assembly declared France to be in danger, and during the night of 9 August the mob (sans-culottes) instituted a "revolutionary commune" with the status of an organ of government; the next day the Tuileries were sacked and 600 of the Swiss Guards massacred. The Assembly responded by depriving the king of his few remaining responsibilities and confining him with his family in the tower of the Templar Prison (Tour du Temple).

Soon after, the "September Massacres" began; 1 200 prisoners, some "politicals", but most of them common offenders, were hauled from the city's jails and arbitrarily executed on the Buci crossroads in a frenzy of fear and panic precipitated by fear of invasion. This grisly event marked the beginning of the Terror. On 21 September, the day after the French defeat at the Battle of Valmy, the Legislative Assembly gave way to the Convention.

The Convention – At its very first meeting, the new assembly, now in the hands of the Girondins, formally abolished the monarchy and proclaimed the **Republic**. This day, 21 September 1792, became Day 1 of Year One in the new revolutionary calendar (which remained in force until 31 December 1805). At the end of May, beset by difficulties at home and abroad and bereft of popular support, the Girondins fell, to be replaced by the "Mountain" (the extreme Jacobin faction, so-called because they occupied the upper tiers of seating in the Assembly).

In one of its first acts, the monarch was guillotined on 21 January 1793 in Place de la Concorde. On 17 September, the Law of Suspects was passed, legalising **the Terror**. The first to be executed by the revolutionary tribunals were the Girondins, in October 1793. On 8 June 1794, Robespierre the "Incorruptible" presided over the Festival of the Supreme Being. The event was orchestrated by the painter David, beginning in the Tuileries Gardens and proceeding to the Champ-de-Mars.

On 10 June (9 Prairial), the Great Terror began. Over a period of two months, the "national razor", as the guillotine was known, was to slice off 2 561 heads. Among those executed was Lavoisier, former Farmer-General and eminent chemist, responsible for the formulation of the theory of the conservation of mass on which much of modern chemistry rests, and André Chénier, the lyric poet who had condemned the excesses of the regime in his verse. The end of the Terror came with the fall and execution of Robespierre himself, on 27 July (9 Thermidor).

The Thermidorian Convention now attempted to put the sickening spectacle of the scaffold behind it with a policy calculated to promote stability. Among its most important achievements were measures designed to advance science and learning, including the founding of the École Polytechnique (School of Engineering); the creation of the Conservatoire des Arts et Métiers (National Technical Institution), and the setting up of the École Normale (the prestigious college). In 1795, the metric system was adopted and the Office of Longitudes founded. Just before the Assembly's dissolution on 25 October, public education was instituted and the Institut de France founded, embracing the nation's learned academies (including the Académie Française).

The Directory and the Consulate – The period of the Directory was marked, in 1798, by the very first Universal Exhibition, but was brought to an end with the *coup d'état* of 9 November (18 Brumaire) 1799, when the Council of Elders persuaded the legislature to move to St-Cloud as a precautionary measure against Jacobin plots. On the following day, **Napoleon Bonaparte** entered the chamber to address the delegates, but was booed; he was saved by the presence of mind of his brother Lucien, who used the guard to disperse the members. By the same evening, power was in the hands of three consuls; it was the end of the Revolution. In less than five years, the Consulate allowed Napoleon to centralise power, opening the way to the realisation of his Imperial ambitions.

The Empire – Proclaimed Emperor of the French by the Senate on 18 May 1804, Napoleon I was anointed on 2 December by Pope Pius VII at Notre-Dame, though it was he himself who actually put the crown on his head in a ceremony immortalised by David. His reign was marked by the promulgation in 1804 of the Civil Code, which he had helped draft himself when he was still First Consul, and which, as the *Code Napoléon*, has since formed the legal basis of many other countries. In order to make Paris into a truly imperial capital, Napoleon ordered the erection of a great column in the Place Vendôme; cast from the melted-down metal of guns taken at the Battle of Austerlitz (Slavkov), it commemorated the victories of his *Grande Armée*. Vignon was commissioned to design a temple which nearly became a railway station before ending up as the Madeleine Church; Chalgrin was put to work drawing up plans for a great triumphal arch (Arc de Triomphe); Brongniart built the Stock Exchange (Bourse); Percier and Fontaine, the promoters of the Empire style, constructed the north wing of the Louvre and the Carrousel Arch (Arc du Carrousel); Gros painted the battles and Géricault the cavalry of the *Grande Armée*.

On 31 March 1814, despite the strong resistance offered by Daumesnil at Vincennes, the Allies occupied Paris. On 11 April, the Emperor, "the sole obstacle to peace in Europe", put his signature to the document of abdication at Fontainebleau.

The Restoration
(May 1814-February 1848)
The reign of Louis XVIII – 1814-24.

The period of rule of Louis XVI's brother was interrupted by the Hundred Days of Napoleon's attempt to re-establish himself between his sojourn on Elba and his final exile to St Helena. During the years of Louis XVIII's reign, Laënnec invented the stethoscope, wrote his *Treatise on Mediate Auscultation* and founded the anatomo-clinical school together with Bayle and Dupuytren; Pinel studied mental illness at the Salpêtrière Hospital; Cuvier put biology on a sounder footing, formulated the principles of subordination of organs to their function and established a zoological classification; Bertholet studied the composition of acids, Sadi Carnot thermodynamics and temperature equilibrium, and Arago electromagnetism and the polarisation of light; Daguerre laid the foundations of his fame with his dioramas, and Lamartine conquered literary society with his *Méditations Poétiques* – its elegaic rhythms soothed Talleyrand's sleepless nights.

The reign of Charles X – 1824-30.

Painting flourished with the brilliant sweep of Delacroix' great canvases and Corot's landscapes. At the same time, Laplace was establishing the fundamental laws of mathematical analysis and providing a firm basis for astronomical mechanics, and Berlioz was composing his *Fantastic Symphony*, the key work of the Romantic Movement in music.

On 21 February 1830, Victor Hugo's drama *Hernani* provoked a literary battle between "moderns" and "classicals" in which the latter were temporarily routed. In the summer, Charles' press ordinances provoked a crisis which led to his abdication; he was succeeded by Louis Philippe, a member of the cadet branch of the Bourbons.

Coronation of Napoleon, by Jacques-Louis David

Reign of Louis-Philippe – 1830-48.
During the 1830s, the mathematician Evariste Galois put forward the theory of sets; Victor Hugo wrote *Notre-Dame de Paris* and Alfred de Musset *Caprices*. Chopin, the darling of Parisian society, composed scherzos, waltzes and his celebrated Polonaises. In 1838, while on holiday in Paris, Stendhal wrote *The Charterhouse of Parma*, a masterpiece of psychological observation which can be read on a number of levels. The first news agency was founded by Charles Havas. In 1839, a railway line was opened between Paris and St-Germain. The 1840s saw the publication of the *Mysteries of Paris* by Eugène Sue, the *Count of Monte Cristo and the Three Musketeers* by Dumas and many of the works of Balzac's prodigious Human Comedy as well as the *Treatise on Parasitology* by Raspail; the abuses of the July monarchy were satirised in the drawings of Daumier.

At the age of 79, Chateaubriand brought his finely chiselled *Memories from beyond the Tomb* to a triumphant conclusion. On 23 February in 1848, the barricades went up on the Boulevard des Capucines and the monarchy fell; the next day, at the City Hall, amid scenes of wild enthusiasm, Lamartine saluted the tricolour "the flag which has spread the name of France, freedom and glory around the wide world".

Second Republic and Second Empire (1848-1870)

Second Republic – The abolition of the National Workshops in June 1848 led to rioting in the St-Antoine district, in which the archbishop of Paris was killed. In 1849, Léon Foucault proved the rotation and spherical nature of the earth by means of a pendulum (the experiment was repeated in 1855 from the dome of the Panthéon). On 2 December 1851 the short life of the Second Republic was ended by a *coup d'état*.

Second Empire – 1852-70. Two great exhibitions (in 1855 and 1867) proclaimed the prosperity France enjoyed under the rule of Bonaparte's nephew, Napoleon III. **Baron Haussmann**, Prefect of the *Département* of the Seine, was responsible for an ambitious programme of public works which transformed the capital, giving it many of the features which now seem quintessentially Parisian. Among them were the laying out of the Bois de Boulogne and the Bois de Vincennes, and the building of railway stations and the North Wing of the Louvre. But the Baron is remembered above all for the ruthless surgery he performed on the capital's ancient urban tissue, opening up new focal points (Place de l'Opéra) and linking them with great axial roadways (Grands Boulevards), splendid exercises in traffic engineering and crowd control.

In 1852, Alexandre Dumas wrote *The Lady of the Camellias* at the same time as Rudé was working on the memorial to Marshal Ney, which was to be placed on the spot where the great soldier had been executed in 1815; in Rodin's opinion, it was Paris' finest statue. In 1857 Baudelaire, the first poet of the teeming modern metropolis, published *Les Fleurs du Mal (The Flowers of Evil)*. In 1859, Gounod presented *Faust* at the Opéra Lyrique. In 1860, Étienne Lenoir registered his first patent for the internal combustion engine.

The year 1863 was marked by the scandals caused by Manet's *Déjeuner sur l'herbe* and *Olympia*; Baltard masked the masterly iron structure of the St-Augustin Church with the stone cladding still obligatory in a religious building. In 1896 Pierre de Coubertin created the International Olympic Committee.

Republican Continuity (1870 to the present day)

On 4 September 1870, the mob which had invaded the National Assembly was led by Gambetta to the City Hall where the Republic was proclaimed. The new government busied itself in preparing to defend Paris against the advancing Prussians; the St-Cloud château was set on fire and a fierce battle took place at Le Bourget.

The ensuing siege subjected the population of Paris to terrible hardships; food ran out and the winter was exceptionally severe. The city surrendered on 28 January 1871. The revolutionary **Commune** was ruthlessly suppressed by military force, not before the Communards had burnt down the City Hall, the Tuileries and the Audit Office (Cours des Comptes – on the site of what is now the Orsay Museum), pulled down the column in the Place Vendôme and shot their prisoners at the Hostages' Wall in the Rue Haxo. They made their last stand in the Père-Lachaise Cemetery, where those of their number who had survived the bitter fighting were summarily executed at the Federalists' Wall (Mur des Fédérés). But political institutions were re-established and the nation revived; the Republic was consolidated as France's political regime, notwithstanding Mar-

Baron Haussmann

shal Pétain's so-called French State (État Français), Nazi occupation and the provisional government following the end of the Second World War.

Third Republic – Carpeaux sculpted the Four Corners of the World for the Observatory Fountain, and Émile Littré completed the publication of his renowned *Dictionary of the French Language*. Bizet wrote *L'Arlésienne (the Woman of Arles)* for the Odéon theatre and followed it with *Carmen*, based on a short story by Mérimée.

In 1874, Degas painted *The Dancing Class* and Monet *Impression: Rising Sun*, which, when exhibited by his dealer Nadar, led to the coining of the initially derisive term Impressionism. Later, Renoir worked at the Moulin de la Galette, and Puvis de Chavannes decorated the walls of the Panthéon. The public applauded Delibes' innovatory *Coppélia* and *Lakmé*. Rodin created the *Thinker*, followed by figures of Balzac and Victor Hugo.

In 1879, Seulecq put forward the principle of sequential transmission on which television is based and Pasteur completed his vast body of work. Seurat's *Grande Jatte* heralded the establishment of the Pointillist school of painting. In the following year, 1887, Antoine founded the Free Theatre (Théâtre libre) based on spontaneous expression. The engineer Gustave Eiffel completed his great tower, centrepiece of the Universal Exhibition of 1889. In the century's final decade, Toulouse-Lautrec painted cabaret scenes and Pissarro Parisian townscapes, and Forain gained fame as a marvellous caricaturist. In the Catholic Institute, Édouard Branly discovered radio-conductors.

In 1891, René Panhard built the first petrol-engined motor car, which drove right across Paris.

In 1898, the 21-year-old Louis Renault built his first car, then founded his Billancourt factory; in 1902 he patented a turbocharger. The factory turned out cars, lorries, planes and, in 1917, light tanks which contributed to the German defeat in 1918. Nationalised at the end of the Second World War, the firm continued to produce vehicles in large numbers.

In October 1898 Pierre and Marie Curie succeeded in isolating radium and established the atomic character of radioactivity; their laboratory was a shed which has since disappeared, but its outline is shown in the paving pattern in the courtyard of the school at No 10 Rue Vauquelin. At the same time, Henri Bergson was teaching philosophy at the Collège de France and Langevin was conducting his investigations into ionised gases (in 1915, he was to use ultrasonic waves in the detection of submarines); a combination of steel, stone and glass was employed by Girault in the construction of the exhibition halls (the Grand Palais and the Petit Palais) for the 1900 Exhibition; this occasion also saw the bridging of the Seine by the great flattened arch of the Pont Alexandre III.

In 1900, Gustave Charpentier put on a musical romance *Louise*; with its lyrical realism and popular appeal it was a great "hit" of the time. In 1902, Debussy's *Pelléas et Mélisande* was produced at the Salle Favart of the Comic Opera. In 1906, Santos-Dumont succeeded in taking off in a heavier-than-air machine, staying aloft for 21 seconds, and covering a distance of 220m – 720ft. Dalou's bronze group entitled *The Triumph of the Republic* graced the Place de la Nation, while at Montparnasse the re-erected Wine Pavilion from the 1900 Exhibition provided lodgings and studios for Soutine, Zadkine, Chagall, Modigliani and Léger; other innovative artists included the sculptor Maillol and the painter Utrillo, while Brancusi's work was evolving away from cubism towards abstraction *(The Sleeping Muse)*; the Perret brothers built the Théâtre des Champs-Élysées in reinforced concrete; its façade was adorned with eight relief panels by Bourdelle. The theatre was opened in 1913 with a performance of Stravinsky's *Rite of Spring*; its music and choreography outraged an unprepared public.

In 1914 the construction of the Sacré-Cœur Church (begun in 1878 by the architect Abadie) on the Montmartre heights was completed. On the evening of 31 July, the eve of general mobilisation, Jean Jaurès was assassinated.

The World Wars

World War I (1914-18) put civilians as well as soldiers to the severest of tests; after three years of conflict, Clemenceau was made head of government, and, by restoring the country's confidence, earned the title of "Father of Victory".

In 1920, the interment of an unknown soldier at the Arc de Triomphe marked France's recognition of the sacrifices made by her ordinary soldiers, the unshaven "poilus" of the trenches.

In the course of the 1920s, Le Corbusier built the La Roche Villa, and Bourdelle sculpted *"France"* at the Palais de Tokyo; Georges Rouault, with his predilection for religious themes, completed his *Miserere*, and Landowsky carved the

Archive Laboratoire Curie, Paris

Marie Curie

figure of St Genevieve for the Tournelle Bridge; in the course of a fortnight, Maurice Ravel composed *Boléro* for the dancer Ida Rubinstein; with its subtle instrumentation and rhythmic precision it popularised the name of this aristocratic composer; Poulbot created the archetypal Montmartre urchin; Cocteau wrote *Les Enfants Terribles*; the dynamism of the theatrical scene was marked by many fine actors and producers, notably the Cartel of Four (Cartel des Quatre) consisting of Charles Dullin (at the Sarah Bernhardt Theatre), Gaston Baty (at the Montparnasse), Louis Jouvet (at the Champs-Élysées then the Athénée) and Georges Pitoëff (at the Mathurins).

At the end of the 19C, Émile Roux had studied the causes of and cure for diphtheria; he was now in charge of the Pasteur Institute, and brought to Paris the scientists Calmette and Guérin who had worked on vaccination against tuberculosis.

In 1934, André Citroën brought out the Traction Avant (Front-Wheel Drive) car; 15 years previously, his Type A had been Europe's first mass-produced car; 21 years later, he was to unveil the innovative DS 19.

In 1940, during World War II, Paris was bombed, then **occupied** by the German army. Between 16 and 17 July 1942, numerous French Jews, victims of the Nazi racial myth, were rounded up at the Vélodrome d'Hiver prior to their deportation eastwards for extermination; 4 500 members of the Resistance also met their deaths in the clearing on Mount Valérien where the National Memorial of Fighting France now stands. Finally, on 19 August 1944, Paris was **liberated**.

Fourth and Fifth Republics – In 1950, Alfred Kastler, working in the laboratories of the École Normale Supérieure, succeeded in verifying the principle of "optical pumping", which has subsequently become the basis of one of the methods of producing a laser beam. The *Symphony for a Single Man* by Maurice Béjart, presented at the Étoile Theatre on 3 August 1955, was danced to *musique concrète* composed by Pierre Henry and

Morris Column

Pierre Schaeffer, and led to many innovations in ballet throughout Europe.

Since 1945 the influence of Le Corbusier (there are few examples of his genius in Paris: Villa La Roche, Cité Universitaire pavilions...), has given a new impetus to architecture: new forms (Maison de Radio-France), structures on piles (UNESCO), sweeping rooflines (CNIT building). The present trend is for glass buildings (GAN and Manhattan towers, Centre Georges-Pompidou, Institut du Monde Arabe). The use of pre-stressed concrete led to technical advances (Palais des Congrès, Tour Montparnasse). But in the main architecture becomes an integral part of town planning: buildings are designed to fit into an overall plan: remodelling of an area (Maine-Montparnasse, les Halles, la Villette, Bercy) or new project (la Défense).

Grand new town-planning initiatives have also been implemented: the Opera house at la Bastille, the Ministry of Finance buildings at Bercy, the Grande Arche at la Défense and the Bibliothèque nationale de France François-Mitterand at Tolbiac are distinctive modern landmarks.

The City's Monuments

Civil architecture

Palais du Louvre★★★

👁 *See also The Great Museums.* Neither the Merovingians nor the Carolingians, nor even the Capet kings lived in the old Louvre, which then lay beyond the city limits; instead, they preferred the Law Courts (Palais de Justice), their *hôtels* in the Marais, the manor at Vincennes, their own châteaux or those of their liegemen in the Loire Valley.

Contributions of the Heads of State

Floor plan below shows the evolution of the Louvre Palace. It was **François I** who had the old Louvre pulled down, and, in 1546, commissioned Pierre Lescot to build the palace which was to become the residence of the kings of France. Lescot's work 1 is regarded as the most prestigious part of the Louvre; it was he who brought the Italian Renaissance style, already flowering on the Loire, to the banks of the Seine; to the façade he built, sculptor Jean Goujon added the nymphs of the Fountain of the Innocents.

When Charles IX came to the throne at age ten, the Florentine **Catherine de' Medici** was made Regent. At first she lived in the Louvre on the floor since known as the Queens' Lodging (Logis des Reines), but ordered Philibert Delorme (succeeded by Jean Bullant) to build the Tuileries. The site of this new palace was some 500m – 550yd away, just beyond the fortifications built by Charles V, and, to link it with the Louvre, Catherine requested a covered way following the line of the Seine, with a smaller gallery at right angles.

Charles IX completed the southwestern part of the Cour Carrée, the courtyard which is the most impressive part of the Old Louvre to remain, embellishing it with his monogram (K = Carolus).

Henri III was responsible for the southeastern part of the Cour Carrée (which bears the monogram H). **Henri IV**, from 1595, had the work on the Great Gallery (Grande Galerie) continued by Louis Métezeau. He also had the Flora Pavilion (Pavillon de Flore) built by Jacques II Androuet Du Cerceau, completed the Small Gallery (Petite Galerie) (its first floor was occupied by Marie de' Medici and Anne of Austria, hence the monogram AA), and erected the upper part of the Henri III wing in the Cour Carrée, marked by his monogram.

Louis XIII continued with the construction of the Cour Carrée. At the same time as he was building the Sorbonne and the Palais-Royal, the architect Lemercier erected the Clock Pavilion (Pavillon de l'Horloge) together with the northwest corner of the courtyard, a Classical

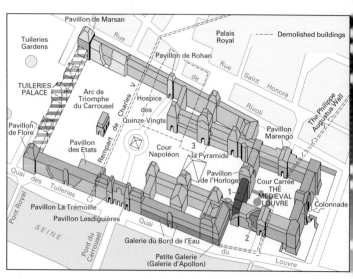

The Louvre colonnade

J.P. Clapham/MICHELIN

response to Lescot's work (the mono-gram LA = Louis and Anne). Anne of Austria lived in the Queens' Lodging; the bathroom designed for her by Lemercier now houses the Venus de Milo. In 1638, Charles V's rampart was razed and the moat filled in.

On the death of Louis XIII, Anne became Regent and moved to the Palais-Royal with the young **Louis XIV**. Nine years later, however, having been made aware of the palace's vulnerability by the upris-ing of the nobility (the Fronde), she took up residence in the Louvre again.The young king, who had married Maria-Theresa, moved into the Tuileries in 1664 for three years. The architect Le Vau, working on the Louvre, his per-sonal style evident in the Small Gallery, started again after a fire in 1661, and in the Apollo Gallery; he continued the enclosure of the Cour Carrée by adding a storey onto the western part of the north wing (monogram LMT = Louis, Maria-Theresa) and by building the Marengo Pavilion (Pavillon Marengo) (with the monogram LB = Louis XIV de Bourbon).

But the palace still needed a monu-mental façade facing the city; **Colbert** had refused permission for a number of projects designed with this in mind. An appeal was made to the master-architect of the Italian Baroque, Bernini, already 67 years old. But his proposals were turned down too, since they would have either destroyed or clashed with Lescot's

façade. In the end it fell to Claude Per-rault, aided by Le Brun and Le Vau, to design an imposing colonnaded façade. In 1682, the king left Paris for Versailles. The Louvre now housed the Academy as well as a less desirable population. In 1715, the Court returned to Paris for a period of seven years; the young King Louis XV lived in the Tuileries and the Regent in the Palais-Royal. Coustou con-tinued the work on the colonnade.

After the **Revolution**, the Convention used the Louvre theatre for its delibera-tions. The Committee of Public Safety (Comité du Salut public) convened in the state rooms of the Tuileries, which were subsequently appropriated for his own use by Napoleon.

Napoleon I took up residence in the Tuileries. Percier and Fontaine com-pleted the Cour Carrée by adding a second floor to the north and south wings. They also provided a wing link-ing the Rohan and Marsan Pavilions and gave it a façade identical to Du Cerceau's Grande Galerie, as well as enlarging the Place du Carroussel to enable Napoleon to review his legions and embellishing it with a triumphal arch commemorating the Emperor's victories, its design based on the Arch of Septimus Severus.

All of the "restored" monarchs lived in the Tuileries, as did **Napoleon III,** who decided to enclose the large courtyard on the north, confiding the task to Visconti, then to Lefuel, whose design was intended to conceal the disparity

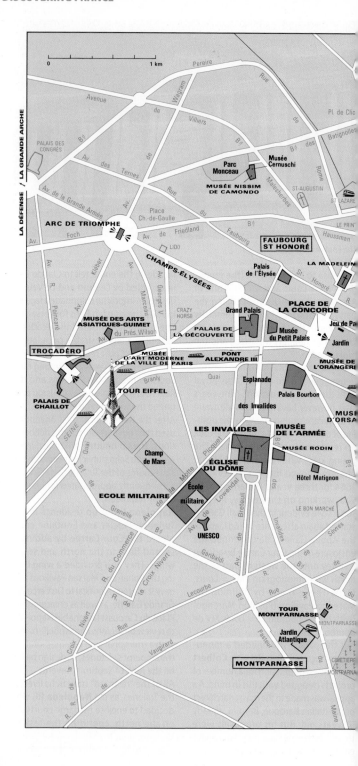

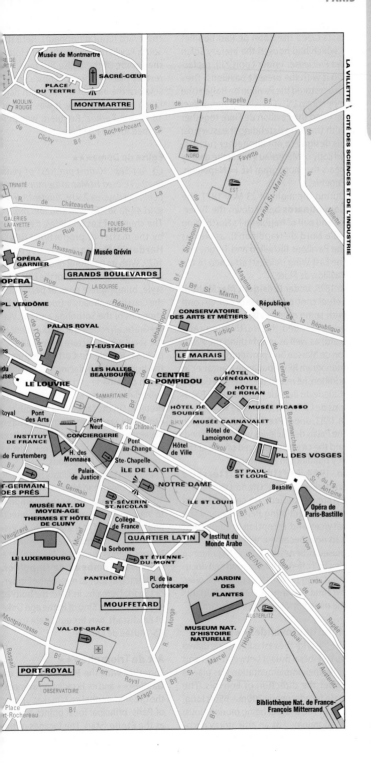

Musée de Montmartre

SACRÉ-CŒUR

PLACE
DU TERTRE

MOULIN
ROUGE

MONTMARTRE

B⌀ de la Chapelle B⌀

de
Clichy B⌀ de Rochechouart

B⌀

de Fayette

NORD

la

EST

Canal St-Martin

Villette

TRINITÉ

R. de Châteaudun

La

de Strasbourg

Magenta

GALERIES
LAFAYETTE

Rue

FOLIES-
BERGÈRES

B⌀ Haussmann Musée Grévin

OPÉRA
GARNIER

GRANDS BOULEVARDS

B⌀ St Martin

République

B⌀ de la République

OPÉRA

Rue

LA BOURSE

Réaumur

PL. VENDÔME

de l'Opéra

CONSERVATOIRE
DES ARTS ET MÉTIERS

St Honoré

PALAIS ROYAL

Sébastopol

Turbigo

B⌀ du Temple

ST-EUSTACHE

R.

LE MARAIS

usel

LES HALLES
BEAUBOURG

CENTRE
G. POMPIDOU

HÔTEL
GUÉNÉGAUD

LE LOUVRE

SAMARITAINE

B⌀

HÔTEL
DE ROHAN

HÔTEL DE
SOUBISE

MUSÉE PICASSO

Royal Pont
des Arts

Pont
Neuf

B.H.V.

MUSÉE CARNAVALET

Beaumarchais

INSTITUT
DE FRANCE

CONCIERGERIE

PL. du Châtelet

Hôtel de
Lamoignon

de Furstemberg

H. des
Monnaies

Pont
au Change

Hôtel
de Ville

Rivoli

PL. DES VOSGES

Palais
de Justice

Ste-Chapelle

ÎLE DE LA CITÉ

ST PAUL-
ST LOUIS

T-GERMAIN
DES PRÉS

St Germain

NOTRE-DAME

Bastille

R. du Fg.
St. Antoine

MUSÉE NAT. DU
MOYEN-AGE
THERMES ET HÔTEL
DE CLUNY

ST-SÉVERIN-
ST-NICOLAS

ÎLE ST LOUIS

B⌀ Henri IV

Opéra de
Paris-Bastille

Collège
de France

QUARTIER LATIN

Institut du
Monde Arabe

R. de Lyon

Vaugirard

Michel

la Sorbonne

SEINE

LE LUXEMBOURG

ST ÉTIENNE-
DU-MONT

PANTHÉON

Pl. de la
Contrescarpe

JARDIN
DES
PLANTES

LYON

de la Rapée

MOUFFETARD

R. Monge

AUSTERLITZ

Montparnasse

B⌀

VAL-DE-GRÂCE

MUSEUM NAT.
D'HISTOIRE
NATURELLE

Quai d'Austerlitz

Raspail

de

Port

R.

Marcel

de l'Hôpital

PORT-ROYAL

Royal

St.

OBSERVATOIRE

Arago

B⌀

Place
rt-Rocher eau

Bibliothèque Nat. de France-
François Mitterrand

between the two wings; the architects razed the Hôtel de Rambouillet 3 which had housed the literary *Salon des Précieuses* under Louis XIII, replacing it with the present pavilions. They also restored the Pavillon de Rohan (the monogram LN = Louis Napoléon). Lefuel restored the Pavillon de Flore together with the wing extending it eastwards; his design is a not altogether successful copy of Métezeau's work; the gallery bears the monogram NE (= Napoleon, Eugénie).

During the night of 23 May 1871, the **Communards** burnt down the Tuileries and half of Napoleon I's North Wing (Aile Nord de Napoléon I), as well as the Pavillons Richelieu and Turgot and the East Wing (Aile Est) attached to the Pavillon de Flore.

In 1875, under **President MacMahon**, Lefuel continued the work of Visconti with some modifications; he restored and extended the North Wing (Aile Nord) as well as refurbishing the Pavillon de Marsan and providing it with the monogram RF (République Française); in addition, he rebuilt the Riverside Gallery (Galerie du Bord de l'Eau) and the Pavillons de La Trémoille and de Flore.

In 1883, under **President Jules Grévy**, the Palais des Tuileries was demolished; and the city was deprived of one of the key buildings in its history.

In 1984 **President Mitterrand** embarked on the "Grand Louvre and Pyramide" project. He commissioned the architect Ming Pei to expand the services and reception area of what had now become a world-famous art museum. Beneath the Cour Napoléon, a vast hall offering information and documentation services is lit up by the glass pyramid **(Pyramide**★★**)** which marks the main entrance to the museum.

Hôtel des Invalides★★★

The plans for the vast edifice were drawn up by Libéral Bruant between 1671 and 1676; their implementation was placed under the direction of Louvois. The main façade, nearly 200m – 650ft long, is majestic without being monotonous; it is dominated by an attic storey decorated with masks and dormer windows in the form of trophies. Napoleon used to parade his troops in the main courtyard (Cour d'honneur); here the South Pavilion (Pavillon du Midi) forms the façade of the Église St-Louis, the resting-place of some of France's great soldiers; the interior is hung with flags taken from the enemy. It was here, in 1837, that Berlioz' Requiem was performed for the first time.

Église du Dôme★★★

🕐 *Apr-Sep: 10am-6pm (rest of year: 5pm).* 🕐 *Closed 1st Mon in the month, and public holidays.* 👁 *7.50€ (under 18: free).* ☎ *01 44 42 38 77. www. invalides.org.*

The church of Les Invalides, designed by the master of proportion, **Jules-Hardouin Mansart,** was begun in 1677. With its beautiful gilded dome, it is one of the great works of the Louis XIV style, bringing to a peak of perfection the Classicism already introduced in the churches of the Sorbonne and the Val-de-Grâce, an ecclesiastical equivalent of the secular architecture of Versailles.

In 1735, Robert de Cotte completed the building by replacing the planned south colonnade and portico with the splendid vista offered by the Avenue de Breteuil. On the far side he laid out the Esplanade, and set up the guns captured at Vienna in 1805 by Napoleon to defend the gardens and fire ceremonial salvoes on great national occasions.

The church became a military necropolis after Napoleon had Marshal Turenne (d 1675) buried here. Note the memorial to Vauban, the great military architect, and the tomb of Marshal Foch. In Visconti's crypt of green granite from the Vosges stands the "cloak of glory", the unmarked **Tombeau de Napoleon** completed in 1861 to receive the Emperor's mortal remains. In 1940, the body of Napoleon's son, King of Rome and Duke of Reichstadt, was brought here too.

▶ Musée de l'Armée

Arc de Triomphe★★★

Together with the **Place Charles de Gaulle**★★★ and its 12 radiating avenues, the great triumphal arch makes up one of Paris' principal focal points, known as the **Étoile** (Star). The façades of the buildings around were designed in a

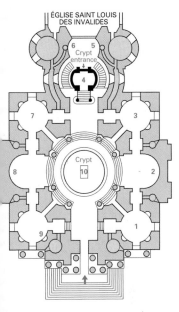

ÉGLISE SAINT LOUIS DES INVALIDES

1) Tomb of Joseph Bonaparte, elder brother of Napoleon, King of Spain.
2) Monument to Vauban by Etex. The Emperor himself commanded that the military architect's heart be brought to the Invalides.
3) Marshal Foch's tomb by Landowsky.
4) Ornate high altar surrounded by twisted columns and covered by a baldaquin by Visconti. Vaulting decoration by Coypel.
5) General Duroc's tomb.
6) General Bertrand's tomb.
7) At the back – the heart of La Tour d'Auvergne, first grenadier of the Republic; in the centre, the tomb of Marshal Lyautey.
8) Marshal Turenne's tomb by Tuby.
9) St Jerome's Chapel (carvings by Nicolas Coustou). The tomb at the foot of the wall is Jerome Bonaparte's, Napoleon's younger brother and King of Westphalia.
10) The Emperor's tomb.

harmonious style by Hittorff as part of Haussmann's plans for the metropolis. The Arc de Triomphe was the scene on 14 July 1919 of the great victory parade and, on 11 November 1920, of the burial of the Unknown Soldier. Three years later the flame of remembrance was kindled for the first time. The arch is ornamented with sculpture, notably Rude's masterpiece of 1836 known as the *Marseillaise,* depicting volunteers departing to defend France from the invading Prussians (1792).

Place de la Concorde★★★

A perfect expression of the Louis XV style, it was designed by Ange-Jacques Gabriel in 1755 and completed over a period of 20 years. On 21 January 1793, near where the statue of Brest now stands, the guillotine was set up for the execution of Louis XVI and other victims of the Terror.

The square owes its monumental character to the colonnaded buildings defining it to the north, to its octagonal plan, and to the massive pedestals intended for allegorical statues of French cities. Two great urban **axes**★★★ intersect here: one runs from the Église de la Madeleine to the Palais-Bourbon, the other from *Coysevox's Winged Horses (Chevaux ailés),* which mark the entrance to the Tuileries,

to the magnificent marble sculptures (copies) by Nicolas and Guillaume Coustou which flank the Champs-Élysées. The pink granite Luxor obelisk (Obélisque de Louksor), 3 300 years old, covered with hieroglyphics, was brought here from Egypt in 1836. The square's fountains adorned with statues are particularly fine.

Tour Eiffel★★★

Kids ⏱ *Lift: mid-Jun to end Aug: daily 9am-midnight; Jan to mid-Jun: daily 9.30am-11pm. Sep-Dec: daily 9.30am-6pm.* 🚇 *4.20€ (1st floor), 7.70€ (2nd floor), 11€ (3rd floor). Stairs: 1st and 2nd floors only, 3.80€.* ☎*01 44 11 23 23. www.tour-eiffel.fr.*
11 fold 28 – J7. The Eiffel Tower is Paris' most famous symbol. The first proposal for a tower was made in 1884; construction was completed in 26 months and the tower opened in March 1889 for the Universal Exhibition (Exposition universelle) of that year.
The structure is evidence of Eiffel's imagination and daring; in spite of its weight of 7 000 tonnes and a height of 320.75m – 1 051ft and the use of 2.5 million rivets, it is a masterpiece of lightness. It is difficult to believe that the tower actually weighs less than the volume of air surrounding it and that the pressure it exerts on the ground is that of a man sitting on a chair.

Palais de Justice and Conciergerie★★

Palais: ⏱ *daily except Sun 8.30am-6pm.* ⏱ *Closed public holidays. Visitors are nor-*

MICHELIN

Église du Dôme

mally allowed to attend a civil or criminal hearing. (⊶The sculpture gallery and children's tribunal are not open to the public.) ☎01 44 32 52 52.

Conciergerie: 🕐 *Mar-Oct: daily 9.30am-6pm; Nov-Feb: daily 9.30am-5pm. Last entry 30 min before closing.* 🕐 *Closed 1 Jan, 1 May and 25 Dec.* 🎟 *6.10€ (under 17 years: no charge).* ☎01 53 40 60 80.

Known as the Palace (Palais), this is the principal seat of civil and judicial authority. Before becoming the royal palace of the rulers of medieval France, it had been the residence of Roman governors, Merovingian kings and the children of Clovis, the mint of Dagobert and Duke Eudes' fortress.

The Capetian kings built a chapel and fortified the palace with a keep. Philippe le Bel (the Fair) entrusted Enguerrand de Marigny with the building of the Conciergerie as well as with the extension and embellishment of the palace; its Gothic halls of 1313 were widely admired. Later, Charles V built the Clock Tower (Tour de l'Horloge), the city's first public clock; he also installed Parliament here, the country's supreme court. Survivals from this period include the Great Hall (Salle des gens d'Armes) with its fine capitals, the Guard Room (Salle des Gardes) with its magnificent pillars, and the kitchens with their monumental corner fireplaces.

The great hall on the first floor was restored by Salomon de Brosse after the fire of 1618; it was refurbished again

in 1840 and once more after the fire of 1871.

The First Civil Court is in the former Parliamentary Grand Chambe (Grand'chambre du parlement), the place where the kings dispensed justice, where the 16-year-old Louis XIV dictated his orders to Parliament, where that body in its turn demanded the convocation of the States-General in 1788 and where the Revolutionary Tribunal was set up under the public prosecutor Fouquier-Tinville.

The entrance to the royal palace was once guarded by the twin towers gracing the north front of the great complex this is the oldest part of the building albeit now hiding behind a 19C neo Gothic façade.

The **Conciergerie** served as antechamber to the guillotine during the Terror housing up to 1200 detainees at any one time. The Prisoners' Gallery (Galerie des Prisonniers), Marie-Antoinette's cell (cachot) and the Girondins' Chapel (chapelle des Girondins) are particularly moving.

Palais-Royal★★

In 1632, Richelieu ordered Lemercier to build the huge edifice which came to be known as the Cardinal's Palace (Palais Cardinal) when it was extended in 1639. It is remarkable for its impressive central façade, surmounted by allegorical statues and a curved pediment. On his deathbed, Richelieu bequeathed it to Louis XIII, whereupon its name was changed to the Palais-Royal. In 1783, Victor Louis laid out the charming formal gardens and the arcades which enclose them and which house a number of specialist shops and boutiques.

In 1986, Daniel Buren designed the arrangement of 260 columns, all of different height, which occupy the outer courtyard.

École Militaire★★

Though the original design could not be fully implemented because of lack of financial resources, the Military Academy by Jacques-Ange Gabriel is one of the outstanding examples of French 18C architecture. It was begun in 1752 financed in part by Mme de Pompadour

Place de la Concorde, previously Place Louis XV

and completed in 1773. Under the Second Empire, cavalry and artillery buildings of nondescript design were added, together with the low-lying wings which frame the main building. True to its original function, it now houses the French Army's Staff College.

The superb main courtyard (**cour d'honneur★**), lined on either side by beautiful porticoes with paired columns, is approached via an exercise yard; the imposing central section and the projecting wings form a harmonious composition.

Panthéon★★

🕐 *Apr-Sep: daily 9.30am-6.30pm; Oct-Mar: daily 10am-6.15pm.* 🕐 *Closed public holidays.* ⊚ *7.50€.* ☎*01 44 32 18 00.*

In 1744, Louis XV had made a vow at Metz to replace the half-ruined church of St Genevieve's Abbey. Fourteen years later Soufflot began the construction of the new building on the highest point of the Left Bank. The scale of the building was such that its collapse was confidently predicted and the pretensions of its architect ridiculed. The present building has been much changed since Soufflot's day; its towers have gone, its pediments have been remodelled, its windows blocked up. In 1791, the Constituent Assembly closed the church to worshippers in order to convert it into the last resting place of the "great men of the epoch of French liberty". Successively a church, a necropolis, headquarters of the Commune, a lay temple, the Panthéon is representative of the time in which churches lost their dominant position in the urban landscape. Still crowned by Soufflot's dome, the great edifice is built in the shape of a Greek Cross. It has a fine portico with Corinthian columns and a pediment carved by David d'Angers in 1831. In the crypt are the tombs of the famous.

Opéra Garnier★★

🕐 *Daily 10am-5pm (unless matinée or special event taking place). Guided tours ☜ (1hr15min) of the public entrance halls and museum, daily at noon (meet at 11.45pm in the entrance hall, next to Rameau's statue).* ⊚ *7€.* 🕐 *Closed 1 Jan and 1 May.* ☎*0892 899 090. www.operadeparis.fr.*

This is the National Academy of Music, and was until 1990 France's premier home of opera. It opened in 1875 and it is the work of Charles Garnier, who had dreamed of creating an authentic Second Empire style. But the huge edifice, "more operatic than any opera" (Ian Nairn), magnificent though it was, lacked sufficient originality to inspire a new school of architecture. The interior, with its Great Staircase, foyer and auditorium, is of the utmost sumptuousness. Garnier used marble from all the quarries of France, and there is a ceiling by Chagall.

Palais de Chaillot★★

This remarkable example of inter-war architecture was built for the 1937 Exhibition. Its twin pavilions are linked by a portico and extended by wings which curve to frame the wide terrace with its statues in gilded bronze. From here there is a wonderful **view**★★★ of Paris; in the foreground are the Trocadero Gardens with their spectacular fountains, and beyond the curving river the Eiffel Tower, the Champ-de-Mars, and the École Militaire.

The Palais houses the Théâtre de Chaillot, the Musée de l'Homme★★, Musée de la Marine★★, Musée des Monuments Français★★ and Musée du Cinéma Henri-Langlois★.

Ecclesiastical architecture

Cathédrale Notre-Dame★★★

Notre-Dame is the point from which distances to Paris are measured.

People have worshipped here for 2 000 years and the present building has witnessed the great events of French history.

Work on the cathedral was begun by Maurice de Sully in 1163. Notre-Dame is the last great galleried church building and one of the first with flying buttresses. In 1245 the bulk of the work was complete and St Louis held a ceremony for the knighting of his son and also placed the Crown of Thorns in the cathedral until the Sainte-Chapelle was ready to receive it. In 1250 the twin towers were finished.

In 1430, the cathedral was the setting for the coronation of the young Henry VI of England as King of France; in 1455, a ceremony was conducted to rehabilitate Joan of Arc; in 1558, Mary Stuart was crowned here on becoming Queen of France by her marriage to François II and, in 1572, the Huguenot Henri IV waited at the door as his bride, Marguerite of Valois, stood alone in the chancel; in 1594 the king converted to the Catholic faith.

The great building was not spared mutilations of various kinds; in 1699 the choir screen was demolished, and later some of the original stained glass was removed to let in more light, and the central portal demolished (18C) to allow processions to move more freely. During the Revolution statues were destroyed and the cathedral declared a Temple of Reason. It was in a much-dilapidated building that Napoleon Bonaparte crowned himself Emperor and the King of Rome was baptised. In 1831, public opinion was alerted by Hugo's novel Notre-Dame de Paris to the state of the building, and in 1841 Louis-Philippe charged Viollet-le-Duc with its restoration. In the space of 24 years, he completed his work in accordance with his own, idealised vision of the Gothic style; though open to criticism, it needs to be seen in the context of the wholesale demolition of the medieval Île-de-la-Cité and its replacement with administrative buildings.

The magnificent Cloister Portal (Portail du Cloître – north transept) is 30 years later than the west front portals; with its richly carved gables and smiling figure of the Virgin – the only original large sculpture to have survived – it demonstrates clearly how far the art of sculpture had advanced over the period.

At the beginning of the 14C, the bold array of flying buttresses was sent soaring over ambulatory and galleries to hold in place the high vaults of the east end.

Above the Kings' Gallery is the great rose window, still with its medieval glass. An enterprise of considerable daring – it was the largest such window of its time – its design is so accomplished that it shows no sign of distortion after 700 years and has often been imitated. Inside, the rose window has particularly fine stained glass of a deep bluish-mauve.

Sainte-Chapelle★★★

🕐 *Daily 9.30am-6pm. Last admission 30min before closing.* 🕐 *Closed 1 Jan, 1 May, 1 and 11 Nov, 25 Dec.* ⊘ *6.10€.* ☎*01 53 40 60 80.*

Only 80 years separate this definitive masterpiece of the High Gothic from the Transitional Gothic of Notre-Dame, but the difference is striking; in the lightness and clarity of its structure, the Sainte-Chapelle pushes Gothic ideas to the limit. The chapel was built

Notre-Dame, east view

on the orders of St Louis to house the recently acquired relics of the Passion within the precincts of the royal palace; it was completed in the record time of 33 months.

The upper chapel resembles a shrine with walls made almost entirely of remarkable **stained glass** covering a total area of 618m2 – 6 672sq ft; 1 134 different scenes are depicted, of which 720 are made of original glass. The windows rise to a height of 15m – nearly 50ft. By 1240, the stained glass at Chartres had been completed, and the king was thus able to call on the mastercraftsmen who had worked on them to come to Paris; this explains the similarity between the glass of cathedral and of chapel, in terms of the scenes shown and the luminous colour which eclipses the simplicity of the design.

The theme is Christ's Passion, including its foretelling by the Prophets and by John the Baptist, together with the episodes which lead up to it. The original rose window is shown in a scene from the *Très Riches Heures du Duc de Berry*; the present rose window is a product of the Flamboyant Gothic, ordered by Charles VII, and showing the Apocalypse of St John. It is characteristic of its age in the design of its tracery and in the subtle variations of colour which had replaced the earlier method of juxtaposing a great number of small coloured panes. The glass of the Sainte-Chapelle has been much imitated, even in architecturally inappropriate situations.

Abbaye de St-Germain-des-Prés★★

This most venerable of the city's churches reveals more than visual delights to those who know something of the history of its ancient stones. With the exception of Clovis, the Merovingian kings were buried here. The church was subsequently destroyed by the Normans, but restored in the course of the 10C and 11C. Understandably, the tower rising above the west front has a fortress-like character. Around 1160, the nave was enlarged and the chancel rebuilt in the new Gothic style. "Improvements" followed in the 17C (triforium and chancel windows) and in 1822 a somewhat overzealous restoration took place.

But the church's years of glory were between 1631 and 1789, when the austere Congregation of St Maur made it a centre of learning and spirituality: the monks studied ancient inscriptions (epigraphy) and writing (paleography); the Church Fathers (Patristics), archeology, cartography… Their library was confiscated at the time of the French Revolution.

Église St-Séverin-St-Nicolas★★

This much-loved Latin Quarter Church has features from a number of architectural styles. The lower part of the portal and the first three bays of the nave are High Gothic; while much of the rest of the building was remodelled in Flamboyant style (upper part of the tower, the remainder of the nave, the secondary aisle, the highly-compartmentalised vaulting of the chancel and the famous spiral pillar in the ambulatory). In the 18C, the pillars in the chancel were clad in wood and marble.

Église St-Eustache★★

This was once the richest church in Paris, centre of the parish which included the areas around the Palais-Royal and the Halles market; its layout was modelled on that of Notre-Dame when building began in 1532. But St-Eustache took over a hundred years to complete; tastes changed, and the Gothic skeleton of the great building is fleshed out with Renaissance finishes and detail.

The Flamboyant style is evident in the three-storeyed interior elevation, in the vaulting of the choir, crossing and nave, in the lofty side aisles and in the flying buttresses. The Renaissance is exemplified in the Corinthian columns and in the return to the use of semicircular arches, and Classicism in P de Champaigne's choir windows and in Colbert's tomb, designed by Le Brun in collaboration with Coysevox and Tuby. In the Chapelle St-Joseph is the English sculptor Raymond Mason's colourful commemoration of the fruit and vegetable market's move out of Paris in 1969.

Église Notre-Dame-du-Val-de-Grâce★★

After many childless years, Anne of Austria commissioned François Mansart to design a church in thanksgiving for the birth of Louis XIV in 1638. The work was completed by Lemercier and Le Muet. The church recalls the Renaissance architecture of Rome; the dome, rising above the two-tier west front with its double triangular pediment, is particularly ornate and obviously inspired by St Peter's. Inside, the spirit of the Baroque prevails; there is polychrome paving, highly-sculptured vaulting over the nave, massive crossing pillars and a monumental baldaquin with six wreathed columns. The **cupola**★★ was decorated by Mignard with a fresco featuring 200 figures.

Urban Design

Since the sweeping away of much of medieval Paris in the 19C, three central districts have come to typify particular stages in the city's evolution.

Le Marais★★★

Renaissance, Louis XIII and Louis XIV Charles V's move to the Hôtel St-Paul in the Marais district in the 14C signalled the incorporation of a suburban area into Paris. The area soon became fashionable, and Rue St-Antoine the city's finest street. It was here that that characteristic French town house, the hôtel, took on its definitive form with the collaboration of the finest architects and artists; it became the setting for that other distinctive feature of Parisian life the literary or philosophical salon.

The **Hôtel Lamoignon**★ of 1584 is a typical example of a mansion in the Henri III style. For the first time in Paris, its architect, Jean-Baptiste Androuet Du Cerceau, used the Giant Order with its flattened pilasters, Corinthian capitals and sculpted string-course.

The Henri IV style makes its appearance in the **Place des Vosges**★★★ designed by Louis Métezeau and completed in 1612. The 36 houses retain their original symmetrical appearance with arcades, two storeys with alternate brick and stone facings and steeply-pitched slate roofs pierced with dormer windows. The King's Pavilion (Pavillon du Roi) is sited at the southern end of the square, balanced by the Queen's Pavilion (Pavillon de la Reine) at the sunnier northern end.

Louis XIII's reign heralds the Classical style. In 1624, Jean Androuet Du Cerceau built the **Hôtel de Sully**★ with a gateway framed between massive pavilions and a main courtyard **(cour d'honneur**★★★) with triangular and curved pediments complemented by the scrolled dormer windows; beyond is an exquisite inner courtyard. The early-

Louis XIV style is seen in Mansart's **Hôtel Guénégaud**★★ of 1648, with its plain harmonious lines, majestic staircase, and small formal garden one of the finest houses of the Marais; in Le Pautre's **Hôtel de Beauvais**★ with its curved balcony on brackets and its ingenious internal layout; in the **Hôtel Carnavalet**★, a Renaissance house rebuilt by Mansart in 1655; and in Cottard's **Hôtel Amelot-de-Bisseuil**★ of somewhat theatrical design with its cornice and curved pediment decorated with allegorical figures.

The later-Louis XIV style features in two adjoining *hôtels* built by Delamair: the **Hôtel de Rohan**★★ with its wonderful sculpture of the *Horses of Apollo (Chevaux frémissants d'Apollon à l'abreuvoir)* by Robert Le Lorrain; and the **Hôtel de Soubise**★★ with its horseshoe-shaped courtyard and double colonnade. They are characterised by their raised ground floors, massive windows, roof balustrades and by the sculpture of their projecting central sections.

La Voie Triomphale (From the Tuileries to the Arc de Triomphe)★★★

A great axis leading from the courtyard of the Louvre to St Germain had been planned by Colbert, but today's "Triumphal Way" was laid out under Louis XVI, Napoleon III and during the years of the Third Republic.

Arc de Triomphe du Carrousel★

This delightful pastiche of a Roman arch is decorated with statues of Napoleonic military men in full uniform. An observer standing in the Place du Carrousel commands an extraordinary perspective which runs from the Louvre, through the arch, to the obelisk in the Place de la Concorde, then onward and upward to the Grande Arche at the Défense.

Jardin des Tuileries★

The gardens were first laid out in the 1560s by Catherine de' Medici in the Italian style. A century later, they were remodelled by Le Nôtre, who here created the archetypal French garden, a formal setting for the elegant pleasures of outdoor life. The Riverside Terrace (Terrasse du Bord de l'Eau) became the playground of royal princes and of the sons of the two Napoleons, then of all the children of Paris.

Champs-Élysées★★★

In 1667, Le Nôtre extended the axis from the Tuileries to a new focal point, the

Place des Vosges

A. Eli/MICHELIN

Rond-Point, which he laid out himself. The avenue was then a service road for the houses facing the Rue du Faubourg-St-Honoré, but very soon refreshment stalls were set up and crowds flocked to the area. In 1724, the Duc d'Antin planted rows of elms to extend the "Elysian Fields" up to the Étoile. In 1729, street lanterns lit the evening scene. Forty-eight years on, and the avenue had descended the gentle slope beyond the Étoile to reach the Seine at the Pont de Neuilly. The buildings lining it included taverns and wine-shops, the later haunt of Robespierre and his friends. Finally, in 1836, the **Arc de Triomphe**★★★ was completed by Louis-Philippe.

The Champs-Élysées became fashionable during the reign of Louis-Napoléon, when high society flocked to the restaurants (like Ledoyen's), to the theatres (like the Folies Marigny and the Bouffes d'Été where Offenbach's operettas were performed), or to receptions in the grand houses (like no 25, today occupied by the Travellers' Club, with its doors of bronze and its onyx staircase).

The avenue has undergone much change since 1914. Its character nowadays is determined by its luxury shops, expensive cafés, and motor showrooms; but it nevertheless remains the capital's rallying point at times of high national emotion (the Liberation, 30 May 1968, the funeral of De Gaulle in 1970, and annually on July 14).

La Défense★★

An outstanding architectural achievement, La Défense has nothing in common with the traditional business districts found in most city centres.

A 1 200m – 4 000ft terraced podium, pleasantly punctuated with gardens, fountains and shaded spots, runs from the Seine up to La Grande Arche. It is lined with an impressive ensemble of huge towers (Tour Fiat: 178m – 583ft) that compose a dazzling tableau of radiant light.

It is also noted for many outdoor works by distinguished modern sculptors, which turn the district into an informal, open-air museum.

La Grande Arche★★

🕐 Apr-Sep: 10am-8pm. Oct-Mar: 10am-7pm (last admission 30min before closing). ☞ 7€ (children: 5.50€). ☎01 49 0▮ 27 27. www.grandearche.com.

The Danish architect Johan Otto von Spreckelsen designed this vast hollow cube which stands at the end of the esplanade and houses private firms a well as several ministries. The Cathédrale Notre-Dame with its spire could fit into the space between the walls of the arch. Each side of the cube is 110m – 360ft long. Towering 100m – 328ft above the esplanade, the 1 ha (2.4 acres) terrace roof is partly taken up by temporary exhibition rooms. From the belvedere visitors will also be able to admire Paris and its suburbs. At the foot of the arch lies the Palais de la Défence **(CNIT)**: it was the first to be built (1958) and has been "rejuvenated". Now it is an important business centre focusing on three main areas of activity: technology, world trade and corporate communication. Nearby stands a car museum **(Musée de l'Automobile de la Colline de la Défense**★★**)** and the glass sphere of a cinema **(Dôme Imax** with a giant panoramic screen.

Bercy

The modernised Bercy district boasts a **Palais Omnisports** by architects Andrault, Parat and Gavan; the imposing buildings of the **Finance Ministry** designed by Chemetow and Huidobro – part of the structure rises above the Seine and the **Jardins de la Mémoire** with three planted areas. Across the river, the **Bibliothèque nationale de France-François-Mitterrand**★ by Dominique Perrault – four tower blocks in the shape of open books – was the last of the "great projects" carried out under the former President.

La Villette★★

The **Parc**★ de la Villette is the largest architectural ensemble within the city. The 55ha – 135 acre site houses an impressive urban complex featuring the City of Science and Industry (Cité de la Sciences et de l'Industrie) and its cinema La Géode, the Zenith concert hall, the Paris-Villette Theatre, La Grande Halle and the Cité de la Musique.

The Intellectual Life

Political and Intellectual Sights

In addition to the city's famous monuments, churches and modern structures, other buildings and districts have come to be identified with the political and intellectual aspects of Paris.

Hôtel de Ville★

It is from here that central Paris is governed. Municipal government was introduced in the 13C, under the direction of leading members of the powerful watermen's guild appointed by Louis IX. The place has long been the epicentre of uprising and revolt. Throughout the French Revolution it was in the hands of the Commune, and in 1848 it was the seat of the Provisional Government. The Republic was proclaimed from here in 1870, and, on 24 March 1871, the Communards burnt it down. It was rebuilt from 1874.

Institut de France★★

The Institute originated as the College of Four Nations founded by Mazarin for scholars from the provinces incorporated into France during his ministry Piedmont, Alsace, Artois and Roussil-

lon). Dating from 1662, its building was designed by Le Vau and stands on the far side of the river from the Louvre. The Institute is made up of five academies: The Académie Française, founded 1635; Académie des Beaux-Arts, 1816; Académie des Inscriptions et Belles Lettres, 1663; Académie des Sciences, 1666; and Académie des Sciences morales et politiques, 1795.

Montmartre★★★

The "Martyrs' Hill" was a real village before becoming the haunt of artists and Bohemians in the late 19C, and it still has something of the picturesque quality of a village in its steep and narrow lanes and precipitous stairways. The "Butte", or mound, rises abruptly from the city's sea of roofs; at its centre is the **Place du Tertre**★★ with the former town hall at no 3, still enjoying some semblance of local life, at least in the morning; by the afternoon, tourism has taken over, and the "art market" is in full swing.

Not far away from all this activity rises the exotic outline of the **Basilique du Sacré-Cœur**★★, a place of perpetual pilgrimage. From here, particularly from the gallery of the dome, there is an incomparable **panorama**★★★ over the whole metropolitan area.

Palais du Luxembourg

J.P. Clapham/MICHELIN

Palais de l'Élysée

The palace has been the Paris residence of the President of France since 1873. It was built in 1718 by Henri de La Tour d'Auvergne.

Palais Bourbon★

The palace of 1722 has been the seat of the Lower House of France's parliament, the Assemblée Nationale, for more than 150 years.

Palais du Luxembourg★★

This is the seat of the Senate, the French Upper House. The president of the Senate exercises the functions of Head of State if the Presidency falls vacant.

It was constructed in the early 17C by the Regent, Marie de' Medici, who wished to have a palace of her own which would remind her of the Pitti Palace in Florence.

Quartier Latin★★★

Lying on the left bank of the Seine, and on the slopes of the mount, **"Montagne" Ste-Geneviève,** and the surrounding area are concentrated many of the capital's most venerable institutions, notably the Sorbonne, the country's most illustrious university, founded 1253. Around them is the ebb and flow of a perpetually youthful tide, the students and other young people who make up the population of the "Latin" Quarter (so-called because Latin was the language of instruction right up to the French Revolution). The area abounds in publishing houses, bookshops, and terrace cafés, including the legendary Flore, Deux-Magots and Procope.

Quartier de St-Germain-des-Prés★★

Antique dealers, literary cafés, the night life of side streets all combine to create the reputation of this former centre of international Bohemian life.

City of Entertainment

This section outlines the city's wide range of entertainment and cultural attractions. Consult publications such as *L'Officiel des Spectacles, Une Semaine à Paris and Pariscope*, and the daily press for details of time and place.

The monthly booklet *"Paris Selection"* edited by the Paris Tourist Office, lists exhibitions, shows and other events in the capital.

Entertainment

Paris may be said to be one huge "living stage", as it boasts a total of 100 **theatres** and other venues devoted to the performing arts, representing altogether a seating capacity of 56 000. Most of these are located near the Opéra and the Madeleine but from Montmartre to Montparnasse, from the Bastille to the Latin Quarter and from Boulevard Haussmann to the Porte Maillot, state-funded theatres (Opéra-Garnier, Opéra-Bastille, Comédie Française, Odéon, Chaillot, La Colline) are to be found side by side with local and private theatres, singing cabarets and *cafés-théâtres*.

Not to mention television studios and the large auditoriums where radio and TV programmes are regularly recorded in public.

Famous artists

On 19 December 1915, Giovanna Gassion was born to abject poverty on the steps of no 72, rue de Belleville. She later sang in the streets, before becoming a radio, gramophone and music-hall success in 1935 under the name of **Édith Piaf**. Beloved for the instinctive but deeply moving tones of her voice, she came to embody the spirit of France *(La vie en rose, Les cloches)*.

Another famous figure was Maurice Chevalier (1888 – 1974), film star, entertainer and cabaret singer *(chansonnier)*; he paired with Jeanne Mistinguett at the Folies Bergères (1909) and sang at the Casino de Paris between the wars. Before attaining fame on Broadway in blacktie and boater, he was known at home for songs that are rooted in Belleville: *Ma pomme, Prosper and Marche de Ménilmontant*.

S. Sauvignier/MICHELIN

Exhibition Centre Georges-Pompidou, rue Beaubourg

Cinemas, more than 400 in number, are to be found in every part of the city, with particular concentrations in the same areas as the theatres and on the Champs-Élysées.

Music-hall, variety shows and **reviews** can be enjoyed at such places as the Alcazar de Paris, the Crazy Horse, the Lido, the Paradis Latin, the Casino de Paris, the Folies Bergère and the Moulin Rouge.

As well as the Opéra-Garnier, the Opéra-Bastille and the Comic Opera (Opéra-Comique), there are a number of **concert halls** with resident orchestras like the Orchestre de Paris at the Salle Pleyel, the Ensemble Orchestral de Paris at the Salle Gaveau, and the orchestras of the French Radio at the Maison de Radio-France. In addition there are many other halls in which full-scale performances are put on (Théâtre des Champs-Élysées, Châtelet, Salle Cortot, Espace Wagram, Maison de la Chimie, Palais des Sports, Palais Omnisports de Bercy, Palais des Congrès, Théâtre de la Ville, Zénith...). There are also nightclubs, cabarets, dens where *chansonniers* can be heard, *café-théâtres*, television shows open to the public, concerts and recitals in churches, circuses, and other entertainment.

Exhibitions

The city has a total of 87 museums and over 100 art galleries. In addition, there are around 30 places where temporary exhibitions are held and a whole array of studios (particularly around the Rue St-Honoré, Avenue Matignon and the Rue de la Seine), as well as libraries and other institutions. Between them, they offer the visitor a continuously changing view of past and present artistic achievement and aspiration. The most famous include the Grand Palais, the Palais de Tokyo, the Pavillon des Arts, the Petit Palais, the Pompidou Centre and the Grande Halle de la Villette.

The Great Museums

Paris Museum Pass, valid for 2, 4 or 6 consecutive days (*price 30€, 45€ and 60€ respectively*), provides unlimited access to more than 60 museums in and around Paris. It is on sale at each of the museums and at city tourist offices. Perhaps the greatest advantage: passholders do not have to wait in line for admission. www.parismuseumpass.fr.

Musée du Louvre★★★

See previous Civil Architecture for the history of the Louvre Palace.

Daily except Tue and some public holidays 9am-6pm (Wed and Fri 9am-9.45pm). Temporary exhibitions under the pyramid: 9am-6pm (Wed and Fri 9am-9.45pm). Permanent collection and temporary exhibits (same ticket, except for temporary exhibits in the hall Napoléon)

381

8.50€ before 4pm, 6€ after 4pm (under 18 years: no charge, under 26 years: no charge every Fri after 4pm), no charge 1st Sun in the month and 14 Jul. Ticket also gives access to the musée Delacroix. Last ticket sold at 5.15pm (9.15pm Wed and Fri). Tickets can be bought in advance at FNAC (☎ 08 92 68 46 94) or at Ticketnet (☎ 08 92 69 70 73) with 1.10€ surcharge. Tickets do not expire. www.louvre.fr.

When the Grand Louvre was opened to the public in 1994, the different collections were divided into three large departments, **Sully, Denon** and **Richelieu**, which are located in the two wings and around the Cour Carrée.

🛈 **Information:** ☎ 01 40 20 53 17. www.louvre.fr.

▶ **Orient Yourself:** The main entrance to the museum is near the Pyramid. There is also an entrance through the shopping mall of the Carrousel du Louvre, accessed by metro stop Palais-Royal-Musée-du-Louvre (lines 1 and 7), on either side of the Arc du Carrousel, or at 99 rue de Rivoli. You will find yourself in the well-lit **Napoleon Hall,** which orients you towards the three wings of the museum: **Denon, Richelieu and Sully**. There is a bookstore, restaurant "Le Grand Louvre", and an auditorium.

🕐 **Organizing Your Time:** The Louvre cannot be enjoyed in its entirety even in several visits, let alone one. From the list of artworks below, decide what you would like to see and head for your selections. The information desks offer a variety of aids and amenities to enhance your visit. For 5€ you can rent an Audio guide, or choose one of the thematic trails (provided on leaflets) designed for all ages that allow you to discover both masterpieces and less well-known works while exploring a particular theme.

🅿 **Parking:** The closest underground car park is **Parking Carrousel-Louvre**, located on avenue du Général Lemonnier. It is open daily from 7 a.m. to 11 p.m. After parking, enter the museum via the shopping mall

of the Carrousel by the fortifications of Charles V.

Kids **Especially for Kids:** Children age 4 and up can take part in one of the many workshops for young people or follow a Children's Route through the museum. Call or check the web site for details.

👁 **Don't Miss:** Of all the artworks inside the museum, probably the most famous are Leonardo's masterpiece, The Mona Lisa (here called La Joconde) and among the classical works, the Victoire de Samothrace and the Vénus de Milo. All three are in the Denon section.

Choose which section of the museum to visit:

Sully
History of the Louvre Entresol
Medieval Louvre Entresol
Egyptian Antiquities
    Ground and 1st floor
Greek Antiquities (Salle des Caryatides, Hellenistic Period)
    Ground floor
Oriental Antiquities (Levantine Art)
    Ground floor
Greek Antiquities (Bronzes) 1st floor
Objets d'art (Restoration and 18C)
    1st floor
French Painting (17C and 19C)
    2nd floor
Beistegui Collection 2nd floor

Denon
Greek antiquities Ground and 1st floors
Etruscan Antiquities Ground floor
Roman and Paleo-Christian Antiquities
    Ground floor
Italian Sculpture Entresol and
    ground floor
Northern Schools: Sculpture Entresol
    and ground floor
Objets d'art (Galerie d'Apollon, Crown
    Jewels) 1st floor
Italian Painting 1st floor
Large Format 19C French Painting
    1st floor
Spanish Painting 1st floor

Richelieu
Special Exhibitions Entresol
Islamic Art Entresol

French Sculpture *Ground floor, Cour Marly and Cour Puget*
Oriental Antiquities *Ground floor*
Objets d'art *1st floor*
French Painting (14C-17C) *2nd floor*
Northern Schools Painting *2nd floor*

Select what to see within the chosen section:

Oriental Antiquities
Statues of *Gudea* and *Ur-Ningirsu* – Mesopotamia: c 2150 BC
Code of Hammurabi – Babylon: c 1750BC
Frieze of the Archers from Darius' palace – Susa: 6C BC
Low-reliefs from Nineveh and Khorsabad – Assyria: 7C BC
Vase from Amathus – Cyprus: early 5C BC

Egyptian Antiquities
Gebel-el-Arak knife – Egypt: end of prehistoric times
Sphinx of the Crypt – Egypt: end of the Old Kingdom
Jewellery of Rameses II – middle of second millennium
Seated Scribe from Sakkara – Egypt: Fifth Dynasty
Funerary chapel of Akhout-Hetep – Fifth Dynasty
Fragments from the Coptic monastery of Bawit – 5C

Classical Antiquities
Kore from the Temple of Hera at Samos – Greece: archaic period
La Dame d'Auxerre (Lady of Auxerre) – Greece: archaic period
Apollo of Piombino – Greece: archaic period
Venus de Milo – Greece: Hellenistic period
Parthenon fragments (metopes) – Greece: Classical period
Etruscan terracotta sarcophagus from Cerveteri, Italy: 6C BC
Victoire de Samothrace (Winged Victory) – Greece: Hellenistic period

Sculpture
Limewood *Madonna* from the Church of the Antonites, Isenheim – late 15C

Diana the Huntress (fountain) from Château d'Anet – French Renaissance
The Three Graces (funerary monument for Henri II) by Germain Pilon
The Four Evangelists by Jean Goujon
Madonna and Child (terracotta) by Donatello – Florence c1450
Marble bust of *Voltaire* by Houdon: 1778
The Slaves by Michelangelo – Florence: early 16C

Painting
Malouel's circular *Pietà* – Dijon: early 15C
St Denis Altarpiece by Henri Bellechose – Dijon: 15C
Avignon *Pietà* by Enguerrand Quarton – c 1440
Portrait of *François* I by Jean Clouet – Loire Valley School
St Thomas by Georges de La Tour – 17C
Gilles by Watteau – 18C
Portrait of *Mme Récamier and Sacre de Napoléon I (The Coronation of Napoleon)* by David
La Baigneuse de Valpinçon (The Turkish Bath) and *Grande Odalisque* by Ingres
Les Massacres de Chios (Scenes of the Massacres of Chios) by Delacroix – 1824
Le Radeau de la Méduse (Raft of the Medusa) by Géricault – 1819
Vierge aux anges (Virgin with Angels) by Cimabue – Florence: 13C
Couronnement de la Vierge (Coronation of the Virgin) by Fra Angelico – Florence: 15C
La Joconde (The Gioconda – Mona Lisa) by Leonardo da Vinci – Florence: early 16C
Les Noces de Cana (The Wedding at Cana) by Veronese – Venice: 16C

Rameses II's breastplate (19th dynasty)

RMN

The Fortune-Teller by Caravaggio (c1590)

La Mort de la Vierge (Death of the Virgin)
    by Caravaggio – Naples: early 17C
Jeune mendiant (Young Beggar)
    by Murillo – Seville: mid-17C
Vierge d'Autun (Madonna)
    by Jan van Eyck – Dijon: 15C
Charles I of England
    by Van Dyck – England: 17C
Vie et règne de Marie de Médicis – allegorical paintings of the *Life of Marie de' Medici*
    by Rubens
Les Pèlerins d'Emmaüs (Pilgrims at Emmaus)
    by Rembrandt

Objets d'art

The Regent Diamond and Crown
    Jewels of France
Ivory figure of the Virgin Mary from
    the Sainte-Chapelle, Paris: middle
    of the 13C
The *Hunts of Maximilian* tapestries
    – Brussels: 1537
The study of the Elector of Bavaria
    by Boulle – early 18C
Clock in ebony case inlaid with tortoise-
    shell by Boulle – early 18C
Monkey commode (gilded bronze)
    by Charles Cressent – 1740
The *Loves of the Gods* tapestries –
    Gobelins: middle 18C
Writing-desk, table and commode in the
    Oeben room – middle 18C
Medici vase (Sèvres porcelain, bronzes
    by Thomire)

Other Major Museums

Musée d'Orsay★★★

🕐 *daily 9.30am-6pm (Thu 9.45pm)Last admission 1 hr before closing.* 🕐 *Closed Mon, 1 Jan, 1 May, 25 Dec.* 👁 *7.50€ (Sun 7.50€), no charge 1st Sun in the month.* 🚽 ☎*01 40 49 48 14. www.musee-orsay.fr.*
The focus of the museum is the period 1848 to 1914. The upper floor is dedicated to the Impressionists, with one of the world's finest collections. There is a considerable collection of pre- and post-Impressionist works. Other sections include decorative arts and photography. Highlights include:
La Source (The Spring) by Ingres
Un enterrement à Ornans (Burial at Ornans) by Courbet – 1849
Les Glaneuses (Gleaners) and *L'Angélus du Soir (Angelus)*
    by Jean-François Millet
Le Déjeuner sur l'herbe and *Olympia*
    by Manet
La Danse (The Dance), sculpture
    by Jean-Baptiste Carpeaux – 1869
L'Estaque vue du port et du golfe de Marseille (L'Estaque from Marseille Bay)
    by Cézanne – 1878
Les Danseuses bleues (Blue Dancers)
    by Degas
L'Église d'Auvers-sur-Oise (The church at Auvers-sur-Oise) and *Autoportrait (Self-Portrait)* by Van Gogh
Le Cirque (The Circus) by Seurat
Aréarea joyeusetés (Women of Tahiti)
    by Gauguin – 1892

Jane Avril dansant (Jane Avril Dancing)
by Toulouse-Lautrec
Balzac by Rodin – 1897
The Mediterranean by Maillol – 1902
Pendant and chain by René Lalique
Héraclès Archer (Hercules the Archer)
in bronze by Antoine Bourdelle
– 1909
Les Baigneuses (Women Bathing)
by Renoir – 1918

Musée National d'Art Moderne (Centre George Pompidou)★★★

🕓 *Daily except Tue 11am-10pm (last admission 1hr before closing); Museum and exhibitions 11am-9pm, Thu 11am-11pm.* 🕓 *Closed 1 May.* 💬 *10€, no charge 1st Sunday in the month.* ♿ ☎*01 44 78 12 33. www.cnac-gp.fr.*

The Centre seeks to demonstrate that there is a close correlation between art and daily activities. For both the specialists and the general public, this multipurpose cultural centre offers an astonishing variety of activities and modern communication techniques encouraging curiosity and participation. The Centre includes four departments: the **Bibliothèque Publique d'Information** (BPI), offering a wide variety of French and foreign books, slides, films, periodicals and reference catalogues; the **Musée National d'Art Moderne – Centre de Création Industrielle** (MNAM – CCI), the former presenting collections of paintings, sculptures and drawings from 1905 to the present time, and the latter demonstrating the relationship between individuals and spaces, objects and signs through architecture, urbanism, industrial design and visual communication; the **Institut de Recherche et Coordination Acoustique/Musique** (IRCAM), bringing together musicians, composers and scientists for the purpose of sound experimentation.
Highlights include:
La Rue pavoisée (Street Bedecked with Bunting) by Dufy – Fauvism:
early 20C
Le Guéridon (Table) by Braque –
Cubism: 1911
Nus de dos (Nudes) by Matisse –
beginnings of Abstraction: 1916
Arlequin (Harlequin) by Picasso
– mature Cubism: 1923

La Vache spectrale (Spectral Cow) by Dali –
beginnings of Hyper-realism: 1928
Le Phoque (Seal), sculpture by Brancusi
– Surrealism in sculpture: 1935
Outside the museum, re-creation of the workshop of the sculptor Constantin Brancusi

Hôtel de Cluny (Musée du Moyen Âge)★★

🕓 *Daily except Tue 9.15am-5.45pm. Last admission 30min before closing.* 🕓 *Closed 1 Jan, 1 May and 25 Dec.* 💬 *6.50€, no charge 1st Sunday in the month.* ☎*01 53 73 78 16. www.musee-moyenage.fr.*
Highlights include:
Ivory casket –
Constantinople: early 11C
Gilt altar-front made for Henri II –
Basle cathedral: 11C
29 medallions from the stained glass of
the Sainte-Chapelle – Paris: 13C
Limoges reliquaries in *champlevé*
enamel – 13C
Golden rose given by Pope Clement V
to the Prince-Bishop of
Basle: early 14C
Eagle of St John (brass lectern) –
Tournai cathedral: 1383
Life of St Stephen tapestry –
Arras: middle 15C
Altarpiece from Limburg in painted and
gilded wood – late 15C
Lady and the Unicorn tapestries –
Brussels: late 15C
Mary Magdalene (probable likeness of
Mary of Burgundy) – Flanders

The Lady and the Unicorn, "Sight" 15C

Musée de l'Orangerie★★

🕐 *Daily except Tue 12.30-7pm (Fri 9pm) – 6.50€ (possibly increased for temporary exhibitions), no charge 1st Sunday in the month.* ☎01 44 77 80 07. www.musee-orangerie.fr

Highlights include:

Portrait of Mme Cézanne by *Cézanne*
Baigneuse aux cheveux longs (Woman Bathing) and *Femme à la lettre (The Letter-Writer)* by Renoir
Nude on red background by Picasso – 1906
La Carriole du père Junier (Père Junier's Cart) by Douanier Rousseau – 1908
Maison de Berlioz (Berlioz' House) and *Église de Clignancourt* by Utrillo
Antonia by Modigliani
Nymphéas (Water-lilies) from Giverny by Claude Monet
Les Trois Soeurs (The Three Sisters) by Matisse
Le Petit Pâtissier (The Little Pastry-cook) and *Garçon d'étage (The Attendant)* by Soutine – 1922
Arlequin à la guitare (Harlequin with Guitar) and *Le Modèle blond (Blond Model)* by Derain

Musée de l'Armée (Hôtel des Invalides)★★★

🕐 *Apr-Sep: Mon-Sat 10am-6pm, Sun 10am-6.30pm; Oct-Mar: Daily 10am-5pm. Last admission 15min before closing.* 🕐 *Closed 1st Mon in the month, 1 Jan, 1 May, 1 Nov and 25 Dec.* ⊚ *7.50€.* ♿ ☎01 44 42 51 73. www.invalides.org.

Highlights include:

Seussenhofer's suit of armour for François I – 1539
Model of the city of Perpignan (one of a series ordered by Vauban in 1696)
Napoleon's flag of farewell flown at Fontainebleau on 20 April 1814
The room where Napoleon died on St Helena (reconstruction)
The Armistice Bugle (which sounded the cease-fire at 9pm on 7 November 1918)

Cité des Sciences et de l'Industrie★★★

Kids 🕐 *Daily except Mon 10am-6pm (Sun. 7pm).* 🕐 *Closed 1 May and 25 Dec.* ⊚ *7.50€ (under 25s: 5.50€, under 7 years: no charge). Planetarium: extra 3€.* ♿ ☎0892

697 072 (0.34 €/mn + 1.60 € reserv. fee). www.cite-sciences.fr.

Built in response to the growing need of young and old alike to have a better understanding of the scientific and industrial world, this living museum encourages visitors to investigate, learn and have fun through a wide range of edifying and entertaining scenarios.

Highlights include:

L'Argonaute (a submarine formerly in use with the French Navy)
Le Nautile (full-size model of research submarine)
Voyager 2 space probe
Model of Ariane 5 rocket (scale 1:5)
Le Robot-mouche (a glimpse into the future development of bionics)

Cité des enfants★

Kids *As above.* ⊚ *5€.*

The ground floor of the Cité is designated especially for young, encouraging scientific discovery through experimentation and play. It's cleverly divided into two sections: ages 2-7, and ages 5-12.

La Géode★★★

Kids 🕐 *10.30am-9.30pm (special times Mon, call in advance), 1 program every hour.* ⊚ *7€ per program. Reservations recommended.* ♿. 😊 *Children under 3 and women over 6 months pregnant prohibited.* ☎01 40 05 79 99. www.lageode.fr.

The Cité's extraordinary reflective spherical cinema and its circular screen (diameter: 36m – 118ft), which rests on a sheet of water, is a remarkable technical achievement, whose bold conception and perfect execution is the work of the engineer Chamayou.

Palais de la Découverte★★

Kids 🕐 *Tue-Sat: 9.30am-6pm; Sun and public holidays: 10am-7pm.* ⊚ *6.50€ (under 18 years: 4€), 3.50€ supplementary cost for the planetarium.* 🕐 *Closed 1 Jan, 1 May, 14 Jul, 25 Dec. .* ☎01 56 43 20 21. www.palais-decouverte.fr.

Located inside the Grand Palais, this children's museum is a marvel of ingenuity and interest, with clever animators to bring the exhibits to life.

Highlights include:

School of Rats

The Planetarium

Lunakhod (Soviet moon buggy) –
   12 November 1970

Fragment of moon-rock –
   Apollo Mission XVII: 1972

The number Pi and the 703 prime
   numbers of the 16 000 000 deci-
   mals calculated

Conservatoire des Arts et Métiers (Musée National des Techniques)★★

Kids ⏰ *Tue-Sun 10am-6pm (closes at 9.30pm Thu).* ⏰ *Closed Mon and public holidays.* ⊚ *6.50€ (under 18 years: no charge).* ☎*01 53 01 82 00. www.arts-et-metiers.net.*

Highlights include: Microscope
   belonging to the Duke of Chaulnes
   – middle 18C

Cugnot's steam-carriage of 1771

Marie-Antoinette's automaton "Dulci-
   mer-Player" – 1784

Jacquard loom

Thimonnier's sewing-machine – 1825

Foucault's pendulum (proving the rotation of the Earth)

L'Obéissante automobile
   by Amédée Bollée Snr – 1873

The Lumière brothers' cinematographic
   apparatus – 1895

Transmitting station from the
   Eiffel Tower

Blériot's No 9 aeroplane (in which
   he made the first cross-Channel
   flight)

◯◯ Other important museums:

   Musée Picasso

   Musée Rodin

   Musée Carnavalet

   Musée d'Art et Histoire du Judaïsme

   Kids **Musée de la Curiosité et de la Magie**

   Musée Marmottan

   Musée d'Art moderne de la Ville de Paris

Shopping

Shopping districts

Most major stores are concentrated in a few districts whose name alone is suggestive of Parisian opulence.

Champs-Elysées

All along this celebrated avenue and in the surrounding streets (avenue Montaigne, avenue Marceau), visitors can admire dazzling window-displays and covered shopping malls (Galerie Elysée Rond-Point, Galerie Point-Show, Galerie Elysée 26, Galerie du Claridge, Arcades du Lido) devoted to fashion, cosmetics and luxury cars.

Rue du Faubourg-St-Honoré

Here haute couture and ready-to-wear clothing are displayed alongside perfume, fine leather goods and furs.

Place Vendôme

Some of the most prestigious jewellery shops (Cartier, Van Cleef & Arpels, Boucheron, Chaumet) stand facing the Ritz Hotel and the Ministry of Justice.

Place de la Madeleine and rue Tronchet

An impressive showcase for shoes, ready-to-wear clothing, luggage, leather goods and fine tableware.

Department stores

⌖*See map following.*

For locals and visitors alike, the city's great department stores are the ideal way to find a vast choice of high-quality fashions and other goods under one roof. Most leading names are represented. Some have free fashion shows. Department stores are usually open from 9.30am to 7pm Monday to Saturday.

Bazar de l'Hôtel de Ville (4th arrondissement)

Galeries Lafayette (9th)

Magasins du Printemps (9th)

Samaritaine (1st)

Au Bon Marché (7th)

Antique shops and dealers

Le Louvre des Antiquaires (1st), Le Village Suisse (15th), the Richelieu-Drouot auction room and the rues Bonaparte and La Boétie specialise in antique objects and furniture. Good bargains can also be found by browsing through the flea market at the Porte de Montreuil and Porte de St-Ouen (Saturdays, Sundays and Mondays).

Fairs and Exhibitions

Paris hosts a great number of trade fairs and exhibitions all year round. The following events are among the most important.

Paris – Expo

(Porte de Versailles) International Agricultural Show and World Fair of Tourism and Travel in March; Book Fair in April; Foire Internationale de Paris in April; International Fair of Photography, Video and Sound in late September; International Motor Show in early October (even years); International Boat Show in mid-December.

Parc International d'Expositions

(Paris-Nord Villepinte) International Fair of Farming Machinery (SIMA) in March; World Exhibition of Computer Science, Office Equipment and Technology (SICOB) in October.

Parc des Expositions

(Le Bourget aerodrome) International Fair of Space and Aeronautics (odd years).

Sports Capital

Among the most popular sporting events held in and around Paris are the International Roland Garros Tennis Championships, the Paris Marathon, the legendary **Tour de France** with its triumphant arrival along the Champs-Elysées, and several prestigious horse races (Prix du Président de la République in Auteuil, Prix d'Amérique in Vincennes, Prix de l'Arc de Triomphe in Longchamp). The **Parc des Princes** stadium is host to the great football and rugby finals, attended by an enthusiastic crowd, and the **Palais Omnisport de Paris-Bercy (POPB)** organises the most unusual indoor competitions: indoor surfing, North American rodeos, ice figure-skating, tennis championships (Open de Paris), moto-cross races, martial arts, Six-day Paris Cycling Event, and also pop concerts by international stars.

Parks and Gardens

The city has as many as 450 parks, public gardens and green spaces, some perfect for a rest and some fresh air, or a place for children to play; other parks are prestigious and historic, and perhaps adorned with fine sculpture.

Among the highlights:

Bois de Vincennes, 995 ha including the Parc Floral.

Bois de Boulogne, 846 ha with the Bagatelle, iris and rose gardens.

Jardin des Plantes, historic Botanic Gardens of Paris.

Jardin des Tuileries, with its ancient and modern stauray.

Jardin du Luxembourg, very agreeable Latin Quarter park with a circular pond alongside a palace, popular with students and with big play areas for children.

Parc Montsouris and **Square des Batignolles**, examples of "Jardins Anglais", with less formal layout.

Parc paysager des Buttes-Chaumont, without doubt the most picturesque.

Jardin du Palais-Royal, a haven of silence and elegance in the very heart of Paris.

Jardin Japonais de l'Unesco.

Jardin du Musée Rodin, ideal spot to prolong the museum visit and discover magnificent city view along its pathways.

Parc Monceau, where it is enjoyable to encounter statues of Musset, Maupassant, Chopin and others.

Parc André-Citroën, the most sophisticated.

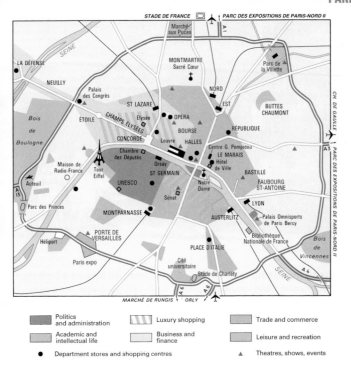

Legend:

- Politics and administration
- Luxury shopping
- Trade and commerce
- Academic and intellectual life
- Business and finance
- Leisure and recreation
- ● Department stores and shopping centres
- ▲ Theatres, shows, events

Parc de La Villette, the largest in Paris.

Parc de Belleville, with views across the whole city.

Parc de Bercy, recalling the wine-dealing past of this modernised district.

Around Paris

50km – 30mi radius from Notre-Dame Cathedral (See Michelin Green Guide Northern France and the Paris Region).

Barbizon★★

The landscapes of the Forest of Fontainebleau and the Bière plateau inspired a group of landscape painters who worked directly from nature (1830-60) and came to be known as the Barbizon School. Together with their leader, Théodore Rousseau (1812-67), these forerunners of Impressionism favoured dark tones, soft light and stormy skies. The old inn **(Auberge du Père Ganne★)** where they used to stay is now a museum **(Musée de l'École de Barbizon)**.

"Coco" Chanel's headquarters

At the end of 1910, Gabrielle Chanel (1883-1971), the descendant of a family of stall-holders from the Cévennes, and well versed in financial dealings and horse racing, set up shop as a milliner in a basement at 21 rue Cambon. Ten years later she moved to no 31. With her keen business sense, she launched in 1920 the famous "Number 5" perfume, a stable, subtle scent blending floral and animal extracts and artificial stabilisers. Her essential talent, however, was in fabric-cutting and dress-making, applied with skill in the use of "humble" fabrics such as jersey, tweed and plaid. She had an expert eye for colour and designed clothes that relied on line rather than ornament for effect. The reputation of this independent career woman, who was a popular figure in the world of poetry, painting and dance, is based in the main on the success of her tailored suits.

Les Deux Magots

Château de Champs★★

An 18C mansion and landscape. The **park**★★ was designed in typically French style, while the internal layout of the **château** broke new ground in its time: the rooms are no longer directly connected with one another and each is provided with a closet and dressing-room; a separate dining room makes its appearance. There is fine Rococo wainscoting **(boiseries★)** and a Chinese Room **(Salon chinois★★)**.

Château de Chantilly★★★ – *See Château de CHANTILLY.*

Château d'Écouen ★★

The château is a good example of the progress made in architecture between the Early and High Renaissance. It houses a **Musée de la Renaissance**★★ which has furniture, tapestries and embroidery, ceramics, enamels…

Château de Gros-Bois★

The early-17C château houses a fascinating **furniture collection**★★ of the Classical and Empire periods; it includes a mahogany bed with gilded bronze decoration, porphyry candelabra and bronzes by Thomire, and furniture by Jacob.

Château de Maisons-Laffitte★

Built 1642-51 by Mansart in early-Louis XIV style, the château subordinates considerations of domestic well-being to the creation of grandiose effects (dominance of its site, majestic scale, use of columns and pilasters, lofty pediments).

Port-Royal-des-Champs★

At the Musée National des Granges de Port-Royal, the spirit of Jansenism is captured in a magnificent painting by Philippe de Champaigne, Ecce Homo, whose power lies in its restraint and profound acceptance of suffering to come. The museum also has a copy of the Augustinius. Below the museum there are remains of the famous abbey in the valley, scene of the struggle between Jesuits and Jansenists.

Rambouillet★

The small town attracts many visitors because of its **château** (Rococo **woodwork★**), its **park**★ with formal parterres, water gardens, Royal Dairy **(Laiterie de la Reine★)**, Shell Cottage **(Chaumière des Coquillages★)** and the splendid walks offered by its vast forest. The château is the summer residence of the President of France.

Abbaye de Royaumont★★

Founded by Louis IX in 1228. The extent of the original abbey church is indicated by the still-extant bases of its columns, while the splendid Gothic refectory and the 14C Madonna of Royaumont evoke the spirit of the Middle Ages.

Rueil-Malmaison★★

Malmaison is a place of pilgrimage for all those fascinated by the figure of Napoleon. In 1799, three years after her marriage to Bonaparte, Josephine bought the château and its park from the actor Talma. The First Consul spent much of his free time here with her; it was the happiest period of their life together and it was to Malmaison that Josephine returned after their divorce (1809). In June 1815, at the end of the Hundred Days (Josephine had been dead for more than a year), Napoleon fled here, staying with her daughter Hortense until his final departure from France.

Lemercier worked on the château around 1625; the building is interesting for its decoration by Percier and Fontaine and for its **collections**★★, which include busts of the Imperial family, Jacob furniture and many other ornamental objects.

The **Château de Bois-Préau**★ has many moving mementoes of Bonaparte's exile and of the eventual return of his remains to France.

Cathédrale (or Basilique) St-Denis ★★★

St-Denis is an important manufacturing centre in the northern suburbs of Paris. It owes its name to the great missionary who became the first bishop of Paris when it was still Roman Lutetia.

St Denis was beheaded at Montmartre around AD 250; legend has it that he walked all the way here with his head in his hands before finally expiring.

The basilica, begun in 1136 by Abbot Suger, is of central importance in the evolution of the Early Gothic style. A century later, the upper parts of the chancel and transept, and nave, were rebuilt by Pierre de Montreuil as masterpieces of High Gothic.

The many royal tombs (tombeaux★★★) in chancel and pre-chancel make the cathedral a veritable museum of funerary art from the Middle Ages to the Renaissance. Note the splendid crypt★★.

St-Germain-en-Laye★★ – ⚲ See ST-GERMAIN-EN-LAYE.

Senlis★★ – ⚲ See SENLIS.

Sèvres★★

Sèvres owes its fame to the porcelain made here. In 1756, on the orders of Louis XV, the original factory at Vincennes was moved to Sèvres, half-way between Paris and Versailles; the government saw the move as an opportunity to assuage the concerns that had arisen as a result of the beginnings of the development of industry. Not unnaturally, Sèvres products are featured in the **Musée National de Céramique**★★, which also has examples of the work from the world's other great porcelain makers. On the ground floor is an "Etruscan vase" (19C), while the first floor has plates, cups, dinner services and a range of objects illustrating the differences between hard- and soft-paste porcelain from 1770 onwards.

Château de Vaux-le-Vicomte★★★

– ⚲ See Château de VAUX-LE-VICOMTE.

Ph. Gajic/MICHELIN

Keep, Château de Vincennes

Château de Versailles★★★ – 🕭
See Château de VERSAILLES.

Château de Vincennes★★
This "Versailles of the Middle Ages" originated in the manor house built by Philippe Auguste. Louis IX was wont to dispense justice here in the shade of an oak-tree. The fortress begun by Philippe VI was completed by Charles V whose place of birth it was.

In the 17C, Mazarin ordered Le Vau to build the King and Queen Pavilions (Pavillons du Roi et de la Reine) with a portico linking them. The **château** subsequently became a state prison.

Built in 1337, the keep (**donjon★★**) is a masterpiece of 14C military architecture. Henri II completed the chapel (**chapelle★**); the choir has fine stained glass (**vitraux★**) made in 1556 in Paris.

Films Set in Paris

Hôtel du Nord (1938) directed by Marcel Carné – This film contains the famous line spoken by Arletty. "Atmosphere, atmosphere, do I look like I've got atmosphere?" The Hôtel du Nord still exists, near the Canal St-Martin whose bridges and locks are inseparably linked to the film, although it was, in fact, shot on a studio set.

Les Enfants du Paradis (Children of Paradise, 1943-45) directed by Marcel Carné – Arletty/Garance, Jean-Louis Barrault/Baptiste, Frédéric Lemaître/Pierre Brasseur, Maria Casarès, dialogue by Prévert – This film is one of cinema's all-time classics.

Gigi (1948) directed by Claude Dolbert – This period movie is full of local colour. It's the story of a young girl who is brought up by an aunt and is married off to a rake. Not to be confused with the musical version.

Zazie dans le métro (Zazie on the Underground, 1959) directed by Louis Malle – A burlesque comedy that is a screen adaptation of an idea by Raymond Queneau.

A bout de Souffle (Breathless, 1959) – A light touch on the camera and natural settings. Jean-Luc Godard's film laid down the principles of the New Wave.

Les Quatre cents coups (The 400 blows, 1959) directed by François Truffaut – A lively spontaneous Parisian lad, Antoine Doinel, ends up in a Borstal-type institution. The unforgettable shots of the streets of Paris are reminiscent of the photographic art of Doisneau.

Charade (1962) directed by Stanley Donen – Audrey Hepburn is chased through Paris by a gang of ruffians and helped by Cary Grant. Is he or is he not interested in the missing 250 000 dollars?

Last Tango in Paris (1972) – Bernardo Bertolucci directs this fateful story of obsessive love in Paris. Stars include Marlon Brando and Maria Schneider.

Le locataire (The Tenant, 1976) directed by Roman Polanski – A lonely young man falls victim to a conspiracy in an apartment block full of hostile neighbours.

Le dernier Métro (The Last Métro, 1980) directed by François Truffaut – The oppressive atmosphere of Paris during the German Occupation.

La passante de Sans-Souci (1981) directed by Jacques Rouffio – A moving performance by Romy Schneider in her last film. Having fled to Paris (Hôtel George V then Pigalle) to escape Nazi killers, she is finally caught.

Diva (1981) directed by Beineix – Paris serves as a refined context for two very different themes. A beautiful black opera singer gets indirectly entangled with the harsh and violent underworld.

Subway (1985) directed by Luc Besson – This was filmed like a video clip, with musical backing by Eric Serra. The leading actors (Isabelle Adjani and Christophe Lambert) express their love in the labyrinthine world of the Paris métro.

Les amants du Pont-Neuf (1991) directed by Léo Carax – The décors are artificial and heighten the unreal atmosphere of the life led by two young homeless lovers in the middle of the Pont-Neuf while work is being carried out on the bridge.

Le Fabuleux destin d'Amélie Poulain, better known simply as *Amelie* (2001) directed by Jean-Pierre Jeunet – Enchanting tale of an eccentric young woman who wanders around Paris making others happy.

PAU★★

MICHELIN MAP 342 J 3 –POPULATION 85 766
GREEN GUIDE FRENCH ATLANTIC COAST

Overlooking the Gave de Pau torrent, the town has guarded an important route to Spain since Roman times. Since 1450 it has been the capital of the Béarn country, in touch with both the lowlands and the high mountains of this ancient southwestern province of France.

- **Information:** Place Royale, ☎05 59 27 27 08. www.pau-pyrenees.com.
- **Orient Yourself:** Pau lies just off the A64 between Biarritz and Toulouse.
- **Parking:** On arrival head for Place Clemenceau or Plade de Verdun in the city centre, and park the car.

A Bit of History

The Béarn and its people

The province has an attractively varied landscape of hills, vineyards, orchards and pasture. Houses are large, with steep slate roofs. **Gaston IV Fébus** (1331-91), an authoritarian ruler who surrounded himself with men of letters; was the first to fortify Pau. **Jean II d'Albret** acquired the Foix country through his marriage to Catherine de Foix in 1484, but was obliged to abandon southern Navarre to the King of Spain. In 1527, his son Henri II married Marguerite d'Angoulême, the sister of François I: it was she who brought the art of the Renaissance to the castle, and, fired with Reformation zeal, made the place one of the intellectual centres of Europe. Their daughter, **Jeanne d'Albret,** married Antoine de Bourbon, a descendant of Louis IX; this enabled her own son Henry of Navarre (the future Henri IV) to garner the inheritance of the House of Valois on the extinction of the line, thereby "incorporating France into Gascony by way of the Béarn" (Henri IV).

Sight

Boulevard des Pyrénées★★

From this splendid panoramic avenue running along a high ridge between the chateau and the park, there is a famous view★★★ over the valley to the Pyrenean foothills, and, in clear weather, far beyond, to the Pic du Midi de Bigorre and the Pic d'Anie.

- **Château★★** ◷ *Guided tours (1hr15min) mid-Jun to mid-Sep: daily 9.30am-12.15pm, 1.30-5.15pm; Apr to mid-Jun and mid-Sep to end Oct: daily 9.30am-11.45pm, 2-5pm; Nov-Mar: daily 9.30am-11.45am, 2-4.15pm.* ◷ *Closed 1 Jan, 1 May, 25 Dec.* *4.50€, no charge 1st Sunday in the month.* ☎05 59 82 38 07– **tapestry collection★★★**.
  Musée des Beaux-Arts★ ◷ *Daily Wed-Sun 10am-noon, 2-6pm.* ◷ *Closed Tue, 1 Jan and 1 May, 14 Jul, 1 Nov and 25 Dec.* *3€.* ☎05 59 27 33 02.

GROTTE DU **PECH-MERLE**★★★

MICHELIN MAP 337 F 4
GREEN GUIDE DORDOGNE BERRY LIMOUSIN

Sited high above the River Célé just before it flows into the Lot, the Pech-Merle cave is one of the most fascinating in terms of prehistory and speleology.

- **Information:** Place du Sombral, St. Cirq-Lapopie, ☎05 65 31 29 06. www.saint-cirqlapopie.com

▶ **Orient Yourself:** The cave is located 7km/4.5mi north of St. Cirq-Lapopie and 32km/20mi east of Cahors.

Visit

🕐 *Guided tours* 🚶 *(1hr) mid-Apr to end Oct: 9.30am–noon, 1.30-5pm. Tour limited to 700 visitors per day (reservations recommended 3 days in advance in Jul and Aug).* 👓 *7€ (children: 4.50€).* ☎*05 65 31 27 05. www.pechmerle.com.*

On the lower level of the cave **(grotte)** are paintings of a fish, two horses covered in coloured dots, and of "negative hands" (made by stencilling around hands placed flat against the rock). Something like a three-dimensional effect is produced by the way in which the Late Perigordian artists integrated their work with the irregularities of the rock surface. There are also representations of bisons and mammoths, as well as petrified human footprints from the Early Magdalenian. The upper level has strange, disc-like concretions, "cave pearls", and eccentrics with protuberances defying the laws of gravity.

POINTE DE **PENHIR**★★★

MICHELIN MAP 308 D 5
GREEN GUIDE BRITTANY

Penhir Point is the most impressive of the four headlands of the Crozon Peninsula, which has some of the finest coastal landscapes in the whole of Brittany.

▶ **Orient Yourself:** Crozon Peninsula (Presqu'île de Crozon) lies between the Brest roadstead to the north and Douarnenez Bay to the south.

Visit

The high cliffs and deep inlets of the peninsula are the result of the faulting and fracturing of this part of the Armorican plateau. The processes of coastal erosion have worn away the sandstone matrix from which the cliffs were formed, exposing the seams of quartzite. In rough weather, the violence of the waves crashing against the variously-coloured rocks makes a magnificent spectacle. Offshore, the line of isolated rocks known as the Tas de Pois marks where the ancient coastline used to be; there is an unusual view of them from the grassy strip called the Chambre Verte.

▶ **Other sites on the Crozon Peninsula**
Pointe des Espagnols★★
Pointe de Dinan★★
Grottes de Morgat★
Cap de la Chèvre★

PÉRIGUEUX★★
MICHELIN MAP 329 F 4–POPULATION 63 539
GREEN GUIDE DORDOGNE BERRY LIMOUSIN

The ancient town, with its distinctive domed churches, is attractively sited in the valley of the River Isle.

Information: 26, place Francheville, Tour Mataguerre, ☎05 53 53 10 63. www.tourisme-perigueux.fr.

▶ **Orient Yourself:** Périgueux is 49km/30mi north of Bergerac.

Parking: The town has three large underground car parks: pl. Montaigne, pl. Francheville and Esplanade du Théâtre.

Guided Tours: The tourist office offers 2hr discovery tours of the Gallo-Roman town (including a visit to the temple of Vesone, which is not open to the public otherwise) or the medieval and Renaissance town (including a visit to the hôtel la Joubertie and the Tour Mataguerre which are also not normally open to the public). *Jun-Sep: daily except Sun*

A Bit of History

Five distinct historical periods have contributed to the formation of this ancient town. First was the Gaulish settlement which prospered in Roman times under the name of Vesunna; its site, the "Cité", is marked by the amphitheatre gardens and St Stephen's Church (St-Étienne). In the Middle Ages, the quarter known as "Puy St-Front" became established on a rise to the north; the cathedral was built here and the area became the heart of Périgueux, eventually in 1251 absorbing the older Cité. In the 18C, the provincial governors, the Intendants, were responsible for a planned northward extension of the city, which linked the two districts by means of broad streets lined with public buildings. At the end of the 19C, the station area was developed, and more recently vast modern suburbs have grown up on the outskirts.

Address Book

For coin ranges, see the Legend on the cover flap .

WHERE TO EAT

⊜ **Au Temps de Vivre** – *10 r. St-Silain – ☎ 05 53 09 87 18 . Closed evenings, Sun and Mon – reserv. recommended.* Tucked away in a pleasant street in the old town, this restaurant serves daily specials, plus savoury and sweet pies. In the afternoon, tea and pastries are served here. The decor includes attractive wooden tables and painted chairs.

⊜ **Au Bien Bon** – *15 r. des Places – ☎05 53 09 69 91. Closed during Feb school hols and in early Nov, Sat lunchtime, Sun, Mon and public hols – .* The menu here is firmly influenced by seasonal local products. Dine in the rustic interior or outdoors on the summer terrace.

⊜⊜ **Le Clos Saint-Front** – *5 r. de la Vertu – ☎05 53 46 78 58. Closed part of Nov.* This old house, with its exposed beams, fireplace and Louis XVI furniture, is now home to an elegant restaurant which is resolutely devoted to Périgourdine cuisine with an inventive twist. Attractive summer terrace with shade provided by linden, banana and liquidambars trees.

⊜⊜⊜ **Hercule Poireau** – *2 r. de la Nation – ☎05 53 08 90 76. Vlosed 24-27 Dec, 31 Dec-3 Jan and Sat-Sun.* In a vaulted 16C cellar, this place is popular with locals, who come here for the varied menu which includes several healthy options.

WHERE TO STAY

⊜⊜ **Comfort Hôtel Régina** – *14 r. Denis-Papin (opposite the train station) –* ☎*05 53 08 40 44 – comfort.periguex@wanadoo.fr. 45 rooms.* It is easy to spot this hotel, thanks to its yellow façade. The rooms are small, functional and colourful. Buffet breakfast, friendly service and good location.

⊜⊜ **Hôtel-Restaurant L'Écluse** – *at Antonne-et-Trigonant – 10km/6mi NE of Périgueux –* ☎*05 53 06 00 04 – contact@ ecluse-perigord.com. 43 rooms.* The River Isle flows gently past the hotel's small waterfront. Rooms on the main façade have balconies which overlook the river. Dine on the terrace in summer.

SHOPPING

Le Relais des Caves – *44 r. du Prés.-Wilson –* ☎*05 53 09 75 00.* The friendly proprietor sells a wide selection of wines from across France, including a few very special vintages. Other local specialities such as fruit preserved in Bergerac wine, wine jam and foie gras are also sold here.

Stéphane Malard – *8 r. de la Sagesse –* ☎ *05 53 08 75 10.* Behind the window arcades of his shop, Stéphane sells the region's finest delicacies, including confits, foies gras, duck magret and wines. What he doesn't prepare himself, he sources with the greatest care.

Markets – Pl. de Clautre: Wed and Sat morning; pl. de la Clautre (food), pl. Bugeaud and pl. Franche-Ville (clothing): every morning; pl. du Coderc (food); duck and goose product market *(marché au gras)* from Dec-Feb.

Sights

St-Étienne-de-la-Cité★

Two of the domes of the original sanctuary have survived. The earlier is thought to have been built in 1117. The second dome, half a century later, is altogether lighter.

Cathédrale St-Front★

Of the original early-Romanesque church there remain only two small octagonal domes at the eastern end of the nave. The church was an important stopping-place for pilgrims on their way to Santiago de Compostela since it was here that the remains of St Front, the apostle of Périgord, could be seen. His tomb dates from 1077. The cathedral was virtually rebuilt from 1852 onwards by Abadie, the architect who designed the Sacré-Cœur in Paris.

▶ Quartier du Puy-St-Front★.
   Rue Limogeanne★.
   Musée du Périgord★

PÉROUGES★★

MICHELIN MAP 328 E 5–POPULATION 1 103
GREEN GUIDE AUVERGNE THE RHÔNE VALLEY

Tightly contained within the ramparts, the tortuous streets and ancient houses of the old town of Pérouges have formed the perfect setting for many a period film.

🛈 **Information:** Entrance of the old Cité, ☎04 74 46 70 84. www.perouges.org.
▶ **Orient Yourself:** The town is just beyond the north-east outskirts of Lyon.

Sight

Cité ancienne★★

On its hilltop site dominating the Ain valley, this fortified town was originally founded by settlers who came from Perugia in central Italy long before Caesar's invasion of Gaul. It was virtually rebuilt in its entirety after the war of 1468 with Savoy. The older buildings are timber-framed with projecting upper storeys. The modest artisans' houses contrast with those of the richer townsfolk and gentry, which have mullioned windows and basket-handle arches. The Upper Gate (**Porte d'en Haut★**) is the principal entrance to the town; the main square, the **Place de la Halle★★★**, has a splendid old hostelry and the **Musée du Vieux-Pérouges**, as well as a Liberty Tree planted in 1792.

PERPIGNAN★★

MICHELIN MAP 344 I 6–POPULATION 105 115
GREEN GUIDE LANGUEDOC ROUSSILLON TARN GORGES

Lively, attractive Perpignan is Catalonia's second city, after Barcelona, and is bursting with vibrant local culture.

🛈 **Information:** Palais des Congrès, pl. Armand Lanoux, ☎04 68 66 30 30. www.perpignantourisme.com
▶ **Orient Yourself:** The most southerly city in mainland France, Perpignan lies on the banks of the River Têt and its tributary the Basse. The city centres on Place de la Loge and Place Arago.
📷 **Guided Tours:** The tourist office runs guided tours through the summer.
🛍 **Shopping:** Clothing boutiques are found near rue Mailly. Avenue Gén.-de-Gaulle is also good for shopping, while the "rue des Olives" (rue de l'Adjudant-Pilot-Paratilla) is well-known for fine foods.

A Bit of History

In the 13C the city prospered from growing trade with the eastern Mediterranean. In 1276, it became capital of Roussillon, part of the Catalan kingdom of Majorca. When the kingdom broke up, Roussillon became part of the principality of Catalonia. From 1463, the French crown tried in various ways to take posession of Roussillon, but met fierce resistance from the local inhabitants. The province was briefly given to the monarchs of Spain, who fortified it heavily. Local people rebelled against Spanish rule too, and in 1640, Richelieu offered Roussillon a degree of autonomy if it would become part of France, which it agreed to do, leading to the Seige of Perpignan as the Spanish tried to retain the city. The French victory was ratified by the Treaty of the Pyrenees.

Sights

Palais des rois de Majorque★

🕐 *Daily. Jun-Sep: 10am-6pm; Oct-May: 9am-5pm. Last admission 30min before closing.* 🕐 *Closed 1 Jan, 1 May, 1 Nov and 25 Dec.* ▨ *4€.* ☎ *04 68 34 96 26.*

The origin of this characteristically Catalan palace lay in the desire of James I of Aragon to make his younger son ruler of the "Kingdom of Majorca" with its mainland seat in Perpignan. Flints and pebbles are used to make decorative patterns in the brickwork. See the great hall known as the Salle de Majorque, the lower Queen's Chapel (Chapelle de la Reine) with traces of medieval frescoesand the royal apartments.

Rue de la Loge ★

The civic buildings make a fine architectural group along Rue de la Loge.

The **Loge de Mer**★ once housed the tribunal regulating Perpignan's sea-trade. Its walls are of the finest stonework with tall Gothic arches at ground level. The Town Hall (**Hôtel de Ville**★) has been rebuilt a number of times. The upper floor is made of bands of pebbles held in place by brick coursing. The Renaissance courtyard has arcades and 18C wrought-iron grilles. The **Députation**★, once the seat of the Catalan "Corts"; has a high arched doorway and window-openings with delicate marble columns.

Castillet★

This pink brick citadel dates from the reign of Peter IV of Aragon, while the adjacent Notre-Dame Gate was built during the occupation of the city by Louis XI. The **Casa Pairal** (🕐 *May-Sep: daily exc. Tue 10am-6pm; Oct-Apr: Wed-Mon 11am-5.30pm;* 🕐 *closed 1 Jan, 1 May, 1 Nov and 25 Dec.* ▨ *4€.* ☎ *04 68 35 42 05)* is now a Catalan folk museum.

Cathédrale St-Jean★

Work on the cathedral was begun by Sancho of Aragon in 1324 but the building was completed only in 1509. The bell-tower is topped by an 18C wrought-iron cage housing a great 15C bell. Inside, the altarpieces of the high altar and the north chapels are fine work of the 15C and 16C. In an outside chapel is a touching carved wood **Crucifixion**★, known as the Devout Christ.

Excursions

Musée de Tautavel (Centre européen de préhistoire) ★★

25km – 15mi northwest of Perpignan, 9km – 5.5mi from Estagel. After the discovery in in the 1970s of fragments of human skull at Tautavel, this little village gave its name to **"Tautavel man"**, hunters living about 450 000 years ago. Highlights of the excellent museum are a reconstruction of his skeleton and a copy of the cave where ithe bones were found.

La Côte Vermeille★★

Between Argelès Beach and the Spanish border, small towns and ports huddle in bays along the mountainous coast. The picturesque port **Collioure**★★, below its royal castle, attracted artists of the Fauve School in the early 20C. **Banyuls** is famous for its sweet wine. In the hills above, the Madeloc Tower enjoys a wide **panorama**★★ of the Côte.

Fort de Salses ★★

Rising strangely above the surrounding vine-covered plain north of Perpignan, this huge and intriguing brick fortress, originally 15C, was adapted by Vauban in the 17C to meet the demands of modern artillery.

CHÂTEAU DE **PEYREPERTUSE**★★★

MICHELIN MAP 344 G 5

GREEN GUIDE LANGUEDOC ROUSSILLON TARN GORGES

The dramatic barrier of the Corbières was defended by a number of strongholds of which the ruins of the Château de Peyrepertuse, separated into two distinct castles on their rocky promontory, are the most imposing.

▶ **Orient Yourself:** The site is 47km north-west of Perpignan. On D14, south of Duilhac, look out for the 3.5km / 2mi narrow access road that leads to the site.

🕒 **Organizing Your Time:** Allow 30min for walk up to the castle and back, and an hour to explore.

🐝 **Caution:** Take great care when walking up to the castle, especially if it is windy. Good footwear is needed. Use the chains, which serve as a handrail.

Visit

🕒 *Jun-Sep: daily 8.30am-8pm; Apr-May and Oct: daily 9am-7pm; Nov-Mar: daily 10am-5pm.* 🕒 *Closed Jan. No visits during stormy weather.* ⊛ *5€.* ☎ *04 68 45 40 55. www.chateau-peyrepertuse.com.*

The Lower Castle (Château Bas) to the east came under Aragonese rule in 1162. In 1240, it surrendered to the Seneschal of Carcassonne acting in the name of the king. Under the terms of the Treaty of Corbeil in 1258, it became part of the fortified French border facing Spanish Roussillon.

The northern curtain wall running to a dramatic point, together with the ruins of the main building, the keep and

chapel, give an idea of the changes that took place over the centuries.

On the far side of the open area separating the two castles, a monumental stairway has been hewn into the rock. The royal castle raised on this western height is known as St George's Castle. It was built in the course of a single campaign, probably by Philip the Bold. There are remains of a cistern and a chapel. From its western extremity the view extends over the fortifications capping the neighbouring crests.

In 1659, the incorporation of Roussillon into France by the Treaty of the Pyrenees stripped Peyrepertuse of its strategic importance, but improvements in artillery had already made it obsolete.

D. Fazery/MICHELIN

Peyrepertuse

POITIERS★★

MICHELIN MAP 322 H -I 5–POPULATION 119 371

GREEN GUIDE FRENCH ATLANTIC COAST

Key events in France's history have occurred in and around this city. The medieval districts in its heart have much of interest to sightseers.

🔲 **Information:** 45 pl. Charles-de-Gaulle, ☎05 49 41 21 24.

▶ **Orient Yourself:** The city is 102km/64mi south of Tours. The old town centre sits on a promontory almost surrounded by the rivers Boivre and Clain.

☞ **Guided tours:** 5.40€. Contact the tourist office for further information.

📷 **Especially for Kids:** Just 12km from Poitiers, the science-themed leisure park Futuroscope is popular with children.

A Bit of History

Poitiers was established in Gallo-Roman times on the promontory overlooking a bend in the River Clain, a site which commanded the "Gate of Poitou", the almost imperceptible rise in the land some 30km – 20mi south that divides the Paris Basin from Aquitaine. It was here in 732 that Charles Martel (688-741) won a great victory against invading Arab forces at **Moussais-la-Bataille** on the banks of the Clain, thereby saving Europe from Islamic rule.

Poitiers was under English domination twice: in the 12C and the 14C. On 19 September 1356, a famous episode in Hundred Years War took place at **Nouaillé-Maupertuis** on the steep banks of the River Miosson. Jean II le Bon (the Good) was fighting with the French forces, who were defeated. The French king surrendered and was taken to London, where he remained in comfortable exile. The result was the signing four years later of the Treaty of Brétigny under which the French agreed to give Poitiers to the English. In 1372 Gen. Bertrand du Guesclin retook the town, presenting it to the king's representative, Duke Jean de Berry, brother of Charles V. In 1418, the fleeing Charles VII set up his court and parliament here; four years later he was proclaimed king. In March 1429, in the Gothic Great Hall **(Grande Salle★)** of Poitiers' recently rebuilt Law Courts **(Palais de Justice)**, Joan of Arc was subjected to a humiliating investigation by an ecclesiastical commission.

In the 16C the city played host to Rabelais, then Calvin and the writers of the Pléiade. In 1569, the place was besieged for seven weeks by a Protestant army under Coligny. In the 18C, under the rule of the centrally-appointed governors known as Intendants, Poitiers became a tranquil provincial capital.

Sights

Baptistère St-Jean★

🕐 Jul and Aug: daily 10.30am-12.30pm, 2.30-6pm; Apr-Jun and Sep: daily except Tue 10.30am-12.30pm, 3-6pm; Oct-Mar. daily except Tue 2.30-4.30pm; 🕐 closed 1 Jan, 25 Dec; ☜ 0.80€; ☎ 05 49 41 21 24.

This is one of France's most venerable Christian buildings. It goes back to the 4C, when St Hilary was elected Bishop of Poitiers, 27 years after the Edict of Constantine. Hilary played a leading role in the conversion of Gaul.

The narthex and baptistery proper have the characteristic architecture of 4C Gaul. The narthex was restored in the 10C and is polygonal in form; there are panels of Roman brickwork under its windows, and beneath the gables are strange pilasters with capitals carved in low relief.

Inside are marble columns and arcades with richly-decorated capitals. Right up until the 17C, the octagonal pool was the city's sole place of baptism, originally by total immersion.

Address Book

🪙For coin ranges, see the Legend on the cover flap.

WHERE TO EAT

⊜ **L'Orée des Bois** – 86280 St-Benoît – ☎ 05 49 57 11 44. Closed Sat noon, Sun eve and Mon. This building covered in Virginia creeper is a restful place for a meal away from the bustle of the city centre. There are two country-style dining rooms, one with a fireplace. Traditional local fare.

⊜ **Jasmin Citronnelle** – 32 r. Gambetta – ☎ 05 49 41 37 26. This delightful tea-room situated opposite a flower-filled courtyard serves a wide variety of teas, pastries and ice cream, as well as quiches and salads at lunchtime. Attractive terrace in summer. Exhibitions of paintings.

⊜⊜ **Poitevin** – 76 r. Carnot – ☎ 05 49 88 35 04. Closed 19 Apr–2 May, 11 Jul–3 Aug, 23 Dec–3 Jan and Sun. The accent is on traditional regional cuisine in this busy restaurant which is popular with locals. Sample specialities such as mouclade charentaise or farci poitevin in one of four comfortable contemporary-style dining rooms.

⊜⊜ **Les Bons Enfants** – 11 bis r. Cloche-Perse – ☎ 05 49 41 49 82. Closed 20–29 Feb, Sun eve and Mon. Amid the many schools of this neighbourhood, this little restaurant with a green façade boasts a large painting of a group of late-19C schoolchildren. The restaurant specialises in regional cuisine. Friendly ambience.

⊜⊜ **Maxime** – 4 r. St-Nicholas – ☎ 05 49 41 09 55. Closed 13 Jul–18 Aug, Sat (except eve Nov–Feb) and Sun. Situated near the Musée de Chièvres in a quiet street in the city centre, this restaurant serves traditional French cuisine. Attractive mix of red and yellow hues in the contemporary-style dining room.

⊜⊜⊜ **Le Chalet de Venise** – in the village – 86280 St-Benoît – 4km/2.4mi S of Poitiers via the D 88 – ☎ 05 49 88 45 07. Closed 1–10 Mar, 23 Aug–2 Sep, Sun eve and Mon. This charming restaurant is situated just outside Poitiers in the village of St-Benoît. The outdoor terrace overlooking a peaceful garden with a stream is the perfect spot for a meal in summer, while the comfortable dining room has a cosy ambience in winter.

WHERE TO STAY

⊜⊜ **Hôtel Gibautel** – rte de Nouaillé – ☎ 05 49 46 16 16 – hotel.gibautel@ wanadoo.fr – 36 rms. This modern hotel situated opposite a clinic on the outskirts of Poitiers has small, modern and well-equipped rooms.

⊜⊜ **Chambre d'hôte Château de Vaumoret** – r. du Breuil Mingot – 10km/6mi NE of Poitiers. Take the D3 towards La Roche-Posay, then the D 18 to Sèvres-Anxaumont – ☎ 05 49 61 32 11 – 3 rms. Although only a few kilometres from Poitiers, this B&B is surrounded by peaceful countryside. Housed in a delightful 17C château in grounds of 15ha/37 acres, the guestrooms here are attractively furnished in traditional style. The perfect place to unwind.

⊜⊜ **Hôtel Château de Périgny** – Périgny – 86190 Vouillé – 17km/12mi NW of Poitiers via the N 149 and a secondary road – ☎ 05 49 51 80 43 – info@ château-perigny.cim – 39 rms. Right in the middle of a park, this 15C château is a haven of peace and tranquillity. The rooms are furnished in period or modern style; those in the annexe are a little more basic. Attractive patio-terrace. Contemporary cuisine.

MARKET

The main food market takes place (daily except Sun) in the market hall near Église Notre-Dame-la-Grande. There is an excellent choice of fruit and vegetables, fish, meat, cheese and bread.

Église St-Hilaire-le-Grand★★

This great Romanesque edifice was built in 1049; it was an important staging-post on the pilgrimage route to Santiago de Compostela and in architectural terms is Poitiers' most interesting church. In 1100, it was given stone vaults to replace the original wooden roof which had been destroyed by fire. The distance it was possible to span in

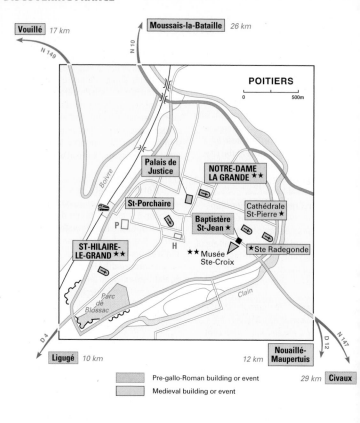

Vouillé 17 km · N 149

Moussais-la-Bataille 26 km · N 10

POITIERS

0 — 500m

Palais de Justice

NOTRE-DAME LA GRANDE ★★

St-Porchaire

Cathédrale St-Pierre ★

Baptistère St-Jean ★

ST-HILAIRE-LE-GRAND ★★

★★ Musée Ste-Croix

★ Ste Radegonde

Boivre

Clain

Parc de Blossac

D 4

Ligugé 10 km

12 km

Nouaillé-Maupertuis

D 12

N 147

29 km Civaux

Pre-gallo-Roman building or event

Medieval building or event

stone was naturally shorter than in timber, and the designer thus had to reduce the width of the nave and increase the number of aisles; he set up a double row of columns linked ingeniously with the original walls and carrying a series of domes. The final arrangement is the unusual one of a nave flanked by three aisles on either side.

Église Notre-Dame-la-Grande★★

The church is a good example of the local version of the Romanesque style as it had developed around 1140. Its harmonious appearance is due to the great height of its rib-vaulted aisles. It has a splendid 12C west **front**★★★, richly decorated with sculpture. Six round columns hold up the choir vault, which was painted in the 12C with a fresco depicting the Virgin in Majesty and Christ in Glory.

Palais de Justice

🕐 Mon–Fri 8.45am–noon, 1.45–5.30pm; 🕐 closed Sat–Sun and public holidays; no charge; ☎ 05 49 50 22 00. The **Grande Salle**★ of Poitiers' recently rebuilt Law Courts was where Joan of Arc was questioned about her vsisions and her instructions from God. The vast hall, scene of solemn audiences, great trials and the sessions of the Provincial Estates, was built under the Plantagenets and restored by Jean de Berry. It has a great gable wall with monumental chimneys, a balcony and Flamboyant windows

▶ Cathédrale St-Pierre★.
   Musée Ste-Croix★★ www.musees-poitiers.org – archeology, ethnology, fine arts.
   Église Ste-Radegonde★.

PONTARLIER

MICHELIN MAP 321 I 5–POPULATION 18 360
GREEN GUIDE BURGUNDY JURA

Between the 13C and 17C this proud upland town, which still commands the internationally important Besançon-Lausanne highway, was the capital of the area known as the Baroichage. This statelet, consisting of Pontarlier and the 18 surrounding villages, enjoyed an independent regime of republican character which was only extinguished by Louis XIV's conquest of the Franche-Comté. Today, Pontarlier is a busy resort and commercial centre.

Information: 14bis rue de la Gare, ☎03 81 46 48 33.

▶ **Orient Yourself:** The town lies near the Swiss border at the foot of the Jura mountains.

Excursions

Cluse de Pontarlier★★

5km – 3mi south. The Jura has many such cluses—lateral clefts through the high ridges separating two valleys that facilitates communication between valley communities. This example, with the road and railway tightly squeezed together in the narrow defile, is strategically located on the route to Switzerland and overlooked by the Larmont and Joux forts high above (The Cluse de Joux is one of the Jura's most beautiful cluses).

Lac de St-Point★

8km – 5mi south. Nearly 7km – 4mi long and covering an area of 398ha – 983 acres, it is the largest lake in the Jura, fed by the waters of the River Doubs and attractively sited among mountain pastures and firwoods.

Source de la Loue★★★

16km/10mi west. The River Loue rises in one of the blind valleys that penetrate deeply into the high plateau of the Jura. In its setting of high cliffs and luxuriant vegetation, it is one of the region's finest natural sites.

LE PONT DU GARD★★★

MICHELIN MAP 339 M 5
GREEN GUIDE PROVENCE

This superb aqueduct and road bridge was built between AD 40 and 60. It formed part of a water-supply system with a total length of 49km – 30mi, stretching from its source near Uzès via a whole series of cuttings, trenches, bridges and tunnels to supply the growing Roman city of Nîmes with up to 20 000 cubic metres—nearly 3/4 million cubic feet of fresh water every day.

Information: Tourist offices throughout the region (*see Planning Your Trip*) have information on the Pont du Gard .

▶ **Orient Yourself:** The site is in the countryside close to the A9 autoroute at Remoulins, west of Avignon. The road bridge is closed to motor traffic, so you must choose from which bank you want to view the Pont du Gard.

P **Parking:** Both banks of the river have a large car park. They are open 7am-1am (5€ per day, fixed charged).

Pont du Gard

Visit

Free access to the bridge at the beginning of the Mémoires de garrigue footpath and at the médiathèque. ☎ *0825 01 30 30.*

The three great rows of arches of the aqueduct rise 49m – 160ft above the valley of the Gardon. One can imagine the effect such a structure must have had on the imagination of the local Gauls, impressing with the power and prestige of Roman achievement, as indeed it still does today. A slight curve in the upstream direction increases its ability to withstand seasonal high waters, while the independent construction of the arches lends a certain flexibility to the whole. Careful calculation of the dimensions of the huge blocks o[f] stone (some of them weighing more than six tonnes) meant that they could be put in place without the use of mortar. The channel on the topmost level was faced with stone in order to maintain water quality, and alongside it ran the carriageway of a Roman road. The Pont du Gard fulfilled its function until the 9C, when lack of maintenance and blocking by deposits of lime finally put it out of use.

GOLFE DE **PORTO**★

MICHELIN MAP 345 A-B 6
GREEN GUIDE CORSE (IN FRENCH)

The Bay of Porto is one of the most splendid destinations on the Corsican coast, owing to its sheer size, range of colours and varied natural sights. Imposing cliffs of red granite contrast with the deep-blue waters. The area is part of a nature park, Parc naturel régional de Corse, listed as a World Heritage Site.

🗎 **Information:** Place de la Marine, ☎04 95 26 10 55. www.porto-tourisme.com.
▶ **Orient Yourself:** The Gulf is the large bay on the shores of which the town o[f] Porto stands, in western Corsica.

Excursions

Calanche de Piana★★★

Boat trips (1hr30min) leaving from Porto.
🕐 *Apr-Sep: departure 2pm, 4pm, 6pm.*

The deep creeks (*calanche*) dominating the Bay of Porto are remarkable; the cha[otic] landscape is shaped by erosion o[f] the granite, jagged rocks and spherica[l] cavities known as "taffoni". A road (D 81) which runs through the calanche for 2km – 1mi, affords splendid viewpoints ove[r] the rock piles and the sea. Starting from the terrace of the **Chalet des Roches** bleues, several walks lasting about one hour allow visitors to admire at close range the distinctive form of some of the rocks: the Turtle, the Bishop, a human head (Tête de Poincaré) and a castle.

Réserve Naturelle de Scandola★★★

The Scandola Peninsula (Presqu'île de Scandola) rises to a height of 560m – 1 837ft between the Punta Rossa to the south and the Punta Nera to the north. The majestic massif is of volcanic origin. It is the habitat of the last surviving pairs of ospreys in France. The large cavities known locally as **"taffoni"**, piercing the bare rocks along the coast, are an integral feature of the picturesque landscape of Corsica. In prehistoric times, they were used as burial places.

PROVINS★★

MICHELIN MAP 312 I 4–POPULATION 11 667
GREEN GUIDE ALSACE LORRAINE CHAMPAGNE

The ancient fortified city of Provins sits atop a ridge overlooking the Seine valley and the Champagne chalklands, roughly equidistant from both Paris and Troyes. The town has a famous outline (once painted by Turner), dominated by a tower (Tour de César) and the dome of Église St-Quiriace. Provins' role as an important centre of commerce was confirmed in the 12C when it became one of the two capitals of the County of Champagne. Its annual fairs were renowned, part of a round of such events which also took place at Lagny, Bar-sur-Aube and Troyes. For a number of years in the 13C, Edmund of Lancaster was lord of Provins, at a time when the place was known for its roses, in those days a rare flower. He incorporated a red rose into his emblem; a century-and-a-half later it was this flower which triumphed over the white rose of York in the Wars of the Roses.

Information: Maison du visiteur, Chemin de Villecran, ☏0 64 60 26 26 www.provins.net.

▶ **Orient Yourself:** Provins is in the Ile de France region, south east of Paris. It can be easily reached by road or rail from the capital. On arrival, head for the Ville Haute. The tourist office offers a choice of guided tours on summer weekends, costing around 6.10€.

Visit

Ville Haute★★

Still protected to north and west by its 12C and 13C walls★★, its most splendid feature is the **Tour de César★★**, a massive 12C keep with an additional rampart built by the English in the Hundred Years War as an artillery emplacement. There is also a roughly-built 13C tithe barn (Grange aux Dîmes), which belonged to the canons of St-Quiriace.

▶ Église St-Ayoul – group of statues★★.

Tour de César

Excursion

Église de St-Loup-de-Naud★

11km – 6mi southwest. The church belonged to a Benedictine priory of the Archbishopric of Sens, and was one of the first in the area to be vaulted in stone.

Erected in the 11C and 12C, it demonstrates the gradual evolution of the Romanesque into Early Gothic (in 1874, the vaulting was subjected to major restoration). The choir dates from the 11C, as does the early-Romanesque cradle-vault next to it. The dome over the crossing, the barely-projecting transepts and the first two bays of the nave were built at the beginning of the 12C. Finally, around 1160, the last two bays of the nave were completed; they are square in plan and have alternating pillars and twin columns on the model of Sens cathedral. The well-preserved doorway (**portail★★**), under the main porch, shows similarities with the Royal Doorway (Portail royal) of Chartres Cathedral; Christ in Majesty surrounded by symbols of the Evangelists on the tympanum, apostles in arched niches on the lintel, statue-columns in the splays, figures in between the arch mouldings. The sculptures of St-Loup mark the beginning of a transition which gave birth to Gothic Realism.

LE **PUY DE DÔME**★★★

MICHELIN MAP 326 E 8

GREEN GUIDE AUVERGNE THE RHÔNE VALLEY

At 1 465m – 4 806ft, this peak is the highest of the peaks in the volcanic landscape known as the Puys. The Gauls erected a sanctuary to their god Lug here, the Romans built a temple to Mercury. In 1648, Pascal conducted an experiment here proving Torricelli's theory about atmospheric weight, taking readings of the height of a column of mercury while his brother-in-law simultaneously did the same in Clermont-Ferrand; the difference was a decisive 8.4cm. On 7 March 1911, aviator Eugène Renaux landed on the top of the Puy de Dôme 5 hours 11 minutes after leaving Paris, thereby winning the Michelin Grand Prix of 100 000 francs.

- **Information:** pl. de la Victoire, Clermont-Ferrand, ☎04 73 98 65 00. www.clermont-fd.com.
- ▶ **Orient Yourself:** It is easy to drive almost to the summit (there is a car park), but more spectacular is the shuttle service running between Clermont-Ferrand and Le Puy de Dôme.
- **Especially for Kids:** Vulcania, close to Le Puy de Dôme, is a dramatic and entertaining leisure park on the theme of volcanoes. *19.5€ (6-16 years: 12€). www.vulcania.com.*

Visit

Panorama★★★

From the summit there is a vast panorama over the city of Clermont-Ferrand, the Grande Limagne basin and the Puys themselves. The Puys, or the Monts Dômes as they are sometimes known, extend over an area 30km – 19mi long and 5km – 3mi wide; in it, there are a total of 112 extinct volcanoes, all more than 50 000 years old.

If visibility is good, the view extends over 11 départements, one-eight of the total surface area of France. At sunset the view is the most spectacular.

Puy de Pariou and Puy de Dôme

J. Damase/MICHELIN

LE **PUY DE SANCY**★★★

MICHELIN MAP 326 D 9

GREEN GUIDE AUVERGNE THE RHÔNE VALLEY

The Puy de Sancy, the highest peak in central France, rises to 1 885m – 6 184ft from the set of extinct volcanoes called the Mont Dore massif, one of the most picturesque areas in the Auvergne.

▶ **Orient Yourself:** Sancy station sits 4km/2.5mi along D983. Take the cable-car ride (3min), then 20min on foot to the summit.

Visit

Panorama★★★

1hr 30min to the summit and back on foot by a rough path from the top station of the cable railway. With the heights of the Mont Dore massif in the foreground, the immense views extend northeastwards over the Puys and to the Cantal massif in the south. The hedged fields of the valley bottoms give way, between 1 100 and 1 400m (3 600 – 4 600ft), to forest of beech, spruce and fir, while the landscape as a whole is enhanced by the presence of volcanic lakes.

Besse-en-Chandesse★

On the eastern slopes of the massif. This is a mountain village, made of lava, with picturesque **streets** and houses, a barbican and a severe little church (**église**★) with sturdy columns, rough capitals, and a choir screen and stalls decorated with Italian-style grotesques of the 16C.

Around the village are a number of volcanic lakes, each with its own character. The **Lac Pavin**★★ occupies a crater which was formed by the explosion of a pocket of gas on the slopes of the **Puy de Montchal**★★; Lake Chauvet has filled the void left by the effects of an implosion, while Lake Montcineyre and the **Lac Chambon**★★ were formed when the volcano Tartaret erupted into the Vallée de la Couze's floor and blocked the outflow of water.

LE **PUY DU FOU**★★★

MICHELIN MAP 316 K 6

GREEN GUIDE FRENCH ATLANTIC COAST

This impressive theme park based around a real château and its grounds takes visitors on a journey of adventure and fun through 2000 years of Vendean hisotry. On summer evenings its château sparkles under the lights of a famous Son et Lumière show in which a cast of hundreds stages an open-air historical pageant; by day the museum, Écomusée de la Vendée★★, evokes the past of the Vendée region, while various attractions along a trail (Grand Parcours★★) lure visitors into the 12ha – 30 acres of grounds. The name Puy du Fou comes from Latin and means "beech hill".

- **Information:** ☎02 51 64 11 11. www.puydufou.com
- ▶ **Orient Yourself:** Puy du Fou is at Les Epesses, south-west of Cholet.
- ◑ **Organizing Your Time:** There is a hotel and restaurant on the site, ideal for an unhurried visit including the evening show.
- Kids **Especially for Kids:** Many of the attractions are for children.

Visit

Grand Parc★★

◑*From approximately mid-Apr to mid-Sep 10am-7pm (9pm on certain dates). Also open to 10pm or 10.30pm on selected dates for Cinéscénie, fireworks evenings (Feux Follets) and late evenings (Nocturnes).* ◉ *Grand Parc only 25€ (child 15€), or with Cinéscénie 42€ (child 24€), or with Nocturnes 5€ supplement, or with Feux Follets 36€ (child 21€). Audio headsets in English: 7€.* Numerous paths surround the chateau, skirting lakes or passing through dense chestnut woods, with many attractions.

Château

It is likely that the original castle, built in the 15C and 16C, was never completed; it was in any case partly destroyed during the Wars of the Vendée. There remains a fine late-Renaissance pavilion at the end of the courtyard, preceded by a peristyle with engaged Ionic columns. This now serves as an entrance. The left wing of the château is built over a long gallery.

Cinéscénie★★★

◑ *Early Jun to end Jul: show (1hr45min) Fri and Sat at 10.30pm (last admission 10pm); Aug: Fri and Sat at 10pm; first two Saturdays in Sep.* ◉ *Book together with the Grand Park – see above. Visitors must reserve.* ☎ *02 51 64 11 11.*

The terrace below the rear façade of the château, together with the ornamental lake below it, makes an agreeable background for the spectacular *"Cinéscénie"* in which "Jacques Maupillier, peasant of the Vendée" directs a company of 700 actors and 50 horsemen in a dazzling show. The history of the Vendée is relived with the help of an impressive array of special effects, fountains, fireworks, laser and other lighting displays.

LE **PUY-EN-VELAY**★★★

MICHELIN MAP 331 F 3–POPULATION 20 490
GREEN GUIDE AUVERGNE THE RHÔNE VALLEY

The town occupies one of the most amazing sites in France, its most striking landmark being the huge statue of the Virgin Mary atop a tall column of volcanic rock. The town is famous for pilgrimages and its fine lace.

- **Information:** pl. du Clauzel, ☎04 71 09 38 41.
- **Orient Yourself:** In the summer there is a tourist train that introduces you to the many curiosities of Puy-en-Velay. Saturday is the market day when the place du Breuil and the surrounding streets come alive with activity.
- **Don't Miss:** The fantastic views from the upper rim of the basin, especially during sunset.

Visit

Rocher Corneille

This is an outlier of the volcano of which the Rocher St-Michel was the vent. It is topped by a 16m – 52ft statue of Notre-Dame of France made in 1860 from melted-down cannons captured at the siege of Sebastopol. The terrace at the foot of the statue offers the best viewpoint over the extraordinary **site**★★★ of Le Puy.

La cité épiscopale (Cathedral Quarter)★★★

The city's growth dates from the 11C, when it took over the urban functions of nearby St-Paulien and when it formed an important destination on the pilgrimage road to Santiago de Compostela in Spain.

The cathedral's fortifications are evidence of the bishops' quarrels with the local lords (the Polignacs, Montlaurs, Mercœurs...) over sovereignty and over the taxes raised from the pilgrims.

In the centre of the old town, the area around the cathedral has a sombre air, with its buildings of granite and lava, narrow arcaded entranceways, mullioned windows, heavy iron grilles and paving stones.

Cathédrale Notre-Dame★★★

Guided tours available, contact the Tourist Office. ☎ *04 71 09 38 41.*

The first building to occupy the site was a Roman temple. This was followed

St-Michel-d'Aiguilhe and Rocher Corneille

J.Damase/MICHELIN

around 430 by a sanctuary dedicated to the Virgin Mary, built at the same time as Santa Maria Maggiore at Rome. Rebuilding and extension took place from the 10C on, and in the 19C major restoration was carried out.

The lofty west front rises from its monumental steps to dominate the Rue des Taules. The windows in the third storey mark the extension to the nave which took place at the end of the 12C and which is supported on massive arcading. The overall impression is a highly ornamental one, due to the pierced or blind Romanesque arches, the use of polychrome granite and basalt stonework, the mosaics in the gables and the columns with carved lava capitals.

The steps continue to rise, giving a good view of the carved doors (which were once painted) of the Golden Doorway (Porte Dorée) with, on the left, a depiction of the Nativity, and on the right, Christ's Passion. In the 10C and 11C, the apse was rebuilt and the transepts and first two bays of the nave erected. At the beginning of the 12C the two adjacent bays were built and vaulted with splendid domes; here there is a carved 14C figure of Christ and a 17C pulpit. The two last bays were added at the end of the 12C.

Dating from the 11C and 12C, the cathedral **Cloisters** ★★ have polychrome mosaics, an allegorical Romanesque frieze at the base of the roof, a fine 12C wrought-iron grillea and, in the Reliquary Chapel (Chapelle des Reliques), a celebrated Renaissance fresco depicting the Liberal Arts.

Chapelle St-Michel-d'Aiguilhe★★

🕐 *May-Sep 9am-6.30pm (mid-Jul to end Aug, 6.45pm); mid-Mar to end Apr and Oct to mid-Nov: 9.30am-noon, 2-5.30pm;* *Feb to mid-Mar and Christmas school hol* *days: 2-5pm.* 🕐 *Closed 1 Jan and 25 De* 🕮 *3€.* ☎ *04 71 09 50 03.*

268 steps lead to the chapel perche on its 82m – 270ft lava pinnacle. Ara besques and polychrome mosaics Byzantine inspiration decorate th chapel doorway. Inside, the comple vaulting gives some indication of th difficulties the 11C architect had overcome in transforming the origin. Carolingian sanctuary; one of his contr butions was the addition of a gallery the narthex. Note two capitals re-used the smaller gallery, the 10C murals in th apse depicting the heavenly kingdom and a Romanesque Christ-reliquar carved in wood.

▸ **Trésor de la cathédrale**★★ (Treasury).
Trésor d'art religieux★★ (Religiou Art Collection in the cloisters).
Musée Crozatier (with a **lace collection**★ of great richness).

Excursions

Château de Polignac

5km – 3mi northwest. There is a stri ing view of this medieval fortress fror the N 102 main road. Its defences wer so strong that its lords were known a the "Kings of the Mountain". From th 17C to the 19C, their descendants hel prominent positions in political an diplomatic life.

The ruined walls and keep rise from basalt platform, a fragment of one the lava flows from the Mont-Denis volcano which poured along the floo of an ancient valley and then solidifiec The strata beneath it were thus pro tected from erosion, while the materia all around was being carried away b

---

Lace

Lace-making was widespread in the area around Le Puy as early as the 17C, though its high point was reached in the 19C, in part due to the efforts of Théodore Falcon (1804-56), who encouraged high standards in both design and quality. Before the First World War, bobbin lace and needlepoint lace were equally popular, but after 1919, the former (also known as pillow lace) became dominant, with threads of linen, silk and wool used to form patterns of great variety and delicacy.

he waters of the Loire, the Borne and heir tributaries. The resulting tableland tands nearly 100m – some 300ft above he surrounding land, a good example f relief inversion.

.ac du Bouchet★

1km – 13mi southwest. The clear waters f the lake, surrounded by coniferous woodland, occupy the almost perfectly circular crater of an ancient volcano. Around it stretch the extensive Devès uplands, formed by a series of fissure-eruptions and overlying the even older granite foundation of the landscape.

LE **PUY MARY**★★★

MICHELIN MAP 330 E 4
GREEN GUIDE AUVERGNE RHÔNE VALLEY

t 1 787m – 5 863ft, Puy Mary is one of the main peaks of the once immense Cantal volcano, which had a circumference of 60km – 37 miles and a cone rising o 3 000m – nearly 10 000ft.

▶ **Orient Yourself:** These peaks are north-east from the town of Aurillac. The summit is reached by a steep path from Pas-de-Peyrol – 1hr30min round trip on foot.

Geography

harp ridges divide the country up into series of amphitheatres, in each of vhich the same set of activities is care-ully staged. Meadows and cropland fill he valley bottoms, where the villages are lso sited, though in areas less exposed to he sun there are birchwoods, grown for uel. On the middle slopes are beeches, used for a range of purposes, and recently lanted conifers. Higher still come the pland pastures, dotted with stone-built uts used until lately as summer-dwell-ngs by shepherds or for cheese-making. Known as burons, they are planted round vith ash-trees, a useful source of fodder n times of drought.

The basaltic lava (unlike the trachytes of Mont Dore) yields rich herbage which is grazed by the reddish Salers cattle, who in their turn yield the milk for which Cantal cheese is famous.

Visit

Panorama★★★

Glacial action has decapitated the vol-cano and worn it down. The view from the top takes in a landscape punctu-ated by the remains of volcanic vents and lava flows which seem to have only just cooled. The **Pas-de-Peyrol**★★ too affords fine views.

he ridge along the top of Le Puy Mary

J. Damase/MICHELIN

QUIMPER★★

MICHELIN MAP 308 G 6-7–POPULATION 120 441
GREEN GUIDE BRITTANY

Quimper is in Brittany's far west and is the capital of Finistere. It lies in a pretty valley at the junction of (kemper in Breton) of two rivers, the Steir and the Odet.

🔲 **Information:** 7 r. de la Déesse, ☎02 98 53 04 05. www.quimper-tourisme.com.
▶ **Orient Yourself:** A large ring-road skirts the town. The old centre lies between the two rivers close to the confluence.
☞ **Guided tours:** The tourist office offers 1hr30min discovery tours and other options including nocturnal tours.

A Bit of History

The town was first of all a Gaulish foundation, sited on the north bank of the Odet estuary 16km – 10 miles inland at the tidal limit. Towards the end of the 5C BC, Celts sailed over from Britain (hence the area's name of Cornouaille, i.e. Cornwall) and drove out the original inhabitants. This was the era of the legendary King Gradlon and of the fabulous city of Ys which is supposed to have sunk beneath the waves of Douarnenez Bay. The town had a long tradition of making faience (fine earthenware), and is a centre of Breton folk art.

Visit

Cathédrale St-Corentin★★

🕐 *Open daily from about 8.30am.* The choir being out of alignment with the nave is particularly striking. This is due to using the foundations of earlier buildings on the site. The choir itself is remarkable for deeply-moulded pillars,

an imposing triforium and the design of the vault spanning both the ambulatory and radiating chapels.

Le Vieux Quimper★

The medieval town lies between the cathedral and the Odet and its tributary the Steyr. There are fine old houses with granite ground floors and timber-framed projecting upper storeys, notably in the Rue Kereona.

⊙⊙ **Musée des Beaux-Arts★★** 🕐 *Daily exc. Tue: Jul and Aug: 10am–7pm; Apr-Jun and Sep-Jun: 10am–noon, 2-6pm. Nov-Mar: 10am-noon 2-6pm (Sun pm only).* 🕐 *Closed public holidays.* ⊛ *4€.* ☎02 98 95 45 20.
Musée Départemental Breton★ 🕐 *Jun-Sep: daily 9am-6pm; Oct-May daily except Sun morning and public holidays 9am-noon, 2-5pm.* 🕐 *Closed Easter Mon, 1 and 8 May, 25 Dec.* ⊛ *3.80€, no charge Sun after (Oct-May.* ☎02 98 95 21 60– local history.
Musée de la Faïence★ 🕐 *Mid-Apr to end Oct: daily except Sun 10am-6pm.* 🕐 *Closed public holidays. Call in advance for guided tour.* ⊛ *4€.* ☎02 98 90 12 72 www.quimper-faiences.com.

Excursion

La Cornouaille★★

Although the area today is limited to the coast and immediate hinterland west of its capital Quimper, Cornouaille was once the Duchy of medieval Brittany, stretching as far north as Morlaix. Brittany's "Cornwall" juts out into the

Dish decorated with Breton figures, HB faïence works (late 19C)

Jean-Yves Uguet / Musée de la Faïence, Quimper

Atlantic just like its counterpart across the Channel. The spectacular coastline with its two peninsulas, **Presqu'île** de Penmarch★ and **Cap Sizun**★★, culminates in the breathtaking **Pointe du Raz**★★★.

POINTE DU **RAZ**★★★
MICHELIN MAP 308 C 6
GREEN GUIDE BRITTANY

Raz Point is one of France's most spectacular coastal landscapes. Its jagged cliffs, battered by the waves and seamed with caves, rise to over 70m – 220ft.

▶ **Orient Yourself:** The point is at the farthest tip of Brittany's Cornouaille peninsula, west of Quimper.

Visit

The **view**★★ extends over the fearsome Raz de Sein with its multitude of reefs and rocky islands (on the outermost of which is sited the lighthouse, Phare de la Vieille). The outline of the Île de Sein can be seen on the horizon. To the north lies the headland, Pointe du Van, perhaps less impressive, but having the distinct advantage of being off the tourists' beaten track.

A coastal path *(difficult in places, 1hr 30min round trip on foot –* 🚷 *to be avoided in bad weather or high winds)* leads round the Point; the sheer walls of the Plogoff Inferno (Enfer de Plogoff) dropping down to the boiling ocean are particularly impressive *(safety rope)*. To the north of the Point, **baie des Trépassés** cuts into the schists; it was from here that the bodies of Druids are supposed to have been taken over to Île de Sein for burial.

REIMS★★★
MICHELIN MAP 306 G 7–POPULATION 215 581
GREEN GUIDE ALSACE LORRAINE CHAMPAGNE

The ancient university town on the banks of the river Vesle is famous for its magnificent and important cathedral, where French kings were traditionally crowned. It has a wealth of other architectural masterpieces. Reims is also (along with Epernay) the capital of champagne's wine industry. Most of the great champagne houses' cellars are open to the public.

🛈 **Information:** 2 rue Guillaume de Machault, ☎03 26 77 45 00. www.reims-tourisme.com.

▶ **Orient Yourself:** Reims is 143km/89mi north-east of Paris on the A4 autoroute, and 275km /171mi from Calais on the A26, which skirts the town. Take any turning for Centre Ville.

🚶 **Guided Tours:** Tours are available from the tourist office.

A Bit of History

Under the Romans, Reims was the capital of the province which was to become Belgium. It was at Reims, in 496, that Clovis, King of the Franks, was baptised by St Remigius (St Rémi). This was a political event of some significance, since it made the ambitious 35-year-old warrior the only Christian ruler in the chaotic times folowing the collapse of the Roman Empire. it was he who halted the advance of the Visigoths at Poitiers, subsequently pushing them back, first to Toulouse, then all the way into Spain. With him, the source of political authority in Gaul passed from Provence to the north.

At the time of the Carolingians, a feeling for beauty became evident at Reims; ancient texts were carefully copied, manuscripts illuminated, ivory carved and masterpieces of the goldsmith's art created. The period produced Charlemagne's Talisman (now in the Bishops' Palace) as well as the Épernay Gospel. In 816, Louis I the Pious had himself crowned here, as Charlemagne had done at Rome 16 years before. It was from this point that the dynasty acquired a sort of religious character, though it was not until the crowning of Louis VIII, four 400 years later, that the city became the recognised place for coronations, with a ceremonial ever more elaborate and charged with symbolism. By the time of Charles X, 25 kings had been crowned here. The most moving coronation was that of Charles VII on 17 July 1429, which took place in the middle of the Hundred Years War in the presence of Joan of Arc; the Maid of Orléans had given Frenchmen the first inklings of national identity, and had persuaded the king to make his way to Reims, even though this involved him in crossing the hostile Burgundian territory of Philippe le Bon (the Good).

On 7 May 1945, in a modern technical college near the station, the document was signed which marked the surrender of Germany. Confirmed the day after in Berlin, this brought to an end the Second World War in Europe.

Sights

Cathédrale Notre-Dame★★★

Illustration 👁 *see Introduction: Art – Architecture.* The present building was begun in 1211. It is one of the great cathedrals of France, built in the Lanceo late Gothic style pioneered at Chartres but with more sophisticated ornamentation, its window tracery above all. The west front has wonderfully soaring lines and superb 13C sculpture, whose masterpiece is the world-famous Smiling Angel (in a splay of the north portal). Inside is one of the greatest achievements of the Gothic, the west end of the nave, best seen towards the end of the afternoon when the sun lights up the two rose windows.

Reims was occupied by the German army between 3 and 12 September 1914 and for four years remained in the battle zone. By the end of the war, out of a total of 14 130 houses, only 60 remained habitable. The cathedral, one of the country's most precious buildings in terms of both artistic and historic value, was in ruins. The artillery bombardments of 19 September 1914 and April 1917 had been particularly destructive. The skilful restoration has largely been financed by the Rockefeller Foundation.

Champagne

Though covering only 2% of the total area planted with vines in France, this northernmost of the country's wine-growing regions is perhaps its most prestigious. The product was known in Roman times, when it was a still wine. It was Dom Pérignon (1638-1715), cellar-master of Hautvillers Abbey (Abbaye de Hautevilliers), who had the idea of making it sparkle by means of double fermentation, a process carried out today by the use of cane sugar and yeasts.

The vines are spread over an area totalling 30 000ha – nearly 74 000 acres, on the lower slopes of the chalk escarpment of the Côte de l'Île-de-France for preference. The most renowned vineyards are the Montagne de Reims (robust, full-bodied wines), the valley of the Marne (fruity wines with plenty of bouquet) and the Côte des Blancs (fresh and elegant wines). Champagne is a blended, branded wine, the prestige of the great labels dependent on the expertise of the master-blenders.

Some 215 million bottles are produced in an average year, with over 75 million of them for export.

Address Book

💶 *For coin ranges, see the Legend on the cover flap.*

WHERE TO EAT

🍽️ **Brasserie Le Boulingrin** – 48 r. Mars – ☎03 26 40 96 22 – boulingrin@wanadoo.fr. This Art Deco-style restaurant dating from 1925 has become an institution in Reims life. The owner is much in evidence, overseeing the operations and creating a congenial atmosphere. The menu is inventive and the prices reasonable.

🍽️ **La Table Anna** – 6 r. Gambetta – ☎03 26 89 12 12. Champagne takes pride of place in the window of this establishment next door to the music conservatory. Some of the paintings adorning the walls are the work of the owner. Traditional dishes renewed with the seasons.

🍽️ **La Vigneraie** – 14 r. de Thillois – ☎03 26 88 67 27. La Vigneraie, in the heart of the nightlife area, boasts a fantastic collection of carafes. Tasty classical menu and fine wine list. Excellent value-for-money.

🍽️ **Café du Palais** – 14 pl. Myron-Herrick – ☎ 03 26 47 52 54. This lively café near the cathedral was founded in 1930. With its original glass roof and a warm red decor, it serves generous portions of salad and other daily dishes, which are much appreciated, as are the home-made pastries. You can also enjoy a reasonably priced glass of champagne.

🍽️ **Au Petit Comptoir** – 17 r. de Mars – ☎ 03 26 40 58 58. Closed 1-5 Jan, 1-7 Mar, 1-15 Aug, 24-31 Dec. This imposing restaurant with its wooden terrace is right behind the town hall. Inside, the black and white decor and studied lighting lend a cosy atmosphere. Traditional cooking and spit-roast dishes.

🍽️ **Da Nello** – 39 r. Cérès – ☎ 03 26 47 33 25. Closed Aug. A Mediterranean welcome awaits you at this Italian restaurant where the tables look onto the kitchen and the pizzas are baked in the oven in the centre of the room. Fresh pasta, grilled dishes and daily specials according to what the market has to offer… and all served with an authentic Italian accent.

WHERE TO STAY

🛏️ **Ardenn Hôtel** – 6 r. Caqué – ☎03 26 47 42 38. Closed Dec-early Jan – 14 rooms.

€5.50. This hotel, behind an attractive brick façade in a quiet little town-centre street, has tastefully decorated rooms and smiling service.

🛏️ **Grand Hôtel du Nord** – 75 pl. Drouet-d'Erlon – ☎03 26 47 39 03 – grandhoteldunord-reims@wanadoo.fr. Closed Christmas period. – 50 rooms – €9.50. Mostly refurbished rooms in a 1920s building set in a pedestrians-only square. The rooms facing the back are quieter. Many restaurants and lots going on nearby.

🛏️ **Hôtel La Cathédrale** – 20 r. Libergier – ☎03 26 47 28 46 – 17 rooms – €7. This smart, welcoming hotel stands in a street lead ingto the cathedral has small bright and cheerful rooms with comfortable beds, while the breakfast room is decorated with old engravings.

🛏️ **Crystal** – 86 pl. Drouet-d'Erlon – ☎03 26 88 44 44 – hotelcrystal@wanadoo.fr – 31 rooms – €9. A haven of greenery right in the centre of town is the main sales argument of this 1920s house. The renovated bedrooms all have excellent bedding. Breakfast is served in a delightful flowered courtyard/garden in summer.

🛏️ **Hôtel Continental** – 93 pl. Drouet-d'Erlon – ☎ 03 26 40 39 35– grand-hotel-continental-restaurant@wanadoo.fr. Closed 21 Dec-7 Jan – 50 rooms – €11.50. The attractive façade of this central hotel adorns one of the city's liveliest squares. The rooms, renovated in varying styles, are reached by a splendid staircase (avoid the rooms overlooking Bd du Gén-Leclerc). Elegant Belle Epoque sitting rooms.

🛏️ **Hôtel Porte Mars** – 2 pl. de la République – ☎ 03 26 40 28 35 – hotel.porte-mars@wanadoo.fr – 24 rooms – €10. Drink tea in the cosy sitting room, or enjoy a drink in the sophisticated bar. A delicious breakfast is served in the attractive glass-roofed dining room decorated with photographs and old mirrors. The comfortable, well sound-proofed rooms all have a personal touch.

ON THE TOWN

Place Drouet-d'Erlon – This square is the prime starting point for anyone wanting to go out on the town. There is something for everyone, whether you are looking for a bar, pub, restaurant, tearoom or brasserie.

La Chaise au Plafond – *190 av. d'Épernay* – ☎ *03 26 06 09 61*. Founded in 1910, this bar and tobacconists is famous for the chair that has remained stuck to the ceiling ever since a shell hit the establishment on 12 September 1914. Terrace in summer. Selection of 150 cigars (Cuban, Honduran or from Santo Domingo).

SHOPPING

Deleans – *20 r. Cérès* – ☎ *03 26 47 56 35 Closed Aug.* Cocoa-based specialities have been made here in the old-fashioned way since 1874. Those to try include Néluskos (chocolate-coated cherries in cognac) and petits bouchons de champagne enclosed in a giant champagne cork made of chocolate.

Fossier – *25 cours Jean-Baptiste Langlet* – ☎ *03 26 47 59 84*. Founded in 1756, the biscuit and chocolate maker Fossier creates the ultimate in Reims confectionary (biscuits roses and croquignoles). Pay a visit to the shop and factory and learn how to "piouler" (stir) your glass of champagne correctly!

La Petite Friande – *15 cours J.-B. Langlet* – ☎ *03 26 47 50 44* – *hjw@sirtem. fr.* For over 170 years, the establishment has prided itself on being the specialists in authentic bouchons de champagne, made with marc de champagne.

Another of their delicious creations are bulles à la vieille fine de la Marne.

CALENDAR

Fêtes johanniques – *2nd weekend in June.* 2,000 walk-ons in period costume accompany Joan of Arc and Charles VII during a massive street festival.

Flâneries musicales d'été – *Jul and Aug.* Over 150 street concerts throughout the town, including shows by major international stars in some of the town's most prestigious and unlikely venues.

CHAMPAGNE HOUSES

Several of the world's most renowned champagne makers have their cellars in Reims, and offer guided tours, tastings and discount purchases.

Mumm, 34 r. du Champ-de-Mars – ☎03 26 49 69 67 – www.mumm.com

Piper-Heidsieck, 51 bd Henry-Vasnier – ☎03 26 84 43 44 www.piper-heidsieck.com

Pommery, 5 pl. du Gén.-Gouraud – ☎03 26 61 62 56 www.pommery.com

Ruinart, 4 r. des Crayères – ☎03 26 77 51 21 – www.ruinart.com

Taittinger, 9 pl. St-Nicaise – ☎03 26 85 84 33 – www.taittinger.fr

Veuve Clicquot-Ponsardin, 1 pl. des Droits-de-l'Homme – ☎03 26 89 53 90 – www.veuve-clicquot.fr

Palais du Tau★★

🕐 *May–Aug: daily except Tue 9.30am-6.30pm; Sep–Apr: daily except Mon 9.30am-12.30pm, 2-5.30pm. Last admission 30min before closing.* 🕐 *Closed public holidays.* ⊕ *6.50€.* ☎ *03 26 47 81 79.* Dating from 1690, the former palace of the bishops of Reims was built by Mansart and Robert de Cotte. In it is housed some of the cathedral's original statuary and tapestries, among them two huge 15C Arras tapestries depicting scenes from the life of Clovis.

The treasury has many objects of outstanding interest, such as the 9C Talisman of Charlemagne, the 11C cut-glass Holy Thorn reliquary, the 12C coronation chalice, the St Ursula reliquary with its cornelian casket, the Holy Ampulla reliquary, and a collar of the Order of the Holy Ghost.

Basilique St-Rémi★★

Dating from 1007, this is the city's most venerable church, though restoration have left little that is Romanesque and less that is Carolingian. The west front was rebuilt during a major restoration in 1170; it is remarkable for its Romanesque south tower. The façade of the south transept with its statue of St Michael was reconstructed in the 14C and 15C.

The sombre interior (**intérieur★★★**) is remarkable for it length (122m – 400ft) in proportion to its width (26m – 85ft). The oldest part of the church is the 11C transepts. In the 12C, the choir was rebuilt in the Early Gothic manner and the whole nave given Gothic vaulting.

▸ Musée-abbaye St-Rémi★★
   Centre historique de l'automobile française★

RENNES★★

MICHELIN MAP 309 L-M 6–POPULATION 272 263
GREEN GUIDE BRITTANY

The city of artistic, architectural and historical interest, founded by the Gauls, became capital of Brittany in the 16C.

- **Information:** 11 r. St Yves, ☎02 99 67 11 11. www.tourisme-rennes.com.
- **Orient Yourself:** Rennes, capital of Brittany, is skirted by a large ring road. The old centre lies on the right bank of the River Vilaine where it is joined by the Ille-et-Rance canal. The tourist office runs guided tours.

A Bit of History

Du Guesclin's Beginnings (14C)

See Dinan. **Bertrand Du Guesclin** was born in a castle (no longer in existence) southwest of Dinan. The eldest of 10 children, he entered a tournament at Rennes at age 17 and unseated several opponents. From this humble victory, he went on to defeat far greater opponents during the Hundred Years War. In the service of France, he freed Périgord from English rule in 1370 and Normandy in 1378.

Great Fire of 1720

In the 18C there was no running water in the town and therefore, no way of fighting fires. In December 1720 an accidental fire caused by a lamp falling into a carpenter's shavings destroyed much of the town. Architect Jacques Gabriel's rebuilding plan resulted in the fine rectangular street pattern and uniform granite houses of today (*see below*).

Sights

Palais du Parlement★★

Guided tours ⌁ daily except Sat-Sun. Closed 1 Jan, 1 May and 25 Dec. ⌁ 5.10€. Call the Tourist Office in advance.
This is the former seat of the Breton Parliament. The splendid south front of the building is an early and characteristically severe example of the Classical style of architecture.

Le vieux Rennes★

The old town was devastated in 1720 by a great fire that raged for eight days and engulfed almost 1 000 houses. Enough buildings were spared to make a walk through the old part of Rennes an architecturally rewarding experience. The medieval houses crowd picturesquely together in the narrow streets, identifiable, like the Early Renaissance (pre-1580) houses among them, by their timber construction, their projecting upper floors and their sculptured decoration. 3 rue St-Guillaume, called the **Du Guesclin** House (although it actually dates from a later period than the Breton hero), has a deeply-carved door flanked by figures of St Sebastian and one of his tormentors.

In the 17C, oversailing upper floors were abandoned and ground-floor walls sometimes built in granite; exuberant timber patterning still found favour. The city's notables had houses built in which the granite ground floor supports one or two upper floors with walls of tufa or Charentes limestone. The **Hôtel de Brie**★ (8 rue du Chapitre) is of such refinement that it has been attributed to Mansart.

After the great fire, the streets were realigned and widened and lined with new buildings with granite ground floors, frequently in the form of arcades, and upper floors of stone.

- Musée de Bretagne★ – the history of Brittany.
  Musée des Beaux-Arts★ – fine picture collection. *www.mbar.org.*
  Cathédrale St-Pierre – interior★; altarpiece★★.
  Jardin du Thabor★ – at former St Mélaine abbey.

RIOM★★

MICHELIN MAP 326 F 7–POPULATION 18 548

GREEN GUIDE AUVERGNE RHÔNE VALLEY

The old town of Riom, market centre of the Limagne district, still reflects the splendour of bygone days.

- **Information:** 16 r.du Commerce, ☎04 73 38 59 45. www.riom.auvergne.com.
- ▶ **Orient Yourself:** A ring of boulevards is built on the former ramparts enclosing the old town.
- **Don't Miss:** Be sure to have a leisurely wander in the Old Town.

Sights

Quartier Ancien (Old Town)

The medieval town is was the capital of the Duchy of Auvergne, then in the 16C and 17C an administrative and legal centre, giving it a heritage of fine houses. Note 16C **Maison des Consuls ★** at 5 Rue de l'Hôtel de Ville; and the Renaissance **clock tower** and 16C **Hôtel Guimoneau★** in Rue de l'Horloge.

Rue du Commerce

The modern sculptures made of lava contrast with the traditional decoration of the houses using the same material (no 36 has 17C caryatids). 16C **Église Notre-Dame-du-Marthuret★**, houses the splendid late 14C sculpture – **Virgin with a bird★★★**, a masterpiece of harmonious proportion.

◐◑ Ste-Chapelle★ – remarkable 15C stained glass windows.
Musée régional d'Auvergne★ – folk art and local customs.
Musée Mandet★ – 17-18C French and Flemish painting and decorative arts.

Excursions

Église de Mozac★

2km – 1mi west. This ancient abbey was founded towards the end of the 7C by St Calminus, becoming subordinated to Cluny in 1095. Until its collapse in 1460, the abbey church was one of the finest in Auvergne. Of the building of 1095, all that remains are arches and pillars and the north aisle, together with the

47 capitals **(chapiteaux★★)** which are the oldest and perhaps the most beautiful in the whole of the province. They are products of a workshop which was active from the end of the 11C until the middle of the 12C and which enjoyed considerable influence. Those depicting Jonah (1st bay of the nave), the Apocalypse (on the ground in the choir), and the Centaur (3rd pillar on the left), are justly famous, but it is the capital showing the Resurrection which is truly outstanding (on the ground at the end of the nave); it is a faithful account of St Mark's text, but in its sober depiction of pose, gesture and expression, goes beyond the telling of a story to convey inner truths.

The Shrine of St Calminus **(châsse de Saint Calmin★★)** in champlevé enamel is an exquisite example of Limoges work with chased and gilded inlay figures.

Église de Marsat

3km – 2mi southwest. The church here has one of Auvergne's great works of medieval art, a 12C **Black Virgin★★** (in the choir of the north chapel). Few will be untouched by this depiction of Mary as a simple countrywoman, holding out the Child in a maternal gesture of great dignity.

Château de Tournoël★★

8km – 5mi west. This is one of the province's most celebrated castles. It dominates the town of Volvic, famous not only for its lava quarry, but also for its spring water, whose exceptional purity is due to the filtering effect of one of the lava flows from the Puy-de-la-Nugère. Picturesquely perched on a crag, the castle has two keeps, one round, one square, joined together by ancillary buildings now in ruins. Mullioned windows of Renaissance date look down onto the courtyard, some of them blocked up to avoid the payment of window tax.

Gour de Tazenat★

22km – 14mi northeast. This lovely upland lake (32ha – 79 acres, 60m – 200ft deep) in its wooded setting marks the northern limit of the Auvergne volcanoes, one of whose craters it now fills.

RIQUEWIHR★★★

MICHELIN MAP 315 H 8–POPULATION 1 212
GREEN GUIDE ALSACE LORRAINE CHAMPAGNE

Situated along the Route des Vins *(see map following)*, **the tiny village of Riquewihr prides itself on its fine Riesling; the vintners' houses in its picturesque streets were designed with the production of wine in mind .**

- **Information:** 2 r. de la 1re Armée, ☎ 03 20 36 09 22. www.ribeauville-riquewihr.com
- ▶ **Orient Yourself:** Rue du Général-de-Gaulle is the main road running east to west from which the museum and the old houses are easily accessed.
- ◔ **Organizing Your Time:** Allow 2hr, and time to try a glass of the region's famous Riesling.
- **Parking:** Use the parking facilities on the outside of the town: place des Charpentiers, rue de la Piscine, rocade Nord and près de la Poste.

Visit

Brick, red sandstone, timber or paint enliven the façades of the houses, adorned with balconies filled with flowers. Some of the dwellings (like the De Hugel house of 1494) go back to the end of the 15C, others to Renaissance times

---

Address Book

♨ *For coin ranges, see the Legend on the cover flap.*

WHERE TO EAT

▱ **Auberge St-Alexis** – 68240 St-Alexis 6km W of Riquewihr on minor road and path – ☎ 03 89 73 90 38. Closed Fri. It's worth venturing into the forest along a dirt track to this former 17C hermitage. You will be rewarded with simple dishes, as authentic as the site, made from local farm produce.

▱▱ **Le Sarment d'Or** – 4 r. du Cerf – ☎ 03 89 86 02 86. Closed 5 Jan-11 Feb, 28 Jun-6 Jul, Sun evening, Tue lunchtimes and Mon. Pale wood panelling, copper light-fittings, fireplace and huge beams create a lovely warm atmosphere in this restaurant. The cooking is traditional and uses seasonal ingredients. Plush, comfortable rooms.

WHERE TO STAY

▱ **Chambre d'hôte Schmitt** – 3 chemin des Vignes – ☎ 03 89 47 89 72. Closed Jan-Mar – ⊟ – 2 rooms. A house with a garden in the higher part of the village, on the edge of a vineyard. The wood-panelled rooms have sloping ceilings. High standard of cleanliness and reasonable prices.

▱▱▱ **Hôtel L'Oriel** – 3 r. des Écuries-Seigneuriales – ☎ 03 89 49 03 13 – hotel.oriel@wanadoo.fr – 19 rooms – ⊡ €9.50. This 16C hotel is easily recognised by its wrought-iron sign. The lack of straight lines in the building, combined with simple decor and old Alsatian furniture and exposed beams, creates a romantic atmosphere. The three new rooms nestled in the annexe are smarter and more modern.

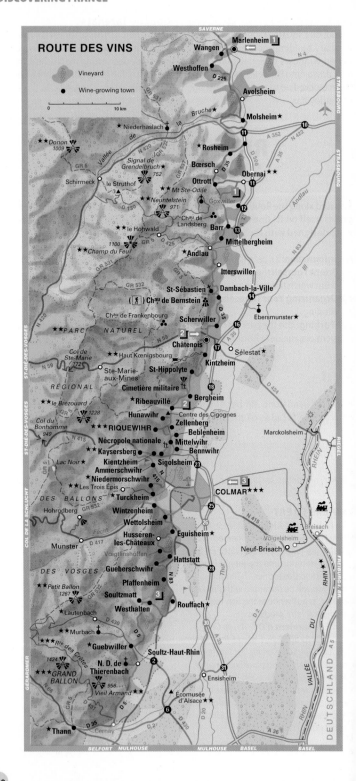

ROUTE DES VINS

Vineyard
● Wine-growing town

0   10 km

Riquewihr

(like the Cour de Strasbourg house of 1597); most of them, however, are of 17C date, but they are all ornamented in the Rhineland Renaissance style which persisted longer in Alsace than elsewhere. Other notable houses are Maisons Lie-

brich (1535), Kiener (1574), Dissler (1610) and Preiss-Zimmer (1686)★.

◗◗ Porte Dolder★ (1291) – local history museum. .

ROCAMADOUR★★★
MICHELIN MAP 337 F 3–POPULATION 614
GREEN GUIDE DORDOGNE BERRY LIMOUSIN

Clinging dramatically to the sheer cliffs of the gorge cut by the little River Alzou, the tiny medieval town of Rocamadour is one of the most visited places in the Dordogne. All around stretches the **Causse de Gramat**★, a vast limestone plateau, known as good sheep country and for its pâté de foie gras.

🛈 **Information:** The tourist office is at L'Hospitalet. ☎05 65 33 22 00.
▶ **Orient Yourself:** Rocamadour itself is approached through a separate small community, almost joined on to it, called L'Hospitalet. You can only enter Rocamadour on foot so park on the plateau and walk into town (or pay and take the elevator) or take the little train (fee). To reach the Place St-Amadour (and the seven sanctuaries), take the stairway at Via Sancta or the elevator.
☺ **Don't Miss:** View Rocamadour from the Hospitalet belvedere *(2km – 1.5mi northeast)*, or from the Couzou road. The castle, rising 125m – 420ft above the valley floor, towers over a picturesque confusion of old houses, stepped streets, towers, gateways, churches and chapels. It's especially lovely at night.

A Bit of History

Long ago, Rocamadour was chosen by a hermit, Saint Amadour, as his place

of retreat. From the 12C onwards, and above all during the 13C, Rocamadour was one of the most popular places of pilgrimage in the whole of Christendom. Just as they do today, souvenir stalls tempted the throngs of tourists, among them Henry III of England, who experienced a miraculous cure here.

Visit

A stairway with 216 steps leads to the Place St-Amadour (**or Parvis des églises**) around which are grouped

seven sanctuaries, including the Chapel of Notre-Dame or Miraculous Chapel. The stream of pilgrims eventually dried up, unsurprisingly, in view of the destruction which was caused by the great rock-fall of 1476 and completed by the Huguenots a century later. In the 19C, the place was restored by the Bishops of Cahors in an attempt to revive the pilgrimages.

ROCHEFORT★★

MICHELIN MAP 324 E 4–POPULATION 25 797
GREEN GUIDE FRENCH ATLANTIC COAST

Rochefort takes pride in an illustrious maritime past. There is still something exotic in the air around the arsenal, where great expeditions were masterminded.

- 🛈 **Information:** avenue Sadi-carnot, ☎05 46 99 08 60. www.tourisme.fr/rochefort.
- ▶ **Orient Yourself:** Rochefort is 38km/24mi south-east of La Rochelle.
- 👁 **Don't Miss:** the Arsenal district.

A Bit of History

In 1665, Colbert chose a site 22km – 14mi up the River Charente and commissioned Vauban to extend the defences of the fort already built there. Though the place had few natural advantages as a port, the presence of easily fortifiable islands and promontories facilitated the great engineer's task.

Seven years later, the work, which included a harbour for the navy, was complete, and by 1690 Rochefort rivalled the naval bases of Toulon and Brest. The increasing draught of modern vessels led to the harbour's obsolescence, however, and on 31 December 1926, the base was closed down.

Visit

Rochefort's history has left many richly ornamented houses; the former rope-walk (**corderie**★★), 374m – 1 200ft long; the great timber hall built by naval carpenters (now a covered market and conference centre), and the Sun Gateway (Porte du Soleil) which formed the entrance to Colbert's **Arsenal**. Admirers of the writer Pierre Loti (1850-1923), a native of Rochefort and lover of the exotic, should pause at the **Maison de Pierre Loti**★ *(45min guided tours.* 👛 *7.65€)*, now a museum evocative of his travels.

- ▶ Musée Naval★.
  Musée d'Art et d'Histoire★.

Pierre Loti (1850-1923)

The author Pierre Loti, whose real name was Julien Viaud, was born in Rochefort at No 141 of the street that now bears his nom-de-plume. He was the son of a municipal official. Loti, a much-travelled naval officer, accomplished sportsman and something of a dandy with a distinguished bearing, was also a novelist of great sensitivity and an exceptional story-teller. Inspired by his voyages to exotic destinations, he wrote *Pêcheur d'Islande* (Iceland Fisherman), *Aziyadé, Ramuntcho* and *Madame Chrysanthème*, books that were instrumental in his acceptance as a member of the élite Académie Française at the unusually young age of 41.

CHÂTEAU DE LA **ROCHEFOUCAULD**★★

MICHELIN MAP 324 M 5

GREEN GUIDE FRENCH ATLANTIC COAST

This elegant Renaissance château, reminiscent of the Loire, stands outside a pucturesque village of the same name.

- **Information:** 1 r. des Tanneurs, ☎05 45 63 07 45.
- ▶ **Orient Yourself:** The chateau and village are in the Charente, north-east of Angoulême.

A Bit of History

The property is the seat of a noble family which gave the name François to all its first-born sons and which produced many a very distinguished soldier, statesman, artist and churchman. **François VI** (1613-1680) established his reputation as the greatest of France's maxim-writers. In his younger days, he thad been a brave soldier but a somewhat inept plotter; he had been imprisoned by Richelieu, fought on the wrong side in the Fronde and was almost blinded by a blast from a harquebus. With a perception of the world sharpened by an understandable pessimism, he produced the *Maxims* for which he is famous, for example: "Hypocrisy is the tribute vice pays to virtue", and "We are all brave enough to bear other people's misfortunes."

Visit

François I de la Rochefoucauld transformed the severe fortress into a sophisticated Renaissance residence, albeit retaining the medieval towers, with its chapel, terrace and 16C façades.

LA **ROCHELLE**★★★

MICHELIN MAP 324 D 3–POPULATION 116 157

GREEN GUIDE FRENCH ATLANTIC COAST

The port of La Rochelle is a lively place, much frequented by artists. It owes its origin to the fort built in the 11C during the centuries of English rule.

- **Information:** pl. de la Petite-Sirene, ☎05 46 41 14 68.
- ▶ **Orient Yourself:** Rochefort is on the west coast of France, easily reached from Bordeaux, Poitiers and Nantes. The town centre lies around the Vieux Port.
- Kids **Especially for Kids:** Take them to the Aquarium (*www.aquarium-larochelle.com*), the Musée des Automates and Musée des Modèles Reduit (*www.museeslerochelle.com*).
- ◷ **Organizing Your Time:** Francofolies is La Rochelle's huge popular music festival celebrating French music and culture for about a week around 14 July.

A Bit of History

La Rochelle was one of the first places in France where the Reformation took hold. After the St Bartholomew's Day Massacre, La Rochelle became one of the main centres of Protestant resistance.

The religious freedoms secured by the Edict of Nantes in 1598 brought several years of peace. By 1627, however, the town's continued adherence to Protestantism had become intolerable to Richelieu, not least because of its English connection. Richelieu personally directed a siege of La Rochelle that took

Address Book

For coin ranges, see the Legend on the cover flap.

WHERE TO EAT

Le Mistral – *10 pl. Coureauleurs, in the Le Gabut district* – ☏ 05 46 41 24 42. *Closed 23 Feb-8 Mar, 23 Oct-4 Nov and Sun to Thu eve except Jul-Aug.* This wood-clad house is located a stone's throw from the tourist office. The maritime-style dining room is on the first floor; the terrace, on the same level, overlooks the old fishing port.

André – *pl. de la Chaîne* – ☏ 05 46 41 28 24. A visit to La Rochelle is not complete without a meal at André! On the old docks, facing the Tour de la Chaîne, this enormous restaurant is comprised of a dozen bistro-style dining rooms where customers sit elbow to elbow to feast on seafood. Nautical ambience and marine paintings.

À Côté de chez Fred – *32-34 r. St-Nicolas* – ☏ 05 46 41 65 76. *Reser. recommended.* Here the fish couldn't be fresher! This little restaurant gets its provisions from its neighbour and sister…the fishmonger. Result: a slate menu that changes as the fishing boats come to moor and an authentic atmosphere just behind the docks.

Le Boute-en-Train – *7 r. des Bonnes-Femmes* – ☏ 05 46 41 73 74. *Closed 26 Aug-9 Sep, Sun and Mon.* Near the markets, this charming restaurant serves a variety of quiches and food fresh from the marketplace. Children's drawings adorn the walls of the bistro dining room…grab a crayon and add to their collection. More mature customers may prefer to visit the vaulted cellar to choose their bottle of wine.

Le Petit Rochelais – *25 r. St-Jean-du-Pérot* – ☏ 05 46 41 28 43. A friendly and competent team has taken over this ex-pizzeria cum bistro. The menu chalked on slate and the inviting atmosphere complement food prepared with brio, cooked fresh each day and served with enjoyable wines.

WHERE TO STAY

Hôtel France-Angleterre et Champlain – *20 r. Rambaud* – ☏ 05 46 41 23 99 – *hotel@france-champlain.com* – *36 rooms.* ☐7€. A spot of the country in the city. On a busy street near the historic district, this old 16C convent features a discrete, pleasant garden – a marvellous place to unwind after a busy day in town. In this genteel setting, the rooms, some quite spacious, are decorated with period pieces.

Hôtel Les Brises – *Chemin digue Richelieu, (av. P.-Vincent)* – ☏ 05 46 43 89 37 -46 rooms. ☐12€. How delightful to open one's windows in the morning, contemplate the ocean and breathe the sea air… This 1960s hotel is well situated between earth and water. Lovely views.

Hôtel de la Monnaie – *3 r. de la Monnaie* – ☏ 05 46 50 65 65 – *info@ hotel-monnaie.com* – *31 rooms.* ☐12€. Right behind the Tour de la Lanterne, this splendid 17C mansion where coins used to be made is an agreeable address. You'll appreciate the serenity of the rooms between courtyard and garden, as well as their modern furnishings and spaciousness.

BARS AND CAFÉS

Cave de la Guignette – *8 r. St-Nicolas* – ☏ 05 46 41 05 75. This charming and colourful wine bar used to be the watering hole of the local fishermen (who have since changed towns). Try the house speciality, Guignette, an aperitif made of wine and fruit.

Café de la Paix – *54 r. Chaudrier* – ☏ 05 46 41 39 79. Behind its carved wood facade, this big café covered with mirrors and mouldings has a long history. A hospital in 1709, a theatre during the Revolution, since 1900 it has been a café popular with visiting artists such as Colette.

LEISURE ACTIVITIES

Casino de la Rochelle – *Allée du Mail* – ☏ 05 46 34 12 75 – *www.lucienbarriere. com. Open daily 10am-5am.* Le Casino awaits with 120 slot machines. From 9pm you can also try your hand at traditional blackjack or roulette.

15 months to starve the town into submission. 23 000 citizens perished. The 5 000 who survived were spared, though a number of their leaders, including the mayor, Jean Guiton, were banished for a period of several months.

La Rochelle contributed more than its share to the opening up of the world beyond Europe; in the 15C, it was from here that the first colonists embarked for Canada and Jean de Béthencourt sailed to discover the Canary Islands; in the 16C, the La Rochelle fishing fleet operated in the rich fishing grounds off Newfoundland. Other explorers to set out from here were de la Salle, who sailed down the Mississippi to the Gulf of Mexico in 1681-12, and René Caillié, the first European to get back from Timbuktu alive. La Rochelle's shipowners profited from international trade, and above all with the West Indies, where they owned vast plantations; they drew wealth too from the triangular trade involving the selling cloth to Africa, transporting African slaves to the Americas, and bringing American products to Europe.

Visit

Vieux Port★★
The old port was originally laid out by Eleanor of Aquitaine; its entrance is guarded by two towers, probably built by the English in the 14C and once forming part of the town's ring of fortifications. **La Tour St Nicolas** ★ (◔ Open daily . ◔ Closed 1 Jan, 1 May, and 25 Dec.

◉ 4.60€, or 10€ ticket combined with the Tour de la Chaine and Tour de la Lanterne. ☎ 05 46 34 11 81) to the east has rested on its foundation of oak piles for six centuries; 42m – 138ft high and with immensely thick walls, it is a fortress in its own right.

Vieux Ville ★★
The 18C **Porte de la Grosse-Horloge**★ leads into the Old Town. As well as timber-framed medieval houses and fine Renaissance residences, there are substantial 18C stone town houses adorned with astonishing gargoyles. The splendid **Hôtel de ville**★, built in Tuscan style, has a courtyard **façade**★ of 1606, with an arcaded gallery.

▶ Museum d'Histoire Naturelle★★.
Musée du Nouveau-Monde★
Musée des Beaux-Arts
Musée d'Orbigny-Bernon★ – local history, ceramics.
Tour de la Lanterne★
Musée des Automates★ Kids – hundreds of automatic figures in life-like set-pieces.
Parc Charruyer★.

Excursion

Île de Ré★
The island, which is also known as White Island and has been linked to the mainland by a viaduct since 1988, is a popular resort. Part of the salt-marshes to the north has been set aside as a bird sanctuary.

ROCROI★

MICHELIN MAP 306 J 3–POPULATION 2 420
GREEN GUIDE ALSACE LORRAINE CHAMPAGNE

First laid out in the 16C in a clearing in the Ardennes forest, Rocroi is a typical Renaissance fortified town.

- **Information:** pl. d'Armes, ☎03 24 54 20 06. www.otrocroi.com.
- **Orient Yourself:** The small town stands close to the Belgian border.
- **Don't Miss:** Vauban's ramparts are a fine example of the great engineer's mastery of his art.

A Bit of History

After the principality of Sedan had been incorporated into France in 1642, the death of Richelieu and the ill health of Louis XIII made a long period of uncertain rule by a regent seem likely. The prospect whetted the expansionist appetites of Philip IV of Spain, for whom the capture of Rocroi would open the way to Paris via the valleys of the Aisne and the Marne.

On 19 May 1643, three days after the death of Louis XIII, a bold manœuvre by the Duke d'Enghien – the future **Grand Condé** – routed the redoubtable Spanish infantry which never succeeded in regrouping. This, the first French victory over the Spaniards for more than a century, reverberated around Europe (it is commemorated by a monument in the leafy countryside 3km – 2 miles to the south). Fortune now began to smile on France, and Mazarin was able to implement Richelieu's foreign policy, using the generation of officers trained by the far-sighted Cardinal.

Later, after his involvement in the disturbances known as the Fronde, Condé went over to the Spaniards, and, in 1658, was responsible for capturing Rocroi for them. But in the following year, the Treaty of the Pyrenees gave the fortress town back to France and Condé to his king.

Visit

Ramparts

The ramparts **(remparts)** of Rocroi were improved by **Vauban**. With their glacis, bastions, demi-lunes and deep defensive ditches they are a fine example of the great engineer's mastery of his art.

RODEZ★

MICHELIN MAP 338 H 4 –POPULATION 23 707
GREEN GUIDE LANGUEDOC ROUSSILLON TARN GORGES

The ancient town stands on a rocky spur high above a meanders of the river Aveyron. Its layout reflects the medieval rivalry of secular and ecclesiastical power: the cathedral and castle districts were both fortified.

- **Information:** pl. Foch, ☎05 65 75 76 77. www.ot-rodez.fr.
- **Orient Yourself:** The town is on a meeting of highways between Langudoc and Auvergne.

Visit

Cathédrale Notre-Dame★★

The 13C red sandstone edifice has a fortress-like west front, once a bastion in the city wall. It has Flamboyant Gothic portals and a **bell-tower** ★★★ that is magnificent. The interior was completed in the 16C but still in the style of the 13C. Note the 15C former **rood screen**★ and the superb 17C carved wooden **organ case** ★. The choir stalls **(stalles**★) are by André Sulpice (15C).

Cathedral of Notre-Dame

A. Thuillier/MICHELIN

- Musée Fenaille★★ – prehistoric and medieval collections.

CHAPELLE DE **RONCHAMP**★★

MICHELIN MAP 314 H 6

GREEN GUIDE BURGUNDY JURA

Built by **Le Corbusier** (1887-1965), the Chapelle Notre-Dame-du-Haut on its hilltop site is one of few great works of religious architecture produced by the early 20C Modern Movement. The characteristically Corbusian use of fluid appears here to great effect.

Information: 14 pl. du 14 juillet, ☎03 84 63 50 82.

▶ **Orient Yourself:** Ronchamp is a small former mining town on Burgundy's border with Alsace.

Visit

The apparent simplicity of the building's curving lines and asymmetrical surfaces can be deceptive, as can the architect's subtle use of light falling from the "periscopes" in the side chapels, filtering in from the base of the convex vault or streaming through the irregular wall-openings which constitute the building's main decoration. Only slowly does one come to appreciate the fusion of feeling and technology which is the measure of the greatness of this unique work of art.

Notre-Dame-du-Haut

B. Kaufmann/MICHELIN

CHÂTEAU DE **ROQUETAILLADE**★★

MICHELIN MAP 335 J 8

GREEN GUIDE FRENCH ATLANTIC COAST

This imposing medieval castle, built in 1306, is part of a compound made up of two forts dating from the 12C and the 14C within a single walled enclosure.

Information: in Bazas at 1 pl. de la Cathédrale, ☎05 56 25 25 84. www.ville-bazas.fr.

▶ **Orient Yourself:** The château is south of Langon on the River Garonne, on the edge of the Landes region.

Visit

🕐 *Guided tours* 🚶 *(1hr) Jul-Aug 10.30am-7pm; mid-Apr to end Jun and Sep-Oct: 2.30-6pm; Nov to mid Apr: Sun, public holidays and school holidays 2.30-5pm. Last admission 1hr before closing.* 🕐 *Closed 25 Dec.* ⌨ *6.50€.* ☎ *05 56 76 14 16. www.chateauderoquetaillade.com.*

Six enormous round towers, crenellated and pierced with arrow slits, frame a rectangular main structure. In the courtyard stands a powerful square keep and its turret. There are also vast vaulted rooms and monumental chimneys. Inside, the decorative paintings and the furnishings are a good example of the restoration of medieval buildings by Viollet-le-Duc during the Second Empire.

ROUEN★★★

MICHELIN MAP 304 G 5–POPULATION 389 862
GREEN GUIDE NORMANDY

With its skyline of towers and spires and fine buildings, Rouen offers a wealth of artistic delights.

- 🛈 **Information:** 25 pl. de la Cathédrale, ☎02 32 08 32 40. www.rouentourisme.com
- ▶ **Orient Yourself:** The city stands on both banks of a curve in the River Seine. The quays on the north bank and the surrounding streets are the city centre. The other bank of the river contains the city's administrative buildings, as well as extensive residential and commercial districts and shopping centres.
- ⊘ **Don't Miss:** Notre-Dame cathedral.
- 🕐 **Organizing Your Time:** Take 1hr 30min for the cathedral and 30min for a walk through Old Rouen with its beautiful 15C-18C half-timbered houses.

A Bit of History

Rouen has been important since Roman times owing to its position as the lowest bridging-point on the Seine; the alignment of its two main streets (Rue du Gros-Horloge and Rue des Carmes) still reflects the layout of the early city.

AlthoughRouen is the birthplace of a number of scientists, it is men of letters and artists who have contributed most to Rouen's fame. **Gustave Flaubert** (1821-80) was the son of Rouen's chief surgeon and lived in and around the city. His major works include *Madame Bovary* (1857), in which the village of Ry (20km – 12mi east) is described under the name of Yonville.

Sights

Cathédrale Notre-Dame★★★

🚹 *Illustration see Introduction: Art – Architecture.* This is one of the finest achievements of the French Gothic. It was rebuilt after a fire in 1200. Thanks to the generosity of John Lackland, Duke of Normandy as well as King of England, reconstruction was swift; the transepts were extended and the choir enlarged

Rouen's cathedral

S. Sauvignier/MICHELIN

Address Book

For coin ranges, see the Legend on the cover flap.

WHERE TO EAT

Pascaline – *5 r. de la Poterne – ☎ 02 35 89 67 44. Reserv. advisable.* Located next to the courthouse, this restaurant with a bistro façade is very nice. Brasserie decor with handsome wood counters, long seats and yellow walls. Choice of attractive fixed-price menus.

Les Maraîchers – *37 pl. du Vieux-Marché – ☎ 02 35 71 57 73.* A restaurant with Parisian bistro airs in a half-timbered house. Wall seats, a bar, tables set close to one another, old advertising plaques, hat and jug collections – nothing's missing! Improvised cuisine. Norman-style second dining room on the ground floor.

La Couronne – *31 pl. du Vieux-Marché – ☎ 02 35 71 40 90.* The decor of this 14C house on the market place is simply superb: beams, carved woodwork, hearths and frescos. It is said to be France's oldest inn. True or false? No one knows, but one thing is certain, their *canard rouennais* (Rouen-style duck) is superlative!

Le Beffroy – *15 r. Beffroy – ☎ 02 35 71 55 27 . Closed Sun evening and Tue. Reserv. required.* This 16C Norman half-timbered house offers the choice between three pretty dining rooms, all equally inviting. A fine address for savouring plentiful fare prepared with quality ingredients.

WHERE TO STAY

Hôtel des Carmes – *33 pl. des Carmes – ☎ 02 35 71 92 31 – h.des.carmes@ mcom.fr – 12 rooms – 6.90€.* Situated in the town centre, not far from the cathedral, this hotel is an appealing halt. The delightfully decorated reception area hints of Bohemia, and the clutter-free bedrooms are charming and well fitted out. A very good address for budget-conscious travellers.

Hôtel Versan – *3 r. Jean-Lecanuet – ☎ 02 35 07 77 07 – hotel-versanrouen@ aol.com – 34 rooms – 9€.* A practical address on a busy boulevard not far from the town hall. The rooms are all similar, functional and well equipped.

Hôtel Dandy – *93 bis r. Cauchoise – ☎ 02 35 07 32 00 – contact@ hotels-rouen.net – Closed 26 Dec to 2 Jan – 18 rooms - 9€.* Situated in a pedestrian street downtown, close to place du Vieux-Marché, this little hotel decorated with care has a certain charm. The rooms, rather too cluttered for some tastes, are quite cosy. Breakfast served in a pretty little room.

ON THE TOWN

Le Bateau Ivre – *17 r. des Sapins – ☎ 02 35 70 09 05 – Open Wed-Sat 10pm-4am. Closed Aug.* Ever on the lookout for new talents, this bar has been livening up Rouen night life for the past 20 years. Concerts Fridays and Saturdays, ballads and poetry Thursdays, café-theatre or French songs Tuesday evenings. A few programmes are available at the tourist office.

Bar de la Crosse – *53 r. de l'Hôpital – ☎ 02 35 70 16 68. Closed Sun, Mon, and early to mid-Aug and public holidays.* When spending time in Rouen, pay a visit to this small, unpretentious bar. It owes its fine reputation to its singular atmosphere; between concerts and exhibits, laughter abounds, and it isn't unusual to see tourists and regulars chatting here like old friends.

Taverne St-Amant – *11 r. St-Amant – ☎ 02 35 88 51 34. Open until 2am. Closed 3 weeks in Aug.* Transformed into a bar 30 years ago, this 17C house attracts painters, writers, actors and other regular patrons. Convivial atmosphere.

SHOWTIME

Théâtre de l'Écharde – *16 r. Flahaut – ☎ 02 35 15 33 05 – tickets: at the theatre before performance.* Theatre with 100 seats where the troupe's creations and shows for young theatre-goers are performed.

Théâtre des Deux Rives – *48 r. Louis Ricard – ☎ 02 35 70 22 82 – www. theatredes2rives.com . Ticket office open Tue-Sat 2-7pm . Closed Jul-Aug.* Classical and modern theatre.

SHOPPING

Markets – Place Saint-Marc (Tue, Fri and Sat all day); Place des Emmurés (Tue and Sat all day); Place du Vieux-

Marché (daily except Mon, mornings).
Faïencerie Augy-Carpentier – *26 r. St-Romain* – ☎ *02 35 88 77 47*. The last handmade and hand-decorated earthenware workshop in Rouen! They offer copies of many traditional motifs on white and pink backgrounds, from blue monochrome to multicoloured, and from lambrequin to cornucopia. Personalized pieces available.
Hardi –*22 pl. du Vieux-Marché* – ☎*02 35 71 81 55. Closed Sun-Mon*. In this alluring delicatessen, the Hardis offer Rouen specialities such as terrine de canard, duck being a highly prized fowl in this city (also known for its mutton). Mr Hardi's andouilles de Vire and his Caen tripe cooked in calvados and cider, specialities from Normandy, have clinched his reputation.
Chocolatier Auzou – *163 r. du Gros-Horloge* – ☎ *02 35 70 59 31*. Located in a half-timbered house, this renowned chocolatier will tempt you with his specialities, such as Les Larmes de Jeanne d'Arc (Joan of Arc's Tears: lightly roasted almonds covered with nougatine and chocolate) or L'Agneau Rouennais (a sort of sponge cake) and candied apples.

The spaciousness of the interior is striking. The choir, with its 14 soaring pillars and delicate triforium, is a masterpiece of harmonious proportion.

The great edifice seems to have been under repair for most of its existence for varied reasons: the Hundred Years War, another fire in 1514, the Religious Wars, the hurricane of 1683, the French Revolution, the burning-down of the spire in 1822 and the aerial bombardment of the night of 19 April 1944. This most recent disaster threatened the whole structure, and restoration work still goes on today.

Vieux Rouen★★★

All around the cathedral and the Rue du Gros Horloge approaching it is Vieux Rouen. The old town's narrow streets, many of them pedestrianised, are lined with more than 800 timber-framed houses, large and small, elegant or picturesquely askew, all characteristic examples of medieval building techniques. Until 1520, the upper floors jutted out for reasons of economy and greater floor-space.

Bustling **Rue du Gros-Horloge★★**, lined with old houses and given over to pedestrians, is one of the city centre's main attractions. **The Gros-Horloge clock** on its arch has only one hand; next to it is the belfry from the top of which there is a fine view over the city and its surroundings.

Rue St-Romain★★ is one of the most fascinating streets, with many timber-framed houses dating from the 15C to the 18C. No 74 is a Gothic building with 15C windows.

Place du Vieux-Marché★

This modern complex on the edge of the Old Town occupies the site where Joan of Arc, aged 19, was burned at the stake following her trial as a heretic; 25 years later she was rehabilitated. In the centre of the square is the great Cross of Rehabilitation, marking the place where Joan of Arc was burnt. There is also a covered market and a church incorporating stained-glass windows (**verrière★★**) of 16C date.

Église St-Maclou★★

When compared to the cathedral, the church provides striking evidence of the evolution of the Gothic style. It was begun in 1437 and is a fine example of the Flamboyant style at its purest. Nevertheless its decoration is of the Renaissance (doors, stairs, gallery and organ-case). At the north corner of the west front is a fountain with two manikins performing the same act as their counterpart at Brussels, albeit with somewhat less finesse.

Aître St-Maclou★★

This is a rare example of a medieval plague cemetery. It is enclosed by half-timbered buildings decorated with macabre carvings showing the Dance of Death, skulls and crossbones, grave-diggers' tools...

Église St-Ouen★★

Built in the 14C, this former abbey church marks the peak of achievement of the High Gothic style. Its architect was complete master of the forces acting on his building, leading them at will via ogee arches on to flying buttresses weighted by pinnacles, thence to foundations beyond the walls. The structural problem solved, he was then able to concentrate on designing the shell of the building. With no structural role, walls could become windows, flooding the interior with light and thereby encouraging an increasingly literate congregation to follow the service with the missals now coming into use.

A few years on, and the Gothic had fulfilled its architectural potential; its final phase, the Flamboyant, is a virtuoso style, delighting in ornamental excess rather than structural innovation.

Musée des Beaux-Arts★★★

🕓 Daily 10am-6pm (South wing closed 1-2pm). 🕓 Closed Tue and certain public holidays. ♿ ⌨ 3€, no charge 1st Sun in the month. ☎ 02 35 71 28 40. www.rouen-musees.com.

The museum has a magnificent collection of 15C-20C painting, especially in the earlier period, as well as fine sculpture, and other pieces including furniture and gold-work. See Gérard David's *Virgin and Saints*, an oil painting on wood, one of the masterpieces of Flemish Primitive art, as well as several choice pieces from the French School: *Diana Bathing* by François Clouet, The *Concert of Angels* by Philippe de Champaigne, and *Venus Arming Aeneas* by Nicolas Poussin. Other outstanding works from European countries are *The Adoration of the Shepherds* by Rubens, *St Barnabé Healing the Sick* by Veronese, and especially *Democritus* by Velasquez.

Palais de Justice

Musée de la Céramique★★

🕓 Wed-Mon 10am-1pm, 2-6pm. 🕓 Closed Tue and certain public holidays. ⌨ 2.30€, no charge 1st Sun in the month. ☎ 02 35 50 31 74.

The 17C Hotel d'Hocqueville houses this museum, which presents the history of Rouen pottery with outstanding faience collections. The work of **Masséot Abaquesne**, the first faience-maker in Rouen in the mid 16C, represented here. Rouen pottery enjoyed great popularity in the 18C. The liking for chinoiserie and lambrequin ornament, and a desire to replace metal plates and dishes with ceramics (⚫ *see Index*), helped assure Rouen's success with ewers, fountains, spice pots. The fine bust of Apollo of c 1740 from the Fouquay workshop exemplifies both taste and technique.

▸ Palais de Justice★★
Musée Le Secq des Tournelles★★
– wrought-ironwork.
Panorama★★★ from Côte-Ste-Catherine
Jardin des Plantes★.

ROUTE DES CRÊTES★★★

MICHELIN MAP 315 G 8, F 8, F 9 AND G 9

GREEN GUIDE ALSACE LORRAINE CHAMPAGNE

In the First World War, the French and German armies confronted each other along the old frontier between the two countries formed by the crest-line of the Vosges. Hugging the ridge is the strategic north-south road planned by French military engineers to serve the front; today it forms a fine scenic route, the Vosges Scenic Road, running for 63km – 39 miles from the Bonhomme Pass (Col du Bonhomme) in the north to Thann in the south. It offers the visitor a splendid introduction to the varied landscapes of these uplands, which include the sweeping pasturelands of the summits, an array of lakes, and the broad valleys of the Fisch and the Thur.

▶ **Orient Yourself:** The route starts 30km/18.6mi west of Colmar and heads south to Thann.

⊙ **Don't Miss:** There are stunning panoramas between Le Hohneck and the Grand Ballon.

Driving Tour

Col du Bonhomme

949m – 3 114ft high, this is the pass linking the provinces of Alsace and Lorraine.

Col de la Schlucht

1 139m – 3 737ft. This is the steepest, but also one of the busiest of the routes through the Vosges. The eastern slopes are subject to intense erosion because of the gradient of the torrential rivers; at a distance of only 9km – 5mi from the pass, the town of **Munster**★ lies 877m – 2 877ft below, while Colmar, 26km – 16mi away is 1 065m – 3 494ft lower.

Hohneck★★★

1 362m – 4 469ft. Rising near the central point of the range, this is one of the most visited of the Vosges summits. From the top there are superb **views**★★★; to the east, the **Munster Valley**★★ plunges steeply down towards the broad expanses of the Alsace plain, while to the west is the Lorraine plateau, cut into by the valley of the Vologne.

Grand Ballon★★★

1 424m – 4 672ft. The Grand Ballon forms the highest point of the Vosges. From the top *(30min round trip on foot)* the magnificent **panorama**★★★ extends over the southern part of the

Summer pastures

range, whose physiognomy can be fully appreciated. The eastern and western slopes are quite unlike each other; the drop to the Alsace plain is abrupt, while to the west the land falls away gently to the Lorraine plateau. Glacial action in the Quaternary era is responsible for many features like the massive rounded humps of the summits (ballons), and the morainic lakes in the blocked valleys.

Above the tree-line, the forest clothing the hillsides gives way to the short grass of the wide upland grazing grounds known as the Hautes-Chaumes.

Vieil-Armand★★

The war memorial (monument national) marks one of the most bitterly-contested battlefields of the First World War.

ROUTE DES GRANDES ALPES★★★

MICHELIN MAPS 332, 334, 340 AND 341
GREEN GUIDE FRENCH ALPS

Among the many routes which invite the visitor to explore the French Alps, this high-altitude road is the most famous. Rarely far from the frontier, the Great Alpine Road links Lake Geneva with the Riviera, crossing 25 passes in all as it leaps from valley to valley. It is open from end to end during the summer months only.

- **Information:** Association Grande Traversée des Alpes, 14 r. de la République, ☎04 76 42 41 41. www.routesdesgrandesalpes.com.
- **Orient Yourself:** Streching 600km/375mi from Thonon to Menton, the route crosses 16 mountain passes.

Driving Tour: Thonon to Menton

734km – 458mi
Thonon★★
From the Place du Château the view extends over the great sweep of Lake Geneva (**Lac Léman★★★**). On the Swiss shore to the north rise the terraces of the great Lavaux vineyard, and beyond are the mountains of the Vaudois Alps (to the east) and the Jura. Saint Francis of Sales once preached in St Hippolytus' Church (Église St-Hippolyte); its vault (**voûte★**) has retained its original stucco and 18 painted medallions, together with the stucco decoration of its false pillars (visible from the adjoining basilica), all done by the Italian craftsmen who restored the interior in Rococo style in the 18C. The road rises in a series of steps through the damp beech woodland of the gorges cut by the River Dranse de Morzine. This marks the transition between the gently rolling hill country fringing the great

lake and the **Chablais★★** massif, a complex of high ridges and peaks, with rich pastures grazed by Abondance cattle. The most spectacular part of the route is known as the Devil's Bridge Gorge (**Gorges du Pont du Diable★★**), marked by a number of rock-falls, one of which has formed the bridge attributed to the Evil One.

Morzine★★

The valleys around the resort are dotted with hamlets; the chalets have patterned balconies. All around grow sombre forests of spruce.
After the pass at Les Gets, the small industrial town of Tanninges marks the beginning of the **Faucigny★★** country. Drained by the Giffre, this is a landscape of pastures and sprucewoods, fashioned by the action of glacial moraines on calcareous rocks deposited here far from their point of origin.

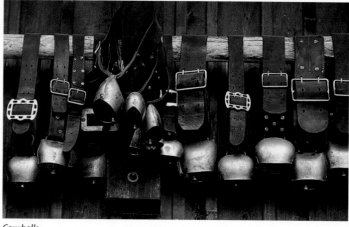

Cow bells

Cluses

The town commands the most important lateral valley *(cluse)* in the French Alps. The River Arve has cut down directly through the folded rocks of the **Aravis** range to make its gorge. Clocks and watches and precision metal products are made here.

The upland Sallanches basin is bounded to the north by the dramatic peaks of a number of ranges, but dominating all is the great mass of Mont Blanc itself, the "Giant of the Alps".

La Clusaz★★

The most important ski resort in the **Massif des Aravis** owes its name to the deep gorge or cluse, downstream of it, through which the Nom torrent gushes. The village, situated in the middle of pine forests and mountain pasture, is tightly huddled around the big church characterised by its onion-dome tower. The jagged outlines of the Aravis mountains can be seen in the distance.

In the summer, La Clusaz offers excellent walking, and in winter plenty of thrills for ski enthusiasts.

At the top of the climb out of the valley, Val d'Arly, the Notre-Dame de Bellecombe road gives good views, first of the whole Aravis massif, then of the wooded gorges cut by the Arly.

Col des Saisies

At this point that the route leaves the Sub-Alpine Furrow (Sillon alpin); from here as far as St-Martin-d'Entraunes to the south of the Cayolle Pass (Col de Cayolle), its course lies entirely within the High Alps (Grandes Alpes).

The broad depression of the Saisies Pass, 1 633m – 5 358ft high, is one of the most characteristic alpine grazing grounds to be seen along the route; it is browsed by sturdy little reddish-brown cattle as well as by the dark-brown Tarines breed and the white-spotted Abondances. The landscape is studded with innumerable chalets.

Beaufort

This little crossroads town (its church has fine woodcarvings and interesting sculptures) has given its name to the **Beaufortain**★★ country, an area of folded limestone beds on a base of ancient crystalline rocks. Virtually continuous forest cover forms a background to sweeping alpine pastures. Above the 1 450m – 4 750ft contour, the pastoral economy is marked by the seasonal movement of the herds up and down the slopes. The village of **Boudin**★ *(7km – 4mi south)* is particularly picturesque.

Cormet de Roselend★

This long valley, 1 900m – 6 200ft high, links the Roselend and Chapieux valleys. It is a vast, treeless, lonely place, dotted with rocks and a few shepherds' huts. A rushing mountain stream descends the steep valley, **Vallée des Chapieux**★, in a series of abrupt steps towards **Bourg-St-Maurice**. This strategically-sited town commands the routes coming down from the Beaufortain country and the Little St Bernard (Petit-St-Bernard) and Iseran Passes. Around it is the **Tarentaise**★★ country of the upper Isère valley where transhumance is still practised. By the time the route reaches Ste-Foy in the upper Tarentaise, the landscape has become more mountainous in character. The Tignes valley (Val de Tignes) is characterised by gorges and glacial bars; the avalanche protection works are impressive, as is the **Tignes Dam** ★★, a major engineering feat of the 1950s.

Val d'Isère★★★

In its high valley 1 000m – 3 300ft above Bourg-St-Maurice, this is the most important town in the upper Tarentaise. With an excellent sunshine record, the resort is surrounded by splendid mountain landscapes; to the south and west are the glaciers and peaks (several rising to more than 3 500m – 11 500ft) of the

Vanoise National Park, much favoured by walkers.

As the road climbs amid the crystalline massifs, it gives views of the imposing peaks of the Gran Paradiso in Italy to the left and of the Vanoise massif (Grande Motte peak) to the right.

Col d'Iseran★

2 770m – 9 088ft. The road across this high pass is the only link between the Tarentaise and the **Maurienne** country to the south which centres on the long valley of the River Arc. Industry is more important here than agriculture. The location of settlements has been determined by the sharp breaks in slope marked by glacial bars.

Modane

This is a border town at the French end of rail and road tunnels into Italy.

D. Hée/MICHELIN

View of La Meije from the Oratoire du Chazelet

At Valloire, the route once more enters the ancient Hercynian mountains and begins to climb towards the Galibier Pass.

Col du Galibier★★★

2 642m – 8 668ft. From the viewing table there is a superb panorama which takes in the Maurienne country (to the north), and the Pelvoux region (to the south), which is separated from the Briançonnais country by the high ridge of the Massif des Écrins. The pass marks the dividing line between the northern and southern part of the French Alps.

At the pass, **Col du Lautaret★★**, with its fine views of the Meije mountains, turn right in the direction of La Grave in the Romanche valley, then turn left at the entrance to the second tunnel.

Oratoire du Chazelet★★★

From the viewing table, the view extends over the high peaks of the Écrins National Park from the Col des Ruillans on the right to the broken ridges of the Meije (including le Doigt de Dieu – The Finger of God – at 3 974m – 13 025ft). The upper course of the glacier, fed by frequent snowfall, is of a staggering whiteness.

La Grave★

The village has a particularly fine **site★★** in the Romanche valley at the foot of the Meije. A two-stage cable-car ride takes the visitor to a height of 3 200m – 10 500ft at the col on the western flank of Mont du Râteau, from where there are unforgettable views over the Meije and the Écrins glaciers.

Back at the Col du Lauteret, the route now enters the southern part of the French Alps. At Monêtier in the Guisanne valley, it re-enters the sedimentary zone of the High Alps; oak, beech and ash reappear, the valleys open out and the whole landscape takes on a lighter air.

Briançon★★

◔ *See BRIANÇON.*

Col d'Izoard★★

2 361m – 7 746ft. The pass is in a desolate setting fringed by dramatic peaks. From the viewing tables magnificent views extend over the Briançonnais to the north and the Queyras country to the south.

The road descends in a series of hairpin bends through a strange landscape of screes and jagged rocks known as the **Casse Déserte★★**. At this high altitude, the processes of erosion are greatly accelerated by the extremes of temperature to which the rocks are exposed.

The high **Queyras★★** country is centred on the valley of the River Guil. Closed off downstream from the outside world by a series of narrow gorges, and cut off from main communication routes, it has fine examples of alpine houses. Above Château-Queyras, the valley sides are sharply differentiated; the gentler south-facing slopes are covered with well-watered meadows, while the north-facing slopes grow only larches and Arolla pines.

St-Véran★★

Lying between the 1 990m – 6 530ft contour and the 2 040m – 6 690ft contour, this is the highest community in Europe. Its chalets, timber-built on a basement of schist, are a unique example of adaptation to the rigours of a high-altitude mountain life which combines arable cultivation and grazing, forestry, and the exercise of craft skills during the long winters. The south-facing dwellings are sited in groups, most with hay-barns and balconies on which cereals are ripened. The village has a strange sculpture showing Christ's Agony.

The little town of **Guillestre**, with its church characterised by a beautiful **porch★** is situated at the end of the **Combe du Queyras★★**, a canyon carved out by the clear waters of the Guil.

Embrun★

24km – 15mi southwest of Guillestre. High up on its terrace overlooking the River Durance as it emerges from the mountains, the little town was once the seat of an archbishop. From the Place de l'Archevêché there are fine views over the valley slopes with their well-cultivated terraced fields. The torrents entering the main valley have spread their debris over its floor in alluvial fans.

The upper slopes are gouged by deep ravines, while dominating the scene are sombre high mountain crests.

The former **Notre-Dame Cathedral**, the finest church in the whole of the Dauphiné Alps, dates from the 12C. It has fine black and white marble stonework and the **north porch**★ is supported on pretty pink columns.

Col de Vars

2 111m – 6 893ft. This pass forms the gateway to the Ubaye valley. The valley floor, littered with boulders and studded with ponds, is grazed by sheep.

Beyond the pass, the south-facing slopes with their scattered hamlets are given over to stock-farming. In its upper reaches, the River Ubaye has cut deeply into the dark schists. Near La Condamine, the 19C Fort Tournoux seems part of the high rock on which it is built. After Jausiers, the route enters the Barcelonnette basin; the valley pastures are interspersed with woodland and the scene becomes more cheerful.

Barcelonnette★

The little capital of the Ubaye district was laid out as a bastide on a regular plan in 1231 by Raimond Béranger, Count of Barcelona. It belonged to the House of Savoy until passing to France under the provisions of the Treaty of Utrecht in 1713. On the edge of town are the houses of the "Barcelonnettes" or "Mexicans", locals who made their fortunes in the textile trade in Mexico before returning home. A museum, **Musée de la Vallée**, traces the history of the migrations.

The road climbs around the flank of Mont Pelat, the highest (3 035m – 10 164ft) peak in the Provence Alps.

Col de la Cayolle★★

2 327m – 7 635ft. This pass links the Ubaye country and the Upper Verdon to the upper reaches of the Var. From the top there are views over the deep valley of the Var towards the Grasse Pre-Alps in the far distance.

The Upper valley of the River Var★★

The source of the Var is on the left as the road drops away from the pass to follow the river through the sombre mountains. At St-Martin-d'Entraunes, the route passes from the High Alps into the sedimentary zone, the Pre-Alps of Provence. Downstream from Villeneuve, water coursing through drainage channels draws attention to the changes that take place in the landscape of the countryside around Guillaume.

Gorges de Daluis★★

These deep gorges have been cut by the river into thick beds of red porphyry and Urgonian limestone, giving striking colour effects. The road from **Guillaume** to **Beuil** leads to the **Gorges du Cians** in the upper stretch of the river Var.

The road climbs steadily to the Col de Valberg offering views of the different sides of the valley: woody to the north, compared to the southern one covered with vineyards and fruit trees. The descent towards **Roubion** from the **Col de Couilloie** (1 678m – 5 503ft) reveals the valleys of **La Vionèse** and **La Tinée**.

After the impressive **site**★★ of Roubion (the village is perched 1 300m – 4 264ft up on a ridge), the road travels through a red schistose landscape, enlivened by several waterfalls.

Roure★

This village is characterised by its architectural unity: houses with red schist walls and limestone tile roofs *(lauze)*.

The route then follows the river Vionèse until it flows into the river Tinée at **St-Sauveur-sur-Tinée**. Outside the village, on the left, a small road leads to the striking **site**★ of **Ramplas**, a village built on a ridge.

La Bolline

This pleasant summer resort is situated in the middle of a chestnut grove.

La Colmiane

The chalets and hotels of this winter sports resort are set amidst a wonderful larch forest. From the **Col de St-Martin**, there is a possibility of taking a chairlift up to the **Pic de Colmiane**★★ (beautiful **panorama**★★ from the top).

St-Martin-Vésubie★

From this famous mountaineering centre, visitors can go rambling in the **Vallon du Boréon**★★ or the **Vallon de la Madone de Fenestre**★.

La Bollène-Vésubie

The concentric streets of this peaceful village, in the middle of a beautiful chestnut grove, converge on the church, which crowns the hill. The forest, Fôret de Turiniaa, which spreads across the valleys of the Vésubie and of the Bévéra, demarcates the southern border of the Parc national du Mercantour.

Le Massif de l'Authion★★

North of the **Col de Turini**, this massif constitutes a wonderful natural fortress which seems to stand guard over the roads between the Vésubie and Roya valleys. This strategic value has caused it to be, throughout the centuries, the stage for several conflicts. In April 1945, it was the last sector of France to be liberated. A stele commemorates the fierceness of the combat.

After crossing the forest of Turini, the river Bévéra winds its way towards the **Gorges du Piaon**★★ where the corniche road overlooks the river. Before reaching the gorges, the road goes through **Moulinet**, a charming village set in a verdant valley before passing the **Chapelle de Notre-Dame-La-Menour** with its Renaissance façade on the left.

Sospel★

This Alpine resort was once a bishopric, during the Great Schism. On the Nice road, 1 km – 0.6 miles from the centre of the village, stands the **Fort St-Roch** one of the last elements of the "Alpine Maginot line" built in the 1930s.

The road follows the old railway line which used to link Sospel to Menton, along the course of the Merlanson, a tributary of the Bévéra. On the opposite side of the valley, the road to Nice via the **Col de Braus** winds its way, amidst olive groves, towards the capital of the French Riviera.

Menton★★
👒 See MENTON.

ROUTE NAPOLÉON★★

MICHELIN MAP 341 B 5-D 6
GREEN GUIDE FRENCH RIVIERA

This scenic highway follows the route taken by Napoleon on his return from Elba in 1815. it leads from the Riviera northwest through the Pre-Alps and is marked along its length by the flying eagle symbol inspired by Napoleon's remark: "The eagle will fly from steeple to steeple until he reaches the towers of Notre-Dame".

🔲 **Information:** ☎04 93 36 66 66. www.route-napoleon.com
▶ **Orient Yourself:** The route starts at Golfe-Juan and ends at Grenoble. The highway following the route is mainly the D6085.

A Bit of History

The Emperor escaped from Elba on 26 February 1815, landing on the beach at Golfe-Juan on 1 March.

2 March: After a brief overnight stop at Cannes, Napoleon and his band halted outside Grasse and took to the mule tracks. The next night was spent at Seranon.

3 March: Midday halt at Castellane and overnight in Barrème.

4 March: The party rejoined the highway at Digne, and passed the night at the Château de Malijai.

5 March: The Emperor lunched at Sisteron, then continued. Overnight at Gap.

6 March: At Les Barraques, Napoleon declined the offer of the local peasants to join his force. Overnight at Corps.

7 March: Near Laffrey, the way was barred by troops. Ordered to fire, they hesitated, then broke ranks to shouts of "Vive l'Empereur!" Escorted by the men of the 7th Regiment, Napoleon made a triumphal entry into Grenoble at 7pm.

Driving Tour: Golfe-Juan to Grenoble

336km – 209mi – allow a whole day. Leading across the southern Pre-Alps to the long valley known as the Sub-Alpine Furrow, the route can be followed throughout the year.

▶ *Leave Golfe-Juan on D6007 (former N7).*

Antibes★★

The first settlement here was a trading-post founded by Greek merchants from Marseille in the 4C BC. Reconstructed in the 16C, the castle (**Château Grimaldi**) dates from the 12C, when it was built on the site of a Roman encampment to protect the coast from the incursions of Barbary pirates. Inside, the Picasso Museum (**Musée Picasso★**) has a superb selection of the master's works, including ceramics, drawings, prints and tapestries *(The Lobster, Two Nudes and a Mirror)*, as well as paintings *(Still Life with Watermelon)*... The town was purchased from the Grimaldi family by Henri IV because of its strategic position in relation to the Kingdom of Savoy. It was fortified first by François I, then by Vauban. To the west of the **Cap d'Antibes★★** stretches the fine sandy beach of Golfe-Juan.

Grasse★★

Prettily located on the slopes of the Grasse Pre-Alps, the old town (**vieille ville★**) has picturesque streets lined with tall Provençal houses. Grasse's most famous son was **Jean-Honoré Fragonard** (1732-1806), a painter known for witty depictions of the frivolities of 18C court life. The Salle Fragonarda in the Villa-Musée Fragonard has two of the artist's self-portraits as well as his *Landscape with washerwomen* and *Three Graces*.

For the past three centuries, Grasse has been the world's most important centre of the perfume industry, with perfume manufacturers open to the public and two museums, the **Musée international de la Parfumerie** and the **Musée d'Art et d'Histoire de Provence**.

To the north of the **Pas de la Faye** with its **view★★** over mountains and Mediterranean, the road enters Upper Provence (Haute Provence) through the Seranon valley.

Castellane★

The sheep-grazed valley in which the town is situated is overlooked by the "Roc", a limestone cliff 184m – 604ft high.

The Castellane Pre-Alps extend over a wide area; they consist of a series of bare ridges through which the River Asse has cut a deep valley. To the north rise the Digne Pre-Alps, a harsh landscape with a meagre mantle of garrigue

Perfume bottle

C.J.Muzzin / Musée international de la parfumerie, Grasse

vegetation, deeply scored by the beds of torrents. A complex geological history has produced a series of folded ridges through which the rivers have cut deep gorges, as well as long crests of pale rock to the east and broad fertile valleys to the north.

Digne-les-Bains★

Digne spreads out along its valley **site**★ at the foot of the rise on which its old town is situated. There are dramatic **views**★ of the whole area from the hilltop village of **Courbons**★, 6km – 4mi to the north. In the Place General-de-Gaulle is a memorial to **Pierre Gassendi** (1592-1655), born at nearby Champtercier. This natural philosopher was provost of the cathedral here; much of his scientific work was devoted to studying the properties of sound.

At **Malijai**, the route enters the **Durance basin**, an alluvial plain 6km – 4mi wide in places, lying between the Valensole plateau to the east and the Vaucluse to the west. The Durance is the great river of the southern Alps, tracing its meanders through the gravel terraces on which a prosperous agricultural pattern has developed, favoured by the mildness of the climate. The best crops are grown on those sites which have been effectively drained; the wetter areas are occupied by woodland.

Sisteron★★

💧 See SISTERON.

Gap★

Gap is pleasantly sited in the valley carved out by the glacier which was the ancestor of the Durance. The town's prosperity was built on the rich soils of its agricultural hinterland, one of the most fertile areas of the southern Alps. Founded by the Gauls, Gap became a staging-post along the Roman road

from Turin to Valence, then a fortified cathedral town.

The **Col Bayard** (1 246m – 4 088ft) links the southern and northern Alps. From the viewing table at Chauvet on the south side of the pass the view extends over the valley around Gap. To the north is the beginning of the Sub-Alpine Furrow which the road enters by way of the Drac valley, hollowed out in the beds of schist by the action of the Quaternary glaciers. This is an ancient highway, once travelled by merchants on their way to the fairs at St-Bonnet. Terraced villages line the route, their roofs tiled in brown stone. To the left are the precipitous slopes and savage peaks of the Dévoluy Massif, to the right the Valgaudemar valley threading its way deep into the Écrins National Park.

Corps

A small bustling town in the Sub-Alpine Furrow. The road passes through areas of well-cultivated farmland interrupted by glacial bars, one of which has been used in the siting of the Sautet Dam (**Barrage de Sautet**★★ – *5km – 3 miles west*), with its deep lake hemmed in by high canyon-like walls; far below its surface is the hidden confluence of the Drac with the Souloise.

Around La Mure, the Trièves country is overlooked by the broad summit of Mont Aiguille (2 086m – 6 880ft), also known as the "unclimbable mountain" though it was actually conquered as long ago as 1492.

Laffrey★

Just south of the village lies the spot known as **"Prairie de la Rencontre★,"** where the vain attempt was made to bar Napoleon's progress northwards. The road now descends towards **Vizille**★ and Grenoble.

ABBAYE DE ST-BENOÎT-SUR-LOIRE★★

MICHELIN MAP 318 K 5

GREEN GUIDE CHÂTEAUX OF THE LOIRE

Enthralling by its majestic size, exquisite harmony and utter simplicity, St-Benoît abbey is justly one of the most famous Romanesque buildings in France.

- **Information:** 44 r. Orléanais, ☎02 38 35 79 00.
- **Orient Yourself:** The abbey is at the village of St-Benoît, beside the Loire between Gien and Orléans. A pretty way to approach it is along the riverside road, D 60.
- **Organizing Your Time:** Allow about 2h for the basilica and village.
- **Don't Miss:** In addition to the abbey, be sure to visit the lovely church of Germigny-des-Près.

A Bit of History

AD 675, the original abbey founded here on a river terrace well above flood level was presented with the remains of St Benedict and of his sister, St Scholastica, brought from Monte Cassino in Italy. Hitherto known as Fleury Abbey – which in fact is still its name – the monastery now rededicated itself to the founder of Western monasticism (St Benedict = St-Benoît in French). The abbey's influence waxed at the beginning of the 9C with the appointment of Theodulf by the Emperor Charlemagne; this great abbot served his master by introducing the study of the Scriptures and of Roman law, and by promoting the conservation of ancient texts.

Visit

Basilique★★

6.30am-10pm. Closed during services, which are held each evening and Sun am. ☎02 38 35 72 43. www.abbaye-fleury.com.

Built between 1067 and 1108, the Romanesque basilica has a fine crypt **(crypte★)** with a double ambulatory and a massive central pillar containing the relics of St Benedict. The choir **(chœur★★)** is remarkable for its paving (a Roman mosaic brought here from Italy) and for the elegant arcading.

Outside, the belfry porch **(clocher-porche★★)** is one of the finest examples of Romanesque art in France. Originally free-standing, it was joined to the basilica when the nave was extended in the middle of the 12C.

Excursions

Germigny-des-Prés★

5.5km – 3mi northwest. The much-restored church is the oratory **(oratoire)** which Abbot Theodulf built for himself. It is a typical example of Carolingian architecture of the 9C, with an unusual plan, alabaster window-panes filtering the light, and a remarkable **mosaic★★**.

Studio 3bis/MICHELIN

Porch of the basilica, St-Benoît-sur-Loire

ST-BERTRAND-DE-COMMINGES★★

MICHELIN MAP 343 B 6–POPULATION 237

GREEN GUIDE LANGUEDOC ROUSSILLON TARN GORGES

This is one of the most picturesque and charming villages in the Pyrenean foot hills, perched on an isolated hilltop, encircled by ancient ramparts and dominated by an imposing cathedral.

- **Information:** Office de tourisme intercommunal de Montréjeau, 22 pl. Valentin Abeille, Montréjeau, ☎05 61 95 80 22. http://otimontrejeau.ifrance.com
- ▶ **Orient Yourself:** Saint-Bertrand lies south of autoroute A64, junction 17. The cathedral – visible from afar – is the centre.
- **Parking:** In July and August, access to the upper part of the village is closed. Park either under the trees in Grand Place and take the steps, or park near Porte Majou, from which a 'little train' (1€) makes the climb easy!

A Bit of History

A substantial town was founded here in 72 BC by Pompey. In AD 585 the Burgundians descended on the place and laid it waste. For centuries the site lay abandoned, until in 1073 St Bernard saw its potential for the building of a cathedral and monastery. Here the rules of the religious reforms of Pope Gregory VII were applied, making the little city the spiritual centre of Comminges, endowing the awkwardly-shaped county (sandwiched as it was between the territories belonging to the House of Foix-Béarn and dotted with enclaves) with a religious significance far outweighing its political importance.

Visit

Cathédrale Ste-Marie-de-Comminges★

Paid access to the cloisters and on the right of the church (treasury, choir stalls) Free access to the rest of the cathedral. ⏱ Jun Sep: 9am-7pm: Feb-Apr and Oct: 10am noon, 2-6pm; Jan and Nov-Dec: 10am noon, 2-5pm. No visit Sun morning and religious holidays. Call ahead for guided tour (cathedral, terraces, and treasury) ☎05 61 89 04 91.

Medieval sculpture here reaches a high point in its development. The Romanesque portal of the cathedral is made up of several independently sculpted panels showing the Adoration of the Magi and a figure of St Bertrand without a halo (i.e. before his canonisation in 1218), recalling the work of the School of Toulouse at St Sernin. The cloister (cloîtreaa) are built over the 12C-15C ramparts; the south side is open, giving fine views over the Upper Garonne countryside, and there is a famous pillar in primitive style with statues of the four Evangelists. There are splendid choir stallsaa of 1535 in Italian Renaissance style; features to note particularly include the bishop's throne, a Jesse Tree and a Madonna and Child.

ST-ÉMILION★★

MICHELIN MAP 335 K 5 –POPULATION 2 345

GREEN GUIDE FRENCH ATLANTIC COAST

St-Émilion offers both simple and sophisticated attractions to art lovers and gourmets alike. The town is divided into two hill sites with the Royal Castle and Deanery (Doyenné) symbolising the age-old rivalry between the civil and religious authorities. Its sun-baked, pantile-roofed stone houses nestle in an amphitheatre★★ on the slope of a limestone plateau. Apart from its wines, the town is known for its strange underground church.

- **Information:** Place des Créneaux, ☎05 57 55 28 28. www.saint-emilion-tourisme.com.
- **Orient Yourself:** The town is 10km/6mi east of Libourne. It has to be explored on foot, so wear comfortable shoes suitable for steep cobbled lanes. Place du Marché is the focal point.
- **Guided Tour:** The Catacombes, St Emilion's Hermitage, Chapelle de la Trinité and the Eglise Monolithe can all be visited on a 45-minute guided tour from the tourist office (5.50€).

Visit

Eglise Monolithe★

This extraordinary underground church was hollowed out of a single rock between the 8C and the 12C. It's an impressive size: the nave and two aisles are 38m – 125ft long, 20m – 65ft wide and 11m – 33ft high.

ST-FLOUR★★

MICHELIN MAP 330 G 4–POPULATION 6 625

GREEN GUIDE AUVERGNE RHÔNE VALLEY

Occupying a spectacular site★★, St-Flour is really two little towns; one, atmospheric historic lanes and old buildings perched on a huge rock; the other a modern, busy place at its foot.

- **Information:** Cours Spy-des-Ternes, ☎04 71 60 22 50 . www.saint-flour.com.
- **Orient Yourself:** Although all the interest is in the Upper Town, it is more convenient to park, eat and stay in the Lower Town.

Visit

At the eastern end of the upper town with its old lava-built houses stands the 15C **cathedral**★. From the Terrasse des Roches nearby there are extensive **views** over the rich grasslands of the Planèze de St-Flour, an inclined plateau.

Excursions

Viaduc de Garabit★★

12km – 7mi south. This daring steel structure carries the Clermont-Ferrand-Millau railway across the Truyère valley with its many hydro-electric works built in the **gorges**★★ gouged in the granite plateaux. Its central arch is 116m – 381ft across. The viaduct was built between 1882 and 1884 by Gustave Eiffel using plans drawn up by Boyer.

Viaduc de Garabit

Site du Château d'Alleuze★★

26km – 16mi west from Garabit via the Mallet viewpoint and the Grandval Dam. The square keep and round towers of this most romantic of ruins loom menacingly over the lake held back by the Grandval Dam.

ST-GERMAIN-EN-LAYE★★

MICHELIN MAP 311 I 2–POPULATION 39 926
GREEN GUIDE NORTHERN FRANCE AND THE PARIS REGION

A residential suburb of Paris, and also a popular weekend resort, St-Germain's attractions are a château with delightful terraces and gardens, and a forest with pleasant walks.

- **Information:** Maison Claude Debussy, 38 r. au Pain, ☎01 34 51 05 12.
- ▶ **Orient Yourself:** The town is on the west side of Paris and easily reached from the city on the RER (line A1). The main area of interest is by the château.

A Bit of History

Now a residential town forming part of the Paris suburbs, St-Germain's significance in the course of French history goes back hundreds, if not thousands, of years. A strategic site 60m – 200ft above a bend in the Seine persuaded Louis VI le Gros (the Fat) to build a stronghold here. Later, when the Hundred Years War was at its height, the castle was restored by Charles V.

Three French kings were born here (Charles IX, Henri II, Louis XIV), as well as several princes, writers, historians, composers... Louis XIII died here. It was here that in 1641 Richelieu promulgated the edict limiting the rights of the French parliament.

On 28 February 1837, the first passenger railway in France was inaugurated, running to Paris.

Sight

Château★

Its appearance is still much as it was when François I had it rebuilt by Pierre de Chambiges in the taste of the 16C. Louis XIV brought in Mansart to replace the corner turrets with pavilions, and Le Nôtre, who designed the park, laid out the very long terrace (terrasse★★), and replanted the forest.
The château houses the **Musée des Antiquités nationales★★** (⏱Open daily except Tue. ☞ 4€. ♿ ☎ 01 39 10 13 00; www.musee-antiquitesnationales.fr); its priceless collection of archeological exhibits traces French history through space and time from the Paleolithic to the Middle Ages.

▶ Ste-Chapelle★ (in the château). Musée départemental Maurice-Denis★ ⏱ Daily exc. Mon. ⏱ Closed 1 Jan, 1 May and 25 Dec. ☞ 3.80€. ☎01 39 73 77 87. www.musee-mauricedenis.fr – paintings of the Pont-Aven School and of the Nabis' movement.

ST-GUILHEM-LE-DÉSERT★★

MICHELIN MAP 339 G 6–POPULATION 245
GREEN GUIDE LANGUEDOC ROUSSILLON TARN GORGES

In its remote and dramatic site★ where the Val de l'Infernet runs into the valley of the Hérault, this 9C village★ grew up around an abbey founded by William of Aquitaine, one of Charlemagne's most valiant lieutenants.

🛈 **Information:** 2 r. de la Font du Portal, ☎04 67 57 44 33.
▶ **Orient Yourself:** The village in the Hérault gorge, and can be approached via villages Gignac and Aniane if coming from the east or south, via St-Félix and Montpeyroux if coming from the north or west.
🅿 **Parking:** All cars must be left in the village's large car park.

Sights

Église abbatiale★

This is a Romanesque structure of striking simplicity, famed for its possession of a fragment of the True Cross (in the south transept). It has a doorway with dog-tooth moulding, and an apse with massive buttresses and an elegant little arcade. Inside, the width of apse and transept is the result of a rebuilding undertaken in the 11C.
Of the 11C-12C cloisters, nothing remains apart from the ground floor of the north walk and part of the west walk. The vigorously-sculpted 13C capitals which once graced the galleries are now among the treasures of the Cloisters Museum, high above the Hudson in New York.

Grotte de Clamouse★★

3km – 2mi south. ⏱ 1h guided visits only. ⏱ daily 10am-7pm (Jun and Sep: 6pm, Mar-May and Oct: 5pm). ☞8€ (children 4.50€). ☎04 67 57 71 05. The caves run beneath the Larzac plateau and were carved by an extensive network of underground streams. There are remarkable stalactites and stalagmites, but above all it are the splendid crystallisations in varied evocative shapes (flowers, bushes, bunches of grapes etc). Take a sweater, the temperature inside is 17 °C.

D.Pazery/MICHELIN

Crystallisations in the Grotte de Clamouse

ST-JEAN-DE-LUZ★★

MICHELIN MAP 342 C 2–POPULATION 13 247
GREEN GUIDE FRENCH ATLANTIC COAST

A popular beach resort and harbour town at the mouth of the river Nivelle, St-Jean-de-Luz is one of the principal centres of the French Basque country.

🛈 **Information:** Place du Maréchal Foch, ☎05 59 26 03 16. www.saint-jean-de-luz.com
▶ **Orient Yourself:** The town is on the Atlantic seafront just south of Biarritz, close to the Spanish border. The centre is on the right bank of the Nivelle.
☺ **Don't Miss:** Be sure to explore the port area.

A Bit of History

The main event to occur in the town was the marriage of Louis XIV of France to the infanta of Spain Maria-Theresa. The wedding was initially held up by the king's passion for Marie Mancini, but in the end was solemnised here, on 9 June 1660. The king had been staying since 8 May in an imposing dwelling belonging to the ship-owner Lohobiague, which ever since has been known as the **Maison Louis-XIV**★(🕐 open daily for 30min guided tours from 10.30am. ☎05 59 26 01 56). The interior is particularly interesting, with a sturdy staircase built by ships' carpenters, 18C furniture in the drawing room and fine panelling in the dining room. Maria-Theresa was lodged in an elegant brick and stone house now known as the **Maison de l'infante**, nearby. For a while in this brief period, St-Jean-de-Luz became in effect the capital of France. Court and government moved here, and days and nights were spent in feasting and revelry.

Sights

The Port and Barre district

This is the original St-Jean-de-Luz. As early as the 11C, its sailors were hunting whale off Labrador. By the 15C, their quarry had changed to the abundant cod of the great fishing grounds off Newfoundland. When the Treaty of Utrecht forbade this activity, they turned to piracy, creating a fearsome reputation for their home port. Eventually they returned to more law-abiding ways, fishing for sardines off the coasts of Portugal and Morocco and for tuna off Senegal and Mauritania.

The part of the town known as **La Barre** was where the ship-owners lived; its growth was intimately linked to the fortunes of its fleet. The 16C and 17C brought good times, though the place was burned down by the Spaniards in 1558, then ravaged by high tides in 1749 and 1785. Among the fine old houses, the most venerable is the one which survived the 1558 fire, once the property of Carquiou Kailu.

Église St-Jean Baptiste★★

Work on enlarging the church, begun in 1649, had still not been completed when the royal wedding took place here in 1660. It is the finest church in the French Basque country, with a resplendent 17C gilded altarpiece **(retable**★) attributed to Martin de Bidache, a painted wooden ceiling and oak-built galleries on several levels. The main altar is raised above the sacristy, a feature of churches in the Basque provinces of Labourd (in France) and Guipuzcoa (in Spain).

Excursions

Corniche basque★★

4km – 9mi south, then extending southward to Hendaye. The Socoa cliff (**Falaise de Socoa★**), an unusual example of coastal relief, is best seen at low tide. Following the drowning of the former coastline by the waters released by the melting of the Quaternary glaciers, the beds of highly laminated schists were attacked by wave action; the strata dip sharply seaward, projecting sharp sawtooth ridges of the more resistant rock from the wave-cut platform at the foot of the cliffs.

La Rhune ★★

14km – 9mi southeast, then as far as Sare. Towards the end of the 6C, the Basques were probably pushed northwards by the Visigoths. Those of their number who settled in the plains of Aquitaine intermarried with the other local people, eventually to become the Gascons. But those who remained in the mountains kept their independence and their enigmatic language, thus guaranteeing their very distinct identity.

The mountain called La Rhune ("good grazing" in Basque) is one of the symbols of the Basque country; its **summit** (accessible by rack-and-pinion railway) rises to a height of 900m – c 3 000ft, offering a wonderful **panorama★★★** of the Bay of Biscay, the Landes and the ancient provinces of Labourd, Navarre and Guipuzcoa.

At the foot of the mountain lie the villages of **Ascain★** and **Sare★**, both with many characteristically Basque features. The houses are timber-framed; the white rendering of the walls makes a pleasant contrast to the reddish-brown colour usually applied to the timber, while the cemeteries adjoining the churches have the typical discoidal tombstones arranged in a circle.

If visitors are lucky, they may see the local people dancing the chaste but passionate fandango or taking part in pigeon-hunts.

ST-MALO★★★

MICHELIN MAP 309 J 3–POPULATION 50 675
GREEN GUIDE BRITTANY

The **site★★★** of the walled town of St Malo on the east bank of the Rance is unique in France, making the ancient port one of the country's great tourist attractions.

- ▮ **Information:** Esplanade St-Vincent, ☎02 99 56 64 48. www.saint-malo-tourisme.com.
- ▶ **Orient Yourself:** St Malo is on Brittany's north coast. The walled town projects into the waters of the English Channel. Inland, it extends far beyond the port and historic walled Old Town.
- ⏱ **Organizing Your Time:** Starting at the Esplanade St-Vincent, it is possible to walk right around the town on top of the ramparts in about 2hr. Spend another 2hr seeing the château and cathedral. There are also several companies that offer a variety of boat tours in the bay of St-Malo (varying prices and times; contact the tourist office for more info, ☎02 99 56 64 48).
- **Kids Especially For Kids:** Le Grand Aquarium.
- 🅿 **Parking:** Park near the port by the Esplanade St-Vincent.

A Bit of History

The town's prosperity began in the 16C. In 1534, **Jacques Cartier** had set out from here on the voyage which led to the discovery and naming of Canada; very soon a thriving commerce had begun, based on furs and fish. Local ship-owners began to build themselves fine manor houses in the surrounding countryside, as well as tall timber-built residences in the town itself. By the 1660s their boats were trading in the Pacific, and their ever-increasing wealth enabled them to build in granite. Parisian architectural fashions began to prevail over local traditions. Anticipating the coming naval rivalry between England and France, Colbert became aware of the vulnerability of his country's western coasts; in 1689, Vauban was commissioned to strengthen the defences of St-Malo.

In the 19C, the invention of floating docks ended the advantage which the great tidal range of the port had long given its ship-builders and -repairers.

Sights

Old Town and Ramparts★★★

From the ramparts there are fine views of the Rance valley and towards Dinard on the far side of the estuary. Within the walls is the old town, almost entirely rebuilt in their original form after near-total destruction in 1944. Solid walls of granite, relieved by horizontal bands between each storey, steep mansard roofs and formidable chimney stacks combine to give an effect of harsh dignity and strong identity. The houses along the Rue de Dinan and those facing the walls are particularly fine.

Château★★

This still has the façades of the 17C and 18C barracks.

Cathédrale St-Vincent

The nave vault of 1160 is one of the oldest in Brittany, albeit rebuilt after the last war. Note the **stained-glass windows**★ by Jean Le Moal.

Le Grand Aquarium★★

The aquarium offers a fascinating experience as well as presenting collections of great scientific interest, as visitors trace the history of great sailors from St-Malo. Attractions are of special interest include the ring **(Anneau)**, a remarkable round aquarium containing 600 000 litres in which shoals of pelagic species of fish swim endlessly; and a life-size reconstruction of a sunken wreck **(Vaisseau englouti)** with sharks.

Fort National at low tide

▶ **Musée d'histoire de la ville et d'Ethnographie du Pays Malouin**★ – history of the town and its famous men.
Quic-en-Groigne Tower★ – wax museum.
Fort National★.

Excursion

Côte d'Émeraude★★★
The name Emerald Coast has been given to Brittany's picturesque northern shore

from Cancale (**headland – Pointe du Grouin**★★) to **Le Val André**★★. The Emerald Coast scenic road runs through the major resorts (Dinard, St-Malo) and offers detours to the tips of the numerous headlands, including **Fort de Latte**★★, **Cap Fréhel**★★★ and **Cap d'Erquy**★ from which the views of the jagged coastline are in places quite spectacular.

ST-MARTIN-DU-CANIGOU★★

MICHELIN MAP 344 F 7
2.5KM – 1.5MI SOUTH OF VERNET-LES-BAINS
GREEN GUIDE LANGUEDOC ROUSSILLON TARN GORGES

The abbey of St Martin on Mont Canigou , an eagle's eyrie at 1 055m – 3 460ft above sea-level, is one of the great sights of the easter Pyrenees.

🛈 **Information:** Contact the tourist office at Vernet-les-Bains ☎04 68 05 55 35.
▶ **Orient Yourself:** The abbey can be reached on foot from Casteil, or by jeep from Vernet-les-Bains (🚐 6.50€ round trip, ☎04 68 05 64 61).
🅿 **Parking:** Park the car in Casteil, then follow a steep road uphill (over 1hr round trip).

Visit

Site★★★
To appreciate St-Martin's unusual site, after reaching the abbey (30min on foot round trip) take a stairway to the left (itinerary no 9) which climbs through the woods. Turn left past the water outlet. There is an impressive view of the abbey, which lies in the shadow of the Canigou until the late morning. It stands in an imposing site dominating the Casteil and Vernet valleys.

Abbey
🕐 Guided tours 🔊 (1hr) Jun-Sep: daily exc. Tue, almost hourly 10am-5pm (winter:, 4pm). 🕐 Closed Jan. 🚐 4€ (ages 12-18 years: 3€). ☎04 68 05 50 03.
The abbey, built on a rocky pinnacle at an altitude of 1 094m – 3 589ft, grew up around a monastic community founded here in the 11C. After falling into disuse

at the Revolution, it was restored from 1902 to 1932 and extended from 1952 to 1972. At the beginning of the 20C, all that remained of the **cloisters** was three galleries with crude semicircular arches. As part of the restoration a south gallery has been rebuilt overlooking a ravine. The **lower church** (10C) dedicated to Notre-Dame-sous-Terre in accordance with an early-Christian tradition, forms the crypt of the **upper church** (11C). The latter, consisting of three successive aisles with parallel barrel vaults, conveys an impression of great age with its rugged, simply carved capitals. On the north side of the chancel stands a bell-tower crowned by a crenellated platform. Near the church, two tombs have been hollowed out of the rock: the tomb of the founder, Count Gulfred de Cerdagne, which he dug out with his own hands, and that of one of his wives.

ÉGLISE DE **ST-NECTAIRE**★★

MICHELIN MAP 326 E 9
GREEN GUIDE AUVERGNE THE RHÔNE VALLEY

This little Romanesque church enjoys a spectacular location on the eastern slopes of the Dore mountains (Monts Dore). Built around 1160 as a dependency of the great Chaise-Dieu monastery, it suffered much damage during the French Revolution, and underwent major restoration (towers, west front) in 1875.

- **Information:** Les Grands Thermes, St-Nectaire, ☎04 73 88 50 86.
- ▶ **Orient Yourself:** The church dominates St-Nectaire-le-Haut, the old village. The lower village, St-Nectaire-le-Bas, is a thermal spa, spreading along a green valley.

Visit

🕐 *Apr-Oct: 9am-7pm; Nov-Mars: 10am-12.30pm, 2pm-6pm. Jul-Aug: guided tours daily except Sun and public holidays 3pm and 5pm ☎04 73 88 50 67.*

The church has a number of notable features, including a massive **narthex**. The 103 **capitals**★★ (most are 12C) are justly famous. The treasury (**trésor**★★ – north transept) houses a statue of Notre-Dame-du-Mont-Cornadore (a Virgin in Majesty of the 12C), **a reliquary bust of St Baudime**★★, a 12C Limoges masterpiece, as well as a reliquary arm of St Nectaire in repoussé silver and a pair of Limoges book-plates of about 1170.

Excursion

Château de Murol★★

6km – 4mi east. The ruined castle rises from a basalt platform formed by a lava flow from the Tartaret volcano. The site with its polygonal keep was fortified as early as the 12C because of its strategic position between Auvergne and Cantal. At the end of the 14C, it became one of the main seigneurial residences of the province; Guillaume de Murol was responsible for those features which still distinguish the stronghold today (internal courtyard, main tower, and north and east walls) and which serve to remind us both of the medieval obsession with security and of the fiercely guarded independence of the Auvergnat nobility.

A century later, the castle was brought into line with Renaissance tastes. But the Wars of Religion led to the place being modernised in a military sense, with the building of bastions, watch-towers, as well as an outer wall rising directly from the cliff, all reinforcing the site's natural defensive ability to withstand bombardment or sapping. Now impregnable, the fortress was spared by Richelieu's demolition programme, but fell into ruin in the 19C.

ST-NICOLAS-DE-PORT★★

MICHELIN MAP 307 J 7–POPULATION 7 702
GREEN GUIDE ALSACE LORRAINE CHAMPAGNE

The splendid 15C-16C Church of St Nicolas rises somewhat incongruously from the workaday surroundings of this industrial town.

- **Information:** Place C. Croué-Friedman, ☎03 83 48 58 75.
- ▶ **Orient Yourself:** The town is on the River Meurthe and Marne-Rhine canal.

Sight

Basilique★★

🕐 Jul to mid-Sep: guided tours (1hr) Sun 3pm. ☜ 5€. Organ concerts every Sunday in August 5.30pm. No charge. Audioguided visit daily except Sun and Mon. 10am-noon, 2- 5pm, Sat 2-5pm. Enquire at the Tourist Office. ☎03 83 48 58 75. This is perhaps the finest example of Flamboyant Gothic in Lorraine. It was built between 1481 and 1560, at a time when the style had passed its peak and was indulging in extravagant embellishment, much in evidence at this church. The transept is lit by windows with unusually complex tracery. The side chapels were built in Renaissance style after the completion of the main part of the building.

ST-OMER★★

MICHELIN MAP 301 G 3–POPULATION 15 747
GREEN GUIDE NORTHERN FRANCE AND THE PARIS REGION

A market centre of some importance, St-Omer has kept many fine town houses dating from the Classical period. The town lies at the junction of Inland Flanders, with its watery landscapes of poplars, elms and willows, and Coastal Flanders, won from the sea in medieval times and now dominated by industry and arable farming.

- **Information:** 4 r. du Lion, ☎03 21 98 08 51. www.tourisme-saintomer.com.
- ▶ **Orient Yourself:** This northern town is 43km from Calais. Its centre is Place Maréchal Foch.

A Bit of History

A border town, St-Omer was in turn part of the Holy Roman Empire, Flanders, Burgundy and then Spain, finally passing into French hands in 1677. The town's industry, predominantly metalworking, chemicals and glass-making, is concentrated in the Arques district. 38km – 24 miles to the south lies the site of the Battle of **Agincourt** (Azincourt), where, on 25 October 1415, France suffered its worst defeat of the Hundred Years War at the hands of Henry V of England. Ten thousand French noblemen were killed, while English casualties were negligible.

Sight

Cathédrale Notre-Dame★★

Completed at the end of the Hundred Years War, the building shows signs of the influence of the English Perpendicular style. There are numerous high quality **works of art**★★, including 18C woodwork, and very rare 13C floor tiles.

- ▶ Hôtel Sandelin★ – decorative arts. Ancienne Chapelle des Jésuites★. Jardin Public★ (gardens).

ST-POL-DE-LÉON★

MICHELIN MAP 308 H 2–POPULATION 7 121

GREEN GUIDE BRITTANY

St-Pol is one of the main market-gardening centres of the rich band of fertile soils running all round the Breton coast from St-Malo to St-Nazaire. Where the wind can be kept out, the otherwise mild climate allows excellent crops of vegetables to be grown, artichokes, onions, early potatoes, cauliflowers, salad vegetables... eagerly bought in the markets of Paris and on the far side of the English Channel. Mechanisation means that much of the characteristic pattern of tiny fields bounded by stone walls is doomed to disappear.

- **Information:** Place de l'Evêché, ☎02 98 69 05 69.
- **Orient Yourself:** The town is in western Brittany, close to the port of Roscoff.

Sights

Chapelle du Kreisker★

The chapel was rebuilt around 1375; in the 15C, when the coastal towns were prospering from their sea-borne trade, it housed the meetings of the town council. In about 1430, Duke John V of Brittany, who had spent his boyhood at the Burgundian court, then married Joan of France, felt it opportune to introduce the Gothic style into Brittany in order to boost his prestige. But the response of the Breton architects was to adapt Flamboyant Gothic to local ways; they shunned highly designed and decorated façades which were difficult to reconcile with the dour qualities of the granites of the region, and favoured a flattened apse (a reflection of the influence of both English architecture and that of the mendicant orders). They thereby eliminated the problems caused by vaults with a circular or polygonal plan, as well as enabling the interior to be lit by a single large window. In addition, the use of a coffered ceiling and a lightweight slate roof allowed them to dispense with flying buttresses.

The chapel was subsequently enlarged, and, between 1436 and 1439, given its belfry (**clocher**★★), the finest in the province. Interest in it has increased owing to the loss of the tower of Notre-Dame-du-Mur at Morlaix on which it is supposed to have been modelled. In its vertical emphasis, it is reminiscent of the churches of Normandy; it has a pointed steeple and pinnacles so delicate they had to be tied into the main structure by braces to enable them to resist the force of the wind. The tall openings below reinforce this impression. The English Perpendicular style is recalled by the mullions of the windows, by the overhanging balustrade and by the entablatures expressing the different levels.

Ancienne cathédrale★

The old cathedral was erected on 12C foundations in the 13C and 14C. This fine building with its characteristically Breton balustraded belfry was restored by the Dukes of Brittany from 1431 onwards. Seven bays of the nave still have their original vaults; the nave itself, unlike most of the rest of the cathedral where local granite was used, was built in Caen stone, a clear indication of Norman influence. Norman too is the inspection gallery which runs below the triforium.

In the north side of the chancel, below the funerary niches, are a number of wooden reliquaries with skulls dug up in a nearby cemetery, while in the sanctuary a palm tree carved in wood contains a ciborium for the Host (1770).

ST-RÉMY-DE-PROVENCE

Excursion

Roscoff★

5km – 3mi north. The harbour town with its fishing fleet and important export trade (vegetables) to Britain also has ferry services linking Brittany to Plymouth and Cork. It is a flourishing resort and a medical centre using sea-water treatment.

Not far from the harbour in the town centre is the church of **Notre-Dame-de-Kroaz-Batz★** with its remarkable lantern-turret belfry (**clocher★**) of Renaissance date. Inside, four alabaster **statues★** grace the altarpiece of one of the altars in the south aisle.

ST-RÉMY-DE-PROVENCE★

MICHELIN MAP 340 D 3–POPULATION 9 806
GREEN GUIDE PROVENCE

Just to the north of the jagged peaks of the Alpilles, St-Rémy encapsulates the character of inland Provence; plane trees shade its boulevards from the intense light and there are charming old alleyways. The Place de la République is Renaissance in style.

- **Information:** Place Jean-Jaurès, ☎04 90 92 05 22. www.saintremy-de-provence.com.
- ▶ **Orient Yourself:** The little town is just north of Les-Baux-de-Provence.

Sight

Les Antiques★★

1km/0.5mi south of the town. These fascinating remains mark the site of the prosperous Roman city of Glanum.

The mausoleum (**mausolée★★**) of the 1C BC is the best preserved of its kind in the Roman world; it was erected in memory of the Emperor Augustus' grandsons Gaius and Lucius, whose early death deprived them of their Imperial inheritance.

The triumphal arch (**arc municipal★**), which is much damaged, dates from the beginning of Augustus' reign and is one of the oldest such structures in the south of the country. Its decorative sculpture (garlands of flowers, groups of prisoners and symbols of victory) demonstrates the continued existence of Greek art in Provence.

The ruined site (**ruines de Glanum★**) have revealed the city's history. The original settlement here was founded by the Celts because of the existence of a spring. Later, in the 6C BC, it was extended by Greek merchants, and fine houses in Hellenic style were erected in the following centuries. The place was destroyed by the Teutons, probably not long before their defeat by Marius near Aix in 125 BC; it was restored by Caesar, only to be laid waste again by Germanic tribes in the 3C AD.

From this time on the city was more or less abandoned, and its streets and canals slowly filled up with material washed down from the Alpilles.

ST-SAVIN★★

MICHELIN MAP 322 L 5–POPULATION 1 009
GREEN GUIDE FRENCH ATLANTIC COAST

St-Savin lies among the pasturelands of the eastern border of the old province of Poitou, an area of sandy clay soils known as Les Brandes. Its former abbey church still draws many visitors in spite of the depredations of the centuries. It is now difficult to imagine how the place must have looked in its days of glory before the Hundred Years War, when the whole interior glowed with Romanesque wall-paintings, when none of the furnishings had been removed, and when the impact of insensitive restoration had not been felt.

🛈 **Information:** 20 pl. de la Libération, ☎05 49 48 11 00.

▸ **Orient Yourself:** The abbey is on the west bank of the River Gartemps, 42km/26mi east of Poitiers.

Visit

L'Abbatiale★★

🕒 *Open all day. Use discretion in visiting during religious services. Guided tour (1hr15min plus 30min for the film): call in advance.* 🕒 *Closed Jan, 11 Nov, 25 and 31 Dec.* ◉ *6€.* ☎*05 49 84 30 00.*

The abbey church was mostly built in the space of 50 years, between 1040 and 1090. The base of the tower dates from the 11C; above it rise two storeys added in the 12C and a slender 14C steeple (rebuilt in the middle of the 19C). Inside, tall columns divide the nave from the transepts, and in the six chapels which open off the choir and transepts are Romanesque altar-tables still with their original carved inscriptions.

The fame of St-Savin rests on its Romanesque **murals**★★★, the finest in the whole of France. They seem to have been painted around 1100 by a single team of artists over a period of only three to four years. Some of the paintings have withstood the ravages of time better than others; they include a monumental treatment of the Apocalypse (in the narthex), the Creation (nave), and the Book of Abraham...

ENCLOS PAROISSIAL DE
ST-THÉGONNEC★★

MICHELIN MAP 308 H 3
GREEN GUIDE BRITTANY

The parish close at St-Thégonnec is among the most famous of these typically Breton monumental groupings of church, cemetery, calvary and ossuary.

▸ **Orient Yourself:** The village lies 12km south-west of the town of Morlaix, in northern Brittany. Enter the parish close via Place de l'Eglise.

Visit

The magnificent 17C parish close at St-Thégonnec was to be the last of the great parish closes of Brittany. By good fortune, the village has managed to preserve it in fine condition.

Although of older origin, parish closes began to develop in this form during the second half of the 16C. They formed a useful tool for the Catholic Church, trying to promote a veneration of apostles and saints in opposition to Brittany's heritage of local cults. Their effectiveness was increased by the presentation of their subject matter somewhat in the manner of a strip cartoon, with exaggerated features and dramatic gestures.. This parish close is approached through a Renaissance triumphal arch (**porte triomphale**★) (1587), lavishly decorated with cannon balls, shells, pilasters and little lanterns. The calvary (**calvaire**★★) dates from 1610. It is the work of Roland Doré, and the last of its type to be carved from the mica-rich igneous rock known as **kersanton**. On the lower arm of the cross are figures of angels collecting Christ's blood, while the base shows scenes of the Passion and Resurrection. Note particularly the depiction of Christ's tormentors and also the symbolic use of clothing, with Our Lord and His followers dressed according to Christian tradition, while the representatives of worldly power wear the fashions of the time of Henri IV. The funerary chapel (**chapelle funéraire**★) of 1676 illustrates traditional decorative motifs in the province (altarpiece with spiral columns and a Holy Sepulchre in painted oak).

The 15C church (**église**★) was rebuilt and refurnished several times in the 17C and early 18C. The pulpit (**chaire**★★) has a polygonal base (1683) carved by master carpenters from the naval yards at Brest, as well as a fine medallion at the back and a Louis XV sounding-board.

Excursion

Enclos paroissial de Guimiliau★★

8km – 5mi southwest. This example of a parish close pre-dates the one at St-Thégonnec by some 30 years. The calvary (**calvaire**★★, 1581) has an attractively naïve quality; its 200 figures are full of a sense of vigorous movement and are carved in a robust way which recalls the sculpture of the Romanesque period. Also of interest is the terrifying sculpture showing the Gates of Hell, with the struggling figure of Catel Gollet (Lost Kate in Breton), the flirtatious serving-girl who failed to reveal all at Confession. The funerary chapel of 1642 has an outdoor pulpit of earlier (15C) date.

The church (**église**★) has a Renaissance **porch**★★ dating from 1606; the arching depicts scenes from the Old and the New Testaments. Panelled vaulting is a feature of the interior, which has a Baroque baptistery (**baptistère**★★) with a canopy and spiral columns decorated with pampres and foliage. With its sculpted panels of about 1675, the pulpit (**chaire**★) is also in the Baroque style.

ST-TROPEZ★★

MICHELIN MAP 340 O 6–POPULATION 5 444

GREEN GUIDE FRENCH RIVIERA

After half a century of fame, the little town of St-Trop' (as the locals call it) is still in fashion, thanks to an exquisitely picturesque harbour, a stunning location, and a constant stream of artists, journalists and photographers.

- **Information:** Quai Jean-Jaurès (the harbour), ☎08 92 68 48 28 (0.34€/mn). www.ot-saint-tropez.com
- **Orient Yourself:** St-Tropez can be reached from west or south on the congested road that encircles the St Tropez Peninsula. There can be a long tail-back to enter the town. The easiest and most enjoyable way to approach is on the water, especially the short passenger ferry crossing from the marina resort of Port Grimaud, on the other side of the bay. The real centre of town is Place des Lices. For visitors, the focus is the quayside.
- **Parking:** It is difficult to park in the street. Use the large car parks on the edge of town.

Visit

Although celebrities are rarely, if ever, seen here nowadays (it's much too crowded), the atmosphere is created by an impressive array of luxury charter yachts moored in the picturesque harbour, which teems with life. The old fishing village which was discovered by writer **Guy de Maupassant** and his friend painter **Paul Signac,** and went on to attract Matisse and major Post-Impressionist artists as well as the writer **Colette**, remains a fashionable resort frequented by writers and artists and more recently by celebrities from the entertainment world. Two Bravades, or "acts of defiance", take place each year. The first is a religious procession in honour of St Tropez, the second commemorates an event of local history which took place in 1637.

Musée de l'Annonciade★★

🕐 *Jul-Oct: daily 10am-1pm, 3-7pm; Dec-Jun: daily exc Tue 10am-noon, 2-6pm;* 🕐 *closed Nov, 1 Jan, 1 May, Ascension Day, 25 Dec;* ✆ *Jul-Aug 5.50€, rest of year 4.50€.* ☎ *04 94 97 04 01).* The museum, in an old house delightfully positioned on a bend in the quayside, has an impressive permanent collection, including post-Impressionist pictures of St-Tropez. In addition, the museum puts on remarklable temporary exhibitions often of works by major 20C artists.

🔵🔵 Citadelle★– 16C fortifications. Maison des Papillons (musée Dany-Lartigue) – collection of 4500 types of butterlies.

Excursions

St Tropez Peninsula★★

St-Tropez is located is on the north coast of the peninsula. Its east coast is fringed with popular sandy beaches, notably the famous **Plage de Pampelonne**. The south coast has some scenic rocky headlands. The interior is hilly and rustic, with small vineyards, pine copses and two charming old villages commanding wide views, **Ramatuelle** and smaller **Gassin**. A **footpath** extends around the coast of the whole peninsula.

Massif des Maures★★★

The long, low parallel ranges of the massif unfold from Fréjus to Hyères. Its fine forests of pine, cork oak and chestnut trees have often been devastated by fire. Chapels, monasteries and small villages are dotted in the hinterland, while the coast is fringed by coves, bays and small beach resorts.

Address Book

For coin ranges, see the Legend on the cover flap.

WHERE TO EAT

🍽 **Leï Salins** – *Plage des Salins* – ☎*04 94 97 04 40. Closed 15 Oct-31 Mar.* Open-air beach restaurant offering a tasty bill of fare consisting of salads and grilled, freshly caught fish. Charming seaside location coupled with attractive surroundings.

🍽🍽 **La Table du Marché** – *38 Rue Georges-Clemenceau* – ☎*04 94 97 85 20.* Gourmets will love this temple of gastronomy located near Place des Lices, open at all hours of the day. In addition to the restaurant offering traditional French cuisine, La Table du Marché is also known for its homemade pastries that can be purchased on the premises.

🍽🍽🍽 **Leï Mouscardins** – *Port (Tour du Portalet)* – ☎*04 94 97 29 00. Closed 9 Jan-4 Feb, 14 Nov-17 Dec, and Tue off-season.* Tucked away behind the harbor, near Tour du Portalet, this restaurant pays homage to Mediterranean tradition. It has a faithful following of food lovers, lured by its creative and lovingly prepared cuisine, presented to you in two dining rooms opening out onto St-Tropez Bay.

🍽🍽🍽 **Régis Restaurant** – *19 Rue de la Citadelle* – ☎*04 94 97 15 53. Closed 30 Oct-15 Mar.* Pasta in all shapes and sizes, cooked in various ways, as well as sushi and wok stir-frys, attract a regular clientele to this restaurant located on a steep, narrow street in St-Tropez. The food is served on the terrace or inside one of the small dining areas decked out in white.

WHERE TO STAY

Hôtel Lou Cagnard – *Avenue Paul-Roussel* – ☎*04 94 97 04 24. Closed 3 Nov-27 Dec* – *19 rooms* – ⌑*8€*. Enjoy breakfast in the shade of a mulberry tree in the tiny garden of this pretty Provençal house, just off Place des Lices. At night you'll be lulled to sleep by the chirping of cicadas. Modest prices, for St-Tropez.

Bello Visto – *Place deï-Barri – Gassin* – ☎*04 94 56 17 30 or 04 94 56 47 33. Closed Jan and Nov* – *9 rooms* – ⌑*8€*. There's truth in the name of this small family-run out-of-town hotel and restaurant at the top of Gassin village. Most rooms, like the terrace, profit from a "beautiful vista" over the Massif des Maures and the gulf of St-Tropez. Dining room with Provençal cuisine.

Hôtel Ponche – *Place Révelin* – ☎*04 94 97 02 53 – www.laponche. com. Closed 1 Nov-13 Feb* – *18 rooms* – ⌑*19€*. The rooms of this cosy hotel occupy four village houses formerly belonging to fishermen; the blue one was a favourite of Romy Schneider's. You will be under the charm of the rooftop terraces nestling between the citadel and the bell-tower. The warm, bright hues and considerate service make the Hôtel Ponche an absolute must.

ON THE TOWN

Bar du Château de la Messardière – *Route de Tahiti* – ☎*04 94 56 76 00. www.messardiere.com. Closed mid-Oct to mid-Mar*. This bar belongs to one of the Riviera's most prestigious hotels. Cosy ambience in the piano bar of this former 18C private residence. The terrace has good views of St-Tropez Bay.

Bar Sube – *15 quai de Suffren* – ☎*04 94 97 30 04. Closed 5-31 Jan*. Right on the quayside, one of the most beautiful bars in town. Model boats decorate the interior, where the leather armchairs and fireplace make a cordial and comfortable setting.

La Tarte Tropézienne – *Place des Lices* – ☎*04 94 97 71 42. www.tarte-tropezienne.com*. It was in this pâtisserie that the famous tarte tropézienne saw the light of day, invented in 1955 by Polish baker Alexandre Micka: a round delightfully moist, brioche cake flavored with orange blossom, filled with custard and sprinkled with crystallised suger.

Sénéquier – *Quai Jean-Jaurès* – ☎*04 94 97 00 90. Closed mid-Nov to mid-Dec*. The sidewalk terrace and crimson chairs of this tea room are famous throughout the world or so say the locals! Renowned personalities such as Jean Marais, Errol Flynn and Colette would come here for a cup of delicately fragrant tea, an iced coffee, a delicious ice cream or a few squares of homemade nougat.

SHOPPING

Markets – Tuesdays and Saturdays on Place des Lices.

Shopping streets – Rue Clemenceau, Rue Gambetta and Rue Allard offer an impressive selection of local arts and crafts: pottery, glassware etc.

Les Sandales Tropéziennes – *16 Rue Georges Clemenceau* – ☎*04 94 97 19 55 – www.nova.fr*. The Rondini house has been crafting St-Tropez sandals since 1927. The distinctive, namesake model in natural leather is the most popular, but the snakeskin version sells well, too!

Le Petit Village – *La Foux – near the commercial center just outside Gassin* – ☎*04 94 56 32 04*. This showroom brings together the wines from eight prestigious vineyards on the St-Tropez peninsula in a location just off the busy La Foux intersection. Includes the famous Château de Pampelonne vineyard. Free tastings and many regional products for sale.

SAINTES★★

MICHELIN MAP 324 G 5–POPULATION 25 595

GREEN GUIDE FRENCH ATLANTIC COAST

With its plane trees, white houses and red-tiled roofs, Saintes has a curiously Mediterranean feel. This pleasant regional capital on the River Charente has a rich cultural and historical heritage.

- **Information:** 62 Cours National, ☎05 46 74 23 82.
- ▶ **Orient Yourself:** The town is just off the A10 autoroute between Cognac and Royan. The main central streets are Avenue Gambetta, Cours National and Cours Lemercier.

A Bit of History

Saintes was already a regional capital in Roman times, with a bridge over the Charente aligned on today's Rue Victor-Hugo. In the Middle Ages, the town was an important stop on the pilgrims' route to Santiago de Compostela. Two great religious establishments developed on its outskirts, St-Eutrope on the west bank of the river, the Abbey for Women (Abbaye aux Dames) on the east bank. The historic core of the town, built on the site of the Gallo-Roman city, has been restored and pedestrianised.

Sights

The Arena and the Arch of Germanicus★

The arch was built in AD 19 at a point on the east bank of the Charente where the roads from Poitiers and Limoges converged on the Roman bridge. An archeological museum houses objects saved when the ruins of the Roman city were demolished. To the west, on the slopes of the west bank of the river, is an amphitheatre (**arènes★**), one of the oldest (1C AD) in the Roman world.

Église St-Eutrope

On the west bank, the crypt (**crypte**) of this church once served as a parish church (**église inférieure★**) to the pilgrimage church above. This upper part of the building was monastic in origin.

Abbaye aux Dames

🕒 Apr-Sep: daily 10am-7pm; Oct-Mar: daily except Mon in early Nov 1-6pm; 🕒 closed between Christmas and New Year's Day; ◎ 3€. ☎05 46 97 48 48

The church (**église★**) of the Abbaye aux Dames is a notable achievement of Romanesque local style, with fine carving in the excellent local stone.

◖◖ Musée des Beaux-Arts ★ 🕒 May-Sep: daily 1.30-6pm; Oct-Apr: daily 1.30-5pm. 🕒 Closed Mon, 1 May. ◎ 1.50€, no charge Sun and Wed. ☎ 05 46 93 03 94.

SALERS★★

MICHELIN MAP 330 C 4–POPULATION 401
GREEN GUIDE AUVERGNE THE RHÔNE VALLEY

High up among the vast grazing-grounds of the volcanic Cantal uplands, Salers has long been a market centre and staging-post for travellers. The tiny town seems to have been laid out to confuse possible attackers, with a maze of tortuous streets leading to the main square.

- **Information:** Place Tyssandier d'Escous, ☎04 71 40 70 68. www.pays-de-salers.com.
- **Orient Yourself:** In the heart of the Cantal region, the village is 43km north of Aurillac.
- **Don't Miss:** Salers is also a locally produced tasty farmhouse cheese made from unpasteurised cows' milk.

Visit

This square (**Grande-Place★★**) is something of a stage-set, overlooked by the corner-towers and turrets of the grandiose 16C lava-built **houses** of the local notables. The Renaissance **Ancien Bailliage** has typically Auvergnat window-mouldings and angle-towers, while the **Hôtel de la Ronade** is distinguished by a Gothic turret rising five storeys high. The church (**église★**) has a 12C porch and, inside, a fine 15C polychrome sculpture of the **Entombment★**.

ÉGLISE **SAN MICHELE DE MURATO**★★

MICHELIN MAP 345 E 4
GREEN GUIDE CORSE (IN FRENCH)

On its hilltop site just north of the village of Murato, this 13C Romanesque church is in Pisan style, of uneven stripes of beautiful green serpentine and white limestone blocks.

- **Orient Yourself:** The church and village of Murato are 28km south-west of Bastia.

SAORGE★★

MICHELIN MAP 341 G 4 –POPULATION 396
GREEN GUIDE FRENCH RIVIERA

The **gorges★★** of the Upper Roya form a spectacular **setting★★** for the village clinging to the steep south-facing slopes which rise abruptly from the river far below.

- **Information:** at the Mairie, or ☎04 93 04 92 05. www.royabevera.com.
- **Orient Yourself:** The village is high in the back country of the Riviera close to the Italian border.

Visit

The place is dominated by the belfries of its churches and monasteries, which overlook terraces and balconies, tall old houses with open-fronted drying lofts and roofs tiled with heavy stone slabs. A maze of stepped and tunnelled streets completes this highly picturesque townscape.

Excursion

Notre-Dame-des-Fontaines★★
17km – 11mi northeast via St-Dalmas-de-Tende. The key to the chapel is kept at

La Brigue. A temple dedicated to water gods once stood in this lonely valley at the foot of Mont Noir (Black Mountain). The chancel of the present building dates from the 12C; the nave added in the 15C was raised in height in the 18C and given a new ceiling. Most of the chapel's well-preserved **frescoes★★★** were painted by the Piedmontese artist Giovanni Canavesio between 1472 and 1492.

SARLAT-LA-CANÉDA★★★

MICHELIN MAP 329 I 6–POPULATION 9 909
GREEN GUIDE DORDOGNE BERRY LIMOUSIN

This attractive old Dordogne market town has narrow medieval streets lined with restored Gothic and Renaissance houses.

- ⓘ **Information:** Rue Tourny, ☎05 53 31 45 45. www.ot-sarlat-perigord.fr.
- ▸ **Orient Yourself:** The town is on a north-south axis. The old town is accessible by the avenue Thiers and Gambetta. In the summer, the old town is closed to motor vehicles during the day.
- ☺ **Don't Miss:** If possible, be here for the famous Saturday market which fills the town centre with a glorious array of local produce.
- 🅿 **Parking:** There are 12 car parks, but it's usually possible to find space in the streets surrounding the old town, except on market day.

Town house, Rue Montaigne

S. Sauvignier/MICHELIN

A Bit of History

Sarlat is the capital of the Périgord Noir (Black Périgord) country, a fortunate and abundant region between the Dordogne and Vézère rivers. The town grew up around the Benedictine abbey founded in the middle of the 9C. The wealth of the surrounding countryside poured into the town, enabling it to support a prosperous population of merchants, clerics and lawyers. Sarlat reached its peak during the 13C and 14C. The town long played host to fairs and markets, which still takes place every Saturday, when the stalls are loaded with seasonal produce, poultry, cereals, horses, nuts, geese, foie gras, truffles and other goods.

Sights

Vieux Sarlat (Old Town)★★★
For over 40 years a conservation pro-gramme has protected Sarlat's excep-tional townscape, which was unfortu-nately damaged in earlier years, notably by the 19C addition of Rue de la Répub-

lique. There are houses of great charm all over the town. The finest include: **Maison de la Boétie**★, a Renaissance building of 1525; **Hôtel de Malleville**★, three medieval dwellings knocked into one another in the 16C; **Hôtel de Pla-mon**★, every storey of which was built in a different century.

SARTÈNE★

MICHELIN MAP 345 C 10–POPULATION 3 410
GREEN GUIDE CORSE (IN FRENCH)

The writer Prosper Mérimée thought Sartène, 305m – 1 000ft above the Bay of Valinco, the "most Corsican of Corsican towns".

- **Information:** Cours Soeur Amélie, ☎04 95 77 15 40.
- ▶ **Orient Yourself:** The town is 12km south-east from Propriano.

Sights

Place de la Libération
The shady square is the focus of local life. It is overlooked by the **Église Ste-Marie**, built in granite. To the left of the main entrance are the chains and the heavy cross of oak borne by Catenacciu, the anonymous red-robed penitential figure at the centre of the nocturnal procession on Good Friday. This procession **(proces-sion du Catenacciu**★★**)** is probably the island's most ancient ceremony.

Vieille ville (Old Town)★★
Go through the arch of the Town Hall (Hôtel de ville) and take the street oppo-site (Rue des Frères-Bartoli). The narrow stone-flagged alleyways, occasionally stepped or vaulted, are lined by tall gran-ite-built houses with a fortress-like air. The **Quartier de Santa Ann**★★★ has a particularly characteristic townscape of this kind.

 Musée de préhistoire corse★.

SAUMUR★★

MICHELIN MAP 317 I 5–POPULATION 857
GREEN GUIDE CHÂTEAUX OF THE LOIRE

Dominated by its imposing château on a chalky spur overlooking the meet-ing-point of the Thouet with the Loire, Saumur is especially famous for its fine wines.

- **Information:** Place de la Bilange, ☎02 41 40 20 60.
  www.saumur-tourisme.com.
- ▶ **Orient Yourself:** Saumur straddles the Loire about midway between Angers and Tours, also taking in an island in midstream. The town centre is on the south side of the river, around Place St-Pierre. For an overview, take a 45-minute ride on the 'little tourist train' (summer only, 6€).
- **Don't Miss:** One of the equestrian shows that take place throughout the year; a stroll around the Old Town; a boat excursion on the Loire.
- Kids **Especially for Kids:** Zoo de Doué★★ (see Excursions).

A Bit of History

The town owed its early prosperity to the wooden bridge which crossed the Loire via two islands (the Île d'Offrand and the Île Millocheau, now joined together). It formed the only crossing point over the river between Tours and Ponts-de-Cé downstream from Angers, at the time of pilgrimages to Santiago de Compostela. In the 13C, the monks from the Abbaye de St Florent undertook to replace the original structure by one of stone, constructed at the rate of one arch a year. Though often carried away by floods, this bridge was always rebuilt.

Like all the towns along the great river such as Decize, Nevers, La Charité, Cosne, Gien, Orléans and Blois, Saumur's site was chosen, regardless of orientation, on whichever bank offered the better protection from high waters. The attractive old houses facing the Loire have walls of pale tufa and steeply-pitched slate roofs.

Saumur's long association with the horse began in 1763, when the crack corps known as the Carabiniers Regiment was sent here, under the command of Louis XV's brother ("Monsieur"). It was a time when the refinement of riding technique which had begun under de Pluvinel (Louis XIII's Master of the Horse) had become fashionable among the aristocracy. The National Equitation Centre (École Nationale d'Équitation) was founded in 1972, incorporating the famous **Cadre Noir** (Black Squad) which had originally consisted solely of army instructors. This aspect of the town's identity is evoked in the museum in the Château, and in the **Musée de l'École de Cavalerie**★ (*presently closed; the museum will reopen in a new location; call the Tourism office for information; ☏02 41 40 20 60*) which has displays on post-18C military history and on the development of horsemanship. In addition, there is a **Musée des Blindés**★★ (🕐 *May-Sep: daily 9.30am-6.30pm; Oct-Apr: daily 10am-5pm; last admission 1hr before closing;* 🕐 *closed 1 Jan and 25 Dec.* 🎫 *6€.* ♿ ☏*02 41 53 06 99; www.musee-des-blindes.asso.fr*), with displays of armoured vehicles both French and foreign from 1918 onwards.

Sight

Château★★

☛ *Château's interior closed for maintenance until 2008. Visit of the exterior only.* 🕐 *daily exc. Tue; Jul-Aug 10am-6pm, Apr-Jun, and Sep 10am-1pm, 2-5.30pm.* 🚶 *30min tours Jul-Aug at 10h15, 11h15, 12h15, 14h15, 15h, 15h45 et 16h45.* 🎫 *2€.* ☏*02 41 40 24 40. www.saumur.fr*

In the 14C, the château was rebuilt on the foundations of the medieval fortress originally erected by Philippe Auguste and Louis IX. As a consequence, it has a somewhat irregular layout. In the 15C, with the return of more peaceful times following the end of the Hundred Years War, Good King René (🕮 *see Index*) endowed his "castle of love" with sumptuous decorative detail in late-Gothic style. The château is shown in this state, albeit in a somewhat idealised landscape, in one of the miniatures from the *Très Riches Heures du Duc de Berry* (🕮 *see Index*). In the late 16C, at the time of the Wars of Religion, the place was refortified, as Saumur was one of the strongholds of French Protestantism.

There are two museums in the château, the **Musée du Cheval**★ with fascinating collections of riding equipment and a number of pictures (including work by Stubbs), and the **Musée des Arts décoratifs**★★, which has a fine display of works of art from the Middle Ages and Renaissance, including a collection of faience and French porcelain from the 17C and 18C.

During the Military Tattoo (Carrousel) held in July, the Musée des Blindés presents a number of armoured vehicles restored at the school and driven by cadets.

Excursion

Zoo de Doué★★

🧒 *20km southwest of Saumur.* The zoo is situated on the western edge of Doué-la-Fontaine on the road to Cholet (D 960). Some 500 animals roam more or less freely in this remarkable cave setting enhanced by acacia trees and bamboo groves, cascades and rocky overhangs. Visitors can walk among the

SENLIS

birds of prey in the vulture pen (fosse aux charognards) while in the large quarry reserved for leopards (canyon aux léopards), there are observation posts to view three sets of cats: snow leopards, Persian leopards and jaguars. A school of penguins disport themselves in a creek (crique aux manchots). A gallery (Galerie des Faluns) gives a glimpse of the fauna which existed on the site some 10 million years ago.

SENLIS★★

MICHELIN MAP 305 G5–POPULATION 16 327
GREEN GUIDE NORTHERN FRANCE AND THE PARIS REGION

Senlis derives a romantic charm from its picturesque Old Quarter streets, with many old dwellings and paved with big flagstones.

- **Information:** Place du Parvis Notre-Dame, ☎03 44 53 06 40.
- **Orient Yourself:** Senlis is on autoroute A1, 50km/31mi north of Paris. There is easy access to Senlis from Paris and the Channel.
- **Don't Miss:** The cathedral is the town's unmissable sight.
- **Especially for Kids:** The big Parc Asterix★★ theme park is south of town.

A Bit of History

At the centre of a rich agricultural region, Senlis was already a prosperous place in Gallo-Roman times. Eventually it became the kernel of the Île-de-France, core of the future kingdom of France.

Sight

Cathédrale Notre-Dame★★

Illustration Art: Architecture. Begun in 1153, the cathedral was consecrated in 1191. Of this first building only a few features survive. Changes in the 13C substantially destroyed the continuity of the pattern previously established. At the same time, the south tower was given its tall spire (**flèche★★**), 78m – 256ft, its verticality emphasised by the gables. The Flamboyant Gothic appearance of the cathedral is the result of the restoration undertaken between 1513 and 1560, following a great fire in 1504.

Old town, Senlis

◑◑ Musée d'Art et d'Archéologie★
Chapelle royale St-Frambourg★
Fondation Cziffr★
(*www.fondation-cziffra.org*).

SENS★★

MICHELIN MAP 319 C 2–POPULATION 26 904

GREEN GUIDE BURGUNDY JURA

The once-important old town is girded by boulevards that replaced the ancient ramparts. In the city centre stands the first of France's great Gothic cathedrals.

🛈 **Information:** Place Jean-Jaurès, ☎03 86 65 19 49. www.office-de-tourisme-sens.com.

▶ **Orient Yourself:** Approach the town from the west for the finest views. The town centre is around the cathedral. There's good shopping along pedestrianised Grande-Rue, and outdoor cafe tables in Place de la République.

◉ **Don't Miss:** The great Gothic cathedral.

A Bit of History

Its central position in relation to Burgundy, Champagne and the Île-de-France gave Sens considerable importance for centuries; for a long time it was the Bishop of Sens who crowned French kings.

Sight

Cathédrale St-Étienne★★

In its general conception this is the very first of France's great Gothic cathedrals, its foundations laid in the years 1128-30, though most building took place between 1140 and 1168.

The influence of the Romanesque can still be discerned in a number of features, like the slightly pointed "Burgundian" arches of the nave, a series of twin openings at tribune level with a false gallery, as yet no triforium, and, in the side chapels, a combination of rounded and pointed arches. But it is the Gothic which is decisive. There is use throughout of quadripartite vaulting; the choir has sexpartite vaults of square plan

resting on massive pillars alternating with slender columns, and the ambulatory has pointed arches, still awkwardly asymmetrical.

Following the collapse of the south tower of the west front in 1268, the building was restored and altered, with the probable addition of flying buttresses. In the 13C and 14C, the clerestory windows were given extra height; then, in the 15C and 16C, the transepts were built in Flamboyant style.

Outside, the decorative features include the pier of the central portal, the famous statue of St Stephen, and the Flamboyant gable of the north portal.

Inside, the eye is drawn to the **stained glass**★★; which is 12C in the ambulatory and north side of the choir, while the Jesse Tree and St Nicholas in the south transept and the rose window of the north transept are all Renaissance works by master glaziers from Troyes. The ambulatory, the chapels opening off it, and the choir all have very fine grilles of wrought and gilded ironwork (18C).

◖◖ Musée, Trésor (treasury) and Palais Synodal (Bishops' Palace)★

PRIEURÉ DE **SERRABONE**★★
MICHELIN MAP 334 G 7
GREEN GUIDE LANGUEDOC ROUSSILLON TARN GORGES

In a wild and stony setting among austere mountains, the former priory contains superb Romanesque sculpture, its severity relieved by delicate pink marble.

- **Information:** From the Priory, ☎04 68 84 09 30, or regional website www.cg66.fr.
- **Orient Yourself:** The steep winding road up to Serrabonne is a turning (near Ille-sur-Têt) off the mountain highway from Perpignan to Font-Roméu.
- **Organizing Your Time:** On summer Sundays at 6pm, there are unusual and imaginative concerts in the priory, with classical and traditional folk performances and other music relevant to the theme of Catalonia and the culture of the Pyrenees.

Visit

🕐 10am-6pm. Last admission 30min before closing. 🕐 Closed public holidays. 🏛 3€.

The chapel gallery (**tribune**★★) of about 1080, originally intended to serve as the choir, was moved to the centre of the nave at the beginning of the 19C. It is an unusual feature to have survived and has wonderful decoration in low relief as well as exceptionally richly carved capitals. A delightful south-facing **gallery**★ (Promenoir des Chanoines) overlooks the ravine far below.

SISTERON★★
MICHELIN MAP 334 D 7–POPULATION 6 964
GREEN GUIDE FRENCH ALPS

The lofty citadel of Sisteron, sternly guarding a narrow ravine and looking down on the clustered lanes of the 14C town, make an impressive spectacle.

- **Information:** pl. de la République, ☎04 92 61 36 50. www.sisteron.com.
- **Orient Yourself:** Sisteron is located on the Route Napoleon between Gap and Digne.

Geography

Sisteron lies between the Laragne valley to the north and the valley of the middle Durance to the south. As well as marking the historic boundary between Dauphiné and Provence, this is also the northern limit of the cultivation of the olive.

Sight

Citadelle★
🕐 Daily Apr-11 Nov, 9am-7pm (Jul-Aug: 7.30pm; Apr, May, Oct: 6.30pm). 🏛 4.80€. ☎04 92 61 27 57..

Following WW2 bombing in August 1944, little remains of the fortress other than the 12C keep and 16C ramparts, with excellent **views**★.

◑◑ The old quarter★ ;
Église Notre-Dame★

SOLIGNAC★★

MICHELIN MAP 325 E 6–POPULATION 1 367
GREEN GUIDE DORDOGNE BERRY LIMOUSIN

The 12C abbey church, robust and harmonious, has multiple domes. As well a
being among the last of their kind to be built in Aquitaine, are some of the fines
examples to be seen. There is an extraordinarily deformed dome over the choi
and one of ovoid shape covering the north transept.

🅸 **Information:** pl. Georges Dubreuil, ☎05 55 00 42 31.
▸ **Orient Yourself:** Solignac is 10km/6mi from Limoges.

Sight

Eglise abbatiale★★
Rebuilt around 1175, the abbey church shows Limoges influence in its use of granite, but its domes are based on the ones at Souillac in Quercy. From th steps of the porch, there is a view c the interior, beautifully proportioned Among the last of their kind, the pointe arches and pendentives are some of th finest examples in the region.

LA HAUTE **SOULE**★★

MICHELIN MAP F-G-H 4-5
GREEN GUIDE FRENCH ATLANTIC COAST

One of the original seven Basque provinces, the Upper Soule has retained th
dances and folk traditions most characteristic of the region.

▸ **Orient Yourself:** The region is in the high Pyrenees near the Spanish border.

Visit

This is ideal country for forest walks (and cross-country skiing) in rough terrain. At **Ahusquy**, a mountain inn stands in a panoramic **site**★★. At **Col d'Aphanize**, wild horses graze on the slopes around the pass. The pastureland here is the summer home of many flocks of sheep **Forêt des Arbailles**★★ and **Fôre d'Iraty**★ are extensive beech forest cov ering the higher reaches. Care is neede when exploring the impressive gorge of **Crevasses d'Holçarté**★ (on footpat GR 10) and grandiose **Gorges de Kakou etta**★★ (tiring and difficult path).

STRASBOURG★★★

MICHELIN MAP 315 K 5–POPULATION 427 245

GREEN GUIDE ALSACE LORRAINE CHAMPAGNE

his important modern city, with a busy river port and renowned university, is
ot just the lively capital of Alsace. It is also where the Council of Europe and
uropean Parliament are located. At the same time, the historic centre around
he cathedral, has been listed as a World Heritage Site since 1988.

- **Information:** 17 pl. de la Cathédrale, ☎03 88 52 28 28; pl. de la Gare, ☎03 88 32 51 49; Pont de l'Europe, ☎03 88 61 39 23. www.strasbourg.com.
- **Orient Yourself:** On the banks of the river Ill, Strasbourg was built around its famous cathedral whose exterior can be enjoyed best from rue Mercière. If you follow the rue des Grandes Arcades you will come across Place Kléber, the most famous square in the city.
- **Guided Tours:** A 1hr 30min audio-guided tour enables visitors to discover the cathedral, the old town and the Petite France at their own speed. Audio devices available in the tourist office for 6€ (30€ deposit).
- **Don't Miss:** Notre-Dame Cathedral and the Musée de l'Œuvre Notre-Dame.
- **Organizing Your Time:** Allow a whole day to see the old town. A choice of different passes (*Unipass, Strasbourg Pass, etc*) is available from the tourist office.
- **Parking:** Eight parking areas along the outskirts of Strasbourg allow you to leave your car and travel into the town centre by tram.

A Bit of History

trasbourg's name comes from the German meaning "city of the roads", and he place is indeed a meeting point for he highways, railways and waterways inking the Mediterranean with the Rhineland, Central Europe, the North Sea and the Baltic via the Belfort Gap nd the Swabian Basin.

On 14 February 842, the **Strasbourg Oaths** were sworn by two of the sons of Louis the Pious (son of Charlemagne). Brothers Charles and Louis undertook to be loyal to one another in their attempt to frustrate the ambitions of their elder brother Lothair. Protocol demanded that each declare the oath in a language comprehensible to his brother's entourage; thus it was that the text read out by Louis the German is considered to be the oldest such document in a Romance language, the first written example of the language which has evolved into modern French. The same can be said for the German text.

Strasbourg remained a **free city** within the Holy Roman Empire even after the virtual incorporation of the rest of Alsace into France by the Peace of Westphalia in 1648, but eventually submitted to annexation by Louis XIV in 1681.

On 24 April 1792, Frédéric de Dietrich, Strasbourg's first constitutional mayor, threw a farewell celebration for the volunteers of the Army of the Rhine. The conversation turned to the need for a marching song to match the troops' enthusiasm. Rouget de Lisle was asked to compose "something worth singing"; by morning he had finished, and sang his "marching song for the Army of the Rhine". Not long after, it was adopted by the Federates of Marseille, and ever since has been known as the **Marseillaise**.

In 1870, Strasbourg was seized by Germany after a long siege. It continued to grow, under the influence of Prussien culture. It became French at the 1918 Armistice, but was again taken by Germany from 1940 to 1944.

Sights

Cathédrale Notre-Dame★★★

In 1176, the cathedral was rebuilt in red Vosges sandstone on a site above flood-level but nevertheless using bundles of oak piles as a foundation (these were recently reinforced with concrete).

Externally, this is still a Romanesque building as far as choir, transept and lantern-tower are concerned. The famous Gothic **spire**★★★ (3€) is an architectural masterpiece, its verticality emphasised by its forward position immediately over the west front. An unmistakable landmark, visible over much of the Alsace plain, it rises to a height of 142m – 466ft. The openwork octagon supporting it was erected between 1399 and 1419 by a Swabian architect and given an extra 7m – 23ft in height during the course of construction for reasons of prestige. Its final stage was designed and built between 1420 and 1439 by a Cologne architect, using techniques from the previous century; it is particularly notable for the projecting structures carrying the external staircases.

The High Gothic west front **(façade**★★★**)** was the work of Erwin von Steinbach. It is decorated with a wealth of sculpture (statues and low-reliefs of many different periods), especially in the central portal **(portail central)** with its double gable and delicate lancets masking part of the rose window. The three lower levels of the tympanum have particularly fine 13C work, including depictions of the Entry into Jerusalem, scenes of the Passion and Resurrection, and the Death of Judas; in the arching can be seen the Creation, the story of Abraham, the Apostles, the Evangelists and the Martyrs.

In the south doorway **(portail Sud)** is a famous portrayal of the Seducer about to succeed in tempting the most daring of the Foolish Virgins (she is undoing her dress). The statues of the Church and Synagogue (copies) on the south side of the cathedral are equally celebrated.

Inside, the nave elevation is a straightforward example of the High Gothic style of the 14C, with an openwork triforium and wide aisles lit by elegant window-openings.

In the south transept is the 13C Angel pillar **(pilier des Anges**★★**)** or Last Judgement **(du Jugement dernier)**; its delicate statuary, on three levels, raises Gothic art to a peak of perfection. **Stained-glass windows**★★★ from the 12C, 13C, and 14C are remarkable. The **astronomical clock**★ (clock chimes at 12.30pm) nearby, dating from 1838, continues to draw crowds with its automata ringing out the quarter-hours (the figure of Death has the privilege of sounding the hours) and the crowd of figures brought out to mark midday (12.30pm).

Musée de l'Œuvre Notre-Dame★★

🕐 Daily 10am-6pm. 🚫 Closed Mon, Jan, Good Friday, 1 May, 1 and 11 Nov, 2 Dec. 🎫 4€ (under 18 years: no charge, no charge 1st Sun in the month. ☎03 8. 52 50 00. www.musees-strasbourg.org/F oeuvre_nd.html.

Housed in a number of old dwellings just to the south, this museum greatly enhances the visitor's appreciation of the cathedral. Its great treasure is the famous Head of Christ **(Tête de Christ**★★**)** from Wissembourg in northern Alsace. In addition, there is the oldest stained glass in existence and above all, many of the cathedral's original statues, including the Church and the Synagogue, the Wise and Foolish Virgins. The architect's drawings of the west front and the spire are here too.

Palais Rohan★

Residence of the Prince-Bishops of Strasbourg, the palace was built between 1732 and 1742, a fine building in the Classical manner, with a curving entrance colonnade ornamented with statues and trophies, a main courtyard defined by balustraded galleries, a façade with dressings of pale limestone, a fine entablature, and mansard roofs lit by bull's-eye windows. The Prince-Bishops' state rooms are considered to be among the finest French interiors of the 18C. The building's most elegant façade is the one overlooking the River Ill; it has tall Corinthian columns, a dome and a balustraded terrace.

The palace houses several **museums**★★ (🕐 Wed-Mon 10am-6pm. 🚫 Closed Tue, 1 Jan, Good Friday, 1 May, 1 and 11 Nov, 25 Dec. 🎫 4€ (under 18 years: no charge), no charge 1st Sun in the month. ♿ ☎03 88 52 50 00. www.musees-strasbourg.org)

Musée des Arts Décoratifs★★

Includes the State Apartments (**Grands Appartements**) and tells the story of the city's crafts and craftsmen. It has one of the finest **ceramic collections★★** in France, particularly rich in Strasbourg and Niderwiller faience and porcelain.

Musée des Beaux-Arts★

Known for its Italian paintings (Primitives and Renaissance), its Spanish works (Zurbaran, Murillo and Goya) and 15C-17C Netherlandish Old Masters. Don't miss Nicolas de Largillière's 1703 portrait of *La Belle Strasbourgeoise*, the elegant, black-robed beauty.

Musée archéologique★★

Covers the period between the Quaternary era and the end of the first millennium AD. There are displays on prehistory, extinct animals, ceramics, and on Roman and Merovingian times.

The Old City (La Cité Ancienne)★★★

Two parts of the old city evoke the delightful spectacle of a bygone Alsace of timber-framed houses with the whole array of traditional features, wooden galleries, loggias on brackets, windows with tiny panes of coloured glass, as well as the overhanging upper storeys which continued to be built here in the post-1681 years even though they had been banned in France proper. Each house can be enjoyed for its own sake; together, they compose the most ravishing of townscapes.

Quartier de la Cathédrale★★★

In the cathedral quarter, two especially attractive buildings give onto the **Place de la Cathédrale**★; at the corner with the Rue Mercière there is the Pharmacie du Cerf (**F**) of 1268, supposedly the oldest pharmacy in France, and on the north corner is the Kammerzell House (**Maison Kammerzell**★) of the same date with frescoes and wooden sculptures. Other streets and squares, like the Place du Marché-aux-cochons-de-lait (Sucking-Pig Market Square), Rue Mercière and Rue des Cordiers, complete the pleasures of a stroll.

Place Kléber

R. Mattès/MICHELIN

Petite France★★

This is the city's well-preserved historic core. It owes its name to a former French hospital and was once the abode of fishermen, tanners and millers. The arms of the Ill were provided with locks giving shipping from the Rhine access to the back door of virtually every shop. With its gabled Renaissance houses reflected in the green waters of the river, it forms a charming urban scene, notably in the **Rue du Bain-aux-Plantes★★.**

Place Kléber

This is the city's most famous square, named after Jean Kléber (1753-1800), the hero of the battles of Mainz (1793), Fleurus and Maastricht, who was assassinated in the course of Napoleon's campaign in Egypt.

▶▶ Cour du Corbeau★.
Covered Bridges★.
View from the Barrage Vauban★★
Musée d'Art Moderne et contemporain ★★
Musée historique.
Église St-Thomas – mausoleum of Marshal de Saxe★★.
Orangerie★.
Palais de l'Europe★.

Address Book

For coin ranges, see the Legend on the cover flap.

WHERE TO EAT

😊 **Pommes de Terre et Cie** – *4 r. de l'Écurie* – ☎*03 88 22 36 82 – booking advisable.* If you want a change from choucroute, this friendly restaurant mainly serves dishes with jacket potatoes and meat, fish or cheese.

😊 **Aux Fines Gourmandises** – *5 pl. Corbeau-* ☎*03 88 36 09 92 – booking advisable in summer.* Internet enthusiasts will love this spacious restaurant-tea room with its internet café. Wde choice of dishes including tartes flambées and choucroute and a delicious selection of pastries.

😊 **Flam's** – *29 r. des Frères, (quartier historique)* – ☎*03 88 36 36 90 – booking advisable at weekends.* This half-timbered house very close to the cathedral houses a restaurant specialising in flam-mekueches. The three dining rooms and two cellars have been redecorated in lovely bright colours. Note the superb 15C painted ceiling.

😊 **Au Hanneton** – *5 r. Ste-Madeleine* – ☎ *03 88 36 93 76 – closed Tue lunchtime and Mon – booking advisable.* This tiny winstub faithfully follows Alsace tradition with its warm, intimate country decor, its friendly atmosphere and regional specialities such as fish choucroute and Munster cordon bleu. Lovely terrace for sunny days.

😊 **Zum Strissel** – *5 pl. de la Grande-Boucherie* – ☎*03 88 32 14 73 – closed 27 Jan-7 Feb, 3 Jul- 2 Aug, Sun and Mon.* An authentic wine bar, run by the same family since 1920. The much-loved decor consists of wood panelling, decorative wrought iron, stained-glass windows depicting Bacchus and a 14C wine press. Regional cooking accompanied by Alsace wines, including the famous kaefferkopf d'Ammerschwihr.

😊 **Le Pigeon** – *23 r. des Tonneliers* – ☎ *03 88 32 31 30 – closed 3 weeks in Jan and 18 Jul-12 Aug.* This typical winstub, which takes its name from the two pigeons sculpted on the façade, is situated in one of the oldest residences in Strasbourg (take a minute to look at the listed wooden staircase). Decor and cuisine in keeping with Alsace tradition.

😊😊 **La Choucrouterie** – *20 r. St-Louis* – ☎*03 88 36 52 87 – closed Aug, Sat and Sun lunchtimes.* This 18C coaching inn was the last place in Strasbourg to make pickled cabbage. Feast and have fun in a slightly chaotic setting, with music, cabaret or theatre dinners, as you like. Alsace cuisine served with local white wine.

😊😊 **Caveau Gurtlerhoft** – *13 pl. de la Cathédrale* – ☎*03 88 75 00 75.* Sample regional and traditional cooking in the lovely cellars of this 14C canonical building near the cathedral, with their splendid vaulting and massive pillars. Mouth-watering menus and fixed-price lunch. Unhurried service.

😊😊 **La Coccinelle** – *22 r. Ste-Madeleine* – ☎*03 88 36 19 27 – closed 15 Jul-15 Aug, Sat lunchtime and Sun – booking advisable.* Wood panelling, beams, copperware, stained-glass windows and old photos lend this winstub (in the family since 1976) its typical Alsace feel. Regional cooking with choucroute, quenelles de foie (liver quenelles), jambonneau rôti (roast knuckle of ham) and bœuf gros sel (beef).

😊😊 **Pont St-Martin** – *13-15 r. des Moulins* – ☎*03 88 32 45 13 – booking advisable.* This ever-popular restaurant in a venerable half-timbered building is in the heart of the picturesque Petite France district, just above the water. Typical Alsace interior of panelling, wainscoting and checked tablecloths. Regional cooking.

😊😊 **La Taverne du Sommelier** – *Ruelle de la Bruche (Krutenau distict)* – ☎*03 88 24 24 10 – closed fortnight in Aug, Christmas and New Year's Day – booking essential.* The type of little restaurant it's always a pleasure to discover. The decor of yellow walls and lithographs is perfect to set off the intimate atmosphere. The cooking follows the seasons, while the wine list features wines from the Languedoc region and the Rhône Valley.

😊😊 **Petit Ours** – *3 r. de l'Écurie (quartier des Tonneliers)* – ☎*03 88 32 13 21 – booking advisable.* Great little restaurant decorated with Tuscany-inspired colours. Light floods through the bay windows of one room, and the non-smoking cellar is also very pleasant. Each dish (mostly fish) is characterised by a particular herb or spice.

🍴 **Au Renard Prêchant** – *34 r. de Zürich – ☎03 88 35 62 87 – closed lunchtime on Sat, Sun and public holidays.* A 16C chapel in a pedestrian-only street, which takes its name from the murals decorating its walls telling the story of the preaching fox. Rustic dining room, pretty terrace in summer, and reasonable fixed-price lunches.

WHERE TO STAY

🏨 **Patricia** – *R. du Puits – ☎03 88 32 14 60. www.hotelpatricia.fr – booking advisable – 20 rooms – ☑€5.* Two small wooden printers are a reminder that this venerable residence (listed façade) was the home of the regional printers' in the 19C. It is now a hotel with quiet, bright rooms where TV is banished and smoking not permitted.

🏨 **Hôtel de L'Ill** – *8 r. des Bâteliers – ☎03 88 36 20 01 – www.hotel-ill.com – closed 29 Dec-6 Jan – 27 rooms – ☑ €6.* Renovated hotel with family atmosphere. The rooms are of differing sizes and impeccably clean, while the traditional-style breakfast room has a cuckoo clock. You can take a boat trip on the River Ill just a stone's throw away.

🏨 **Couvent du Franciscain** – *18 r. du Fg-de-Pierre – ☎03 88 32 93 93. www.hotel-franciscain.com – closed 24 Dec-9 Jan – 43 rooms – ☑ €8.50.* At the end of a cul-de-sac, these two buildings are joined by a pleasant hall. We recommend the rooms in the new wing. The breakfast room is in the cellar. A good option within walking distance of the old city.

🏨 **Hôtel des Rohan** – *17 r. Maroquin – ☎03 88 32 85 11. www.hotel-rohan.com – 36 rooms – ☑ €10.* Named after the nearby palais de Rohan, this little hotel is also near the cathedral. Its quiet, pleasant rooms are furnished in Louis XV style, and those on the south side have air conditioning.

🏨 **Hôtel Pax** – *24 r. du Fg-National – ☎03 88 32 14 54. www.paxhotel.com – closed 23 Dec-4 Jan – 106 rooms – ☑*

€7. A family hotel in a busy street on the edge of the city's old district. Its plain rooms are well kept, and its restaurant serves regional dishes. You can eat in the vine-shaded courtyard in summer.

🏨 **Hôtel Beaucour** – *5 r. des Bouchers – ☎03 88 76 72 00 . www.hotel-beaucour.com – 49 rooms – ☑€11.* Those who like staying in lovely places will enjoy this city-centre hotel spread out in several old houses. Attractions include the flower-decked courtyard, cosy rooms and regional furniture in an inviting decor.

ON THE TOWN

Demandez le programme! – To find out the programme of theatres, concerts, seminars, exhibitions and sporting events, get a copy of the monthy Strasbourg actualités or Hebdoscope, with weekly listings fro arts and shows.

L'Opéra-café (in the public opera house) – *Pl. Broglie – ☎03 88 75 48 26 – daily 11-1.30am except Sun 2-8pm – closed 25 Jul- 16 Aug, 24-26 Dec and 31 Dec.* The purple and gold decor in this theatre bar evokes the world of the stage. A classy setting for an intimate date over a glass of whisky or wine – or a hot chocolate with the family. Painting and photography exhibitions.

SHOPPING

Markets – The markets are generally open from7am-1pm. Traditional market Tue and Fri place Kléber, Wed rue Krutenau and rue de St-Gothard. Direct from the grower market on Sat, pl. du Marché-aux-Poissons. Flea market (9am-6pm) Wed and Sat, r. du Vieil-Hôpital and pl. de la Grande-Boucherie. Book market (9am-6pm) Wed and Sat, pl. and r. Gutenberg and r. des Hallebardes. Christmas market in Dec.

Un Noël en Alsace – *10 r. des Dentelles, Petite France – ☎03 88 32 32 32 – www.noelenalsace.fr – daily except Sun morning 10am-12.30pm, 1.30-7pm (from Jul, Sun 2-6pm) – closed Jan-Feb.* It's Christmas every day in this 16C building in the heart of the Petite France district. Tinsel, little wood figurines, twinkling stars and coloured baubles: you name it, they have it!

Au Paradis des Pains d'Epices – *14 r. des Dentelles, Petite France* – ☎*03 88 32 33 34 32* – *www.paindesoleil.com* – *daily 9am-7pm except Mon mornings.* Scents of orange, honey, cinnamon and cardamom greet you as you enter this tiny shop located in a timber-framed house dating from 1643. Heaven on earth for gingerbread fans: soft or crunchy, sweet or savoury, even iced varieties to tempt you.

BOAT TRIPS

Boat trips on the Ill – ♿ Guided trips (1hr 10min)along the River Ill *(departure from the Palais Rohan pier)* taking in the Petite France, past Barrage Vauban, then the Faux Rempart moat as far as Palais de l'Europe. *Apr to Oct: 1hr 10min, departure every half-hour 9.30am-9pm; Nov-Dec and Jan-Mar: 4 departures a day 10.30am, 1pm, 2.30pm and 4.30pm. €6.80 (children €3.40).*

Boat trips on the Rhine and tour of the **harbour** – ♿ Departure from the Promenade Dauphine pier. *Jul-Aug: guided trip (2hr 15min) at 2.30pm. €8 (children €4).* ☎*03 88 84 13 13, www. strasbourgport.fr*

CALENDAR

Folklore shows – *Mid-Jul to early Aug, Square Louise-Weiss. Local, national and international dancing.* ☎*03 88 60 97 14.*
European Fair – *Early Sep, Parc des Expositions du Wacken.* Over 1000 exhibitors representing a wide range of activities. *Enquiries:* ☎*03 88 37 21 21.*
Strasbourg, Christmas Capital – Countless events and shows all over town: Christmas market (Christkindelsmärik), illuminations, giant Christmas tree, exhibitions, nativity scene and concerts. *Programme available from tourist office.*

Excursion

Wine Villages
Some of the most picturesque villages in Alsace are a short drive from the city.

Saverne★
The town at the entrance to the Vosges uplands has **old house**s★ and a splendid red sandstone **château**★ with a

monumental Louis XVI **façade**★★ giving onto the park.

Église de Marmoutier★★
This 12C former abbey church has a fine **west front**★★ in the red sandstone o the region, in Romanesque style incorporating Carolingian and Rhineland influences.

La Petite France

GORGES DU **TARN**★★★

MICHELIN MAPS 330 H-J 8-9 AND 338 L-N 5
GREEN GUIDE LANGUEDOC ROUSSILLON TARN GORGES

The deep gorges cut by the Tarn through the harsh limestone plateaus (causses) to the south of the Massif Central make up one of France's most spectacular natural landscapes. The source of the Tarn lies high (1 575m – 5 167ft) in the granitic uplands of Mount Lozère; tumbling torrent-like down the slopes of the Cévennes, the river then enters the most spectacular section of its course at Florac.

- **Information:** at the village of Le Rozier: Route de Meyrueis, ☎05.65.62.60.89. www.officedetourisme-gorgesdutarn.com.
- **Orient Yourself:** The River Tarn rises on Mont Lozère, and runs through the Cevennes before reaching the Causses country where it has carved its plunging gorge between the limestone plateaus. The road runs at the top of the cliffs, not in the ravine itself. There are small villages, notably St Enimie, along the gorge, but no communities of any great size.
- **Organizing Your Time:** The road along the gorge is narrow, difficult, and in season can be congested. Allow several hours to cover the full distance.
- **Don't Miss:** Pause at the Point Sublime to get the full impressive picture of the Tarn gorge.

Driving Tour: From Florac to Millau

83km – 52 miles – allow about 4hr.

The river flows through a deep canyon, joined by side valleys like those of the Jonte and the Dourbie. Escape from the valley bottom is by means of roads which twist and turn up the precipitous slopes to join the roughly-planed surface of the Méjean causse; its porous limestone is deeply fissured and hollowed out to form the caves for which the region is famous.

Most visitors come here when the summer sun is beating down, but the scene is best appreciated in spring and autumn, when the vegetation is better able to assert itself and local life is flourishing. Nor should the spectacle of winter be missed, when every feature has its frosty outline.

The hostile landscape here has been humanised by centuries of determined human effort. Thus there are villages on the flatter patches of cultivable land which occur on the valley bottom and sides (Ste-Énimie, La Malène, Les Vignes...) and the castles of lords and robber-barons on the more easily-defended sites overlooking the river. On the plateau above are isolated farms

based on the better soils of the little depressions known as dolinas; the drystone walls once made by piling up the boulders collected laboriously from the fields are now supplemented by electric

Tarn Gorge

A.Thuillier/MICHELIN

fences, and the thoughtless forest clearance of the 19C is being made good by the planting of Austrian pines.

No trace of the underground realm of chasms (**Aven Armand**★★★) and caverns is visible at the surface; those who venture into this unsuspected world are rewarded by the extraordinary spectacle presented by the dissolution of the limestone, and by the strange forms of the stalactites and stalagmites.

Les Détroits (The Straits)★★

This is the narrowest part of the valley, hemmed in by plunging cliffs of coloured limestone.

Cirque des Baumes★★★

Below Les Détroits, the gorge widens forming this magnificent natural amphitheatre.

Le Point Sublime ★★★

(adds 26km/16mi to the journey between La Malène and Les Vignes.) This splendid viewpoint above the Cirque des Baumes overlooks both canyon and causse.

ABBAYE DU **THORONET**★★

MICHELIN MAP 340 M 5
GREEN GUIDE FRENCH RIVIERA

Of the "three Cistercian sisters of Provence" (the others being Silvacane and Sénanque), Le Thoronet is the earliest; it was founded in 1136, when St Bernard was still alive. It is one of the most characteristic of Cistercian abbeys, as well as one of the most austere.

▶ **Orient Yourself:** The abbey is set deep in the Provencal backcountry, close to the River Argens, between Brignoles and Draguignan. It can be reached from autoroute A8, junction 13.

Visit

The plain architecture of the abbey is unrelieved by decoration, save in the chapter-house, where just two roughly-sculpted capitals relieve the prevailing rigour. The abbey **church**★ has a simple beauty. Built from 1160 onwards, it has remarkable stonework which was cut and assembled without the use of mortar (notably in the oven-vaulted apse). The **cloisters**★ of about 1175 have kept their four barrel-vaulted walks; the change of level is more obvious here than in the church and is still causing problems of subsidence.

TOUL★

MICHELIN MAP 307 G 6–POPULATION 16 945
GREEN GUIDE ALSACE LORRAINE CHAMPAGNE

On the banks of the River Moselle, the handsome fortified town occupies a strategic position at the intersection of highways and waterways.

🔲 **Information:** parvis de la Cathedrale, ☎03 83 64 11 69.

▶ **Orient Yourself:** The town is in Lorraine. The walled old quarter, almost enclosed by water, is entered by Porte de France on the west side or Porte de la Moselle on the east.

A Bit of History

Together with Metz and Verdun, the city was one of the three Imperial Bishoprics which were annexed by Henri II in 1552 and were finally recognised as belonging to the French crown by the Peace of Westphalia in 1648.

Sight

Cathédrale St-Étienne★★

Built from 1221 to 1496, cathedral has a very simple elevation. The highly pointed arches of the first five bays of the nave are in the High Gothic style of the 14C. The west front (**façade★★**), almost overloaded with architectural ornament, lost its statuary at the time of the French Revolution. The **cloisters★**, adorned with fine gargoyles, are among the most extensive in France.

◖◗ Église St-Gengoult★ and its Cloisters★★.
Musée d'Art et d'Histoire★.

TOULON★★

MICHELIN MAP 340 K 7–POPULATION 519 640
GREEN GUIDE FRENCH RIVIERA

Backed by high hills whose summits are crowned by forts, Toulon is France's second most important naval base, set in one of the Mediterranean's most beautiful harbours.

🔲 **Information:** pl. Raimu, ☎04 94 18 53 00. www.toulontourisme.com.

▶ **Orient Yourself:** The city is 64km east of Marseille. Autoroute A50 passes through the centre.

🌀 **Don't Miss:** A boat trip around the immense natural harbour (*rade*) is especially enjoyable (9€. ☎04 94 93 07 56).

Sights

La rade★★

Construction of Toulon's Old Port (Vieille darse) began under Henri IV. Richelieu appreciated the strategic advantages of the roadstead and ordered the building of the first naval installations. In the reign of Louis XIV, the base was extended and the New Port (Darse Neuve) laid out by Vauban. In the 19C, the Mourillon extension and the Castigneau basin were built, completing the naval base which had become the home port of the French Mediterranean Fleet.

Beyond the harbour lies the magnificent Outer Roadstead (Grande Rade), approached via the Inner Roads (Petite

Rade), guarded to the north by the Royal Tower (Tour Royale) and the main jetty, to the south by Vieille Point; it is here that the naval base with all its installations and repair yards is located. The still-considerable remains of the French fleet had anchored here after the disaster of Mers-el-Kébir in 1940, when the Royal Navy had turned its guns on the ships of its defeated ally in order to prevent them falling into German hands. The same danger threatened in July 1942; in response to the Allied landings in North Africa, the Germans had swiftly overrun the hitherto-unoccupied part of France. Caught by surprise and unable to escape, 60 warships scuttled themselves, only a few submarines managing to make their way to the open sea.

Port★

To the west of the Quai Cronstedt (landing-stage for boat-trips) is the Navy Museum (Musée de la Marine). Once the entrance to the old Arsenal, its doorway is a Louis XV masterpiece; it is flanked by sculptures of Mars and Bellona and has marble columns with Doric capitals framing tableaux of maritime motifs. The balcony of the former Town Hall (Hôtel de ville) is supported by two splendidly muscular **Atlantes**★, the work of Pierre Puget.

Mont Faron★★★

This distinctive peak rising behind the town is the easternmost of the limestone ranges which were raised up in Provence on the fringe of the great earth movements associated with the formation of the Alps in Tertiary times. A telepherique travels to the summit, an exciting experience, with thrilling views (*follow signs to téléphérique on Boulevard Sainte-Anne. 6€*).

Musée-mémorial du Débarquement en Provence★

🕐 *Jul-mid Sep: daily exc 10am-1pm, 2 6.30pm. Rest of year: closed Mon. Oct-Apr closes 5.30pm. Last admission 1hr before closing.* 🚾 *3.80€.* ♿ ☎*04 94 88 08 09.*
From the tower, Tour Beaumont (507m – 1 663ft), there are fine views inland as well as a magnificent seaward **panorama**★★★ over the Hyères Islands, the Toulon roadstead and the whole of the coast between Sanary and Bandol. The diorama explains the course of the landings which took place on the night of 14 15 August 1944, and of the subsequent liberation of the coast between Antheo and Marseille. This second front supplemented the one already opened up by the Normandy landings, and forced the Wehrmacht to beat a rapid retreat to avoid being cut off.

◗◗ Corniche du Mont Faron★★ (corniche road).
Musée de la Marine★
www.musee-marine.fr.
Vieille ville★ (old town).
Navire de débarquement "La Dives" (landing craft) – museum.

TOULOUSE★★★

MICHELIN MAP 343 G 3—POPULATION 761 090

GREEN GUIDE LANGUEDOC ROUSSILLON TARN GORGES

A vibrant regional capital, attractive with its red-brick architecture, Toulouse is a lively university town with a thriving high-tech industrial sector and, at the same time, plenty of attractions for the visitor to enjoy.

- **Information:** Donjon du Capitole, Square du Général-de-Gaulle, ☎05 61 11 02 22. www.toulouse-tourisme-office.com.
- ▶ **Orient Yourself:** The city is enclosed by a circle of autoroutes and expressways, while the city centre, sitting on the right bank of the River Garonne around Place du Capitole, is also ringed by busy boulevards. The east side of the Place du Capitole is the main meeting place for local residents.
- **Don't Miss:** From the St-Michel bridge, there's a great view of the city, especially towards the end of the day when the sun picks up the warm red tones of the brickwork.
- **Organizing Your Time:** If you plan on visiting most of the museums, check the tourist office for special passes that guarantee reduced rates. Take the 2hr guided tour of Toulouse first to get a better idea of where you want to spend your time in France's sixth-largest urban centre.
- **Parking:** Cars can be parked free of charge in the "transit car parks" and you can then take the bus or metro into the city.

A Bit of History

Toulouse has long been the focus of very diverse influences. The city was the capital of the Visigothic kingdom, and enjoyed considerable prosperity between the 9C and 13C under the Raymond dynasty, whose court was considered to be one of the most cultured in Europe. Their extensive territories were known as the "Langue d'Oc". In the 13C, the whole domain of the Raymonds —most of present-day Languedoc and parts of the Midi-Pyrenees and Provence —embraced Catharism. This stance gave the Capetian kings an opportunity, with the authority of the Pope, to launch the Albigensian Crusade against Catharism. The Crusade put an end to the power of the Raymonds, broke up their territories, and enabled the Capetian kings to push their frontier southwards into Languedoc.

In 1323, Europe's oldest literary society was founded here to further the cause of the language of southern France (Langue d'Oc). Later, in the 16C, the city flourished again because of a boom in what at the time was the most widely-cultivated of all dye plants, woad, which yielded a blue-black colour.

As early as 1917, strategic industries like aircraft manufacturing were being set up in southwestern France, as far away as possible from the country's vulnerable eastern border. In the inter-war period, Toulouse became the starting-point of France's first scheduled air service. The city has remained the focus of France's aeronautics industry.

Sights

Basilique St-Sernin★★★

The great church was built to honour the memory of the Gaulish martyr St Sernin (or Saturninus). A first phase of construction lasting from around 1080 to 1118 was in a mixture of brick and stone, a second phase in brick alone.

St-Sernin was one of a number of major Romanesque pilgrimage churches on the route to Compostela. St-Sernin's octagonal bell-tower is particularly characteristic of the area, with five levels of twin arches built in brick, the upper two of which are provided with little pediments.

Address Book

For coin ranges, see the Legend on the cover flap.

WHERE TO EAT

La Faim des Haricots – *3 r. du Puits Vert* - ☎ *05 61 22 49 25. Closed Sun* - 🖼. A mere stone's throw from the Capitole, this vegetarian restaurant gives diners a choice of varied, plentiful fixed-price menus at painless prices. The warm decor blends brick and yellow shades; the mezzanine is also very appealing.

Jean Chiche – *3 r. St-Pantaléon* - ☎ *05 61 21 80 80. Closed evenings*. This pleasant patisserie and tearoom is close to the Capitole. The menu offers a choice of around a dozen light meals, plus cakes and ice creams.

La Madeleine de Proust – *11 r. Riquet* - ☎ *05 61 63 80 88* - 🖼. Childhood memories inspire the original, carefully designed decor of this restaurant featuring yellow walls, waxed tables, antique toys, an old school desk, a time-worn cupboard. The cuisine gives the starring role to vegetables that have fallen out of common use.

La Cave des Blanchers – *29 r. des Blanchers* - ☎ *05 61 22 47 47. Closed Tues*. An attractive spot, situated among other restaurants on a street which is very popular in the evenings. Vaulted ceiling and pink brick inside, while in summer diners can eat on the pavement terrace. Regional cuisine blending characteristic sweet and sour flavours.

La Régalade – *16 r. Gambetta* - ☎ *05 61 23 20 11. Closed Sat lunch, Sun and 2 weeks in Aug*. Located between the Capitole and the Garonne, this small restaurant's pink brick facade leads to a pleasant interior of exposed beams, modern art, wood furniture and bistro chairs. Bountiful traditional fare.

Bon Vivre – *15 bis pl. Wilson* - ☎ *05 61 23 07 17* - 🖼. With its terrace giving onto Place Wilson and an attractive interior decorated with photos of Gers (where the proprietor was born), this is an appealing spot with a solid traditional menu.

Le Mangevins – *46 r. Pharaon* - ☎ *05 61 52 79 16. Closed Aug and Sun*. In this local tavern where salted foie gras and beef are sold by weight, the bawdy, fun atmosphere is enhanced by ribald songs. There is no menu, but a set meal for hearty appetites. Anyone in search of peace and quiet should look elsewhere!

Colombier – *14 r. Bayard* - ☎ *05 61 62 40 05. Closed Aug, 1 Sep. 25 Dec, Sat lunch, Sun - reservation recommended*. Opened in 1874, this is an essential stopping point for culinary pilgrims in search of authentic cassoulet. Delightful dining room with pink bricks and wall paintings. Friendly and efficient service.

Le Châteaubriand – *42 r. Pargaminières* - ☎ *05 61 21 50 58. Closed end Jul-21 Aug*. The atmosphere in this little restaurant in old Toulouse is particularly pleasant. Cosy interior with a parquet floor, red brick walls, a huge mirror and houseplants. Southwestern cooking on the menu.

L'Envers du Décor – *22 r. des Blanchers* - ☎ *05 61 23 85 33. Closed Sun and Mon* - 🖼. Cuisine of the southwest with some exotic touches is served in this restaurant in a small, busy street not far from the Garonne. Dice, cards, and theatre contribute to the playful ambience; perhaps you will win yourself a second meal. Good luck!

7 Place St-Sernin – *7 pl. St-Sernin* - ☎ *05 62 30 05 30. Closed Sat lunch, Sun*. This pretty 19C house typical of Toulouse stands opposite the basilica. Bright red and yellow Catalan colours, contemporary furniture and a display of paintings from a local art gallery garnish the dining room. Contemporary cuisine.

Brasserie de l'Opéra – *1 pl. du Capitole* - ☎ *05 61 21 37 03. Closed Sun*. The brasserie of the Grand Hôtel de l'Opéra is the essential place to go and see and be seen. The inviting decor, leather wall seats and autographed photos of the many artists who have spent time here create a special atmosphere. Cuisine of southwest France.

Brasserie "Beaux Arts" – *1 quai Daurade* - ☎ *05 61 21 12 12*. The atmosphere of a 1930s brasserie is recreated here with bistro-style chairs, wall seats, retro lighting, wood panelling and mirrors. The cuisine, in keeping with the decor, features seafood, sauerkraut and a few regional specialities.

⊜⊜⊜⊜ **Brasserie de l'Opéra** – *1 pl. du Capitole* – ☏ *05 61 21 37 03. Closed 1-7 Jan., 29 Jul-28 Aug, Mon lunch and Sun.* The excellent restaurant of the Grand Hôtel de l'Opéra. Sophisticated cuisine in luxurious surroundings. Where to see and be seen.

WHERE TO STAY

⊜⊜ **Hôtel de France** – *5 r. d'Austerlitz* - ☏ *05 61 21 88 24 - www.hotel-france-toulouse.com - 64 rms.* ⊡ *7€* In business since 1910, this attractive hotel is situated a few steps from the Place Wilson. The rooms are of various sizes; though not luxurious, they are shipshape and affordable. Some of the largest come with a balcony.

⊜⊜ **Hôtel le Capitole** – *10 r. Rivals* - ☏ *05 61 23 21 28 - hotelcapitolewanadoo.fr* - ⊡ *9€.* Situated very near to the Place du Capitole, this old mansion has a brick facade that has just been redone. Some of the spacious bedrooms are sparkling new, and half are air-conditioned. A bonus: breakfasts are served 'til noon.

⊜⊜ **Hôtel St-Sernin** – *Pl. St-Sernin* - ☏ *05 61 21 73 08 - book in advance* – *18 rms.* ⊡ *8€.* Some rooms at this family hotel have fine views of the famous basilique St-Sernin; all are simply decorated with yellow or pale pink walls and well presented. Open fireplace in the breakfast room.

⊜⊜ **Hôtel de l'Ours Blanc** – *25 pl. Victor-Hugo* - ☏ *05 61 23 14 55 - www.hotel-oursblanc.com* – *38 rms.* ⊡ *8€.* Situated opposite the marché Victor-Hugo, this hotel has simple yet comfortable rooms (recently renovated) which are air conditioned and sound proofed; bright breakfast room with some attractive pictures embellishing its walls.

⊜⊜ **Hôtel Castellane** – *17 r. Castellane* - ☏ *05 61 62 18 82 - 49 rms.* ⊡ *7.50€.* This small hotel close to the Capitole is slightly set back from the main thoroughfare. The simple, practical rooms are housed in three different buildings; some rooms are particularly well suited to families. Breakfast is served on the veranda.

⊜⊜⊜ **Hôtel Mermoz** – *50 r. Matabiau* - ☏ *05 61 63 04 04 - www.hotel.mermoz. com - 52 rms.* ⊡ *10€.* The inner flower garden of this hotel near the city centre provides a haven of calm. Many decorative touches, notably portraits of pilots, bring aviation's early years to mind. Spacious rooms in 1930s style.

SIT BACK AND RELAX

Maison Octave – *11 allée Franklin-Roosevelt* - ☏ *05 62 27 05 21.* Come to this famous ice cream parlour for an overwhelming choice of sherbets, ice cream, *vacherins*. Over thirty different flavours to enjoy in the parlour or take home.

ON THE TOWN

The magazine *Toulouse Cultures* (monthly) list all current and upcoming events.

Place du Capitole – The famous central square of the city is a pedestrians-only meeting place surrounded by alluring brasserie terraces. **Le Bibent** – *5 pl. du Capitole* - ☏ *05 61 23 89 03.* Classified as an historic monument because of its Belle Époque decor, this roomy café has a superb terrace giving onto the Place du Capitole.

Au Père Louis – *45 r. des Tourneurs* - ☏ *05 61 21 33 45. Closed 1 week in Spring, 3 weeks in Aug, Christmas-1 Jan and public holidays.* First opened in 1889 and now a registered historical building, this wine bar is a local institution. The portrait of Père Louis, the founding father, conspicuously observes goings-on from above; his debonair visage also adorns wine bottle labels. Wine is sipped around fat-bellied barrels; an appetizing choice of open-faced sandwiches is available evenings.

SHOPPING

Markets – **Saturday mornings:** organic farmers' market in Place du Capitole. **Sunday morning:** farmers' market around Eglise St-Aubin; L'Inquet, a renowned flea market around the Basilique St-Sernin. **Wednesday and Friday** (Nov-Mar): geese, ducks and foie gras are sold in Place du Salin.

Shopping streets – The main shopping streets are Rue d'Alsace-Lorraine, Rue Croix-Baragnon, Rue St-Antoine-du-T., Rue Boulbonne, Rue des Arts and the pedestrian sections of Rue St-Rome, Rue des Filatiers, Rue Baronie and Rue de la Pomme. There is also a shopping mall, St-Georges, in the centre of the city.

Busquets – *10 r. Rémusat - ☎ 05 61 21 22 16 – www.extrawine.com.* Connoisseurs of wines from the southwest, *foie gras, cassoulet, confit,* and other regional specialities will be in seventh heaven in this shop founded in 1919.

La Maison de la Violette – *Bd de Bonrepas - Canal du Midi - ☎ 05 61 99 01 30.* The celebrated Toulouse violet is the star of this shop housed on a pastel-coloured barge. The very hospitable owner's enthusiasm for this noble flower is contagious – let her guide you through an array of violet-scented perfumes, liqueurs, sweets and cosmetics.

Librairie des Arcades – *16 pl. du Capitole - ☎ 05 61 23 19 49.* This shop specialises in comic books.

Atelier du Chocolat de Bayonne – *1 r. du Rempart-Villeneuve - ☎ 05 61 22 97 67. Closed early-mid Aug, Christmas, New Year.* All the chocolates in this shop are guaranteed 100 % pure cocoa with no added fat. Faced with such abundance, it is difficult to make a choice: chocolate flavoured with cinnamon, orange or ginger, or rather chocolate from Madagascar, Java or Ecuador??

Olivier Confiseur-Chocolatier – *20 r. Lafayette - ☎ 05 61 23 21 87.* Olivier, a master chocolate maker, produces irresistible specialities, including the famous candied violets, capitouls (almonds covered in dark chocolate), *Clémence Isaure* (Armagnac-soaked grapes covered in dark chocolate), *brindilles* (nougatine covered in chocolate praline) and *Péché du Diable*, The Devil's Sin, (dark chocolate ganache with orange peel and ginger).

RECREATION

Le Capitole – *Quai de la Daurade - ☎ 05 61 25 72 57. Daily at 10.30am, 3pm and 4.30pm (May-Sep: also at 6pm) - 8€; Jul-Aug: night cruises, 9pm, 10pm - 5€.* Embark upon this pleasure steamer for a cruise on the Garonne.

Péniche Baladine – *Quai de la Daurade - ☎ 05 61 80 22 26 or 06 74 64 52 36 – www.bateaux-toulousains.com .* Oct-May: open Wed, Sat, Sun and public holidays; Jun-Sep and school holidays: open every day, Canal du Midi cruises (1hr 15mins) depart at 10.50am and 4pm, Garonne cruises (1hr 15mins) depart at 2.30pm, 5.30pm and 7pm. 7€. Details of night cruises on request.

Parc toulousain – Set on an island in the river Garonne, the Parc toulousain offers four swimming pools, three outdoors and one covered; the Stadium, where the Stade Toulousain rugby team plays; the Parc des Expositions and the Palais des Congrès.

CALENDAR OF EVENTS

Fête de la violette – *First or second weekend in Feb - ☎ 05 62 16 31 31.* Growing, selling, exhibiting… the ideal opportunity to learn all about the flower that is the city's emblem.

Printemps du rire – *Late Mar - ☎05 62 21 23 24, www.printemps-du-rire.com.* Spring comedy festival.

Garonne le Festival – *Late Jun - ☎ 05 61 32 77 28, www.garonne-rioloco.org.* Visitors from all over the world congregate for concerts and other events.

Piano aux Jacobins – *Sep - ☎ 05 61 22 40 05, www.pianojacobins.com*

Le Printemps de Septembre – *Late Sep - ☎ 01 43 38 00 11, www. printempsdeseptembre.com.* Festival of photography and visual arts.

Festival Occitania – *Oct - ☎ 05 61 11 24 87, www.ieotolosa.free.fr.* Regional culture celebrated through various media (cinema, poetry, song etc).

Jazz sur son 31 – *Oct - ☎ 05 34 45 05 92, www.jazz31.com.* Large jazz festival established 18 years ago.

Cinespaña – *Octobre - ☎ 05 61 12 12 20, www.cinespagnol.com.* Spanish cinema.

Église des Jacobins★★

Daily 9am-7pm. Possibility of a guided tour (1hr). 3€, no charge 1st Sun in the month. 05 61 22 21 92. www.jacobins.mairie-toulouse.fr.

This was the first church of the Preaching Friars, an order founded in 1215 by St Dominic, and intended to help in the fight against Catharism. To the poverty demanded by St Francis of his followers, Dominic added a knowledge of theology and a training in eloquence which enabled his disciples to attempt to overcome their opponents in argument.

The church is the key building in the evolution from 1230 onwards of Southern French Gothic as influenced by the mendicant orders.

The size of the edifice, combined with the impossibility of providing it with external support (because of ownership and circulation problems), ruled out the construction of a single nave. The architect resorted to the expedient of a marvellous ribbed vault and the **"palm-tree"** of the chancel with its splendid array of 22 radiating arches. All this in 1292, 170 years before the great pointed vaults of the Late Gothic.

The tower dates from 1298. With its great height, octagonal plan, pedimented arches and rhomboid openings, it became the model for the towers of the major churches of Southern France.

Capitole★

This is Toulouse's City Hall, its name being derived from the "capitouls" or consuls who administered the city when it was ruled by the Raymonds. With its Ionic pilasters and alternating use of brick and stone, it is a fine example of the urban architecture of the 18C.

Cathédrale St-Étienne★

There is a fascinating contrast here between the nave completed in 1212, a vast hall in the Mediterranean tradition designed to accommodate large numbers of people, and the chancel, begun 60 years later on the pattern of the Gothic churches of Northern France. The architect of this later addition was Jean Deschamps, who took it upon himself to propagate this style throughout Languedoc once it had become part of the Capetian realm.

The nave and chancel are not aligned on the same axis and hardly seem to form part of a whole. The original plan had envisaged a more or less total reconstruction, but in the event the old nave was retained, and the link between it and the chancel cleverly improvised by some architectural virtuosity in what should have been the north transept.

Musée des Augustins★★

Daily 10am-6pm (Wed 9pm). Possibility of a guided tour (1hr15min). Closed 1 Jan, 1 May, 25 Dec. 3€, no charge 1st

Quai de la Daurade

J.Malburet/MICHELIN

Sun in the month. ♿ ☎ *05 61 22 21 82.*
www.augustins.org.
The museum is housed in the former convent, with a famous **Pietà** and superb collection of **Romanesque sculpture**★★★ (mostly 12C), much of it in grey Pyrenean marble.

◖◗ Hôtel d'Assezat★★ – 16C mansion considered the most beautiful in Toulouse.
Musée St-Raymond★★ – archeology.
Muséum d'Histoire naturelle★★ ⚮ *reopening 2008* – natural history.
Musée Paul-Dupuy★ – applied arts from medieval times to the present.

Violets

According to tradition violets, which originate in Parma, were brought back to Toulouse in the 19C by French soldiers returning from the Napoleonic wars in Italy. They proved very popular with the locals and in particular with florists, perfumers, and confectioners who specialised in the famous crystallised violets. At the beginning of the 20C some 600 000 bunches were despatched each year to Paris, Northern Europe and even as far as Canada. Unfortunately the delicate flower succumbed to disease. From 1985 scientists made a determined attempt to save the little mauve flower. Ten years later in vitro cultivation was a success. Nowadays the glasshouses of Lalande, north of Toulouse, are once more filled with the characteristic perfume of violets and Toulouse has regained its emblem.

LE **TOUQUET**★★★

MICHELIN MAP 301 C 4–POPULATION 5 299
GREEN GUIDE NORTHERN FRANCE AND THE PARIS REGION

With its casinos, grand villas, immense beach, designer stores, gourmet restaurants and luxury hotels, the "Pearl of the Opal Coast" enjoys an international reputation.

- **Information:** Palais de l'Europe, pl. de l'Hermitage, ☎03 21 06 72 00 - www.letouquet.com
- ▶ **Orient Yourself:** The town is on the Channel coast south of Boulogne. It is divided into two: the well-treed residential area with its luxury villas, some of them modern, but many in a hybrid style known as "Anglo-Norman"; then there is the resort itself, stretching out along the magnificent beach of fine sand. The town centre is laid out on a grid pattern and the main shopping streets are Rue St-Jean and Rue de Paris.
- **Don't Miss:** The forest, which provides a refreshing backdrop to the town – hire a bike to explore.
- **Especially for Kids:** Boolaboo (pedal-boat hire); Aqualud (water park); and lots of kids' attraction of the beach.

A Bit of History

In 1837, a stretch of empty sand dunes was purchased by a speculator who planted it with maritime pines and later, in 1876, divided it into residential plots. At the beginning of the 20C, a British company, the "Le Touquet Syndicate" moved in and built exclusive holiday dwellings. By 1912 the place had become so fashionable among the leisured classes of England but also of Paris, that it took on the name Paris Plage.

Seaside

Along the seafront, the **promenade** is edged by gardens and car parks. The south end leads to a yachting club and a thalassotherpy centre. The fine sand beach stretches as far as the mouth of the River Authie. The **coast road** follows the line of the dunes and leads to the marina and the water sports club, well sheltered by Pointe du Touquet.

TOURS★★

MICHELIN MAP 317 N 4–POPULATION 297 631
GREEN GUIDE CHÂTEAUX OF THE LOIRE

With a civilised air, under dazzling Loire valley skies, built in bright white tufa and roofed in black slate, the ancient city of Tours makes a perfect base for excursions into the châteaux country.

- **Information:** 78 r. Bernard-Palissy, ☏02 47 70 37 37. www.ligeris.com.
- **Orient Yourself:** Tours spans the Loire and fills the isthmus between the Loire and its tributary the Cher. The Old Town lies along the left bank of the Loire, reaching from the lively Place Plumereau area to the peaceful Cathedral district.

A Bit of History

The place originated in Gaulish times, becoming an important centre of trade and administration under the Romans. Throughout the Middle Ages it was an important religious centre.

Sights

Château★

Not camparable in grandeur to the more typical Loire châteaux, this is a heterogeneous collection of buildings from the 4C to the 19C. The lower parts of the wall on the west side go back to Roman times and here too is the 11C residence of the Counts of Anjou; the Guise Tower (Tour de Guise) with its machicolations and pepper-pot roof is of the 13C-15C, while the dormer-windowed Governor's Lodging (Logis du Gouverneur) is 15C and other additions were made as recently as the 17C-19C.

Cathédrale St-Gatien★★

Following a fire, the cathedral was rebuilt from 1235 onwards. The work lasted all of 250 years. As a result it

Tours - Place Plumereau

S.Sauvignier/MICHELIN

Address Book

For coin ranges, see the Legend on the cover flap.

WHERE TO EAT

🍴 **Bistrot de la Tranchée** – 103 av. Tranchée – ☎ 02 47 41 09 08. Closed 5-26 Aug, Sun and Mon. Dark wood panelling, bottles of wine, comfortable wall sofas and old-fashioned pizza ovens (remnants of the previous restaurant) make up the decor of this pleasant bistro. Enjoy a good selection of small dishes typical to this type of restaurant. Definitely worth a visit.

🍴 **Cap Sud** – 88 r. Colbert - ☎ 02 47 05 24 81. Closed 12 Aug-7 Sep., 24 Dec-8 Jan and weekends. This little restaurant has a Mediterranean atmosphere, both in its warm decorr with sunny colours and up-to-date cuisine. Short, well-selecetd wine list.

🍴 **Léonard de Vinci** – 19 r. de la Monnaie – ☎ 02 47 61 07 88. Closed Sun evening and Mon – reservation required in evenings – A taste of Tuscany in the heart of the Touraine. This Italian restaurant's claim to fame is that it doesn't serve pizzas! A chance to discover different Italian dishes, in a decor that highlights models of Leonardo da Vinci's inventions.

🍴 **La Roche Le Roy** – 55 rte de St-Avertin – ☎ 02 47 27 22 00. Closed Feb school holidays, 1-25 Aug, Sun and Mon. The restaurant in this Touraine manor house was created under a lucky star and will be much appreciated by gourmets. Sample the cooking, which varies with the seasons, in the intimate dining room or the pretty enclosed courtyard in summer, and enjoy fine wines from the cellar hewn into the cliff face.

WHERE TO STAY

🛏 **Chambre d'hôte Le Moulin Hodoux** – 37230 Luynes – 14km/8.75mi W of Tours on N 152 and minor road – ☎ 02 47 55 76 27 – 🚫 – 4 rooms. In a peaceful country setting not far from Tours, near the castle at Luynes, this 18C-19C watermill provides comfortable, well-equipped rooms. In the lovely garden there are tables, chairs and a barbecue for visitors' use, as well as a swimming pool.

🛏 **Hôtel Le Cygne** – 6 r. du Cygne - ☎ 02 47 66 66 41 – Closed Christmas. – 16 rooms. - 🍽 7 €. One of Tours' oldest hotels (18C). Rooms have been renovated, but their character has been preserved. In winter, a fine 16C fireplace warms the little lounge. There is a pleasant family atmosphere.

🛏 **Hôtel du Relais St-Éloi** – 8 r. Giraudeau - ☎ 02 47 38 18 19 - relais-ste-loi2@wanadoo.fr - 56 rooms. 🍽 8 €. Recent building with small, practical rooms. Some, with a mezzanine, are particularly suitable for families. No-frills decor and regular maintenance. Modern dining room, but traditional culinary repertoire. .

🛏 **Central Hôtel** – 21 r. Berthelot – ☎ 02 47 05 46 44 – 40 rooms – 🍽 12€. A quiet, comfortable hotel in the old part of Tours, near the busy pedestrian-only districts. The staff are reserved but pleasant. There is a small, peaceful garden to enjoy behind the hotel in summer, and you can eat breakfast on the terrace.

SIT BACK AND RELAX

Le Vieux Mûrier – 11 pl. Plumereau – ☎ 02 47 61 04 77 – 🕐 Tue 2pm-2am, Wed-Sat 11am-2am, Sun 2pm-1am. This is one of the oldest cafés in place Plumereau, and it has that extra hint of character that is so often missing from modern establishments, with a decor reminiscent of a museum. Lovely terrace in the square.

SHOPPING

Markets – Second-hand goods: 1st and 3rd Fri of the month, r. de Bordeaux; 4th Sun in the month, bd Bérange; Wed and Sat mornings, pl. de la Victoire. **Flowers** –Wed and Sat, all day, bd Béranger.

Au Vieux Four – 7 pl. des Petites-Boucheries, ☎ 02 47 66 62 33. www.auvieuxfour-mahou.com. Closed Sun and Mon. This boulangerie and museum reveals the secrets of traditional bread-making.

La Chocolatière – 6 r. de la Scellerie, ☎ 02 47 05 66 75. www.la-chocolatiere.com. Closed Mon. 'Le pavé de Tours' is one of the great specialities of the exceptional maker of pâtisseries, confectionery and top-of-the-range chocolates.

La Livre Tournois – 6 r. Nationale, ☎02 47 66 99 99. Speciality of the house is of course Livre Tournois, delicious bitter chocolate with coffee and orange, but there are plenty of other delicious temptations here to taste ... and you can watch them being made too.

demonstrates the complete evolution of the Gothic style, from a chevet in the early phase, to a Flamboyant west front, and even a lantern crowning the twin towers that is characteristic of the Early Renaissance. The stained glass ranges in date from the 13C (high windows in the chancel) via the 14C (transept rose windows) to the 15C (rose window of the west front).

La Psalette★

🕐 May-Sep: 9.30am-12.30pm, 2-6pm (Sun closed in morning). Apr: 10am-12.30pm, 2-5.30pm (Sun closed in morning). Oct-Mar: daily exc. Mon and Tue 9.30am-12.30pm, 2-5pm (Sun closed in morning). 🕐 Closed 1 Jan, 1 May and 25 Dec. ⊚ 2.80€. ☎ 02 47 47 05 19.

This is the name given to the cathedral cloisters where canons and choir-master used to meet. The tiny Archive Room (Salle des Archives) of 1520 and the vaulted Library (Librairie) are reached by means of a spiral staircase, Gothic in structure but Renaissance in the way in which it is detailed.

Place Plumereau★

This busy and picturesque square is located at the old "meeting of the ways" (carroi); it is bordered by fine 15C residences built of stone and timber. On the corner with the Rue du Change and the Rue de la Monnaie is a carved corner post with a somewhat mutilated depiction of the Circumcision.

Musée des Beaux-Arts★★

🕐 9am-12.45pm, 2-6pm. 🕐 Closed Tue, 1 Jan, 1 May, 14 Jul, 1 and 11 Nov, 25 Dec. ⊚ 4€. ☎ 02 47 05 68 73.

In the former Bishops' Palace (17C-18C), its rooms are beautifully decorated with Louis XVI panelling and silk hangings made locally. It houses works of art from the châteaux at Richelieu and Chanteloup (now demolished) as well as from the great abbeys of Touraine. The collection of paintings consists mostly of French works of the 19C-20C, but there are also two outstanding Mantegnas, a Resurrection and Christ in the Garden of Olives (late 15C).

Musée du Compagnonnage★★

Entrance via 8 r. Nationale and a walkway. 🕐 Jun-mid Sep: daily 9am-12.30pm, 2-6pm. Rest of year: daily exc Tue 9am-12, 2-6pm. Last entry 30min before closing. 🕐 Closed public holidays. ⊚4.80€. ☎ 02 47 61 07 93.

The city long prided itself on its craftsmen, and even at the end of the 19C there were still three guilds jealously guarding their traditions. The museum contains many fine examples of the work of master craftsmen like roofers and slaters, blacksmiths and locksmiths, saddlers and carpenters.

▶▶ Rue Briçonnet★.
Place Grégoire-de-Tours★.
Hôtel Gouin★
Musée de la Société archéologique de Touraine★.
Historial de Touraine★
(in the castle).
Jardin de Beaune-Semblançay★.
Musée des Équipages militaires et du Train★

TRÉGUIER★★

MICHELIN MAP 309 C 2–POPULATION 2 679
GREEN GUIDE BRITTANY

Tréguier is a little medieval city, overlooking the wide estuary of the Jaudy and Guindy rivers, one of the drowned valleys known as abers which are so characteristic of the Breton coast.

▫ **Information:** 67 r. Ernest Renan, ☎02 96 92 22 33. www.paysdetreguier.com.
▶ **Orient Yourself:** The town lies half-way between Lannion and Paimpol.

A Bit of History

The place was converted to Christianity in the 6C by St Tugdual, a monk of Welsh origin, and soon became the seat of a bishop. The most popular Breton saint, **Saint-Ives** (1253-1303), lived here; he was often depicted in the act of even-handedly dispensing justice between rich and poor alike and hence became the patron saint of lawyers.

The town and its surroundings were no strangers to misfortune. In 1345-47 the area was devastated by the English allies of Jean de Montfort in retribution for having supported Jeanne de Penthièvre in the War of the Breton Succession. In 1592 it was pillaged by the Catholic Leaguers for having taken the part of Henri IV, then punished again in 1789 for its oppostion to taxes and reforms introduced at the French Revolution.

Sights

Cathédrale St-Tugdual★★

Begun in 1339, this is one of the finest buildings of its kind in Brittany, Anglo-Norman in style in spite of the use of the local granite. The exterior is notable for its Romanesque Hastings Tower (Tour d'Hastings) and the balustrades adorning the slate roofs, as well as for the two porches on the south side; the larger one with its statues of the Apostles is known as the People's Porch (Porche du Peuple), the other with its much-eroded statuary is the Bell Porch (Porche des Cloches). Within, the Lanceolate version of the Gothic survives in the three-storeyed elevation. A frieze sculpted in white tufa runs underneath the blind triforium, while in the south transept there is a graceful window (**Grande Verrière★**) with Flamboyant Gothic lancets (**fenêtre★**) adorned with a depiction of the Mystic Vine symbolising the Church in Brittany. In the ambulatory is a 13C wooden figure of Christ, and the nave has a copy of the tomb of St Ives built by Duke John V.

The cathedral's **cloisters (cloître)**★ of 1458 are among the few to survive in Brittany. Timber-roofed and with a carved frieze, it has 48 elegant arches giving onto a hydrangea-planted courtyard. ◷ *Jul-Aug: daily 9.30am-6.30pm; Low season: 10am-noon, 2-6pm.* ◷*Closed Sun morning.* ☜ *3€ (Oct-Mar: no charge).* ☎ *02 96 92 22 33.*

FORÊT DE **TRONÇAIS**★★★

MICHELIN MAP 326 D 3

GREEN GUIDE AUVERGNE RHÔNE VALLEY

This splendid oak forest, "one of the finest in France, indeed in Europe" (JL Reed), lies at the southeastern end of the great plains of central France, bounded by the rivers Allier and Cher.

🛈 **Information:** Place du Champ-de-Foire, Cérilly, ☎04 70 67 55 89. http://paysdetroncais.free.fr/.

▶ **Orient Yourself:** The forest lies north of Montluçon, and is easily reached on autoroute A71. For information on tourist activities, contact the Association du Pays de Tronçais in Cérilly. ☎ 04 70 67 55 89.

A Bit of History

Today's forest covers a total area of 10 954ha – 27 067 acres. It passed into the hands of the French Crown when François I put an end to the independence of the Bourbonnais in 1527.

A steady process of deterioration set in, which was reversed by the great Colbert in 1670; anxious to maintain the supply of ship timber for the expanding French navy, he instituted measures for the conservation and renewal of the woodland. However, in 1788 an iron foundry was opened, and to satisfy its demands for charcoal, two-thirds of the area was converted from high forest to a coppice regime, thereby destroying much of the resource slowly built up over the preceding century.

In 1832 a new policy of conservation was adopted, and since 1928 six blocks of high forest totalling 650ha – 1 606 acres have been managed on a long rotation of 225 years.

Visit

The forest consists largely of sessile oak. The finest stands are called the **Hauts-Massifs**★★★; here there are a number of exceptional individuals with their own names, some of them more than 300 years old. To the east of the Gardien clearing are the Carré, Émile-Guillaumin and Charles-Louis-Philippe oaks, and to the west of the Buffévent clearing in the Richebout block other venerable trees bearing the names Jacques-Chevalier, de la Sentinelle and des Jumeaux. The Tronçais region straddles the boundary between the north and south of France. To the north is the country of langue d'oïl, four-wheeled carts, and slate or flat-tiled roofs; to the south, langue d'oc, carts with only two wheels, and roofs covered with pantiles in the Roman fashion.

◖◖ Séries de l'Ouest★ – Western forest stands.
Futaie Colbert★ – Colbert Stand .
Étangs de St-Bonnet★
Pirota et Saloup★ – ponds.

TROYES★★★

MICHELIN MAP 313 E 4–POPULATION 128 945
GREEN GUIDE ALSACE LORRAINE CHAMPAGNE

The lively centre of this distinguished old trading town is a charming collection of picturesque half-timbered houses, many beautifully restored.

- 🚇 **Information:** 16 bd. Carnot (by the station) and rue Mignard (pedestrian zone, opposite Saint Jean church), ☎03 25 82 62 70. www.ot-troyes.fr
- ▶ **Orient Yourself:** The town is on the border of Champagne and Burgundy, and is at the meeting of autoroutes A5 (from Paris) and A26 (from Calais). Rue de la Republique is the main street, and Place Alexandre Israël is the town centre, where activities are organized throughout the year.
- 🎧 **Guided Tours:** Guided tours, including audio tours, can be booked all year round at the tourist office, who also sell the useful Pass'Troyes (from 12€).
- 🕐 **Organizing Your Time:** Allow 4hr to visit Vieux Troyes.
- 🚫 **Don't Miss:** Allow time for a leisurely stroll in the lanes of Vieux Troyes. For shopping bargains, visit the big factory outlet malls on the edge of town.
- 🅿 **Parking:** If you are visiting the old town, park the car behind the town hall (place Alexandre-Israël or along boulevard Gambetta.

A Bit of History

Today Troyes shares with Reims the distinction of being one of the capitals of theprovince of Champagne, though historically the city looks southeast towards Burgundy rather than northwards to the Ardennes. The town developed in the Seine valley on the great trade route between Italy and the cities of Flanders. It had a considerable Jewish population,

Maison du Boulanger and Tourelle de l'Orfèvre

among them the influential scholar Rashi (1050-1105). in the Middle Ages the town hosted two huge annual fairs, each lasting for three whole months, and attracting merchants and craftsmen from all over Europe. But by the end of the 14C the pattern of commercial exchanges had changed, and these great gatherings fell into decline.

Troyes has long been (and is still) France's most important centre of hosiery manufacture. The industry was introduced here at the very beginning of the 16C, followed by cloth-making, dyeing, paper-making. The city's wealth enabled it to overcome the great fire of 1524; houses and churches were quickly rebuilt in a style showing both the Italianate influence of the artists who came here from Fontainebleau around 1540 as well as the persistence of local, medieval traditions.

Sights

Le Vieux Troyes★★

The outline of the old part of the city bears a curious resemblance to a champagne cork, with the area around the cathedral forming the head. The majority of the old houses are timber-framed, with vertical members held together by

Address Book

For coin ranges, see the Legend on the cover flap.

WHERE TO EAT

⊜⊜ **Aux Crieurs de Vin** – *4-6 pl. Jean-Jaurès* – ☎ *03 25 40 01 01 – Closed Sun and Mon.* Wine connoisseurs will appreciate this establishment, which is part wine and spirits shop, part atmospheric pre-1940s style bistro. The cuisine will also please enthusiasts, with produce fresh from the market and a good choice of fish.

⊜⊜ **Bistrot DuPont** – *5 pl. Charles-de-Gaulle – 10150 Pont-Ste-Marie – 3km/1.8mi NE of Troyes on N 77* – ☎ *03 25 80 90 99 – Closed Sun evening and Mon.* Flowers and smiles from the staff provide a fine welcome. In a simple but carefully planned setting, the cheap and cheerful dishes suit the style of the bistro. Terrace in summer.

⊜⊜ **Auberge de la Cray'Othe** – *31 Grande-Rue – 10190 Messon - 12km/7.5mi W of Troyes on N 60, Sens direction and D 83 to the left* - ☎ *03 25 70 31 12 – Closed 2 weeks in Jan, 2 weeks in Sep; open from Thu-Sun lunchtime – booking necessary.* This beautiful farm houses a pleasant restaurant decorated with paintings of the village and surrounding area. Connoisseurs will love the authentic local dishes such as coq au cidre du pays d'Othe and the tasty farmhouse terrines.

⊜⊜⊜ **Le Bistroquet** – *Pl. Langevin* – ☎ *03 25 73 65 65 – Closed Sun except lunchtimes from Sep-June.* This restaurant is situated in the centre of the pedestrianised part of Troyes, and is reminiscent of a Parisian brasserie. The large dining room is attractively lit by a decorated glass ceiling, and has leather seats, indoor plants and a lively atmosphere. All dishes are based on fresh ingredients. Terrace with shrubs and garden lights.

WHERE TO STAY

⊜ **Motel Savinien** – *87 r. Fontaine, at Ste-Savinien - 3km/1.5mi W of city centre - 60 rooms* – ☐€8 . ☎ *03 25 79 24 90 – closed Sun and Mon.* This conveniently placed motel by the ring road on the west of the city centre is a large, quiet,

well-maintained 1970s building. Rooms are practical, regularly updated. There's a sauna, jacuzzi and small gym. Traditional cuisine served on the terrace.

⊜⊜ **Les Comtes de Champagne** – *56 r. de la Monnaie* - ☎ *03 25 73 11 70 - 36 rooms* - ☐€6. It is said that the four 12C houses which make up this hotel used to belong to the counts of Champagne who minted their coins here. Renovated rooms; those with kitchen facilities could be ideal for families. The impressive fireplace in the breakfast room testifies to the age of the premises.

⊜⊜ **De La Bonne Fermière** – *Pl. de l'Église - 10450 Bréviandes - 5 km/3mi S of Troyes* - ☎ *03 25 82 45 65 - 13 rooms* - ☐ €7. This peaceful little hotel has just been given a new look with gay springtime colours and new beds. Friendly service and excellent value.

SHOPPING

Specialities – First and foremost, andouillettes (chitterling sausages)… grilled, unaccompanied or drizzled with olive oil flavoured with browned fines herbes and garlic. Try them with mustard au vin de champagne or Meaux mustard and accompanied by mashed potatoes, kidney beans or fried onion rings, dipped in milk or beer, then in flour. Other specialities include Chaource cheese, cider or champagne choucroute, rosé des Riceys, and cacibel (aperitif made with cider, blackcurrant and honey).

Market – Daily market in the Place St-Remy halls. The main market is held on Saturdays. There is another in the Chartreux area on Wed and on Sun morning. A country market is held every third Wed of the month on Boulevard Jules-Guesde.

La Boucherie Moderne – *Halle de l'Hôtel-de-ville* ☎ *03 25 73 32 61/03 25 73 32 64 - Tue-Thu 7.30am-12.45pm, 3.30-7pm, Fri-Sat 9.30am-7pm, Sun 9am-12.30pm.* Stock up on andouillettes made by Gilbert Lemelle, the largest French manufacturer of these sausages.

Charcuterie Audry-Chantal – *Halles de l'Hôtel-de-Ville-Case 37* – ☎ *03 25 73 27 74 – Mon-Thu 8am-12.45pm, Fri-Sat*

7.30am-7pm, Sun 9am-12.30pm - closed 3 weeks in Jul and 2 weeks in Feb. A good place to buy real home-made Troyes andouillettes (chitterling sausages).

Jean-Pierre-Ozérée – *Halles de l'Hôtel-de-Ville -* ☎ *03 25 73 72 25 – Tue, Wed, Thu 7.30am-12.45pm, 3.30-7pm, Fri-Sat 7.30am-7pm, Sun 9am-12.30pm.* Maturing of cheeses, including Chaource, Mussy and Langres. A useful alternative if you don't have time to go to the production site yourself.

Patrick Maury – *28 r. du Gén.-de-Gaulle -* ☎ *03 25 73 06 84 – Tue-Fri 8.30am-12.45pm, 2.45-7pm; Sat 7.30am-8pm.* Opposite the market you will find this tiny boutique prized for its specialities. Andouillette de Troyes is of course the star buy, but black pudding and other home-made charcuterie come a close second.

Le Palais du Chocolat – *2 r. de la Monnaie -* ☎ *03 25 73 35 73 – www.pas-cal-coffet.com – Tue-Fri 9am-12.15pm, 2-7.15pm; Sat 9am-7.15pm; Sun and public holidays 9am-1pm.* An emporium of chocolate, as well as ice cream, sorbets and pastries. Among the specialities are tuiles chocolatées et aux amandes (chocolate almond thins), cristallines de Troyes and liquorice ganache which taste all the better in this magnificent setting.

Marques Avenue – *114 bd de Dijon –* ☎ *03 25 82 00 72 – Mon 2-7pm, Tue-Fri from 10am, Sat from 9.30am.* With 120 boutiques, Marques Avenue is the biggest centre for discount fashion stores in Europe. Here you will find all the big brand names, both French and foreign.

Marques City – *Pont-Ste-Marie - Mon 2-7pm, Tue-Fri 10am-7pm, Sat 9.30am-7pm.* Stores offering almost 200 labels at discount prices in a mall of 15 000 m², ranging across sportswear, formal wear and quality accessories. Three restaurants on site.

Mc Arthur Glen – *Voie des Bois - 10150 Pont-Ste-Marie -* ☎ *03 25 70 47 10 – Mon 2-7pm, Tue-Fri 10am-7pm, Sat 9.30am-7pm. Closed 1 May.* Opened in 1995, the village includes 84 end-of-line shops along an outside covered gallery.

ON THE TOWN

La Chope – *64 av. du Gén.-de-Gaulle -* ☎ *03 25 73 11 99.* Wide selection of beers, whiskies and cocktails.

La Cocktaileraie – *56 r. Jaillant-Deschainets - BP 4102 -* ☎ *03 25 73 77 04– Tue-Sat 5pm-3am.* The clientele of this smart bar ranges from businessmen discussing stock options and the Dow Jones to young lovers whispering sweet nothings. A hundred or so cocktails are on offer, around 45 whiskies and many prestigious champagnes, as well as ice cream. A small reception room can be hired for private parties and meetings.

Le Bougnat des Pouilles – *29 r. Paillot-de-Montabert –* ☎ *03 25 73 59 85 – Open 6pm-3am.* The high-quality vintages in this wine bar are sought out by the young proprietor himself, among the smaller producers in the region. The walls are often hung with exhibitions of painting and photography. The atmosphere is very peaceful and the music an easygoing blend of jazz, blues and world music. Concerts twice a month.

Le Chihuahua – *8 r. Charbonnet –* ☎ *03 25 73 33 53 – Mon-Sat 6pm-3am.* This fashionable cellar bar also has dancing. Each Thursday a theme night takes place (e.g. tequila, techno) and a rock concert is organised once a month. The barman's Tex-Mex cocktails are brilliant.

Le Tricasse – *16 r. Paillot-de-Montabert –* ☎ *03 25 73 14 80 – Mon-Sat 3pm-3am – Closed Sun.* This most famous of Troyes' nightspots is in a smart area and offers a glorious mix of music, from jazz to salsa to house (DJ every Saturday night). It is frequented by students from the business school and engineers, among others. Rum, champagne, cocktails and wines are the house specialities.

SHOWTIME

Théâtre de Champagne – *R. Louis-Mary -* ☎ *03 25 76 27 60 / 61 - Mon-Fri 10am-12.30pm, 2-6pm, Sat 10am-12.30pm, 2-5pm – Closed Jul-Aug.* Opera, comedy, arthouse theatre, variety shows.

Théâtre de la Madeleine – *R. Jules-Lebocey -* ☎ *03 25 43 32 10 – Mon-Sat 10am-12.30pm, 2-6pm.* Arthouse theatre, comedy, variety shows.

horizontal beams rather than by timbers set obliquely or in the form of a St Andrew's cross as elsewhere in France. The most elegant infill is the characteristic local chequer-board pattern made from brick, slate or chalk rather than the cob or daub commonly employed.

The streets with the best examples of such houses are Rue Champeaux, Ruelle des Chats, Rue de Vauluisant, as well as the Cour du Mortier d'Or.

Maison de l'Outil et de la Pensée ouvrière★★

🕐 10am-6pm. 🎫 6.50€ (children under 12 years: no charge). 🕐 Closed 1 Jan and 25 Dec. ☎ 03 25 73 28 26. www.maison-de-l-outil.com.

Housed in the Hôtel du Mauroy, it is a fine architectural setting for the fascinating range of objects displayed. The dignity of labour is celebrated here in the subtle but never gratuitous diversity of forms as much as in the individual character and highly specialised function of each object. Though some are conventionally beautiful or pleasingly ornamented, one is more touched in the end by the way in which tools like hammers have been shaped over time by the hand that has used them as well as by the material they have been in contact with.

Église Ste-Madeleine

This church is Troyes' oldest place of worship. Much rebuilt in the 16C, it is famous for the rood screen (jubé★★) made by Jean Gailde; this has scalloped ogee arches with no intermediate supports, fine glass (verrières★) – the Passion, the Creation, a Jesse Tree – as well as a statue of St Martha (statue de Sainte Marthe★) of striking gravity.

Musée de Vauluisant★

🕐 Jun-Sep: daily except Tue 10am-1pm, 2-6pm; Oct-May: daily except Mon and Tue 10am-noon, 2-6pm. 🕐 Closed public holidays. 🎫 3€ (under 25 years: no charge). No charge 1st Sun in the month (except during special exhibits). ☎ 03 25 73 05 85.

The fine 16C Renaissance Hôtel de Vauluisant★ contains a museum of local art and a museum of hosiery with exhibits depicting the industry's evolution, including historic looms and other machinery and a variety of products, some of which go back to the 18C.

Cathédrale St-Pierre et St-Paul★★

The cathedral was begun in 1208 and continued until the 17C, enabling the regional Gothic style to be traced over the whole period of its evolution. The building has remarkable proportions, exceptionally rich decoration and a beautiful nave.

The stained-glass windows (vitraux★★) of the cathedral cover a total area of 1 500m2 – about 16 000sq ft. One of the supreme achievements of this art form, they transform the building into a cage of glass.

Musée d'Art moderne★★

🕐 Daily exc Mon 11am-6pm. 🕐 Closed public holidays. 🎫 5€. ♿ ☎ 03 25 76 26 80.

This is the collection built up since 1939 by Pierre and Denise Lévy, noted hosiery manufacturers. It comprises thousands of items dating from 1850 to 1950, many of them donated to the State and now on display in the former Bishops' Palace.

Lévy was on good terms with many artists, visiting their studios and becoming firm friends with some of the great figures of our age. Particularly well represented here are the Fauves, who, together with Braque, Dufy, Matisse and Van Dongen "made colour roar". Derain too, one of the first to appreciate the art of Africa, is very much present, as is Maurice Marinot, a local artist and glass-maker.

◗◗ Basilique St-Urbain★ – 13C Gothic architecture.
Église St-Pantaléon★– Collection of religious statuary.
Musée St-Loup – Fine art and archeology★.
Pharmacie★ de l'Hôtel-Dieu – Rich collaction of 18C earthenware.

VAISON-LA-ROMAINE★★

MICHELIN MAP 332 D 8–POPULATION 5 904

GREEN GUIDE PROVENCE

This charming and picturesque old market town in the hills near Mont Ventoux has outstanding and extensive ruins of the original Gallo-Roman town, as well as a Romanesque cathedral and cloisters.

- **Information:** Avenue du Chanoine Sautel, ☎04 90 36 02 11. www.vaison-la-romaine.com.
- ▶ **Orient Yourself:** The town is on the north slopes of the Dentelles de Montmirail hills, some 30km east of the Rhoen valley and the town of Orange.
- **Don't Miss:** Make sure to visit the Puymin ruins; and walk across the sturdy Roman bridge over the Ouvèze river.

A Bit of History

Founded 60 years before Caesar's conquest of Gaul, Vaison was the capital of a Celtic tribe, the Vocontii. Under Roman rule it became the seat of great landed proprietors, a flourishing city possibly as large as Arles or Fréjus, one of the centres of Transalpine Gaul and subsequently of Narbonensis. It fell into ruin at the time of the barbarian invasions, and was covered in debris.

In the Middle Ages the town grew again, but around the castle of the Counts of Toulouse on the other side of the river. In the 17C and 18C, new dwellings were built on the right bank, on top of the Roman site. Its ruins were discovered in the 19C, and began to be excavated in the early 20C.

In 1992, torrential rains caused a disastrous flood in and around Vaison. The Ouvèze rose to the point where it flowed over the top of the Roman bridge (which was undamaged, although the 16C parapet had to be replaced). The Roman and medieval sites were virtually undamaged. A campsite, and modern houses and commercial premises by the river were entirely swept away. 37 people lost their lives.

Visit

Ruines romaines★★

The layout of modern Vaison has allowed two parts of the Roman city to be excavated. The La Villasse quarter **(quartier de la Villasse)** lies to the southwest of the Avenue Général-de-Gaulle on either side of a paved central street; there are shops, houses and a basilica. The Dolphin House (Maison du Dauphin) dating from 30 BC is particularly interesting, as is the House of the Silver Bust (Maison du Buste-d'argent). The Puymin quarter **(quartier de Puymin)** lies to the east of the avenue. Here there is the House of the Messii (Maison des Messii) with its atrium, peristyle and baths, as well as the Roman Theatre.

The latter structure *(approached via a tunnel)* dates from the time of the Emperor Augustus; the pits containing the machinery and curtain have been well preserved and the tiers of seating were reconstructed in 1932.

◗◗ Musée archéologique Théo-Desplans★. Ancienne cathédrale Notre-Dame – High Altar★, cloisters★ – Chapelle de St-Quenin.

CHÂTEAU DE **VALENÇAY**★★

MICHELIN MAP 318 G 9
GREEN GUIDE CHÂTEAUX OF THE LOIRE

Vast and superbly proportioned, richly furnished, and standing in an exquisite park, this is a place dedicated to the good life.

- **Information:** Château de Valençay, ☎02 54 00 15 69. www.chateau-valencay.com
- **Orient Yourself:** The château is on D956, between Tours and Vierzon and south of Blois.
- **Organizing Your Time:** Many events are held here, notably the re-enactments of 19C life in period costume in the afternoons, and evening Son et Lumière (*April to August*).
- **Don't Miss:** On July 21 or August 11 or 18, take the opportunity to see the château and gardens illuminated by thousands of candles.

A Bit of History

The original medieval castle was rebuilt in the 16C, the defensive features being retained purely as decoration. The Early Renaissance is well represented too. The west wing was added in the 17C and altered in the 18C. In 1803, the estate was acquired by **Charles-Maurice de Talleyrand-Périgord** (1754-1838), paid for almost entirely by Napoleon, at the time still First Consul.

For almost a quarter of a century, the château served as a glittering background to international diplomacy conducted by its owner, who held high offices of state from the time of Louis XVI to the Restoration.

Visit

🕐 *25 Mar-end May and Sep: 10.30am-6pm; Jun: 9.30am-6pm; Jul-Aug: 9.30am-7pm; Oct-Nov: 10.30am-5.30pm. . ☞ 9€ château and show (children: 4.50€).*
Inside are opulent furnishings of the Régence and Empire periods, including 18C Savonnerie carpets and the round table from the Congress of Vienna.

VANNES★★

MICHELIN MAP 308 O 9–POPULATION 51 759
GREEN GUIDE BRITTANY

Vannes is a pleasant city in the shape of an amphitheatre, at the highest point to which tides flow at the head of the Morbihan Gulf.

- **Information:** 1 rue Thiers, ☎02 97 47 24 34.
- **Orient Yourself:** Vannes is a lively, popular resort on the south-east coast of Brittany. The historic centre is by the cathedral and Pl. Henri IV.
- **Don't Miss:** A boat trip on the Gulf.

A Bit of History

In pre-Roman times, it was the capital of the **Veneti** tribe. One of Gaul's most powerful peoples, they were intrepid sailors, crossing the seas to trade with the inhabitants of the British Isles. They nevertheless suffered a terrible defeat at sea in 56 BC at the hands of the Romans, losing 200 ships in a single day. As a result, Brittany's fate was to remain a backwater for a very long time.

In the 9C, Vannes was where Breton unity was achieved under Nominoé, who made Vannes his capital.

Sights

Vieille Ville (Old Town)★★

Surrounded by ramparts (**remparts**★), the area around the cathedral, the successor to a much more ancient place of worship, still has the air of a medieval town.

Among the old half-timbered houses built over a granite ground floor with pillars, arcades and lintels is a 14C market hall known as **La Cohue**★. Its upper floor served as the ducal law-court right up until 1796, the ground floor as a market until 1840.

There are fine houses bordering **Place Henri IV**★ and in the adjoining streets. Note the timber cross-braces, corbelling, granite pilasters and 16C slate-hung gables.

Cathédrale St-Pierre★

Of robust granite construction, it has a north aisle with a balustraded terrace and sharply-pointed granite gables in Breton Flamboyant style separating the chapels. Inside, the 15C nave is covered by a heavy ribbed vault of the 18C, concealing the original timber roof.

Ramparts★.
Musée d'Histoire et d'Archéologie★
Aquarium du Golfe★ Kids
www.incontournables56.com.

Excursions

Golfe du Morbihan★★

This little inland sea was formed when the land sank and the sea-level rose as a result of the melting of the great Quaternary glaciers, drowning the valleys occupied by the Vannes and Auray rivers. The indented coastline and the play of the tides around the countless islands make this one of Brittany's most fascinating maritime landscapes.

Château de Suscinio★

This was once the summer residence of the Dukes of Brittany. There is a rare 13C decorated tiled floor (accessible via a spiral staircase with 94 steps). The massive buildings lining the courtyard are now partly ruined.

A gun-emplacement at the foot of the northwest tower may well date from the time of the War of the Breton Succession.

Restoration has saved the Château de Suscinio from the complete ruin

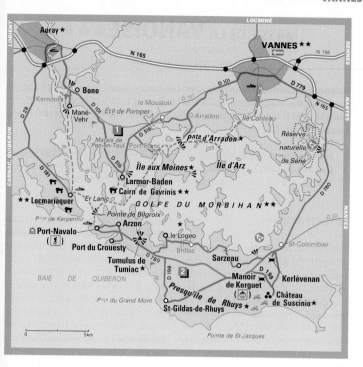

Port-Navalo★

The little port and seaside resort guards the entrance to the Gulf. There are fine views.

Ensemble mégalithique de Locmariaquer★★

This group of megaliths is an important part of a programme of conservation and restoration of megalithic sites. Three megaliths can be found on this site: the **Grand Menhir brisé** (probably broken on purpose into five pieces, after it had served as a landmark for sailors); the **Table des Marchands** (a recently restored dolmen as well as the tumulus underneath) and the **Tumulus d'Er-**

Grah (where excavations are presently under way).

Presqu'île de Quiberon★

Quiberon used to be an island, but over the years sand has accumulated north of Penthièvre Fort to form an isthmus linking it to the mainland. The peninsula's rocky and windswept western shore is known as the **Côte Sauvage** (Wild Coast), but to the east there are sheltered sandy beaches. The ferries for **Belle-Île★★** leave from Quiberon harbour.

◖◖ Cairn de Gavrinis★★. Golfe de Morbihan en bateau★★★ (boat trips).

MASSIF DE LA **VANOISE**★★★

MICHELIN MAP 333 M-N-O 4-5-6

GREEN GUIDE FRENCH ALPS

Numerous Neolithic monuments, cairns and stone roads high on the mountains show that this magnificent landscape has been a centre of human activity for many tens of thousands of years. Today it is one of the most important skiing areas in the world.

🏛 **Information:** Maison de la Vanoise, Termignon, ☎04 79 20 51 67. www.vanoise.com

▶ **Orient Yourself:** The Vanoise extends from the Isère valley in the north to the Arc valley in the south, and to the east runs up to the Italian border.

Geography

This famous massif lies between the valleys of the Arc and the Isère. It was proclaimed a national park in 1963 and consists of two concentric areas. The outer zone (1 450km2 – 560sq miles) includes some of the largest skiing resorts in the world, including the Three Valleys (les 3 Vallées – Courchevel, Méribel, Les Menuires-Val Thorens), and l'Espace Killy (Tignes and Val d'Isère). The central zone (530km2 – 205sq miles), accessible to ramblers, is a remarkable natural site subject to strict regulations. La Vanoise Massif, which is dotted with charming villages and lovely forests, remains nonetheless a high mountain area: 107 summits exceed 3 000m – 9 900ft and the glaciers cover a total surface of 88km2 – 34sq miles. The massif is noted for the extreme diversity of its fauna (marmots, ibexes, chamois) and flora (around 2 000 species).

Visit

Val-d'Isère★★★ – a prestigious winter sports resort with an impressive views.
Rocher de Bellevarde★★★ 🚡 *Access by cable railway.* Views of the Tarentaise and Mont-Blanc.
Refuge de Prariond★★ *2hr round trip on foot.* A pleasant walk with varied landscapes (gorges, rock faces).
Réserve naturelle de la Grande Sassière★★ A backdrop of lakes and glaciers frames Tignes Dam. The park boasts a wealth of animal and plant species which may be easily observed. From

the Saut car park, walks to **Lac de la Sassière**★★ (1hr on foot) and the **Glacier de Rhême-Golette**★★ (2hr30min), at an altitude of 3 000m – 9 900ft.
Tignes★★★ *Alt. 2 100m – 6 890ft.* Resort around a lake in a **site**★★ dominated by the breath-taking view of the Grande Motte Glacier (3 656m – 12 052ft). Seasoned ramblers may want to tackle **Col du Palet**★★, **Pointe du Chardonnet**★★★ (very steep slope) or the **Col de la Croix des Frêtes**★★, the **Lac du Grattaleu**★, **Col de Tourne**★.
Peisey-Nancroix★ This village, nestling in the lush **Vallée de Ponturin**★, opens onto the park and is linked to the skiing area of Les Arcs.
Lac de la Plagne★★ *4hr round trip on foot.* A route in a delightful, flowery setting, at the foot of the Bellecôte summit (3 417m – 11 269ft) and Mont Pourri (3 779m – 12 398ft).
Pralognon★ *Alt. 1 400m – 4 600ft.* One of the main stopping-places for ramblers in La Vanoise Massif.
Col de la Vanoise★★ *Alt. 2 517m – 8 260ft. 4hr round trip.* Views of the Grande Casse (3 855m – 12 705ft).
Col d'Aussois★★★ *Alt. 3 015m – 9 950ft. Ascent 5hr.* Sweeping panorama. These two passes may also be reached from Termignon and Aussois en Maurienne.
La Saulire★★ *Alt. 2 738m – 7 986ft.* 🚡 *Access by cable-car.* View of La Vanoise Massif and the Oisans.
Réserve naturelle de Tuéda★ Beautiful pine forest by Tuéda Lake.
Cime de Caron★★★ *Alt. 3 198m – 10 550ft.* 🚡 *2hr 30min round trip by cable car and cable railway.* Panorama of the Écrins, Tarentaise and Mont-Blanc.

CHÂTEAU DE **VAUX-LE-VICOMTE**★★★

MICHELIN MAP 312 F 4

GREEN GUIDE NORTHERN FRANCE AND THE PARIS REGION

This splendid château, one of the masterpieces of the 17C, lies at the heart of French Brie, a countryside of vast fields broken with occasional copses.

▶ **Orient Yourself:** Vaux-le-Vicomte is south-east of Paris.

Don't Miss: A walk through the gardens laid out by Le Nôtre offers an unforgettable experience.

🕐 **Organizing Your Time:** Plan to enjoy a thrilling tour of the château by candlelight *(May to mid-Oct: Sat 8pm-midnight; Jul-Aug: Fri and Sat. ☞ 15€)*, or a Fountains Show *(every second and last Sat of the month, Mar-Oct, 3-6pm).*

Kids Especially for Kids: Vaux le Vicomte puts on many activities just for children, such as Easter egg hunts, quizzes, treasure hunts and more.

A Bit of History

Nicolas Fouquet had been Superintendent of Finances since the days of Mazarin and built a vast personal fortune. In 1656, he decided to construct at Vaux a palace to symbolise his success. As architect, he chose Louis Le Vau, as interior decorator, Charles Le Brun, as landscaper, André Le Nôtre. By 1661, Vaux looked as it does today. A connoisseur, a man of lavish tastes, but sadly lacking in political judgement, Fouquet had counted on being appointed in Mazarin's place right up to the moment when Louis XIV decided to take power into his own hands. Furthermore, he had alienated Colbert, and, even worse, had made advances to one of the King's favourites, Mlle de La Vallière.

By May, the decision to place him under arrest had already been taken. On 17 August, the unwitting Fouquet threw the most sumptuous of festivities among the Baroque splendours of Vaux. Hoping to impress the young Louis, he succeeded only in offending his monarch more deeply by the unparalleled extravagance of the proceedings. Dinner was presented on a solid gold service, at a time when the royal silverware had been melted down to repay the expenses of the Thirty Years War! On 10 September, Fouquet was arrested at Nantes, his property confiscated, and his brilliant team of designers put to work on Versailles.

Visit

🕐 *Mid-Mar to early Nov: daily 10am-6pm. ☞ 12.50€. ☎ 01 64 14 41 90. www.vaux-le-vicomte.com.*

Le Vau's château is the definitive masterpiece of the early Louis XIV style. It is majestic in its impact. It is to be understood as the central feature of a grandiose designed landscape, an archetype of immense influence over the whole of Europe in the course of the following century and a half.

Le Brun's talent is here made manifest in all its richness and diversity. His King's Bedroom anticipates the splendour of the Royal Apartments at Versailles.

In the **gardens** ★★★, Le Nôtre showed himself to be a master of perspective.

◗◗ Musée des Équipages★

Château de Vaux-le-Vicomte

A. Cassaigne/MICHELIN

VENDÔME ★★

MICHELIN MAP 318 D 5—POPULATION 17 707
GREEN GUIDE CHÂTEAUX OF THE LOIRE

At the foot of a steep bluff, which is crowned by a castle, the River Loir divides into several channels. Vendôme stands on a group of islands crowded with bell-towers, gables and steep slate roofs.

🛈 **Information:** Hotel du Saillant, Parc Ronsard, ☎02 54 77 05 07.

▶ **Orient Yourself:** The River Loir, flows parallel to the Loire, to its north. The town's setting is complicated and unusual , the islands fitting together like a jigsaw puzzle. Rue Poterie runs north-south across the town centre.

Sight

Ancienne Abbaye de la Trinité★

Founded in 1040 by Geoffroy Martel, Count of Anjou, the Benedictine abbey expanded considerably and became one of the most powerful in France. It became a pilgrimage centre where pilgrims flocked to venerate the supposed Holy Tear which Christ had shed at Lazarus' tomb and which Geoffroy Martel had brought back from a Crusade.

The **abbey church★★** is a remarkable example of Flamboyant Gothic. The remarkable west front highlighted by a great incised gable contrasts with the plain Romanesque tower.

The transept, all that is left of the 11C building, leads to the chancel and ambulatory with its five radiating chapels. In the 14C chancel are fine late-15C stalls **(stalles★)** decorated with naïve scenes The axial chapel contains a window dating from 1140 depicting the Virgin and Child (Majesté Notre-Dame).

◗◗ Abbey Museum★ .

MONT VENTOUX ★★★

MICHELIN MAP 332 E 8
GREEN GUIDE PROVENCE

Mount Ventoux enjoys an isolated position far from any rival summit, making it a commanding presence in north-western Provence, visible over vast distances especially when topped in winter with a sparkling coat of snow.

▶ **Orient Yourself:** The massif is served by a scenic route 67km – 42mi long between Vaison and Carpentras. The road was used for motor racing until 1973, and the ascent is a major challenge in those years when it features as part of the Tour de France.

🕐 **Organizing Your Time:** The mountain's upper section is blocked by snow from 15 November to 15 March.

Driving Tour

Vaison-la-Romaine★★

👣 See VAISON-LA-ROMAINE.

Shortly after leaving the little town of Malaucène, the road passes close to the Le Groseau Vauclusian Spring (Source vauclusienne du Groseau) which emerges from several fissures at the foot of an escarpment. Forests of fir trees follow, interspersed with grazing land, and the view then opens out over the Toulourenc valley. Mount Serein (1 428m – 4 685ft) appears, followed by the curiously jagged Dentelles de Montmirail and the Baronies Massif.

Summit★★★

1 909m – 6 263ft. The top of the mountain consists of a vast field of white shingle from which protrudes numerous masts and instruments, radar equipment, a TV transmitter, a weather station... Mount Ventoux, the Windy One, is so named because of the Mistral which blasts it with a force unequalled elsewhere. On average, the temperature here is 11C – 52F lower than in the valley. The flora even includes polar vegetation.

In the early morning and late afternoon, as well as in autumn, the vast **panorama**★★★ extends from the Écrins Massif to the northeast to the Cévennes and the shore of the Mediterranean.

Below the resort of Chalet-Reynard on the descent southward are fine stands of Aleppo and Austrian black pine and Atlantic cedar, as well as beeches and oaks. Finally, beyond St-Estève, vines and fruit-trees make their appearance.

MASSIF DU **VERCORS**★★★

MICHELIN MAP 332 F-G 2-3

GREEN GUIDE FRENCH ALPS

Rising above Grenoble like a fortress, the massive limestone plateau of the Vercors forms the largest regional park in the northern Alps.

- **Information:** Rue du Cinema, Autrans, ☎04 75 48 22 54. www.vercors-net.com.
- ▶ **Orient Yourself:** The area is to the west and south-west of Grenoble.

Geography

The Vercors is the most extensive of the Pre-Alpine massifs. Protected by sheer cliffs, it is a natural citadel, inside which grow fine forests of beech and conifers interspersed with lush pasturelands. In places, the immensely thick limestone has been cut into by the rivers to form deep and spectacular gorges.

A Bit of History

In 1944, the Resistance in these mountains numbered several thousand. In June of that year, the Wehrmacht stepped up its assault on the Resistance, and brought in parachute troops on 21 July. With many of their number lost, the surviving members of the Resistance were given the order to disperse on 23 July. 700 of the inhabitants and defenders of the Vercors had died; several of its villages lay in ruins.

North of the rebuilt village of Vassieux-en-Vercors is a National Cemetery with the graves of some of those who died during that terrible summer, and at the Col de Lachan stands a monument to the fallen (Mémorial du Vercors).

The Grands Goulets

S. Sauvignier/MICHELIN

499

Driving Tour

Gorges de la Bourne★★★

The unusually regular walls of the gorge open out downstream. its entrance is marked by the old cloth town of Pont-en-Royans with its houses clinging picturesquely to the rock face.

Combe Laval★★★

One of the finest sights in the Vercors. The road clings dizzily to a vast limestone wall rising 600m – some 2 000ft above the upper valley of the Cholet.

Grands Goulets★★★

An epic piece of construction dating from 1851, the narrow road was hewn directly into the rock. From its upper section it is possible to see the river beginning the process of eroding an as yet intact geological formation. The village of Les Barraques-en-Vercors was destroyed by enemy action in 1944.

Col de Rousset★★

Go as far as the southern entrance to the disused tunnel. The pass marks the climatic as well as the morphological boundary between the northern and southern Alps. There are spectacular views, not only of the road twisting its way downwards, but also of the great limestone walls protecting the Vercors, of the Die valley 960m – 3 150ft below, and of a succession of bare ridges extending into the far distance.

GRAND CANYON DU **VERDON**★★★

MICHELIN MAP 334 E-F 10

GREEN GUIDE FRENCH ALPS

The modest-looking River Verdon has cut Europe's most spectacular canyon through a remote, wild landscape.

▪ **Information:** Maison des Gorges du Verdon, La Palud-sur-Verdon, ☎04 92 77 32 02. www.lapaludsurverdon.com.

▸ **Orient Yourself:** The gorge is best reached from Castellane on the east side or Moustiers-Ste-Marie on the west. On the north side, the canyon can be followed on D952 and D23, while the D71 (the Corniche Sublime) runs along the south side.

🕐 **Organizing Your Time:** The road on either side is slow and tiring. Don't rush it – allow a full day, especially if you enjoy a hike.

Geography

The canyon extends 26km – 16 miles from the meeting-point of the Verdon with the Jabron in the east to where it flows into Ste-Croix Lake in the west at the Galetas bridge.

The opposite rims of the canyon are between 200-1 500m (about 650-5 000ft) apart. Its depth varies from 250-600m (about 800-2 000ft), while the width of its floor ranges from 8-90m (about 25-300ft). The dizzy height of the canyon's walls impresses on one the sheer scale of the Jurassic sedimentation, in terms of both time and the quantity of material deposited.

Visit

La Corniche Sublime★★★

South bank scenic route. The steep and twisting (20km – 12mi) road was engineered so as to open up the most spectacular views. They include: the **Balcons de la Mescla**★★★ overlooking the swirling waters where the Verdon is joined by the Artuby; the bridge, Pont de l'Artubya, linking sheer walls of rock; the Fayet tunnels above the Étroit des Cavaliers (Knights' Narrows), and the **Falaise des Cavaliers**★ (Knights' Cliff) 300m – 1 000ft high.

La route des Crêtes★★★

North bank scenic route. The road (23km – 14mi long) links a series of viewpoints overlooking the most spectacular section of the canyon. Farther to the east, the viewpoint known as the **Point Sublime**★★★ dominates the downstream section of the canyon and the impressive narrows, the **Couloir de Samson**★★★.

Castellane★

See ROUTE NAPOLÉON.

Moustiers-Ste-Marie★★

The small town is the centre for the Valensole plateau. It has an extraordinary **site**★★ at the foot of a cleft in the limestone cliff, across which a knight returning from the Crusades stretched the chain which can still be seen today. The church has a **tower**★ with arcading in Lombard style. Faience was introduced here in 1679; the most sought-after pieces were fired at high temperatures (*see LIMOGES*) and have charming hunting scenes in blue.

VERDUN★★

MICHELIN MAP 307 D 4–POPULATION 20 733
GREEN GUIDE ALSACE LORRAINE CHAMPAGNE

This ancient stronghold occupies a strategic position on the Meuse. The Upper Town with its cathedral and citadel is poised on an outcrop overlooking the river.

Information: Place de la Nation, ☎03 29 86 14 18.
www.verdun-tourisme.com.
Orient Yourself: The town is in the north, just off the A4 autoroute.

A Bit of History

Gauls were the first to build a fortress here on the left bank of the Meuse. They were followed by the Romans, but Verdun entered the mainstream of history with the signing of the **Treaty of Verdun** in 843. By its terms, Charlemagne's realm was divided up among his grandsons, contrary to their father's wish for its preservation as a single unit. The Emperor, Lothair, received the central zone (Northern Italy, Provence, the Rhineland and the Low Countries); Louis, the Germanic countries, and Charles the Bald, Gaul. The repercussions have been felt throughout the centuries, and the treaty has been referred to as "the most significant in all the continent's history", partly because Louis was dissatisfied with his portion and launched what might be considered the first of all Franco-German wars in 858 following the death of Lothair.

The town was besieged in 1870 at the start of the Franco-Prussian War, then occupied for three years. In the First World War, Verdun was the scene of some of the bloodiest fighting of the Western Front, in a battle that lasted 18 months (*See:* Champ de Bataille de Verdun).

Sight

Ville haute★

The seat of a bishop, the fortified upper town rises in stages from the banks of the river. The city's historic buildings include **Cathédrale Notre-Dame**★, laid out like the great Romanesque basilicas of the Rhineland, and the Bishop's Palace **(Palais épiscopal**★) constructed by Robert de Cotte in the 18C.

▶▶ Citadelle souterraine (Underground Citadel) – self-guided vehicle travels 7km/4.3mi of tunnels equipped to fulfil the needs of the army.

CHAMP DE BATAILLE DE **VERDUN**★★★

The name of Verdun is indissolubly linked to the decisive struggle on which turned the outcome of the Great War (1914-1918). The gaze of the world was fixed for a year and a half on the paroxysm of violence endured by both sides, in a battle which brought forth the uttermost in steadfastness and courage.

- **Information:** Place de la Nation, Verdun, ☎03 29 86 14 18. www.verdun-tourisme.com.
- ▶ **Orient Yourself:** The battlefields are 10km – 6mi northeast of Verdun.
- **Guided Tours:** The Circuit Découverte is a bus tour of the battlefields (*2-6pm, starts from Verdun tourist office. ☞25.50€*).

A Bit of History

At the outbreak of war in August 1914, Verdun lay a mere 40km – 25 miles from the Franco-German frontier. The 21 February 1916 dawned bright but cold. A devastating bombardment preceded the Germans' frontal assault on the French lines. Within four days Douaumont Fort had fallen. This was the moment at which General Pétain took effective charge of the battle; by the time of his replacement in April 1917, it was clear that the German attempt to break the staying-power of the French army had failed. Verdun, the hinge of the whole Western Front, could not be taken.

A series of battles raged throughout March and April in the Argonne, around Les Éparges; and, closer to Verdun, on Hill 304 and the other eminence known chillingly as the Mort-Homme (Dead Man's Hill). On 11 July, the final German offensive ground to a halt in front of the Souville fort, a mere 5km – 3 miles from the city. The French counter-offensive began in October 1916. By 20 August 1917, the Hell of Verdun, which had cost the lives of over 700 000 men, was over.

Douaumont Ossuary

CHÂTEAU DE **VERSAILLES**★★★

MICHELIN MAP 311 I 3

GREEN GUIDE NORTHERN FRANCE AND THE PARIS REGION

Versailles is the creation of the French monarchy at the moment of its greatest splendour. Consisting of the **château**, the gardens, and the Trianon, it is a wonderfully harmonious composition of building and landscape, the definitive monument of French Classicism.

- **Information:** 2bis avenue de Paris, ☎01 39 24 88 88. www.versailles-tourisme.com.
- ▶ **Orient Yourself:** Versailles is only 18km-11mi from Paris, easily reached by road or train (*take line C of the RER to Versailles-Rive gauche, or SNCF rail link from the stations St-Lazare to Versailles-Rive droite or from Montparnasse to Versailles-Chantiers*). The château and park form one side of the town of Versailles. Place du Marché is the town's focal point, offering a variety of delightful restaurants, shops, cafés, brasseries and weekly markets.
- **Guided Tours:** Take one of the tours offered by the tourist office to get better acquainted with not only the château and its gardens, but also the town itself. There is a choice of guided tours at the château, each starting at a different entrance.
- **Don't Miss:** The Grand Canal – rent a rowing boat and enjoy an impressive view of the palace and its gardens.
- **Organizing Your Time:** A variety of guided tours for the interior of the palace are offered, ranging from 1-2hr. Allow 3hr for the gardens, and even more time if you wish to visit the Grand and Petit Trianons. The park is best seen when the Grands Eaux (fountains) are in operation (*weekends and holidays in summer*).
- **Especially for Kids:** Beyond the Petit Trianon is the Queen's Hamlet (**Le Hameau de la Reine**) where farm animals (ducks, black pigs, goats) roam about, serving as a great attraction for children.

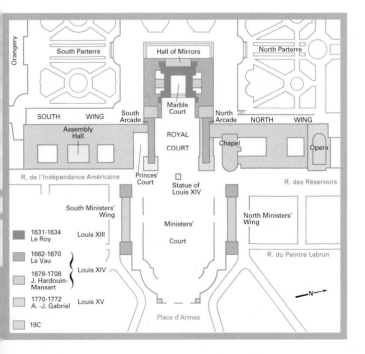

A Bit of History

1624 Louis XIII has a hunting lodge built in this game-rich area.

1631 Philibert Le Roy designs the first château, built of brick, stone and slate.

1661 Le Brun is made responsible for the interior, supervising a gifted team of painters, sculptors, carvers and interior decorators.

1666 The gardens' splendid fountains are inaugurated.

1667 The Grand Canal is dug.

1668 Le Vau extends the palace, builds the **Grand Apartments**★★★ lays out a spacious terrace overlooking the gardens and restores the **cour de Marbre**★★.
The **gardens**★★★ are laid out by Le Nôtre.

1671 Le Brun decorates the State Apartments using the choicest materials.

1672 Boulle delivers the first items of his furniture featuring showy marquetry of tortoiseshell and brass.

1674 Lavish summer festivals are held. Le Brun designs 24 statues for the gardens.

1678 Desjardins, Le Hongre and the Marsy brothers work on the Diana Fountain (Fontaine de Diane). Jules Hardouin-Mansart, a nephew by marriage of François Mansart, adds to the palace, giving it a grand first floor over the raised ground floor, columns, fine windows and roof sculptures. He completes the **Galerie des Glaces**★★★ begun by Le Brun.

1680 The King's Kitchen Garden (Potager du Roi) is laid out.

1684 Jules Hardouin-Mansart designs the Orangerie.

1688 Hardouin-Mansart builds the Grand Trianon (or Marble Trianon)

1699 The Royal Chapel is built by Hardouin-Mansart (completed in 1710 by Robert de Cotte and decorated by Van Cleve and Claude Lorrain, with frescoes by Coustou and Coypel).

1701 The King's Suite is designed by Hardouin-Mansart; the room is laid out around the axis formed by the course of the sun (shown today with its summer furnishings of 1723).

1712 Hercules' Salon (Salon d'Hercule) on the site of the former chapel, is

Address Book

For coin ranges, see the Legend on the cover flap.

WHERE TO EAT

Place du Marché – This agreeable square is marked out by bars, crêperies, pizzerias and restaurants, with outdoor tables in summer.

 La Brasserie du Théâtre – *15 r. des Réservoirs –* ☎ *01 39 50 03 21 – reserv. advisable evenings.* The walls of this 1895 brasserie situated next to the theatre, as its name would suggest, are covered with photos of artists who have frequented it over the years. 1930s style décor, covered terrace and traditional cuisine.

 Le Bœuf à la Mode – *4 r. au Pain, (Pl. du Marché Notre-Dame) –* ☎ *01 39 50 31 99.* A typical 1930s bistro with a con-vivial, relaxed atmosphere. The decor – red wall-seats, knick-knacks, posters, mirrors – is a hit and the regional specialities are delicious. Very busy on market days.

 Au Chapeau Gris – *7 r. Hoche –* ☎ *01 39 50 10 81. Closed 22 Jul to 22 Aug, Tue evening and Wed – reserv. required.* This restaurant, said to date back to the 18C, is a veritable institution hereabouts. Quintessential Versailles ambience and décor are the setting for appetizing, traditional cuisine. Nothing too wild, just a reliable, very much sought-after establishment.

 Valmont – *20 r. au Pain -* ☎ *01 39 51 39 00 . Closed Sun evening and Mon.* This nicely restored old house on the Place des Halles is bound to catch your eye. Venture inside and appreciate the first-rate reception, charming decora-tion, modern colours, elegant tables and succulent cookery. A meal to look forward to!

WHERE TO STAY

 Hôtel Versailles – *7 r. Ste-Anne, Petite Place –* ☎ *01 39 50 64 65. www. hotel-le-versailles.fr – 46 rms –* 🖵 *12€.* This renovated hotel is situated in a quiet side street not far from the château. The Art Deco style rooms are spacious, bright and elegant. Cosy bar-lounge and terrace where breakfast is served in summer.

 Résidence du Berry – *14 r. d'Anjou –* ☎ *01 39 49 07 07. www.hotel-berry.com – 39 rms –* 🖵 *12€.* Located in the Saint-Louis quarter, this 18C edifice has been entirely restored by Les Bâtiments de France. Comfort and top-quality materials await you in rooms with time-worn beams overhead. In summer breakfast is taken on a veranda that opens onto the patio.

ON THE TOWN

Fenêtres sur cour – *Passage de la Geôle, Quartier des Antiquaires –* ☎ *01 39 51 97 77. Closed 3 wks Aug.* A restaurant-salon de thé under a glass roof. The bric-a-brac décor - tile floor, carpets, lamps, chandeliers, plaster statues and paintings – is in perfect harmony with the neighbourhood antique shops. Appetizing wine menu. In summer, tables are set outdoors on the Place de la Geôle.

SHOPPING

Shops – The principal shopping streets are the Rue de la Paroisse and the Place du Marché, the Rue Royale and the Rue du Général-Leclerc. One may also stroll through Les Manèges, opposite the Rive-Gauche station. You'll find many antique dealers in the Passage de la Geôle, near La Place du Marché.

Major stores – From the FNAC (books, CDs, cameras, etc.) to Printemps or BHV (department stores), the shopping complex Le Centre Commercial de Parly II, on your way out of Versailles toward St-Germain, has it all.

begun. Completed in 1736, it has a ceiling by Lemoyne.

1729 The Queen's Bedchamber is completed by Boucher.

1768 Ange-Jacques Gabriel builds the Royal Opera with its splendid auditorium.

1769 The King's celebrated roll-top desk is completed, a masterpiece by Oeben and Riesener.

1774 Ange-Jacques Gabriel completes the Petit Trianon and, together with the sculptor Rousseau, creates the King's Library.

1783 The Hamlet (Hameau) is laid out in the gardens of the Petit Trianon. 14 July: the Fall of the Bastille.

1789 A mob force the royal family to return to Paris.

1791 Louis XVI swears loyalty to the Revolutionary Constitution.

1792 Fall of the monarchy.

1793 Louis XVI guillotined.

1833 The Apartments are demolished (with the exception of the central section of the first floor) in order to house a museum.

1837 The palace becomes a museum of the history of France.

Visit

The enjoyment of even the shortest of visits will be greatly enhanced if the Michelin Green Guide Northern France and the Paris Region is used.

Highlights of the Château and Gardens

Full appreciation of Versailles demands a knowledge of Classical mythology and its symbols, the château and its gardens being in effect a temple dedicated to worship of the Sun God.

Grands Appartements★★★

Apr-Oct: daily except Mon 9am-6.30pm; Nov-Mar: daily 9am-5.30pm. Last admission 30min before closing. 7.50€ (under 18 years: no charge). ☎ 01 30 83 76 20)

Château de Versailles

These comprise the King's Suite on the north and the Queen's Suite to the south, facing the sun.

Cour de Marbre★★

Built in brick with stone dressings and reserved for the King's private use, it has fine raised paving in black and white marble, façades graced by 40 busts (some of them by Coysevox), mansard roofs decorated with urns, and a colonnaded portico supporting the wrought-iron balcony of the King's Bedchamber.

Galerie des Glaces (Hall of Mirrors)★★★

Jules Hardouin-Mansart completed this splendid reception room begun by Le Brun, and built over Le Vau's terrace. It lies between the War Salon and the Peace Salon; its mirrors catch the rays of the setting sun. Its decoration was completed in 1687.

The gardens (Jardins★★★)

Laid out by Le Nôtre, these are a masterpiece of the French landscape style, going beyond the evocation of the idea of majesty (as at Vaux-le-Vicomte) to celebrate the supreme authority of the monarch by the systematic use of Classical symbolism. Among the 200 statues of this open-air sculpture museum are Keller's bronzes in the Water Gardens (Parterres d'eau), the Latona Basin (Bassin de Latone), Tuby's splendid Apollo in his chariot, bas-reliefs by Girardon..

Ville de Versailles★★

The town of Versailles was built as an annex to the château to house the numerous titled and untitled people who served the court. It has retained a certain austere charm. It was originally conceived in the symbol of the sun, with the château at the centre and the three main avenues radiating away like rays of light. There are very few 17C houses left in Versailles; most of the old town dates from the 18C. The pedestrianised rue Satory, in the heart of old town, has become as lively as Quartier Notre-Dame, where antique dealers and outdoor cafés abound.

D. Hée/MICHELIN

VÉZELAY★★★

MICHELIN MAP 319 F 7–POPULATION 492

GREEN GUIDE BURGUNDY JURA

The quiet and picturesque little village of Vézelay climbs a steep slope among the northern foothills of the Morvan countryside, overlooking the Cure valley. Its fame is due to the majestic basilica which numbers among the greatest treasures of France.

- ▮ **Information:** Rue St-Étienne,☎03 86 33 23 69. www.vezelaytourisme.com.
- ▶ **Orient Yourself:** Vézelay is west of Avallon. Grande-Rue leads up to the basilica from Place du Champ-de-Foire at the foot of the village.

A Bit of History

The Celts were the first to settle this hill-top site. In 878 an abbey was founded here, and in 1050 it was dedicated to Mary Magdalene, whose remains were supposedly here, and the place soon became one of France's great pilgrimage destinations. It suffered destruction by fire more than once. It was here that St Bernard preached the Second Crusade in 1146.

In 1279, however, the monks of St-Maximin in Provence claimed to have discovered the bones of Mary Magdalene in a cave; the certification of the relics as authentic led to the decline of Vézelay as a place of pilgrimage; it was pillaged by the Huguenots, razed at the time of the French Revolution and given its coup de grâce by lightning.

In 1840, Prosper Mérimée, who was in charge of the national survey of the country's heritage, came to Vézelay; recognising the value and significance of the ruin, he appointed the young Viollet-le-Duc as architect in charge of its restoration.

Sight

Basilique Ste-Madeleine★★★

First built between 1096 and 1104 and restored following the fire of 1120. The principal external features are the fine Romanesque body of the church (to which flying buttresses were added in the 13C), St Antony's Tower (Tour St-Antoine), and a particularly harmonious chevet with radiating chapels. From the terrace, there is a fine **view**★ over the valley of the River Cure.

In the dimly-lit narthex (1140-60) is the marvellous tympanum (**tympan**★★★) of the central doorway, dating from around 1125. Proportion is used to reinforce the meaning of the composition; for example, the figure of Christ is of superhuman size.

The Romanesque nave is unusually large and well lit. The greatest contribution to the basilica's decoration is made by the many capitals (**chapiteaux**★★★) adorning the pillars; these were sculpted from 1106 onwards. The magnificent Gothic **choir** (1185-1215) seems to have been influenced by the great new churches of the North of France.

VICHY★★★

MICHELIN MAP 326 H 6–POPULATION 26 528
GREEN GUIDE AUVERGNE RHÔNE VALLEY

Pleasantly sited in the Allier valley, and well-endowed with lush parks and luxurious thermal establishments, as well as high-quality entertainment, racing, a casino and good shopping, Vichy is a world-famous spa town. The virtues of the waters drew visitors here in Roman times and in the 17C, while it is primarily to Napoleon III that the place owes its reputation as a luxury health resort.

Information: 19 r. du Parc, ☎04 70 98 71 94. www.ville-vichy.fr.

▶ **Orient Yourself:** The town is north-east of Clermont-Ferrand.

A Bit of History

The Roman spa town here was relatively small. In medieval times, the river crossing was commanded by a castle. Later, the town grew during the reign of Henri IV. It began to flourish as a spa resort from the 17C onwards. More recently, Vichy gave its name to the Nazi collaborationist government of France led by Marshal Pétain, whose regime ruled the country from Vichy under close German supervision from 12 July 1940 until 20 August 1944.

Sight

Le Quartier Thermal (Spa)★

The florid spa architecture of the second half of the 19C is well represented by a number of constructions such as the Grand Casino of 1865, the Napoleon Gallery (Galerie Napoléon) of 1857, the covered galleries bordering the park (Parc des Sources) which formed part of the 1889 Paris Universal Exhibition before being re-erected here, and the Great Baths (Grand établissement thermal) of 1900.

VIENNE★★

MICHELIN MAP 333 C 4–POPULATION 29 975
GREEN GUIDE AUVERGNE RHÔNE VALLEY

Vienne is favoured with a sunny **site**★ on the east bank of the Rhône. The town overlooks the bend formed by the river as it makes its way through the crystalline rocks marking the last outcrops of the Massif Central.

Information: Cours Brillier, ☎04 74 53 80 30. www.vienne-tourisme.com.

▶ **Orient Yourself:** The town is 38km/24mi south of Lyon.

A Bit of History

Originally the capital of the Allobroges tribe, Vienne came under Roman rule 60 years before Caesar's conquest of Gaul. In the 3C and 4C, the city was the centre of the vast province known as the Viennoise stretching from Lake Geneva to the mouth of the Rhône. Great public buildings were erected at the foot of Mount Pipet, opposite **St-Romain-en-Gal**, the Gallo-Roman city (**cité gallo-romaine**★) with its houses and shops. In the 5C, Vienne became the capital of the Burgundians, who ruled over the east bank of the Rhône before being chased away by the Franks in 532. Ruled subsequently by its archbishops, the city became the object of the rivalry between the Kingdom of France and the Holy Roman Empire, until its final incorporation into France at the same time as the Dauphiné, in 1349.

Sights

Temple d'Auguste et de Livie★★

This Classical temple was first built in the reign of Emperor Augustus shortly before the beginning of the Christian era; it seems likely that it was then reconstructed, somewhat carelessly, under Claudius, about 50 years later. At the time it would have dominated the Forum to the east. Its good state of preservation is due to its successive re-use as a public building of various kinds (Church, Jacobin club, tribunal, museum, library), and subsequently to its restoration by Prosper Mérimée in 1850.

It is identifiable as Roman work by the way in which its 16 Corinthian columns rise from a podium rather than directly from the ground in the Greek manner. In the pediment are traces of a bronze inscription to the glory of Augustus and Livia.

Cathédrale St-Maurice ★★

Built from the 12C to the 16C, the cathedral combines Romanesque and Gothic elements. Only 35 years after its completion, the cathedral suffered much mutilation during the Wars of Religion. It underwent extensive restoration in the 19C (vaults, arching of the portals, rose window). But much remains to be admired, including the fine Renaissance window in the south aisle (to the right of the choir), the 13C low-relief between the sixth and seventh chapels in the north aisle depicting Herod and the Magi, and the rare 11C Bishop's Throne (in the apse behind the high altar).

◖◗ Théâtre romain★.
Église St-André-le-Bas★
Cloître de St-André-le-Bas★
Ancienne église St-Pierre★
Musée Lapidaire★

JARDINS ET CHÂTEAU DE **VILLANDRY**★★★

MICHELIN MAP 317 M 4
GREEN GUIDE CHÂTEAUX OF THE LOIRE

In 1536, Jean Le Breton, who had been France's ambassador in Italy, rebuilt the château here on the foundations of an earlier one. The new building had a number of features which made it unusual in Touraine: ditches and canals, an esplanade and a terrace, rectangular pavilions in place of round towers, and, above all, its gardens.

🛈 **Information:** Le Potager, Villandry, ☎02 47 50 12 66. www.tourisme-en-confluence.com.

▶ **Orient Yourself:** Coming from Langeais, take D16, which has scenic views. Coming from Tours, take D288, which crosses the Loire at Savonnières.

⊛ **Don't Miss:** The 13 Mudejar ceiling in the chateau.

🕓 **Organizing Your Time:** The château tour takes 2hrs. Allow another 1hr to stroll through the gardens.

Visit

Château★★

🕓 Jul and Aug: 9am-6.30pm; Apr-Jun and Sep-Oct: 9am-6pm; Mar: 9am-5.30pm; Feb and early Nov to mid-Nov: 9am-5pm; Christmas vacation: 9.30am-4.30pm. 🕓 Closed the rest of the year. ⚘ 2hr guided tours available (call for times) except in Feb, Dec and Sundays May-Sep (during which time you can take a self-guided tour with a leaflet). ⊛ 8€ (château and gardens). ☎ 02 47 50 02 09. www. chateauvillandry.com.

The interior is distinguished by Louis XV panelling in the Great Salon and Dining Room, by the fine ramped staircase in wrought iron, and by a surprising 13C Mudejar ceiling from Spain, brought here by Joachim de Carvallo.

The Gardens of Château de Villandry

Jardins★★★

⏱ *Daily. Jul-Aug 9am-7.30pm; Apr to mid-Jun and mid-Sep to end Sep 9am-7pm; Oct 9am-6.30pm; Mar 9am-6pm; Feb and early Nov to mid-Nov 9am-5.30pm; mid-Nov to end Jan 9am-5pm. ✍ 5.50€ (8€ château and gardens. ☎ 02 47 50 02 09. www.chateauvillandry.com.*

In 1906, Dr Carvallo, founder of the French Historic Houses Association (Demeure Historique), bought the Villandry estate and began to restore the gardens. The plan of the gardens shows both the influence of the agricultural writer **Olivier de Serres**, and the synthesis of the monastery garden with the Italian garden proposed by Jacques II Androuet du Cerceau.

Covering a total area of 7ha – 17 acres, the gardens have many fascinating features. There are three terraces one above the other, separated by shady avenues of limes and vines; the highest is the water garden with its mirrorlike stretch of water, then comes an ornamental garden with box clipped into patterns symbolising the varieties of love: tragic (sword and dagger blades), fickle (butterflies and fans), tender (masks and hearts), and passionate (broken hearts). Finally there is a kitchen garden with 85 000 plants contained in clipped-box beds. The use of the humblest of vegetables (cabbage, celery...), chosen for their culinary value, symbolism, therapeutic value or colour, is here raised to an art form of great delicacy and seasonal interest.

VILLEFRANCHE-DE-ROUERGUE★

MICHELIN MAP 338 E 4–POPULATION 11 919
GREEN GUIDE LANGUEDOC ROUSSILLON TARN GORGES

The ancient bastide of Villefranche, with its rooftops clustered around the foot of the massive tower of its church, lies at the bottom of a green valley surrounded by hills, at the confluence of the Aveyron and the Alzou.

- **Information:** Promenade de Guiraudet, ☎05 65 45 13 18. www.villefranche.com
▶ **Orient Yourself:** On the western edge of the Massif Central, the town is at a meeting point of three highways. The town centre is Place Notre-Dame, beside the church.

Sight

Bastide★

The old town on the north bank of the River Aveyron has kept many of the typical features of a planned urban foundation of the 13C. Its cobbled streets, connected by narrow alleyways, are laid out on a grid pattern, and there is a central square **(Place Notre-Dame★)** with covered walks, dominated by a large metal figure of Christ. The tall, severe houses are characteristic of the Rouergue area; a number of them have high open balconies with provision for drying grain. The President Raynal House (Maison du Président Raynal) with its 15C façade is particularly striking, and the Dardennes House (Maison Dardennes) has a fine galleried courtyard. The fortified church **(Église Notre-Dame★)** has splendid ironwork around the font.

◗◗ Chartreuse St-Sauveur★– *Take D922 towards Najac.* 15C Gothic charterhouse, with 'Great' and 'Small' cloisters. The little cloisters are a masterpiece of Flamboyant architecture.

YVOIRE★★

MICHELIN MAP 328 K 2 - POPULATION 639

GREEN GUIDE FRENCH ALPS

This picturesque village bedecked with flowers has retained its medieval character. It enjoys a magnificent site on the shores of Lake Geneva (Lac Léman), at the tip of a headland separating the Petit Lac and the Grand Lac, and has a very popular marina.

- **Information:** Place de la Mairie, ☎04 50 72 80 21.
- ▸ **Orient Yourself:** Approach the town from Douvaine, passing through the village of Nernier, or come from Exevenex.
- **Parking:** Leave your car in the car park just outside the town wall on the Thonon road.

Sights

Village Médieval (Old Town)★

Pedestrian access only. Rebuilt in the 14C on the site of a former fortress, Yvoire has kept part of its original ramparts including two gates protected by towers and its castle (○━ *not open*) with a massive square keep framed by turrets. The bustling streets lined with old houses and craft shops lead to delightful squares decked with flowers which afford fine views of the lake.

From the end of the pier there are views of the Swiss coast, the town of Noyon and the Jura mountains.

Jardin des Cinq-Sens★

🕐 *Mid-May to mid-Sep: daily 10am-7pm; mid-Apr to mid-May: daily 11am-6pm; mid-Sep to mid-Oct: daily 1-5pm. Summer:* ⊚ *9€ (4-16 years: 5.50€); Spring and Autumn:* ⊚ *8€ (4.50€).* ♿ ☎ *04 50 72 88 80. www.jardin5sens.net*

The former kitchen garden of the castle has been turned into a reconstruction of a medieval enclosed garden where monks would grow vegetables and herbs.

◗◗ Boat trips on the lake.

For the best little places, follow the leader.

Looking for the latest news on today's best hotels and restaurants? Pick up the Michelin Guide and look for the Bib Gourmand and Bib Hotel symbols. With 45,000 addresses in Europe, in every category and price range, the perfect place to dine or stay is never far away.

A better way forward

INDEX

INDEX

INDEX

WHERE TO EAT

INDEX

WHERE TO STAY

MAPS AND PLANS

LIST OF MAPS AND PLANS

COMPANION PUBLICATIONS

LOCAL MAPS

For each site in this guide, you will find map references which correspond to local maps (nos 301 to 345) of France.

MAPS OF FRANCE

For all of France, there are 5 formats at a 1:1 000 000 scale to choose from: France no 721, the whole country on a single sheet with an index of place names; no 722, reversible, divided north/south; no 724, northern France; no 725 southern France; and the collection of atlases. Atlases to France are published in several formats for your convenience: spiral, paperback and hardback all include the Paris region, town plans and an index of place names. Now available in a mini format as well. You may also wish to consult no 728 France Administrative, showing regions, departments, main roads, distance tables, universities.

MOTORWAYS

Other useful maps include no 726 Route Planning, with motorways, alternative routes, journey times and 24-hour service stations.

ROUTE PLANNING VIA INTERNET

Michelin is pleased to offer a route-planning service on the Internet: **www. Via Michelin. com**. Choose the shortest route, a route without tolls, or the Michelin recommended route to your destination; you can also access information about hotels and restaurants from The Michelin Guide, and tourist sites from The Green Guide.

Bon voyage!

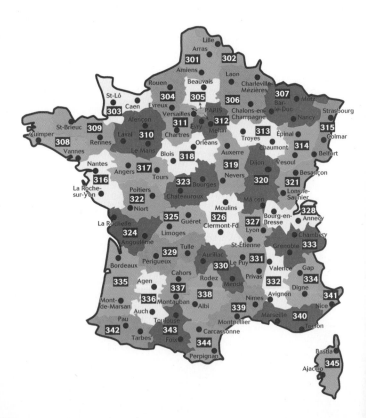

LEGEND

★★★ **Highly recommended**

★★ **Recommended**

★ **Interesting**

Tourism

Sightseeing route with departure point indicated	Map co-ordinates locating sights
Ecclesiastical building	Tourist information
Synagogue – Mosque	Historic house, castle – Ruins
Building (with main entrance)	Dam – Factory or power station
Statue, small building	Fort – Cave
Wayside cross	Prehistoric site
Fountain	Viewing table – View
Fortified walls – Tower – Gate	Miscellaneous sight

Recreation

Racecourse	Waymarked footpath
Skating rink	Outdoor leisure park/centre
Outdoor, indoor swimming pool	Theme/Amusement park
Marina, moorings	Wildlife/Safari park, zoo
Mountain refuge hut	Gardens, park, arboretum
Overhead cable-car	
Tourist or steam railway	Aviary, bird sanctuary

Additional symbols

Motorway (unclassified)	Post office – Telephone centre
Junction: complete, limited	Covered market
Pedestrian street	Barracks
Unsuitable for traffic, street subject to restrictions	Swing bridge
Steps – Footpath	Quarry – Mine
Railway – Coach station	Ferry (river and lake crossings)
Funicular – Rack-railway	Ferry services: Passengers and cars
Tram – Metro, underground	Foot passengers only
Bert (R.)... Main shopping street	Access route number common to MICHELIN maps and town plans

Abbreviations and special symbols

A	Agricultural office (Chambre d'agriculture)	**P**	Local authority offices (Préfecture, sous-préfecture)
C	Chamber of commerce (Chambre de commerce)	**POL.**	Police station (Police)
H	Town hall (Hôtel de ville)		Police station (Gendarmerie)
J	Law courts (Palais de justice)	**T**	Theatre (Théâtre)
M	Museum (Musée)	**U**	University (Université)
			Hotel
			Park and Ride

Some town plans are extracts from plans used in the Green Guides to the regions of France.

Michelin Apa Publications Ltd

A joint venture between Michelin and Langenscheidt

Suite 6, Tulip House, 70 Borough High Street, London SE1 1XF, United Kingdom

No part of this publication may be reproduced in any form
without the prior permission of the publisher.

© 2007 Michelin Apa Publications Ltd
ISBN 978-1-906261-16-0
Printed: October 2007
Printed and bound in Germany